T0202453

Information Security and Cryptography

More information about this series at http://www.springer.com/series/4752

Yehuda Lindell
Editor

Tutorials on the Foundations of Cryptography

Dedicated to Oded Goldreich

Editor
Yehuda Lindell
Department of Computer Science
Bar-Ilan University
Ramat Gan, Israel

ISSN 1619-7100   ISSN 2197-845X   (electronic)
Information Security and Cryptography
ISBN 978-3-319-86064-0   ISBN 978-3-319-57048-8   (eBook)
DOI 10.1007/978-3-319-57048-8

Printed on acid-free paper

This Springer imprint is published by Springer Nature
The registered company is Springer International Publishing AG
The registered company address is: Gewerbestrasse 11, 6330 Cham, Switzerland

To Oded, who is a continual inspiration to us

Benny Applebaum
Boaz Barak
Andrej Bogdanov
Iftach Haitner
Shai Halevi
Yehuda Lindell
Alon Rosen
Salil Vadhan

Preface

This tutorial book is dedicated to Oded Goldreich by his students and mentorees on the occasion of his 60th birthday. This is an opportune time to celebrate Oded's fundamental contributions to the foundations of cryptography. As one of the founders of the field, Oded's work has influenced the way we think about, define, and construct cryptographic schemes. Oded's research contributions are so numerous and wide-ranging that attempting to enumerate even just the most important of them would span many pages. Nevertheless, we would be amiss not to mention at least Oded's classic results on achieving pseudorandom functions, zero knowledge for *NP*, secure two-party and multiparty computation, hard-core predicates for all one-way functions, private information retrieval, lower bounds for black-box simulation, limitations of the random-oracle methodology, oblivious RAM, and multiple definitional works.

Having said the above, Oded's contributions to cryptography have gone *far* beyond his numerous novel scientific results. In particular, I would like to elaborate on his enormous influence on the role and character of the field of theoretical cryptography and what he has termed the *foundations of cryptography*.

At *CRYPTO'97*, Oded gave an invited talk "On the Foundations of Modern Cryptography" in which he articulated his vision for this subfield of cryptography. In the talk and accompanying essay, he describes modern cryptography as comprising *definitional activity* (formulating what "secure" means) and *constructive activity* (constructing schemes that fulfill the definitions). Furthermore, he differentiates between three types of results: *feasibility results, introduction of paradigms and techniques that may be applicable in practice*, and *presentation of schemes that are suitable for practical applications*. (Of course, as Oded mentions in the essay, the field also includes other activities such as establishing lower bounds and impossibility results.) This essay and Oded's lecture notes and seminal two-volume book *Foundations of Cryptography*, have significantly influenced the way that we and others look at and understand our field. Needless to say, there was active research being carried out on the foundations of cryptography before Oded published his essay. However, Oded was the first to articulate the importance of this work and create an identity for this subfield of cryptography.

The success of this approach as articulated by Oded has been outstanding. He was immensely influential in establishing a flourishing research community devoted to studying the foundations of cryptography and the fundamental questions outlined in his 1997 essay. Oded was one of the founders of the Theory of Cryptography Conference in 2004 (together with Mihir Bellare and Shafi Goldwasser), and chaired its steering committee from 2006 to 2012. Although many cryptography theory papers are published at other venues, the TCC conference grew under Oded's leadership to be a natural home for such work.

The importance of this approach and the research carried out on the foundations of cryptography has intrinsic scientific value, related to the theory of computer science in general. The questions asked are fundamental in nature and of importance, irrespective of any specific application. However, in his essay, Oded also discussed the eventual utility of theoretical cryptography to practical constructions, and this has been unequivocally demonstrated. One example of this utility is the fact that all new proposed standards for modes of encryption, signatures, key-exchange protocols, and so on are accompanied with a proof of security. However, a far more striking illustration is the transition of purely theoretical notions to tools that are frequently used by the applied cryptography and security communities. One particularly interesting example is the paper "Towards a theory of software protection and simulation by oblivious RAMs" published by Oded at STOC 1987 (and later merged into a single journal paper with Rafi Ostrovsky). This paper introduced a new theoretical notion and construction and is a clear example of what one would call "pure theory" today. Three decades later, oblivious RAM is a widely studied primitive, from both a theoretical and practical perspective. Papers on oblivious RAM are published at the top security conferences and constructions are implemented. Furthermore, the theoretical model of a *secure processor with external memory* is exactly the model that Intel has adopted in its new SGX architecture and is one that also fits many cloud computing scenarios where storage is held externally. The introduction of this notion three decades ago, and the proof of feasibility provided back then, informed the applied cryptography and security communities and formed the basis they needed when this concept became of practical interest.

Due to the great importance of the "foundations approach" to the field, Oded did not stop at writing a short essay. Rather, he also distributed widely used lecture notes, and expanded these into the two-volume treatise *Foundations of Cryptography* (published by Cambridge University Press in 2001 and 2004, respectively). This work presented a truly comprehensive "bottom-up" approach, starting from minimal assumptions and working up to construct higher-level primitives and applications. It is important to note that many of the results appearing in the *Foundations of Cryptography* were never fully proven prior to the work (most notably, those in the chapter on secure computation), and thus this involved a monumental effort. In fact, new results were uncovered in this process, including an exact formulation of the sufficient assumptions for obtaining oblivious transfer and noninteractive zero knowledge.

The two volumes of the *Foundations of Cryptography* are the most used books on my bookshelf, and are an absolute necessity in my research. The books also provide students and beginning researchers with the ability to enter the world of theoretical cryptography. I cannot imagine how one would learn the topic of zero knowledge in depth without Chapter 3 of the *Foundations of Cryptography*, and likewise all the other topics covered.

It is therefore most appropriate that, in celebration of Oded's 60th birthday (and 20 years since the publication of that essay), we present a book in his honor that focuses on the foundations of cryptography. The chapters in this book consist of *tutorials* that are inspired by the "foundations of cryptography" approach:

Chapter 1 – Garbled Circuits as Randomized Encodings of Functions: a Primer (Benny Applebaum): Yao's garbled circuit construction is a central cryptographic tool with numerous applications. This chapter reviews garbled circuits from a foundational point of view under the framework of randomized encoding of functions, including positive and negative results and a sample of basic applications.

Chapter 2 – The Complexity of Public-Key Cryptography (Boaz Barak): This chapter surveys what is known (and the many things that are not known) about the computational assumptions that can enable public-key cryptography, and the qualitative differences between these assumptions and those that are known to enable private-key cryptography.

Chapter 3 – Pseudorandom Functions: Three Decades Later (Andrej Bogdanov and Alon Rosen): Pseudorandom functions are an extremely influential abstraction, with applications ranging from message authentication to barriers in proving computational complexity lower bounds. This chapter surveys various incarnations of pseudorandom functions, giving self-contained proofs of key results from the literature.

Chapter 4 – The Many Entropies in One-Way Functions (Iftach Haitner and ˌSalil Vadhan): This chapter introduces two recent computational notions of entropy, shows that they can be easily found in any one-way function, and uses them to present simpler and more efficient constructions of pseudorandom generators and statistically hiding commitments from one-way functions.

Chapter 5 – Homomorphic Encryption (Shai Halevi): Fully homomorphic encryption is a relatively new discovery and has gained much attention. This chapter provides a tutorial on the topic, from definitions and properties, to constructions and applications.

Chapter 6 – How to Simulate It — A Tutorial on the Simulation Proof Technique (Yehuda Lindell): The simulation paradigm is central to cryptographic definitions and proofs. This chapter consists of a systematic tutorial on how simulation-based proofs work, from semantic security through zero knowledge and finally secure computation.

Chapter 7 – The Complexity of Differential Privacy (Salil Vadhan): Differential privacy is a theoretical framework for ensuring the privacy of individual-level data when performing statistical analysis of privacy-sensitive datasets. The goal of this chapter is to convey the deep connections between differential privacy and a variety of other topics in computational complexity, cryptography, and theoretical computer science at large.

Oded has quoted his mother as saying "there are no privileges without duties", and this is a message that Oded has also infused into his students by his personal example. I feel greatly privileged to have had Oded as my Ph.D. advisor, and I am sure that the same is true of all the authors of this book (and many others who Oded has advised and mentored over the years). This privilege indeed comes with duties. We hope that the tutorials in this book are helpful to those who are interested in pursuing the foundations of cryptography approach, and as such will constitute a very small part of the fulfillment of our obligations.

In the name of all the authors of this book, I would like to wish Oded a very happy 60th birthday. There is great happiness in being able to look back at a life full of accomplishments, to see the positive influence that you have had on so many people, and to appreciate the continuing influence your work will have in the future. Happy birthday!

Israel,   *Yehuda Lindell*
April 2017

Contents

Contents

List of Contributors

Benny Applebaum
School of Electrical Engineering, Tel Aviv University, Israel
e-mail: bennyap@post.tau.ac.il

Boaz Barak
School of Engineering and Applied Sciences, Harvard University, USA
e-mail: b@boazbarak.org

Andrej Bogdanov
Department of Computer Science, Chinese University of Hong Kong, China
e-mail: andrejb@cse.cuhk.edu.hk

Iftach Haitner
Department of Computer Science, Tel Aviv University, Israel
e-mail: iftach.haitner@cs.tau.ac.il

Shai Halevi
IBM T.J. Watson Research Center, USA
e-mail: shaih@alum.mit.edu

Yehuda Lindell
Department of Computer Science, Bar-Ilan University, Israel
e-mail: lindell@biu.ac.il

Alon Rosen
School of Computer Science, Herzliya Interdisciplinary Center, Israel
e-mail: alon.rosen@idc.ac.il

Salil Vadhan
School of Engineering and Applied Sciences, Harvard University, USA
e-mail: salil@seas.harvard.edu

Chapter 1
Garbled Circuits as Randomized Encodings of Functions: a Primer*

Benny Applebaum

Abstract Yao's garbled circuit (GC) construction is a central cryptographic tool with numerous applications. In this tutorial, we study garbled circuits from a foundational point of view under the framework of *randomized encoding* (RE) of functions. We review old and new constructions of REs, present some lower bounds, and describe some applications. We also discuss new directions and open problems in the foundations of REs.

1.1 Introduction

Garbled circuits were introduced by Yao (in oral presentations of [86]) as a two-party protocol for secure function evaluation. At the heart of Yao's protocol stands a non-interactive *garbling* technique that became a central tool in the design of constant-round secure computation protocols [86, 21, 43, 80, 66, 75]. Over the years, the garbled circuit technique has found a diverse range of other applications to problems such as computing on encrypted data [84, 35], parallel cryptography [10, 11], verifiable computation [46, 14], software protection [55, 58, 25], functional encryption [83, 56], key-dependent message security [19, 2], code obfuscation [5, 38], and others. Correspondingly, it is currently evident that the *garbling technique* should be treated as a stand-alone abstract object.

The first such abstraction was introduced by Ishai and Kushilevitz [66, 67] under the algebraic framework of *randomizing polynomials*, and was later extended and abstracted under the terminology of *randomized encoding of functions* [10, 11]. In this framework we view garbled circuits as an encoding (or encryption) of a computation. Roughly speaking, we would like to represent a function $f(x)$ by a randomized function $\hat{f}(x; r)$ such that the following hold:

School of Electrical Engineering, Tel-Aviv University, e-mail: bennyap@post.tau.ac.il

* This paper subsumes the short survey [3].

- (Correctness) For every fixed input x and a uniformly random choice of r, the output distribution $\hat{f}(x;r)$ forms a "randomized encoding" of $f(x)$, from which $f(x)$ can be efficiently decoded. Namely, there exists an efficient decoding algorithm Dec, referred to as a *decoder*, such that for every x and r, it holds that $\text{Dec}(\hat{f}(x;r)) = f(x)$. In particular, this means that, if $f(x) \neq f(x')$, then the random variables $\hat{f}(x;r)$ and $\hat{f}(x';r')$, induced by a uniform choice of r and r', should have disjoint supports. (We will later discuss relaxations in which the supports are "almost disjoint" and decoding succeeds for most r's.)
- (Privacy) The distribution of this randomized encoding depends only on the encoded value $f(x)$ and essentially does not reveal further information on x. Namely, there exists an efficient randomized algorithm Sim, referred to as a *simulator*, which, given $f(x)$, samples the distribution $\hat{f}(x;r)$ induced by a random choice of r. Ideally, the simulator's output should be identically distributed to the encoding, but we will also consider variants in which the two distributions are only statistically or computationally close. Note that the privacy requirement implies that, if $f(x) = f(x')$, then the random variables $\hat{f}(x;r)$ and $\hat{f}(x';r')$ are close to each other, or even identical when the simulator is perfect.
- (Efficiency/simplicity) To be useful, the encoding $\hat{f}$ should be "simpler" or more "efficient" than the original function with respect to some measure of complexity.

Observe that privacy can be trivially satisfied by the constant function $\hat{f}(x) = 0$ whereas correctness can be trivially satisfied by the identity function $\hat{f}(x) = x$. However, the combination of privacy and correctness forms a natural relaxation of the usual notion of computing. The last, "efficiency" requirement ensures that this relaxation is nontrivial. As we will later see, the use of randomness is necessary for achieving all three goals. For the sake of concreteness consider the following examples:

Example 1.1.1 (Encoding modular squaring). *Let N be a (public) integer and consider the modular squaring function $f(x) = x^2 \bmod N$. Then, f can be encoded by the function $\hat{f}(x;r) = x^2 + r \cdot N$, where computation is over the integers and r is a random integer in $[0,B]$ for some large integer $B \gg N$. To see that the encoding is correct consider the decoder Dec which, given an integer $\hat{y}$ (supposedly in the image of $\hat{f}$), outputs $\hat{y} \bmod N$. Clearly, $\text{Dec}(\hat{f}(x;r)) = f(x)$ for every x and r. Privacy holds since any pair of inputs x and x' for which $f(x) = f(x') = y$ are mapped to a pair of distributions $\hat{f}(x;r)$ and $\hat{f}(x';r)$ which are (N/B)-statistically close. In particular, given $y = f(x)$, the simulator Sim outputs $y+rN$ for a uniformly chosen $r \xleftarrow{R} [0,B]$. It is not hard to show that the resulting distribution D_y is (N/B)-statistically close to $\hat{f}(x;r)$. Finally, the encoder $\hat{f}$ avoids modular reduction, which in some cases, may be considered an expensive operation.*

Let us briefly explain how Yao's garbled circuit fits into the randomized encoding framework. (Readers who are not familiar with Yao's construction may safely skip the following example; a full and modular description of this construction appears later in Section 1.3.)

Example 1.1.2 (Yao's construction as randomized encoding). *Given a Boolean circuit* $C : \{0,1\}^n \rightarrow \{0,1\}^m$ *and secret randomness* r, *Yao's construction generates a "garbled circuit"* $\hat{C}$ *(which consists of several ciphertexts per logical gate of* C*), together with* n *pairs of "short" keys* (K_i^0, K_i^1), *such that for any (a priori unknown) input* x, *the garbled circuit* $\hat{C}$ *together with the* n *keys* $K_x = (K_1^{x_1}, \ldots, K_n^{x_n})$ *reveal* $C(x)$ *but give no additional information about* x. *Therefore, the mapping* $g : (x; r) \mapsto (\hat{C}, K_x)$ *forms a randomized encoding of the computation* $C(x)$. *The decoder* Dec *takes* $(\hat{C}, K_x)$ *as an input and recovers the value* $C(x)$. *(This is done by gradually decrypting, for each gate of* C, *a ciphertext of* $\hat{C}$, *starting with the input layer for which the keys* K_x *are used for decryption, and ending up in the output layer from which the actual output* $C(x)$ *is recovered.) The construction also admits a simulator which, given* $y = C(x)$, *samples a distribution* Sim(y) *which is computationally indistinguishable from the encoder's distribution* $(\hat{C}, K_x)$. *The encoding satisfies several notions of simplicity. In particular, each output of* g *depends on at most a single bit of* x. *Moreover, most of the output entries (the ones that correspond to the "garbled circuit" part* $\hat{C}$*) depend only on the randomness* r, *and so they can be computed in an "offline phase" before the actual input* x *is known. As we will later see, these efficiency properties are extremely useful for several applications.*

Note that, in the above examples, the saving in efficiency of the encoder has some cost: the decoder itself performs expensive operations (i.e., modular reduction in Example 1.1.1, and, in Example 1.1.2 an evaluation of a garbled version of the circuit C). This is inherent, as the computation $f(x)$ can be written as Dec($\hat{f}(x; r)$) and so we do not expect to simultaneously reduce the complexity of the encoder and decoder, since this would allow us to "speed up" the computation of f. Nevertheless, the ability to decompose the computation into an easy part ($\hat{f}$) and complicated part (Dec), while preserving privacy, can be useful in many cases, as demonstrated by the following example:

Example 1.1.3 (Simple usage scenario). *Imagine a scenario of sending a weak device* U *into the field to perform some expensive computation* f *on sensitive data* x. *The computation is too complex for* U *to quickly perform on its own, and since the input* x *is sensitive,* U *cannot just send the entire input out. Randomized encoding provides a noninteractive solution to this problem:* U *simply sends out a single (randomized) message* $\hat{f}(x; r)$. *The rest of the world can, at this point, recover* $f(x)$ *(by applying the decoder) and nothing else (due to the privacy property). In fact, one could define* RE *as a noninteractive solution to the above problem.*

Remark 1.1.4 (FHE vs. RE). *It is instructive to compare the use of RE in the above scenario (Example 1.1.3) with a solution based on fully homomorphic encryption (FHE) [47]. Using FHE, the client can send an encryption* FHE(x) *to an outside server, which can generate, in turn, the value* FHE($f(x)$). *However, in order to publish* $f(x)$, *another round of interaction is needed, since* U *has to decrypt the output. More generally, the power of RE stems from the ability to reveal* $f(x)$ *to anyone (while hiding* x*).*

This chapter   The abstract framework of randomized encoding (RE) is quite general and can be instantiated in several ways, including computational and information-theoretic variants and different forms of efficiency/simplicity requirements. In this tutorial, we use this framework to study garbled circuits from a foundational point of view. As we will see, the use of a general and abstract framework is beneficial, even if one is interested in concrete forms of REs (e.g., ones that correspond to "standard garbled circuits"). Our presentation emphasizes the properties of REs and the way that basic REs can be combined and manipulated to produce better ones. Naturally, this leaves several important aspects uncovered. Most notably, this includes many useful direct information-theoretic randomization techniques. Such techniques are thoroughly covered in the survey of Ishai [64]. We also focus on asymptotic analysis and leave out the concrete efficiency of REs.

Organization   The rest of this chapter is organized as follows: In Section 1.2, we formally define REs and present their basic properties. A general template for constructing randomized encodings appears in Section 1.3, together with basic feasibility results. Recent constructions of REs which provide better efficiency or stronger security are presented in Section 1.4. Some basic applications of REs are sketched in Section 1.5. Section 1.6 is a summary with suggestions for further reading. A brief comparison of REs with the "garbling scheme" framework of Bellare et al. [26] appears in Section 1.7.

Acknowledgements   This chapter is written in honor of the 60th birthday of Oded Goldreich. As a student, I enthusiastically read Oded's introductory texts and was excited to encounter a combination of the technical with the conceptual (and sometimes even the philosophical). Later, I was fortunate to interact with Oded as an editor, mentor, and friend. In many aspects, my scientific view is rooted in Oded's insightful oral and written discussions. I also thank Yehuda Lindell for initiating this tutorial, and for his useful comments on this manuscript. Finally, I am grateful to Yuval Ishai and Eyal Kushilevitz for introducing me to the notion of randomized encoding and for fruitful and enjoyable collaborations. The author was supported by the European Union's Horizon 2020 Programme (ERC-StG-2014-2020) under grant agreement no. 639813 ERC-CLC, ISF grant 1155/11, and the Check Point Institute for Information Security.

1.2 Definitions and Basic Properties

Notation   For a positive integer $n \in \mathbb{N}$, let $[n]$ denote the set $\{1, \ldots, n\}$. A function $\varepsilon : \mathbb{N} \to [0, 1]$ is negligible if it tends to zero faster than $1/n^c$ for every constant $c > 0$. The term "efficient" refers to probabilistic polynomial time. For a finite set (resp., probability distribution) X, we let $x \xleftarrow{R} X$ denote an element that is sampled uniformly at random from X (resp., according to the distribution X). We let U_n denote the uniform distribution over n-bit strings. The statistical distance between a pair of random variables X and Y over a finite range R is defined by $\frac{1}{2} \sum_{r \in R} |\Pr[X = r] - \Pr[Y = r]|$.

1.2.1 Syntax and Basic Definition

We begin with a formal definition of randomized encoding of functions. In the following let X, Y, Z, and R be finite sets (typically taken to be sets of fixed-length strings).

Definition 1.2.1 (Randomized encoding [10, 11]). *Let $f : X \to Y$ be a function. We say that a function $\hat{f} : X \times R \to Z$ is a δ-correct, (t, ε)-private randomized encoding of f if there exist a pair of randomized algorithms, decoder* Dec *and simulator* Sim, *for which the following hold:*

- *(δ-correctness) For any input $x \in X$,*

$$\Pr_{r \xleftarrow{R} R} [\mathsf{Dec}(\hat{f}(x; r)) \neq f(x)] \leq \delta.$$

- *$((t, \varepsilon)$-privacy) For any $x \in X$ and any circuit[2] $\mathcal{A}$ of size t*

$$\left| \Pr[\mathcal{A}(\mathsf{Sim}(f(x))) = 1] - \Pr_{r \xleftarrow{R} R} [\mathcal{A}(\hat{f}(x; r)) = 1] \right| \leq \varepsilon.$$

We refer to the second input of $\hat{f}$ as its random input, *and a use semicolon (;) to separate deterministic inputs from random inputs. We will sometimes write $\hat{f}(x)$ to denote the random variable $\hat{f}(x; r)$ induced by sampling $r \xleftarrow{R} R$. We refer to $\log |R|$ and $\log |Z|$ as the* randomness complexity *and the* communication complexity *of $\hat{f}$, respectively. By default, we measure the* computational complexity *of $\hat{f}$ by its circuit size.*

Infinite functions and collections Definition 1.2.1 naturally extends to infinite functions $f : \{0, 1\}^* \to \{0, 1\}^*$, and, more generally, to *collections of functions*. Let $\mathcal{F}$ be a collection of functions with an associated representation (by default, a boolean or arithmetic circuit). We say that a class of randomized functions $\hat{\mathcal{F}}$ is a $\delta(n)$-correct, $(t(n), \varepsilon(n))$-private RE of $\mathcal{F}$ if there exists an efficient algorithm (compiler) which gets as an input a function $f : X \to Y$ from $\mathcal{F}$ and outputs (in time polynomial in the representation length $|f|$) three circuits $(\hat{f} \in \hat{\mathcal{F}}, \mathsf{Dec}, \mathsf{Sim})$ which form a $(t(n), \varepsilon(n)$-RE of f where n denotes the input length of f, i.e., $n = \log |X|$.

Remark 1.2.2. *We use n both as an input length parameter and as a cryptographic "security parameter" quantifying computational privacy. When describing some of our constructions, it will be convenient to use a separate parameter k for the latter, where computational privacy will be guaranteed as long as $k = n^\epsilon$ for some constant $\epsilon > 0$.*

---

[2] For simplicity, throughout the chapter we model adversaries as non-uniform circuits. However, all the results presented here also hold in a uniform model where adversaries are modeled as probabilistic polynomial-time Turing machines. A uniform treatment of REs can be found in [11, 15].

Variants   Several variants of randomized encodings have been considered in the literature. Correctness is said to be *perfect* when $\delta = 0$ and *statistical* if $\delta(n)$ is negligible (i.e., $\delta(n) = n^{-\omega(1)}$). We say that the encoding is ε-private if it satisfies (t, ε)-privacy for every t, namely, the simulator output $\mathsf{Sim}(f(x))$ is ε-close in statistical distance to the encoding $\hat{f}(x, U_m)$. Under this convention, *perfect privacy* corresponds to 0-privacy and *statistical privacy* corresponds to $\varepsilon(n)$-privacy for some negligible ε. An encoding is *computationally private* if it is $(t, 1/t)$-private for every polynomial $t(n)$. Throughout this chapter, we mainly focus on *computational encodings* which are both computationally private and perfectly correct. However, we will also mention basic feasibility results regarding *perfect encodings* which achieve perfect correctness and perfect privacy.

1.2.2 Efficiency and Simplicity

So far, the notion of RE can be trivially satisfied by taking $\hat{f} = f$ and letting the simulator and decoder be the identity functions.[3] To make the definition nontrivial, we should impose some efficiency constraint. The most obvious efficiency measure is sequential time; i.e., we would like to encode functions computable by large circuits (or by Turing machines with large time complexity) via relatively small circuits (or fast Turing machines). In addition to sequential time, several other notions of efficiency/simplicity have been considered in the literature. Here we review only a few of them.

Online/offline complexity   We would like to measure separately the complexity of the outputs of $\hat{f}$ which depend solely on r (*offline* part) from the ones which depend on both x and r (*online* part).[4] Without loss of generality, we assume that $\hat{f}$ can be written as $\hat{f}(x; r) = (\hat{f}_{\mathsf{off}}(r), \hat{f}_{\mathsf{on}}(x; r))$, where $\hat{f}_{\mathsf{off}}(r)$ does not depend on x at all. We can therefore split the communication complexity (resp., computational complexity) of $\hat{f}$ into the *online communication complexity* (resp., *online computational complexity*), which corresponds to the online part $\hat{f}_{\mathsf{on}}(x; r)$, and the *offline communication complexity* (resp., *offline computational complexity*), which corresponds to the offline part $\hat{f}_{\mathsf{off}}(r)$.

Efficient online encodings   Let $\hat{\mathcal{F}}$ be an encoding of the collection $\mathcal{F}$. We say that $\hat{\mathcal{F}}$ is *online efficient* if, for every function $f \in \mathcal{F}$, the online computational complexity of the encoding $\hat{f}$ is *independent* of the computational complexity (i.e., circuit size) of the encoded function f (but grows with the bit length of the input of f). We may further require *online universality*, which means that the computation of

---

[3] The omission of efficiency requirements from Definition 1.2.1 is not accidental. We believe that, at a definitional level, it is best to leave such requirements unspecified and adopt appropriate efficiency requirements in an application-dependent context. Moreover, the ability to treat inefficient encodings as "legal REs" turns out to be useful. Indeed, as we will later see, some constructions start with a trivial RE and gradually convert it into a more efficient one.

[4] The online/offline terminology hints towards applications in which f is known ahead of time in an "offline phase", whereas x becomes available only later in an "online phase".

the online part $\hat{f}_{\text{on}}$ corresponds to some universal computation which is independent of the encoded function f. In such a case, we may think of the encoding of $\mathcal{F}$ as being composed of two mappings: One that maps the function $f \in \mathcal{F}$ and the randomness r to $\hat{f}_{\text{off}}(r)$, and one that maps the input x and the randomness r to $\hat{f}_{\text{on}}(x; r)$. (Indeed, this view is taken in [26].) In the context of garbled circuits, $\hat{f}_{\text{off}}(r)$ is typically referred to as the *garbled circuit* part, and $\hat{f}_{\text{on}}(x; r)$ is typically referred to as the garbled input. It is sometimes useful to think of $\hat{f}_{\text{off}}(r)$ as a ciphertext and $\hat{f}_{\text{on}}(x; r)$ as a key K_x that "opens" the ciphertext to the value $f(x)$.

Remark 1.2.3. *The distinction between the online part of the encoding and its offline part naturally gives rise to a stronger form of adaptive privacy in which the adversary may choose the input x based on the offline part of the encoding. This form of security is discussed later, in Section 1.4.5. For now, we use the online/offline terminology only as an efficiency requirement without imposing any additional requirement on privacy; That is, all we require is standard privacy as per Definition 1.2.1.*

Affinity and decomposability Some of the applications of REs further require some form of algebraic simplicity. Assume that the function f is an arithmetic function whose input $x = (x_1, \ldots, x_n)$ is a vector of elements of some ring R. We say that an RE $\hat{f} : \mathsf{R}^n \times \{0, 1\}^m \to \mathsf{R}^s$ of f is an *affine randomized encoding* (ARE) if, for every fixing of the randomness r, the online part of the encoding $\hat{f}_{\text{on}}(x; r)$ becomes an affine function over the ring R, i.e., $\hat{f}_{\text{on}}(x; r) = M_r \cdot x + v_r$, where M_r (resp., v_r) is a matrix (resp., vector) that depends on the randomness r. We say that $\hat{f}$ is a *decomposable* randomized encoding (DRE) if each output of the online part of $\hat{f}$ depends on at most a single input x_i. Namely, $\hat{f}_{\text{on}}(x; r)$ decomposes to $(\hat{f}_1(x_1; r), \ldots, \hat{f}_n(x_n; r))$, where $\hat{f}_i$ may output several ring elements. An RE which is both decomposable and affine is called a DARE. Observe that, in the binary case where $\mathsf{R} = \mathbb{Z}_2$, decomposability implies affinity and so any DRE is also a DARE, although this is not the case for general rings.

Algebraic degree and output locality Affinity and decomposability essentially require simple dependency on x. One can strengthen these notions by also placing restrictions on the way $\hat{f}$ depends on the randomness r. Specifically, one can require that the *algebraic degree* of each output of $\hat{f}(x; r)$, viewed as a polynomial in r and x, will be small (e.g., constant). Similarly, one may require that each output of $\hat{f}(x; r)$ will depend on a constant number of inputs (including the r's), namely that $\hat{f}$ should have constant *output locality*. Over the binary ring $\mathbb{Z}_2$, constant locality implies constant degree (since over the binary ring, polynomials may be assumed to be multilinear).

The necessity of randomness For any of the above notions of simplicity, randomness is necessary in order to obtain a "simple" encoding for a "nonsimple" boolean function. To see this, assume that $f : \{0, 1\}^n \to \{0, 1\}$ has a deterministic encoding $\hat{f} : \{0, 1\}^n \to \{0, 1\}^s$. The privacy of the encoding promises that there exists a pair of strings $y_0, y_1 \in \{0, 1\}^s$ such that, for every $x \in \{0, 1\}^n$, we have $\hat{f}(x) = y_{f(x)}$. Also, by correctness, y_0 and y_1 disagree in some position, say the first. Hence, we can compute $f(x)$ by computing the first bit of $\hat{f}(x)$ or its negation. We conclude that if $\hat{f}$ is simple then so is f, assuming that "simplicity" is closed under projection (which is the case for affinity, decomposability, locality, and degree).[5]

1.2.3 Useful Properties

REs satisfy several natural properties which hold regardless of their efficiency. First, just like in the case of string encodings, if we take an encoding $\hat{f}$ of f, and re-encode it by $\hat{\hat{f}}$, then the resulting encoding also encodes the original function f. Second, an encoding of a tuple $(f_1(x), f_2(x))$ can be obtained by encoding each element of the pair separately and concatenating the result. Finally, given an encoding $\hat{f}(y; r)$ of $f(y)$, we can encode a function of the form $f(g(x))$ by encoding the outer function and substituting y with $g(x)$, i.e., $\hat{f}(g(x); r)$. We summarize these properties via the following lemmas [10]. For simplicity, we restrict our attention to perfectly correct encodings and refer to perfectly correct (t, ε)-private encodings as (t, ε)-encodings.

Lemma 1.2.4 (Composition). *Suppose that $g(x; r_g)$ is a (t_1, ε_1)-encoding of $f(x)$ with decoder Dec_g and simulator Sim_g, and that $h((x, r_g); r_h)$ is a (t_2, ε_2)-encoding of the function $g(x, r_g)$, viewed as a single-argument function, with decoder Dec_h and simulator Sim_h. Then, the function $\hat{f}(x; (r_g, r_h)) = h((x, r_g); r_h)$ together with the decoder $\mathsf{Dec}(\hat{y}) = \mathsf{Dec}_g(\mathsf{Dec}_h(\hat{y}))$ and the simulator $\mathsf{Sim}(y) = \mathsf{Sim}_h(\mathsf{Sim}_g(y))$ forms a $(\min(t_1 - s, t_2), \varepsilon_1 + \varepsilon_2)$-encoding of $f(x)$ where s upper-bounds the circuit complexity of h and its simulator Sim_h.*

Proof: Perfect correctness follows by noting that $\Pr_{r_g, r_h}[\mathsf{Dec}(\hat{f}(x; r_g, r_h)) \neq f(x)]$ is upper-bounded by

$$\Pr_{r_g, r_h}[\mathsf{Dec}(h(x, r_g; r_h)) \neq g(x, r_g)] + \Pr_{r_g}[\mathsf{Dec}(\hat{g}(x; r_g)) \neq f(x)] = 0.$$

To prove privacy, consider a t-size adversary $\mathcal{A}$ which, for some x, distinguishes the distributions $\mathsf{Sim}(f(x))$ from $\hat{f}(x)$ with advantage ε, where $\varepsilon > \varepsilon_1 + \varepsilon_2$ and $t < \min(t_1 - s, t_2)$. We show that we can either violate the privacy of the encoding g or the privacy of the encoding h. Indeed, by considering the "hybrid" distribution $\mathsf{Sim}_h(g(x))$, we can write

---

[5] This argument relies heavily on the fact that f is a boolean function. Indeed, the claim does not hold in the case of non-boolean functions. Suppose, for example, that $f : \{0, 1\}^n \to \{0, 1\}^n$ is a permutation. Then it can be trivially encoded by the identity function. Moreover, if f can be computed and inverted in polynomial time, then the encoding allows efficient decoding and simulation.

$$\varepsilon_1 + \varepsilon_2 < \left| \Pr[\mathcal{A}(\mathsf{Sim}_h(\mathsf{Sim}_g(f(x)))) = 1] - \Pr_{r_g, r_h}[\mathcal{A}(h((x, r_g); r_h)) = 1] \right| \quad (1.1)$$

$$= \left| \Pr[\mathcal{A}(\mathsf{Sim}_h(\mathsf{Sim}_g(f(x)))) = 1] - \Pr_{r_g}[\mathcal{A}(\mathsf{Sim}_h(g(x; r_g))) = 1] \right| \quad (1.2)$$

$$+ \left| \Pr_{r_g}[\mathcal{A}(\mathsf{Sim}_h(g(x; r_g))) = 1] - \Pr_{r_g, r_h}[\mathcal{A}(h((x, r_g); r_h)) = 1] \right|. \quad (1.3)$$

It follows that either (1.2) is larger than ε_1 or (1.3) is larger than ε_2. In the first case, we get, for some fixing of the coins of Sim_h, an adversary $\mathcal{A}(\mathsf{Sim}_h(\cdot))$ of complexity $t + s < t_1$ which violates the privacy of the encoding g. In the second case, there exists an input (x, r_g) for which $\mathcal{A}$ violates the privacy of h. $\blacksquare$

Lemma 1.2.5 (Concatenation). *Suppose that $\hat{f}_i(x; r_i)$ is a (t, ε)-encoding of the function $f_i : \{0, 1\}^n \to \{0, 1\}^{\ell_i}$ with decoder Dec_i and simulator Sim_i for every $i \in [c]$. Then the function $\hat{f}(x; (r_1, \ldots, r_c)) = (\hat{f}_i(x; r_i))_{i=1}^c$ together with the decoder $\mathsf{Dec}(\hat{y}) = (\mathsf{Dec}_i(\hat{y}_i))_{i=1}^c$ and simulator $\mathsf{Sim}(y) = (\mathsf{Sim}_i(y_i))_{i=1}^c$ forms a $(t - cs, c\varepsilon)$-encoding of $f(x) = (f_1(x), \ldots, f_c(x))$ where s is an upper-bound on the complexity of the encodings $\hat{f}_i$.*

Proof: Perfect correctness follows from

$$\Pr_r[\mathsf{Dec}(\hat{f}(x; r)) \neq f(x)] \leq \sum_{i=1}^c \Pr_r[\mathsf{Dec}(\hat{f}_i(x; r_i)) \neq f_i(x)] = 0.$$

Privacy is proved via a standard hybrid argument. Specifically, suppose towards a contradiction, that $\mathcal{A}$ is a $(t - cs)$-size adversary that distinguishes $\hat{f}(x; r)$ from $\mathsf{Sim}(f(x); \rho)$ with advantage $c\varepsilon$. Then, by an averaging argument, for some $j \in \{1, \ldots, c\}$, the adversary $\mathcal{A}$ distinguishes with advantage at least ε between the tuple

$$(\hat{f}_1(x; r_1), \ldots, \hat{f}_{j-1}(x; r_{j-1}), \mathsf{Sim}_j(f_j(x)), \ldots, \mathsf{Sim}_c(f_c(x)))$$

and the tuple

$$(\hat{f}_1(x; r_1), \ldots, \hat{f}_j(x; r_j), \mathsf{Sim}_{j+1}(f_j(x)), \ldots, \mathsf{Sim}_c(f_c(x))).$$

By an averaging argument, $\mathcal{A}$ distinguishes with advantage at least ε between $(w, \mathsf{Sim}_j(f_j(x)), z)$ and $(w, \hat{f}_j(x; r_j), z)$ for some fixing $w = (w_1, \ldots, w_{j-1})$ and $z = (z_{j+1} \ldots z_c)$. Let $\mathcal{B}$ be an adversary that, given a challenge $\hat{y}_j$, calls $\mathcal{A}$ on the input $(w, \hat{y}_j, z)$ and outputs the result. The adversary $\mathcal{B}$ can be implemented by a t-size circuit and it distinguishes $\hat{f}_j(x; r_j)$ from $\mathsf{Sim}_j(f_j(x))$ with advantage ε, in contradiction to our hypothesis. $\blacksquare$

Lemma 1.2.6 (Substitution). *Suppose that the function $\hat{f}(x; r)$ is a (t, ε)-encoding of $f(x)$ with decoder Dec and simulator Sim. Let $h(z)$ be a function of the form $f(g(z))$ where $z \in \{0, 1\}^k$ and $g : \{0, 1\}^k \to \{0, 1\}^n$. Then, the function $\hat{h}(z; r) = \hat{f}(g(z); r)$ is a (t, ε)-encoding of h with the same simulator and the same decoder.*

Proof: Follows immediately from the definition. For correctness we have that, for all z,

$$\Pr_r[\mathsf{Dec}(\hat{h}(z;r)) \neq h(z)] = \Pr_r[\mathsf{Dec}(\hat{f}(g(z);r)) \neq f(g(z))] = 0,$$

and for privacy we have that, for all z, the distribution $\mathsf{Sim}(h(z)) = \mathsf{Sim}(f(g(z)))$ cannot be distinguished from the distribution $\hat{f}(g(z)) = \hat{h}(z)$ with advantage better than ε by any t-size adversary. ∎

Remark 1.2.7 (Composition, concatenation, and substitution with constructive simulators/decoders). *Observe that, in all the above cases, the simulator and the decoder of the new encoding can be derived in a straightforward way based on the original simulators and decoders.*

Remark 1.2.8 (The efficiency of simulation). *In the composition lemma, the loss in security depends, in part, on the complexity of the simulator. Typically, the latter is roughly the same as the complexity of the encoding itself. Indeed, a natural way to define a simulator $\mathsf{Sim}(y)$ is to sample an encoding $\hat{f}(x_y)$ where x_y is some fixed canonical preimage of y under f. The complexity of such a simulator is the same as the complexity of the encoding plus the cost of finding x_y given y. In fact, it is not hard to see that, if $\hat{f}$ is a (t,ε)-private encoding with some simulator Sim', then the canonical simulator defined above is $(t,2\varepsilon)$-private. Of course, in some cases, the canonical simulator may not be efficiently computable, since it may be hard to find a canonical input x_y for some y's (e.g., when f is a one-way permutation).*

1.3 Feasibility Results

In this section we present basic feasibility results regarding the existence of DARE for several rich function classes. We present these constructions via the unified framework of [15].

1.3.1 Perfect DARE for Finite Functions

As a warmup, we consider several examples of DARE for finite functions. (The examples apply to any finite ring.)

Example 1.3.1 (Addition). *The addition function $f(x_1, x_2) = x_1 + x_2$ over some finite ring R is perfectly encoded by the DARE*

$$\hat{f}(x_1, x_2; r) = (x_1 + r, x_2 - r).$$

Indeed, decoding is performed by summing up the two components of the encoding, and simulation is done by sampling a random pair whose sum equals to $y = f(x_1, x_2)$.

Example 1.3.2 (Multiplication). *The product function $f(x_1, x_2) = x_1 \cdot x_2$ over a ring R is perfectly encoded by the ARE*

$$g(x_1, x_2; r_1, r_2) = (x_1 + r_1, x_2 + r_2, r_2 x_1 + r_1 x_2 + r_1 r_2).$$

Indeed, given an encoding (c_1, c_2, c_3), *we can recover* $f(x)$ *by computing* $c_1 \cdot c_2 - c_3$.
Also, perfect privacy holds, since the triple (c_1, c_2, c_3) *is uniform subject to the correctness constraint. Hence, the simulator* $\mathrm{Sim}(y; c_1, c_2) := (c_1, c_2, c_1 c_2 - y)$ *perfectly simulates g. Observe that the above encoding is affine but not decomposable (the last entry depends on both* x_1 *and* x_2). *We can derive a DARE by viewing the last entry* $g_3(x, r) = (r_2 x_1) + (r_1 x_2 + r_1 r_2)$ *as a deterministic function in x and r and re-encoding it via the DARE for addition (Example 1.3.1):*

$$\hat{g}_3(x, r; s) = (r_2 x_1 + s, r_1 x_2 + r_1 r_2 - s).$$

By the concatenation lemma, the function $\hat{g}(x, r; s) = (g_1(x, r), g_2(x, r), \hat{g}_3(x; r))$ *perfectly encodes* $g(x, r)$, *and therefore, by the composition lemma,* $\hat{g}(x; r, s)$ *perfectly encodes* $f(x)$.

Using similar ideas, it can be shown that any polynomial f over a ring R can be encoded by a perfect DARE (whose complexity may be large). In the next section, we show how to achieve complexity which is polynomial in the formula size of f. For this, it will be useful to record the following concrete DARE for the function $x_1 x_2 + x_3$ (MUL-ADD).

Fact 1.3.3 (DARE for MUL-ADD [15]) *The function* $f(x_1, x_2, x_3) = x_1 x_2 + x_3$ *over a finite ring R is perfectly encoded by the DARE* $\hat{f}(x_1, x_2, x_3; r_1, r_2, r_3, r_4)$ *defined by*

$$\left(x_1 \begin{bmatrix} 1 \\ r_2 \end{bmatrix} + \begin{bmatrix} -r_1 \\ -r_1 r_2 + r_3 \end{bmatrix}, \quad x_2 \begin{bmatrix} 1 \\ r_1 \end{bmatrix} + \begin{bmatrix} -r_2 \\ r_4 \end{bmatrix}, \quad x_3 - r_3 - r_4 \right),$$

where r_1, r_2, r_3, r_4 *are random and independent ring elements.*

1.3.2 Perfect DARE for Formulas

Our goal in this section is to construct perfect DARE for arithmetic circuits with logarithmic depth (i.e., formulas). An arithmetic circuit over a ring R is defined similarly to a standard boolean circuit, except that each wire carries an element of R and each gate can perform an addition or multiplication operation over R. We prove the following theorem:

Theorem 1.3.4. *There exists a perfect DARE for the class of arithmetic circuits with logarithmic depth over an arbitrary ring.*[6]

We mention that a stronger version of the theorem (cf. [67, 40, 10]) provides perfect DAREs for arithmetic branching programs over an arbitrary ring. The latter class is believed to be computationally richer than the class of logarithmic-depth arithmetic circuits, and therefore, as a feasibility result, the branching program-based encoding

---

[6] Recall that, by default, a statement like this always means that the encoding is efficiently constructible as defined in Section 1.2.

subsumes the one from Theorem 1.3.4.[7] The existence of efficient perfect or statistical DARE for general polynomial-size circuits, or even for circuits with, say, $\log^2 n$ depth, is wide open.

Proof: [Proof of Theorem 1.3.4] Let C be an arithmetic circuit over a ring R. Instead of individually considering each wire and gate of C (as in Yao's classical garbled circuit construction), we build the encoder by processing one *layer* at a time. For simplicity, we assume that C is already given in a layered form; That is, $C(x) = B_1 \circ B_2 \circ \cdots \circ B_h(x)$, where each B_i is a depth-1 circuit. We further assume that each gate has a bounded fan-out, say of 2. (For circuits of logarithmic depth, such a restriction can be forced with overhead polynomial in the size while keeping the depth logarithmic.) We denote by y^i (values of) variables corresponding to the input wires of layer B_i; That is, $y^i = B_{i+1} \circ \cdots \circ B_h(x)$, where $y^0 = C(x)$ and $y^h = x$. We denote by C^i the function mapping y^i to the output of C; that is, $C^i(y^i) = B_1 \circ \ldots \circ B_i(y^i)$, where $C^0(y^0)$ is the identity function on the outputs.

We build the encoding Enc in an iterative fashion, processing the layers of C from top (outputs) to bottom (inputs). We start with a trivial encoding of the identity function C^0. In iteration i, $i = 1, 2, \ldots, h$, we transform a DARE for $C^{i-1}(y^{i-1})$ into a DARE for $C^i(y^i)$ by first *substituting* $B_i(y^i)$ into y^{i-1}, and then re-encoding the resulting function to bring it into a *decomposable affine form*. The affinization step is performed by adding new random inputs and has the effect of increasing the size of the online part.

Formally, the DARE compiler is described in Figure 1.1. As explained in Figure 1.1, Lemmas 1.2.4, 1.2.5, and 1.2.6 guarantee that, in the i-th iteration, the compiler generates a decomposable affine encoding $\text{Enc}^i(y^i)$ of $C^i(y^i)$, and so, at the final iteration, we derive a DARE for $C^h = C$. Observe that the computational complexity of Enc^i (and, in particular, the length of its online part) is larger by a constant factor than the complexity of Enc^{i-1}. More precisely, the online part grows by a factor of at most twice the fan-out of B_i. Hence, the encoding can be generated in polynomial time as long as the encoded circuit has logarithmic depth. Circuits for the simulator and decoder can be generated with similar complexity due to the constructive nature of the substitution, composition, and concatenation lemmas (see Remark 1.2.7). This completes the proof of the theorem. ∎

Example 1.3.5. *Let us apply the DARE compiler (Figure 1.1) to the formula $ab + cd$ depicted in Figure 1.2. The initial trivial encoding is simply y^0. Then, substitution yields $y_1^1 + y_2^1$, which after affinization becomes $(y_1^1 + r_0, y_2^1 - r_0)$. Another substitution results in the encoding $(x_1 x_2 + r_0, x_3 x_4 - r_0)$. After an additional affinization, we get the final encoding $\hat{f}(x_1, x_2, x_3, x_4; (r_0, r_1, r_2, r_3, r_4, r_1', r_2', r_3', r_4'))$ defined by*

$$x_1 \begin{bmatrix} 1 \\ r_2 \end{bmatrix} + \begin{bmatrix} -r_1 \\ -r_1 r_2 + r_3 \end{bmatrix}, x_2 \begin{bmatrix} 1 \\ r_1 \end{bmatrix} + \begin{bmatrix} -r_2 \\ r_4 \end{bmatrix}, x_3 \begin{bmatrix} 1 \\ r_2' \end{bmatrix} + \begin{bmatrix} -r_1' \\ -r_1' r_2' + r_3' \end{bmatrix}, x_4 \begin{bmatrix} 1 \\ r_1' \end{bmatrix} + \begin{bmatrix} -r_2' \\ r_4' \end{bmatrix}, \begin{bmatrix} r_0 - r_3 - r_4 \\ -r_0 - r_3' - r_4' \end{bmatrix}.$$

---

[7] Arithmetic branching programs can emulate arithmetic circuits of logarithmic depth with only polynomial overhead, whereas the converse is believed to be false (this is equivalent to separating log-space computation from $\mathbf{NC}^1$).

1. Let $\mathsf{Enc}^0(y^0) = y^0$ be the identity function on the variables y^0 (one variable for each output of C).
2. For $i = 1, 2, \ldots, h$, obtain an encoding $\mathsf{Enc}^i(y^i)$ of $C^i(y^i)$ from an encoding $\mathsf{Enc}^{i-1}(y^{i-1})$ of $C^{i-1}(y^{i-1})$ using the following two steps:

   a. **Substitution.** Let $F(y^i) = \mathsf{Enc}^{i-1}(B_i(y^i))$.
      The substitution lemma (1.2.6) guarantees that, if Enc^{i-1} encodes C^{i-1}, then F encodes C^i. Assuming that Enc^{i-1} is a DARE, each output of F can be written as

      $$Q_* = a * (y_\ell^i * y_r^i) + b \quad \text{or as} \quad Q_+ = a * (y_\ell^i + y_r^i) + b,$$

      where a and b depend on the randomness and ℓ and r are some indices of gates in the i-th layer. This means that F is not decomposable anymore, since each of the resulting outputs depends on a pair of input variables of C^i. Moreover, if the i-th layer contains a multiplication gate, then F is also not affine (since Q_* contains a product of two input variables of C^i).

   b. **Affinization.** Turn F into a decomposable affine encoder Enc^i of the same function by applying to each output that depends on two inputs y_j^i a perfect DARE. Here we rely on the fact that the above expressions (Q_+ and Q_*) are finite and thus have a constant-size DARE. Concretely, the term Q_* can be handled by applying the basic gadget of Fact 1.3.3 to $Q_* = z * y_r^i + b$ and substituting ay_ℓ^i into z. The resulting encoding of Q_* can be written in the form $\hat{Q}_* = (a'_\ell y_\ell^i + b'_\ell, a'_r y_r^i + b'_r, w)$, where a'_i, b'_i, w are vectors in $\mathbb{R}^2$ that depend only on random inputs. Similarly, we can handle Q_+ by rewriting it as $Q_+ = z_1 + z_2$, where $z_1 = a * y_\ell^i$ and $z_2 = a * y_r^i + b$, and then applying the encoding for addition (Example 1.3.1), leading to a DARE of the form $(a * y_\ell^i + b', a * y_r^i + b'')$, where $a, b, b'' \in \mathbb{R}$. Applying this transformation to every term Q in the output of F and concatenating different affine functions of the same input, we get, by the concatenation and composition lemmas (1.2.5, 1.2.4), decomposable affine encoding Enc^i of C^i.

3. Output the arithmetic circuit computing $\mathsf{Enc}(x) = \mathsf{Enc}^h(x)$.

Fig. 1.1: DARE compiler for arithmetic circuits of logarithmic depth. For simplicity, we treat encoders as probabilistic circuits and omit their random inputs from the notation

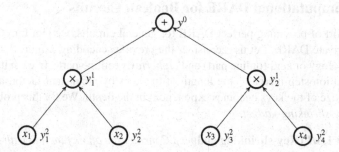

Fig. 1.2: An arithmetic formula computing the function $x_1 x_2 + x_3 x_4$

1.3.3 Generalization: "Simple" Encodings for Formulas

The proof of Theorem 1.3.4 provides a general template for constructing "simple" encodings. Formally, consider a class Simple of single-output (possibly randomized) functions defined over some ring R. Call an encoding $\hat{f}$ *simple* if each of its outputs is computed by a function in Simple.

Theorem 1.3.6 (Simple encodings for formulas (meta-theorem)). *Suppose that the class Simple satisfies the following conditions:*

- Simple *contains the identity function $f(x) = x$.*
- *There exists a simple DARE $\hat{g}$ for every function g obtained by taking some function $f(x; r) \in$ Simple and substituting a deterministic input x_i by the expression $y \diamond z$, where y and z are deterministic inputs and $\diamond \in \{+, *\}$ is a ring operation. Moreover, the circuit complexity of $\hat{g}$ is at most c times larger than the complexity of f for some universal constant c.*

Then, any depth-d arithmetic circuit $C : R^n \to R^\ell$ has a simple perfect encoding of complexity at most ℓc^d.

Theorem 1.3.4 can be derived from Theorem 1.3.6. Indeed, the notion of DARE corresponds to the case where Simple is the class of randomized functions with a single deterministic input x and (possibly many) random inputs r of the form $f(x; r) = x * g(r) + h(r)$, where g and h are arbitrary.

The proof of Theorem 1.3.6 follows the outline of Theorem 1.3.4 except that the affinization gadget is replaced with a simple encoding of $f(x \diamond y)$ (for appropriate f and $\diamond$). The details are left for the reader. We further mention that one can state a more general result by considering circuits over an arbitrary basis $G = \{g\}$, assuming that $f(g(x_1, \ldots))$ admits a simple encoding for every $f \in$ Simple and every $g \in G$. In some cases, this version leads to better concrete efficiency then the current "gate-by-gate" approach.

1.3.4 Computational DARE for Boolean Circuits

Falling short of providing perfect DARE for general circuits, we aim for computationally private DARE. Let us reconsider the previous encoding (Figure 1.1) under the terminology of *keys* (online part) and *ciphertexts* (offline part). In each iteration, the affinization step increases the length of the keys by a constant factor, and as a result the size of the keys becomes exponential in the depth. We fix this problem by using a *key-shrinking gadget*.

Definition 1.3.7 (Key-shrinking gadget). *Consider the affine function with $4k$-long keys over the ring R*
$$f(y, c, d) = yc + d, \qquad y \in R, c, d \in R^{4k}.$$

A key-shrinking gadget *is a computational encoding $\hat{f}$ for f with shorter keys of length k of the form*
$$\hat{f}(y, c, d; r) = (ya + b, W) \qquad y \in R, a, b \in R^k,$$

where a, b, and W may depend on c, d and on the internal randomness of $\hat{f}$ but not on y.

Remark 1.3.8. *The concrete shrinkage factor (4k to k) is somewhat arbitrary. Indeed, it is possible to turn a key-shrinking gadget with minimal shrinkage (k + 1 to k) into a key-shrinking gadget with arbitrary polynomial shrinkage (k^c to k for any constant c > 0) by re-encoding the gadget polynomially many times and applying the composition lemma (1.2.4).*

Given such a gadget, we can fix the key-blowup problem of the previous encoding. First, rearrange the affine encoding obtained from the affinization step terms into blocks (grouping together outputs that depend on the same variable), and then apply the key-shrinking gadget to each output block. As a result, the size of the keys is reduced at the cost of generating additional outputs that do not depend on the inputs and thus can be accumulated in the offline part (as a ciphertext). See Figure 1.3 for a formal description. Again, correctness and privacy follow easily (and modularly) from the substitution, concatenation, and composition properties of randomized encodings (see Section 1.2.3).

---

1. Let $\mathsf{Enc}^0(y^0) = y^0$ be the identity function on the variables y^0 (one variable for each output of C).
2. For $i = 1, 2, \ldots, h$, obtain an encoding $\mathsf{Enc}^i(y^i)$ of $C^i(y^i)$ from an encoding $\mathsf{Enc}^{i-1}(y^{i-1})$ of $C^{i-1}(y^{i-1})$ using the following three steps:

   a. **Substitution.** Let $F(y^i) = \mathsf{Enc}^{i-1}(B_i(y^i))$.
   b. **Affinization.** Turn F into a decomposable affine encoder G^i of the same function by applying to each output that depends on two inputs y^i_j a perfect DARE. (See affinization step in Figure 1.1.)
   c. **Key shrinkage.** To avoid the exponential blowup of keys, the compiler applies the key-shrinking gadget. Partition G^i to $(G^i_1, \ldots, G^i_\ell)$, where $G^i_j = c_j y^i_j + d_j$ is an affine function in the variable y^i_j and ℓ is the number of gates in the i-th level. For every G^i_j whose length is larger than k, the key-shrinking gadget is applied to bring it to the form $(W, a_j y^i_j + b_j)$, where $a_j \in \mathsf{R}^k$, $b_j \in \mathsf{R}^k$, and a_j, b_j, W depend only on random inputs. The W entries are aggregated in the offline part of the encoding. Let $\mathsf{Enc}^i(y^i)$ be the decomposable affine encoding resulting from this step.

3. Output the arithmetic circuit computing $\mathsf{Enc}(x) = \mathsf{Enc}^h(x)$.

Fig. 1.3: Encoding arithmetic circuits via key-shrinking gadget. Think of k as a security parameter which is set it to some polynomial in the input length n. We assume, without loss of generality, that the circuit has fan-out of two

Lemma 1.3.9. *Assume that the key-shrinking gadget is (t, ε)-private and can be computed and simulated by a circuit of size s. Then, the compiler from Figure 1.3 constructs a perfectly correct $(t - |C|s, |C|\varepsilon)$-private DARE for the circuit C with online complexity kn and offline complexity of at most $s|C|$, where n is the input length of C.*

Proof: For brevity, we refer to a perfectly correct (t,ε)-private encoding with on-line complexity of k and offline complexity of m as a (t,ε,k,m)-encoding. Keeping the notation from Theorem 1.3.4, we prove that, in the i-th iteration, the compiler generates a $(t_i,\varepsilon_i,k\ell_i,m_i)$-DARE $\mathsf{Enc}^i(y^i)$ of $C^i(y^i)$, where $t_i = t - s|C^i|$, $\varepsilon_i = \varepsilon|C^i|$, $m_i = s|C^i|$, and ℓ_i denotes the input length of C^i (which is the number of gates in the i-th layer of the circuit C).

The proof is by induction on i. Observe that the claim is trivial for $i = 0$. Let us assume that the claim holds for the $i - 1$ iteration. As in the proof of Theorem 1.3.4, Lemmas 1.2.4, 1.2.5, and 1.2.6 guarantee that the function G^i is a $(t_{i-1},\varepsilon_{i-1},4k\ell_i,m_{i-1})$-DARE of $C^i(y^i)$. Indeed, recall that affinization increases the online complexity by a factor of two (and does not affect the offline complexity). Since the fan-out is assumed to be two, this leads to a total factor of 4 in the online complexity. The key-shrinking gadget provides a (t,ε,k,s) affine encoding for G^i_j (for every $j \in [\ell_i]$). Therefore, by Lemma 1.2.5, the concatenation of these encodings $\mathsf{Enc}^i(y^i)$ is a $(t - \ell_i s, \ell_i\varepsilon, k\ell_i, s\ell_i)$-encoding of G^i. Finally, by the composition lemma (1.2.4), $\mathsf{Enc}^i(y^i)$ is a $(t_i - \ell_i s, \varepsilon_i + \ell_i\varepsilon, k\ell_i, m_{i-1} + s\ell_i)$-DARE of $C^i(y^i)$, as required. ∎

As in Theorem 1.3.4, the compiler implicitly defines a simulator and decoder of complexity $\mathrm{poly}(|C|, s)$ using the constructive version of the substitution, composition, and concatenation lemmas mentioned in Remark 1.2.7.

Shrinking the keys in the binary case Lemma 1.3.9 reduces the construction of DARE compilers to an implementation of the key-shrinking gadget. In the binary case, this can be done quite easily with the help of a standard symmetric encryption scheme. First, observe that, in the binary setting, an affine function $ya + b$ in y operates as a "selection" function which outputs b if $y = 0$, and $a+b$ if $y = 1$. Hence, in order to implement the key-shrinking gadget, we need to encode the selection function

$$\mathrm{Sel}(y, M_0, M_1) := M_y, \qquad \text{where } y \in \{0,1\}, M_0, M_1 \in \{0,1\}^n$$

with n-long vectors (M_0, M_1) by a selection function with shorter vectors (K_0, K_1) (and, possibly, an offline part). Let us start with a slightly easier task and try to encode a variant of the selection function which leaks the "selection bit" y, i.e.,

$$\mathrm{Sel}'(y, M_0, M_1) := (y, M_y).$$

A simple way to implement such an encoding is to employ symmetric encryption, where M_0 is encrypted under the random key K_0 and M_1 under the random key K_1. Formally, we prove the following claim:

Claim 1.3.10. *Let* (E, D) *be a perfectly correct one-time semantically secure symmetric encryption with key length k and message length n. Then, the function*

$$g'(y, M_0, M_1; (K_0, K_1)) = (\mathrm{Sel}'(y, K_0, K_1), \mathsf{E}_{K_0}(M_0), \mathsf{E}_{K_1}(M_1))$$

is a computational DARE for $\mathrm{Sel}'(y, M_0, M_1)$.

Proof: [Sketch] Given the encoding (y, K_y, C_0, C_1), we can decode M_y by applying the decryption algorithm to C_y. The simulator takes (y, M_y) as input, samples a pair of random keys K_0 and K_1, and outputs (y, K_y, C_0, C_1), where $C_y = \mathsf{E}_{K_y}(M_y)$ and $C_{1-y} = \mathsf{E}_{K_y}(0^n)$. It is not hard to show that the simulator's output is computationally indistinguishable from the distribution of the real encoding based on the semantic security of the encryption. ∎

We move on to encode the selection function Sel. For this we have to hide the value of y. One way to achieve this is to remove y from the output of the previous encoding and to randomly permute the order of the ciphertexts C_0 and C_1. The resulting function privately encodes Sel, however, to guarantee correctness we have to assume that the encryption is verifiable (i.e., decryption with an incorrect key can be identified). This variant of the encoding typically leads to a statistically small decoding error (as in the garbled circuit variant of [76]). A perfectly correct solution can be achieved by releasing a "pointer" to the correct ciphertext. (This version corresponds to the garbled circuit variant in [21, 80, 11].) More abstractly, observe that the input to $\mathrm{Sel}(y, M_0, M_1)$ can be randomized to

$$y' = y + r, \quad M_0' = (1 - r) \cdot M_0 + r \cdot M_1, \quad \text{and} \quad M_1' = r \cdot M_0 + (1 - r) \cdot M_1,$$

where the random bit r is treated as a scalar over $\mathbb{Z}_2$, and M_0 and M_1 as vectors over $\mathbb{Z}_2^n$. This means that $\mathrm{Sel}(y, M_0, M_1)$ can be encoded by $\mathrm{Sel}'(y', M_0', M_1')$ (since y' can be released). We can now re-encode $\mathrm{Sel}'(y', M_0', M_1')$ via Claim 1.3.10, and derive an encoding $g(y, M_0, M_1; (r, K_0, K_1))$ for the Sel function whose polynomial representation is

$$(y + r, (1 - (y + r))K_0 + (y + r)K_1, \mathsf{E}_{K_0}((1 - r)M_0 + rM_1), \mathsf{E}_{K_1}(rM_0 + (1 - r)M_1)).$$

It is not hard to see that g satisfies the syntactic requirements of Definition 1.3.7. We therefore obtain a key-shrinking gadget based on a semantically secure encryption scheme. Since the latter can be based on any one-way function, we derive the following corollary (Yao's theorem):

Theorem 1.3.11. *Assuming the existence of one-way functions, there exists an online-efficient DARE for the class of polynomial-size boolean circuits.*

The above encoding provides a modular and, arguably, conceptually simpler derivation of Yao's original result for boolean circuits.

1.3.5 Computational DARE for Arithmetic Circuits

We would like to obtain online-efficient DARE for *arithmetic* circuits. Since arithmetic computations arise in many real-life scenarios, this question has a natural motivation in the context of most of the applications of garbled circuits (to be discussed in Section 1.5). Clearly, one can always encode an arithmetic function $f : \mathsf{R}^n \to \mathsf{R}^\ell$ by implementing an equivalent boolean circuit f' (replacing each R-operation by a corresponding boolean subcircuit) and applying a boolean encoding to the result.

This approach suffers from an overhead which depends on the boolean complexity of ring operations (which may be too high), and requires access to the *bits* of the inputs, which may not be accessible in some scenarios.[8] Instead, we would like to obtain an arithmetic encoding which treats the elements as *atomic* values and manipulates them only via *ring operations* just like the arithmetic encoding of Theorem 1.3.4 for the case of logarithmic-depth arithmetic circuits (i.e., formulas).

Observe that the encoding presented in Figure 1.3 reduces the problem of constructing arithmetic ARE to the construction of an arithmetic key-shrinking gadget, since all other components "arithmetize". Over a large ring, the key-shrinking gadget essentially implements a symmetric encryption scheme with special homomorphic properties that applies both to the keys and to data. Indeed, we can view the offline part of the key-shrinking gadget as an encryption of the long keys $c, d \in \mathsf{R}^n$ under the short keys $a, b \in \mathsf{R}^k$ with the property that the linear combination of the keys $ay + b$ allows one to decrypt the linear combination of the plaintexts $cy + d$ (and hides any other information). Such a gadget was (approximately) implemented over bounded-size integers by [15], leading to the following theorem:

Theorem 1.3.12 (Informal). *Assuming the hardness of the Learning with Errors problem, there exists an efficient compiler that, given an arithmetic circuit $f : \mathbb{Z}^n \to \mathbb{Z}^\ell$ over the integers and a positive integer U bounding the value of circuit wires, outputs (in time polynomial in the size of f and in the binary representation of U) an arithmetic circuit $\hat{f}$ (over the integers) which forms an online-efficient DARE of f.*

We mention that [15] also provide an alternative (less efficient) construction of arithmetic garbled circuits over the integers based on one-way functions.

Mod-p arithmetic encodings   The task of encoding circuits over $\mathbb{Z}_p$ can be reduced to encoding circuits over the integers (e.g., by applying the encoding in Example 1.1.1). The reduction is efficient but "nonarithmetic" since it treats the elements of $\mathbb{Z}_p$ as integers (as opposed to abstract ring elements of $\mathbb{Z}_p$). It would be interesting to obtain a *fully arithmetic encoder* which treats the ring $\mathbb{Z}_p$ in a fully black-box way.[9] We ask:

> Is there an efficient compiler that takes an arithmetic circuit $f : \mathsf{R}^n \to \mathsf{R}^\ell$ which treats the ring in an abstract way and generates an arithmetic circuit $\hat{f}$ over R such that, for any concrete (efficiently implementable) ring R, the function $\hat{f}$ forms an online-efficient ARE of f?

This question is open even for the special case of prime-order fields $\mathbb{Z}_p$. It was recently shown in [8] that, if the decoder is also required to be fully arithmetic (as

[8] E.g., when the input ring elements are encrypted under some cryptographic scheme that supports some limited form of ring operations.

[9] Formally, one should define a set of legal operations (gates) which are available for the encoder. A natural choice is to allow field operations (addition, subtraction, multiplication, and possibly division and zero-checking), access to the constants $\{0, 1\}$, and some form of randomization gate, say allowing to sample random field elements and a random $\{0, 1\}$ elements.

achieved by Theorem 1.3.4 for formulas), then the online complexity must grow with the output length of f and so it is impossible to achieve *online efficiency*. This limitation applies even to the simpler case of prime-order fields $\mathbb{Z}_p$. Extending this impossibility result to single-output functions remains an interesting open problem.

1.4 Advanced Constructions

Having established the feasibility of online-efficient DARE, we move on to study their complexity. In Section 1.4.1, we minimize the parallel-time complexity of the encoding, and in Section 1.4.2, we minimize the online communication complexity. The computational complexity of REs is amortized in Section 1.4.3 by reusing the offline part of REs over many invocations. Then, in Section 1.4.4, we study the possibility of reducing the total complexity even in a single invocation. We end with a discussion on adaptively secure REs (Section 1.4.5).

1.4.1 Minimizing the Parallel Complexity

In this section, we show that any efficiently computable function admits an encoding with constant *locality*; i.e., each of its outputs depends on a constant number of inputs (counting both deterministic and random inputs). Such an encoding can be computed by a constant-depth circuit with bounded fan-in gates (also known as an $\mathbf{NC}^0$ circuit), and so it captures a strong form of constant-parallel-time computation.

We begin with the following theorem from [10]:

Theorem 1.4.1 ($\mathbf{NC}^0$ RE for branching programs). *There exists a perfect degree-3 DARE in which each output depends on four inputs for the class of arithmetic branching programs over an arbitrary ring.*

The theorem is based on a direct randomization technique for branching programs from [67, 40]. Below, we sketch a proof for a weaker version of the theorem that applies to arithmetic circuits of logarithmic depth ($\mathbf{NC}^1$ circuits).

Proof: [Proof of Theorem 1.4.1 restricted to $\mathbf{NC}^1$ functions] We rely on the metatheorem for encoding logarithmic-depth circuits (Theorem 1.3.6). Let Simple denote the class of randomized functions of the form $\{abc + d, b + c + d\}$ where a can be a deterministic or a random input, and b, c, d are either random inputs (possibly with a minus sign) or ring constants. Recall that an encoding $\hat{f}$ is simple if, for every output i, the function that computes the i-th output of $\hat{f}$ is a function in Simple. By Theorem 1.3.6, it suffices to present a perfect simple DARE of finite complexity for the function $Q_+ = (x + y)bc + d$ and for the function $Q_* = (x * y)bc + d$ where x and y are deterministic inputs. (Note that only a is allowed to be a deterministic input, and so we do not have to consider the case where one of the other variables is substituted.)

Indeed, for the case of addition, the function Q_+ can be written as $X + Y$ where $X = xbc + d$ and $Y = ybc$. By applying the encoding for addition (Example 1.3.1), we derive the encoding $(xbc + d + r, ybc - r)$. The first item can be viewed as $X + Y$

where $X = xbc$ and $Y = d + r$, and so, by re-encoding it again, we get the encoding $(xbc + r', d + r - r', ybc - r)$, which is simple.

We move on to the case of multiplication. For simplicity, assume that the ring is commutative. (The more general case can also be treated with slightly more work.) The function Q_* can then be written as $XY + d$ where $X = xbc$ and $Y = ybc$. By applying the MUL-ADD encoding (Fact 1.3.3), we derive an encoding which is simple except for one output of the form $r_0 xb + r_1 r_2 + r_3$. The latter can be brought to simple form via double use of the addition encoding (Example 1.3.1). ∎

In [11] it was shown how to extend the above theorem to the case of polynomial-size circuits. Formally,

Theorem 1.4.2 (NC^0-RE for circuits). *Assuming the existence of one-way functions computable by circuits of logarithmic depth (NC^1), the class of polynomial-size boolean circuits admits an online-efficient DARE of degree 3 and locality 4.*

Proof: [Proof idea] First observe that it suffices to encode a polynomial-size boolean circuit f by an NC^1-computable encoding g. Indeed, given such an encoding, we can apply Theorem 1.4.1 to re-encode the encoding g by an NC^0 encoding $\hat{g}$ and derive (by the composition lemma) an NC^0 encoding for f.

The second observation is that the DARE from Theorem 1.3.11 (Yao's theorem) can be computed by an NC^1 circuit, assuming that the key-shrinking gadget is computable in NC^1. Hence, it suffices to implement the key-shrinking gadget in NC^1. Such an implementation is given in [11] based on the existence of NC^1-computable pseudorandom generators (PRGs) with minimal stretch (i.e., ones that stretch a k-bit seed into a $k + 1$ pseudorandom string). It was shown by [59] that such PRGs follow from the existence of NC^1-computable one-way functions.[10] ∎

The existence of one-way functions in NC^1 follows from most standard cryptographic assumptions including ones that are related to hardness of factoring, discrete logarithm, and lattice problems. Hence, the underlying assumption is very conservative. Still, the question of proving Theorem 1.4.2 based on a weaker assumption (e.g., the existence of arbitrary one-way functions) remains an interesting open question.

We also mention that the concrete degree and locality bounds (3 and 4) are known to be (at least) almost optimal, since most functions do not admit an encoding of degree 1 or locality 2. It is also known that perfectly private encodings require degree 3 and locality 4 ([66], see also [6, Chapter 3]). The existence of statistical (or computational) encodings of locality 3 and degree 2 remains open.

Finally, we mention that stronger notions of constant-parallel-time encodings were studied in [12, 13].

---

[10] Indeed, the original statement in [11], which precedes [59], relied on the existence of minimal-stretch pseudorandom generators (PRGs) in NC^1. See discussion in [6, Chapter 5].

1.4.2 Reducing the Online Complexity

As we saw in Theorem 1.3.11, every function f can be encoded by an online-efficient DARE $\hat{f}(x; r) = (\hat{f}_{\text{off}}(r), \hat{f}_{\text{on}}(x; r))$. In particular, the online communication (and computational complexity) is $O(|x| \cdot k)$, where k is the security parameter. Let us define the *online rate* of DARE to be the ratio

$$\frac{|\hat{f}_{\text{on}}(x; r)|}{|x|}.$$

Using this terminology, the online rate achieved by Theorem 1.3.11 is proportional to the security parameter. In [16], it was shown that this can be significantly improved.

Theorem 1.4.3 (Online-succinct RE). *Under the decisional Diffie–Hellman assumption (DDH), the RSA assumption, or the Learning-with-Errors assumption (LWE), the class of polynomial-size circuits admits an RE with online rate $1 + o(1)$ and with $O(n^{1+\varepsilon})$ online computation, for any $\varepsilon > 0$.*

Theorem 1.4.3 shows that, instead of communicating a cryptographic key per input bit (as in Theorem 1.3.11), it suffices to communicate n bits together with a single cryptographic key (i.e., $n + k$ bits instead of nk bits). A similar result holds for arithmetic mod-p formulas under the LWE assumption. (See [16].)

Proof: [Proof idea] We briefly sketch the proof of Theorem 1.4.3. The starting point is a standard decomposable affine RE, such as the one from Theorem 1.3.11. Since this DARE is defined over the binary field, its online part can be viewed as a sequence of selection operations: For each i, we use the i-th bit of x to select a single "key" $K_i^{x_i}$ out of two k-bit vectors (K_i^0, K_i^1) that depend only on the randomness of the encoding. By the composition theorem, it suffices to encode this online procedure by an encoding such that most of its bits depend on the keys $(K_i^0, K_i^1)_{i \in [n]}$ while few of its bits (say $n + k$) depend on the input x. Put differently, we would like to have a compact way to reveal the selected keys.

Let us consider the following "riddle", which is a slightly simpler version of this problem. In the offline phase, Alice has n vectors $M_1, \ldots, M_n \in \{0, 1\}^k$. She is allowed to send Bob a long encrypted version of these vectors. Later, in the online phase, she receives a bit vector $x \in \{0, 1\}^n$. Her goal is to let Bob learn only the vectors which are indexed by x, i.e., $\{M_i\}_{i:x_i=1}$, while sending only a single message of length $O(n)$ bits (or even $n + k$ bits).[11]

Before solving the riddle, let us further reduce it to an algebraic version in which Alice wants to reveal a 0–1 linear combination of the vectors which are indexed by x. Observe that, if we can solve the new riddle with respect to nk-bit vectors $T = (T_1, \ldots, T_n)$, then we can solve the original riddle with k-bit vectors $(M_1, \ldots, M_n)$. This is done by placing the M_i's in the diagonal of T; i.e., T_i is partitioned to k-size

---

[11] The main difference between the riddle and our actual encoding problem is that, in the latter case, the vector x itself should remain hidden; this gap can be bridged by permuting the pairs and randomizing the vector x; see [16] for details.

blocks with M_i in the i-th block and zero elsewhere. In this case, Tx simply "packs" the vectors $\{M_i\}_{i:x_i=1}$.

It turns out that the linear version of the riddle can be efficiently solved via the use of a symmetric-key encryption scheme with some (additive) homomorphic properties. Specifically, let (E, D) be a symmetric encryption scheme with both key homomorphism and message homomorphism as follows: A pair of ciphertexts $\mathsf{E}_k(x)$ and $\mathsf{E}_{k'}(x')$ can be mapped (without any knowledge of the secret keys) to a new ciphertext of the form $\mathsf{E}_{k+k'}(x + x')$. Given such a primitive, the answer to the riddle is easy: Alice encrypts each vector under a fresh key K_i and publishes the ciphertexts C_i. At the online phase, Alice sends the sum of keys $K_x = \sum K_i x_i$ together with the indicator vector x. Now Bob can easily construct $C = \mathsf{E}_{K_x}(Mx)$ by combining the ciphertexts indexed by x, and since K_x is known, Bob can decrypt the result. Intuitively, Bob learns nothing about a column M_j which is not indexed by x, as the online key K_x is independent of the j-th key. Indeed, the DDH- and LWE-based solutions provide (approximate) implementations of this primitive. (A somewhat different approach is used in the RSA-based construction.)   ∎

A few comments regarding Theorem 1.4.3 are in order.

Reducing the online computational complexity   The online *computational* overhead of the encoding from Theorem 1.4.3 still has multiplicative dependence on the security parameter. It is possible to achieve linear computational complexity (e.g., $O(n + \mathrm{poly}(k))$) based on very strong cryptographic assumptions (such as general-purpose obfuscation). Achieving a linear computational overhead based on weaker assumptions is an interesting open question.

Impossibility of DARE with constant rate   The encoding constructed in Theorem 1.4.3 is not a DARE. Specifically, while the theorem yields affine encodings (e.g., under DDH or LWE), it does not provide decomposable encodings. It turns out that this is inherent: constant-rate DAREs are impossible to achieve even for very simple functions [16].

Rate 1 is optimal   Theorem 1.4.3 provides an asymptotic online rate of 1. It is clear that this is optimal for functions with a long output (such as the identity function). However, the case of boolean functions is slightly more subtle. It is not hard to show that the online rate must be at least 1, if the online part is independent of the encoded function f. (As in the case of affine REs or in the model of [26].) Indeed, for every $i \in [n]$, consider the function $f_i(x) = x_i$, and assume that all these functions admit encodings $\hat{f}_i(x; r)$ whose online parts are all identical to $g(x; r)$. Using the appropriate decoders and the offline parts (which are independent of x), one can recover the value x_i from $g(x; r)$ for every i. The length of $g(x; r)$ must therefore be at least n.

It is not trivial to extend the lower bound to the more general case where the online computation $\hat{f}_{\mathrm{on}}(x; r)$ may fully depend on the code of f. This is especially true in the uniform model, where f has a succinct description (say as a Turing machine).

Interestingly, it was observed in [16] that an encoding with online rate smaller than 1 would allow us to *compress* $f(x)$ in the following sense. Given x we can compute $\hat{f}_{on}(x; r)$ for some fixed r and derive a short string $\hat{x}$ of length smaller than $|x|$ from which the value of $f(x)$ can be recovered. Moreover, the online efficiency of the encoding implies that $\hat{x}$ can be computed much faster than the time complexity of f. Following [60, 41], it was conjectured in [16] that some efficiently computable functions cannot be compressed, and so online rate smaller than 1 cannot be achieved. Later in [7], it was shown that the existence of incompressible functions can be based on relatively standard complexity-theoretic assumptions. A combination of these results yields the following theorem:

Theorem 1.4.4 ([16, 7]). *The class of polynomial-time computable functions does not admit an online-efficient randomized encoding with online rate smaller than 1, unless every function which is computable by a deterministic Turing machine in time $2^{O(n)}$ can be computed by subexponential-size nondeterministic circuits.*[12]

1.4.3 Reusable RE

Having minimized the online communication complexity of the encoding, we move on to a more ambitious goal: Improving the total computational complexity of $\hat{f}$. Recall that Theorem 1.3.11 yields an encoding whose offline complexity is proportional to the circuit size of f. A natural way to reduce this expensive offline cost is to amortize it over many independent inputs. For this, we need a *reusable randomized encoding*.

Definition 1.4.5 (ρ-Reusable randomized encoding). *Let $f : \{0, 1\}^n \rightarrow \{0, 1\}^{\ell}$ be a function. We say that $\hat{f} = (\hat{f}_{off}, \hat{f}_{on})$ is a perfectly correct (t, ε)-private ρ-reusable randomized encoding of f if, for any $i \leq \rho$, the function*

$$\hat{f}^i(x^1, \ldots, x^i; r) := (\hat{f}_{off}(r), \hat{f}_{on}(x^1; r), \ldots, \hat{f}_{on}(x^i; r))$$

is a perfectly correct, (t, ε)-private encoding of the i-wise direct-product function

$$f^i(x^1, \ldots, x^i) = (f(x^1), \ldots, f(x^i)).$$

Remark 1.4.6. *Observe that the definition is monotone: a ρ-reusable RE is always $(\rho - 1)$-reusable, and a 1-reusable RE is simply an RE. Also note that a decoder of $\hat{f}^i$ can always be defined by applying the basic decoder of $\hat{f}$ to the offline part of the encoding and to each coordinate of $\hat{f}^i$ separately. Hence, reusability is essentially a strengthening of the privacy requirement. Finally, note that the above definition is static; i.e., the i-th input x^i is chosen independently of the encodings of the previous inputs. We will discuss stronger (adaptive) versions of security later in Section 1.4.5.*

---

[12] Similar assumptions are widely used in the complexity-theoretic literature. Such assumptions are considered to be strong, and yet plausible—their failure will force us to change our current view of the interplay between time, non-uniformity, and nondeterminism.

As before, the definition naturally extends to infinite functions $f : \{0,1\}^* \to \{0,1\}^*$, and, more generally, to collections of functions via the use of an efficient compiler. Given a description of a function f with input length of n, the compiler should output (the descriptions of) an encoder $\hat{f}$, a decoder, and a $(t(n), \varepsilon(n))$-private $\rho(n)$-reusable simulator. The latter should be uniform over the number of encoded instances. Specifically, we assume that the simulator is given as a Turing machine that takes as an input a sequence of f-outputs and outputs the corresponding simulated encodings. By default, $\rho(n)$ and $t(n)$ should be larger than any polynomial and $\varepsilon(n)$ should be smaller than any polynomial.

Reusable REs with low online complexity   Reusable REs are nontrivial if their online complexity is smaller than the complexity of f. None of the encodings that we have seen so far satisfy this requirement, even for the case of 2-reusability. Recently, Goldwasser et al. [54] (building on the work of Gorbunov et al. [57]) showed that it is possible to construct nontrivial reusable REs whose online complexity depends only on the depth of the encoded function.[13]

Theorem 1.4.7 (Reusable REs). *Assuming the intractability of Learning with Errors, there exists a reusable RE for efficiently computable functions whose online complexity depends only on the input length, output length, and circuit depth of the encoded function f.*

It follows that the amortized complexity of encoding f grows only with its circuit depth and input/output length.

1.4.3.1 Proof Idea of Theorem 1.4.7

The proof of Theorem 1.4.7 consists of two high-level steps. First, we prove the theorem for functions of a certain type, denoted as "conditional disclosure of secrets" (CDS) functions, and then we reduce the general case to the first, via the use of fully homomorphic encryption.

CDS functions   We begin with the definition of CDS functions. For a predicate $P : \{0,1\}^n \to \{0,1\}$, let g_P denote the non-boolean function which maps an n-bit input τ ("tag") and a k-bit string s ("secret") to the value (τ, c), where

$$c = \begin{cases} s & \text{if } P(\tau) = 1 \\ \bot & \text{otherwise.} \end{cases}$$

That is, g_P always reveals the value of the tag, but reveals the secret s only if the tag satisfies the predicate. In this sense, g_P conditionally discloses the secret.[14]

---

[13] In fact, [57] and [54] construct so-called *predicate encryption*, and *functional encryption* which can be viewed as a multi-user variant of randomized encoding.

[14] The term "conditional disclosure of secretes" originates from the work of [50] who considered an information-theoretic variant of this primitive. In a reusable setting, the resulting primitive is closely related to the notion of attribute-based encryption, cf. [68, 45].

Rekeyable encryption Our reusable REs for CDS are based on a special type of public-key encryption scheme with the following rekeying mechanism: For every pair of public keys (A, B) and a target public key C, there exists a special re-encryption key $T_{A,B\to C}$ that allows one to transform a pair of ciphertexts $(\mathsf{E}_A(s), \mathsf{E}_B(s))$ into a ciphertext $\mathsf{E}_C(s)$. Intuitively, the re-encryption key $T_{A,B\to C}$ should be "useless" given only one of the two encryptions $(\mathsf{E}_A(s), \mathsf{E}_B(s))$; For example, given $\mathsf{E}_A(s)$ and $T_{A,B\to C}$, it should be impossible to generate $\mathsf{E}_C(s)$. In fact, this ciphertext should be pseudorandom, and so even if the secret key that corresponds to C is known, s should be hidden. It is shown in [57] that such a rekeyable encryption scheme can be based on the Learning with Errors assumption, where the length of the ciphertext grows linearly with the number of iterated re-encryptions.[15]

From rekeyable encryption to reusable RE for CDS [57] In order to encode the CDS function we would like to encrypt s in a way that is decryptable only if the (public) tag τ satisfies the predicate P. This should be done with a reusable offline part (whose complexity may grow with the complexity of P) while keeping the online part (which depends on s and τ) short, i.e., independent of the circuit size of P. The basic idea is as follows. For each wire i of the circuit that computes P, we will have a pair of public keys $(\mathsf{pk}_{i,0}, \mathsf{pk}_{i,1})$, labeled by zero and one. In the online part, we release the tag τ together with n ciphertexts, one for each input wire, where the i-th ciphertext is $\mathsf{E}_{\mathsf{pk}_{i,\tau_i}}(s)$, i.e., an encryption of s under the key of the i-th wire which is labeled by τ_i. The offline part of the encoding consists of the secret key sk of the output wire which is labeled by 1, together with several re-encryption keys. Specifically, for each internal gate g, we include all four re-encryption keys that correspond to the semantic of the gate. Namely, if the keys of the left incoming wire are (A_0, A_1), the keys of the right incoming wire are (B_0, B_1), and the keys of the outgoing wire are (C_0, C_1), then we include the transformation key $T_{A_a,B_b\to C_{g(a,b)}}$, for every pair of bits $a, b \in \{0, 1\}$.

Given such an encoding, the decoder can propagate the ciphertexts from the inputs to the outputs, and compute for each wire i the ciphertext $\mathsf{E}_{\mathsf{pk}_{i,\sigma_i}}(s)$, where σ_i is the value that the public tag τ induces on the i-th wire. If the predicate is satisfied, the decoder learns an encryption of s under the 1-key of the output wire, and since the corresponding private key appears as part of the encoding, s is revealed. The security properties of the underlying encryption guarantee that s remains hidden when $P(\tau)$ is not satisfied. Moreover, the offline part is reusable and the online part grows linearly with the depth of the circuit that computes P, and is independent of the circuit size.

From CDS to general functions [54] We move on to handle a general (non-CDS) function f. For this step, we employ a fully homomorphic encryption (FHE) which, by [34], can also be based on the intractability of Learning with Errors. In such an encryption, there exists a special Eval algorithm that maps a public key pk, a ciphertext $\mathsf{FHE}_{\mathsf{pk}}(x)$, and a circuit g to a new ciphertext $\mathsf{FHE}_{\mathsf{pk}}(g(x))$.

---

[15] In the original terminology of [57], this is called two-to-one recoding (TOR).

The encoding of f is based on the following basic idea. Encrypt the input x using FHE and include the ciphertext ct in the online part. In addition, provide (ideally in the offline part) some sort of conditional decryption mechanism that decrypts an FHE ciphertext ct' only if ct' is "legal" in the sense that it is the result of homomorphically applying f to ct = $\mathsf{FHE}_{\mathsf{pk}}(x)$. Such an encoding would allow the decoder to transform $\mathsf{FHE}_{\mathsf{pk}}(x)$ to $\mathsf{FHE}_{\mathsf{pk}}(f(x))$ and then decrypt the value $f(x)$, without learning any other information on x.

To implement this approach, we should find a way to push most of the complexity of the conditional decryption mechanism to the offline phase. This is somewhat tricky since the condition depends on the online ciphertext ct. We solve the problem in two steps. First, consider the following naive (and inefficient) encoding:

$$(\mathsf{pk}, \mathsf{ct} = \mathsf{FHE}_{\mathsf{pk}}(x), \hat{D}(\mathsf{sk}, \mathsf{ct}'; r)), \tag{1.4}$$

where $\hat{D}$ is a DARE of the decryption algorithm D, and ct' = $\mathsf{Eval}(\mathsf{pk}, f, \mathsf{ct})$. It is not hard to verify that this is indeed an encoding of $f(x)$. However, the encoding is not even online efficient. Indeed, ct' is computed in the online phase (based on ct) at a computational cost which depends on the circuit size of f.

In order to improve the efficiency, we take a closer look at $\hat{D}(\mathsf{sk}, \mathsf{ct}'; r))$. Since $\hat{D}$ is a DARE, we can decompose it to $\hat{D}_0(\mathsf{sk}; r)$ and to $\hat{D}_i(\mathsf{ct}'_i; r)$ for $i \in [\ell]$, where ℓ is the bit length of ct'. Using the "keys" terminology, for each bit of ct', there exists a pair of keys $(K_{i,0}, K_{i,1})$ where $K_{i,b} = \hat{D}_i(b; r)$, and the encoding $\hat{D}$ reveals, for each i, the key that corresponds to ct'_i. Namely, $K_{i,b}$ is exposed only if the i-th bit of $\mathsf{Eval}_f(\mathsf{ct})$ equals to b. This means that we can re-encode (1.4) by

$$(\mathsf{pk}, \mathsf{ct} = \mathsf{FHE}_{\mathsf{pk}}(x), \hat{D}_0(\mathsf{sk}; r), [g_{i,b}((\mathsf{pk}, \mathsf{ct}), K_{i,b})]_{i\in[\ell], b\in\{0,1\}}),$$

where $g_{i,b}((\mathsf{pk}, \mathsf{ct}), s)$ is the CDS function that releases the secret s only if the pair $(\mathsf{pk}, \mathsf{ct})$ satisfies the predicate "the i-th bit of $\mathsf{Eval}(\mathsf{pk}, f, \mathsf{ct})$ equals to b". Now, we can re-encode $g_{i,b}$ by a re-usable CDS encoding $\hat{g}_{i,b}$, and, by the composition and concatenation lemmas, get a reusable encoding for f. In the online part of the resulting encoding we sample a public/private key pair for the FHE $(\mathsf{pk}, \mathsf{sk})$ and compute $\mathsf{ct} = \mathsf{FHE}_{\mathsf{pk}}(x), \hat{D}_0(\mathsf{sk}; r)$ together with the online parts of $\hat{g}_{i,b}$. Overall, the online complexity is independent of the circuit size of f. (The dependence on the circuit depth is inherited from that of the CDS encoding.) This completes the proof of Theorem 1.4.7. ∎

1.4.4 Reducing the Computational Complexity of REs

Theorem 1.4.7 implies that the amortized complexity of encoding f grows only with its parallel complexity (i.e., circuit depth) and input/output length. This result does not leave much room for improvements. Still, one can ask whether it is possible to obtain an encoding whose complexity is independent of the complexity of the encoded function f in a non-amortized setting, i.e., even for a single use of $\hat{f}$. This question makes sense only if the encoded function f has a succinct representation whose length is independent of its time complexity. Indeed, let us move to a uniform setting and assume that f can be computed by a Turing machine (whose description length is independent of its time complexity). We will show that, under sufficiently strong cryptographic assumptions, one can obtain an encoding whose complexity is completely independent of the time complexity of f and depends only on the input/output length of f. We refer to such an encoding as a *fast RE*. The construction will employ a powerful cryptographic tool: the general-purpose program obfuscator.

Obfuscators   General-purpose program obfuscation allows us to transform an arbitrary computer program into an "unintelligible" form while preserving its functionality. Syntactically, an obfuscator for a function family $\mathcal{F} = \{f_K\}$ is a randomized algorithm that maps a function $f_K \in \mathcal{C}$ (represented by an identifier K) into a "program" $[f] \in \{0, 1\}^*$. The obfuscated program should preserve the same functionality as f_K while hiding all other information about f_K. The first property is formalized via the existence of an efficient universal evaluation algorithm Eval which, given an input x and an obfuscated program $[f]$, outputs $f_K(x)$. The second property has several different formulations. We will rely on *indistinguishability obfuscation* (iO), which asserts that, given a pair of functionally equivalent functions f and f', it is hard to distinguish between their obfuscated versions $[f]$ and $[f']$.

Obfuscators versus REs   As a cryptographic primitive, obfuscators are stronger than REs. Intuitively, an obfuscator provides the adversary the ability to compute the function by herself, while REs provide only access to encodings that were computed by the encoder (which is out of the adversary's control). Indeed, given an iO for a function class $\mathcal{F}$, we can easily get an RE for the same class by obfuscating the constant function $g = f(x)$ (x is hardwired) and letting the simulator $\mathsf{Sim}(y)$ be an obfuscated version of the constant function $h = y$. We can therefore trivially get fast REs based on "fast" obfuscators whose complexity is independent of the time complexity of the obfuscated function (and depends only on its description length). The following theorem provides a stronger result: Fast REs (for Turing machines) can be based on *standard* obfuscators whose complexity is proportional to the circuit complexity of the obfuscated function.

Theorem 1.4.8 (Fast RE from circuit obfuscators [28, 37, 72]). *Assuming the existence of iO for circuits and the existence of one-way functions, the class of polynomial-time computable functions* **P** *admits an RE with computational complexity of* $\mathrm{poly}(n, \ell)$, *where n and ℓ denote the input and output length of the encoded function.*

Fast REs were first constructed by Goldwasser et al. [53] based on a stronger assumption. Bitansky et al. [28] and Canetti et al. [37] concurrently relaxed the assumption to iO, but their results yield REs whose complexity grows with the space complexity of f. The dependence on the space complexity was later removed by Koppula et al. [72]. We mention that Theorem 1.4.8 was further used to obtain fast obfuscators. (For more on the relation between REs and obfuscators see [74].) The proof of Theorem 1.4.8 is beyond the scope of this chapter. The interested reader is referred to the original papers.

Optimality of Theorem 1.4.8   Theorem 1.4.8 provides REs whose complexity depends on the input length and on the output length of the encoded function. We already saw in Theorem 1.4.4 that one cannot go below the input length. The following theorem (from [16]) shows that one cannot go below the output length either:

Theorem 1.4.9 (Communication of RE is larger than the output length). *Assuming that one-way functions exist, for every constant c there exists a function* $f : \{0,1\}^n \to \{0,1\}^{n^c}$ *such that every* $(n^{\omega(1)}, 1/3)$-*private RE of f has communication complexity of at least* n^c *bits. Furthermore, there are at least* n^c *bits in the output of the simulator* $\mathsf{Sim}(y)$ *that depend on the input* y *(as opposed to the randomness).*

Note that some complexity-theoretic assumption is necessary for Theorem 1.4.9. In particular, if, say $\mathbf{P} = \mathbf{NP}$, then one can obtain an encoding with total complexity n. Indeed, this can be done by letting $\hat{f}(x; r) = x'$, where x' is a random sibling of x under f, and taking the decoder to be $\mathsf{Dec}(x') = f(x')$, and the simulator to be $\mathsf{Sim}(y) = x'$, where x' is a random preimage of y. If $\mathbf{P} = \mathbf{NP}$, then this encoding can be implemented efficiently.[16]

Proof: Fix some constant c, and let $f : \{0,1\}^n \to \{0,1\}^\ell$ be a pseudorandom generator with output length $\ell = n^c$. (The existence of such a pseudorandom generator follows from the existence of one-way functions [61].) It suffices to prove the "furthermore" part, as the online complexity of the simulator lower-bounds the communication complexity of the encoding. Let $\hat{f}(x; r)$ be an RE of f with decoder Dec and simulator Sim such that the number of bits of $\mathsf{Sim}(y)$ that depend on y is smaller than ℓ. Then, we distinguish the output of f from a truly random string via the following test: Given a string $y \in \{0,1\}^\ell$, we accept if and only if the outcome of $\mathsf{Dec}(\mathsf{Sim}(y))$ is equal to y.

First we claim that, when y is random, the test accepts with probability at most $\frac{1}{2}$. Indeed, fix some value r for the randomness of the simulator and some value d for the randomness of the decoder. Then the image of $\mathsf{Sim}(y; r) = (z_r, \mathsf{Sim}_{\mathsf{on}}(y; r))$ can take at most $2^{\ell-1}$ values, and therefore the decoder $\mathsf{Dec}(\cdot; s)$ recovers y successfully for at most half of all y's in $\{0,1\}^\ell$.

On the other hand, if y is in the image of f, the test accepts with probability at least $2/3 - \mathrm{neg}(n)$. Indeed, let x be a preimage of y, then by definition $\mathsf{Dec}(\hat{f}(x; r))$ outputs $y = f(x)$ with probability 1. Since $\hat{f}(x; r)$ is $(t, 1/3)$-indistinguishable from $\mathsf{Sim}(f(x))$, it follows that $\mathsf{Dec}(\mathsf{Sim}(y)) = y$ with probability at least $2/3 - \mathrm{neg}(n)$.
∎

Remark 1.4.10 (Inefficient simulation). *Theorem 1.4.9 exploits the efficiency of the simulator to "compress" an "incompressible" source. This argument does not hold if we allow inefficient simulation. The resulting notion corresponds to the*

---

[16] In fact, if one-way functions do not exist, then it can be shown that the aforementioned encoding achieves a relaxed version of privacy (against uniform adversaries).

following indistinguishability-based definition of privacy. The encodings $\hat{f}(x)$ and $\hat{f}(x')$ should be indistinguishable for any pair of inputs x and x' which are mapped by f to the same output, i.e., $f(x) = f(x')$. Indeed, based on iO, one can get fast REs with inefficient simulation whose complexity grows only with the input length of the encoded function (see [28, 37, 72]).

1.4.5 On Adaptive Security

The standard security definition of REs can be captured by the following game: (1) The challenger secretly tosses a random coin $b \xleftarrow{R} \{0, 1\}$; (2) the adversary chooses an input x, submits it to the challenger, and gets as a result the string $\hat{y}$ which, based on the secret bit b, is either sampled from the encoding $\hat{f}(x; r)$ or from the simulator $\mathsf{Sim}(f(x))$. At the end, the adversary outputs his guess b' for the bit b. The security of REs says that t-bounded adversaries cannot win the game (guess b) with probability better than $\frac{1}{2} + \varepsilon/2$.

In some scenarios (e.g., the online/offline setting or the reusable setting) it is natural to consider an *adaptive* version of this game in which the adversary chooses its input x based on the previous part of the encodings. Let us focus on the simpler online/offline setting. Syntactically, this requires an online/offline simulator $\mathsf{Sim}(y; r) = (\mathsf{Sim}_{\mathsf{off}}(r); \mathsf{Sim}_{\mathsf{on}}(x; r))$ whose offline part does not depend on its input $f(x)$, and has the same length as the offline part of the encoding. Adaptive security can be defined as follows:

Definition 1.4.11 (Adaptively secure RE [25]). *Let f be a function and $\hat{f}(x; r) = (\hat{f}_{\mathsf{off}}(r), \hat{f}_{\mathsf{on}}(x; r))$ be a perfectly correct RE with decoder Dec and online/offline simulator $\mathsf{Sim}(y; r) = (\mathsf{Sim}_{\mathsf{off}}(r), \mathsf{Sim}_{\mathsf{on}}(y; r))$. We say that $\hat{f}$ is (t, ε) adaptively private if every t-bounded adversary $\mathcal{A}$ wins the following game with probability at most $\frac{1}{2} + \varepsilon$:*

1. The challenger secretly tosses a random coin $b \xleftarrow{R} \{0, 1\}$, chooses randomness r, and outputs

$$\hat{y}_{\mathsf{off}} = \begin{cases} \hat{f}_{\mathsf{off}}(r) & \text{if } b = 1, \\ \mathsf{Sim}_{\mathsf{off}}(r) & \text{if } b = 0. \end{cases}$$

2. Based on $\hat{y}_{\mathsf{off}}$, the adversary $\mathcal{A}$ chooses an input x, submits it to the challenger, and gets as a result the string

$$\hat{y}_{\mathsf{on}} = \begin{cases} \hat{f}_{\mathsf{on}}(x; r) & \text{if } b = 1, \\ \mathsf{Sim}_{\mathsf{on}}(f(x); r) & \text{if } b = 0. \end{cases}$$

3. At the end, the adversary outputs his guess b' and wins if $b' = b$.

It turns out that the online complexity of adaptively secure REs must grow with the output length of the encoded function and thus cannot be online efficient. Indeed, this follows directly from Theorem 1.4.9.

Corollary 1.4.12 (Adaptive security requires long online communication [16]).
Assuming one-way functions exist, for every constant c there exists a function f :
$\{0, 1\}^n \to \{0, 1\}^{n^c}$ *such that every RE of f has online communication complexity of*
at least n^c bits.

Proof: By Theorem 1.4.9, there exists a function f for which the online part of the
simulator must be longer than n^c. Privacy ensures that the online communication
complexity of $\hat{f}$ satisfies the same bound.   ∎

Remark 1.4.13 (Adaptive security with inefficient simulation). *The output length*
limitation does not seem to apply to inefficient simulators (just like in Remark 1.4.10),
and so, in this case, one may hope to achieve online efficiency. In fact, such a con-
struction of adaptive REs with inefficient simulation easily yields efficiently simulat-
able adaptive REs: To encode f : $\{0, 1\}^n \to \{0, 1\}^s$ encode the related function

$$g(x, b, y) = \begin{cases} f(x) & \text{if } b = 0 \\ y & \text{otherwise} \end{cases},$$

via an adaptive encoding $\hat{g}(x, y, b; r)$ with inefficient simulation. Now, the function
$\hat{g}(x, y, b; r)$ with b fixed to zero and y fixed to, say, the all zero string, forms an adap-
tive encoding for `f` with the (efficient) simulator $\text{Sim}(y; r) := \hat{g}_{\text{off}}(r), \hat{g}_{\text{on}}(x, y, b; r))$
with $b = 1$ and $x = 0^n$. Note that the input length of g equals the sum of the input
and output lengths of f. Hence, the above transformation incurs an overhead which
is (at least) as large as the output length, as expected due to Corollary 1.4.12.

Constructions   Any standard RE can be viewed as an adaptive one by including
all the encoding in the online part. Yao's construction (Theorem 1.3.11) therefore
provides an adaptive RE based on one-way functions whose online part depends
on the circuit of the encoded function f. An encoding whose online part depends
only on the size of the circuit was constructed by Bellare et al. [25]. This is done by
taking Yao's encoding $\hat{f} = (\hat{f}_{\text{off}}, \hat{f}_{\text{on}})$, encrypting its offline part via a one-time pad,
and releasing the key in the online part of the encoding. This yields an encoding
whose online complexity is proportional to the circuit size of f based on one-way
functions.

Using a (programmable) random oracle, it is possible to "compress" the key of
the one-time pad and get an online-efficient adaptive encoding. Alternatively, such
an encoding can be obtained via "complexity leveraging". Indeed, any (t, ε) adaptive attack against an encoding $\hat{f}$ with offline communication complexity of s immediately translates into a $(t, \varepsilon \cdot 2^{-s})$ static attack against $\hat{f}$ by guessing the offline
part and calling the adaptive adversary. Hence, a sufficiently strong static encoding
(e.g., Yao's construction instantiated with subexponential secure encryption) yields
an adaptively secure RE.

In the standard model, Theorem 1.4.8 provides an adaptively-secure encoding
with an optimal total complexity (proportional to the input and output length) based
on the existence of general-purpose indistinguishability obfuscation. Based on general one-way functions, Hemenway et al. [62] constructed an adaptive encoding

whose online complexity is proportional to the width of the encoded circuit (or exponential in its depth). Achieving an online complexity which depends only on the input and output lengths of f (based on one-way functions) remains an interesting open problem.

1.5 Applications

The ability to encode complex functions by simple ones is extremely useful. In the next subsections we will demonstrate several interesting ways in which this tool can be employed. We consider the archetypal cryptographic setting where Alice and Bob wish to accomplish some computational goal (e.g., a functionality f) in the presence of an adversary. We will see that REs can be beneficial when they are applied to each component of this system: to the functionality, to the honest parties, and even to the adversary.

1.5.1 Encoding the Functionality

Delegating computations Suppose that Bob is a computationally weak device (client) who wishes to compute a complex function f on an input x. Bob is too weak to compute f on his own, and so he delegates the computation to a computationally strong server Alice. Since Bob does not trust Alice, he wishes to guarantee the following: (1) *secrecy*: Alice should learn nothing on the input x; and (2) *verifiability*: Bob should be able to verify the correctness of the output (i.e., a cheating Alice should be caught w.h.p.). Similar problems have been extensively studied in various settings, originating from the early works on interactive proofs, program checking, and instance-hiding schemes.

Let us start with secrecy and consider a variant where both parties should learn the output $f(x)$ but x should remain private. As we saw in the introduction (Example 1.1.3), a randomized encoding $\hat{f}$ immediately solves this problem via the following single-round protocol: Bob selects private randomness r, computes $\hat{f}(x; r)$, and sends the result to Alice, who applies the recovery algorithm and outputs the result. The privacy of the RE guarantees that Alice learns nothing beyond $f(x)$. We refer to this protocol as the *basic RE protocol*. Jumping ahead, we note that the protocol has a nontrivial correctness guarantee: even if the server Alice deviates from the protocol and violates correctness, she cannot force an erroneous output which violates privacy; that is, it is possible to simulate erroneous outputs solely based on the correct outputs.

It is not hard to modify the basic protocol and obtain full secrecy: instead of encoding f, encode an encrypted version of f. Namely, define a function $g(x, s) = f(x) \oplus s$, where s plays the role of a one-time pad (OTP), and apply the previous protocol as follows: Bob uniformly chooses the pad s and the randomness r, and sends the encoding $\hat{g}(x, s; r)$ of g to Alice, who recovers the result $y = g(x, s) = f(x) \oplus s$, and sends it back to Bob. Finally, Bob removes the pad s and terminates with $f(x)$. (See [11] for more details.)

Achieving verifiability is slightly more tricky. The idea, due to [14], is to combine an RE with a private-key signature scheme (also known as message authentication code or MAC) and ask the server to sign the output of the computation under the client's private key. Here the privacy property of the RE will be used to hide the secret key. Specifically, given an input x, Bob asks Alice to compute $y = f(x)$ (via the previous protocol) and, in addition, to generate a signature on $f(x)$ under a private key k which is chosen randomly by the client. The latter request is computed via the basic RE protocol that hides the private key from Alice. More precisely, Bob, who holds both x and k, invokes an RE protocol in which both parties learn the function $g(x, k) = \text{MAC}_k(f(x))$. Bob then accepts the answer y if and only if the result of the protocol is a valid signature on y under the key k. (The latter computation is typically cheap.) The soundness of the protocol follows by showing that a cheating Alice, which fools Bob to accept an erroneous $y^* \neq f(x)$, can be used to either break the privacy of the RE or to forge a valid signature on a new message. For this argument to hold, we crucially rely on the ability to simulate erroneous outputs based on the correct outputs.

The main advantage of this approach over alternative solutions is the ability to achieve good soundness with low computational overhead; For example, a soundness error of $2^{-\tau}$ increases the communication by an additive overhead of τ, whereas the overhead in competing approaches is multiplicative in τ. (See [14] for a more detailed comparison.) Instantiating these approaches with known constructions of REs leads to protocols with highly efficient clients; For example, Theorems 1.4.1 and 1.4.2 yield an NC^0 client for either log-space functions or poly-time functions depending on the level of security needed (information-theoretic or computational). In the computational setting, we can use online-efficient REs (Theorem 1.3.11) to get a client whose online computational complexity does not grow with the complexity of f, at the expense of investing a lot of computational resources in a preprocessing phase before seeing the actual input x.[17] Moreover, we can achieve optimal online communication via the use of online-succinct REs (Theorem 1.4.3), amortize the cost of the offline phase by employing reusable REs (Theorem 1.4.7), or even avoid the offline cost at all via the use of fast REs (Theorem 1.4.8).

We also mention that REs can achieve other related properties such as *correctability* [14]: i.e., Bob is able to *correct* Alice's errors as long as Alice is somewhat correct with respect to a predefined distribution over the inputs. In the latter case, REs yield NC^0 correctors for log-space computations, strengthening the results of [52].

Secure computation [66]   Let us move on to a more general setting where the roles of Alice and Bob are symmetric and neither of them is computationally weak. The main observation is that, instead of securely computing f, it suffices to securely compute the randomized encoding $\hat{f}(x; r)$. Indeed, if Alice and Bob learn a sample from $\hat{f}(x; r)$ then they can locally recover the value of $f(x)$ and nothing else. In other

---

[17] The standard privacy of REs guarantees security only if the input x is chosen independently of the offline part. Adaptively secure REs can be used to deal with the case where the input is (adversarially) chosen based on the offline part.

words, the task of securely computing f *reduces* to the task of securely computing a simpler randomized functionality $\hat{f}(x; r)$. As protocol designers, we get a powerful tool which allows us to construct a complex interactive object (protocol) by arguing about a simpler *noninteractive* object (RE).

This paradigm, which was introduced in [66] (and motivated the original definition of REs), yields several new results in the domain of secure computation. As an example, if the algebraic degree of $\hat{f}$ is constant, then it can be computed in a constant number of rounds [27, 39]. By instantiating this approach with known perfect-RE constructions (Theorem 1.4.1), we derive constant-round protocols for boolean or arithmetic log-space functions with information-theoretic security. In the computational setting, constant-degree REs (Theorem 1.4.2) yield a new constant-round protocol for poly-time functions, providing an alternative construction to the classical protocol of [21].[18]

The above paradigm was implicitly used by Yao to prove the feasibility of general secure computation based on oblivious transfer (OT) [85]. Indeed, consider a two-party functionality $f(x, y)$, where x is given to Alice and y is given to Bob. A DARE $\hat{f}$ for f can be written as $\hat{f}(x, y; r) = (\hat{f}_1(x_1, y; r), \ldots, \hat{f}_n(x_n, y; r))$, and therefore it can be privately computed (with semi-honest security) by using n calls to an OT functionality. For each $i \in [n]$, Bob prepares a pair of "keys": $K_{i,0} = \hat{f}_i(0, y; r)$ and $K_{i,1} = \hat{f}_i(0, y; r)$, and lets Alice choose the key K_{i,x_i} that corresponds to her input by using the OT. After collecting all the n keys, Alice can recover the output by applying the decoder. The existence of DARE for any efficiently computable function f (Theorem 1.3.11) therefore gives a direct noninteractive reduction from securely computing f to OT. Other classical completeness results (e.g., for the multiparty case [51] and for the malicious case [69]) can also be proved using the above paradigm.

1.5.2 Encoding the Primitive: Parallel Cryptography

Suppose now that we already have an implementation of some cryptographic protocol. A key observation made in [10] is that we can "simplify" some of the computations in the protocol by replacing them with their encodings. Consider, for example, the case of public-key encryption: Alice publishes a public/private key pair (pk, sk); Bob uses the public key pk and a sequence of random coins s to "garble" a message m into a ciphertext $c = \mathsf{E}(\mathsf{pk}, m, s)$; Finally, Alice recovers m by applying the decryption algorithm to the ciphertext $\mathsf{D}(\mathsf{sk}, c)$. Suppose that Bob sends an encoding of his ciphertext $\widehat{\mathsf{E}}(\mathsf{pk}, m, s; r)$ instead of sending c. This does not violate semantic security as all the information available to an adversary in the modified protocol can be emulated by an adversary who attacks the original protocol (thanks to the simulator of the RE). On the other hand, Alice can still decrypt the message: first she recovers the original ciphertext (via the recovery algorithm) and then she applies the original decryption algorithm. As a result, we "pushed" the complexity of the sender (encryption algorithm) to the receiver (decryption algorithm).

---

[18] The RE-based solution requires a slightly stronger assumption—one-way function computable in log-space rather in poly-time—but can also lead to efficiency improvements, cf. [41].

By employing REs with some additional properties, it is possible to prove similar results for many other cryptographic protocols (e.g., one-way functions, pseudorandom generators, collision-resistance hash functions, signatures, commitments, and zero-knowledge proofs) and even information-theoretic primitives (e.g., ε-biased generators and randomness extractors). In the case of stand-alone primitives (e.g., one-way functions and pseudorandom generators) there is no receiver and so the gain in efficiency comes for "free".

Being security preserving, REs give rise to the following paradigm. In order to construct some cryptographic primitive $\mathcal{P}$ in some low-complexity class $\mathcal{WEAK}$, first encode functions from a higher-complexity class $\mathcal{STRONG}$ by functions from $\mathcal{WEAK}$; then, show that $\mathcal{P}$ has an implementation f in $\mathcal{STRONG}$, and finally replace f by its encoding $\hat{f} \in \mathcal{WEAK}$ and obtain a low-complexity implementation of $\mathcal{P}$. This approach was used in [10, 11, 13] to obtain cryptographic primitives in $\mathbf{NC^0}$ and even in weaker complexity classes. The fact that REs preserve cryptographic hardness has also been used to reduce the complexity of cryptographic *reductions* [10, 11] and to reduce the complexity of complete problems for subclasses of statistical zero-knowledge [42].

1.5.3 Encoding the Adversary: Key-Dependent Security

Key-dependent message (KDM) secure encryption schemes [36, 29] provide secrecy even when the attacker sees encryptions of messages related to the secret key sk. Namely, we say that an encryption is KDM secure with respect to a function class $\mathcal{F}$ if semantic security holds even when the adversary can ask for an encryption of the message $f(\mathsf{sk})$ where f is an arbitrary function in $\mathcal{F}$. Several constructions are known to achieve KDM security for simple linear (or affine) function families [31, 9, 32]. To improve this situation, we would like to have an *amplification* procedure which starts with an $\hat{\mathcal{F}}$-KDM secure encryption scheme and boosts it into an $\mathcal{F}$-KDM secure scheme, where the function class $\mathcal{F}$ should be richer than $\hat{\mathcal{F}}$. It was shown in [33, 19] that a strong form of amplification is possible, provided that the underlying encryption scheme satisfies some special *additional* properties. Below we show how to use REs in order to achieve a *generic* KDM amplification theorem [2].

Let $f(x)$ be a function and let us view the encoding $\hat{f}(x; r)$ as a *collection* of functions $\hat{\mathcal{F}} = \left\{ \hat{f}_r(x) \right\}_r$, where each member of the collection corresponds to some possible fixing of the randomness r, i.e., $\hat{f}_r(x) = \hat{f}(x; r)$. Now suppose that our scheme is KDM secure with respect to the family $\hat{\mathcal{F}}$, and we would like to immunize it against the (more complicated) function f. This can be easily achieved by modifying the encryption scheme as follows: To encrypt a message m we first translate it into the $\hat{f}$-encoding by applying the RE simulator $\mathsf{Sim}(m)$, and then encrypt the result under the original encryption scheme. Decryption is done by applying the original decryption algorithm, and then applying the decoding algorithm Dec to translate the result back to its original form. Observe that an encryption of $f(\mathsf{sk})$ in the new scheme is the same as an encryption of $S(f(\mathsf{sk})) = \hat{f}(\mathsf{sk}; r)$ under the original scheme. Hence, a KDM query for f in the new scheme is emulated by an old KDM query for a *randomly chosen* function $\hat{f}_r$. It follows that the KDM security of the new scheme with respect to f reduces to the KDM security of the original scheme with respect to $\hat{f}$.

This idea easily generalizes to the case where, instead of a single function f, we have a class of functions $\mathcal{F}$ which are all encoded by functions in $\hat{\mathcal{F}}$. Moreover, the simple structure of the reduction (i.e., a single KDM query of the new scheme translates to a single KDM query of the original scheme) allows one to obtain a strong amplification theorem which is insensitive to the exact setting of KDM security, including the symmetric-key/public-key setting, the cases of chosen-plaintext/chosen-ciphertext attacks, and the case of multiple keys. Using known constructions of REs (Theorem 1.3.11), we can amplify KDM security with respect to linear functions (or even bit projections) into functions computable by circuits of arbitrary fixed polynomial size (e.g., n^2).

Interestingly, here we essentially encoded the adversary and used the simulator in the construction rather than in the proof. A similar approach ("encoding the adversary") was used by [20] to obtain strong impossibility results for concurrent non-malleable secure computation.

1.6 Summary and Suggestions for Further Reading

Randomized encodings form a powerful tool with a wide range of applications. Since Yao's original construction in the early 1980s, the complexity of REs has been significantly improved, especially in the last decade. Many of these improvements are based on encryption schemes which suggest various forms of *homomorphism*. (This includes Theorems 1.3.12, 1.4.3, 1.4.7, and 1.4.8 as well as works which are not covered here, cf. [49, 4, 30].) It is interesting to find out whether this use of homomorphism is necessary. In particular, we ask:

> Is it possible to achieve highly efficient REs (such as the ones constructed in Section 1.4) based on weaker assumptions, e.g., one-way functions?

An even more basic question is to understand the power of information-theoretic REs:

> Are there efficiently computable perfectly secure DAREs for polynomial-size circuits?

The question is interesting also for other notions of simplicity such as constant algebraic degree or constant output locality. Coming up with a positive result, or developing tools for proving nontrivial lower bounds, is an important problem in the context of information-theoretic cryptography.

Another interesting direction for future research is to explore stronger forms of security for REs. This direction is being extensively pursued by the study of primitives such as functional encryption (and its variants) and even program obfuscators. Indeed, these primitives can be viewed as REs which offer richer functionalities and stronger security guarantees (cf. [83, 56]).

Suggestions for Further Reading

We end by briefly mentioning some of the aspects of REs that were omitted from this chapter.

Encoding RAM computation   A relatively recent line of work, initiated by Lu and Ostrovsky [78], studies the possibility of encoding stateful computations modeled as RAM programs. Roughly speaking, such a computation is defined by a (large) memory D, a (typically small) program P, and an input x. The computation $P^D(x)$ generates an output y and updates the memory D (typically only at a small number of locations). The goal is to obtain a *stateful RE* that initializes the memory $\hat{D}$ based on D, and then, given a program/input pair (P, x), generates an encoding $(\hat{P}, \hat{x})$ that together with $\hat{D}$ forms an encoding of the original computation. The complexity of $(\hat{P}, \hat{x})$ is allowed to depend on the time complexity of P and the input length x but should have only a minor (say poly-logarithmic) dependence on the size of the memory. The security definition allows one to sequentially execute many programs, and so the initialization cost of the memory is amortized. Following [78], several constructions of garbled RAM have been presented, including ones which are based solely on one-way functions [48, 44].

Concrete efficiency and practical implementations   Starting with the work of Malkhi et al. [79], computational DAREs (garbled circuits) were implemented on various platforms, and their concrete efficiency was extensively studied. These constructions are typically formalized under the garbling-schemes framework of Bellare, Hoang, and Rogaway [26], and offer a wide range of concrete tradeoffs between computational complexity, communication complexity, and intractability assumptions (cf. [80, 77, 71, 81, 63, 73, 24, 70, 87]). A partial summary of these results can be found in [82].

Communication complexity treatment   Feige, Kilian, and Naor [43] and Ishai and Kushilevitz [65] studied REs in a communication complexity framework. In this model, the input $x \in \{0, 1\}^n$ is partitioned between several parties (typically two or n) who also have access to shared randomness r. Each party should send a single message $M_i(x_i; r)$, based on her input x_i and on the randomness r, to a referee, who should be able to recover the value of $f(x)$ and nothing else. All parties are computationally unbounded, and the goal is to minimize the communication. In the two-party setting, such a *private simultaneous message* (PSM) protocol naturally defines a *two-decomposable* RE $\hat{f}(x; r) = (M_1(x_1; r), M_2(x_2; r))$, and in the multiparty setting it corresponds to a DARE $\hat{f}(x; r) = (M_1(x_1; r), \ldots, M_n(x_n; r))$. The best known protocols (for an arbitrary function) appear in [23]. This model and its variants (e.g., for conditional disclosure of secrets) are further studied in [68, 45, 18, 22].

Complexity-theoretic treatment   From a complexity-theoretic perspective, the notion of "simple" computation may be associated with probabilistic polynomial-time computation. Hence, the question of encoding a complex function by a "simpler" one naturally corresponds to polynomial-time computable encodings. We can now ask which functions can be statistically encoded by efficiently computable encodings, and define a corresponding complexity class **SRE**. To avoid trivialities, we allow the decoder to be inefficient. Going back to Example 1.1.3, this corresponds to the setting where a weak (polynomial-time) client who holds an input x wishes to release the value $f(x)$ to a computationally unbounded server without leaking the value of x. It is not hard to show that the resulting complexity class **SRE** contains **BPP** and is contained in the class of languages that admit statistical zero-knowledge protocols (**SZK**) [6]. The exact relation between these three classes is further studied in [1] and [17].

1.7 Appendix: Randomized Encodings Versus Garbling Schemes [26]

In this section we briefly compare the RE framework with the notion of *garbling schemes* introduced by Bellare, Hoang, and Rogaway (BHR) in [26].

Roughly speaking, garbling schemes can be viewed as a concrete variant of RE which is required to satisfy some additional syntactic properties. In particular, the encoding $\hat{f}(x; r)$ is partitioned into three parts (F, d, X), where X is the online part, and (F, d) essentially corresponds to the offline part of the encoding. (The d part is viewed as a "decoding key", and it allows one to consider a designated decoding variant as opposed to public decoding). The BHR framework decomposes the encoder into two algorithms $(\mathsf{Gb}, \mathsf{En})$, and decomposes the decoder into two algorithms $(\mathsf{De}, \mathsf{Ev})$ as follows:

Syntax   The probabilistic garbling algorithm Gb is given a security parameter 1^k and a description of a function f (under some fixed representation scheme) and returns a triple of strings $(F, e, d) \overset{R}{\leftarrow} \mathsf{Gb}(1^k, f)$. Think of F as an offline encoding, and e and d as encoding and decoding keys, respectively. The strings e, d and the length of F are allowed to depend on the syntactic properties of f (i.e., its input length, output length, and description length), but, otherwise, should be independent of f. The (deterministic) *input encoding* algorithm, $\mathsf{En}(\cdot, \cdot)$, takes an encoding key e and an input $x \in \{0, 1\}^n$ and outputs a garbled input $X = \mathsf{En}(e, x)$. The decoding proceeds in two steps: first the algorithm $\mathsf{Ev}(F, X)$ maps F and a garbled input X to a "garbled output" $Y = \mathsf{Ev}(F, X)$, and second the decoding algorithm $\mathsf{De}(d, Y)$ maps a decoding key d and a garbled output Y to a final output $y = \mathsf{De}(d, Y)$. Correctness asserts that $\mathsf{De}(d, \mathsf{Ev}(F, \mathsf{En}(e, x))) = \mathsf{ev}(f, x)$, where ev is a universal evaluation algorithm that maps a description f of a function, and an input x to the value of the corresponding function on the input x. Overall, BHR define a *garbling scheme* as the five-tuple $(\mathsf{Gb}, \mathsf{En}, \mathsf{De}, \mathsf{Ev}, \mathsf{ev})$.

Security   Garbling schemes can satisfy different variants of security. The most central one is a parameterized version of privacy which, in addition to standard privacy (as defined for REs), may support some notion of "function hiding" for the encoded function f (the exact level of hiding depends on a leakage parameter). Other notions of security include *obliviousness* and *authenticity*. Obliviousness means that decoding can be performed only given a secret key d (i.e., (F, X) do not reveal $y = f(x)$). Authenticity essentially means that, given (F, X), it is hard to generate Y', which leads to an undetected decoding error (i.e., $\mathsf{De}(d, Y') \notin \{f(x), \bot\}$).

Comparison   Syntactically, garbling schemes and REs are quite different. These differences reflect two conflicting goals. The garbling scheme framework offers a concrete and highly detailed treatment of garbled circuits which can be almost given to a programmer as an API. As a result, efficiency requirements (e.g., on-line efficiency) are hard-wired into the syntax itself. Moreover, in order to keep the framework wide enough (while keeping it concrete), the syntax has to take into account several different usage scenarios (e.g., the possibility of designated decoding) which, inevitably, make the definition more complicated (e.g., the decomposition of the decoder into an evaluator and decoder). In contrast, the RE framework strives for minimalism. It deals only with basic correctness and privacy, and deliberately leaves efficiency issues to be determined in an application-dependent context.[19] As a result, the RE framework offers a high-level view which misses some practical aspects but highlights the general properties of REs which are independent of efficiency concerns (cf. Section 1.2.3).

References

[1] S. Agrawal, Y. Ishai, D. Khurana, and A. Paskin-Cherniavsky. Statistical randomized encodings: A complexity theoretic view. In M. M. Halldórsson, K. Iwama, N. Kobayashi, and B. Speckmann, editors, *ICALP 2015, Part I*, volume 9134 of *LNCS*, pages 1–13. Springer, Heidelberg, July 2015.

[2] B. Applebaum. Key-dependent message security: Generic amplification and completeness. In K. G. Paterson, editor, *EUROCRYPT 2011*, volume 6632 of *LNCS*, pages 527–546. Springer, Heidelberg, May 2011.

[3] B. Applebaum. Randomly encoding functions: A new cryptographic paradigm - (invited talk). In S. Fehr, editor, *ICITS 11*, volume 6673 of *LNCS*, pages 25–31. Springer, Heidelberg, May 2011.

[4] B. Applebaum. Garbling XOR gates "for free" in the standard model. In A. Sahai, editor, *TCC 2013*, volume 7785 of *LNCS*, pages 162–181. Springer, Heidelberg, Mar. 2013.

[5] B. Applebaum. Bootstrapping obfuscators via fast pseudorandom functions. In P. Sarkar and T. Iwata, editors, *ASIACRYPT 2014, Part II*, volume 8874 of *LNCS*, pages 162–172. Springer, Heidelberg, Dec. 2014.

---

[19] This is also the case with more refined security variants. Indeed, function hiding, obliviousness, and authenticity can all be reduced to basic privacy via simple transformations with a polynomial overhead (e.g., by encoding a universal circuit $g(\langle f \rangle, x) = f(x)$, encoding an encrypted circuit $g(s, x) = f(x) \oplus s$, or encoding a MAC-ed circuit $g(s, x) = \mathsf{MAC}_s(f(x))$; see Section 1.5.1). Of course, direct study of these notions may lead to solutions with better efficiency.

[6] B. Applebaum. *Cryptography in Constant Parallel Time*. Information Security and Cryptography. Springer, 2014.

[7] B. Applebaum, S. Artemenko, R. Shaltiel, and G. Yang. Incompressible functions, relative-error extractors, and the power of nondeterministic reductions (extended abstract). In *30th Conference on Computational Complexity, CCC 2015, June 17-19, 2015, Portland, Oregon, USA*, pages 582–600, 2015.

[8] B. Applebaum, J. Avron, and C. Brzuska. Arithmetic cryptography: Extended abstract. In T. Roughgarden, editor, *ITCS 2015*, pages 143–151. ACM, Jan. 2015.

[9] B. Applebaum, D. Cash, C. Peikert, and A. Sahai. Fast cryptographic primitives and circular-secure encryption based on hard learning problems. In S. Halevi, editor, *CRYPTO 2009*, volume 5677 of *LNCS*, pages 595–618. Springer, Heidelberg, Aug. 2009.

[10] B. Applebaum, Y. Ishai, and E. Kushilevitz. Cryptography in NC^0. In *45th FOCS*, pages 166–175. IEEE Computer Society Press, Oct. 2004.

[11] B. Applebaum, Y. Ishai, and E. Kushilevitz. Computationally private randomizing polynomials and their applications. *Computational Complexity*, 15(2):115–162, 2006.

[12] B. Applebaum, Y. Ishai, and E. Kushilevitz. Cryptography with constant input locality. In A. Menezes, editor, *CRYPTO 2007*, volume 4622 of *LNCS*, pages 92–110. Springer, Heidelberg, Aug. 2007.

[13] B. Applebaum, Y. Ishai, and E. Kushilevitz. Cryptography by cellular automata or how fast can complexity emerge in nature? In A. C.-C. Yao, editor, *ICS 2010*, pages 1–19. Tsinghua University Press, Jan. 2010.

[14] B. Applebaum, Y. Ishai, and E. Kushilevitz. From secrecy to soundness: Efficient verification via secure computation. In S. Abramsky, C. Gavoille, C. Kirchner, F. Meyer auf der Heide, and P. G. Spirakis, editors, *ICALP 2010, Part I*, volume 6198 of *LNCS*, pages 152–163. Springer, Heidelberg, July 2010.

[15] B. Applebaum, Y. Ishai, and E. Kushilevitz. How to garble arithmetic circuits. In R. Ostrovsky, editor, *52nd FOCS*, pages 120–129. IEEE Computer Society Press, Oct. 2011.

[16] B. Applebaum, Y. Ishai, E. Kushilevitz, and B. Waters. Encoding functions with constant online rate or how to compress garbled circuits keys. In R. Canetti and J. A. Garay, editors, *CRYPTO 2013, Part II*, volume 8043 of *LNCS*, pages 166–184. Springer, Heidelberg, Aug. 2013.

[17] B. Applebaum and P. Raykov. On the relationship between statistical zero-knowledge and statistical randomized encodings. In *CRYPTO 2016, part III*, LNCS vol. 9816, Springer, 2016.

[18] B. Applebaum and P. Raykov. From private simultaneous messages to zero-information Arthur-Merlin protocols and back. LNCS, pages 65–82. Springer, Heidelberg, 2016.

[19] B. Barak, I. Haitner, D. Hofheinz, and Y. Ishai. Bounded key-dependent message security. In H. Gilbert, editor, *EUROCRYPT 2010*, volume 6110 of *LNCS*, pages 423–444. Springer, Heidelberg, May 2010.

[20] B. Barak, M. Prabhakaran, and A. Sahai. Concurrent non-malleable zero knowledge. In *47th FOCS*, pages 345–354. IEEE Computer Society Press, Oct. 2006.

[21] D. Beaver, S. Micali, and P. Rogaway. The round complexity of secure protocols (extended abstract). In *22nd ACM STOC*, pages 503–513. ACM Press, May 1990.

[22] A. Beimel, A. Gabizon, Y. Ishai, and E. Kushilevitz. Distribution design. In M. Sudan, editor, *ITCS 2016*, pages 81–92. ACM, Jan. 2016.

[23] A. Beimel, Y. Ishai, R. Kumaresan, and E. Kushilevitz. On the cryptographic complexity of the worst functions. In Y. Lindell, editor, *TCC 2014*, volume 8349 of *LNCS*, pages 317–342. Springer, Heidelberg, Feb. 2014.

[24] M. Bellare, V. T. Hoang, S. Keelveedhi, and P. Rogaway. Efficient garbling from a fixed-key blockcipher. In *2013 IEEE Symposium on Security and Privacy*, pages 478–492. IEEE Computer Society Press, May 2013.

[25] M. Bellare, V. T. Hoang, and P. Rogaway. Adaptively secure garbling with applications to one-time programs and secure outsourcing. In X. Wang and K. Sako, editors, *ASIACRYPT 2012*, volume 7658 of *LNCS*, pages 134–153. Springer, Heidelberg, Dec. 2012.

[26] M. Bellare, V. T. Hoang, and P. Rogaway. Foundations of garbled circuits. In T. Yu, G. Danezis, and V. D. Gligor, editors, *ACM CCS 12*, pages 784–796. ACM Press, Oct. 2012.

[27] M. Ben-Or, S. Goldwasser, and A. Wigderson. Completeness theorems for non-cryptographic fault-tolerant distributed computation (extended abstract). In *20th ACM STOC*, pages 1–10. ACM Press, May 1988.

[28] N. Bitansky, S. Garg, H. Lin, R. Pass, and S. Telang. Succinct randomized encodings and their applications. In R. A. Servedio and R. Rubinfeld, editors, *47th ACM STOC*, pages 439–448. ACM Press, June 2015.

[29] J. Black, P. Rogaway, and T. Shrimpton. Encryption-scheme security in the presence of key-dependent messages. In K. Nyberg and H. M. Heys, editors, *SAC 2002*, volume 2595 of *LNCS*, pages 62–75. Springer, Heidelberg, Aug. 2003.

[30] D. Boneh, C. Gentry, S. Gorbunov, S. Halevi, V. Nikolaenko, G. Segev, V. Vaikuntanathan, and D. Vinayagamurthy. Fully key-homomorphic encryption, arithmetic circuit ABE and compact garbled circuits. In P. Q. Nguyen and E. Oswald, editors, *EUROCRYPT 2014*, volume 8441 of *LNCS*, pages 533–556. Springer, Heidelberg, May 2014.

[31] D. Boneh, S. Halevi, M. Hamburg, and R. Ostrovsky. Circular-secure encryption from decision Diffie-Hellman. In D. Wagner, editor, *CRYPTO 2008*, volume 5157 of *LNCS*, pages 108–125. Springer, Heidelberg, Aug. 2008.

[32] Z. Brakerski and S. Goldwasser. Circular and leakage resilient public-key encryption under subgroup indistinguishability - (or: Quadratic residuosity strikes back). In T. Rabin, editor, *CRYPTO 2010*, volume 6223 of *LNCS*, pages 1–20. Springer, Heidelberg, Aug. 2010.

[33] Z. Brakerski, S. Goldwasser, and Y. T. Kalai. Black-box circular-secure encryption beyond affine functions. In Y. Ishai, editor, *TCC 2011*, volume 6597 of *LNCS*, pages 201–218. Springer, Heidelberg, Mar. 2011.

[34] Z. Brakerski and V. Vaikuntanathan. Efficient fully homomorphic encryption from (standard) LWE. In R. Ostrovsky, editor, *52nd FOCS*, pages 97–106. IEEE Computer Society Press, Oct. 2011.

[35] C. Cachin, J. Camenisch, J. Kilian, and J. Muller. One-round secure computation and secure autonomous mobile agents. In U. Montanari, J. D. P. Rolim, and E. Welzl, editors, *ICALP 2000*, volume 1853 of *LNCS*, pages 512–523. Springer, Heidelberg, July 2000.

[36] J. Camenisch and A. Lysyanskaya. An efficient system for non-transferable anonymous credentials with optional anonymity revocation. In B. Pfitzmann, editor, *EUROCRYPT 2001*, volume 2045 of *LNCS*, pages 93–118. Springer, Heidelberg, May 2001.

[37] R. Canetti, J. Holmgren, A. Jain, and V. Vaikuntanathan. Succinct garbling and indistinguishability obfuscation for RAM programs. In R. A. Servedio and R. Rubinfeld, editors, *47th ACM STOC*, pages 429–437. ACM Press, June 2015.

[38] R. Canetti, H. Lin, S. Tessaro, and V. Vaikuntanathan. Obfuscation of probabilistic circuits and applications. In Y. Dodis and J. B. Nielsen, editors, *TCC 2015, Part II*, volume 9015 of *LNCS*, pages 468–497. Springer, Heidelberg, Mar. 2015.

[39] D. Chaum, C. Crépeau, and I. Damgård. Multiparty unconditionally secure protocols (extended abstract). In *20th ACM STOC*, pages 11–19. ACM Press, May 1988.

[40] R. Cramer, S. Fehr, Y. Ishai, and E. Kushilevitz. Efficient multi-party computation over rings. In E. Biham, editor, *EUROCRYPT 2003*, volume 2656 of *LNCS*, pages 596–613. Springer, Heidelberg, May 2003.

[41] I. Damgård and Y. Ishai. Scalable secure multiparty computation. In C. Dwork, editor, *CRYPTO 2006*, volume 4117 of *LNCS*, pages 501–520. Springer, Heidelberg, Aug. 2006.

[42] Z. Dvir, D. Gutfreund, G. N. Rothblum, and S. P. Vadhan. On approximating the entropy of polynomial mappings. In B. Chazelle, editor, *ICS 2011*, pages 460–475. Tsinghua University Press, Jan. 2011.

[43] U. Feige, J. Kilian, and M. Naor. A minimal model for secure computation (extended abstract). In *26th ACM STOC*, pages 554–563. ACM Press, May 1994.

[44] S. Garg, S. Lu, R. Ostrovsky, and A. Scafuro. Garbled RAM from one-way functions. In R. A. Servedio and R. Rubinfeld, editors, *47th ACM STOC*, pages 449–458. ACM Press, June 2015.

[45] R. Gay, I. Kerenidis, and H. Wee. Communication complexity of conditional disclosure of secrets and attribute-based encryption. In R. Gennaro and M. J. B. Robshaw, editors, *CRYPTO 2015, Part II*, volume 9216 of *LNCS*, pages 485–502. Springer, Heidelberg, Aug. 2015.

[46] R. Gennaro, C. Gentry, and B. Parno. Non-interactive verifiable computing: Outsourcing computation to untrusted workers. In T. Rabin, editor, *CRYPTO 2010*, volume 6223 of *LNCS*, pages 465–482. Springer, Heidelberg, Aug. 2010.

[47] C. Gentry. Fully homomorphic encryption using ideal lattices. In M. Mitzenmacher, editor, *41st ACM STOC*, pages 169–178. ACM Press, May / June 2009.

[48] C. Gentry, S. Halevi, S. Lu, R. Ostrovsky, M. Raykova, and D. Wichs. Garbled RAM revisited. In P. Q. Nguyen and E. Oswald, editors, *EUROCRYPT 2014*, volume 8441 of *LNCS*, pages 405–422. Springer, Heidelberg, May 2014.

[49] C. Gentry, S. Halevi, and V. Vaikuntanathan. i-Hop homomorphic encryption and rerandomizable Yao circuits. In T. Rabin, editor, *CRYPTO 2010*, volume 6223 of *LNCS*, pages 155–172. Springer, Heidelberg, Aug. 2010.

[50] Y. Gertner, Y. Ishai, E. Kushilevitz, and T. Malkin. Protecting data privacy in private information retrieval schemes. *JCSS: Journal of Computer and System Sciences*, 60, 2000.

[51] O. Goldreich, S. Micali, and A. Wigderson. How to play any mental game or a completeness theorem for protocols with honest majority. In A. Aho, editor, *19th ACM STOC*, pages 218–229. ACM Press, May 1987.

[52] S. Goldwasser, D. Gutfreund, A. Healy, T. Kaufman, and G. N. Rothblum. A (de)constructive approach to program checking. In R. E. Ladner and C. Dwork, editors, *40th ACM STOC*, pages 143–152. ACM Press, May 2008.

[53] S. Goldwasser, Y. T. Kalai, R. A. Popa, V. Vaikuntanathan, and N. Zeldovich. How to run Turing machines on encrypted data. In R. Canetti and J. A. Garay, editors, *CRYPTO 2013, Part II*, volume 8043 of *LNCS*, pages 536–553. Springer, 2013.

[54] S. Goldwasser, Y. T. Kalai, R. A. Popa, V. Vaikuntanathan, and N. Zeldovich. Reusable garbled circuits and succinct functional encryption. In D. Boneh, T. Roughgarden, and J. Feigenbaum, editors, *45th ACM STOC*, pages 555–564. ACM Press, June 2013.

[55] S. Goldwasser, Y. T. Kalai, and G. N. Rothblum. One-time programs. In D. Wagner, editor, *CRYPTO 2008*, volume 5157 of *LNCS*, pages 39–56. Springer, Heidelberg, Aug. 2008.

[56] S. Gorbunov, V. Vaikuntanathan, and H. Wee. Functional encryption with bounded collusions via multi-party computation. In R. Safavi-Naini and R. Canetti, editors, *CRYPTO 2012*, volume 7417 of *LNCS*, pages 162–179. Springer, Heidelberg, Aug. 2012.

[57] S. Gorbunov, V. Vaikuntanathan, and H. Wee. Attribute-based encryption for circuits. In D. Boneh, T. Roughgarden, and J. Feigenbaum, editors, *45th ACM STOC*, pages 545–554. ACM Press, June 2013.

[58] V. Goyal, Y. Ishai, A. Sahai, R. Venkatesan, and A. Wadia. Founding cryptography on tamper-proof hardware tokens. In D. Micciancio, editor, *TCC 2010*, volume 5978 of *LNCS*, pages 308–326. Springer, Heidelberg, Feb. 2010.

[59] I. Haitner, O. Reingold, and S. P. Vadhan. Efficiency improvements in constructing pseudorandom generators from one-way functions. In L. J. Schulman, editor, *42nd ACM STOC*, pages 437–446. ACM Press, June 2010.

[60] D. Harnik and M. Naor. On the compressibility of NP instances and cryptographic applications. In *47th FOCS*, pages 719–728. IEEE Computer Society Press, Oct. 2006.

[61] J. Håstad, R. Impagliazzo, L. A. Levin, and M. Luby. A pseudorandom generator from any one-way function. *SIAM Journal on Computing*, 28(4):1364–1396, 1999.

[62] B. Hemenway, Z. Jafargholi, R. Ostrovsky, A. Scafuro, and D. Wichs. Adaptively secure garbled circuits from one-way functions. In *CRYPTO 2016, part III*, LNCS vol. 9816, Springer, 2016.

[63] Y. Huang, D. Evans, J. Katz, and L. Malka. Faster secure two-party computation using garbled circuits. In *20th USENIX Security Symposium*, 2011.

[64] Y. Ishai. Randomization techniques for secure computation. In M. Prabhakaran and A. Sahai, editors, *Secure Multi-Party Computation*, volume 10 of *Cryptology and Information Security Series*, pages 222–248. IOS Press, 2013.

[65] Y. Ishai and E. Kushilevitz. Private simultaneous messages protocols with applications. In *ISTCS*, pages 174–184, 1997.

[66] Y. Ishai and E. Kushilevitz. Randomizing polynomials: A new representation with applications to round-efficient secure computation. In *41st FOCS*, pages 294–304. IEEE Computer Society Press, Nov. 2000.

[67] Y. Ishai and E. Kushilevitz. Perfect constant-round secure computation via perfect randomizing polynomials. In P. Widmayer, F. T. Ruiz, R. M. Bueno, M. Hennessy, S. Eidenbenz, and R. Conejo, editors, *ICALP 2002*, volume 2380 of *LNCS*, pages 244–256. Springer, Heidelberg, July 2002.

[68] Y. Ishai and H. Wee. Partial garbling schemes and their applications. In J. Esparza, P. Fraigniaud, T. Husfeldt, and E. Koutsoupias, editors, *ICALP 2014, Part I*, volume 8572 of *LNCS*, pages 650–662. Springer, Heidelberg, July 2014.

[69] J. Kilian. Founding cryptography on oblivious transfer. In *20th ACM STOC*, pages 20–31. ACM Press, May 1988.

[70] V. Kolesnikov, P. Mohassel, and M. Rosulek. FleXOR: Flexible garbling for XOR gates that beats free-XOR. In J. A. Garay and R. Gennaro, editors, *CRYPTO 2014, Part II*, volume 8617 of *LNCS*, pages 440–457. Springer, Heidelberg, Aug. 2014.

[71] V. Kolesnikov and T. Schneider. Improved garbled circuit: Free XOR gates and applications. In L. Aceto, I. Damgård, L. A. Goldberg, M. M. Halldórsson, A. Ingólfsdóttir, and I. Walukiewicz, editors, *ICALP 2008, Part II*, volume 5126 of *LNCS*, pages 486–498. Springer, Heidelberg, July 2008.

[72] V. Koppula, A. B. Lewko, and B. Waters. Indistinguishability obfuscation for Turing machines with unbounded memory. In R. A. Servedio and R. Rubinfeld, editors, *47th ACM STOC*, pages 419–428. ACM Press, June 2015.

[73] B. Kreuter, a. shelat, and C. hao Shen. Billion-gate secure computation with malicious adversaries. Cryptology ePrint Archive, Report 2012/179, 2012. http://eprint.iacr.org/2012/179.

[74] H. Lin, R. Pass, K. Seth, and S. Telang. Output-compressing randomized encodings and applications. LNCS, pages 96–124. Springer, Heidelberg, 2016.

[75] Y. Lindell and B. Pinkas. A proof of security of Yao's protocol for two-party
computation. *Journal of Cryptology*, 22(2):161–188, Apr. 2009.

[76] Y. Lindell and B. Pinkas. An efficient protocol for secure two-party computation in the presence of malicious adversaries. *Journal of Cryptology*,
28(2):312–350, Apr. 2015.

[77] Y. Lindell, B. Pinkas, and N. P. Smart. Implementing two-party computation
efficiently with security against malicious adversaries. In R. Ostrovsky, R. D.
Prisco, and I. Visconti, editors, *SCN 08*, volume 5229 of *LNCS*, pages 2–20.
Springer, Heidelberg, Sept. 2008.

[78] S. Lu and R. Ostrovsky. How to garble RAM programs. In T. Johansson
and P. Q. Nguyen, editors, *EUROCRYPT 2013*, volume 7881 of *LNCS*, pages
719–734. Springer, Heidelberg, May 2013.

[79] D. Malkhi, N. Nisan, B. Pinkas, and Y. Sella. Fairplay - secure two-party
computation system. In *13th USENIX Security Symposium*, pages 287–302,
2004.

[80] M. Naor, B. Pinkas, and R. Sumner. Privacy preserving auctions and mechanism design. In *1st EC*, pages 129–139. ACM Press, Nov. 1999.

[81] B. Pinkas, T. Schneider, N. P. Smart, and S. C. Williams. Secure two-party
computation is practical. In M. Matsui, editor, *ASIACRYPT 2009*, volume
5912 of *LNCS*, pages 250–267. Springer, Heidelberg, Dec. 2009.

[82] M. Rosulek. A brief history of practical garbled circuit optimizations. Securing
Computation workshop, Simons Institute, June 2015. Available at http://
web.engr.oregonstate.edu/~rosulekm/.

[83] A. Sahai and H. Seyalioglu. Worry-free encryption: functional encryption with
public keys. In E. Al-Shaer, A. D. Keromytis, and V. Shmatikov, editors, *ACM
CCS 10*, pages 463–472. ACM Press, Oct. 2010.

[84] T. Sander, A. Young, and M. Yung. Non-interactive cryptocomputing for NC1.
In *40th FOCS*, pages 554–567. IEEE Computer Society Press, Oct. 1999.

[85] A. C.-C. Yao. Protocols for secure computations (extended abstract). In *23rd
FOCS*, pages 160–164. IEEE Computer Society Press, Nov. 1982.

[86] A. C.-C. Yao. How to generate and exchange secrets (extended abstract). In
27th FOCS, pages 162–167. IEEE Computer Society Press, Oct. 1986.

[87] S. Zahur, M. Rosulek, and D. Evans. Two halves make a whole - reducing
data transfer in garbled circuits using half gates. In E. Oswald and M. Fischlin,
editors, *EUROCRYPT 2015, Part II*, volume 9057 of *LNCS*, pages 220–250.
Springer, Heidelberg, Apr. 2015.

Chapter 2
The Complexity of Public-Key Cryptography

Boaz Barak

Abstract We survey the computational foundations for public-key cryptography. We discuss the computational assumptions that have been used as bases for public-key encryption schemes, and the types of evidence we have for the veracity of these assumptions.

2.1 Introduction

Let us go back to 1977. The first (or fourth, depending on your count) "Star Wars" movie was released, ABBA recorded "Dancing Queen" and in August, Martin Gardner described in his *Scientific American* column the RSA cryptosystem [110], whose security relies on the difficulty of integer factoring. This came on the heels of Diffie, Hellman, and Merkle's 1976 invention of public-key cryptography and the discrete-logarithm based Diffie–Hellman key exchange protocol [41].

Now consider an alternative history. Suppose that, in December of that year, a mathematician named Dieter Chor discovered an efficient algorithm to compute discrete logarithms and factor integers. One could imagine that, in this case, scientific consensus would be that there is something *inherently impossible* about the notion of public-key cryptography, which anyway sounded "too good to be true". In the ensuing years, people would occasionally offer various alternative constructions for public-key encryption, but, having been burned before, the scientific and technological communities would be wary of adapting them, and treat such constructions as being *insecure* until proven otherwise.

This alternative history is of course very different from our own, where public-key cryptography is a widely studied and implemented notion. But are the underlying scientific facts so different? We currently have no strong evidence that the integer factoring and discrete logarithm problems are actually hard. Indeed, Peter Shor [115] has presented an algorithm for this problem that runs in polynomial time

Boaz Barak
Harvard John A. Paulson School of Engineering and Applied Sciences, e-mail: b@boazbarak.org

on a so-called "quantum computer". While some researchers (including Oded Goldreich [52, 54]) have expressed deep skepticism about the possibility of physically implementing this model, the NSA is sufficiently concerned about this possibility to warn that government and industry should transition away from these cryptosystems in the "not too far future" [1]. In any case we have no real justification to assume the nonexistence of a *classical* (i.e., not quantum) algorithm for these problems, especially given their strong and not yet fully understood mathematical structure and the existence of highly non-trivial subexponential algorithms [84, 35].

In this tutorial I want to explore the impact on the *theory* of cryptography of such a hypothetical (or perhaps not so hypothetical) scenario of a breakthrough on the discrete logarithm and factoring problems, and use this as a launching pad for a broader exploration of the role of hardness assumptions in our field. I will discuss not just the *mathematical* but also the *social* and *philosophical* aspects of this question. Such considerations play an important role in any science, but especially so when we deal with the question of which unproven assumptions we should believe in. This is not a standard tutorial or a survey, in the sense that it is more about *questions* than *answers*, and many of my takes on these questions are rather subjective. Nevertheless, I do think it is appropriate that students or anyone else who is interested in research on the foundations of cryptography consider these types of questions, and form their own opinions on the right way to approach them.

Acknowledgements This survey is written in honor of Oded Goldreich's 60th birthday. I was first exposed to the beauty of the foundations of cryptography through Oded, and while we may not always agree on specific issues, his teachings, writing, and our discussions have greatly influenced my own views on this topic. Oded wrote many essays worth reading on issues related to this survey, such as subjectivity and taste in science [48], computational assumptions in cryptography [51, 49], as well as the distinction between pure and applied (or "intellectual" versus "instrumental") science [50, 53]. I also thank Benny Applebaum, Nir Bitansky, and Shai Halevi for extremely insightful comments on earlier versions of this survey that greatly improved its presentation.

2.1.1 What Is Special About Public-Key Cryptography?

Perhaps the first instance of an unjustified subjective judgment in this chapter is my singling out of the integer factoring and discrete logarithm problems, as well as other "public key type" assumptions, as particularly deserving of suspicion. After all, given that we haven't managed to prove $P \neq NP$, essentially *all* cryptographic primitives rest on unproven assumptions, whether it is the difficulty of factoring, discrete log, or breaking the AES cipher. Indeed, partially for this reason, much of the work on theoretical cryptography does not deal directly with particular hard problems but rather builds a *web of reductions* between different primitives. Reduction-based security has been a resounding success precisely because it allows to *reduce* the security of a great many cryptographic constructions to a relatively small number of simple-to-state and widely studied assumptions. It helped change cryptography from an alchemy-like activity which relied on "security by obscurity" to a science with well-defined security properties that are obtained under precisely stated conjectures, and is often considered the strongest component in secure applications.

Given the above, one can think of the canonical activity of a theoretical cryptographer as constructing a new (typically more sophisticated or satisfying stricter security notions) cryptographic primitive from an old primitive (that would typically be simpler, or easier to construct).[1] The "bottommost layer" of such primitives would have several *candidate constructions* based on various hardness assumptions, and new developments in cryptanalytic algorithms would simply mean that we have one fewer candidate.

The intuition above is more or less accurate for *private-key cryptography*. Over the last three decades, cryptographers have built a powerful web of reductions showing constructions of a great many objects from the basic primitive of *one-way functions*.[2] And indeed, as discussed in Section 2.2 below, we do have a number of candidate constructions for one way functions, including not just constructions based on factoring and discrete logarithms, but also constructions based on simple combinatorial problems such as planted clique [78], random SAT [2], Goldreich's expander-based candidate [57], as well as the many candidate block ciphers, stream ciphers, and hash functions such as [39, 98, 20, 21] that are widely used in practice and for many of which no significant attacks are known despite much cryptanalytic effort.

However, for *public-key* cryptography, the situation is quite different. There are essentially only two major strains of public-key systems.[3] The first family consists of the "algebraic" or "group-theoretic" constructions based on integer factoring and the discrete logarithm problems, including the Diffie–Hellman [41] (and its elliptic curve variants [94, 81]), RSA [110], Rabin [106], Goldwasser–Micali [64] schemes and more. The second family consists of the "geometric" or "coding/lattice"-based systems of the type first proposed by McEliece [88] (as well as the broken Merkle–Hellman knapsack scheme [91]). These were invigorated by Ajtai's paper on *lattices* [5], which was followed by the works of Ajtai–Dwork [6], Goldreich–Goldwasser–Halevi [58], and Hoffstein et al. [68] giving *public-key* systems based on lattices, and by the later work of Regev [109] who introduced the *Learning With Errors (LWE)* assumption and showed its equivalence to certain hardness assumptions related to lattices.[4]

The known classical and quantum algorithms call into question the security of schemes based on the algebraic/group-theoretic family. After all, as theoreticians,

---

[1] For example, by my rough count, out of the nearly 800 pages of Goldreich's two-volume canonical text [55, 56], fewer than 30 deal with concrete assumptions.

[2] These include some seemingly *public-key* notions such as digital signatures which were constructed from one-way functions using the wonderful and surprising notion of pseudorandom functions put forward by Goldreich, Goldwasser, and Micali [59], as well as universal one-way hash functions [97, 111].

[3] I think this is a fair statement in terms of all systems that have actually been implemented and widely used (indeed by the latter metric, one might say there is only one major strain). However, as we will discuss in Section 2.5 below, there have been some alternative suggestions, including by this author.

[4] Admittedly, the distinction into "geometric" versus "algebraic" problems is somewhat subjective and arbitrary. In particular, lattices or linear codes are also Abelian groups. However, the type of problems on which the cryptographic primitives are based are more geometric or "noisy" in nature, as opposed to the algebraic questions that involve exact group structure.

we are interested in schemes for which efficient attacks are not merely *unknown* but are *nonexistent*. There is very little evidence that this first family satisfies this condition. That still leaves us with the second family of lattice/coding-based systems. Luckily, given recent advances, there is almost no primitive achieved by the group-theoretic family that cannot be based on lattices, and in fact many of the more exciting recent primitives, such as fully homomorphic encryption [47] and indistinguishability obfuscation [45], are only known based on lattice/coding assumptions.

If, given these classical and quantum algorithms, we do not want to trust the security of these "algebraic"/"group theoretic" cryptosystems, we are left in the rather uncomfortable situation where all the edifices of public-key cryptography have only one foundation that is fairly well studied, namely the difficulty of lattice/coding problems. Moreover, one could wonder whether talking about a "web of abstractions" is somewhat misleading if, at the bottommost layer, every primitive has essentially only a single implementation. This makes it particularly important to find out whether pubic key cryptography can be based on radically different assumptions. More generally, we would like to investigate the "assumption landscape" of cryptography, both in terms of concrete assumptions and in terms of relations between different objects. Such questions have of course interested researchers since the birth of modern cryptography, and we will review in this tutorial some of the discoveries that were made, and the many open questions that still remain.

Remark 2.1.1. *One way to phrase the question we are asking is to understand what type of structure is needed for public-key cryptography. One-way functions can be thought of as a completely unstructured object, both in the sense that they can be implemented from any hard-on-the-average search or "planted" problem [73], as well as that they directly follow from functions that have pseudorandom properties. In contrast, at least at the moment, we do not know how to obtain public-key encryption without assuming the difficulty of structured problems, and (as discussed in Remark 2.3.1) we do not know how to base public-key encryption on private-key schemes. The extent to which this is inherent is the topic of this survey; see also my survey [12] for more discussion on the role of structure in computational difficulty.*

2.1.2 Organization

In the rest of this tutorial we discuss the assumption landscape for both private and public-key cryptography (see Sections 2.2 and 2.3, respectively). Our emphasis is not on the most efficient schemes, nor on the ones that provide the most sophisticated security properties. Rather we merely attempt to cover a sample of candidate constructions that represents a variety of computational hardness assumptions. Moreover, we do not aim to provide full mathematical descriptions of those schemes— there are many excellent surveys and texts on these topics— but rather focus on their *qualitative* features.

Many of the judgment calls made here, such as whether two hardness assumptions (that are not known to be equivalent) are "similar" to one another, are inherently *subjective*. Section 2.6 is perhaps the most subjective part of this chapter, where we attempt to discuss what it is about a computational problem that makes it hard.

2.2 Private-Key Cryptography

Before talking about public-key cryptography, let us discuss *private-key* cryptography, where we have a much cleaner theoretical and practical picture of the landscape of assumptions. The fundamental theoretical object of private-key cryptography is a *one-way function*:

Definition 2.2.1 (One-way function). *A function* $F : \{0, 1\}^* \to \{0, 1\}^*$ *is a* one-way function *if there is a polynomial-time algorithm mapping* $r \in \{0, 1\}^*$ *to* $F(r)$ *and for every probabilistic polynomial-time algorithm A, constant c, and sufficiently large n,*

$$\Pr_{w=F(r);r \leftarrow_R \{0,1\}^n} [F(A(w)) = w] < n^{-c}.$$

We denote by OWF the conjecture that one-way functions exist.

While a priori the definition of one-way functions does not involve any secret key, in a large body of works it was shown (mainly through the connection to psuedo-randomness enabled by the Goldreich–Levin theorem [62]) that OWF is *equivalent* to the existence of many cryptographic primitives including:

- Pseudorandom generators [67]
- Pseudorandom functions and message authentication codes [59]
- Digital signatures [111][5]
- Commitment schemes [96].
- Zero knowledge proofs for every language in NP [63].[6]

(See Goldreich's text [55, 56] for many of these reductions as well as others.)

Thus, OWF can be thought of as the central conjecture of private-key cryptography. But what is the evidence for the *truth* of this conjecture?

2.2.1 Candidate Constructions for One-Way Functions

"From time immemorial, humanity has gotten frequent, often cruel, reminders that many things are easier to do than to reverse", Leonid Levin.

The main evidence for the OWF conjecture is that we have a great number of candidate constructions for one-way functions that are potentially secure. Indeed, it seems that "you can't throw a rock without hitting a one-way function" in the sense

---

[5] While from the perspective of applied cryptography, digital signatures are part of *public-key* cryptography, from our point of view of computational assumptions, they belong in the private-key world. We note that the current constructions of digital signatures from symmetric primitives are rather inefficient, and there are some negative results showing this may be inherent [16].

[6] Actually, zero-knowledge proofs for languages outside of **P** imply a slightly weaker form of "non-uniform" one-way functions, see [100].

that, once you cobble together a large number of simple computational operations then, unless the operations satisfy some special property such as linearity, you will typically get a function that is hard to invert (indeed, people have proposed some formalizations of this intuition, see Sections 2.2.1.4 and 2.2.1.5). Here are some example candidate constructions for one-way functions:

2.2.1.1 Block Ciphers, Stream Ciphers and Hash Functions

Many practical constructions of symmetric key primitives such as block ciphers, stream ciphers, and hash functions are believed to satisfy the security definitions of pseudorandom permutations, pseudorandom generators, and collision-resistant hash functions, respectively. All these notions imply the existence of one-way functions, and hence these primitives all yield candidate one-way functions. These constructions (including DES, AES, SHA-x, etc.) are typically described in terms of a fixed finite input and key size, but they often can be naturally generalized (e.g., see [93]). Note that practitioners often require very strong security from these primitives, and any attack faster than the trivial 2^n (where n is the key size, block size, etc.) is considered a weakness. Indeed, for many constructions that are considered weak or "broken", the known attacks still require exponential time (albeit with an exponent much smaller than n).[7]

2.2.1.2 Average Case Combinatorial Problems: Planted SAT, Planted Clique, Learning Parity with Noise

A *planted distribution* for an **NP** problem can be defined as follows:

Definition 2.2.2 (NP relations and planted problems). *A relation $R \subseteq \{0, 1\}^* \times \{0, 1\}^*$ is an* **NP** *relation if there is a polynomial $p(\cdot)$ such that $|y| \leq p(|x|)$ for every $(x, y) \in R$ and there is a polynomial-time algorithm M that on input (x, y) outputs 1 iff $(x, y) \in R$.*

A probabilistic polynomial-time algorithm G is a sampler for R if, for every n, $G(1^n)$ outputs with probability 1 a pair (x, y) such that $(x, y) \in R$.

We say that an algorithm A solves the planted problem corresponding to (G, R) if, for every n, with probability at least 0.9, $(x, A(x)) \in R$ where (x, y) is sampled from $G(1^n)$.

We say that the planted problem corresponding to (G, R) is hard if there is no probabilistic polynomial-time algorithm that solves it.

The following simple lemma shows that hard planted problems imply the OWF conjecture:

---

[7] The claim that it is easy to get one-way functions might seem contradictory to the fact that there have been successful cryptanalytic attacks even against cryptographic primitives that were constructed and widely studied by experts. However, practical constructions aim to achieve the best possible efficiency versus security tradeoff, which does require significant expertise. If one is fine with losing, say, a factor 100 in the efficiency (e.g., build a 1000-round block cipher instead of a 10-round one), then the task of constructing such primitives becomes significantly easier.

Lemma 2.2.3. *Suppose that there exists a hard planted problem (G, R). Then there exists a one-way function.*

Proof: We will show that a hard planted problem implies a *weak* one-way function, which we define here as a function F such that for every probabilistic polynomial-time A and sufficiently large m,

$$\Pr_{x=F(r); r \leftarrow_R \{0,1\}^m} [F(A(x)) = x] < 0.9 . \tag{2.1}$$

That is, we only require that an adversary fails to invert the function with probability larger than 90%, as opposed to nonnegligible probability as required in Definition 2.2.1. It is known that the existence of weak one-way functions implies the existence of strong ones (e.g., see [73], [55, Sec 2.3]). Let G be a generator for a hard planted problem and let R be the corresponding relation. By padding, we can assume without loss of generality that the number of coins that G uses on input 1^n is n^c for some integer $c \geq 1$. For every $r \in \{0,1\}^*$, we define $F(r) = x$ where $(x, y) = G(1^n; r_1 \ldots r_{n^c})$ where $n = \lfloor |r|^{1/c} \rfloor$, and $G(1^n; r)$ denotes the output of G on input 1^n and coins r.

We now show that F is a weak one-way function. Indeed, suppose towards a contradiction that there exists a probabilistic polynomial-time algorithm A violating (2.1) for some sufficiently large m, and let $n = \lfloor m^{1/c} \rfloor$. This means that

$$\Pr_{(x,y)=G(1^n; r_{1,\ldots,n}); r \leftarrow_R \{0,1\}^m} [G(1^n; A(x)) = x] \geq 0.9 ,$$

which in particular implies that, if we let $A'(x) = G(1^n; A(x))$, then with probability at least 0.9, $A'(x)$ will output a pair (x', y') with $x' = x$ and $(x', y') \in R$ (since the latter condition happens with probability 1 for outputs of G). Hence we get a polynomial-time algorithm to solve the planted problem with probability at least 0.9 on length n inputs. ∎

Using this connection, there are several natural planted problems that give rise to candidate one way functions:

The planted clique problem: It is well known that, in a random Erdős–Rényi graph $G_{n,1/2}$ (where every pair gets connected by an edge with probability $1/2$), the maximum clique size will be $(2 - o(1)) \log n$ [66, 27]. However, the greedy algorithm will find a clique of only $1 \cdot \log n$ size, and Karp asked in 1976 [79] whether there is an efficient algorithm to find a clique of size $(1 + \epsilon) \log n$. This remains open till this day. In the 1990s, Jerrum [76] and Kucera [82] considered the easier variant of whether one can find a clique of size $k \gg \log n$ that has been *planted* in a random graph by selecting a random k-size set and connecting all the vertices in it. The larger k is, the easier the problem, and at the moment no polynomial-time algorithm is known for this question for any $k = o(\sqrt{n})$. By the above discussion, if this problem is hard for any $k > 2 \log n$, then there exists a one-way function. Juels and Peinado [78] showed that, for $k = (1 + \epsilon) \log n$, the planted distribution is *statistically* *close* to the uniform distribution. As a result there is a hard planted distribution (and hence a one-way function) as long as the answer to Karp's question is negative.

Planted constraint satisfaction problems: A (binary alphabet) *constraint satisfaction problem* is a collection of functions $C = \{C_1, \ldots, C_m\}$ mapping $\{0, 1\}^n$ to $\{0, 1\}$ such that every function C_i depends on at most a constant number of the input bits. The *value* of C w.r.t. an assignment $x \in \{0, 1\}^n$ is defined as $\frac{1}{m} \sum_{i=1}^{m} C_i(x)$. The *value* of C is its maximum value over all assignments $x \in \{0, 1\}^n$.

There are several models for random constraint satisfaction problems. One simple model is the following: for every predicate $P : \{0, 1\}^k \rightarrow \{0, 1\}$ and numbers n, m, we can select $C_1, \ldots, C_m$ by choosing every C_i randomly and independently to equal $P(y_1, \ldots, y_k)$ where $y_1, \ldots, y_k$ are random and independent *literals* (i.e., equal to either x_j or to $1 - x_j$ for some random j). Using standard measure concentration results, the following can be shown:

Lemma 2.2.4. *For predicate $P : \{0, 1\}^k \rightarrow \{0, 1\}$ and every $\epsilon > 0$ there exists some constant α (depending on k, ϵ) such that, if $m > \alpha n$ and $C = (C_1, \ldots, C_m)$ is selected at random from the above model, then with probability at least $1 - \epsilon$, the value of C is in $[\mu - \epsilon, \mu + \epsilon]$ where $\mu = \mathbb{E}_{x \leftarrow_R \{0,1\}^k}[P(x)]$.*

There are several *planted* models where, given $x \in \{0, 1\}^n$, we sample at random an instance C such that the value of C w.r.t. x is significantly larger than μ. Here is one model suggested in [15]:

Definition 2.2.5. *Let P, n, m be as above, let $x \in \{0, 1\}^n$, and D be some distribution over $\{0, 1\}^k$. The (D, δ, x) planted model for generating a constraint satisfaction problem is obtained by repeating the following for $i = 1, \ldots, m$: with probability δ sample a random constraint C_i as above; otherwise sample a string d from D, and sample $y_1, \ldots, y_k$ to be random literals as above conditioned on the event that these literals applied to x yield d, and let C_i be the constraint $P(y_1, \ldots, y_k)$.*

Analogously to Lemma 2.2.4, if C is sampled from the (D, δ, x) model, then with high probability the value of C w.r.t. x will be at least $(1 - \delta)\mu_D - \epsilon$ where $\mu_D = \mathbb{E}_{x \leftarrow_R D}[P(x)]$. If $\mu_D > \mu$, then we can define the planted problem as trying to find an assignment with value at least, say, $\mu_D/2 + \mu/2$. [15] conjectured that this planted problem is hard as long as D is a *pairwise independent* distribution. This conjecture immediately gives rise to many candidate one-way functions based on predicates such as k-XOR, k-SAT, and more.

It was shown by Friedgut [44] that every random constraint satisfaction problem satisfies a *threshold* condition in the sense that, for every ϵ, as n grows, there is a value $m(n)$ such that the probability that a random instance of $(1 - \epsilon)m(n)$ constraints has value 1 is close to 1, while the probability that a random instance of $(1 + \epsilon)m(n)$ has value 1 is close to 0. It is widely believed that the value $m(n)$ has the value $\alpha^* n$ for some constant α^* depending on the problem (and are concrete guesses for this constant for many predicates) but this has not yet been proven in full generality and in particular the case of $3SAT$ is still open. It is also believed that, for k sufficiently large (possibly even $k = 3$ is enough), it is hard to find a satisfying (i.e., value 1) assignment for a random k-SAT constraint satisfaction problem where $m(n)$ is very close (but below) the threshold. Using a similar reasoning to [78] (but much more sophisticated techniques), Achlioptas and Coja-Oghlan [2] showed that this conjecture implies the hardness of a certain planted variant and hence yields another candidate for one-way functions.

2.2.1.3 Unsupervised Learning and Distributional One-Way Functions

Unsupervised learning applications yield another candidate for one-way functions. Here one can describe a *model M* as a probabilistic algorithm that, given some parameters $\theta \in \{0, 1\}^n$, samples from some distribution $M(\theta)$. The models studied in machine learning are all typically efficiently computable in the forward direction. The challenge is to solve the *inference* problem of recovering θ (or some approximation to it) given s independent samples $x_1, \ldots, x_s$ from $M(\theta)$.[8]

Consider s that is large enough so that the parameters are *statistically identifiable*.[9] For simplicity, let us define this as the condition that, for every θ, with high probability over the choice of $x = (x_1, \ldots, x_s)$ from $M(\theta)$, it holds that

$$P_{\theta'}(x) \ll 2^{-n} P_\theta(x) \qquad (2.2)$$

for every $\theta' \neq \theta$, where for every set of parameters ϑ and $x = (x_1, \ldots, x_s)$,

$$P_\theta(x) = \prod_{i=1}^{s} \Pr[M(\vartheta) = x_i] .$$

Now, suppose that we had an algorithm A that, given $x = (x_1, \ldots, x_s)$, could sample uniformly from the distribution on uniform parameters θ' and random coins $r_1, \ldots, r_s$ conditioned on $M(\theta'; r_i) = x_i$ for all $i \in \{1, \ldots, s\}$. Then (2.2) implies that, if the elements in x itself were sampled from $M(\theta)$ then with probability $1 - o(1)$ the first output θ' of A will equal θ. Thus, if there is a number of samples s where the unsupervised learning problem for M is statistically identifiable but computationally hard, then the process $\theta, r_1, \ldots, r_s \mapsto M(\theta; r_1), \ldots, M(\theta; r_s)$ is hard to invert in this distributional sense. But Impagliazzo and Luby [73] showed that the existence of not just weak one-way functions but even *distributional one-way functions* implies the existence of standard one-way functions, and hence any computationally hard unsupervised learning problem yields such a candidate.

The *Learning Parity with Noise* (LPN) problem is one example of a conjectured hard unsupervised learning problem that has been suggested as a basis for cryptography [60, 24]. Here the parameters of the model are a string $x \in \{0, 1\}^n$ and a

---

[8] This is a very general problem that has been considered in other fields as well, often under the name "parameter estimation problem" or "inverse problem", e.g., see [116].

[9] In many applications of machine learning, the parameters come from a continuous space, in which case they are typically only identifiable up to a small error. For simplicity, we ignore this issue here, as it is not very significant in our applications.

sample consists of a random $a \in \{0, 1\}^n$ and a bit $b = \langle a, x \rangle + \eta \pmod 2$, where η is chosen to equal 0 with probability $1 - \delta$ and 1 with probability δ for some constant $\delta > 0$. Using concentration of measure one can show that this model is statistically identifiable as long as the number of samples s is at least some constant times n, but the best known "efficient" algorithm requires $\exp(\Theta(n/\log n))$ samples and running time [25] ([86] improved the number of samples at the expense of some loss in error and running time). Thus, if this algorithm cannot be improved to work in an optimal number of samples and polynomial time, then one-way functions exist.[10]

2.2.1.4 Goldreich's One-Way Function Candidate

Goldreich has proposed a very elegant concrete candidate for a one-way function [57] which has caught several researchers' interest. Define an (n, m, d) graph to be a bipartite graph with n left vertices, m right vertices, and right degree d. Goldreich's function $Gol_{H,P} : \{0, 1\}^n \to \{0, 1\}^m$ is parameterized by an (n, m, d) graph H and a predicate $P : \{0, 1\}^d \to \{0, 1\}$. For every $x \in \{0, 1\}^m$ and $j \in [m]$, the jth output bit of Goldreich's function is defined as $Gol_{H,P}(x)_j = P(x_{\overleftarrow{\Gamma}_H(j)})$, where we denote by $\overleftarrow{\Gamma}_H(j)$ the set of left-neighbors of the vertex j in H, and x_S denotes the restriction of x to the coordinates in S.

Goldreich conjectured that this function is one way as long as P is sufficiently "structureless" and H is a sufficiently good expander. Several follow-up works showed evidence for this conjecture by showing that it is not refuted by certain natural families of algorithms [34, 75]. Other works showed that one needs to take care in the choice of the predicate P and ensure that it is *balanced*, as well as not having other properties that might make the problem easier [26]. Later works also suggested that Goldreich's function might even be a *pseudorandom generator* [10, 8, 99]. See Applebaum's survey [9] for more about the known constructions, attacks, and applications of Goldreich's function and its variants.

2.2.1.5 Random Circuits

Perhaps the most direct formalization of the intuition that if you cobble together enough operations, then you get a one-way function comes from a conjecture of Gowers [65] (see also [70]). He conjectured that for every n, there is some polynomial $m = m(n)$ such that, if we choose a sequence $\overline{\sigma} = (\sigma_1, \ldots, \sigma_m)$ of m *random local permutations* over $\{0, 1\}^n$, then the function $\sigma_1 \circ \cdots \sigma_m$ would be a *pseudorandom function*. We say that $\sigma : \{0, 1\}^n \to \{0, 1\}^n$ is a *local permutation* if it is obtained by applying a permutation on $\{0, 1\}^3$ on three of the input bits. That is, there exist $i, j, k \in [n]$ and a permutation $\pi : \{0, 1\}^3 \to \{0, 1\}^3$ such that $\sigma(x)_\ell = x_\ell$ if

---

[10] Clearly, the lower the noise parameter δ, the easier this problem, but the best known algorithm requires δ to be at most a logarithmic factor away from the trivial bound of $/1n$. As δ becomes smaller, and in particular smaller than $1/\sqrt{n}$, the problem seems to acquire some *structure* and becomes more similar to the *learning with errors problem* discussed in Section 2.4.2 below. Indeed, as we mention there, in this regime Alekhnovich [7] showed that the learning parity with noise problem can yield a *public-key* encryption scheme.

$\ell \notin \{i, j, k\}$ and $\sigma(x)_{i,j,k} = \pi(x_i, x_j, x_k)$. The choice of the sequence $\overline{\sigma}$ consists of the *seed* for the pseudorandom function. Since pseudorandom functions imply one-way functions, this yields another candidate.

2.2.1.6 Private-Key Cryptography from Public-Key Assumptions

While it is an obvious fact, it is worth mentioning that all the assumptions implying *public-key* cryptography also imply *private-key* cryptography as well. Thus one can obtain one-way functions based on the difficulty of integer factoring, discrete logarithm, learning with errors, and all of the other assumptions that have been suggested as bases for public-key encryption and digital signatures.

2.3 Public-Key Cryptography: an Overview

We have seen that there is a wide variety of candidate private-key encryption schemes. From a superficial search of the literature, it might seem that there are a great many *public-key* systems as well. However, the currently well-studied candidates fall into only two families: schemes based on the difficulty of algebraic problems on certain concrete *Abelian groups*, and schemes based on the difficulty of geometric problems on linear *codes* or integer *lattices*; see Figure 2.1.

Family	Sample cryptosystems	Structural properties
"Algebraic" family: Abelian groups	Diffie–Hellman (ElGamal, elliptic curve cryptography), RSA	Polynomial-time quantum algorithm, subexponential classical algorithms (for all but elliptic curves), can break in **NP ∩ coNP**
"Geometric" family: coding / lattices	Knapsack (Merkle–Hellman), McEliece, Goldreich–Goldwasser–Halevi, Ajtai–Dwork, NTRU, Regev	Can break in **NP ∩ coNP** or **SZK**. Nontrivial classical and quantum algorithms for special cases (knapsack, principal ideal lattices)

Fig. 2.1: The two "mainstream" families of public-key cryptosystems

Do these two families contain all the secure public schemes that exist? Or perhaps (if you think large-scale quantum computing could become a reality, or that the existing classical algorithms for the group-based family could be significantly improved) are lattices/codes the *only* source for secure public-key cryptography? The short answer is that we simply do not know, but in this chapter I want to explore the long answer.

We will discuss some of the alternative public-key systems that have been proposed in the literature (see Section 2.5 and Figure 2.4) and ask what is the evidence for their security, and also to what extent are they *truly different* from the first two families. We will also ask whether this game of coming up with candidates and trying to break them is the best we can do or is there a more *principled* way to argue about the security of cryptographic schemes.

As mentioned, our discussion will be inherently *subjective*. I do not know of an objective way to argue that two cryptographic schemes belong to the "same family" or are "dissimilar". Some readers might dispute the assertion that there is any crisis or potential crisis in the foundations of public-key cryptography, and some might even argue that there is no true difference between our evidence for the security of private and public-key cryptography. Nevertheless, I hope that even these readers will find some "food for thought" in this survey which is meant to provoke discussion more than to propose any final conclusions.

Remark 2.3.1. *One could ask if there really is an inherent difference between public-key and private-key cryptography or maybe this is simply a reflection of our ignorance. That is, is it possible to build a public-key cryptosystem out of an arbitrary one-way function and hence base it on the same assumptions as private-key encryption? The answer is that we do not know, but in a seminal work, Impagliazzo and Rudich [74] showed that this cannot be done via the standard form of black-box security reductions. Specifically, they showed that, even given a random oracle, which is an idealized one-way function, one cannot construct a key-exchange protocol with a black-box proof that is secure against all adversaries running in polynomial time (or even $\omega(n^6)$ time, where n is the time expended by the honest parties). Barak and Mahmoody [17] improved this to $\omega(n^2)$ time, thus matching Merkle's 1974 protocol discussed in Section 2.5.1 below.*

2.4 The Two "Mainstream" Public-Key Constructions

I now discuss the two main families of public-key constructions—ones that have their roots in the very first systems proposed by Diffie and Hellman [41], Rivest, Shamir and Adleman [110], Rabin [106], Merkle and Hellman [91], and McEliece [88] in the late 1970s.

2.4.1 The "Algebraic" Family: Abelian-Group Based Constructions

Some of the first proposals for public-key encryption were based on the *discrete logarithm* and the *factoring* problems, and these remain the most widely deployed and well-studied constructions. These were suggested in the open literature by Diffie and Hellman [41], Rivest, Shamir, and Adleman [110] and Rabin [106], and in retrospect we learned that these scheme were discovered a few years before in the intelligence community by Ellis, Cocks, and Williamson [42]. Later works by Miller [94] and Koblitz [81] obtained analogous schemes based on the discrete logarithm in *elliptic curve* groups.

These schemes have a rich algebraic structure that is essential to their use in the public-key setting, but also enable some nontrivial algorithmic results. These include the following:

- The factoring and discrete logarithm problems both fall in the class **TFNP**, which are **NP** search problems where *every* input is guaranteed to have a solution. Problems in this class cannot be **NP**-hard via a Cook reduction unless **NP** = **coNP** [89].[11] There are also some other complexity containments known for these problems [61, 30].
- The integer factoring problem and discrete logarithm problem over $\mathbb{Z}_p^*$ have subexponential algorithms running in time roughly $\exp(\tilde{O}(n^{1/3}))$, where n is the bit complexity [84].
- Very recently, *quasipolynomial*-time algorithms were shown for the discrete logarithm over finite fields of small characteristic [77].
- There is no general sub-exponential discrete logarithm algorithm for elliptic curves, though sub-exponential algorithms are known for some families of curves such as those with large genus [3]
- Shor's algorithm [115] yields a polynomial time *quantum* algorithm for both the factoring and discrete logarithm problem.

2.4.2 The "Geometric Family": Lattice/Coding/Knapsack-Based Cryptosystems

The second type of public-key encryption candidates also have a fairly extended history.[12] Merkle and Hellman proposed in 1978 their knapsack scheme [91] (which, together with several of its variants, was later broken by lattice reduction techniques [114]). In the same year, McEliece proposed a scheme based on the Goppa code [88]. In a seminal 1996 work, Ajtai [5] showed how to use integer lattices to obtain a one-way function based on *worst-case* assumptions. Motivated by this work, Goldreich, Goldwasser, and Halevi [58], as well as Ajtai and Dwork [6] gave lattice-based public-key encryption schemes (the latter based also on *worst-case* assumptions). Around the same time, Hoffstein, Pipher, and Silverman constructed the NTRU public-key system [68], which in retrospect can be thought of as a [58]-type scheme based on lattices of a particularly structured form. In 2003, Regev [107] gave improved versions of the Ajtai–Dwork cryptosystem. In 2003 Alekhnovich [7] gave a variant of the Ajtai–Dwork system based on the problem of learning parity with (very small) noise, albeit at the expense of using *average-case* as opposed to worst-case hardness assumptions. See the survey [103] for a more comprehensive overview of lattice-based cryptography.

---

[11] The proof is very simple and follows from the fact that, if SAT could be reduced via some reduction R to a problem in **TFNP**, then we could certify that a formula is *not* in SAT by giving a transcript of the reduction.

[12] The terminology of "group based" versus "lattice/code based" is perhaps not the most descriptive, as after all, lattices and codes are commutative groups as well. One difference seems to be the inherent role played by *noise* in the lattice/coding based constructions, which gives them a more geometric nature. However, it might be possible to trade non-commutativity for noise, and it has been shown that solving some lattice-based problems reduces to non-Abelian hidden subgroup problems [108].

Remark 2.4.1 (discreteness + noise = hardness?). *One way to think about all these schemes is that they rely on the brittleness of the Gaussian elimination algorithm over integers or finite fields. This is in contrast to the robust least-squares minimization algorithm that can solve even noisy linear equations over the real numbers. However, when working in the discrete setting (e.g., when x is constrained to be integers or when all equations are modulo some q), no analog of least-squares minimization is known. The presumed difficulty of this problem and its variants underlies the security of the above cryptosystems.*

The Learning with Errors Problem (LWE). The cleanest and most useful formalization of the above intuition was given by Regev [109], who made the following assumption:

Definition 2.4.2. *For functions $\delta = \delta(n)$ and $q = q(n)$, the* learning with error (LWE) *problem with parameters q, δ is the task of recovering a fixed random $s \in \mathbb{Z}_q^n$, from poly(n) examples (a, b) of the form*

$$b = \langle s, a \rangle + \lfloor \eta \rfloor \quad (\text{mod } q) \tag{2.3}$$

where a is chosen at random in $\mathbb{Z}_q^n$ and η is chosen from the normal distribution with standard deviation δq.

The *LWE assumption* is the assumption that this problem is hard for some $\delta(n)$ of the form n^{-C} (where C is some sufficiently large constant). Regev [109] and Peikert [102] showed that it is also equivalent (up to some loss in parameters) to its *decision* version where one needs to distinguish between samples of the form (a, b) as above and samples where b is simply an independent random element of $\mathbb{Z}_q$. Using this reduction, LWE can be easily shown to imply the existence of public-key cryptosystems, see Figure 2.2.

Regev [109] showed that if the LWE problem with parameter $\delta(n)$ is easy, then there is a $\tilde{O}(n/\delta(n))$-factor (worst-case) approximation *quantum* algorithm for the *gap shortest vector problem* on lattices. Note that even if one doesn't consider quantum computing to be a physically realizable model, such a reduction can still be meaningful, and recent papers gave classical reductions as well [102, 28].

The LWE assumption is fast becoming the centerpiece of public-key cryptography, in the sense that a great many schemes for "plain" public-key encryption, as well as encryption schemes with stronger properties such as fully homomorphic [47, 29], identity based, or more, rely on this assumption, and there have also been several works which managed to "port" constructions and intuitions from the group-theoretic world into LWE-based primitives (e.g., see [105, 31]).

Ideal/ring LWE. The *ideal* or *ring* variants of lattice problems correspond to the case when the matrix A has structure that allows to describe it using n numbers as opposed to n^2, and also often enables faster operations using a fast-Fourier-transform like algorithm. Such optimizations can be crucial for practical applications. See the manuscript [104] for more on this assumption and its uses.

PRIVATE KEY: $s \leftarrow_R \mathbb{Z}_q^n$

PUBLIC-KEY: $(a_1, b_1), \ldots, (a_m, b_m)$ where each pair (a_i, b_i) is sampled independently according to (2.3).

ENCRYPT $m \in \{0, 1\}$: Pick $\sigma_1, \ldots, \sigma_m \in \{\pm 1\}$, output (a', b') where $a' = \sum_{i=1}^m \sigma_i a_i$ (mod q) and $b' = \sum_{i=1}^m \sigma_i b_i + \lfloor \frac{q}{2} \rfloor$ (mod q).

DECRYPT (a', b'): Output 0 iff $|\langle s, a' \rangle - b' - \lfloor \frac{q}{2} \rfloor$ (mod q)$| < q/100$.

Fig. 2.2: Regev's simple public-key cryptosystem based on the LWE problem [109]. The scheme will be secure as long as LWE holds for these parameters and $m \gg n \log q$. Decryption will succeed as long as the noise parameter δ is $o(1/\sqrt{m})$

Approximate GCD. While in lattice-based cryptography we typically think of lattices of high dimension, when the numbers involved are large enough one can think of very small dimensions and even *one-dimensional* lattices. The computational question used for such lattices is often the *approximate greatest common denominator* (GCD) problem [71] where one is given samples of numbers obtained by taking an integer multiple of a secret number s plus some small noise, and the goal is to recover s (or at least distinguish between this distribution and the uniform one). Approximate GCD has been used for obtaining analogs of various lattice-based schemes (e.g., [117]).

Structural properties of lattice-based schemes. The following structural properties are known about these schemes:

- All the known lattice-based public-key encryption schemes can be broken using oracle access to an $O(\sqrt{n})$ approximation algorithm for the lattice closest vector problem. Goldreich and Goldwasser showed that such an efficient algorithm exists if the class **SZK** (which is a subset of **AM ∩ coAM**) is in **P** (or **BPP**, for that matter). Aharonov and Regev showed this also holds if **NP ∩ coNP** $\subseteq$ **P** [4]. Note that, while most experts believe that **NP ∩ coNP** is *not* contained in **P**, this result can still be viewed as showing that these lattice-based schemes have some computational *structure* that is not shared with many one-way function candidates.
- Unlike the lattice-based schemes, we do not know whether Alekhnovich's scheme [7] is insecure if **AM ∩ coAM** $\subseteq$ **P** although it does use a variant of the learning parity with very low noise, which seems analogous to the closest vector problem with an approximation factor larger than $\sqrt{n}$. A recent result of Ben-Sasson et al. [19] suggests that using such a small amount of noise might be an *inherent* limitation of schemes of this general type.[13]

---

[13] [19] define a general family of public-key encryption schemes which includes Alekhnovich's scheme as well as Regev's and some other lattice-based schemes. They show that under a certain

- The order-finding problem at the heart of Shor's algorithm can be thought of as an instance of a more general *hidden subgroup problem*. Regev showed a reduction from lattice problem into this problem for diehedral groups [108]. Kuperberg gave a subexponential (i.e., $\exp(O(\sqrt{n}))$ time) quantum algorithm for this problem [83], though it does not yield a subexponential quantum algorithm for the lattice problems since Regev's reduction has a quadratic blowup.
- A sequence of recent results showed that these problems are significantly easier (both quantumly and classically) in the case of *principal ideal* lattices which have a short basis that is obtained by taking shifts of a single vector (see [38] and the references therein).

The bottom line is that these schemes still currently represent our best hope for secure public-key systems if the group-theoretic schemes fail for a quantum or classical reason. However, the most practical variants of these schemes are also the ones that are more structured, and even relatively mild algorithmic advances (such as subexponential classical or quantum algorithms) could result in the need to square the size of the public-key or worse. Despite the fact that this would only be a polynomial factor, this can have significant real-world implications. One cannot hope to simply "plug in" a key of 10^6 or 10^9 bits into a protocol designed to work for keys of 10^3 bits and expect it to work as is, and so such results could bring about significant changes to the way we do security over the Internet. For example, it could lead to a centralization of power, where key exchange will be so expensive that users would share public-keys with only a few large corporations and governments, and smaller companies would have to route their communication through these larger corporations.

Remark 2.4.3 (Impagliazzo's worlds). *In a lovely survey, Russell Impagliazzo [72] defined a main task of computational complexity as determining which of several qualitatively distinct "worlds" is the one we live in, see Figure 2.3. That is, he looked at some of the various possibilities that, as far as we know, the open questions of computational complexity could resolve in, and saw how they would affect algorithms and cryptography.*

As argued in Section 2.2 above, there is very strong evidence that one-way functions exist, which would rule out the three worlds Impagliazzo named as "Algorithmica", "Heuristica", and "Pessiland". This survey can be thought of as trying to understand the evidence for ruling out the potential world "Minicrypt" where private-key cryptography (i.e., one-way functions) exist but not public-key cryptography. Impagliazzo used the name "Cryptomania" for the world in which public-key crypto, secure multiparty computation, and other similar primitives exist; these days people also refer to "Obfustopia" as the world where even more exotic primitives such as indistinguishability obfuscation [45] exist.

---

conjecture from additive combinatorics, all such schemes will need to use noise patterns that satisfy a generalized notion of being $\sqrt{n}$-sparse.

World	Condition	Algorithmic implications	Cryptographic implications
Algorithmica	**P = NP**	Algorithmic paradise, all **NP** and polynomial-hierarchy problems can be solved	Essentially no crypto
Heuristica	No average-case hard **NP** problem	Almost algorithmic paradise (though harder to solve problems in polynomial hierarchy)	Essentially no crypto
Pessiland	No hard *planted* **NP** problem (i.e., one-way functions)	Have hard on average algorithmic problem though can do all un-supervised learning	Essentially no crypto
Minicrypt	No public-key crypto	Algorithmic benefits minimal (can factor large integers, do dis-crete log, solve linear equations with very small noise)	CPA and CCA secure private-key encryp-tion, pseudorandom functions, digital sig-natures, zero-knowledge proofs, etc.
Cryptomania	LWE conjecture holds but not IO	No algorithmic bene-fits known for lack of IO	All of the above plus CPA and CCA se-cure public-key encryption, secure multi-party computation, fully homomorphic en-cryption, private information retrieval, etc.
Obfustopia	LWE and IO		All of the above plus a growing number of applications including functional encryp-tion, witness encryption, deniable encryp-tion, replacing random oracles in certain instances, multiparty key exchange, and many more.

Fig. 2.3: A variant of Impagliazzo's worlds from [72]. We have redefined Cryp-tomania to be the world where LWE holds and denote by "Obfustopia" the world where indistinguishability obfuscators (IO) exist (see also [46])

2.5 Alternative Public-Key Constructions

The group-theoretic and lattice-based families described above represent the main theoretical and practical basis for public-key encryption, as well as the more ad-vanced applications, including secure multiparty computation [118, 63], fully homo-morphic encryption [47, 29], and many other primitives. However, there have been other proposals in the literature. We do not attempt a comprehensive survey here but do give some pointers (for another perspective, see also the NIST report [32]; these days, such alternative constructions are often grouped under the category of "post-quantum cryptography").

Scheme	Computational assumption	Notes
Merkle puzzles [90]	Strong one-way functions	Only quadratic security
Alekhnovich [7]	Solving linear mod 2 equations with $\approx 1/\sqrt{n}$ noise	Mod 2 analog of Regev/Ajtai–Dwork, though not known to be solvable in **NP ∩ coNP/SZK**
ABW Scheme 1 [10]	Planted 3LIN with $n^{1.4}$ clauses and noise $n^{-0.1}$	Similar to refuting random 3SAT with $n^{1.4}$ clauses, has nondeterministic refutation; some similarities to Alekhnovich
ABW Scheme 2 [10]	Planted 3LIN with m clauses and noise δ + unbalanced expansion with parameters $(m, n, \delta m)$	Some similarities to Alekhnovich
ABW Scheme 3 [10]	Nonlinear constant locality PRG with expansion $m(n)$ + unbalanced expansion with parameters $(m, n, \log n)$	At best $n^{\Omega(\log n)}$ security
Couveignes, Rostovtsev, Stolbunov [37, 112]	Isogeny star problem	Algebraic structure, similarities to elliptic curve cryptography, subexponential quantum algorithm
Patarin HFE systems [101]	Planted quadratic equations	Several classical attacks
Sahai–Waters IO based system [113]	Indistinguishality obfuscation or witness encryption	All currently known IO/WE candidates require much stronger assumptions than Lattice schemes

Fig. 2.4: A nonexhaustive list of some "non-mainstream" public-key candidates. See also Section 2.5

2.5.1 Merkle puzzles

The first public-key encryption proposed by an academic researcher was Ralph Merkle's "puzzle-based" scheme which he submitted to the *Communications of the ACM* in 1975 [90] (as well as described in a project proposal for his undergraduate security class in the University of Berkeley), see Figure 2.5.[14]

Merkle's scheme can yield up to a *quadratic* gap between the work required to run the scheme and work required to break it, in an idealized (and not fully specified) model. Biham, Goren and Ishai [23] showed that this model can be instantiated using exponentially strong one way functions.

Merkle conjectured that it should be possible to obtain a public-key scheme with an *exponential* gap between the work of the honest parties and the adversary but was

---

[14] Merkle's scheme, as well as the Diffie–Hellman scheme it inspired, are often known in the literature as *key-exchange protocols*, as opposed to a *public-key encryption schemes*. However, a key-exchange protocol that takes only two messages (as is the case for both Merkle's and Diffie–Hellman's schemes) is essentially the same as a (randomized) public-key encryption scheme, and indeed Diffie and Hellman were well aware that the receiver can use the first message as a public key that can be placed in a "public file" [41]. I believe that this confusion in notation arose from the fact that the importance of randomization for encryption was not fully understood until the work of Goldwasser and Micali [64]. Thus, Diffie and Hellman reserved the name "public-key encryption" for a deterministic map we now call a *trapdoor permutation* that they envisioned as yielding an encryption by computing it in the forward direction and a signature by computing its inverse.

unable to come up with a concrete candidate. (The first to do so would be Diffie and
Hellman, who, based on a suggestion of John Gill to look at modular exponentiation, came up with what is known today as the *Diffie–Hellman key exchange*.) As
mentioned in Remark 2.3.1, [17] (building on [74]) showed that Merkle's original
protocol is *optimal* in the setting where we model the one-way function as a random
oracle and measure running time in terms of the number of queries to this function.

We should note that, although n^2 security is extremely far from what we could
hope for, it is not completely unacceptable. As pointed out by Biham et al. [23], any
superlinear security guarantee only becomes better with technological advances,
since, as the honest parties can afford more computation, the ratio between their
work and the adversary's grows.

ASSUMPTIONS: $f : S \rightarrow \{0,1\}^*$ is an "ideal" 1-to-1 one-way function, that requires
almost $|S|$ times as much time to invert as it does to compute. Let $n = |S|$.

PRIVATE KEY: $x_1, \ldots, x_{\sqrt{n}}$ that are chosen independently at random in S.

PUBLIC-KEY: $f(x_1), \ldots, f(x_{\sqrt{n}})$

ENCRYPT $m \in \{0,1\}$: Pick x at random in S, and if $f(x)$ appears in the public-key then
output $f(x), h(x) \oplus m$ where $h(\cdot)$ is a "hardcore bit function" that can be obtained, e.g.,
by the method of Goldreich–Levin [62]. If $f(x)$ is not in the public-key then try again.
DECRYPT (y, b): Output $h(x_i) \oplus b$ where i is such that $f(x_i) = y$.

Fig. 2.5: In Merkle's puzzle-based public-key encryption, the honest parties make
$\approx \sqrt{n}$ invocation to an ideal one-way function, while an adversary making $\ll n$
invocations would not be able to break it

2.5.2 Other Algebraic Constructions

There were several other proposals made for public-key encryption schemes. Some
of these use *stronger* assumptions than those described above, for the sake of achieving better efficiency or some other attractive property. We briefly mention here
schemes that attempt to use qualitatively different computational assumptions.

Hidden field equations. Patarin [101] (following a work of Matsumoto and
Imai [87]) proposed the *Hidden Field Equations* (HFE) cryptosystem. It is based on
the difficulty of a "planted" variant of the quadratic equation problem over a finite
field. The original HFE system was broken by Kipnis and Shamir [80], and some
variants have been attacked as well. It seems that currently fewer attacks are known
for HFE-based signatures, though our interest here is of course only in public-key
encryption; see [36] for more information about known attacks.

ASSUMPTIONS: **(i)** There is a constant d and some $f : \{0,1\}^d \rightarrow \{0,1\}$ such that, if we choose a random (n,m,d) graph H, then the map $G : \{0,1\}^n \rightarrow \{0,1\}^m$ where $G_H(x)_j = f(x_{\overleftarrow{\Gamma}_H(j)})$ is a pseudorandom generator, where $\overleftarrow{\Gamma}_H(j)$ denotes the left-neighbors of j in H. **(ii)** It is hard to distinguish between a random (n,m,d) graph H and a random (n,m,d) graph where we *plant* a set S of right vertices of size $k = O(\log n)$ such that $|\overleftarrow{\Gamma}_H(S)| = k-1$ where $\overleftarrow{\Gamma}_H(S)$ denotes the set of left-neighbors of S in H.

KEY GENERATION: Choose a random (n,m,d) graph H with a planted nonexpanding set S. The public-key is H, and the private key is S.

ENCRYPT $m \in \{0,1\}$: If $m = 0$ then output a random $y \in \{0,1\}^m$. If $m = 1$ pick random $x \in \{0,1\}^n$ and output $y = G_H(x)$.

DECRYPT y: Output 1 iff $y_S \in \{G_H(x)_{|S} : x \in \{0,1\}^n\}$. By our condition this set has at most 2^{k-1} elements.

Fig. 2.6: The ABW Goldreich-generator-based encryption scheme (a simplified variant)

Isogeny star. Rostovtsev and Stolbunov [112] (see also [37]) proposed a cryptographic scheme based on the task of finding an *isogeny* (an algebraic homomorphism) between two elliptic curves. Although this scheme is inspired by elliptic-curve cryptography, its security does not reduce to the security of standard elliptic-curve based schemes. In particular, there are no known quantum algorithms to attack it, though there have been some related results [33, 22]. Another group-theoretic construction that was suggested is to base cryptography on the conjugacy problem for *braid groups* though some attacks have been shown on these proposals (e.g., see [95] and references therein).

2.5.3 Combinatorial(?) Constructions

Applebaum, Barak and Wigderson [10] tried to explore the question of whether public-key encryption can be based on the conjectured average-case difficulty of *combinatorial* problems. Admittedly, this term is not well defined, though their focus was mostly on *constraint satisfaction problems*, which are arguably the quintessential combinatorial problems.

[10] gave a construction of a public-key encryption scheme (see Figure 2.6) based on the following conjectures:

- A *local pseudorandom generator*: this is a strengthening of the assumption that Golreich's one-way function discussed in Section 2.2.1.4 is secure. Namely, we assume that we can obtain a pseudorandom generator mapping n bits to m bits where every output bit applies some predicate f to a constant number d of input bits. Furthermore, we assume that we can do so by choosing which input bits map into which output bits using a random (n, m, d) bipartite graph as defined in Section 2.2.1.4.[15]

- The *unbalanced expansion problem*: this is the problem of distinguishing between a random (n, m, d) bipartite graph as above, and such a graph where we *plant* a set S of size k of left vertices such that S has at most $k - 1$ neighbors on the right-hand side (as opposed to the $(d - 1 - o(1))k$ neighbors you would expect in a random graph).[16] Expansion problems in graphs have been widely studied (e.g., see [69]), and at the moment no algorithm is known for this range of parameters.

The larger m is compared with n, the stronger the first assumption and the weaker the second assumption. Increasing the parameter k makes the second problem harder (and in fact, depending on m/n, at some point the assumption becomes *unconditionally* true since there would exist such a nonexpanding set with high probability even in a random graph). Moreover, there is always a way to solve the expansion problem in $\binom{n}{k}$ time, and so smaller values of k make the problem quantitatively easier. [10] showed that, if both assumptions hold for a set of parameters (n, m, d, k) where $k = O(\log n)$, then there exists a public-key cryptosystem.

By construction, the above cryptosystem cannot achieve better than $n^{\Omega(\log n)}$ security which is much better than the n^2 obtained by Merkle puzzles but still far from ideal. It also relies on the somewhat subtle distinction between $n^{O(k)}$ and $poly(n)2^{O(k)}$ complexity. [10] showed how to get different tradeoffs if, instead of using a *nonlinear* function f for the pseudo-random generator, we use a linear function with some probabilistic additional noise. The noise level δ should satisfy $\delta k = O(1/\log n)$ for efficient decryption, and so the lower the noise level we consider (and hence the stronger we make our assumption on the pseudo-random generator), the larger value of k we can afford. In particular, if we assume a sufficiently low level of noise, then we can get k to be so large as to avoid the second assumption (on difficulty of detecting nonexpanding sets) altogether. However, there is evidence that at this point the first assumption becomes more "structured" since it admits a non-constructive short certificate [43].

Using such a linear function f raises the question of to which extent these schemes are different from coding-based schemes such as Alekhnovich's. Indeed, there are similarities between these schemes and the main difference is the use of the unbalanced expansion assumption. An important question is to find the extent to which this problem is *combinatorial* versus *algebraic*. We do not yet fully understand this question, nor even the right way to formally define it, but it does seem key to figuring out whether the [10] scheme is truly different from the coding/lattices-based constructions. On one hand, the unbalanced expansion questions "feels" combinatorial. On the other hand, the fact that we require the set S to have fewer than S neighbors implies that, if we define for each right-vertex j in H a linear equation

---

[15] [10] also gave a version of their cryptosystem which only assumed that the function is one way, and more general reductions between these two conditions were given in [8].

[16] One only needs to conjecture that it has to distinguish between these graphs with some constant bias, as there are standard techniques for hardness amplification in this context.

corresponding to the sum of variables in $\overleftarrow{\Gamma}_H(S)$, then the equations corresponding to S are *linearly dependent*. So this problem can be thought of as the task of looking for a short linear dependency.

Thinking about the *noise level* might be a better way of considering this question than the combinatorial versus algebraic distinction. That is, one could argue that the main issue with the coding/lattice-based constructions is not the algebraic nature of the linear equations (after all, both the knapsack and approximating kXOR problems are **NP** hard). Rather, it is the fact that they use a noise level smaller than $1/\sqrt{n}$ (or, equivalently, a larger than $\sqrt{n}$ approximation factor) that gives them some *structure* that could potentially be a source of weakness. In particular, using such small noise is quite analogous to using an approximation factor larger than $\sqrt{n}$ for lattice problems, which is the reason why lattice-based schemes can be broken in **NP** ∩ **coNP**. However, at the moment no such result is known for either the [7] or [10] schemes.

This viewpoint raises the following open questions:

- Can we base a public-key encryption scheme on the difficulty of solving $O(n)$ random kXOR equations on n variables with a planted solution satisfying $1 - \epsilon$ of them for some constant $\epsilon > 0$?
- Does the reliance on the unbalanced expansion problem introduce new *structure* in the problem? For example, is there *a nondeterministic* procedure to certify the *nonexistence* of a short non-expanding subset in a graph?

One way to get evidence for a negative answer for the second question would be to get a *worst-case* **NP** hardness of approximation result for the unbalanced expansion problem with parameters matching those used by [10]. We do not at the moment know whether such a result is likely or not to hold.

2.5.4 Public-key Cryptography from Indistinguishability Obfuscators

From the early writing of Diffie and Hellman [40], it seems that one of the reasons why they believed that public-key cryptography is at least not inherently impossible is the following: Given a block cipher/pseudorandom permutation collection $\{p_k\}$, one could imagine fixing a random key k and letting P_k be a program that on input x outputs $p_k(x)$. Now, if P_k was compiled via some "optimizing compiler" to a low-level representation such as assembly language, one could imagine that it would be hard to "extract" k from this representation. Thus, one can hope to obtain a public-key encryption scheme (or, more accurately, a trapdoor permutation family) by letting the *public encryption key* be this representation of P_k, which enables computing the map $x \mapsto p_k(x)$, and letting the *private decryption key* (or *trapdoor*) be the secret key k that enables computing the map $y \mapsto p_k^{-1}(y)$. It seems that James Ellis, who independently invented public-key encryption at the British intelligence agency GCHQ, had similar thoughts [42].

Diffie and Hellman never managed to find a good enough instantiation of this idea, but over the years people have kept trying to look for such an *obfuscating compiler* that would convert a program P to a functionally equivalent but "inscrutable" form. Many practical attempts at obfuscation have been broken, and the paper [14] showed that a natural definition for security of obfuscation is in fact *impossible* to achieve. However, [14] did give a weaker definition of security, known as *indistinguishability obfuscation* (IO), and noted that their impossibility result did not rule it out. (See the survey [13].)

In a recent breakthrough, a candidate construction for an IO compiler was given by [45]. They also showed that an IO compiler is sufficient to achieve Diffie and Hellman's dream of constructing a public-key encryption scheme based only on one-way functions (see also [113]). Now from a first look, this might seem to make as much sense as a bottle opener made out of diamonds: after all, we can already build public-key encryption from the learning with error assumption, while building IO from LWE would be a major breakthrough with a great many applications. Indeed, many of the current candidate constructions for IO would be easily broken if LWE was easy. (And in fact might be broken regardless [92].)

However, a priori, it is not at all clear that achieving IO requires an *algebraic* approach. While at the moment it seems far removed from any techniques we have, one could hope that a more combinatorial/program transformation approach can yield an IO obfuscator without relying on LWE. One glimmer of hope is given by the observation that despite the great many applications of IO, so far we have not been able to obtain primitives such as fully homomorphic encryption that imply that $\mathbf{AM} \cap \mathbf{coAM} \not\subseteq \mathbf{BPP}$ (see also [11]). In contrast, such primitives do follow from LWE.

2.6 Is Computational Hardness the Rule or the Exception?

As long as the **P** versus **NP** question remains open, cryptography will require unproven assumptions. Does it really make sense to distinguish between an assumption such as the hardness of LWE and assuming hardness of the problems that yield private-key encryption? This is a fair question. After all, many would argue that the only real evidence we have that $\mathbf{P} \neq \mathbf{NP}$ is the fact that a lot of people have tried to get algorithms for **NP**-hard problems and failed. That same evidence exists for the LWE assumption as well.

However, I do feel there is a *qualitative* difference between these assumptions. The reason is that assuming $\mathbf{P} \neq \mathbf{NP}$ yields a *coherent and beautiful* theory of computational difficulty that agrees with all current observations. Thus we accept this theory not only because we do not know how to refute it, but also because, following Occam's razor principle, one should accept the cleanest/most parsimonious theory that explains the world as we know it. The existence of one-way functions, with the rich web of reductions that have been shown between it and other problems, also yields such a theory. Indeed, these reductions have shown that one-way functions are a *minimal* assumption for almost all of cryptography.

In contrast, while LWE has many implications, it has not been shown to be *minimal* for "Cryptomania" in the sense that it is not known to be implied by any primitives such as public-key encryption or even stronger notions such as fully homomorphic encryption. We also do not have a clean theory of average-case hardness that would imply the difficulty of LWE (or the existence of public-key encryptions).

In fact, I believe it is fair to say that we don't have a clean theory of average-case hardness at all.[17] The main reason is that *reductions*—which underpin the whole theory of worst-case hardness, as well as the web of reductions between cryptographic primitives—seem to have very limited applicability in this setting. As a rule, a reduction from a problem A to a problem B typically takes a *general* instance of A and transforms it to a *structured* instance of B. For example, the canonical reduction from 3SAT to 3COL takes a general formula φ and transforms it into a graph G that has a particular form with certain *gadgets* that correspond to every clause of φ. While this is enough to show that, if A is hard in the worst-case then so is B, it does not show that, if A is hard on, say, uniformly random instances, then this holds for B as well. Thus reductions have turned out to be extremely useful for relating the worst-case complexity of different problems, or using the conjectured average-case hardness of a particular problem to show the hardness of other problems on *tailored* instances (as we do when we construct cryptographic primitives based on average-case hardness). However, by and large, we have not been able to use reductions to relate the hardness of natural average-case problems, and so we have a collection of incomparable tasks including integer factoring, discrete logarithms, the RSA problem, finding planted cliques, finding planted assignments in 3SAT formulas, LWE, etc. without any reductions between them.[18]

Even the successful theory of worst-case complexity is arguably more *descriptive* or *predictive* than *explanatory*. That is, it tells us which problems are hard, but it does not truly explain to us *why* they are hard. While this might seem as not a well-defined question, akin to asking "why is 17 a prime?", let me try to cast a bit more meaning into it, and illustrate how an *explanatory* theory of computational difficulty might be useful in situations such as average-case complexity, where reductions do not seem to help.

What makes a problem easy or hard? To get some hints on answers, we might want to look at what algorithmicists do when they want to efficiently solve a problem, and what cryptographers do when they want to create a hard problem. There are obviously a plethora of algorithmic techniques for solving problems, and in particular many clever data structures and optimizations that can make improvements that might be moderate in theory (e.g., reducing an exponent) but make all the difference in the world in practice. However, if we restrict ourselves to techniques that help show a problem can be solved in better than brute force, then there are some themes that repeat themselves time and again. One such theme is *local search*. Starting with

---

[17] Levin [85] has proposed a notion of completeness for average-case problems, though this theory has not been successful in giving evidence for the hardness of natural problems on natural input distributions.

[18] One notable exception is the set of reductions between different variants of lattice problems, which is enabled by the existence of a *worst-case to average-case* reduction for these problems [5]. However, even there we do not know how to relate these problems to tasks that seem superficially similar such as the *learning parity with noise* [60, 24] problem.

a guess for a solution and making local improvements is a workhorse behind a great many algorithms. Such algorithms crucially rely on a structure of the problem where *local* optima (or at least all ones you are likely to encounter) correspond to *global* optima. In other words, they rely on some form of *convexity*.

Another theme is the use of *algebraic cancellations*. The simplest such structure is *linearity*, where we can continually deduce new constraints from old ones without a blowup in their complexity. In particular, a classical example of cancellations in action is the algorithm to efficiently compute the *determinant* of a matrix, which works even though at least one canonical definition of it involves computing a sum on an exponential number of terms.

On the cryptography side, when applied cryptographers try to construct a hard function such as a hash function or a block cipher, there are themes that recur as well. To make a function that is hard to invert, designers try to introduce *nonlinearity* (the function should not be linear or close to linear over any field and in fact have large algebraic degree so it is hard to "linearize") and *nonlocality* (we want the dependency structure of output and input bits to be "expanding" or "spread out"). Indeed, these themes occur not just in applied constructions but also in theoretical candidates such as Goldreich's [57] and Gowers' [65] (where each takes one type of parameters to a different extreme).

Taken together, these observations might lead to a view of the world in which computational problems are presumed hard unless they have a structural reason to be easy. A theory based on such structure could help to *predict*, and more than that to *explain*, the difficulty of a great many computational problems that currently we cannot reach with reductions. However, I do not know at the moment of any such clean theory that will not end up "predicting" some problems are hard where they are in fact solvable by a clever algorithm or change of representation. In the survey [18], Steurer and I tried to present a potential approach to such a theory via the conjecture that the *sum of squares* convex program is *optimal* in some domains. While it might seem that making such conjectures is a step backwards from cryptography as a science towards "alchemy", we do hope that it is possible to extract some of the "alchemist intuitions" practitioners have, without sacrificing the predictive power and the mathematical crispness of cryptographic theory. However, this research is still very much in its infancy, and we still do not even know the right way to formalize our *conjectures*, let alone try to prove them or study their implications. I do hope that eventually an explanatory theory of hardness will emerge, whether via convex optimization or other means, and that it will not only help us design cryptographic schemes with stronger foundations for their security, but also shed more light on the mysterious phenomena of efficient computation.

References

[1] Cryptography today: Memorandum on Suite B Cryptography, 2015. Retrieved on 2/29/16 from `https://www.nsa.gov/ia/programs/suiteb_cryptography/`

[2] D. Achlioptas and A. Coja-Oghlan. Algorithmic barriers from phase transitions. In *49th Annual IEEE Symposium on Foundations of Computer Science, FOCS 2008*, pages 793–802, 2008.

[3] L. M. Adleman, J. DeMarrais, and M. A. Huang. A subexponential algorithm for discrete logarithms over hyperelliptic curves of large genus over $GF(q)$. *Theoretical Computer Science*, 226(1-2):7–18, 1999.

[4] D. Aharonov and O. Regev. Lattice problems in $NP \cap coNP$. *J. ACM*, 52(5):749–765, 2005. Preliminary version in FOCS 2004.

[5] M. Ajtai. Generating hard instances of lattice problems (extended abstract). In *Twenty-Eighth Annual ACM Symposium on the Theory of Computing*, pages 99–108, 1996.

[6] M. Ajtai and C. Dwork. A public-key cryptosystem with worst-case/average-case equivalence. In *Proceedings of the Twenty-Ninth Annual ACM Symposium on the Theory of Computing*, pages 284–293, 1997.

[7] M. Alekhnovich. More on average case vs approximation complexity. *Computational Complexity*, 20(4):755–786, 2011. Published posthumously. Preliminary version in FOCS '03.

[8] B. Applebaum. Pseudorandom generators with long stretch and low locality from random local one-way functions. In *Proceedings of the 44th Symposium on Theory of Computing Conference, STOC*, pages 805–816, 2012.

[9] B. Applebaum. The cryptographic hardness of random local functions - survey. *IACR Cryptology ePrint Archive*, 2015:165, 2015.

[10] B. Applebaum, B. Barak, and A. Wigderson. Public-key cryptography from different assumptions. In *Proceedings of the 42nd ACM Symposium on Theory of Computing, STOC*, pages 171–180, 2010.

[11] G. Asharov and G. Segev. Limits on the power of indistinguishability obfuscation and functional encryption. In *Foundations of Computer Science (FOCS)*, pages 191–209, 2015.

[12] B. Barak. Structure vs. combinatorics in computational complexity. *Bulletin of the European Association for Theoretical Computer Science*, 112, 2014. Survey, also posted on Windows on Theory blog.

[13] B. Barak. Hopes, fears, and software obfuscation. *Commun. ACM*, 59(3):88–96, 2016.

[14] B. Barak, O. Goldreich, R. Impagliazzo, S. Rudich, A. Sahai, S. P. Vadhan, and K. Yang. On the (im)possibility of obfuscating programs. *J. ACM*, 59(2):6, 2012.

[15] B. Barak, G. Kindler, and D. Steurer. On the optimality of semidefinite relaxations for average-case and generalized constraint satisfaction. In *Innovations in Theoretical Computer Science, ITCS '13*, pages 197–214, 2013.

[16] B. Barak and M. Mahmoody-Ghidary. Lower bounds on signatures from symmetric primitives. In *48th Annual IEEE Symposium on Foundations of Computer Science (FOCS*, pages 680–688, 2007.

[17] B. Barak and M. Mahmoody-Ghidary. Merkle puzzles are optimal - an $O(n^2)$-query attack on any key exchange from a random oracle. In *Advances*

in Cryptology - CRYPTO 2009, Springer (LNCS 5677), pages 374–390, 2009.

[18] B. Barak and D. Steurer. Sum-of-squares proofs and the quest toward optimal algorithms, 2014.

[19] E. Ben-Sasson, I. Ben-Tov, I. Damgård, Y. Ishai, and N. Ron-Zewi. On public key encryption from noisy codewords. In *Public-Key Cryptography - PKC 2016*, Springer pages 417–446, 2016.

[20] D. J. Bernstein. The Salsa20 family of stream ciphers. In *New stream cipher designs*, Springer, pages 84–97, 2008.

[21] G. Bertoni, J. Daemen, M. Peeters, and G. Van Assche. The Keccak SHA-3 submission. *Submission to NIST (Round 3)*, 6(7):16, 2011.

[22] J.-F. Biasse, D. Jao, and A. Sankar. A quantum algorithm for computing isogenies between supersingular elliptic curves. In *Progress in Cryptology–INDOCRYPT 2014*, pages 428–442. Springer, 2014.

[23] E. Biham, Y. J. Goren, and Y. Ishai. Basing weak public-key cryptography on strong one-way functions. In *Theory of Cryptography, Fifth Theory of Cryptography Conference, TCC 2008*, pages 55–72, 2008.

[24] A. Blum, M. L. Furst, M. J. Kearns, and R. J. Lipton. Cryptographic primitives based on hard learning problems. In *Advances in Cryptology - CRYPTO '93*, pages 278–291, 1993.

[25] A. Blum, A. Kalai, and H. Wasserman. Noise-tolerant learning, the parity problem, and the statistical query model. *J. ACM*, 50(4):506–519, 2003. Preliminary version in STOC '00.

[26] A. Bogdanov and Y. Qiao. On the security of Goldreich's one-way function. *Computational Complexity*, 21(1):83–127, 2012.

[27] B. Bollobás and P. Erdös. Cliques in random graphs. In *Mathematical Proceedings of the Cambridge Philosophical Society*, volume 80, pages 419–427. Cambridge Univ. Press, 1976.

[28] Z. Brakerski, A. Langlois, C. Peikert, O. Regev, and D. Stehlé. Classical hardness of learning with errors. In *Proceedings of the Forty-Fifth Annual ACM Symposium on Theory of Computing*, pages 575–584. ACM, 2013.

[29] Z. Brakerski and V. Vaikuntanathan. Efficient fully homomorphic encryption from (standard) LWE. In *IEEE 52nd Annual Symposium on Foundations of Computer Science, FOCS*, pages 97–106, 2011.

[30] J. Buresh-Oppenheim. On the TFNP complexity of factoring, 2006.

[31] D. Cash, D. Hofheinz, E. Kiltz, and C. Peikert. Bonsai trees, or how to delegate a lattice basis. *J. Cryptology*, 25(4):601–639, 2012.

[32] L. Chen, S. Jordan, Y.-K. Liu, D. Moody, R. Peralta, R. Perlner, and D. Smith-Tone. Report on post-quantum cryptography. *National Institute of Standards and Technology Internal Report*, 8105, 2016. Available on http://csrc.nist.gov/publications/drafts/nistir-8105/nistir_8105_draft.pdf.

[33] A. Childs, D. Jao, and V. Soukharev. Constructing elliptic curve isogenies in quantum subexponential time. *Journal of Mathematical Cryptology*, 8(1):1–29, 2014.

[34] J. Cook, O. Etesami, R. Miller, and L. Trevisan. Goldreich's one-way function candidate and myopic backtracking algorithms. In *Theory of Cryptography*, pages 521–538. Springer, 2009.

[35] D. Coppersmith, A. M. Odlzyko, and R. Schroeppel. Discrete logarithms in *GF(p)*. *Algorithmica*, 1(1-4):1–15, 1986.

[36] N. T. Courtois, M. Daum, and P. Felke. On the security of HFE, HFEv- and Quartz. In *Public Key CryptographyPKC 2003*, pages 337–350. Springer, 2003.

[37] J. M. Couveignes. Hard homogeneous spaces. *IACR Cryptology ePrint Archive*, 2006:291, 2006.

[38] R. Cramer, L. Ducas, C. Peikert, and O. Regev. Recovering short generators of principal ideals in cyclotomic rings. *IACR Cryptology ePrint Archive*, 2015:313, 2015.

[39] J. Daemen and V. Rijmen. *The design of Rijndael: AES-the advanced encryption standard*. Springer Science & Business Media, 2013.

[40] W. Diffie and M. E. Hellman. Multiuser cryptographic techniques. In *Proceedings of the June 7-10, 1976, National Computer Conference and Exposition*, pages 109–112. ACM, 1976.

[41] W. Diffie and M. E. Hellman. New directions in cryptography. *IEEE Transactions on Information Theory*, 22(6):644–654, 1976.

[42] J. H. Ellis. The history of non-secret encryption. *Cryptologia*, 23(3):267–273, 1999.

[43] U. Feige, J. H. Kim, and E. Ofek. Witnesses for non-satisfiability of dense random 3CNF formulas. In *47th Annual IEEE Symposium on Foundations of Computer Science (FOCS*, pages 497–508, 2006.

[44] E. Friedgut. Sharp thresholds of graph properties, and the k-SAT problem. *Journal of the American Mathematical Society*, 12(4):1017–1054, 1999. With an appendix by Jean Bourgain.

[45] S. Garg, C. Gentry, S. Halevi, M. Raykova, A. Sahai, and B. Waters. Candidate indistinguishability obfuscation and functional encryption for all circuits. In *FOCS*, pages 40–49, 2013.

[46] S. Garg, O. Pandey, A. Srinivasan, and M. Zhandry. Breaking the sub-exponential barrier in Obfustopia. *IACR Cryptology ePrint Archive*, 2016:102, 2016.

[47] C. Gentry. Fully homomorphic encryption using ideal lattices. In *STOC*, pages 169–178, 2009.

[48] O. Goldreich. Lessons from Kant: On knowledge, morality, and beauty. Essay available on `http://www.wisdom.weizmann.ac.il/~oded/on-kant.html`

[49] O. Goldreich. On cryptographic assumptions. Short note available on `http://www.wisdom.weizmann.ac.il/~oded/on-assumptions.html`

[50] O. Goldreich. On intellectual and instrumental values in science. Essay available on
`http://www.wisdom.weizmann.ac.il/~oded/on-values.html`

[51] O. Goldreich. On post-modern cryptography. Short note available on http://www.wisdom.weizmann.ac.il/~oded/on-pmc.html, revised on 2012.

[52] O. Goldreich. On quantum computing. Essay available on http://www.wisdom.weizmann.ac.il/~oded/on-qc.html

[53] O. Goldreich. On scientific evaluation and its relation to understanding, imagination, and taste. Essay available on http://www.wisdom.weizmann.ac.il/~oded/on-taste.html

[54] O. Goldreich. On the philosophical basis of computational theories. Essay available on
http://www.wisdom.weizmann.ac.il/~oded/on-qc3.html

[55] O. Goldreich. *The Foundations of Cryptography - Volume 1, Basic Techniques*. Cambridge University Press, 2001.

[56] O. Goldreich. *The Foundations of Cryptography - Volume 2, Basic Applications*. Cambridge University Press, 2004.

[57] O. Goldreich. Candidate one-way functions based on expander graphs. In *Studies in Complexity and Cryptography. Miscellanea on the Interplay between Randomness and Computation - In Collaboration with Lidor Avigad, Mihir Bellare, Zvika Brakerski, Shafi Goldwasser, Shai Halevi, Tali Kaufman, Leonid Levin, Noam Nisan, Dana Ron, Madhu Sudan, Luca Trevisan, Salil Vadhan, Avi Wigderson, David Zuckerman*, pages 76–87. 2011. Original version published as ECCC TR00-090 in 2000.

[58] O. Goldreich, S. Goldwasser, and S. Halevi. Public-key cryptosystems from lattice reduction problems. In *Advances in Cryptology - CRYPTO '97, 17th Annual International Cryptology Conference, Santa Barbara, California, USA, August 17-21, 1997, Proceedings*, pages 112–131, 1997.

[59] O. Goldreich, S. Goldwasser, and S. Micali. How to construct random functions. *J. ACM*, 33(4):792–807, 1986.

[60] O. Goldreich, H. Krawczyk, and M. Luby. On the existence of pseudorandom generators. *SIAM J. Comput.*, 22(6):1163–1175, 1993. Preliminary versions in CRYPTO '88 and FOCS '88.

[61] O. Goldreich and E. Kushilevitz. A perfect zero-knowledge proof system for a problem equivalent to the discrete logarithm. *J. Cryptology*, 6(2):97–116, 1993.

[62] O. Goldreich and L. A. Levin. A hard-core predicate for all one-way functions. In *Proceedings of the 21st Annual ACM Symposium on Theory of Computing*, pages 25–32, 1989.

[63] O. Goldreich, S. Micali, and A. Wigderson. How to play any mental game or a completeness theorem for protocols with honest majority. In *Proceedings of the 19th Annual ACM Symposium on Theory of Computing*, pages 218–229, 1987.

[64] S. Goldwasser and S. Micali. Probabilistic encryption and how to play mental poker keeping secret all partial information. In *Proceedings of the 14th Annual ACM Symposium on Theory of Computing*, pages 365–377, 1982.

[65] W. Gowers. An almost m-wise independent random permutation of the cube. *Combinatorics, Probability and Computing*, 5(02):119–130, 1996.

[66] G. R. Grimmett and C. J. McDiarmid. On colouring random graphs. In *Mathematical Proceedings of the Cambridge Philosophical Society*, volume 77, pages 313–324. Cambridge Univ Press, 1975.

[67] J. Håstad, R. Impagliazzo, L. A. Levin, and M. Luby. A pseudorandom generator from any one-way function. *SIAM J. Comput.*, 28(4):1364–1396, 1999. Preliminary versions in STOC '89 and STOC '90.

[68] J. Hoffstein, J. Pipher, and J. H. Silverman. Ntru: A ring-based public key cryptosystem. In *Algorithmic number theory*, pages 267–288. Springer, 1998.

[69] S. Hoory, N. Linial, and A. Wigderson. Expander graphs and their applications. *Bulletin of the American Mathematical Society*, 43(4):439–561, 2006.

[70] S. Hoory, A. Magen, S. Myers, and C. Rackoff. Simple permutations mix well. *Theor. Comput. Sci.*, 348(2-3):251–261, 2005.

[71] N. Howgrave-Graham. Approximate integer common divisors. In *Cryptography and Lattices, International Conference, CaLC 2001*, pages 51–66, 2001.

[72] R. Impagliazzo. A personal view of average-case complexity. In *Proceedings of the Tenth Annual Structure in Complexity Theory Conference*, pages 134–147, 1995.

[73] R. Impagliazzo and M. Luby. One-way functions are essential for complexity based cryptography (extended abstract). In *30th Annual Symposium on Foundations of Computer Science*, pages 230–235, 1989.

[74] R. Impagliazzo and S. Rudich. Limits on the provable consequences of one-way permutations. In *Proceedings of the 21st Annual ACM Symposium on Theory of Computing*, pages 44–61, 1989.

[75] D. Itsykson. Lower bound on average-case complexity of inversion of Goldreich's function by drunken backtracking algorithms. In *Computer Science–Theory and Applications*, pages 204–215. Springer, 2010.

[76] M. Jerrum. Large cliques elude the Metropolis process. *Random Structures & Algorithms*, 3(4):347–359, 1992.

[77] A. Joux and C. Pierrot. Technical history of discrete logarithms in small characteristic finite fields - the road from subexponential to quasi-polynomial complexity. *Des. Codes Cryptography*, 78(1):73–85, 2016.

[78] A. Juels and M. Peinado. Hiding cliques for cryptographic security. *Des. Codes Cryptography*, 20(3):269–280, 2000.

[79] R. M. Karp. The probabilistic analysis of some combinatorial search algorithms. *Algorithms and complexity: New directions and recent results*, 1:19, 1976.

[80] A. Kipnis and A. Shamir. Cryptanalysis of the HFE public key cryptosystem by relinearization. In *Advances in Cryptology - CRYPTO '99*, Springer, pages 19–30, 1999.

[81] N. Koblitz. Elliptic curve cryptosystems. *Mathematics of computation*, 48(177):203–209, 1987.

[82] L. Kucera. Expected complexity of graph partitioning problems. *Discrete Applied Mathematics*, 57(2-3):193–212, 1995.

[83] G. Kuperberg. A subexponential-time quantum algorithm for the dihedral hidden subgroup problem. *SIAM J. Comput.*, 35(1):170–188, 2005.

[84] A. K. Lenstra, H. W. Lenstra Jr, M. S. Manasse, and J. M. Pollard. The number field sieve. In *Proceedings of the Twenty-Second Annual ACM Symposium on Theory of Computing*, pages 564–572. ACM, 1990.

[85] L. A. Levin. Average case complete problems. *SIAM J. Comput.*, 15(1):285–286, 1986.

[86] V. Lyubashevsky. The parity problem in the presence of noise, decoding random linear codes, and the subset sum problem. In *Proceedings of the 8th International Workshop on Approximation Algorithms for Combinatorial Optimization Problems APPROX 2005, and 9th International Workshop on Randomization and Computation RANDOM 2005*, pages 378–389, 2005.

[87] T. Matsumoto and H. Imai. Public quadratic polynominal-tuples for efficient signature-verification and message-encryption. In *Advances in Cryptology - EUROCRYPT '88*, Springer, pages 419–453, 1988.

[88] R. McEliece. A public-key cryptosystem based on algebraic coding theory. *Deep Space Network Progress Report*, 44:114–116, 1978.

[89] N. Megiddo and C. H. Papadimitriou. On total functions, existence theorems and computational complexity. *Theor. Comput. Sci.*, 81(2):317–324, 1991.

[90] R. C. Merkle. Secure communications over insecure channels. *Commun. ACM*, 21(4):294–299, 1978. Originally submitted in August 1975.

[91] R. C. Merkle and M. E. Hellman. Hiding information and signatures in trapdoor knapsacks. *IEEE Transactions on Information Theory*, 24(5):525–530, 1978.

[92] E. Miles, A. Sahai, and M. Zhandry. Annihilation attacks for multilinear maps: Cryptanalysis of indistinguishability obfuscation over GGH13. Cryptology ePrint Archive, Report 2016/147, 2016.

[93] E. Miles and E. Viola. Substitution-permutation networks, pseudorandom functions, and natural proofs. In *Advances in Cryptology - CRYPTO 2012*, Springer, pages 68–85, 2012.

[94] V. S. Miller. Use of elliptic curves in cryptography. In *Advances in Cryptology - CRYPTO '85*, Springer, pages 417–426, 1985.

[95] A. D. Myasnikov and A. Ushakov. Length based attack and braid groups: cryptanalysis of anshel-anshel-goldfeld key exchange protocol. In *Public Key Cryptography–PKC 2007*, Springer, pages 76–88, 2007.

[96] M. Naor. Bit commitment using pseudorandomness. *J. Cryptology*, 4(2):151–158, 1991. Preliminary version in CRYPTO '89.

[97] M. Naor and M. Yung. Universal one-way hash functions and their cryptographic applications. In *Proceedings of the 21st Annual ACM Symposium on Theory of Computing*, pages 33–43, 1989.

[98] NIST. Secure hash standard, 2002. Federal Information Processing Standard Publication 180-2. US Department of Commerce, National Institute of Standards and Technology (NIST).

[99] R. O'Donnell and D. Witmer. Goldreich's PRG: evidence for near-optimal polynomial stretch. In *IEEE 29th Conference on Computational Complexity, CCC*, pages 1–12, 2014.

[100] R. Ostrovsky and A. Wigderson. One-way fuctions are essential for nontrivial zero-knowledge. In *ISTCS*, pages 3–17, 1993.

[101] J. Patarin. Hidden fields equations (HFE) and isomorphisms of polynomials (IP): Two new families of asymmetric algorithms. In *Advances in Cryptology - EUROCRYPT96*, Springer, pages 33–48, 1996.

[102] C. Peikert. Public-key cryptosystems from the worst-case shortest vector problem: extended abstract. In *Proceedings of the 41st Annual ACM Symposium on Theory of Computing, STOC 2009*, pages 333–342, 2009.

[103] C. Peikert. A decade of lattice cryptography. Cryptology ePrint Archive, Report 2015/939, 2015. http://eprint.iacr.org/.

[104] C. Peikert. How (not) to instantiate ring-LWE, 2016. Unpublished manuscript; available at web.eecs.umich.edu/~cpeikert/pubs/instantiate-rlwe.pdf.

[105] C. Peikert and B. Waters. Lossy trapdoor functions and their applications. *SIAM Journal on Computing*, 40(6):1803–1844, 2011.

[106] M. O. Rabin. Digitalized signatures and public-key functions as intractable as factorization. MIT technical report, 1979.

[107] O. Regev. New lattice based cryptographic constructions. In *Proceedings of the 35th Annual ACM Symposium on Theory of Computing*, pages 407–416, 2003.

[108] O. Regev. Quantum computation and lattice problems. *SIAM J. Comput.*, 33(3):738–760, 2004.

[109] O. Regev. On lattices, learning with errors, random linear codes, and cryptography. *J. ACM*, 56(6), 2009. Preliminary version in STOC 2005.

[110] R. L. Rivest, A. Shamir, and L. M. Adleman. A method for obtaining digital signatures and public-key cryptosystems. *Commun. ACM*, 21(2):120–126, 1978.

[111] J. Rompel. One-way functions are necessary and sufficient for secure signatures. In *Proceedings of the 22nd Annual ACM Symposium on Theory of Computing*, pages 387–394, 1990.

[112] A. Rostovtsev and A. Stolbunov. Public-key cryptosystem based on isogenies. *IACR Cryptology ePrint Archive*, 2006:145, 2006.

[113] A. Sahai and B. Waters. How to use indistinguishability obfuscation: deniable encryption, and more. In *Symposium on Theory of Computing, STOC*, pages 475–484, 2014.

[114] A. Shamir. A polynomial time algorithm for breaking the basic Merkle-Hellman cryptosystem. In *Advances in Cryptology - CRYPTO'83*, Springer, pages 279–288, 1983.

[115] P. W. Shor. Polynomial-time algorithms for prime factorization and discrete logarithms on a quantum computer. *SIAM J. Comput.*, 26(5):1484–1509, 1997. Preliminary version in FOCS '94.

[116] A. Tarantola. *Inverse problem theory and methods for model parameter estimation*. SIAM, 2005.

[117] M. van Dijk, C. Gentry, S. Halevi, and V. Vaikuntanathan. Fully homomorphic encryption over the integers. In *Advances in Cryptology - EUROCRYPT 2010*, pages 24–43, 2010.

[118] A. C. Yao. Protocols for secure computations (extended abstract). In *23rd Annual Symposium on Foundations of Computer Science*, pages 160–164, 1982.

Chapter 3
Pseudorandom Functions: Three Decades Later

Andrej Bogdanov and Alon Rosen

Abstract In 1984, Goldreich, Goldwasser and Micali formalized the concept of pseudorandom functions and proposed a construction based on any length-doubling pseudorandom generator. Since then, pseudorandom functions have turned out to be an extremely influential abstraction, with applications ranging from message authentication to barriers in proving computational complexity lower bounds.

In this tutorial we survey various incarnations of pseudorandom functions, giving self-contained proofs of key results from the literature. Our main focus is on feasibility results and constructions, as well as on limitations of (and induced by) pseudorandom functions. Along the way we point out some open questions that we believe to be within reach of current techniques.

> *I have set up on a Manchester computer a small programme using only 1000 units of storage, whereby the machine supplied with one sixteen figure number replies with another within two seconds. I would defy anyone to learn from these replies sufficient about the programme to be able to predict any replies to untried values.*
>
> A. TURING (from [64])

Andrej Bogdanov
Dept. of Computer Science and Engineering and Institute of Theoretical Computer Science and Communications, Chinese University of Hong Kong. e-mail: andrejb@cse.cuhk.edu.hk

Alon Rosen
Efi Arazi School of Computer Science, IDC Herzliya. e-mail: alon.rosen@idc.ac.il

3.1 Introduction

A family of functions $F_s\colon \{0,1\}^k \to \{0,1\}^\ell$, indexed by a key $s \in \{0,1\}^n$, is said to be *pseudorandom* if it satisfies the following two properties:

Easy to evaluate: The value $F_s(x)$ is efficiently computable given s and x.

Pseudorandom: The function F_s cannot be efficiently distinguished from a uniformly random function $R\colon \{0,1\}^k \to \{0,1\}^\ell$, given access to pairs $(x_i, F_s(x_i))$, where the x_i's can be adaptively chosen by the distinguisher.

One should think of the key s as being kept secret, and of the running time of evaluation as being substantially smaller than that of the distinguisher. This faithfully models a prototypical attack on a cryptographic scheme: the adversary's running time is bounded but can still exceed that of the system, and he may adaptively adjust his probing of the system's input/output behavior.

The definition of pseudorandom functions (PRFs), along with the demonstration of its feasibility, is one of the keystone achievements of modern cryptography [64]. This owes much to the fact that the definition hits a "sweet spot" in terms of level of abstraction: it is simple enough to be studied and realized, and at the same time is powerful enough to open the door to countless applications.

Notably, PRFs lend themselves to simple proofs of security. Being indistinguishable from a random function means that analysis cleanly reduces to an idealized system in which a truly random function is used instead of the pseudorandom one.

3.1.1 Applications

Perhaps the most natural application of pseudorandom functions is that of *message authentication*. The goal is to allow Bob to verify that a message m was sent to him by Alice and nobody else. To this end, Alice and Bob share a randomly sampled secret key s, known only to them. When Alice wishes to authenticate m, she appends a tag σ that is efficiently computable from m and s. Verifiability of (m, σ) follows from the fact that Bob also knows m and s and so can compute σ efficiently.

An authentication scheme is said to be *unforgeable* if no computationally bounded adversary (not possessing s) can generate a pair (m, σ) that passes verification, where m can be any message that was not previously sent (and hence authenticated) by Alice. To authenticate m using a PRF family F_s, Alice simply sends to Bob the (message, tag) pair

$$(m, F_s(m)). \tag{3.1}$$

Upon receiving (m, σ), Bob uses s to evaluate $F_s(m)$ and verifies that it equals σ. Unforgeability follows from the fact that the probability with which any computationally bounded adversary correctly guesses $\sigma = F_s(m)$ does not noticeably change if $F_s(m)$ is replaced with $R(m)$, where R is a random function. The probability of correctly guessing $R(m)$ is $2^{-\ell}$. This remains true even if the adversary gets to see pairs of the form (m_i, σ_i), where $m \neq m_i$ for all i and the m_i's are adaptively chosen.

Symmetric-key encryption. In the setting of *symmetric-key encryption*, Alice and Bob share a randomly sampled secret key s, which is used along with some other string r to generate an encryption $\text{Enc}_s(m; r)$ of a plaintext m. Alice sends $\text{Enc}_s(m; r)$ to Bob, who can use s in order to compute the decryption $m = \text{Dec}_s(\text{Enc}_s(m; r))$.

An encryption scheme is said to be *secure* if for any two plaintexts m_0, m_1 the distributions $\text{Enc}_s(m_0; r)$ and $\text{Enc}_s(m_1; r)$ cannot be efficiently distinguished. Given a PRF family F_s, one can implement a secure encryption scheme as follows:

$$\text{Enc}_s(m; r) = (r, F_s(r) \oplus m), \qquad \text{Dec}_s(r, c) = F_s(r) \oplus c. \tag{3.2}$$

Similarly to the case of message authentication, security is established by observing that the advantage of any efficient distinguisher between $\text{Enc}_s(m_0; r)$ and $\text{Enc}_s(m_1; r)$ will not noticeably change if we replace $F_s(r)$ with $R(r)$, where R is a random function. In the latter case, the adversary's task is to distinguish between $R(r) \oplus m_0$ and $R(r) \oplus m_1$, which is information-theoretically impossible.

This argument is valid even if the distinguisher gets to see $\text{Enc}_s(m_i; r_i)$ for adaptively chosen m_i's (m_0, m_1 are also allowed), provided that $r_i \neq r$ for all i. In practice, this can be enforced by either deterministically choosing the r's using a counter, or by sampling them independently at random each time. The counter solution does not require including r as part of the encryption, but requires maintaining state between encryptions. The randomized solution does not require state, but has longer ciphertexts and moreover requires r to be long enough so that collisions of the form $r_i = r$ are unlikely.

Interestingly, neither of the above solutions necessitates the full strength of PRFs, in the sense that they do not require security against *adaptive* access to the function. In the counter solution, the PRF adversary only observes the function values on a predetermined set of inputs, whereas in the randomized mode, it observes values on randomly chosen inputs. This motivates two interesting relaxations of PRFs, called *nonadaptive* PRFs and *weak* PRFs, respectively, and opens the door to more efficient constructions.

Key derivation. The following is a convenient method for generating a long sequence of cryptographic keys "on-the-fly". Let F_s be a PRF, and define a key k_i by

$$k_i = F_s(i). \tag{3.3}$$

This method has advantages both in terms of memory usage and in terms of key management, at least as long as one is able to protect the (relatively short) "master-key" s from leaking to an attacker (by definition, F_s remains pseudorandom even if some of the k_i's are leaked). In terms of security, any efficient system that uses the k_i's as secret keys is guaranteed to be no less secure than the same system would have been if it were to use truly random and independent keys.

Storing, protecting, and managing a single short key s is indeed convenient. However, it has the disadvantage that compromise of s results in loss of security for the entire system. One way to mitigate this concern would be to store $\text{FHE}(s)$, where FHE is a *fully homomorphic* encryption scheme [120]. The idea would be to store $c = \text{FHE}(s)$ and erase s, keeping only the FHE decryption key. One can then homomorphically compute $\text{FHE}(F_s(i))$ for any desired i (think of the circuit $C_i(s) = F_s(i)$), and then decrypt the result at the location in which the FHE decryption key is stored (say on a client machine). An attacker who compromises the system learns nothing about the master key s, whereas an attacker who compromises the client alone learns only the FHE key.

While conceptually simple, this solution is still not practical. Currently known FHE schemes can practically support only simple computations, certainly not ones nearly as complex as evaluating a PRF. Can PRFs be made simple enough to allow their fast homomorphic evaluation? Alternatively, could one devise FHE schemes so that efficient homomorphic evaluation of compatible PRFs is enabled?

Hardness of learning. The fundamental task in machine learning is to make future predictions of an unknown concept based on past training data. In the model of *probably approximately correct* (PAC) learning [127, 82] the concept is described by an efficient function F, the data comes in the form of input–output samples $(x, F(x))$, and the objective is for the learner to make almost always correct predictions (with respect to a given distribution on inputs). Statistical considerations show that $O(\log|\mathbf{C}|)$ random samples provide sufficient information to learn any function coming from a given class $\mathbf{C}$ with precision at least 99%.

In particular, a PRF F_s can in principle be learned from $O(n)$ random samples, where n is the size of its key. The learning, however, cannot be carried out efficiently: any learner L that is able to predict the value of F_s at a new input x^* based on past data $(x_1, F_s(x_1)), \ldots, (x_q, F_s(x_q))$ can be applied to distinguish the sequences

$$(x_1, F_s(x_1)), \ldots, (x_q, F_s(x_q)), (x^*, F_s(x^*)) \quad \text{and}$$
$$(x_1, R(x_1)), \ldots, (x_q, R(x_q)), (x^*, R(x^*)),$$

thereby violating the pseudorandomness of F_s. To distinguish, one can use the first q elements as training data for the learner and test the value $F(x^*)$ against the learner's prediction $L(x^*)$. If the learner is probably approximately correct, $L(x^*)$ is likely to agree with $F(x^*)$ when $F = F_s$. On the other hand, when $F = R$, the value $F(x^*)$ is statistically independent of the training data and uncorrelated with $L(x^*)$.

A learning algorithm can thus be viewed as a potential cryptanalytic attack against any PRF. Vice versa, any algorithm that is believed to learn a given concept class should be tested on conjectured PRF constructions that fall within this class.

3.1.2 Feasibility

The construction of PRFs necessitates postulating computational hardness. This is not surprising given that the existence of PRFs requires at the very least ruling out the possibility that P equals NP: distinguishing F_s from a random function R reduces to the NP-search problem of finding a key s consistent with the samples

$(F(1), F(2), \ldots, F(m))$. Such a key always exists when $F = F_s$, but only with small probability when $F = R$ (assuming $m\ell > n$).

The first hardness assumption under which PRFs were constructed is the existence of *pseudorandom generators* [64]. A pseudorandom generator (PRG) is an efficiently computable deterministic function $G: \{0, 1\}^n \to \{0, 1\}^m$ with $m > n$ whose output $G(s) \in \{0, 1\}^m$, where s is sampled uniformly from $\{0, 1\}^n$, cannot be efficiently distinguished from a uniformly random string $r \in \{0, 1\}^m$.

While PRGs and PRFs both map a short random string into a longer pseudorandom string, the definitions differ in the quantity of output bits and in the adversary's access to them. Any PRF family $F_s: \{0, 1\}^k \to \{0, 1\}$ gives rise to a PRG:

$$G(s) = (F_s(1), F_s(2), \ldots, F_s(m)),$$

as long as $n < 2^k$ (assuming, for simplicity, that the distribution on keys s is uniform). In other words, the truth-table of a PRF is an efficiently computable sequence of pseudorandom bits of essentially unbounded length. In contrast, the output length of a PRG is a priori bounded by its running time.

From this perspective, a PRF can be thought of as a PRG whose output length is much larger than the running time of the distinguisher. As this output is too large to be stored in the distinguisher's memory, a definitional choice must be made regarding how these bits are accessed by the adversary. In this respect, the definition of a PRF provides the adversary with imposing power: his access to the pseudorandom bits is *adversarial* and *adaptive*.

Goldreich, Goldwasser, and Micali showed how to use any length-doubling PRG, $G: \{0, 1\}^n \to \{0, 1\}^{2n}$, to construct a PRF family $F_s: \{0, 1\}^k \to \{0, 1\}^\ell$, that is keyed by $s \in \{0, 1\}^n$, for arbitrary k and ℓ. Subsequently, it was shown that PRGs are polynomial-time equivalent to one-way functions [73, 69, 126]. A function $f: \{0, 1\}^n \to \{0, 1\}^\ell$ is *one-way* if f is efficiently computable, but given $y = f(x)$ for a random x, it is infeasible to find any x' such that $f(x') = y$.

Theorem 3.1.1 ([64, 73]). *Pseudorandom functions exist iff one-way functions exist.*

One-way functions are the most rudimentary primitive in modern cryptography. Their existence is necessary for virtually all applications of interest, save a select few in which information-theoretic security is achievable. The definition of a one-way function merely postulates the ability to hide a "secret" that is computationally hard to reconstruct. This encompasses, in particular, the secret key s of any candidate PRF construction. In contrast, the security requirements of a PRF are significantly more stringent: the adversary is given access to multiple input–output samples of its choice and is only asked to detect any form of nonrandom behavior, a seemingly much easier task than reconstructing the secret key s.

Owing to the relatively mild security requirement of one-way functions, candidate constructions abound. Any stochastic computational process that is typically difficult to invert can be modeled as a one-way function. In contrast, pseudorandom functions must exhibit significant internal structure in order to resist the vast variety of distinguishers that they can be tested against (see Section 3.7 for some representative examples). It is thus remarkable that the two notions are equivalent.

3.1.3 Efficiency, Security, and Functionality

The work of Goldreich, Goldwasser, and Micali (GGM) provides an elegant conceptual solution to the problem of constructing PRFs. This has opened the door towards
the finer study of their theory and practice, and has resulted in a large body of work.
In this survey we will focus on the following aspects:

Efficiency. Every evaluation of the GGM PRF on a k-bit input necessitates k sequential invocations to the underlying PRG, while its provable security deteriorates
as k becomes larger. Are there more efficient constructions?

Naor and Reingold gave a construction that has lower parallel evaluation complexity than the GGM construction, but assumes the availability of a pseudorandom
synthesizer, an object (seemingly) stronger than a PRG. In Section 3.3 we present
the two constructions of PRFs, and in Section 3.4 we give concrete instantiations of
PRFs obtained using this paradigm.

On the negative side, the existence of efficient learning algorithms for certain
types of circuits implies inherent lower bounds on the complexity of pseudorandom functions. Razborov and Rudich explain how such learning algorithms arise
naturally from proofs of circuit lower bounds. We discuss these connections in Section 3.6.

Security. Pseudorandom functions are required to be secure against all efficient
distinguishers. It is sometimes useful to consider security against restricted classes
of distinguishers that model specific types of attacks such as differential cryptanalysis. A sufficiently restrictive class of adversaries may allow for a proof of security
that is unconditional. Proofs of security against restricted distinguishers can also
provide confidence in the soundness of heuristic constructions.

In Section 3.7 we discuss some restricted classes of distinguishers arising from
the study of pseudorandomness (bounded query distinguishers, linear distinguishers, space-bounded algorithms), complexity theory (polynomials, rational functions), and learning theory (statistical queries).

Functionality. In Section 3.5 we illustrate the robustness of the definition of PRFs
with respect to domain size and discuss how PRFs provide a basis for implementing "huge random objects", the most notable example of which are pseudorandom
permutations.

For certain cryptographic applications it is useful to have pseudorandom functions with additional functionality. In Section 3.8 we present two such extensions:
key-homomorphic PRFs and puncturable PRFs.

Open questions. In spite of the enormous body of work on pseudorandom functions in the last three decades, many questions of interest remain unanswered. We
mark some of our favorite ones with the symbol ⑦ as they come up in the text. For
convenience, all the open questions are indexed at the end of the chapter.

3.1.4 The Wide Scope of Pseudorandom Functions

Pseudorandom functions permeate cryptography and are of fundamental importance in computational complexity and learning theory. In this survey we do not attempt to provide comprehensive coverage of their applications, but focus instead on a handful of representative settings which highlight their conceptual importance. The following (partial) list gives an indication of the wide scope of PRFs.

Basic cryptographic applications. Pseudorandom functions fit naturally into message authentication and in particular underlie the security of the widely deployed authentication function HMAC [22, 21]. They are also used in constructions of deterministic stateless digital signatures [59], and randomized stateless symmetric-key encryption (see Section 3.1.1).

Pseudorandom permutations (PRPs, see Section 3.5.2), which are closely related to PRFs, model block ciphers such as DES and AES, where the PRP security notion was a criterion in the design [111].

Advanced cryptographic applications. PRFs have been applied to achieve resettable security in protocols [48, 18], to hide memory access patterns in oblivious RAM [60, 66], and to bootstrap fully homomorphic and functional encryption schemes [9, 8]. The construction of authentication schemes from PRFs extends naturally to provide digital signatures from *verifiable PRFs* [23, 97].

Key-homomorphic PRFs are useful for constructing distributed PRFs, proxy re-encryption, and other applications with high relevance to "cloud" security (see Section 3.8.2). The recently introduced notion of puncturable PRFs, in conjunction with indistinguishability obfuscation, has found applications for the construction of strong cryptographic primitives, and demonstrates how to bridge between private-key and public-key encryption (see Section 3.8.2).

Puncturable PRFs have also been recently combined with indistinguishability obfuscation to exhibit hard on the average instances for the complexity classses PPAD [32, 58] and CLS [74].

Other applications. In the realm of data structures, permutation-based hashing, which is inspired by the Feistel construction of PRPs, has been applied to improve the performance of dynamic dictionaries [12]. PRPs were also recently used in the construction of adaptively secure Bloom filters [108]. More generally, PRFs are a basic building block in implementations of huge random objects (see Section 3.5.3).

Lower bounds and barriers. As pointed out in Section 3.1.1, PRF constructions present a fundamental barrier for efficient learning algorithms (see Section 3.6.1) and for our ability to prove circuit lower bounds (see Section 3.6.2).

Finally, pseudorandom functions provide natural examples for "pseudo-entropic" functions that cannot be virtually black-box obfuscated in a strong sense [67, 31].

3.1.5 Intellectual Merit

The evolution in the design and use of PRFs exemplifies how theory affects practice in indirect ways, and how basic conceptualizations free our minds to develop far-reaching and unexpected ideas. The wide array of applications of PRFs can in large part be attributed to their simplicity and flexibility. These traits facilitate the robust design of cryptographic primitives, while relying on clearly stated and well-defined assumptions (compare this with vague terms such as "diffusion" and "confusion").

For instance, while a candidate PRP was already proposed in the mid 1970s (DES), there was no methodology available at the time for capturing the desired security properties. Indeed, rigorous analysis of various modes of operation for block ciphers [24, 85] and Feistel-like constructions [90, 104] only emerged after the 1984 work of Goldreich, Goldwasser, and Micali [64].

From a pedagogical point of view, the study of pseudorandom functions clarifies concepts and sharpens distinctions between notions that arise in the study of cryptographic constructions. Some examples that come to mind are:

Computational indistinguishability. PRFs are a prime example of a distribution that is extremely nonrandom from a statistical perspective, yet indistinguishable from random by computationally bounded observers (see discussion on "A delicate balance" in Section 3.2.1). Moreover, computational indistinguishability in PRF constructions and applications exemplifies the use of the hybrid proof technique, which is prevalent in cryptographic reasoning.

Key recovery, prediction, and distinguishing. For an adversary to break a cryptographic system it does not necessarily have to fully recover the key, which may be underspecified by the system's behavior. A more reasonable notion of security is that of unpredictability of future responses based on past interaction. In the case of PRFs, this type of attack is exemplified by PAC learning algorithms, which reconstruct an approximation of the function based on past input–output data. As explained in Section 3.6.1, unpredictability is implied by indistinguishability from a random function. The converse does not hold in general. The ability to distinguish a system's behavior from random already opens the door to severe security breaches, even if the function cannot be predicted or the key fully recovered.

Modeling access to a system. The definition of PRFs cleanly captures what type of access an adversary can have to a system, be it adaptive, nonadaptive, sequential, or statistically random (see Section 3.2.1). It also clarifies the distinction between the adversary's running time and the number of times it queries the function/system.

How not to model a random function. For the definition of PRFs to make sense, the function's description given by the random key s must be kept secret from the distinguisher. This should be contrasted to the random oracle model [54, 25], whose instantiations (wrongly) assume that the oracle retains its random properties even if its description is fully available to the distinguisher.

3.2 Definitions

> *If you have something interesting to say,*
> *it doesn't matter how you say it.*
>
> LEONID LEVIN (1985)

We give a formal definition of pseudorandom functions, discuss our definitional choices, and try to provide some intuition behind the requirements. We then gain some practice through two "warm-ups": first, we show how to generically increase the range size of a PRF. Second, we give a security analysis of the symmetric-key encryption scheme from Section 3.1.1. Although these types of proofs are standard in cryptography [61, 80], they will serve as compelling motivations to introduce some additional ideas and should help the reader get accustomed to the notation.

For formal definitions of circuits and oracles the reader is referred to Goldreich's textbook on computational complexity [62].

3.2.1 Pseudorandom Functions

Since it does not make sense to require pseudorandomness from a single fixed function $F : \{0, 1\}^k \to \{0, 1\}^\ell$, the definition of pseudorandom functions refers to distributions of functions sampled from a family. Each member of the family is a function $F : \{0, 1\}^n \times \{0, 1\}^k \to \{0, 1\}^\ell$, where the first argument is called the *key* and denoted s, and the second argument is called the *input* to the function. The key is sampled according to some distribution S and then fixed. We are interested in the pseudorandomness of the function $F_s(x) = F(s, x)$ over the distribution S of the keys.

The PRF's adversary is modeled by a Boolean circuit D that is given oracle access to some function F. Namely, throughout its computation, D has access to outputs of the function F on inputs $x_1, x_2, \dots$ of his choice. The type of access can vary depending on the definition of security. By default D is given *adaptive* access, meaning that the input x_j may depend on values $F(x_i)$ for $i < j$. For an oracle F we denote by D^F the output of D when given access to F.

Definition 3.2.1 (Pseudorandom function [64]). *Let S be a distribution over $\{0, 1\}^n$ and $\{F_s : \{0, 1\}^k \to \{0, 1\}^\ell\}$ be a family of functions indexed by strings s in the support of S. We say $\{F_s\}$ is a (t, ε)-pseudorandom function family if for every Booleanvalued oracle circuit D of size at most t,*

$$\left| \Pr_s[D^{F_s} \text{ accepts}] - \Pr_R[D^R \text{ accepts}] \right| \le \varepsilon,$$

where s is distributed according to S, and R is a function sampled uniformly at random from the set of all functions from $\{0, 1\}^k$ to $\{0, 1\}^\ell$.

The string s is called the *key*, the circuit D is called the *distinguisher*, and the above difference in probabilities is its *distinguishing advantage* with respect to F_s. Since D is nonuniform, we may assume that it is deterministic, as it can always hardwire the coin tosses that maximize its distinguishing advantage.

Weak, nonadaptive, and sequential PRFs. In certain settings it is natural to restrict the oracle access mode of the distinguisher. In a *nonadaptive* PRF the distinguisher must make all its queries to the oracle at once. In a *weak* PRF at every invocation the oracle returns the pair $(x, F(x))$ for a uniformly random x in $\{0, 1\}^k$. In a *sequential* PRF the i-th oracle invocation is answered by the value $F(i)$.

Efficiency. We say $\{F_s\}$ has *size* c if s can be sampled by a circuit of size at most c and for every s there exists a circuit of size at most c that computes F_s. We are interested in the parameter regime where the size of $\{F_s\}$ is much smaller than the distinguisher size t and the inverse of its distinguishing advantage $1/\varepsilon$. In the theory of cryptography it is customary to view n as a symbolic *security parameter* and study the asymptotic behavior of other parameters for a function ensemble indexed by an infinite sequence of values for n. The PRF is viewed as efficient if its input size k grows polynomially in n, but its size is bounded by some polynomial of n.

Security. Regarding security, it is less clear what a typical choice of values for t and ε should be. At one end, cryptographic dogma postulates that the adversary be given at least as much computational power as honest parties. In the asymptotic setting, this leads to the minimalist requirement of *superpolynomial security*: for every t that grows polynomially in n, ε should be negligible in n (it should eventually be smaller than $1/p(n)$ for every polynomial p). At the other end, it follows from statistical considerations that $(2^n, 1/2)$ and $(\omega(n), 2^{-n})$-PRFs cannot exist. In an attempt to approach these limitations as closely as possible, the maximalist notion of *exponential* security sets t and ε to $2^{\alpha n}$ and $2^{-\beta n}$, respectively, for some constants $\alpha, \beta \in (0, 1)$. Most cryptographic reductions, including all the ones presented here, guarantee deterioration in security parameters that is at most polynomial. Both super-polynomial and exponential security are preserved under such reductions.

A delicate balance. PRFs strike a delicate balance between efficiency and security. A random function $R \colon \{0, 1\}^k \to \{0, 1\}^\ell$ is ruled out by the efficiency requirement: its description size, let alone implementation size, is as large as $\ell \cdot 2^k$. For the description size to be polynomial in k, the PRF must be sampled from a set of size at most $2^n = 2^{\mathrm{poly}(k)}$, which is a tiny fraction of the total number of functions $2^{\ell 2^k}$. Let **F** be such a set and assume for simplicity that F_s is sampled uniformly from **F**. Which sets **F** would give rise to a PRF? One natural possibility is to choose **F** at random, uniformly among all sets of size 2^n. Then with overwhelming probability over the choice of **F** the function F_s is indistinguishable from random, but the probability that it can be computed efficiently (in terms of circuit size) is negligible.

Uniformity. We model computational efficiency using circuit size. A more common alternative is the running time of some uniform computational model such as Turing machines. Most of the theory covered here carries over to the uniform setting: all reductions between implementations preserve uniformity, but some of the reductions between adversaries may rely on nonuniform choices. We think that the circuit model of computation is a more natural one in the context of PRFs. Besides, proofs of security in the circuit model are notationally simpler.

3.2.2 Computational Indistinguishability

It will be convenient to define a general notion of *computational indistinguishability*, which considers distinguishers D that adaptively interact as part of probabilistic experiments called *games*. When a game is not interactive we call it a *distribution*.

Definition 3.2.2 (Computational indistinguishability). *We say that games H_0, H_1 are (t, ε)-indistinguishable if for every oracle circuit D of size at most t,*

$$\left| \Pr[D^{H_0} \text{ accepts}] - \Pr[D^{H_1} \text{ accepts}] \right| < \varepsilon,$$

where the probabilities are taken over the coin tosses of H_0, H_1.

The definition of pseudorandom functions can be restated by requiring that the following two games are (t, ε)-computationally indistinguishable:

F_s: Sample $s \in \{0, 1\}^n$ from S and give D adaptive oracle access to F_s
R: Sample $R : \{0, 1\}^k \to \{0, 1\}^\ell$ and give D adaptive oracle access to R

Definition 3.2.2 is more general in that it accomodates the specification of games other than those occurring in the definition of a PRF.

Proposition 3.2.3. *Suppose that H_0, H_1 are (t_1, ε_1)-indistinguishable and that H_1, H_2 are (t_2, ε_2)-indistinguishable. Then, H_0, H_2 are $(\min\{t_1, t_2\}, \varepsilon_1 + \varepsilon_2)$-indistinguishable.*

In other words, computational indistinguishability is a transitive relation (up to appropriate loss in parameters). Proposition 3.2.3 is proved via a direct application of the triangle inequality to Definition 3.2.2.

Proposition 3.2.4. *Let H^q denote q independently sampled copies of a distribution H. If H_0 and H_1 are (t, ε)-indistinguishable then H_0^q and H_1^q are $(t, q\varepsilon)$-indistinguishable.*

Proof: For $i \in \{0, \ldots, q\}$, consider the "hybrid" distribution $D_i = (H_0^i, H_1^{q-i})$. We claim that D_i and D_{i+1} are (t, ε)-indistinguishable. Otherwise, there exists a circuit B of size t that distinguishes between D_i, D_{i+1} with advantage ε. We use B to build a B' of size t that distinguishes between H_0, H_1 with the same advantage.

The circuit B' is given an h that is sampled from either H_0 or H_1. It then samples h_0^{i-1} from H_0^{i-1} and h_1^{q-i} from H_1^{q-i} (the samples can be hardwired inducing no overhead in size), feeds the vector $d = (h_0^{i-1}, h, h_1^{q-i})$ to B, and outputs whatever B outputs. If h is sampled from H_0, then d is distributed according to D_i, whereas if it is sampled from H_1, then d is distributed according to D_{i-1}. We get that B' distinguishes between H_0, H_1 with advantage ε, in contradiction to their (t, ε)-indistinguishability. Thus, D_i and D_{i+1} are (t, ε)-indistinguishable.

The claim now follows by observing that $D_0 = H_1^q$ and $D_q = H_0^q$ and invoking Proposition 3.2.3 for q times. $\square$

Two games are (∞, ε)-indistinguishable if they are indistinguishable by any oracle circuit, regardless of its size. In the special case of distributions, (∞, ε)-indistinguishability is equivalent to having statistical (i.e., total variation) distance at most ε.

3.2.3 Warm-Up I: Range Extension

Sometimes it is desirable to increase the size of the range of a PRF. This may for instance be beneficial in applications such as message authentication where one requires a function whose output on a yet unobserved input to be unpredictable. The larger the range, the harder it is to predict the output.

We show that a pseudorandom function with many bits of output can be obtained from a pseudorandom function with one bit of output. Let $F'_s \colon \{0,1\}^k \to \{0,1\}$ be any pseudorandom function family and define $F_s \colon \{0,1\}^{k-\lceil \log \ell \rceil} \to \{0,1\}^\ell$ by

$$F_s(x) = (F'_s(x,1), F'_s(x,2), \ldots, F'_s(x,\ell)),$$

where the integers $1, \ldots, \ell$ are identified with their $\lceil \log \ell \rceil$-bit binary expansion.

Proposition 3.2.5. *If $\{F'_s\}$ is a (t, ε)-pseudorandom function family then $\{F_s\}$ is a $(t/\ell, \varepsilon)$-pseudorandom function family.*

Proof: For every oracle circuit D whose oracle type is a function from $\{0,1\}^{k-\lceil \log \ell \rceil}$ to $\{0,1\}^\ell$, let D' be the circuit that emulates D as follows: when D queries its oracle at x, D' answers it by querying its own oracle at $(x,1), \ldots, (x,\ell)$ and concatenating the answers. The distributions D^{F_s} and $D'^{F'_s}$ are then identical, and so are D^R and $D'^{R'}$ for random functions R and R'.

It follows that D and D' have the same distinguishing advantage. By construction, D' is at most ℓ times larger than D. Therefore, if D is a circuit of size t/ℓ with distinguishing advantage ε, D' has size t with distinguishing advantage ε. By assumption such a D' does not exist so neither does such a D. $\qquad\square$

Proposition 3.2.5 provides a generic secure transformation from a PRF with one bit of output to a PRF with ℓ bits of output for any given value of ℓ. This generality, however, comes at the price of worse complexity and security: implementation size grows by a factor of ℓ, while security drops by the same factor. Such losses are often unavoidable for a construction obtained by means of a generic transformation, and it is indeed desirable to directly devise efficient constructions.

3.2.4 Warm-Up II: Symmetric-Key Encryption

We now state and prove the security of the encryption scheme (Enc, Dec) described in (3.2). Recall that $\text{Enc}_s(m; r) = (r, F_s(r) \oplus m)$.

Proposition 3.2.6. *If $\{F_s \colon \{0,1\}^k \to \{0,1\}^\ell\}$ is a weak $(t + \ell t, \varepsilon)$-pseudorandom function family then for every two messages $m_0, m_1 \in \{0,1\}^\ell$, the following games are $(t, 2\varepsilon + t/2^k)$-indistinguishable:*

E_0: *Sample random $s \in \{0,1\}^n$ and $r \in \{0,1\}^k$ and output $\text{Enc}_s(m_0; r)$*
E_1: *Sample random $s \in \{0,1\}^n$ and $r \in \{0,1\}^k$ and output $\text{Enc}_s(m_1; r)$*

In both games the distinguisher is also given access to an oracle that in the i-th invocation samples a uniform and independent r_i and outputs $\text{Enc}_s(x_i; r_i)$ on input x_i.

Proof: Consider the following two games:

R_0: Sample random $R\colon \{0,1\}^k \to \{0,1\}^\ell$ and $r \in \{0,1\}^k$ and output $(r, R(r) \oplus m_0)$
R_1: Sample random $R\colon \{0,1\}^k \to \{0,1\}^\ell$ and $r \in \{0,1\}^k$ and output $(r, R(r) \oplus m_1)$

In both games the distinguisher is also given access to an oracle that on input x_i samples a uniform and independent r_i and outputs $(r_i, R(r_i) \oplus x_i)$.

Claim 3.2.7. *For* $b \in \{0, 1\}$ *games* E_b *and* R_b *are* (t, ε)*-indistinguishable.*

Proof: Suppose for contradiction that there exists a distinguisher A of size t that distinguishes between E_b and R_b with advantage ε. We use A to build a distinguisher D between F_s and R with the same advantage.

The distinguisher D is given access to an oracle F that is either F_s or R. It emulates A, answering his queries, which are either according to E_b or to R_b, as follows:

- Sample r, query F to obtain $F(r)$, and output $\mathrm{Enc}_s(m_b; r) = (r, F(r) \oplus m_b)$
- On input x_i, sample r_i, query F to obtain $F(r_i)$, and output $(r_i, F(r_i) \oplus x_i)$

Accounting for the ℓ extra $\oplus$ gates incurred by each oracle query (out of at most t queries) of A, the circuit D is of size $t + \ell t$. Note that D^{F_s} and D^R are identically distributed to A^{E_b} and A^{R_b}, respectively, so D distinguishes F_s from R with advantage ε, contradicting the $(t + \ell t, \varepsilon)$-pseudorandomness of F_s.   □

Claim 3.2.8. *Games* R_0 *and* R_1 *are* $(t, t/2^k)$*-indistinguishable.*

Proof: Let A be a potential distinguisher between R_0 and R_1. Note that A's view of the games R_0 and R_1 is identical conditioned on the event that A never makes a query x that is answered by $(r, R(r) \oplus x)$. Since an A of size t makes at most t queries and r_i is chosen uniformly and independently for every query the probability of this event is at most $t/2^k$.   □

Combining the two claims with Proposition 3.2.3, we conclude that E_0 and E_1 are $(t, 2\varepsilon + t/2^k)$-indistinguishable.   □

The analysis above incurs security loss that grows linearly with the number of encryption queries made by the distinguisher D. In this case the number of queries was bounded by t, which is the size of D. However, as we will see later, it is sometimes useful to separately quantify the number of queries made by the distinguisher.

Definition 3.2.9 (Bounded-query PRF). *A* (t, q, ε)*-pseudorandom function is a* (t, ε)*-pseudorandom function in which the distinguisher makes at most q queries.*

We also give an analogous definition for computational indistinguishability.

Definition 3.2.10 (Bounded-query indistinguishability). *We say that games* H_0 *and* H_1 *are* (t, q, ε)*-indistinguishable if they are* (t, ε)*-indisinguishable by distinguishers that make at most q queries.*

Decoupling the number of queries from the adversary's running time (as well as from the function's input size) will turn out to be beneficial in the proofs of security of the GGM and NR constructions (Section 3.3), in the construction of pseudorandom permutations (Section 3.5.2), and in the discussion of natural proofs (Section 3.6.2).

3.3 Generic Constructions

Beware of proofs by induction,
especially in crypto.

ODED GOLDREICH (1990s)

We now present two generic methods for constructing a pseudorandom function. The first method, due to Goldreich, Goldwasser, and Micali (GGM), relies on any length-doubling *pseudorandom generator*. The second method is due to Naor and Reingold (NR). It builds on a stronger primitive called a *pseudorandom synthesizer*.

Both the GGM and NR methods inductively extend the domain size of a PRF. Whereas the GGM method doubles the domain size with each inductive step, the NR method squares it. Instantiations of the NR method typically give PRFs of lower depth. The GGM construction, on the other hand, has shorter keys and relies on a simpler building block.

3.3.1 The Goldreich–Goldwasser–Micali Construction

We start by defining the notion of a pseudorandom generator (PRG). Pseudorandom generation is a relatively well-understood cryptographic task. In particular, it admits many candidate instantiations along with highly efficient implementations.

Definition 3.3.1 (Pseudorandom generator [37, 129]). *Let $G: \{0,1\}^n \to \{0,1\}^m$ be a deterministic function, where $m > n$. We say that G is a (t, ε)-pseudorandom generator if the following two distributions are (t, ε)-indistinguishable:*

- *Sample a random "seed" $s \in \{0,1\}^n$ and output $G(s)$.*
- *Sample a random string $r \in \{0,1\}^m$ and output r.*

A pseudorandom generator $G: \{0,1\}^n \to \{0,1\}^{2n}$ can be viewed as a pseudorandom function $F'_s: \{0,1\} \to \{0,1\}^n$ over one input bit. For this special case the pair of values $(F'_s(0), F'_s(1))$ should be indistinguishable from a truly random pair. This is satisfied if we set $F'_s(0) = G_0(s)$ and $F'_s(1) = G_1(s)$, where $G_0(s)$ and $G_1(s)$ are the first n bits and the last n bits of the output of G, respectively.

The above method extends naturally for larger domains. Suppose for example that we wish to construct a two-bit input PRF $F_s: \{0,1\}^2 \to \{0,1\}^n$, which is specified by its four values $(F_s(00), F_s(01), F_s(10), F_s(11))$. To this end one can define the values of F_s by an inductive application of the pseudorandom generator:

$$G_0(F'_s(0)) \quad G_1(F'_s(0)) \quad G_0(F'_s(1)) \quad G_1(F'_s(1)). \tag{3.4}$$

Since F'_s is pseudorandom we can replace it with a random $R': \{0,1\} \to \{0,1\}^n$, and infer that distribution (3.4) is computationally indistinguishable from the distribution

$$G_0(R'(0)) \quad G_1(R'(0)) \quad G_0(R'(1)) \quad G_1(R'(1)). \tag{3.5}$$

On the other hand the distribution (3.5) can be described as the pair of values obtained by applying G on the independent random seeds $R'(0)$ and $R'(1)$. The pair $(G(R'(0)), G(R'(1))$ is computationally indistinguishable from a pair of uniformly random values. Therefore, distribution (3.4) is computationally indistinguishable from the truth-table of a random function $R: \{0,1\}^2 \to \{0,1\}^n$.

The GGM construction generalizes this idea naturally to larger input lengths. It is described in Figure 3.1.

Building block: A length-doubling pseudorandom generator, $G : \{0,1\}^n \to \{0,1\}^{2n}$
Function key: A seed $s \in \{0,1\}^n$ for G
Function evaluation: On input $x \in \{0,1\}^k$ define $F_s: \{0,1\}^k \to \{0,1\}^n$ as

$$F_s(x_1 \cdots x_k) = G_{x_k}(G_{x_{k-1}}(\cdots G_{x_1}(s) \cdots)),$$

where $G(s) = (G_0(s), G_1(s)) \in \{0,1\}^n \times \{0,1\}^n$.
Size: $k \cdot \text{size}(G)$
Depth: $k \cdot \text{depth}(G)$

Fig. 3.1: The Goldreich–Goldwasser–Micali construction

The construction can be thought of as a labeling of the leaves of a binary tree of depth k, where the leaf indexed by $x \in \{0,1\}^k$ is labeled by the value $F_s(x)$. The value at each leaf is evaluated in the time it takes to reach the leaf but is never stored. Figure 3.2 illustrates the case $k = 3$.

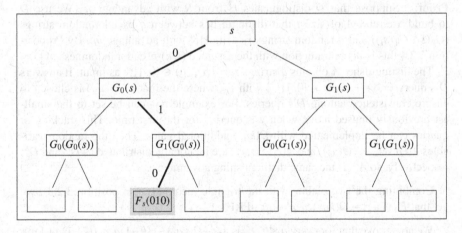

Fig. 3.2: Evaluating $F_s(010) = G_0(G_1(G_0(s)))$

Theorem 3.3.2 ([64]). *If $G: \{0,1\}^n \to \{0,1\}^{2n}$ is a (t, ε)-pseudorandom generator then $\{F_s\}$ is a $(t', kt'\varepsilon)$-pseudorandom function family, as long as $t' = o(\sqrt{t/k})$ and the size of G is at most t'.*

Proof: We prove the theorem by induction on k. Given $F'_s \colon \{0,1\}^{k-1} \to \{0,1\}^n$ define $F_s \colon \{0,1\}^k \to \{0,1\}^n$ as $F_s(x,y) = G_x(F'_s(y))$. For the inductive step we will apply the following claim. Let c denote the circuit size of G.

Claim 3.3.3. *If F'_s is a $(t{-}O(kq^2){+}cq, q, \varepsilon')$-PRF then F_s is a $(t{-}O(kq^2), q, \varepsilon'{+}q\varepsilon)$-PRF.*

Recall that a (t, q, ε)-PRF is a (t, ε)-PRF in which the distinguisher makes at most q queries to the function (Definition 3.2.9).

Proof: Let $(x,y) \in \{0,1\} \times \{0,1\}^{k-1}$ be an oracle query made by a purported distinguisher D between F_s and a random R. Consider the following three games:

F_s: Sample random $s \in \{0,1\}^n$. Answer with $F_s(x,y) = G_x(F'_s(y))$.
H: Sample random $R' \colon \{0,1\}^{k-1} \to \{0,1\}^n$. Answer with $H(x,y) = G_x(R'(y))$.
R: Sample random $R \colon \{0,1\}^k \to \{0,1\}^n$. Answer with $R(x,y)$.

Claim 3.3.4. *Games F_s and H are $(t - O(kq^2), \varepsilon')$-indistinguishable.*

Proof: If D distinguishes F_s from H with advantage ε' then consider the circuit $A^{F'}$ that simulates D by answering D's queries (x,y) with $G_x(F'(y))$. Then $A^{F'_s}$ and $A^{R'}$ are identically distributed to D^{F_s} and D^H, respectively, so A is a circuit of size at most $t - O(kq^2) + cq$ and query complexity q that distinguishes F'_s from R' with advantage ε'. This contradicts $(t{-}O(kq^2){+}cq, q, \varepsilon')$-pseudorandomness of F'_s. $\square$

Claim 3.3.5. *Games H and R are $(t - O(kq^2), q\varepsilon)$-indistinguishable.*

Proof: Suppose that D distinguishes H from R with advantage $q\varepsilon$. We use D to build a circuit A of size t that distinguishes between q pseudorandom strings $(G_0(s_i), G_1(s_i))$ and q random strings $r_i \in \{0,1\}^{2n}$ with advantage $q\varepsilon$. By Proposition 3.2.4 this is in contradiction with the assumed (t, ε)-pseudorandomness of G.

The distinguisher A obtains q strings $z_i = (z_{0i}, z_{1i}) \in \{0,1\}^{2n}$ as input. It answers D's query $(x,y) \in \{0,1\} \times \{0,1\}^{k-1}$ with z_{xi}, where the index $i = i(y)$ is chosen to ensure consistency among D's queries. For example $i(y)$ can be set to the smallest previously unused index when y is queried for the first time. This tracking of queries can be implemented with $O(kq^2)$ additional gates. Then the random variables $A(G(s_1), \ldots, G(s_q))$ and $A(r_1, \ldots, r_q)$ are identically distributed as D^H and D^R, respectively, so A has the same distinguishing advantage as D. $\square$

Combining the two claims with the triangle inequality (Proposition 3.2.3), we get that F_s is a $(t - O(kq^2), q, \varepsilon' + q\varepsilon)$-PRF. $\square$

We now prove that for every $q \leq t$, F_s is a $(t{-}O(kq^2){-}c(k-1)q, q, ((k-1)q+1)\varepsilon)$-PRF by induction on k. In the base case $k = 1$, $F_s(x) = G_x(s)$ and F_s is (t, q, ε)-secure by the assumed security of G. The inductive step is immediate from the claim we just proved.

If we set $q = \alpha \sqrt{t/k}$ for a sufficiently small absolute constant $\alpha > 0$, assume that $c \leq q$, and simplify the expression, we get that F_s is a $(t/2, q, kq\varepsilon)$-PRF. Because $q \leq t/2$, F_s is a $(q, kq\varepsilon)$-PRF. $\square$

The quadratic loss in security can be traced to the distinguisher transformation that enforces the distinctness of its queries. A simple "data structure" for this purpose has size that is quadratic in the number of queries. In other computational models, such as random access machines, more efficient data structures can be used, resulting in better security parameters.

Extensions and properties. The GGM construction readily extends to produce a PRF from $\{1, \ldots, d\}^n$ to $\{1, \ldots, d\}$ from a PRG $G: \{0, 1\}^n \rightarrow \{0, 1\}^{dn}$. The output of such a PRG can sometimes be naturally divided up into d blocks of n bits. This variant is particularly attractive when random access to the blocks is available (see Section 3.4.2 for an example).

The security of the GGM PRF extends to quantum adversaries, where the distinguisher may query the function in superposition [131].

The GGM construction is not *correlation intractable* [63]: it is possible to efficiently find an $x \in \{0, 1\}^k$ that maps to say 0^ℓ given the key s for a suitable instantiation of the PRG G. At the same time, the GGM construction is *weakly one-way* for certain parameter settings [51]: for a nonnegligible fraction of the inputs x it is infeasible to recover x given s and $F_s(x)$.

3.3.2 The Naor–Reingold Construction

Using pseudorandom synthesizers as building blocks, Naor and Reingold give a generic construction of a PRF [106]; see Fig. 3.3. Synthesizers are not as well understood as PRGs, and in particular do not have as many candidate instantiations. Most known instantiations rely on assumptions of a "public-key" flavor. Towards the end of this section we show how weak PRFs give rise to pseudorandom synthesizers, opening the door for basing synthesizers on "private-key" flavored assumptions.

Definition 3.3.6 (Pseudorandom synthesizer [106]). *Let* $S: \{0, 1\}^n \times \{0, 1\}^n \rightarrow \{0, 1\}^n$ *be a deterministic function. We say that* S *is a* (t, q, ε)*-pseudorandom synthesizer if the following two distributions are* (t, ε)*-indistinguishable:*

- *Sample* $a_1, \ldots, a_q, b_1, \ldots, b_q \leftarrow \{0, 1\}^n$. *Output the* q^2 *values* $S(a_i, b_j)$.
- *Output* q^2 *independent uniform random strings in* $\{0, 1\}^n$.

A synthesizer can be seen as an almost length-squaring pseudorandom generator with good locality properties, in that it maps $2q$ random "seed" elements to q^2 pseudorandom elements, and any component of its output depends on only two components of the input seed.

Using a recursive tree-like construction, it is possible to obtain PRFs on k-bit inputs, which can be computed using a total of about k synthesizer evaluations, arranged in $\log k$ levels. Given a synthesizer S and two independent PRF instances F_0 and F_1 on t input bits each, one gets a PRF on $2t$ input bits, defined as

$$F(x_1 \cdots x_{2t}) = S\big(F_0(x_1 \cdots x_t), F_1(x_{t+1} \cdots x_{2t})\big). \tag{3.6}$$

The base case of a 1-bit PRF can trivially be implemented by returning one of two random strings in the function's secret key.

Building block: A synthesizer $S : \{0, 1\}^n \times \{0, 1\}^n \to \{0, 1\}^n$
Function key: A collection of $2k$ strings in $\{0, 1\}^n$, where k is a power of two
Function evaluation: On input $x \in \{0, 1\}^k$ recursively define $F_s : \{0, 1\}^k \to \{0, 1\}^n$ as

$$F_s(x) = \begin{cases} S(F_{s_0}(x_0); F_{s_1}(x_1)), & \text{if } k > 1, \\ s_x, & \text{if } k = 1, \end{cases}$$

where z_0 and z_1 denote the left and right halves of the string z.
Size: $k \cdot \text{size}(S)$
Depth: $\log k \cdot \text{depth}(S)$

Fig. 3.3: The Naor–Reingold construction

The evaluation of F_s can be thought of as a recursive labeling process of a binary tree with k leaves and depth $\log k$. The i-th leaf has two possible labels: $s_{i,0}$ and $s_{i,1}$. The i-th input bit x_i selects one of these labels s_{i,x_i}. The label of each internal node at depth d is the value of S on the labels of its children, and the value of F_s is simply the label of the root; see Fig. 3.4.

This labeling process is very different than the one associated with the GGM construction. First, the binary tree is of depth $\log k$ instead of depth k as in GGM. Second, the labeling process starts from the leaves instead of from the root. Moreover, here each input defines a different labeling of the tree, whereas in GGM the labeling of the tree is fully determined by the key.

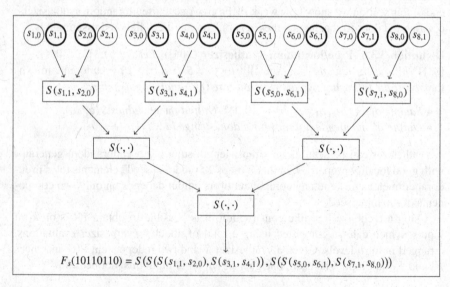

Fig. 3.4: Evaluating $F_s(x)$ at $x = 10110110$

Theorem 3.3.7 ([106]). *If $S : \{0,1\}^n \times \{0,1\}^n \to \{0,1\}^n$ is a (t, q, ε)-pseudorandom synthesizer then $\{F_s\}$ is a $(q, (k-1)\varepsilon)$-pseudorandom function family, as long as the size of S is at most q and that $q = o(\sqrt{t/\max\{k,n\}\log k})$.*

Proof: We prove the theorem by induction on k. Given $F_s' : \{0,1\}^k \to \{0,1\}^n$ define $F_s : \{0,1\}^{2k} \to \{0,1\}^n$ by $F_{s_0,s_1}(x_0, x_1) = S(F_{s_0}'(x_0), F_{s_1}'(x_1))$. Let c be the size of S and $k^\star = \max\{k, n\}$.

Claim 3.3.8. *If F_s' is a $(t + O(k^\star q^2 + ckq), q, \varepsilon')$-PRF then F_s is a $(t, q, 2\varepsilon' + \varepsilon)$-PRF.*

Proof: Let $(x_0, x_1) \in \{0,1\}^k \times \{0,1\}^k$ be an oracle query made by a purported distinguisher D between F_s and a random R. Consider the following four games:

F_s: Sample random $s_0, s_1 \leftarrow \{0,1\}^{2k \times n}$. Answer with $S(F_{s_0}'(x_0), F_{s_1}'(x_1))$.
H: Sample random $R_0, R_1 : \{0,1\}^k \to \{0,1\}^n$. Answer with $S(F_{s_0}'(x_0), R_1(x_1))$.
H': Sample random $R_0, R_1 : \{0,1\}^k \to \{0,1\}^n$. Answer with $S(R_0(x_0), R_1(x_1))$.
R: Sample a random $R : \{0,1\}^{2k} \to \{0,1\}^n$. Answer with $R(x_0, x_1)$.

Claim 3.3.9. *Games F_s and H are (t, q, ε')-indistinguishable.*

Proof: If this were not the case, namely there is a distinguisher D with the corresponding parameters, then F_{s_1}' and R_1 would be distinguishable by a circuit A^F that simulates D and answers each query x by $S(F_{s_0}'(x_0), F(x))$. The key s_0 can be hardwired to maximize the distinguishing advantage between F_{s_1}' and R. The additional complexity of A is $(c + O(1))k$ gates per query, as the evaluation of F_{s_0}' requires $k - 1$ evaluations of S. This contradicts the assumed security of F_{s_1}'. □

Claim 3.3.10. *Games H and H' are (t, q, ε')-indistinguishable.*

Proof: The proof is analogous to the previous claim, except that now A^F answers each query x with $S(F(x_0), R_1(x_1))$. The distinguisher emulates the function $R_1(x_1)$ by answering every new query with a fresh random string (eventually hardwired to maximize the distinguishing advantage). This requires tracking previous queries, which can be accomplished with $O(kq^2)$ additional gates. Another cq gates are sufficient for evaluating the synthesizer. The resulting circuit A has size $t + O(kq^2 + cq)$ and distinguishes F_{s_0}' from R_0 with q queries and advantage ε', violating the assumed security of F_{s_0}'. □

Claim 3.3.11. *Games H' and R are (t, q, ε)-indistinguishable.*

Proof: Suppose that D distinguishes between H' and R in size t and q queries with advantage ε. We will argue that D can be used to break the security of the synthesizer. The challenge of the synthesizer consists of a collection of q^2 strings $u_{ij}, 1 \le i \le j \le q$ coming from one of the two distributions in Definition 3.3.6.

We describe the circuit A that distinguishes these two distributions. The circuit A simulates D, answering query (x_0, x_1) with u_{ij} where the indices $i = i(x_0)$ and $j = j(x_1)$ are chosen in some manner consistent with past queries. For example, $i(x_0)$ can set to the smallest previously unused index when x_0 is queried for the first time, and similarly for $j(x_1)$. This tracking of queries can be implemented with $O(k^\star q^2)$ additional gates. Then A perfectly simulates the games H' and R under the two distributions u_{ij} from Definition 3.3.6, respectively, thereby distinguishing them with advantage ε in size $t + O(k^\star q^2)$. $\qquad\qquad\qquad\qquad\qquad\qquad\qquad\square$

This completes the proof of Theorem 3.3.7. $\qquad\qquad\qquad\qquad\qquad\qquad\qquad\qquad\square$

We now prove by induction on k that F_s is a $(t - O(k^* q^2 + ckq)\log k, q, (k-1)\varepsilon)$-PRF. In the base case $k = 1$, F'_s is perfectly secure, so it is a $(t, q, 0)$-PRF for all t and q. The inductive step from length k to length $2k$ follows from the above claim.

Setting $q = \alpha\sqrt{t/k^\star}\log k$ for a sufficiently small absolute constant $\alpha > 0$ and assuming that $c \le q$, after simplifying we obtain that F_s is a $(t/2, q, (k-1)\varepsilon)$-PRF. Since $q \le t/2$, F_s is in particular a $(q, (k-1)\varepsilon)$-PRF. $\qquad\qquad\qquad\qquad\square$

The NR function can be shown to admit natural time/space tradeoffs, as well as techniques for compressing the key size. These ideas are described in detail in [106]. As in the case of GGM, the NR construction is also secure against quantum distinguishers [131]. We next show that any weak PRF gives rise to a synthesizer.

Proposition 3.3.12. *If* $W_s \colon \{0, 1\}^n \to \{0, 1\}^n$ *is a* (t, ε)-*weak PRF for uniformly distributed keys* $s \in \{0, 1\}^n$ *then the function* $S(s, x) = W_s(x)$ *is a* $(t - cq^2, q, \varepsilon + \binom{q}{2} \cdot 2^{-n})$-*pseudorandom synthesizer for every* q, *where* c *is the circuit size of* W_s.

Proposition 3.3.12 assumes that the weak PRF is length preserving. This assumption is essentially without loss of generality (see Section 3.5.1), though for efficiency it may be desirable to guarantee this property directly by construction.

Proof: The q queries provided to the synthesizer's adversary can be represented as a $q \times q$ matrix. Assume for contradiction that there is a circuit D' of size $t - cq^2$ that distinguishes between the following two distributions with advantage $q\varepsilon$:

S: Sample random $s_i, x_j \in \{0, 1\}^n$. Output the $q \times q$ matrix $S(s_i, x_j) = W_{s_i}(x_j)$.
R: Sample q^2 random entries $r_{ij} \in \{0, 1\}^n$. Output the $q \times q$ matrix r_{ij}.

Let S' be the distribution S with the additional condition that the strings x_j are pairwise distinct. Distributions S and S' are $(\infty, q, \binom{q}{2}2^{-n})$-indistinguishable.

Claim 3.3.13. *Distributions* S' *and* R *are* $(t - cq^2, q, \varepsilon)$-*indistinguishable.*

Proof: Let H_i be the hybrid in which the first $q - i$ rows are sampled from distribution S' and the rest are sampled from distribution R. Then D' distinguishes $H_{i^\star-1}$ and $H_{i^\star}$ with advantage ε for some $i^\star$. This holds even after a suitable fixing of the values s_i for all $i < i^\star$ and r_{ij} for all $i > i^\star$ and j. Consider now the following distinguisher D: First, obtain samples $(x_1, y_1), \ldots, (x_q, y_q)$ from the oracle. Then generate the matrix M whose (i, j)-th entry is $W_{s_i}(x_j)$ for $i < i^\star$, y_j for $i = i^*$ and r_{ij} for $i > i^\star$ and simulate D' on input M. Then D has size at most t and distinguishes W_s from a random function with advantage at least ε. $\qquad\qquad\qquad\qquad\square$

The proposition now follows from the triangle inequality (Proposition 3.2.3). $\qquad\square$

Despite their close relation, in Section 3.7.6 we present evidence that pseudorandom synthesizers are objects of higher complexity than weak PRFs.

3.4 Instantiations

> *Why don't they do all the riots*
> *at the same time?*
> CHARLIE RACKOFF (1980s)

The building blocks underlying the GGM and NR constructions can be instantiated with specific number-theoretic and lattice-based computational hardness assumptions, resulting in efficient constructions of pseudorandom functions. The first class of instantiations is based on the *decisional Diffie–Hellman* (DDH) problem. The second class is based on the *learning with errors* (LWE) problem, via a deterministic variant of LWE called *learning with rounding* (LWR).

Utilizing the structure of the constructions, it is possible to optimize efficiency and obtain PRFs that are computable by constant-depth polynomial-size circuits with unbounded fan-in threshold gates (TC^0 circuits). Beyond giving rise to efficient PRFs that are based on clean and relatively well-established assumptions, these constructions have direct bearing on our ability to develop efficient learning algorithms and prove explicit lower bounds for the corresponding circuit classes (see Section 3.6).

The algebraic structure underlying the PRF instantiations also opens the door to more advanced applications such as verifiability, key homomorphism, and fast homomorphic evaluation. Some of these are described in Section 3.8.

3.4.1 Number-Theoretic Constructions

We consider the availability of public parameters $(\mathbb{G}, g)$, where g is a randomly chosen generator of a group $\mathbb{G}$ of prime order q with $|q| = n$. For concreteness think of $\mathbb{G}$ as being a subgroup of $\mathbb{Z}_p^*$ where p is a prime such that q divides $p - 1$.

The DDH problem. *We say that the DDH problem is (t, ε)-hard in $(\mathbb{G}, g)$ if the following two games are (t, ε)-indistinguishable:*

- *Sample random and independent $a, b \in \mathbb{Z}_q$ and output $(g^a, g^b, g^{ab}) \in \mathbb{G}^3$.*
- *Sample random and independent $a, b, c \in \mathbb{Z}_q$ and output $(g^a, g^b, g^c) \in \mathbb{G}^3$.*

For (t, ε)-DDH hardness to hold it is necessary that the discrete logarithm problem is (t, ε)-hard in the group $\mathbb{G}$; namely no circuit of size less than t can find x given g^x with probability larger than ε. It is not known whether (t, ε)-hardness of the discrete logarithm problem is sufficient for $(\text{poly}(t), \text{poly}(\varepsilon))$-DDH hardness.

The fastest known method for breaking DDH is to find the discrete logarithm of g^a or of g^b.[1] The best classical algorithms for finding discrete logarithms run in time $2^{\tilde{O}(n^{1/3})}$. Thus, given the current state of knowledge, it does not seem unreasonable to assume that there exist $\alpha, \beta > 0$ such that DDH is $(2^{n^\alpha}, 2^{-n^\beta})$-hard.

---

[1] In particular, since discrete logarithms can be found in time $\text{poly}(n)$ by a quantum algorithm [123], then the DDH problem is not $(\text{poly}(n), 1 - \varepsilon)$-hard for quantum algorithms.

Instantiating GGM using a DDH-based PRG. Consider the following family of (effectively) length-doubling functions $G_{g^a} : \mathbb{Z}_q \to \mathbb{G} \times \mathbb{G}$, defined as:

$$G_{g^a}(b) = (g^b, g^{ab}). \tag{3.7}$$

When $g^a \in \mathbb{G}$ and $b \in \mathbb{Z}_q$ are sampled independently at random, the distribution of $G_{g^a}(b)$ is (t, ε)-indistinguishable from a random pair in $\mathbb{G}^2$ if and only if DDH is (t, ε)-hard. This suggests using the function G_{g^a} as a PRG, and instantiating the GGM construction with it. However, the efficiency of the resulting construction is not very appealing, as it requires k sequential exponentiations modulo p.

To improve efficiency, Naor and Reingold [105] proposed the following construction of a DDH-based length-doubling PRG $G_{g^a} : \mathbb{G} \to \mathbb{G} \times \mathbb{G}$:

$$G_{g^a}(g^b) = (G_{g^a}^0(g^b), G_{g^a}^1(g^b)) = (g^b, g^{ab}). \tag{3.8}$$

At a first glance this alternative construction does not appear useful, as it is not clear how to compute $G_{g^a}(g^b)$ efficiently. Nevertheless, a closer look at the proof of security of GGM reveals that efficient public evaluation of the underlying PRG is not actually necessary. What would suffice for the construction and proof of GGM to work is that the underlying PRG can be efficiently computed using the random bits a that were used to sample its index g^a.

The key observation is that, if a is known, then $G_{g^a}(g^b)$ can be efficiently evaluated, and thus satisfies the required property.[2] Invoking the GGM construction with the PRG from (3.8), where at level $i \in [k]$ one uses a generator indexed by g^{a_i} for independently and randomly chosen $a_i \in \mathbb{Z}_q$, one obtains the PRF

$$F_{a_0,\dots,a_k}(x) = G_{g^{a_k}}^{x_k}(G_{g^{a_{k-1}}}^{x_{k-1}}(\cdots G_{g^{a_1}}^{x_1}(g^{a_0})\cdots)). \tag{3.9}$$

The final observation leading to an efficient construction of a PRF is that the k sequential exponentiations required for evaluating $F_{\bar{a}}(x)$ can be collapsed into a single subset product $a_1^{x_1} \cdots a_k^{x_k}$, which is then used as the exponent of g^{a_0}; see Fig. 3.5.

Public parameters: A group G and a random generator g of $\mathbb{G}$ of prime order q with $|q| = n$
Function key: A vector $\bar{a}$ of $k + 1$ random elements $a_0, \dots, a_k \in \mathbb{Z}_q^*$
Function evaluation: On input $x \in \{0, 1\}^k$ define $F_{\bar{a}} : \{0, 1\}^k \to \mathbb{G}$ as

$$F_{\bar{a}}(x_1 \cdots x_k) = g^{a_0 \prod_{i=1}^k a_i^{x_i}}.$$

Size: $k \cdot \text{poly}(\log |\mathbb{G}|)$
Depth: $O(1)$ (with threshold gates)

Fig. 3.5: The Naor–Reingold DDH-based construction

---

[2] In a uniform model of computation (where randomness that maximizes distinguishing advantage cannot be hardwired), it is also necessary to generate the distribution of G_{g^a}'s output given its index g^a (this is in fact also possible since if b is known then $G_{g^a}(g^b)$ can be efficiently evaluated). Such a requirement would have come up in the hypothesis of Proposition 3.2.4.

Theorem 3.4.1 ([105]). *If the DDH problem is $(t, 1/2)$-hard in $(\mathbb{G}, g)$ then $\{F_{\bar{a}}\}$ is a (t', ε')-pseudorandom function family, as long as $t' = o(\varepsilon'^{2/3} t^{1/3} / k)$ and group operations in $\mathbb{G}$ require circuit size at most t'.*

Proof: As seen in (3.9), the function $F_{\bar{a}}$ is based on the GGM construction. Thus, Theorem 3.4.1 follows from Theorem 3.3.2. The PRG from (3.8), which underlies the construction, is (t, ε)-pseudorandom iff the DDH problem is (t, ε)-hard, meaning that security depends on the hardness parameters of the DDH problem.

The DDH problem is *random self-reducible*: If it can be solved on a random instance, then it can be solved on any instance. This can be leveraged to reduce the distinguishing advantage at the cost of increasing the complexity of the distinguisher. Let op be the circuit size of a group operation in $\mathbb{G}$.

Claim 3.4.2. *If DDH is $(t, 1/2)$-hard then it is $(o(\varepsilon^2 t - 10 \cdot \text{op}), \varepsilon)$-hard for all $\varepsilon > 0$.*

Proof: Consider the randomized mapping $T : \mathbb{G}^3 \to \mathbb{G}^3$ defined as

$$T(g^a, g^b, g^c) = \left((g^a)^r \cdot g^{s_1}, g^b \cdot g^{s_2}, (g^c)^r \cdot (g^a)^{r \cdot s_2} \cdot (g^b)^{s_1} \cdot g^{s_1 \cdot s_2} \right),$$

where s_1, s_2, and r are uniformly and independently sampled in $\mathbb{Z}_q$. It can be verified that T is computable using 10 group operations, given g^a, g^b, g^c, s_1, s_2, and r. Letting $(g^{a'}, g^{b'}, g^{c'}) = T(g^a, g^b, g^c)$ and writing $c = ab + e \mod q$, we have that:

$$a' = ra + s_1 \mod q, \qquad b' = b + s_2 \mod q, \qquad c' = a'b' + er \mod q.$$

Using the fact that $c = ab \mod q$ if and only if $e = 0 \mod q$ and that if $e \neq 0 \mod q$ then $er \mod q$ is uniformly distributed in $\mathbb{Z}_q$ (since q is prime), it follows that

- If $c = ab$ then $c' = a'b'$ and a', b' are uniform and independent in $\mathbb{Z}_q$.
- If $c \neq ab$ then a', b', c' are uniform and independent in $\mathbb{Z}_q$.

To obtain the desired parameters, invoke the distinguisher $O(1/\varepsilon^2)$ times independently on the output of the reduction. Accept if the number of times the distinguisher accepts exceeds a threshold that depends on the distinguisher's acceptance probability (this can be determined in advance and hardwired). □

The theorem follows by plugging the parameters into those of Theorem 3.3.2. □

Efficiency. The evaluation of the NR function can be performed by invoking the following two steps in sequence:

1. Compute the "subset product" $a_0 \cdot a_1^{x_1} \cdots a_k^{x_k} \mod q$.
2. Compute the PRF output $F_{\bar{a}}(x) = g^{a_0 \cdot a_1^{x_1} \cdots a_k^{x_k}}$.

As shown in [118], both steps can be computed by constant-depth polynomial-size circuits with threshold gates.[3] Thus, if the DDH problem is indeed hard, PRFs can be computed within the class TC^0, which corresponds to such circuits.

---

[3] The second step reduces to subset product by hardwiring $g_i = g^{2^i} \mod p$ for $i = 1, \ldots, \lceil \log q \rceil$ and observing that $g^x = \prod g_i^{x_i} \mod p$ for $x = \sum 2^i x_i$.

An additional efficiency optimization with interesting practical implications comes from the observation that, for sequential evaluation, efficiency can be substantially improved by ordering the inputs according to a *Gray code*, where adjacent inputs differ in only one position. The technique works by saving the entire state of the subset product $\prod a_i^{x_1}$ from the previous call, updating to the next subset product by multiplying with either a_j or a_j^{-1} depending on whether the j-th bit of the next input is turned on or off (according to the Gray code ordering). This requires only a single multiplication per call (for the subset product part), rather than up to $k - 1$ when computing the subset product from scratch.

Applications and extensions. The algebraic structure of the NR pseudorandom functions has found many applications, including PRFs with "oblivious evaluation" [55], verifiable PRFs [91], and zero-knowledge proofs for statements of the form "$y = F_s(x)$" and "$y \neq F_s(x)$" [106]. Naor and Reingold [106], and Naor, Reingold and Rosen [107] give variants of the DDH-based PRF based on the hardness of RSA/factoring. The factoring-based construction directly yields a large number of output bits with constant computational overhead per output bit. Such efficiency cannot be attained generically (i.e., by applying a PRG to the output of a PRF).

3.4.2 Lattice-Based Constructions

Underlying the efficient construction of lattice-based PRFs are the (decision) learning with errors (LWE) problem, introduced by Regev, and the learning with rounding (LWR) problem, introduced by Banerjee, Peikert, and Rosen (BPR).

The LWE problem ([117]). *We say that the LWE problem is (t, m, ε)-hard if the following two distributions are (t, ε)-indistinguishable:*

- *Sample random $\mathbf{s} \in \mathbb{Z}_q^n$ and output m pairs $(\mathbf{a}_i, b_i) \in \mathbb{Z}_q^n \times \mathbb{Z}_q$, where $\mathbf{a}_i$'s are uniformly random and independent and $b_i = \langle \mathbf{a}_i, \mathbf{s} \rangle + e_i \bmod q$ for small random e_i.*
- *Output m uniformly random and independent pairs $(\mathbf{a}_i, b_i) \in \mathbb{Z}_q^n \times \mathbb{Z}_p$.*

One should think of the "small" error terms $e_i \in \mathbb{Z}$ as being of magnitude $\approx \alpha q$, and keep in mind that without random independent errors, LWE would be easy. While the dimension n is the main hardness parameter, the error rate α also plays an important role: as long as αq exceeds $\sqrt{n}$ or so, LWE is as hard as approximating conjectured hard problems on lattices to within $\tilde{O}(n/\alpha)$ factors in the worst case [117, 112, 94]. Moreover, known attacks using lattice basis reduction [87, 122] or combinatorial/algebraic methods [36, 13] require time $2^{\tilde{\Omega}(n/\log(1/\alpha))}$. Unlike DDH, no nontrivial quantum algorithms are known for LWE.

The learning with rounding problem is a "derandomized" variant of LWE, where instead of adding a small random error term to $\langle \mathbf{a}_i, \mathbf{s} \rangle \in \mathbb{Z}_q$, one deterministically rounds $\langle \mathbf{a}_i, \mathbf{s} \rangle$ to the nearest element of a public subset of p well-separated values in $\mathbb{Z}_q$, where p is much smaller than q. Since there are only p possible rounded values in $\mathbb{Z}_q$, we view them as elements of $\mathbb{Z}_p$ and denote the rounded value by $\lfloor \langle \mathbf{a}_i, \mathbf{s} \rangle \rceil_p \in \mathbb{Z}_p$, where $\lfloor x \rceil_p$ equals $\lfloor (p/q) \cdot x \bmod q \rceil \bmod p$.

The LWR problem ([17]). *We say that the LWR problem is (t, m, ε)-hard if the following two distributions are (t, ε)-indistinguishable:*

- *Sample random $\mathbf{s} \in \mathbb{Z}_q^n$ and output m pairs $(\mathbf{a}_i, b_i) \in \mathbb{Z}_q^n \times \mathbb{Z}_p$, where the $\mathbf{a}_i$'s are uniformly random and independent and $b_i = \lfloor \langle \mathbf{a}_i, \mathbf{s} \rangle \rceil_p$.*
- *Output m uniformly random and independent pairs $(\mathbf{a}_i, b_i) \in \mathbb{Z}_q^n \times \mathbb{Z}_p$.*

The LWR problem can be hard only if $q > p$, for otherwise no error is introduced. The "absolute" error is roughly q/p, and the "error rate" relative to q (the analogue of the parameter α in the LWE problem) is on the order of $1/p$.

An LWE-error distribution is *B-bounded* if for all errors e in the support of the distribution it holds that $e \in [-B, B]$.[4] Let RD be the cost of rounding a single element in $\mathbb{Z}_q$ into an element in $\mathbb{Z}_p$.

Proposition 3.4.3 ([17]). *If the LWE problem is (t, m, ε)-hard for some B-bounded error distribution then the LWR problem is $(t - m \cdot \text{RD}, m, mp(2B + 1)/q) + \varepsilon)$-hard.*

The proof relies on the fact that when e is small relative to q/p we have $\lfloor \langle \mathbf{a}, \mathbf{s} \rangle + e \rceil_p = \lfloor \langle \mathbf{a}, \mathbf{s} \rangle \rceil_p$ with high probability (see Figure 3.6), while $\lfloor x \rceil_p$ for a random $x \in \mathbb{Z}_q$ is random in $\mathbb{Z}_p$ (assuming p divides q). Therefore, given samples $(\mathbf{a}_i, b_i)$ of an unknown type (either LWE or uniform), we can round the b_i terms to generate samples of a corresponding type (LWR or uniform, respectively).

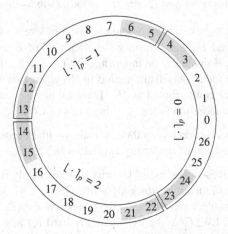

Fig. 3.6: Rounding an LWE sample $\langle a, x \rangle + e$ with $q = 27$, $p = 3$, and $B = 2$. The shaded areas denote the possibility of a rounding error. For instance, when $\langle a, x \rangle = 3$, $\lfloor \langle a, x \rangle \rceil_p = 0$ but it is possible that $\lfloor \langle a, x \rangle + e \rceil_p = 1$, but when $\langle a, x \rangle = 17$, $\lfloor \langle a, x \rangle \rceil_p$ and $\lfloor \langle a, x \rangle + e \rceil_p$ are equal with probability one

---

[4] Under typical LWE error distributions the event $e_i \notin [-B, B]$ does have some positive probability. This probability, however, is usually negligible (think of a Gaussian distribution with $\alpha \approx B/q$), and so one can conduct the analysis conditioning on the event not occurring without substantial loss in parameters.

Proof: Consider the following three distributions:

H_0: Output m pairs $(\mathbf{a}_i, \lfloor \langle \mathbf{a}_i, \mathbf{s} \rangle \rceil_p) \in \mathbb{Z}_q^n \times \mathbb{Z}_p$.

H_1: Output m pairs $(\mathbf{a}_i, \lfloor \langle \mathbf{a}_i, \mathbf{s} \rangle + e_i \rceil_p) \in \mathbb{Z}_q^n \times \mathbb{Z}_p$.

H_2: Output m pairs $(\mathbf{a}_i, \lfloor b_i \rceil_p) \in \mathbb{Z}_q^n \times \mathbb{Z}_p$, where the b_i's are random.

In all the distributions above, the $\mathbf{a}_i$'s are uniformly random and independent in $\mathbb{Z}_q^n$ and the e_i's are chosen independently from the LWE error distribution. For simplicity, we assume that $\mathbf{s}$ is random in the set of nonzero divisors $\mathbb{Z}_q^{n*} = \{x \in \mathbb{Z}_q^n : \gcd(x_1, ..., x_n, q) = 1\}$.

Claim 3.4.4. *Distributions H_0 and H_1 are $(\infty, mp(2B+1)/q)$-indistinguishable.*

Proof: Since the e_i's are selected according to a B-bounded error distribution, it holds that $e_i \in [-B, B]$ for all $i \in [m]$. We thus know that, as long as $\langle \mathbf{a}_i, \mathbf{s} \rangle$ does not fall within $\pm B$ of a multiple of q/p, it is guaranteed that $\lfloor \langle \mathbf{a}_i, \mathbf{s} \rangle + e_i \rceil_p = \lfloor \langle \mathbf{a}_i, \mathbf{s} \rangle \rceil_p$.

For any fixed $\mathbf{s} \in \mathbb{Z}_q^{n*}$ the probability over random $\mathbf{a}_i \in \mathbb{Z}_q^n$ that $\langle \mathbf{a}_i, \mathbf{s} \rangle \in \mathbb{Z}_q$ falls within $\pm B$ of a multiple of q/p is $p(2B+1)/q$. By the union bound:

$$\Pr\left[\exists i \in [m]: \lfloor \langle \mathbf{a}_i, \mathbf{s} \rangle + e_i \rceil_p \neq \lfloor \langle \mathbf{a}_i, \mathbf{s} \rangle \rceil_p\right] \leq mp(2B+1)/q,$$

where probability is taken over random and independent $\mathbf{a}_i \in \mathbb{Z}_q^n$ and $e_i \in [-B, B]$. Since this holds for every fixed $\mathbf{s} \in \mathbb{Z}_q^{n*}$ then it also holds for random $\mathbf{s}$. □

Claim 3.4.5. *Distributions H_1 and H_2 are $(t - m \cdot \text{RD}, \varepsilon)$-indistinguishable.*

Proof: Suppose that there exists an oracle circuit D of size $t - m \cdot \text{RD}$ that distinguishes between H_1 and H_2, and consider the circuit D' of size t that on input m pairs $(\mathbf{a}_i, b_i) \in \mathbb{Z}_q \times \mathbb{Z}_q$ simulates D on input $(\mathbf{a}_i, \lfloor b_i \rceil_p) \in \mathbb{Z}_q \times \mathbb{Z}_p$. If $(\mathbf{a}_i, b_i)$ are LWE samples then the input fed to D is distributed as in H_1, whereas if $(\mathbf{a}_i, b_i)$ are random then the input fed to D is distributed as H_2. Thus, D' has the same distinguishing advantage as D, in contradiction to the (t, ε)-hardness of LWE. □

The theorem follows by combining the two claims with Proposition 3.2.3 and by observing that H_2 is distributed uniformly at random in $\mathbb{Z}_q^n \times \mathbb{Z}_p$. □

Proposition 3.4.3 gives a meaningful security guarantee only if $q \gg mp(2B+1)$. Nevertheless, the state of the art in attack algorithms [36, 13, 87, 122] indicates that, as long as q/p is an integer (so that $\lfloor x \rceil_p$ for a random $x \in \mathbb{Z}_q$ is random in $\mathbb{Z}_p$) and is at least $\Omega(\sqrt{n})$, LWR may be exponentially hard for any $p = \text{poly}(n)$, and superpolynomially hard when $p = 2^{n^\epsilon}$ for any $\epsilon < 1$. It is open whether one could obtain worst-case hardness guarantees for LWR in such parameter regimes. ⊘

In some applications, such as the PRG described below, the parameter m can be fixed in advance, allowing smaller q. Several works have studied LWR in this setting [7, 38, 6]. In other applications, however, m cannot be a priori bounded. It is an open problem whether the dependency of q on m can be removed. ⊘

Instantiating GGM using an LWR-based PRG. The LWR problem yields a simple and practical pseudorandom generator $G_A : \mathbb{Z}_q^n \to \mathbb{Z}_p^m$, where the moduli $q > p$ and the (uniformly random) matrix $A \in \mathbb{Z}_q^{n \times m}$ are publicly known [17]. Given a seed $s \in \mathbb{Z}_q^n$, the generator is defined as

$$G_A(s) = \left\lfloor A^\top \cdot s \right\rceil_p , \tag{3.10}$$

where rounding is performed coordinate-wise. The generator's seed length (in bits) is $n \log_2 q$ and its output length is $m \log_2 p$, which gives an expansion rate of $(m \log_2 p)/(n \log_2 q) = (m/n) \log_q p$. For example, to obtain a length-doubling PRG, we may set $q = p^2 = 2^{2k} > n$ and $m = 4n$. In this case rounding corresponds to outputting the k most significant bits.

When evaluating the GGM construction instantiated with G_A, one can get the required portion of $G_A(s)$ by computing only the inner products of s with the corresponding columns of A, not the entire product $A^\top \cdot s$. This becomes particularly attractive if one considers GGM trees with fan-in $d > 2$.

Instantiating NR using an LWR-based weak PRF. Consider the following weak pseudorandom function $W_s : \mathbb{Z}_q^n \to \mathbb{Z}_p$, indexed by $s \in \mathbb{Z}_q^n$:

$$W_s(a) = \lfloor \langle a, s \rangle \rceil_p . \tag{3.11}$$

Weak (t, m, ε)-pseudorandomness of W_s follows from (t, m, ε)-hardness of the LWR problem, using the fact that the a_i vectors are public [17]. To instantiate the NR construction of PRFs from synthesizers, invoke Proposition 3.3.12, giving a synthesizer from a weak PRF. This requires the weak PRF's output length to match its input length. To this end, one can apply an efficient bijection, $K : \mathbb{Z}_p^{\ell \times \ell} \to \mathbb{Z}_q^{n \times \ell}$, for $\ell \geq n$ such that $p^\ell = q^n$, and modify the weak PRF from Equation (3.11) as follows:

$$W_S(A) := K\left(\lfloor A^\top \cdot S \rceil_p \right) \in \mathbb{Z}_q^{n \times \ell},$$

where $S, A \in \mathbb{Z}_q^{n \times \ell}$. The resulting synthesizer can be plugged into Equation (3.6) to give LWR-based PRFs $F_{\{S_{i,b}\}} : \{0,1\}^k \to \mathbb{Z}_q^{n \times \ell}$. Security assuming $(t, m\ell, \varepsilon)$-hardness of LWE follows from combining Propositions 3.4.3 and 3.3.12 with Theorem 3.3.7. This results in a (t', ε')-pseudorandom function family, where $t' = t - \text{poly}(n, m, \ell)$ and $\varepsilon' = O(\ell(k-1)(mp(2B+1)/q + \varepsilon))$. As a concrete example, the evaluation of this PRF when $k = 8$ (so $x = x_1 \cdots x_8$) unfolds as follows:

$$\left\lfloor \left\lfloor \lfloor S_{1,x_1} \cdot S_{2,x_2} \rceil_q \cdot \lfloor S_{3,x_3} \cdot S_{4,x_4} \rceil_q \rceil_q \cdot \left\lfloor \lfloor S_{5,x_5} \cdot S_{6,x_6} \rceil_q \cdot \lfloor S_{7,x_7} \cdot S_{8,x_8} \rceil_q \rceil_q \right\rceil_q \right\rceil_q ,$$

where for clarity we let $\lfloor S_{i,x_i} \cdot S_{j,x_j} \rceil_q$ stand for $K\left(\lfloor S_{i,x_i} \cdot S_{j,x_j} \rceil_p \right)$.

A direct construction of PRFs. One drawback of the synthesizer-based PRF is that it involves $\log k$ levels of rounding operations, which appears to lower-bound the depth of any circuit computing the function by $\Omega(\log k)$.

Aiming to get around this issue, BPR suggested to imitate the DDH-based construction, where sequential exponentiations are collapsed into one subset product. Since such a collapse is not possible in the case of LWR, they omitted all but the last rounding operation, resulting in a "subset-product with rounding" structure.

Public parameters: Moduli $q \gg p$
Function key: A random $\mathbf{a} \in \mathbb{Z}_q^n$ and k random short (B-bounded) $\mathbf{S}_i \in \mathbb{Z}_q^{n \times n}$
Function evaluation: On input $x \in \{0,1\}^k$ define $F = F_{\mathbf{a},\{\mathbf{S}_i\}} : \{0,1\}^k \to \mathbb{Z}_p^n$ as

$$F_{\mathbf{a},\{\mathbf{S}_i\}}(x_1 \cdots x_k) = \left\lfloor \mathbf{a}^\mathsf{T} \cdot \prod_{i=1}^{k} \mathbf{S}_i^{x_i} \right\rceil_p .$$

Size: $\mathrm{poly}(k,n)$
Depth: $O(1)$ (with threshold gates)

Fig. 3.7: The Banerjee–Peikert–Rosen LWR-based construction

The BPR function can be proved to be pseudorandom assuming that the LWE problem is hard. Two issues that affect the parameters are the distribution of the secret key components $\mathbf{S}_i$, and the choice of q and p. For the former, the proof requires the $\mathbf{S}_i$ to be short. (LWE is no easier to solve for such short secrets [10].) This appears to be an artifact of the proof, which can be viewed as a variant of the LWE-to-LWR reduction from Proposition 3.4.3, enhanced to handle adversarial queries.

Theorem 3.4.6 ([17]). *If the LWE problem is (t, mn, ε)-hard for some B-bounded error distribution then $\{F_{\mathbf{a},\{\mathbf{S}_i\}}\}$ is a (t', m, ε')-pseudorandom function family, where*

$$t' = t - m \max\{n, 2k\}\mathrm{OP} - O(nm^2) - n \cdot \mathrm{RD}, \qquad \varepsilon' = mnp(2n^k B^{k+1} + 1)/q + k\varepsilon n,$$

and OP *is the cost of a group operation in $\mathbb{Z}_q$.*

Proof: Define the function $P : \{0,1\}^k \to \mathbb{Z}_q^n$ as

$$P(x) = P_{\mathbf{a},\{\mathbf{S}_i\}}(x) := \mathbf{a}^\mathsf{T} \cdot \prod_{i=1}^{k} \mathbf{S}_i^{x_i} \tag{3.12}$$

to be the subset product inside the rounding operation. The fact that $F = \lfloor P \rceil_p$ lets us imagine adding independent error terms to each output of P. Consider then a related randomized function $\tilde{P}$ that computes the subset product by multiplying by each $\mathbf{S}_i^{x_i}$ in turn, but also adds a fresh error term immediately following each multiplication.

By LWE-hardness and using induction on k, the randomized function $\tilde{P}$ can be shown to be itself pseudorandom (over $\mathbb{Z}_q$), hence so is $\lfloor \tilde{P} \rceil_p$ (over $\mathbb{Z}_p$). Moreover, for every queried input, with high probability $\lfloor \tilde{P} \rceil_p$ coincides with $\lfloor P \rceil_p = F$, because P and $\tilde{P}$ differ only by a cumulative error term that is small relative to q (this is where we need to assume that $\mathbf{S}_i$'s entries are small). Finally, because $\lfloor \tilde{P} \rceil_p$ is a (randomized) pseudorandom function over $\mathbb{Z}_p$ that coincides with the deterministic function F on all queries, it follows that F is pseudorandom as well.

Specifically, consider the following three games:

R: Give adaptive oracle access to a random function $R: \{0, 1\}^k \to \mathbb{Z}_q^n$.
P: Give adaptive oracle access to $P: \{0, 1\}^k \to \mathbb{Z}_q^n$ defined in (3.12).
$\tilde{P}$: Give adaptive oracle access to $\tilde{P}: \{0, 1\}^k \to \mathbb{Z}_q^n$ inductively defined as:

- For $i = 0$, define $\tilde{P}_0(\lambda) = \mathbf{a}^\top$, where λ is the empty string.
- For $i \geq 1$, and on input $(x, y) \in \{0, 1\}^{i-1} \times \{0, 1\}$, define $\tilde{P}_i: \{0, 1\}^i \to \mathbb{Z}_q^n$ as

$$\tilde{P}_i(x, y) = \tilde{P}_{i-1}(x) \cdot \mathbf{S}_i^y + y \cdot \mathbf{e}_x, \tag{3.13}$$

where $\mathbf{a}, \mathbf{S}_1, \ldots, \mathbf{S}_k$ are sampled at random and the $\mathbf{e}_x \in \mathbb{Z}_q^n$ are all sampled independently according to the B-bounded LWE error distribution.

The function $\tilde{P} = \tilde{P}_k$ is specified by $\mathbf{a}$, $\{\mathbf{S}_i\}$, and exponentially many vectors $\mathbf{e}_x$. The error vectors can be sampled "lazily", since the value of $\tilde{P}(x)$ depends only on $\mathbf{a}$, $\{\mathbf{S}_i\}$, and $\mathbf{e}_x$.

Lemma 3.4.7. *Games $\lfloor P \rceil_p$ and $\lfloor \tilde{P} \rceil_p$ are $(\infty, m, mnp(2n^k B^{k+1}+1)/q)$-indistinguishable.*

Proof: Observe that for $x \in \{0, 1\}^k$

$$\tilde{P}(x) = (\cdots ((\mathbf{a}^\top \cdot \mathbf{S}_1^{x_1} + x_1 \cdot \mathbf{e}_\lambda) \cdot \mathbf{S}_2^{x_2} + x_2 \cdot \mathbf{e}_{x_1}) \cdots) \cdot \mathbf{S}_k^{x_k} + x_k \cdot \mathbf{e}_{x_1 \cdots x_{k-1}} \bmod q$$

$$= \underbrace{\mathbf{a}^\top \cdot \prod_{i=1}^{k} \mathbf{S}_i^{x_i}}_{P(x)} + \underbrace{x_1 \cdot \mathbf{e}_\varepsilon \cdot \prod_{i=2}^{k} \mathbf{S}_i^{x_i} + x_2 \cdot \mathbf{e}_{x_1} \cdot \prod_{i=3}^{k} \mathbf{S}_i^{x_i} + \cdots + x_k \cdot \mathbf{e}_{x_1 \cdots x_{k-1}}}_{\mathbf{e}_x} \bmod q.$$

Now since both $\mathbf{S}_i$ and $\mathbf{e}_i$ are sampled from a B-bounded distribution, then each entry of an "error term" vector $\mathbf{e}_x$ is bounded by $n^k B^{k+1}$ (the magnitude being dominated by the entries of $\mathbf{e}_\varepsilon \cdot \prod_{i=2}^{k} \mathbf{S}_i^{x_i}$). By an analogous argument to the one in the proof of Proposition 3.4.3, it follows that, for every fixed choice of $\mathbf{S}_1, \ldots, \mathbf{S}_k$,

$$\Pr_{\mathbf{a}}\left[\exists x: \ \lfloor P(x) + \mathbf{e}_x \rceil \neq \lfloor P(x) \rceil_p\right] \leq mnp(2n^k B^{k+1} + 1)/q.$$

Since this holds for every choice of $\mathbf{S}_i$'s, it also holds for a random choice. □

Lemma 3.4.8. *Games $\lfloor \tilde{P} \rceil_p$ and $\lfloor R \rceil_p$ are $(t-2mk\textsc{op}-n\textsc{rd}, m, k\varepsilon n)$-indistinguishable.*

Proof: For $i \in [k]$, consider the following games:

R_i: Give adaptive oracle access to a random function $R_i: \{0, 1\}^i \to \mathbb{Z}_q^n$.
$\tilde{P}_i$: Give adaptive oracle access to the function $\tilde{P}_i: \{0, 1\}^i \to \mathbb{Z}_q^n$ as defined in (3.13).
H_i: Give adaptive oracle access to the function $H_i: \{0, 1\}^i \to \mathbb{Z}_q^n$, defined as

$$H_i(x, y) = \mathbf{a}_x \cdot \mathbf{S}_i^y + y \cdot \mathbf{e}_x, \tag{3.14}$$

where $(x, y) \in \{0, 1\}^{i-1} \times \{0, 1\}$, and $\mathbf{a}_x$, $\mathbf{S}_i$, and $\mathbf{e}_x$ are all sampled at random.

We prove inductively that $\tilde{P}_k$ and R_k are $(t-2mk\text{OP}, m, k\varepsilon n)$-indistinguishable. For the induction basis we have that $\tilde{P}_0$ and R_0 are $(\infty, m, 0)$-indistinguishable by definition, and so are in particular $(t, m, 0)$-indistinguishable. For the inductive step, suppose that $\tilde{P}_{i-1}$ and R_{i-1} are $(t - 2m(i-1)\text{OP}, m, (i-1)\varepsilon n)$-indistinguishable.

Claim 3.4.9. *Games $\tilde{P}_i$ and H_i are $(t - 2mi\text{OP}, m, (i-1)\varepsilon n)$-indistinguishable.*

Proof: Suppose that there exists a circuit D of size $t - 2mi\text{OP}$ that distinguishes between $\tilde{P}_i$ and H_i with advantage $(i-1)\varepsilon n$ using m queries. We use D to build an A that $(t - 2m(i-1)\text{OP}, m, (i-1)\varepsilon n)$-distinguishes between $\tilde{P}_{i-1}$ and R_{i-1}.

The distinguisher A starts by sampling a random $\mathbf{S} \in \mathbb{Z}_q^{n \times n}$. Then, given a query of the form $(x, y) \in \{0, 1\}^{i-1} \times \{0, 1\}$ from D, it queries its oracle with input x to obtain $\mathbf{a}_x$, and replies to D with $\mathbf{a}_x \cdot \mathbf{S}^y + y \cdot \mathbf{e}_x$, using a random LWE error $\mathbf{e}_x$.

If A's oracle is distributed according to $\tilde{P}_{i-1}$, then A's replies to D are distributed as $\tilde{P}_i$. On the other hand, if A's oracle is distributed according to R_{i-1}, then $\mathbf{a}_x = R_{i-1}(x)$ is random, and so A's replies are distributed as H_i. Thus, A has the same advantage as D. Accounting for the two additional operations required by A for each of the m queries made by D we get that A is of size $t - 2mi\text{OP} + 2m\text{OP}$. □

Claim 3.4.10. *Games H_i and R_i are $(t - mn\text{OP} - O(nm^2), m, \varepsilon n)$-indistinguishable.*

Proof: Using a hybrid argument (akin to the proof of Proposition 3.2.4) it can be shown that the (t, mn, ε)-hardness of LWE implies that the following two distributions are $(t - mn\text{OP}, m, \varepsilon n)$-indistinguishable:

- Sample a random $\mathbf{S} \in \mathbb{Z}_q^{n \times n}$ and output $((\mathbf{a}_1, \mathbf{b}_1) \ldots, (\mathbf{a}_m, \mathbf{b}_m)) \in (\mathbb{Z}_q^n \times \mathbb{Z}_q^n)^m$, where the $\mathbf{a}_j$'s are uniformly random and $\mathbf{b}_j = \mathbf{a}_j^{\mathsf{T}} \cdot \mathbf{S} + \mathbf{e}_j \bmod q$ for random $\mathbf{e}_j$.
- Output m uniformly random pairs $((\mathbf{a}_1, \mathbf{b}_1) \ldots, (\mathbf{a}_m, \mathbf{b}_m)) \in (\mathbb{Z}_q^n \times \mathbb{Z}_q^n)^m$.

Suppose that there exists a distinguisher D of size $t - mn\text{OP} - O(nm^2)$ that distinguishes between H_i and R_i with m queries and advantage εn. We use D to build a distinguisher A that $(t - mn\text{OP}, m, \varepsilon n)$-distinguishes the two distributions from above.

Given m pairs $(\mathbf{a}_j, \mathbf{b}_j) \in \mathbb{Z}_q^n \times \mathbb{Z}_q^n$, the distinguisher A emulates an oracle for D as follows: for $j \in [m]$, answer the query $(x_j, y_j) \in \{0, 1\}^{i-1} \times \{0, 1\}$ given by D with $\mathbf{a}_j$ if $y_j = 0$ and with $\mathbf{b}_j$ if $y_j = 1$. Similarly to Theorem 3.3.2, $O(nm^2)$ additional gates are required for A to memorize previous answers so that he can answer consistently.

If $\mathbf{b}_j = \mathbf{a}_j^{\mathsf{T}} \cdot \mathbf{S} + \mathbf{e}_j \bmod q$ then the replies given by the above oracle are distributed exactly as in (3.14) (with $\mathbf{S}_i = \mathbf{S}$), and hence according to H_i. On the other hand, if $\mathbf{b}_j$ is random, then the oracle's replies are random and independent and hence distributed according to R_i. Thus A has the same advantage as D. □

Combining the two claims using Propositions 3.2.3 and 3.2.4, we get that games $\tilde{P}_i$ and R_i are $(\min\{t - mn\text{OP} - O(nm^2), t - 2mi\text{OP}\}, m, (i-1)\varepsilon n + \varepsilon n)$-indistinguishable. Thus, games $\tilde{P}_k$ and R_k are $(t - m\max\{n, 2k\}\text{OP} - O(nm^2), m, k\varepsilon n)$-indistinguishable.

Since $\tilde{P}_k = \tilde{P}$ and $R_k = R$, we finally conclude that the games $\lfloor \tilde{P} \rceil$ and $\lfloor R \rceil$ are $(t - m\max\{n, 2k\}\text{OP} - O(nm^2) - n \cdot \text{RD}, m, k\varepsilon n)$-indistinguishable. □

The theorem now follows by combining Lemma 3.4.7 with Lemma 3.4.8 via the triangle inequality (Proposition 3.2.3), and by observing that $F = \lfloor P \rceil$ and that $\lfloor R \rceil$ is a random function from $\{0, 1\}^k$ to $\mathbb{Z}_p^n$ (assuming p divides q). □

Parameters. In the proof, the gap between P and $\tilde{P}$ grows exponentially in k, because noise is added after each multiplication by an $\mathbf{S}_i$. So in order to ensure that $\lfloor \tilde{P} \rceil_p = \lfloor P \rceil_p$ on all queries, we need both q and $1/\alpha$ to exceed $(nB)^{k+1} = n^{\Omega(k)}$. However, as in Proposition 3.4.3, it is unclear whether such large parameters are necessary, or whether $\mathbf{S}_i$ really need to be short. It would be desirable to have a security reduction for smaller q and $1/\alpha$, ideally both $\text{poly}(n)$ even for large k. ⑦

It would be even better if the construction were secure if the $\mathbf{S}_i$ were uniformly random in $\mathbb{Z}_q^{n \times n}$, because one could then recursively compose the function in a k-ary tree to rapidly extend its input length. ⑦

One reason for optimism (beyond the fact that no attacks are known) is that the PRF does not actually expose any low-error-rate LWE samples to the attacker; they are used only in the proof as part of a thought experiment. This appears to be related to the so-called *hidden number* problem (see, e.g., [2]). It would be interesting to investigate whether there exist connections between the problems. ⑦

A closely related PRF, due to Banerjee and Peikert [16], is described in Section 3.8.1. This PRF achieves the tightest known tradeoffs between LWE-based security and parallellism, though if one were to instantiate it with concrete parameters, then it would still be slower than instantiations of the subset product with rounding PRF with comparable security (see description of the SPRING family below).

Efficiency. The fastest instantiations of the PRF use ring elements instead of matrices. In the ring variant, $\mathbf{a}$ is replaced with a uniform $a \in R_q$ for some polynomial ring R_q (e.g., $\mathbb{Z}_q[X]/(X^n + 1)$ for n a power of 2), and each $\mathbf{S}_i$ by some $s_i \in R_q^*$, the set of invertible ring elements modulo q.[5] This function is particularly efficient to evaluate using the discrete Fourier transform, as is standard with ring-based primitives (see, e.g., [93, 94]). Similarly to [106], one can optimize the subset-product operation via preprocessing, and evaluate the function in TC^0.

The functions are amenable to the same key-compression and amortization tehniques as the one used to optimize the performance of the NR DDH-based PRFs.

The SPRING family of PRFs ([15]). The SPRING (Subset Product with Rounding over a Ring) family of functions is a concrete instantiation of the PRF described in Figure 3.7 (aiming for 128-bit security), with parameters

$$n = 128, \quad q = 257, \quad p = 2, \quad k = 128.$$

Using "Gray code" amortization, an implementation of SPRING was shown to perform as much as 4x slower than that of AES-128 (in software) with further potential optimization [15, 46]. We describe the main ideas behind the implementation.

The key, consisting of $a, s_1, \ldots, s_k \in R_q^*$, is stored as vectors in $\mathbb{Z}_q^n$ using the DFT or "Chinese remainder" representation mod q (that is, by evaluating a and the s_i

---

[5] Here, hardness is based on the *ring*-LWE problem [94], in which we are given noisy/rounded ring products $b_i \approx a_i \cdot s$, where s and the a_i are random elements of R_q, and the error terms are "small" in a certain basis of the ring; the goal again is to distinguish these from uniformly random pairs.

as polynomials at the n roots of $X^n + 1 \bmod q$), so that multiplication of two ring elements corresponds to a coordinate-wise product. Then to evaluate the function, one computes a subset product of the appropriate vectors, interpolates the result using an n-dimensional FFT over $\mathbb{Z}_q$, and rounds coordinate-wise. For $k = \omega(\log n)$, the runtime is dominated by the kn scalar multiplications in $\mathbb{Z}_q$ to compute the subset product; in parallel, the arithmetic depth (over $\mathbb{Z}_q$) is $O(\log(nk))$.

The subset-product part of the function might be computed even faster by storing the discrete logs of the Fourier coefficients of a and s_i, with respect to some generator g of $\mathbb{Z}_q^*$. The subset product then becomes a subset sum, followed by exponentiation modulo q, which can be implemented by table lookup if q is relatively small. Assuming that additions modulo $q - 1$ are significantly less expensive than multiplications modulo q, the sequential running time is dominated by the $O(n \log n)$ scalar operations in the FFT, and the parallel arithmetic depth is again $O(\log n)$.

3.5 Transformations

> *Do you have the notion of a refill?*
> SHAFI GOLDWASSER (1995)

The significance of pseudorandom functions can be partly explained by their remarkable robustness and flexibility. In Section 3.2.3 we saw that the size of the function range is essentially irrelevant in the PRF definition. PRFs are similarly robust with respect to the choice of domain size: the domain can be easily enlarged and restricted for strong and weak PRFs alike. Domain extension can be accomplished with the help of *pairwise independence*, a restricted notion of pseudorandomness for which simple, unconditional constructions are available.

With regard to flexibility, PRFs serve as the main building block used in the construction of more complex pseudorandom functionalities. The best-known example is that of *pseudorandom permutations*, but the paradigm can be applied more generally to obtain succinct implementations of various *huge random objects* such as pseudorandom codes and pseudorandom graphs.

3.5.1 Domain Extension (and Restriction)

The domain extension problem is to efficiently construct a PRF on long inputs from a PRF on relatively short inputs. The GGM and NR constructions can be viewed as domain extension procedures in which the input length grows by one bit and doubles in every stage, respectively. Consequently, the complexity of the domain-extended PRF grows with the resulting input size (at different rates in the two constructions).

We present a domain extension procedure of Levin [88] in which the efficiency of the original PRF is essentially preserved. However, unlike in the GGM and NR constructions, the original domain size affects the security of the domain-extended PRF. Levin's construction makes use of pairwise independent functions.

Definition 3.5.1 (Pairwise independence). *A family* $\{H_s : \{0,1\}^k \rightarrow \{0,1\}^{k'}\}$ *of functions is* pairwise independent *if it is perfectly indistinguishable from a random function by any distinguisher that makes at most two queries.*

In other words, $\{H_s\}$ is $(\infty, 2, 0)$-indistinguishable from random. This is a special case of the notion of bounded independence (see Definition 3.7.1 in Section 3.7). Pairwise independent hash families can have size as small as linear in $k + k'$ [78].

Theorem 3.5.2. *If* $H_s : \{0,1\}^k \rightarrow \{0,1\}^{k'}$ *is a pairwise independent family of functions and* $F'_{s'} : \{0,1\}^{k'} \rightarrow \{0,1\}^{\ell}$ *is a* (t, q, ε)-*PRF then the function* $F_{s,s'}(x) = F'_{s'}(H_s(x))$ *is a* $(t - c, q, \varepsilon + \binom{q}{2} \cdot 2^{-k})$-*PRF, where c is the circuit size of* H_s.

Proof: We analyze the advantage of the distinguisher with respect to the following sequence of games:

F': Sample s and s'. Answer query x by $F'_{s'}(H_s(x))$.
R': Sample s and $R' : \{0,1\}^{k'} \rightarrow \{0,1\}^{\ell}$. Answer query x by $R'(H_s(x))$.
R: Sample $R : \{0,1\}^k \rightarrow \{0,1\}^n$. Answer query x by $R(x)$.

Games F' and R' can be shown to be $(t - c, q, \varepsilon)$-indistinguishable using a standard simulation argument.

Claim 3.5.3. *Games* R' *and* R *are* $(\infty, q, \binom{q}{2} \cdot 2^{-k/2})$-*indistinguishable.*

Proof: We will assume, without loss of generality, that the distinguisher's queries are pairwise distinct. We relate R' and R to the following pair of games:

C: Sample s. Answer query x by collision if $H_s(x) = H_s(x')$ for some previously queried x', and by $\perp$ if not.
$\perp$: Answer every query by $\perp$.

If games C and $\perp$ are (∞, q, ε)-indistinguishable so must be R' and R: Unless a collision occurs, the answers of R' and R are identically distributed (to a sequence of independent random strings).

Any distinguisher between C and $\perp$ is essentially nonadaptive: The query sequence $x_1, \dots, x_q$ can be extracted by assuming that the distinguisher interacts with the $\perp$ oracle. Its advantage equals the probability of a collision, which can be bounded by

$$\Pr[\text{collision}] \leq \sum_{1 \leq i < j \leq q} \Pr[H_s(x_i) = H_s(x_j)] = \binom{q}{2} \cdot 2^{-k}.$$

The inequality is obtained by taking a union bound over all pairs of queries, while the equality follows from pairwise independence.   □

The theorem follows by applying the triangle inequality.   □

The security guarantee in Theorem 3.5.2 becomes meaningless when the number of queries exceeds $2^{k/2}$. This is unavoidable by the birthday paradox: A distinguisher that looks for collisions among $2^{k/2}$ random queries has constant advantage. Berman, Haitner, Komargodski, and Naor [28] give a different domain extension procedure with improved security: Their construction uses two independent instances of the PRF F'_s and has security that is independent of the input length k, as long as the number of queries is at most 2^{k-2}.

Domain restriction and range extension for weak PRFs. Domain extension for weak PRFs is rather straightforward: If $F'_s: \{0,1\}^{k'} \rightarrow \{0,1\}^{\ell}$ is a (t, q, ε)-weak PRF then the function $F_s(x, y) = F'_s(x)$ is a $(t, q, \varepsilon + \binom{q}{2} 2^{-k'})$-weak PRF.

Naor and Reingold [105] consider domain *restriction*—namely, the problem of reducing the input length—for weak PRFs. (Their construction applies, more generally, to synthesizers.) They prove the following statement, which follows by an application of Proposition 3.2.4:

Proposition 3.5.4. *If F'_s is a (t, q, ε)-weak PRF and $G: \{0,1\}^k \rightarrow \{0,1\}^{k'}$ is a $(t + c, \varepsilon')$-PRG then the function $F_s(x) = F'_s(G(x))$ is a $(t, q, \varepsilon + \varepsilon')$-weak PRF, where c is the circuit size of F'_s.*

Proposition 3.5.4 can be combined with the following range extension construction to convert a weak PRF with sufficiently long input and one bit of output into a length-preserving weak PRF:

Proposition 3.5.5. *If $F'_s: \{0,1\}^k \rightarrow \{0,1\}$ is a (t, q, ε)-weak PRF then $F_s(x_1, \ldots, x_\ell) = (F'_s(x_1), \ldots, F'_s(x_\ell))$ is a $(t, q/\ell, \varepsilon + \binom{q\ell}{2} \cdot 2^{-k})$-weak PRF.*

3.5.2 Pseudorandom Permutations

Nu, permutaziot!

Abraham Lempel (1981)

A pseudorandom permutation (PRP) is a permutation that is easy to evaluate, but hard to distinguish from a random permutation. PRPs are a model of block ciphers, which are used to implement various modes of operation in symmetric-key encryption and authentication schemes. PRPs will also serve as an illustrative example of the "huge random objects" discussed in Section 3.5.3.

Definition 3.5.6 (Pseudorandom permutation [90]). *A family of permutations $F_s: \{0,1\}^k \rightarrow \{0,1\}^k$ is (t, q, ε)-pseudorandom if the following two games are (t, q, ε)-computationally indistinguishable:*

F_s: Sample a random $s \leftarrow \{0,1\}^n$ and answer query $x \in \{0,1\}^k$ by $F_s(x)$,
P: Sample a random permutation $P: \{0,1\}^k \rightarrow \{0,1\}^k$ and answer x by $P(x)$.

The security requirement of Definition 3.5.6 is met by any pseudorandom *function* family F_s:

Proposition 3.5.7. *If F_s is a (t, q, ε)-PRF then games F_s and P are $(t, q, \varepsilon + \binom{q}{2}2^{-k})$-indistinguishable.*

Proof: Consider the game

R: Sample a random function $R\colon \{0, 1\}^k \to \{0, 1\}^k$ and answer query x by $R(x)$.

Claim 3.5.8. *Games R and P are $(\infty, q, \binom{q}{2}2^{-k})$-indistinguishable.*

Proof: We may assume, without loss of generality, that the distinguisher's queries are pairwise distinct. We analyze the hybrid game H_i in which the first i queries $x_1, \ldots, x_i$ are answered using P and the rest are answered using R. Games H_{i-1} and H_i are identically distributed conditioned on $R(x_i)$ taking a different value from $P(x_1), \ldots, P(x_{i-1})$. The probability this fails is $(i-1)2^{-k}$. The claim follows by the triangle inequality. □

As F_s and R are (t, q, ε)-indistinguishable, Proposition 3.5.7 follows by applying the triangle inequality again. □

In general, the functionality requirement of being a permutation may not be satisfied by certain PRFs such as those obtained via the GGM and NR constructions. Luby and Rackoff [90] describe a generic transformation for constructing a PRP from any length-preserving PRF.

Both of these constructions are based on the Feistel shuffle

$$\mathbf{Fei}[F](x, y) = (y, x + F(y)), \qquad x, y \in \{0, 1\}^{k/2},$$

where F is a function from $\{0, 1\}^{k/2}$ to $\{0, 1\}^{k/2}$ and $+$ is bit-wise XOR. The function $\mathbf{Fei}[F]$ is a permutation on $\{0, 1\}^n$; its inverse is $(x, y) \mapsto (y + F(x), x)$.

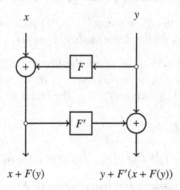

Fig. 3.8: The two-round Feistel network. The intermediate outputs are flipped for clarity

The Feistel permutation is clearly not pseudorandom (regardless of the choice of F) as its output reveals half of its input. The starting point of the PRP construction is the composition $\mathbf{Fei}^2[F, F'] = \mathbf{Fei}[F'] \circ \mathbf{Fei}[F]$ for "independent" functions F and F' (see Figure 3.8). This is the permutation

$$\mathbf{Fei}^2(x, y) = (x + F(y), y + F'(x + F(y))).$$

The permutation $\mathbf{Fei}^2$ also fails to be pseudorandom (regardless of the choice of F and F') as its outputs satisfy the relation

$$\mathbf{Fei}^2(x, y) + \mathbf{Fei}^2(x', y) = (x + x', \text{something}) \qquad (3.15)$$

for any pair of queries of the form (x, y) and (x', y). It turns out that this is the only nonrandom feature of the permutation, in the following sense:

Proposition 3.5.9. *For every q, the following two games are $(\infty, q, q(q - 1) \cdot 2^{-k/2})$-indistinguishable:*

 F: Sample F, F': $\{0, 1\}^{k/2} \to \{0, 1\}^{k/2}$. Answer query (x, y) by $Fei^2[F, F'](x, y)$.
 P: Sample a random permutation P: $\{0, 1\}^k \to \{0, 1\}^k$ and answer with $P(x, y)$,

assuming all queries made by the distinguisher are ynique.

Definition 3.5.10 (ynique sequence). *We call a sequence $(x_1, y_1), \ldots, (x_q, y_q)$ ynique if all y-components are distinct (i.e., $y_i \neq y_j$ when $i \neq j$).*

Proof: We analyze the advantage of the distinguisher with respect to the sequence F, R, P, where R is the game

 R: Sample R: $\{0, 1\}^k \to \{0, 1\}^k$. Answer query (x, y) by $R(x, y)$.

By Proposition 3.5.7, games R and P are $(\infty, q, \binom{q}{2} \cdot 2^{-k/2})$-indistinguishable. It remains to analyze the distinguishing advantage between F and R.

Claim 3.5.11. *Games F and R are $(\infty, q, \binom{q}{2} \cdot 2^{-k/2})$-indistinguishable, assuming the sequence of queries made by the distinguisher is ynique.*

Proof: Consider the hybrid H_i in which the first i queries $(x_1, y_1), \ldots, (x_i, y_i)$ are answered as in F and the rest are answered as in R. We will show that H_i and H_{i-1} are $(\infty, \infty, (i - 1) \cdot 2^{-k/2})$-indistinguishable. The claim then follows by the triangle inequality.

The first i outputs of H_i are

$$(x_j + F(y_j), y_j + F'(x_j + F(y_j)))_{j=1,\ldots,i-1}, (x_i + F(y_i), y_i + F'(x_i + F(y_i)))$$

By yniqueness, $F(y_i)$ is random and independent of $F(y_1), \ldots, F(y_{i-1})$, F', as well as the other $q - i$ outputs of H_i, which can be fixed to maximize the distinguishing advantage. We can therefore represent this distribution as

$$(x_j + F(y_j), y_j + F'(x_j + F(y_j)))_{j=1,\ldots,i-1}, (x_i + r, y_i + F'(x_i + r)).$$

for a random $r \leftarrow \{0, 1\}^k$. The probability that $x_i + r = x_j + F(y_j)$ for some $j < i$ is at most $(i-1) \cdot 2^{-k/2}$. Conditioned on this event not happening, $F'(x_i + r)$ is independent of all the other $j - 1$ evaluations of F and F' and of r. Changing notation again, we can represent the distribution as

$$(x_j + F(y_j), y_j + F'(x_j + F(y_j)))_{j=1,\ldots,i-1}, \ (x_i + r, y_i + r').$$

for a random $r' \leftarrow \{0,1\}^k$. The pair (x_i+r, y_i+r') is uniformly random. By yniqueness it can be replaced with $R(x_i, y_i)$ as in the distribution H_{i-1}.   □

The proposition now follows from the triangle inequality.   □

The Luby–Rackoff and Naor–Reingold constructions. The requirement that all queries have distinct y-coordinates can be enforced by preprocessing the queries. Luby and Rackoff apply another Feistel round for this purpose. Here we describe a variant of Naor and Reingold [104], who use a pairwise independent permutation instead. A family of permutations $H_s: \{0,1\}^k \to \{0,1\}^k$ is *pairwise independent* if it is perfectly indistinguishable from a random permutation by any distinguisher that makes at most two queries. One simple example is the family $H_{a,b}(x) = a \cdot x + b$ where $a \leftarrow \mathbb{F}_{2^k}^\times$, $b, x \leftarrow \mathbb{F}_{2^k}$, and the operations are performed over the field $\mathbb{F}_{2^k}$.

Theorem 3.5.12. *If $\{F_s\}$ is a (t, q, ε)-PRF and H_s is a pairwise independent family of permutations then the function $\mathbf{Fei}^2[F_{s'}, F_{s''}] \circ H_s$ is a $(t - O(kq^2 + ckq), q, \frac{3}{2}q(q-1) \cdot 2^{-k/2} + 2\varepsilon)$-PRP, assuming F_s and H_s have circuit size at most c.*

Proof: We may assume that the distinguisher never makes the same query twice by modifying it to memorize its previous answers. This incurs a loss of at most $O(kq^2)$ in size. Consider the sequence of games

F_s: Sample s, s', s'' independently. Answer by $\mathbf{Fei}^2[F_{s''}, F_{s'}](H_s(x, y))$.
I: Sample s and $F, F': \{0,1\}^{k/2} \to \{0,1\}^{k/2}$. Answer by $\mathbf{Fei}^2[F', F](H_s(x, y))$.
P: Sample H_s and a random permutation P on $\{0,1\}^k$. Answer by $P(H_s(x, y))$.

Games F_s and I are $(t - O(kq^2 + ckq), q, 2\varepsilon)$-indistinguishable by an analysis as in the proof of Theorem 3.3.7. Game P is perfectly indistinguishable from a random permutation. To show indistinguishability of I and P we need the following claim. Let $(x_1, y_1), \ldots, (x_q, y_q)$ denote the query sequence.

Claim 3.5.13. *The probability that the sequence $(H_s(x_i, y_i))_{i=1,\ldots,q}$ is not ynique in game P is at most $\binom{q}{2} \cdot 2^{-k/2}$.*

Proof: By the same argument used in the proof of Theorem 3.5.2, it can be assumed without loss that the distinguisher makes its queries nonadaptively. Writing (x_i', y_i') for $H(x_i, y_i)$,

$$\Pr[(x_i', y_i')_{i=1,\ldots,q} \text{ is not ynique}] \leq \sum_{1 \leq i < j \leq q} \Pr[y_i' = y_j'] = \binom{q}{2} \cdot \frac{2^{-k/2} - 2^{-k}}{1 - 2^{-k}}.$$

The inequality follows from the union bound, and the equality follows from pairwise independence of H_s. After simplifying we obtain the desired bound.   □

Andrej Bogdanov and Alon Rosen

Claim 3.5.14. *Games I and P are* $(\infty, q, \frac{3}{2}q(q-1) \cdot 2^{-k/2})$-*indistinguishable.*

Proof: Consider the following pair of games:

$I^\star$: Same as F, but fail if $H_s(x, y)$ is not ynique.
$P^\star$: Same as P', but fail if $H_s(x, y)$ is not ynique.

By the above claim, $P^\star$ and P are $(\infty, q, \binom{q}{2} \cdot 2^{-k/2})$-indistinguishable. By Proposition 3.5.9, $I^\star$ and $P^\star$ are $(\infty, q, q(q-1) \cdot 2^{-k/2})$-indistinguishable. Applying the triangle inequality, $I^\star$ and P are $(\infty, q, \frac{3}{2}q(q-1) \cdot 2^{-k/2})$-indistinguishable. The distinguishing advantage cannot increase when $I^\star$ is replaced by I, proving the claim.

$\square$

The theorem follows by applying the triangle inequality. $\square$

The pairwise independence of H_s is only used in the proof to ensure that the y-components of the sequence $H_s(x_i, y_i)$ are pairwise pseudorandom. Luby and Rackoff accomplish the same effect with an initial Feistel round.

Strongly pseudorandom permutations. A family of permutations is *strongly pseudorandom* if security holds even against adversaries that are allowed to query both the permutation P and its inverse P^{-1}. This property is required in certain cryptographic applications. The construction from Theorem 3.5.12 may not be strongly pseudorandom as the inverse permutation satisfies relations analogous to (3.15). Strong pseudorandomness can be achieved by adding another hashing step at the output, or via an additional Feistel round (see Figure 3.9).

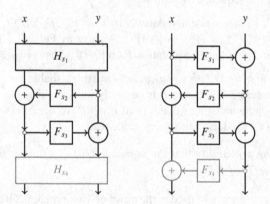

Fig. 3.9: The pseudorandom permutations of Naor–Reingold and Luby–Rackoff. The last layer is needed for strong pseudorandomness

Security versus domain size. In Theorem 3.5.12, the parameter k governs both the input size and the security guarantee of the pseudorandom permutation. The security guarantee is poor for PRPs on small domains, which are useful in practice [33]. This is unavoidable for the Luby–Rackoff construction; Aiello and Venkatesan [1] proved that the four-round Feistel network is not $(\mathrm{poly}(k) \cdot 2^{k/4}, 2^{k/4}, \frac{1}{2})$-pseudorandom. Maurer, Pietrzak, and Renner [96] show that increasing the number of Feistel rounds can improve the dependence on k in the security. However, their security guarantee is still inadequate for small values of k.

While it is not known in general if this dependence between security and input size is necessary for Feistel-type PRP instantiations, it is an inherent limitation of "information-theoretic" security proofs such as the proof of Theorem 3.5.12. There, the security of the PRP is deduced from the security of an idealized game I in which the underlying PRF instances are replaced by truly random functions. It is then shown that the game I is statistically secure: Any q-query adversary, regardless of its size, distinguishes I from a random permutation P with probability at most $O(q^2 \cdot 2^{-k/2})$.

A counting argument shows that the analogues of games I and P for the r-round Feistel network $\mathbf{Fei}^r[F_1, \ldots, F_r]$ are *not* $(\infty, r2^{k/2}, \frac{1}{2})$-indistinguishable [100]. To see this, consider the sequence of permutation values at the lexicographically first q inputs. The permutation $\mathbf{Fei}^r$ is fully specified by the truth-tables of the r underlying PRFs $F_1, \ldots, F_r \colon \{0,1\}^{k/2} \to \{0,1\}^{k/2}$, so the sequence $(\mathbf{Fei}^r(1), \ldots, \mathbf{Fei}^r(q))$ can by described by at most $rk/2 \cdot 2^{k/2}$ bits. On the other hand, for a random permutation P, the sequence $(P(1), \ldots, P(q))$ has min-entropy $\log(2^k)_q \geq q\log(2^k - q)$. The two can be distinguished with constant advantage when $q \geq r2^{k/2}$.

In summary, the security analysis of the Feistel construction is limited by the relatively small input size of the underlying (pseudo)random functions, which is an artifact of its balanced nature—namely, the requirement that x and y should be equally long. It is therefore sensible to investigate the security of unbalanced variants. In the extreme setting $|x| = 1$, $|y| = k - 1$ the analog of the Feistel shuffle is the Thorp shuffle

$$\mathbf{Th}[F](x, y) = (y, x + F(y)), \qquad x \in \{0, 1\}, y \in \{0, 1\}^{k-1}$$

with underlying (pseudo)random function $F \colon \{0,1\}^{k-1} \to \{0,1\}$. Morris, Rogaway, and Stegers [100] show that the r-round Thorp network $\mathbf{Th}^r$ (instantiated with random functions) is $(\infty, q, (q/r^\star) \cdot (4kq/2^k)^{r^\star})$-indistinguishable from a random permutation, where $r^\star = r/(2k + 1)$. In the case $q = 2^k$, Morris [99] proves that $r = O(k^3 \log 1/\varepsilon)$ rounds yield $(\infty, 2^k, \varepsilon)$ security for any k and ε.

The Feistel shuffle $\mathbf{Fei}[F]$ and the Thorp shuffle $\mathbf{Th}[F]$ are examples of *oblivious* card-shuffling procedures: The permutation can be viewed as a rule for shuffling a deck of 2^k cards with the randomness described by the underlying (pseudo)random function F.[6] For the resulting PRP to be efficiently computable, the shuffle should be oblivious in the sense that the new position of every card in the deck can be computed efficiently as a function of only its previous position and the randomness, and not the positions of the other cards in the deck. Oblivious shuffles that enjoy

---

[6] This perspective is attributed to Naor [104], who was the first to propose the Thorp shuffle-based PRP construction.

rapid "local" mixing give rise to PRP constructions with a good tradeoff between efficiency and security.

3.5.3 Implementing Huge Random Objects

A pseudorandom permutation is an example of a huge object that is guaranteed to satisfy the global property of being a permutation, while being "locally" indistinguishable from a random permutation. An implementation of a pseudorandom permutation by a (pseudo)random function would preserve the local indistinguishability (by Proposition 3.5.7), but is likely to violate the global property. This may be relevant in applications where the user of the implementation may rely, for instance, on the existence of inverses.

The distinction is even more prominent in the case of a strong pseudorandom permutation. In a "truthful" implementation, such as the four-round Feistel network, the user is guaranteed that evaluating $P_s^{-1}(P_s(x))$ always outputs x. In contrast, if P is instantiated with an arbitrary PRF, a consistent inverse may not even exist, much less be efficiently computable.

Goldreich, Goldwasser, and Nussboim [65] initiated a general study of efficient implementations of huge random objects of various types. The Luby–Rackoff construction suggests a generic two-step template for this purpose:

1. Starting from a random function R, construct an object O^R that is statistically indistinguishable from a random object of the desired type (for a suitable bound on the number of queries).
2. Replace the random function R by a PRF to obtain an efficient implementation O_s of the object.

Let us call the implementation O_s *truthful* if the object O_s is of the desired type.[7] Goldreich et al. observe that, even if one is willing to tolerate untruthful implementations with some small probability in the second step, the first step must guarantee a truthful random object with probability one. This phenomenon is illustrated in the following example:

Example 3.5.15 (Random injective function). *A random function* $R: \{0,1\}^n \to \{0,1\}^{3n-1}$ *is injective with probability at least* $1 - 2^{-n}$. *However, a PRF* F_s *with the same domain and range need not be injective for any key s. In fact, any PRF can be converted into a noninjective PRF by planting a random collision: If* F_s *is a* (t, q, ε)-*PRF then the family*

$$F_{s,a}(x) = \begin{cases} F_s(x), & \text{if } x \neq a \\ F_s(0), & \text{if } x = a \end{cases}$$

is a $(t, q, \varepsilon + q \cdot 2^{-n})$-*PRF that is not injective for any key* (s,a), $a \neq 0$.

Example 3.5.15 can be explained by the fact that injectivity is a global property of functions, while step 2 only guarantees that local indistinguishability is preserved.

---

[7] Our use of the term deviates slightly from the definition in [65].

In view of this it is interesting to ask if an almost always truthful implementation of a random injective function can be obtained. In this case the answer is positive.

Proposition 3.5.16. *If $F_s \colon \{0,1\}^k \to \{0,1\}^\ell$ is a (t, ε)-PRF and $H_s \colon \{0,1\}^k \to \{0,1\}^\ell$ is a pairwise-independent hash family then $I_{s,s'}(x) = F_s(x) \oplus H_{s'}(x)$ satisfies the following two properties:*

1. *$I_{s,s'}$ is $(t - c, \varepsilon + \binom{2^k}{2} \cdot 2^{-\ell})$-indistinguishable from a random injective function, where c is the size of $H_{s'}$.*
2. *$\Pr_{s,s'}[I_{s,s'}$ is not injective$] \leq \binom{2^k}{2} \cdot 2^{-\ell}$.*

Proof: The first property follows by a hybrid argument (details omitted). We prove that the second property holds for every fixing of s:

$$\Pr_{s'}[I_{s,s'} \text{ is not injective}] \leq \sum_{x \neq x'} \Pr[I_{s,s'}(x) = I_{s,s'}(x')]$$

$$= \sum_{x \neq x'} \Pr[H_{s'}(x) \oplus H_{s'}(x') = F_s(x) \oplus F_s(x')]$$

$$= \binom{2^k}{2} \cdot 2^{-\ell}.$$

The inequality is the union bound, and the last equality follows from the pairwise independence of $H_{s'}$.   □

Can Proposition 3.5.16 be strengthened so as to also provide the distinguisher access to F^{-1}? More generally, $I_{s,s'}$ almost always truthfully implements a random code of linear distance. Goldreich et al. ask if there is an alternative implementation in which the distinguisher can be also furnished with a decoding oracle. ⊘

The work [65] contains many additional results and open questions regarding huge random objects arising from random graph theory and the theory of random Boolean functions.

Efficient implementations of huge random objects can enable an experimentalist to carry out simulations on random objects that are prohibitively large (e.g., random graphs, random codes) with results that are guaranteed to be sound, assuming the availability of a sufficiently strong PRF. In this setting, the stateless nature of PRFs is a desirable feature (as it provides a short description of the huge object) but not entirely necessary.

Bogdanov and Wee [39] introduce the notion of a *stateful implementation*, which may keep state in between queries. Their work gives a stateful implementation of a specification suggested by Goldreich et al. (a Boolean function $f \colon \{0,1\}^n \to \{0,1\}$ in which the distinguisher may query the XOR of all the values of f over a subcube of its choice) for which a stateless implementation is not known. While stateful implementations seem easier to construct than stateless ones, no formal separation between these two notions is known. ⊘

3.6 Complexity of Pseudorandom Functions

Chazak Razborov!
BENNY CHOR (1980s)

The GGM and NR constructions from Section 3.3 are generic methods for obtaining a PRF from a simpler pseudorandom object. The resulting PRF is in general more complex than the underlying primitive. In the specific instantiations discussed in Section 3.4, this increase in complexity was mitigated by careful implementation.

There is however a limit to the amount of efficiency that can be squeezed by further optimizations. PRF implementations inherently require a certain amount of complexity. We discuss two related reasons for this: the availablity of efficient learning algorithms and the existence of "natural" lower-bound proofs for sufficiently simple circuit classes. We then describe some heuristic PRF candidates that are just complex enough to arguably match these limitations.

3.6.1 Learning Algorithms

A learner for a class of functions $\mathbf{F}$ is a two-stage algorithm L that works as follows: In the first stage the algorithm is given oracle access to some function $F \in \mathbf{F}$. In the second stage the algorithm receives an input x and outputs a prediction for the value $F(x)$. The learner has *approximation error* δ if $\Pr[L^F(x) \neq F(x)] \leq \delta$ for x chosen from the uniform distribution on inputs.[8]

Learning algorithms differ depending on the learner's mode of oracle access. A membership query learner may query the oracle adaptively on inputs of its choice. A learner from random examples has only access to random input–output pairs $(x, F(x))$ for independent and uniform inputs x.

The existence of a low-complexity learner for a class of functions implies bounds on the security of any implementation of a pseudorandom function family in this class [113]. We state the result for Boolean-valued functions $F_s \colon \{0,1\}^k \to \{0,1\}$.

Proposition 3.6.1. *If the function family $\{F_s\}$ can be learned from membership queries (resp., random examples) with approximation error $\frac{1}{2} - \varepsilon$ by an algorithm of size t then F_s is not a $(t + O(k), \varepsilon - t/2^k)$-PRF (resp., weak PRF).*

Learning with approximation error $\frac{1}{2}$ amounts to random guessing. Proposition 3.6.1 states that any nonnegligible improvement to the approximation error by an efficient learner rules out pseudorandomness of F_s.

Proof: Consider the distinguisher D^F that simulates L^F and makes one additional random query x to obtain answer $F(x)$ (or, in the case of random examples, obtains one additional example $(x, F(x))$). If $L^F(x) = F(x)$ the distinguisher accepts, and otherwise it rejects.

---

[8] Other distributions on inputs are also studied in learning theory.

By assumption, $L^{F_s}(x)$ equals $F_s(x)$ with probability at least $\frac{1}{2} + \varepsilon$. On the other hand, if R is a random function, $L^R(x)$ is statistically independent of $R(x)$ as long as the oracle has not been queried at x, which fails to happen with probability at most $t/2^k$. The advantage of the distinguisher is therefore at least $(\frac{1}{2} + \varepsilon) - (\frac{1}{2} + t/2^k) = \varepsilon - t/2^k$.   □

We will say a pseudorandom function F_s can be implemented in class **F** if F_s belongs to **F** for all s. Applying Proposition 3.6.1 to different algorithms from the computational learning theory literature yields the following limitations on the implementation complexity of PRFs:

1. Weak PRFs cannot be implemented by linear threshold functions, as such functions can be learned efficiently using the algorithm of Blum et al. [34].
2. PRFs cannot be implemented by polynomial-size formulas in disjunctive normal form (DNF), as these can be learned efficiently (under the uniform distribution) by Jackson's harmonic sieve algorithm [79].
3. Any function family implemented by AND/OR circuits of size s, depth d, and input length k is not $\left(\binom{k}{\leq O(\log s)^{d-1}}, \frac{1}{2}\right)$-weakly pseudorandom, as such circuits can be learned under the uniform distribution by the algorithm of Linial, Mansour, and Nisan [89].

The learning algorithms of Blum et al. and Linial, Mansour, and Nisan can be implemented in the statistical query model that is discussed in Section 3.7.7.

Proposition 3.6.1 can also be applied in the contrapositive form to argue computational limitations on learning. In particular:

1. Polynomial-size circuit families cannot be learned efficiently from membership queries, assuming polynomial-size one-way function families exist. This follows from the equivalence of one-way functions and PRFs discussed in Section 3.1.2.
2. Polynomial-size constant-depth circuit families with linear threshold gates (the class TC^0) cannot be learned efficiently from membership queries, assuming the hardness of DDH or LWE. This follows from the complexity of the constructions in Section 3.4.
3. Polynomial-size constant-depth AND/OR circuit families require quasipolynomial time to learn from membership queries, assuming the exponential hardness of factoring Blum integers [83].

3.6.2 Natural Proofs

> *I asked my wife what is the definition of natural, and she said "anything that does not contain petroleum products."*
>
> LEONID LEVIN (2007)

In an attempt to understand the difficulties inherent in proving lower bounds on the size of Boolean circuits computing explicit functions, Razborov and Rudich introduced a formal framework that captures many of the currently available techniques.

A circuit lower-bound proof can be viewed as a property P of functions that distinguishes between the functions computable by circuits in the given class and the "hard" function.

Razborov and Rudich showed that, in many known proofs, the distinguishing property has the following two features. For convenience let us assume that the domain and range are $\{0, 1\}^k$ and $\{0, 1\}$, respectively.

Smallness: Property P fails not only for the hard function, but for, say, at least half the functions from $\{0, 1\}^k$ to $\{0, 1\}$.[9]

Constructivity: There exists an oracle circuit of size $2^{O(k)}$ that, given oracle access to F, decides if F has property P.

A small and constructive property that holds for all functions in a given class **F** is called *natural* for **F**.

Proposition 3.6.2. *If there exists a property that is natural for the function family* $\{F_s\}$ *then* F_s *is not a* $(2^{O(k)}, \frac{1}{2})$*-PRF.*

It is useful to keep in mind that the (strong) PRF distinguisher can control the input length k of the candidate PRF by fixing some of the input bits.

Proof: Let D be the circuit of size $2^{O(k)}$ that decides if F has property P. By assumption, D^{F_s} always accepts. By smallness, $\Pr[D^R \text{ accepts}] \leq \frac{1}{2}$. Therefore D has distinguishing advantage at least $1/2$. $\quad\square$

Applying Proposition 3.6.2 to various properties implicit in circuit lower-bound proofs, Razborov and Rudich derive the following consequences among others:

1. Any function family implemented by AND/OR circuits of size $\exp o(k)^{1/(d-1)}$ and depth d is not pseudorandom. This follows from the parity circuit lower bound of Hastad [56, 130, 71]. Boppana [42] shows that the following simple distinguisher works: Choose two random inputs x, y that differ on a single coordinate and check if $F(x) = F(y)$. Distinguishers of this type are discussed in Section 3.7.1.

2. Any function family implemented by AND/OR/PARITY circuits of size s and depth d (the class $AC^0[\oplus]$) is not $(\exp(\log s)^{O(d)}, \frac{1}{2})$-pseudorandom. This follows from a "naturalization" of the lower-bound proof of Razborov and Smolensky [115, 124]. The conclusion also holds if PARITY is replaced by the MOD_q function for any constant prime power q. This distinguisher is described as the Razborov–Rudich test in Section 3.7.4.

3. Any function family implemented by AND/OR formulas of size $k^{3-\varepsilon}$ for any $\varepsilon > 0$ and sufficiently large k is not $(2^{O(k)}, \frac{1}{2})$-pseudorandom. This follows from Hastad's proof of hardness for the Andreev function [72].

In summary, PRFs cannot be constructed in any class that is (a) learnable or (b) has a natural property. The latter requirement appears to be weaker as learnability

---

[9] Razborov and Rudich work with the complementary property NOT P and call the corresponding condition largeness.

(by a specific algorithm) is a natural property. Carmosino et al. [49] recently showed a converse: Any class of functions (satisfying certain closure requirements) that has a natural property can be learned efficiently from membership queries. In particular, $AC^0[\oplus]$ circuit families can be learned in quasipolynomial time.

While these results essentially rule out the existence of PRFs of very low complexity, it remains an open question whether similar limitations hold for some of their immediate applications such as symmetric-key encryption schemes or authentication protocols. ⑦

3.6.3 Heuristic Constructions

Propositions 3.6.1 and 3.6.2 indicate that the efficiency of PRFs is of fundamental relevance in computational learning theory and computational complexity. These connections provide extrinsic motivation for a fine-grained study of the complexity of PRF constructions in various computational models.

In practice, the most efficient PRFs for a given level of security are not obtained by means of generic methods such as the ones from Section 3.3. The modular nature of such constructions appears to entail a loss in security which can be potentially avoided with a carefully crafted design. However, claims of security for "direct" PRF constructions can no longer be based on standard assumptions and must rely instead on the collective wisdom of cryptanalysts (motivated in part by social incentives for attacking candidate implementations).

The practical construction of PRFs is an intricate art form that we do not attempt to cover here. We recommend Chapter 5 in the textbook of Katz and Lindell [80] as an introduction to this subject. Our emphasis here is on elementary principles of direct PRF and PRP constructions. We mention some concrete proposals and discuss their relevance to the feasibility of learning and the existence of natural proofs.

Two paradigms that have been applied towards practical implementations of PRPs (called *block ciphers* in the applied cryptography literature) are Feistel networks and substitution-permutation networks. Both of these methods in fact yield (pseudorandom) permutations.

Feistel networks. The most well-known Feistel network-based PRP is DES (the Data Encryption Standard). Despite the long history and prominence of DES (it was designed and standardized in the 1970s and has enjoyed widespread use ever since), it has shown remarkable resilience to cryptanalysis. DES is a permutation family on 64-bit strings with a 56-bit key. Its basic building block is the 16-round Feistel network $\mathbf{Fei}^{16}[F_{s_1}, \ldots, F_{s_{16}}]$ instantiated with some special function F_s that "mixes" the input and its key. The *round keys* $s_1, \ldots, s_{16}$ are not independent; they are derived by applying iterative transformations to the 56-bit *master key* of DES.

This type of *key scheduling* process that injects partial information about the key at different rounds is commonly used in block cipher design. It possibly serves as a mechanism to hinder cryptanalysis by humans, as it makes the inner workings of the function challenging to understand. Generic constructions like the ones from

Section 3.3, on the other hand, are designed so that human analysis is a desirable feature (for the objective is to come up with proofs of security).

Differential and linear cryptanalysis. One class of attacks that is natural to consider in the context of iterated constructions like the Feistel network is differential cryptanalysis [29]. The attacker tries to obtain correlations among pairs of outputs by flipping some bit positions of a (random) input. If the correlations are sufficiently "typical" they may tend to propagate throughout the Feistel network and be used to learn the candidate PRF. Biham·and Shamir [30] designed such an attack to learn DES using 2^{47} queries and a similar amount of time, and other iterated constructions even more efficiently.

Miles and Viola [98] suggest the following formalization of differential cryptanalysis. Here + denotes bit-wise XOR.

Definition 3.6.3 (Differential cryptanalysis). *A family* $\{F_s: \{0,1\}^k \rightarrow \{0,1\}^\ell\}$ *of functions is said to be* ε-*secure against differential cryptanalysis if for all* $\Delta x \neq 0$ *and* Δy, $\Pr_{x,s}[F_s(x) + F_s(x + \Delta x) = \Delta y] \leq \varepsilon$.

The two-round Feistel construction is an example that is insecure against differential cryptanalysis (recall (3.15) in Section 3.5.2).

Linear cryptanalysis [95] is a different type of attack that attempts to find linear relationships between the bits of random input–output pairs. Miles and Viola [98] formalize it as follows. Here $\langle a, x \rangle$ denotes the inner product modulo 2 function $a_1 x_1 + \cdots + a_k x_k$.

Definition 3.6.4 (Linear cryptanalysis). *A family* $\{F_s: \{0,1\}^k \rightarrow \{0,1\}^\ell\}$ *of functions is said to be* ε-*secure against linear cryptanalysis if for all* $a \in \{0,1\}^k$ *and* $b \in \{0,1\}^\ell$, $\mathbb{E}_s[\mathbb{E}_x[(-1)^{\langle a,x \rangle + \langle b, F_s(x) \rangle}]^2] \leq \varepsilon$.

Matsui [95] devised an attack of this type to learn DES using 2^{43} queries.

In spite of these attacks, DES is believed to be a remarkably secure PRP. Its 56-bit key, however, is considered inadequately short for modern applications.

Substitution–permutation networks. Substitution–permutation networks (SPNs) are another blueprint for constructing PRPs. Here the PRP $P_s: \{0,1\}^k \rightarrow \{0,1\}^k$ is obtained by sequentially composing "simple" permutations of the following types:

- **S-boxes** are highly nonlinear fixed (independent of the key) permutations $S: \{0,1\}^c \rightarrow \{0,1\}^c$ where c is a small factor of k. The input is partitioned into k/c blocks of size c, and the S-box is applied to each block in parallel.
- **P-boxes** are linear permutations of the whole input that contain a large number of input–output dependencies.
- **Round key** operations are linear shifts of the input by the round key. As in Feistel network-based constructions, round keys are obtained by applying iterative transformations to the master key.

The nonlinear nature of the S-boxes is meant to guarantee security against "local" attacks such as linear and differential cryptanalysis. The P-boxes ensure that the effect propagates throughout the input positions. Miles and Viola prove general bounds on the security of SPNs against linear and differential cryptanalysis.

AES (the Advanced Encryption Standard) is a highly efficient SPN-based family of permutations on 128 bits. There are three variants of the construction, allowing keys of size 128, 192, and 256, respectively. In spite of the scrutiny this design has received, no significant weakness is known.

Miles and Viola propose several SPN-based constructions of PRP and PRF families on infinitely many input lengths and provide some theoretical evidence for their asymptotic security. If their security conjectures hold, quasilinear-size circuit families, TC^0-type circuit families of size $n^{1+\varepsilon}$, and quadratic-time single-tape Turing machines with a quadratic number of states are hard to learn and have no natural property.

Dodis et al. [52] study a model of SPNs in which the S-boxes are implemented by a random permutation oracle that can be queried both by the construction and by the distinguisher. They observe that 2-round SPNs are insecure in this model and construct a 3-round SPN that is provably $O(n^2 q^2 / 2^c)$-secure against a distinguisher that makes q queries. They also obtain similar security for a 1-round SPN variant with a nonlinear P-box.

Weak pseudorandom functions.   Owing to the severely restricted nature of the distinguisher, weak PRFs ought to be easier to construct than their strong counterparts. Differential cryptanalysis, in particular, does not apply to weak PRFs, although linear cryptanalysis does. We describe two conjectured separations between PRFs and weak PRFs as evidence that weak PRFs are indeed a less complex object.

Blum, Furst, Kearns, and Lipton [35] (Section 2.3) consider the following family of functions $F_{S,T} \colon \{0,1\}^n \to \{0,1\}$:

$$F_{S,T}(x) = \text{MAJORITY}(x|_S) + \text{PARITY}(x|_T),$$

where the key consists of two random $(\log n)$-bit subsets S and T of $\{1, \ldots, n\}$, $x|_S$ is the projection of x on its S-coordinates, and $+$ denotes XOR. They conjecture that this family is a (n^c, n^{-c})-weak PRF for any constant c and sufficiently large k. The best known algorithms for learning such functions from random examples have complexity $n^{\Omega(\log n)}$ [101]. For every S and T, $F_{S,T}$ is a function of $2 \log n$ inputs and can in particular be computed by a DNF of size n^2. In contrast, as discussed in Section 3.6.1, DNFs cannot compute strong PRFs whose security is superpolynomial in their size.

In the regime of exponential security, the binary modulus ($q = 2$) variant of LWE (see Section 3.4.2) is a conjectured example of a *randomized* weak PRF. The noisy parity randomized function family $F_s \colon \{0,1\}^n \to \{0,1\}$ ($s \in \{0,1\}^n$) is given by

$$F_s(x) = \langle s, x \rangle + e(x) = s_1 x_1 + \cdots + s_n x_n + e(x),$$

where the bits $e(x)\colon x \in \{0,1\}^n$ are independent and δ-biased for some $\delta < 1/2$. Blum, Kalai, and Wasserman [36] give an algorithm for this problem with running time $2^{O(n/(\log n - \log\log 1/(1-2\delta)))}$. Lyubashevsky [92] significantly reduces the query complexity of this algorithm but at the cost of increasing its running time.

Noisy parities are attractive owing to their extreme simplicity, but their randomized nature is undesirable. For instance, using F_s as the basis of an encryption scheme like the one in Section 3.2.4 would introduce decryption errors with some probability.

Akavia et al. [3] conjecture that the function family $G_{A,b}\colon \{0,1\}^n \to \{0,1\}$ given by

$$G_{A,b}(x) = g(Ax + b) \tag{3.16}$$

is a weak PRF. Here, A is a random $n \times n$ matrix, b is a random $\{0,1\}^n$ vector, and $g\colon \{0,1\}^n \to \{0,1\}$ is a suitably chosen function of constant depth and size polynomial in n. By the discussion in Section 3.6.2, the security of any strong PRF in this class is at most quasipolynomial.

Akavia et al. propose setting g to equal the tribes function of Ben-Or and Linial [27] XORed with an additional input bit. In Section 3.7.5 we show that this instantiation is insecure. Proposing an explicit choice of g for which the family (3.16) is arguably weakly pseudorandom, or showing that no such choice exists, remains an open problem. ⑦

3.7 Distinguishers

> *There is no intuition.*
> *You just do the calculation.*
> JOHAN HASTAD (1990s)

The security of PRFs is required to hold against arbitrary efficient adversaries. It is however sometimes useful to study distinguishers of restricted computational power. Restricted distinguishers can model specific classes of cryptanalytic attacks. Proofs of security against such distinguishers can provide evidence for the soundness of heuristic constructions, and potentially achieve better parameters even when a generic proof of security is available. Moreover, if the class of distinguishers is sufficiently restrictive, unconditional proofs of security may be possible.

In the first two parts we focus on distinguishers of bounded query complexity and linear distinguishers. These lead to natural requirements on the distribution of outputs of the PRF: bounded independence for the first type and small bias for the second. We then turn to space-bounded distinguishers and several types of "randomness tests" that have found application in computational complexity and learning theory: polynomial correlation tests, rational function representations, cylinder product tests, and statistical query algorithms.

3.7.1 Distinguishers of Bounded Query Complexity

The following is a generalization of pairwise independence (Definition 3.5.1 in Section 3.5.1).

Definition 3.7.1 (Bounded independence). *A function family* $F_s \colon \{0,1\}^k \to \{0,1\}^\ell$ *is q-wise independent if it is* $(\infty, q, 0)$*-pseudorandom.*

Pairwise (2-wise) indepedence guarantees security against linear and differential cryptanalysis in the sense of Definitions 3.6.3 and 3.6.4.

Achieving q-wise independence requires a key of length at least $q\ell$. When $\ell = n$, a key of size $q\ell$ is in fact sufficient: the function $F_s(x) = s_0 + s_1 x + \cdots + s_{t-1} x^{t-1}$, where s is the vector $(s_0, \ldots, s_{t-1}) \in \mathbb{F}_{2^k}^t$ and all algebra is over the field $\mathbb{F}_{2^k}$.[10]

Although the function F_s is perfectly indistinguishable from a random function by a q-query distinguisher, it is not even weakly pseudorandom: since F_s is a polynomial of degree q, after observing $F_s(x_1), \ldots, F_s(x_q)$ at any q points, the value $F_s(x)$ can be computed efficiently for all x using the Lagrange interpolation formula. Therefore, F_s can be distinguished from a random function using any $q + 1$ queries.

Bounded independence tends to be effective against adversaries that do not employ attacks based on linear algebra (over various outputs of the PRF). One model for such adversaries is the class of bounded-depth circuits. Circuits in this class cannot compute linear functions unless they are very large [56, 130, 71]. Bounded independence ensures security against bounded-depth distinguishers: a $(\log s)^{O(d)} \cdot \log(1/\varepsilon)$-wise independent function family is (s, ε)-pseudorandom with respect to distinguishers of size s and depth d [45] (see also [125, 70]).

The notions of bounded independence and cryptographic pseudorandomness are incomparable: not only is bounded independence insufficient for cryptographic pseudorandomness, it is also unnecessary. Even for a single bit of output, bounded independence requires perfect indistinguishability from true randomness. For cryptographic purposes statistical indistinguishability is adequate. This leads to an approximate notion of bounded independence.

Definition 3.7.2 (Approximate bounded independence). $\{F_s\}$ *is* (q, ε)*-wise independent if it is* (∞, q, ε)*-pseudorandom with respect to nonadaptive distinguishers.*

Approximate bounded independence is closely related to the small bias property that we discuss next.

3.7.2 Linear Distinguishers

A linear distinguisher computes some linear function of the values of the PRF. A distribution that is pseudorandom against such distinguishers is called small-biased [102]. We focus on the case of linear tests over the group $\mathbb{Z}_2$, where it is

---

[10] For one bit of output, a key size of $(q \log k)/2 + O_q(1)$ is both necessary and sufficient (see Section 13.2 of [4]).

natural to assume that the PRF is Boolean-valued. The definition can be extended to other Abelian groups.

Definition 3.7.3 (Small bias [102]). *A function family $\{F_s\}$ is (q, ε)-biased if every distinguisher that computes a linear function modulo 2 of at most q bits of the function's output has advantage at most $\varepsilon/2$.*

It is convenient to view the range of the function as a multiplicative group, which allows for easier Fourier analysis [110]. Under this convention, the values of F_s are represented by the square roots of unity 1 and -1. The small bias property then requires that for all distinct inputs $x_1, \ldots, x_r$, $1 \le r \le q$,

$$\left| E[F_s(x_1) \cdots F_s(x_r)] \right| \le \varepsilon.$$

If a function family is $(q, \varepsilon/2)$-wise independent then it is clearly (q, ε)-biased. The two definitions are in fact equivalent up to an exponential loss in q:

Lemma 3.7.4. *If $\{F_s\}$ is (q, ε)-biased then it is $(q, \sqrt{2^q - 1} \cdot \varepsilon/2)$-wise independent.*

It follows from Lemma 3.7.4 that $(q, 2^{-q/2})$-wise independence cannot be achieved when q exceeds the key length. For smaller values of q, the small bias property provides information-theoretic security against distinguishers that make a bounded number of queries. In particular, these include differential attacks.

Proof: Let $D: \{0,1\}^X \to \{-1, 1\}$ be any statistical distinguisher that queries F on the set $X = \{x_1, \ldots, x_q\}$. In the Fourier basis we can write

$$D^F = \sum_{A \subseteq X} \hat{D}(A) \cdot \prod_{x \in A} F(x).$$

Then

$$
\begin{aligned}
\left| E[D^{F_s}] - E[D^R] \right| &= \left| \sum_{A \subseteq X} \hat{D}(A) \cdot \left(E \prod_{x \in A} F_s(x) - E \prod_{x \in A} R(x) \right) \right| \\
&= \left| \sum_{A \subseteq X, A \ne \emptyset} \hat{D}(A) \cdot E \prod_{x \in A} F_s(x) \right| \\
&\le \sum_{A \subseteq X, A \ne \emptyset} |\hat{D}(A)| \cdot \left| E \prod_{x \in A} F_s(x) \right| \\
&\le \varepsilon \cdot \sum_{A \subseteq X, A \ne \emptyset} |\hat{D}(A)|.
\end{aligned}
\tag{3.17}
$$

By the Cauchy–Schwarz inequality and Parseval's identity the last expression is at most $\varepsilon \sqrt{2^q - 1}$. Therefore

$$\left| \Pr[D^{F_s} \text{ accepts}] - \Pr[D^R \text{ accepts}] \right| = \tfrac{1}{2} \cdot \left| E[D^{F_s}] - E[D^R] \right| \le \sqrt{2^q - 1} \cdot \varepsilon/2.$$

$\square$

Generalizing this argument to adaptive distinguishers, it follows that if $\{F_s\}$ is (q, ε)-biased then every adaptive distinguisher that makes at most q queries has advantage at most $2^q \cdot \varepsilon/2$. To prove this, the distinguisher is modeled as a decision tree over variables $F_s(x)$ of depth at most q. The sum of the absolute values of the Fourier coefficients of a decision tree is upper bounded by the number of its leaves, which is at most 2^q. The bound then follows by a calculation similar to (3.17).

There are several efficient constructions of $(2^k, \varepsilon)$-biased families $F_s \colon \{0, 1\}^k \to \{0, 1\}$ of size polynomial in k and $\log 1/\varepsilon$ [102, 5, 26]. As in the case of bounded independence, some of them are cryptographically insecure.

We do not know of any generic methods for obtaining cryptographically secure PRFs that provably exhibit the small bias property. In the case of the GGM construction, it would be interesting to understand which property of the underlying PRG is sufficient to guarantee that the PRF has small bias. As an initial step in this direction, we suggest the problem of constructing an efficient PRG G so that the GGM construction instantiated with G has small bias. ⑦

Regarding concrete constructions, Miles and Viola [98] prove that one of their proposed PRFs is $(3, 2^{-\Omega(k)})$-biased. It would be interesting to prove that the other constructions described in Section 3.4 have the small bias property. ⑦

3.7.3 Space-Bounded Distinguishers

A distinguisher is space-bounded if it has less memory than the key size of the PRF. An algorithm with m bits of memory can be modeled as a branching program of width 2^m whose input is the truth table of the function to be distinguished.

Definition 3.7.5 (Pseudorandomness against bounded space). *A function family $\{F_s \colon \{0, 1\}^k \to \{0, 1\}\}$ is ε-pseudorandom against space m if the distinguishing advantage of any branching program of width 2^m is at most ε.*

The access mode of the branching programs can be sequential, oblivious, or unrestricted, corresponding to the notion of sequential, nonadaptive, and general PRFs, respectively.

The pseudorandom generators of Nisan [109] and Impagliazzo, Nisan, and Wigderson [76] can be viewed as function families of key length $O(k^2 + km + k \log(1/\varepsilon))$ and size polynomial in k, m, and $1/\varepsilon$ that are ε-pseudorandom against space m with sequential access.

Much less is known with respect to other forms of access. In a permutation branching program, the answer to each query induces a permutation of the states. Reingold, Steinke, and Vadhan [119] give a PRF of key length and size polynomial in k, 2^m, and $\log 1/\varepsilon$ that is ε-pseudorandom against space m permutation branching programs with nonadaptive *read-once* access. There is little hope of removing the read-once and permutation restrictions at the same time: By Barrington's theorem [20], polynomial-size branching program families of width 5 have the same computational power as the circuit class NC^1. A PRF against NC^1 with an unconditional proof of security would imply an explicit circuit lower bound against this class, thereby resolving a long-standing open problem in computational complexity.

We are not aware of any results regarding the security of weak PRFs with respect to space-bounded distinguishers. ⑦

3.7.4 Correlation with Polynomials

> *I don't like polynomials.*
> *They are mysterious.*
>
> ODED GOLDREICH (2000s)

One can attempt to detect nonrandom behavior in a function by looking for correlations with some structured class of functions. In this context, the class of low-degree polynomials over a finite field is important in many areas of the theory of computing. On the algorithmic side, there are efficient methods for detecting low-degree correlations in several interesting parameter regimes. On the complexity-theoretic side, functions that correlate with some low-degree polynomial capture several interesting classes of computations, in particular bounded-depth circuits with AND, OR, and PARITY gates [115, 124].

Here we focus on polynomials over the binary field $\mathbb{F}_2$. The results can be extended to other finite fields, but the efficiency of the tests worsens as the field size becomes larger.

Definition 3.7.6 (Proximity to polynomials). *The function* $F\colon \mathbb{F}_2^k \to \mathbb{F}_2$ *is δ-close to degree d if*

$$\Pr_{x \leftarrow \mathbb{F}_2^k}[F(x) \neq p(x)] \leq \delta$$

for some polynomial $p\colon \mathbb{F}_2^k \to \mathbb{F}_2$ *of degree at most d.*

A standard counting argument shows, for example, that the probability of a random function being $1/3$-close to degree $k/3$ is at most $2^{-\Omega(2^k)}$. We now describe some settings in which low-degree correlation can be tested efficiently.

Exact representation.   In the extreme setting $\delta = 0$, we are interested in an exact representation of F as an $\mathbb{F}_2$-polynomial of degree at most d:

$$F(x) = \sum_{S\,:\,|S|\leq d} \tilde{F}(S) \cdot \prod_{i\in S} x_i. \tag{3.18}$$

Every input–output pair $(x, F(x))$ then reveals a linear dependence between the coefficients $\tilde{F}(S)$. Given sufficiently many such linear dependences, the values $\tilde{F}(S)$ can be learned via linear algebra. As there are $\binom{k}{\leq d}$ values to be learned, at least this many queries to F are required. This number of queries is also sufficient: For example, if x ranges over all $\binom{k}{\leq d}$ strings of Hamming weight at most d, then the system of equations (3.18) has full row rank and the coefficients $\tilde{F}(S)$ are uniquely determined.

Using a few additional queries, F can even be learned from independent random samples of the form $(x, F(x))$: $O(2^d \binom{k}{\leq d})$ such pairs are sufficient to ensure full row rank with constant probability. In Section 3.7.5 we will analyze a more general variant of this test. Since every function has a unique canonical multilinear expansion, it can in principle be verified that a given candidate PRF implementation resists these types of attacks.

High correlation. Low-degree polynomials have a dual characterization: A function p has degree at most d if and only if $\sum_{x \in A} p(x) = 0$ for all affine subspaces A of dimension $d + 1$.

This characterization provides a more efficient test for exact representation of F by a polynomial of degree at most d. Moreover, it extends to testing correlation in the regime where δ is smaller than 2^{-d-2}. The test chooses a random $a \leftarrow \mathbb{F}_2^k$ and outputs $\sum_{x \in A+a} F(x)$ for an arbitrary $(d + 1)$-dimensional affine subspace A. Assuming F is δ-close to a polynomial p of degree at most d, it follows from union bounds that

$$\Pr\left[\sum_{x \in A+a} F(x) \neq 0\right] \leq \Pr\left[\sum_{x \in A+a} p(x) \neq 0\right] + \Pr[F(x) \neq p(x) \text{ for some } x \in A + a]$$

$$\leq 0 + \sum_{x \in A} \Pr[F(x + a) \neq p(x + a)]$$

$$= \delta \cdot 2^{-d-1},$$

while $\Pr[\sum_{x \in A+a} R(x) \neq 0] = 1/2$ for a random function R.

The learner for exact degree-d representation from random input–output samples can also be used in a regime of very high correlation: If F is $\delta = 1/O(2^d\binom{k}{\leq d})$-close to degree d, the learner outputs the unique polynomial p that is δ-close to F with constant probability.

Noticeable correlation. In the regime $\delta \geq 2^{-d-1}$ there may be more than one polynomial of degree at most d that is δ-close to F. This imposes additional difficulties in the design and analysis of correlation tests.

The Gowers test. A natural way to test for correlation is to evaluate the expression $\sum_{x \in A} p(x)$ on a *random* affine subspace A of dimension $d + 1$. It is more convenient for the analysis to also allow degenerate subspaces (of lower dimension): The distinguisher chooses $a_0, \ldots, a_{d+1}$ independently and uniformly at random from $\mathbb{F}_2^k$, sets $A = \{a_0 + a_1 x_1 + \cdots + a_{d+1} x_{d+1} : x_1, \ldots, x_{d+1} \in \mathbb{F}_2\}$, and outputs $\sum_{x \in A} p(x)$.

Theorem 3.7.7. *The Gowers test distinguishes functions that are δ-close to degree d from a random function with advantage at least $2 \cdot (2\delta - 1)^{2^{d+1}}$.*

Proof: Gowers [68] showed that if F is δ-close to degree d then

$$\mathsf{E}_A\left[\prod_{x \in A}(-1)^{F(x)}\right] \geq (2\delta - 1)^{2^{d+1}}.$$

On the other hand, $\mathsf{E}_A[\prod_{x \in A}(-1)^{R(x)}] = 0$ for a random function R. Therefore,

$$\Pr\left[\sum_{x \in A} F(x) = 0\right] - \Pr\left[\sum_{x \in A} R(x) = 0\right]$$

$$= 2 \cdot \left(\mathsf{E}\left[\prod_{x \in A}(-1)^{F(x)}\right] - \mathsf{E}\left[\prod_{x \in A}(-1)^{R(x)}\right]\right) \geq 2 \cdot (2\delta - 1)^{2^{d+1}}.$$

$\square$

The analysis is essentially tight, as can be seen by instantiating F to a random function with $\delta 2^k$ ones. Owing to the doubly exponential dependence on d in Theorem 3.7.7, the efficiency of the Gowers test degrades rapidly with the degree.

The cylinder product test described in Section 3.7.6 extends the Gowers test to a larger class of functions. The two have identical soundness guarantees.

In Section 3.7.5 we describe a test of Razborov and Rudich [116] for correlation with rational functions, of which polynomials are a special case. The Razborov–Rudich and Gowers tests have incomparable soundness guarantees.

Weak pseudorandomness. If only random input–output samples are available, the problem of detecting correlation with linear functions (i.e., degree-1 polynomials) is polynomially equivalent to learning noisy parities [53]. For this purpose, the algorithms of Blum, Kalai, and Wasserman and Lyubashevsky discussed in Section 3.6.3 can be applied. We do not know of any results for higher degree. ⑦

3.7.5 Correlation with Rational Functions

A rational function is a ratio of two polynomials with the convention that $0/0$ may represent any value.

Definition 3.7.8. *A function* $F\colon \mathbb{F}_2^k \to \mathbb{F}_2$ *has* rational degree *at most* r *if there exist polynomials* p *and* q *of degree at most* r, *not both identically zero, such that*

$$F(x) \cdot q(x) = p(x) \qquad \text{for all } x \text{ in } \mathbb{F}_2^k. \tag{3.19}$$

Rational degree generalizes polynomial degree, which corresponds to the special case $q \equiv 1$. Representation by rational functions is in fact equivalent to one-sided representation by polynomials in the following sense:

Proposition 3.7.9 ([11]). *F has rational degree at most d if and only if there exists a nonzero polynomial P of degree at most d such that $P(x) = 0$ whenever $F(x) = b$ for some $b \in \{0, 1\}$.*

As in the case of polynomials, we say f is δ-close to rational degree at most d if there exists r of rational degree at most d such that $\Pr[f(x) \neq r(x)] \leq \delta$.

We describe and analyze two tests for correlation with rational functions of low degree. The first one applies to the high-correlation regime and can distinguish even weakly pseudorandom functions. The second one, due to Razborov and Rudich [116], is for strong pseudorandom functions but works even when the proximity parameter δ is close to $1/2$.

Exact representation and high correlation. Functions of low rational degree cannot even be weakly pseudorandom:

Proposition 3.7.10. *If $F_s\colon \mathbb{F}_2^k \to \mathbb{F}_2$ has rational degree at most d for all s then it is not a* $(\mathrm{poly}(2^d\binom{k}{\leq d}), \frac{3}{4})$-weak PRF.

Proof: The test accepts if there exist p and q that are consistent with the equations (3.19) on $m = 4 \cdot 2^d(\binom{k}{\leq d} + 1)$ samples x. This is a linear system in the coefficients of p and q, so the existence of a nonzero solution can be decided by a circuit of size polynomial in m. If $F = F_s$, a nonzero solution always exists. If, on the other hand, F is a random function, the following claim applies:

Claim 3.7.11. *If p, q are polynomials of degree at most d, not both zero, then for a random function R and a random input x, $\Pr_{R,x}[R(x) \cdot q(x) = p(x)] \leq 1 - 2^{-d-1}$.*

Proof: Since p and q are not both zero, it must be that p is nonzero or p and q are different. If p is nonzero,

$$\Pr[R(x) \cdot q(x) \neq p(x)] \geq \Pr[p(x) \neq 0] \cdot \Pr[R(x) = 0 \mid p(x) \neq 0] \geq 2^{-d} \cdot \tfrac{1}{2} = 2^{-d-1},$$

where the inequality $\Pr[p(x) \neq 0] \geq 2^{-d}$ follows by the Schwarz–Zippel lemma. If p and q are different, then $\Pr[R(x) \cdot q(x) \neq p(x)] = \Pr[(R(x)+1) \cdot q(x) \neq p(x)+q(x)]$, and the same argument applies to the functions $R + 1$, q, and $q + p$.   □

By independence and a union bound over all pairs (p, q), the probability that a random function passes the test is at most

$$\left(2^{2\binom{k}{\leq d}} - 1\right) \cdot \left(1 - 2^{-d-1}\right)^m \leq 2^{2\binom{k}{\leq d} - m \cdot 2^{-d-1}} \leq \tfrac{1}{4}$$

by the choice of m.   □

Akavia et al. [3] conjecture that the construction (3.16) instantiated with g equal to the tribes function XORed with an additional input bit is a weak PRF. Their conjecture is false as g can be seen to have rational degree at most $O(\log k)$. By Proposition 3.7.10, the resulting function family is not a $(k^{O(\log k)}, \tfrac{1}{3})$-weak PRF.

The following theorem shows, more generally, that weak PRF constructions in the class DNF $\circ \oplus$ cannot be too secure.

Theorem 3.7.12. *If $F_s \colon \{0, 1\}^k \to \{0, 1\}$ is an OR of at most t ANDs of parities of literals for all s then it is not a $(\mathrm{poly}(tk \cdot 2^{\log t \cdot \log k}), \tfrac{1}{3})$-weak PRF.*

Proof: [sketch] The distinguisher accepts if (1) F passes the test in Proposition 3.7.10 with $d = \log_2 t + 2$ or (2) the number of x such that $F(x) = 0$ is at most $2^k/3$. From the above proof and large deviation bounds, it follows that a random function is accepted with probability at most $1/3$.

When $F = F_s$, we consider two possibilities. If all AND terms of F_s have fan-in more than $\log_2 t + 2$, then by a union bound, $F_s(x)$ is nonzero with probability at most $1/4$ over the choice of x. By a large deviation bound, F_s is then rejected by test (2) with probability at most $1/3$. If, on the other hand, F_s contains an AND term with fan-in at most $\log_2 t + 2$, then this term is a nonzero polynomial of degree at most $\log_2 t + 2$ that evaluates to one whenever F_s does. By Proposition 3.7.9, F_s has rational degree $\log_2 t + 2$ and it is rejected by test (1) with probability one.   □

Proposition 3.7.10 in fact holds under the weaker assumption that F_s is $o(1/2^d \binom{k}{\leq d})$-close to rational degree d, as the probability that such a function triggers a false negative in the test is vanishingly small. Towards understanding the security of (3.16) it would be interesting to investigate the approximate rational degree of AC^0 function families. Akavia et al. show that the tribes function on n inputs is $\Omega(2^d)$-far from polynomial degree d for every $d \leq n - \omega(\log n)$. Does a similar property hold for some AC^0 function family with respect to rational degree? ⑦

Noticeable correlation. Testing for correlation with functions of low rational degree can be reduced to testing for exact representation by a rational function of degree close to $k/2$.

Proposition 3.7.13. *If F is δ-close to rational degree at most r then the linear space of solutions to (3.19) has dimension at least $\binom{k}{\leq d-r} - \delta \cdot 2^k$.*

Proof: If F is δ-close to rational degree r, then there exist polynomials p, q of degree at most r such that $F(x) \cdot q(x) \neq p(x)$ for at most $\delta 2^k$ inputs $x \in \mathbb{F}_2^k$. Consider the linear space Z of polynomials of degree at most $d - r$ that vanish on these inputs. This space has dimension at least $\binom{k}{\leq d-r} - \delta \cdot 2^k$. On the other hand, for every $z \in Z$, it holds that $F(x) \cdot p(x)z(x) = q(x)z(x)$ on all inputs $x \in \mathbb{F}_2^k$, so all pairs of the form $(pz, qz) \colon z \in Z$ are solutions to (3.19). □

We now restrict our attention to the regime $d = (k - o(\sqrt{k}))/2$. Proposition 3.7.13 then has the following asymptotic behavior for every $\delta < 1/2$ and sufficiently large k: If $r = o(\sqrt{k})$ then the dimension of the solution space is at least $(\frac{1}{2} - \delta - o(1)) \cdot 2^k$. In particular, if δ is bounded away from $\frac{1}{2}$ then the system has at least one solution. This gives the following reduction from approximate to exact rational degree:

Corollary 3.7.14. *For every $\delta < 1/2$ there exists an $\varepsilon > 0$ such that for sufficiently large k, if $F \colon \mathbb{F}_2^k \to \mathbb{F}_2$ is δ-close to rational degree at most $\varepsilon\sqrt{k}$, then F has rational degree at most $(k - \varepsilon\sqrt{k})/2$.*

On the other hand, (3.19) is a linear system of 2^k equations in $(1 - o(1)) \cdot 2^k$ unknowns. We may conjecture that, for a reasonable fraction of functions F, the equations should exhibit few linear dependencies and so the system should have no solution. Razborov and Rudich write that they have no easy proof of this conjecture. It was recently observed by Swastik Kopparty and the first author that this property follows from the asymptotic optimality of Reed–Muller codes under random erasures, which was recently proved by Kudekar et al. [86].

Proposition 3.7.15. *For every $\varepsilon > 0$, the probability that a random function $R \colon \mathbb{F}_2^k \to \mathbb{F}_2$ has rational degree at most $(k - \varepsilon\sqrt{k})/2$ approaches zero for large k.*

Proof: Kudekar et al. show that for every $\varepsilon > 0$, if E is a uniformly random subset of $\mathbb{F}_2^k$ (representing a set of erasures), every polynomial P of degree at most $d = (k - \varepsilon\sqrt{k})/2$ is uniquely determined by the evaluations $(x, P(x)) \colon x \notin E$ with probability approaching one for large k. In particular, when $P \equiv 0$, the only polynomial of degree at most d whose zeros cover the set $\overline{E}$ is the zero polynomial with probability approaching one.

For a random function R, the sets $R^{-1}(0)$ and $R^{-1}(1)$ are uniformly random subsets of $\mathbb{F}_2^k$. Therefore the probability that there exists a nonzero polynomial of degree at most d whose zeros cover $R^{-1}(0)$ or $R^{-1}(1)$ approaches zero for large k. By Proposition 3.7.9, this is exactly the probability that R has rational degree at most d.   □

We obtain the following consequence regarding the correlation of pseudorandom functions to functions of low rational degree.

Theorem 3.7.16. *For every $\delta < \frac{1}{2}$ there exists $\varepsilon > 0$ such that for sufficiently large k, if $F_s: \mathbb{F}_2^k \to \mathbb{F}_2$ is δ-close to rational degree at most $(k - \varepsilon\sqrt{k})/2$ for all s, then $\{F_s\}$ is not a $(2^{O(k)}, \frac{1}{2})$-PRF.*

Proof: By Corollary 3.7.14 and Proposition 3.7.15, the probability that a random function $R: \mathbb{F}_2^k \to \mathbb{F}_2$ is δ-close to rational degree at most $(k - \varepsilon\sqrt{k})/2$ is at most $\frac{1}{3}$ for sufficiently large k. Correlation with rational functions is testable in time $2^{O(k)}$ (the time it takes to solve (3.19)). It follows that F_s and R can be distinguished in size $2^{O(k)}$ with advantage $\frac{1}{2}$.   □

Razborov and Rudich prove a weaker version of Proposition 3.7.15. They show that for k odd and $d = (k-1)/2$ the linear space of solutions to (3.19) has dimension at most $\frac{1}{4}2^k$ with probability at least $\frac{1}{2}$ over the choice of a random R.[11] Together with Proposition 3.7.13, this establishes the conclusion of Theorem 3.7.16 under the stronger assumption $\delta < \frac{1}{4}$.

For completeness, we give an elementary proof of an even weaker dimension bound, which yields the conclusion of Theorem 3.7.16 under the assumption $\delta < \frac{1}{2}\log_2 \frac{4}{3} \approx 0.2075$.

Proposition 3.7.17. *For k odd and $d = (k-1)/2$ the linear space (p, q) of solutions to (3.19) has dimension at most $\frac{1}{2}\log_2 \frac{3}{2} \cdot 2^k + 1$ with probability at least $\frac{1}{2}$ over the choice of a random F.*

Proof: For a fixed pair q, p and a random F, the probability that Fq equals r is zero if $q(x) = 0$ and $p(x) = 1$ for any x, and $2^{-|\{x: \, q(x)=1\}|}$ if not. If p and q are chosen independently at random, we have

$$\Pr_{F,p,q} [Fq = p] = \mathop{\mathsf{E}}_{p,q} \left[\mathbf{1}(q(x) = 1 \text{ or } p(x) = 0 \text{ for all } x) \cdot 2^{-|\{x: \, q(x)=1\}|}\right].$$

Let $B = \{x: |x| < k/2\}$ and $\overline{B} = \{x: |x| > k/2\}$. By the Cauchy–Schwarz inequality, we can write

$$\Pr[Fq = r] \le \sqrt{\mathsf{E}_{q,r}[Z(B)]} \cdot \sqrt{\mathsf{E}_{q,r}[Z(\overline{B})]},$$

where

$$Z(S) = \mathbf{1}(q(x) = 1 \text{ or } p(x) = 0 \text{ for all } x \in S) \cdot 2^{-2|\{x \in S: \, q(x)=1\}|}.$$

By symmetry, $\mathsf{E}[Z(B)] = \mathsf{E}[Z(\overline{B})]$, so $\Pr[Fq = p] \le \mathsf{E}[Z(B)]$.

---

[11] In fact, they only show this holds for the q-component of the solution space, which is sufficient.

Every polynomial of degree less than $k/2$ represents a unique function from B to $\mathbb{F}_2$. (The coefficients of an interpolating polynomial for a given function can be calculated iteratively in order of increasing set size. Since the dimensions of the space of functions and the space of polynomials are both 2^{k-1}, the correspondence is one-to-one.) Therefore the values of q and r at different points in B are mutually independent and

$$\mathsf{E}[Z(B)] = \prod_{x \in B} \mathsf{E}[Z(\{x\})].$$

The value of $Z(\{x\})$ is $1/2$ conditioned on $q(x) = 0$ and $1/4$ conditioned on $q(x) = 1$, from where $\mathsf{E}[Z(\{x\})] = 3/8$ and $\mathsf{E}[Z(B)] = (3/8)^{2^{k-1}}$. It follows that the expected number of solutions (q, r) to $Fq = r$ is at most

$$2^{2^k} \cdot \Pr_{F,q,r}[Fq = r] \leq 2^{2^k} \cdot \left(\frac{3}{8}\right)^{2^{k-1}} = 2^{\frac{1}{2}\log_2 \frac{3}{2} \cdot 2^k}.$$

By Markov's inequality, the probability that the number of solutions is more than $2^{\frac{1}{2}\log_2 \frac{3}{2} \cdot 2^k + 1}$ is less than half, implying the bound on the dimension of the solution space.   □

3.7.6 Correlation with Cylinder Products

Cylinder products are functions that exhibit a "product structure" with respect to a fixed partition of the inputs. They play a central role in the study of low-complexity circuits and communication protocols. Pseudorandom synthesizers and their higher-dimensional analogues turn out to be closely related to cylinder products.

Definition 3.7.18 (Cylinder product). *Let $D_1, \ldots, D_d$ be any finite domains. A function $F \colon D_1 \times \cdots \times D_d \to \{-1, 1\}$ is a d-cylinder product[12] if it can be written as a product $F = f_1 \cdots f_d$ where the function f_i does not depend on its i-th input.*

In particular, 2-cylinder products are the functions of the form $F(x, y) = f(x) \cdot g(y)$. It is easily verified that such functions satisfy the relation

$$F(x_1, y_1) \cdot F(x_2, y_1) \cdot F(x_1, y_2) \cdot F(x_2, y_2) = 1$$

for all $x_1, x_2 \in D_1$ and $y_1, y_2 \in D_2$. In general, for a d-cylinder product F, the following expression vanishes for all $x_1, y_1 \in D_1, \ldots, x_d, y_d \in D_d$:

$$\prod_{\sigma_1 \in \{x_1, y_1\}, \ldots, \sigma_d \in \{x_d, y_d\}} F(\sigma_1, \ldots, \sigma_d). \tag{3.20}$$

The cylinder product test [50, 114, 128] evaluates (3.20) on uniformly random inputs $x_1, y_1, \ldots, x_d, y_d$. We next give an analogue of Theorem 3.7.7 for cylinder intersections.

---

[12] This is the class Π_d^* of Viola and Wigderson [128] (Section 3.1), who explain the close relation with the cylinder intersections of Babai, Nisan, and Szegedy [14].

Theorem 3.7.19. *The cylinder product test distinguishes functions that are δ-close to a d-cylinder from a random function with advantage at least $2 \cdot (2\delta - 1)^{2^d}$.*

The cylinder product test is more general than the Gowers test for the purpose of distinguishing from a random function: A degree-$(d - 1)$ polynomial from $\mathbb{F}_2^k$ to $\mathbb{F}_2$ is a d-cylinder product with respect to any product partition $\mathbb{F}_2^{k_1} \times \cdots \times \mathbb{F}_2^{k_d}$ of the input domain (with $k_1, \ldots, k_d > 0$).

The cylinder product test generalizes to functions that take values on the complex unit circle. (This requires conjugating the entries with an odd number of x_i in (3.20).)

On the complexity of synthesizers. As the 2-cylinder product test can be implemented by a two-query distinguisher for a pseudorandom synthesizer, Theorem 3.7.19 has the following corollary:

Corollary 3.7.20. *If F if $\frac{1}{2}(1 - (\varepsilon/2)^{1/4})$-close to some 2-cylinder then F is not a $(O(1), 2, \varepsilon)$-pseudorandom synthesizer.*

As 2-cylinders over $\mathbb{Z}_2^n \times \mathbb{Z}_2^n$ include all linear functions, it follows that all Fourier coefficients of a synthesizer must have negligible magnitude.

Akavia et al. [3] provide evidence that all function families in the class $AC^0 \circ \oplus$ of polynomial-size, constant-depth AND/OR circuits with a bottom layer of PARITY gates have a Fourier coefficient of magnitude at least $E(-\text{poly} \log n)$. Thus, it is conceivable that $AC^0 \circ \oplus$ circuits can compute weak PRFs (see Section 3.6.3) but not synthesizers. In contrast, Proposition 3.3.12 indicates weak PRFs can only be *more* complex than synthesizers.

To resolve this apparent contradiction, recall that the complexity of a weak PRF family $F_s(x)$ is the maximum complexity of the function F_s over all fixings of the key s. The induced synthesizer $S(s, x) = F_s(x)$ is a function of both the key and the input of the original PRF. The function S could have high complexity, but reduce to a function of lower complexity once s is fixed.

This phenomenon is exemplified by the LWR problem from Section 3.4.2: For every fixing of the key $\mathbf{s}$, the function $F_{\mathbf{s}}(\mathbf{a}) = \lfloor \langle \mathbf{a}, \mathbf{s} \rangle \rceil_p$ (see (3.11)) has a large Fourier coefficient over $\mathbb{Z}_q^k$ (the coefficient $\hat{F}_{\mathbf{s}}(\mathbf{s})$), while all the Fourier coefficients of the corresponding synthesizer are small.

3.7.7 Statistical Queries

Random input–output pairs $(x, F(x))$ can be used as samples to estimate statistics $E\phi = E_x[\phi(x, F(x))]$ for various real-valued functions ϕ. If ϕ is bounded in the range $[-1, 1]$, then about $1/\varepsilon^2$ samples are needed to estimate the statistic within error ε with constant probability. Many known algorithms for learning from random examples operate in this manner: The algorithm computes estimates of $E\phi$ for all ϕ in some fixed class of real-valued functions Φ and outputs the value of some function of these estimates only. The algorithm of Linial, Mansour, and Nisan for low-weight Fourier learning is one such example.

The statistical query learning model [81] captures this class of algorithms. The following pseudorandomness property is necessary and sufficient for functions to be hard to learn in this model [47]. It postulates that any statistic of the queried function should be close in value to what is expected for a random function.

Definition 3.7.21 (Pseudorandomness against statistical queries). *The family $\{F_s\}$ is (ε, δ)-pseudorandom against statistical queries Φ if, with probability at least $1 - \delta$ over the choice of s,*

$$\left| \underset{x}{\mathrm{E}}[\phi(x, F_s(x))] - \underset{x,R}{\mathrm{E}}[\phi(x, R(x))] \right| \leq \varepsilon$$

for all ϕ in Φ.

For Boolean-valued functions, pairwise independence is sufficient to ensure pseudorandomness against statistical queries.

Lemma 3.7.22. *Let Φ be any set of $[-1, 1]$-valued functions. If $F_s: \{0,1\}^k \to \{-1, 1\}$ is pairwise independent then it is $(\sqrt{2|\Phi|/\delta 2^k}, \delta)$-pseudorandom against Φ.*

Proof: Any statistical query can be written as a combination of two *correlation queries* [47]:

$$\underset{x}{\mathrm{E}}[\phi(x, F(x))] = \underset{x}{\mathrm{E}}\left[\phi(x, -1) \cdot \frac{1 - f(x)}{2} + \phi(x, 1) \cdot \frac{1 + f(x)}{2}\right]$$

$$= \tfrac{1}{2}\underset{x}{\mathrm{E}}[\phi(x, 1) \cdot F(x)] - \tfrac{1}{2}\underset{x}{\mathrm{E}}[\phi(x, -1) \cdot F(x)] + \tfrac{1}{2}\underset{x}{\mathrm{E}}[\phi(x, 1) + \phi(x, -1)].$$

The last term is independent of F, so we can bound the distinguishing advantage of ϕ by

$$\left| \underset{x}{\mathrm{E}}[\phi(x, F_s(x))] - \underset{x,R}{\mathrm{E}}[\phi(x, R(x))] \right| \leq \tfrac{1}{2}\left|\underset{x}{\mathrm{E}}[\phi(x, 1) \cdot F_s(x)] - \underset{x,R}{\mathrm{E}}[\phi(x, 1) \cdot R(x)]\right|$$

$$+ \tfrac{1}{2}\left|\underset{x}{\mathrm{E}}[\phi(x, -1) \cdot F_s(x)] - \underset{x,R}{\mathrm{E}}[\phi(x, -1) \cdot R(x)]\right|$$

$$= \tfrac{1}{2}\left|\underset{x}{\mathrm{E}}[\phi(x, 1) \cdot F_s(x)]\right| + \tfrac{1}{2}\left|\underset{x}{\mathrm{E}}[\phi(x, -1) \cdot F_s(x)]\right|.$$

It therefore suffices to bound $|\mathrm{E}_x[\psi(x) \cdot F_s(x)]|$ for an arbitrary set of $2|\Phi|$ functions $\psi: \{0,1\}^k \to [-1, 1]$. We apply the second-moment method. Since every bit of F_s is uniformly distributed, $\mathrm{E}_s\, \mathrm{E}_x[\psi(x) \cdot F_s(x)]$ equals zero. For the second moment, write

$$\underset{s}{\mathrm{E}}[\underset{x}{\mathrm{E}}[\psi(x) \cdot F_s(x)]^2] = \underset{s}{\mathrm{E}}[\underset{x,y}{\mathrm{E}}[\psi(x)F_s(x) \cdot \psi(y)F_s(y)]]$$

$$= \underset{x,y}{\mathrm{E}}[\psi(x)\psi(y)\underset{s}{\mathrm{E}}[F_s(x) \cdot F_s(y)]]$$

$$= \underset{x,y}{\mathrm{E}}[\psi(x)\psi(y)\mathbf{1}(x = y)]$$

$$\leq \Pr[x = y].$$

This is the collision probability of the uniform distribution, which equals $1/2^k$. By Chebyshev's inequality, the probability that $|E_s[\psi(x) \cdot F_s(x)]|$ exceeds $\sqrt{2|\Phi|}/\delta 2^k$ is at most $\delta/2|\Phi|$. The lemma follows by taking a union bound over all ψ. □

It would be interesting to investigate if an analogous statement holds for adaptive distinguishers. ⑦

A variant of this proof appears in the work of Akavia et al. [3]. In particular, since the function family $H_{A,b}(x) = Ax + b$ is pairwise independent, construction (3.16) is pseudorandom against statistical queries.

3.8 Contemporary Constructions

> *The dishwasher is a gift of nature!*
> SILVIO MICALI (1980s)

We present two contemporary extensions of PRFs and describe some of their applications. A *key-homomorphic* PRF allows for the efficient evaluation of $F_{s_1+s_2}(x)$ given the values $F_{s_1}(x)$ and $F_{s_2}(x)$. In a *puncturable* PRF the adversary obtains code for evaluating F_s everywhere but at a single input $\mathring{x}$ of its choice and cannot distinguish the value $F_s(\mathring{x})$ from a random one.

Puncturable PRFs are an indispensable tool in applications of *indistinguishability obfuscation*, an intriguing concept that has attracted recent interest. Sahai and Waters used puncturable PRFs together with indistinguishability obfuscation to convert certain private-key encryption schemes into public-key ones. We provide a self-contained treatment of their result.

3.8.1 Key-Homomorphic PRFs

Key-homomorphic PRFs were introduced by Naor, Pinkas, and Reingold [103], who constructed, in the random oracle model, a very simple key-homomorphic PRF family assuming the DDH problem is hard.

Definition 3.8.1 (Key-homomorphic PRF). *Let $\mathbb{S}$ and $\mathbb{G}$ be Abelian groups. We say that a family $\{F_s: \{0,1\}^k \to \mathbb{G}\}$ of functions, indexed by $s \in \mathbb{S}$, is key homomorphic if for every $s_1, s_2 \in \mathbb{S}$ and every $x \in \{0,1\}^k$, it holds that*

$$F_{s_1}(x) + F_{s_2}(x) = F_{s_1+s_2}(x).$$

Recently, Boneh et al. [40] constructed the first (almost) key-homomorphic PRF without random oracles. The construction is based on the LWE problem, and builds upon ideas used in the non-key-homomorphic LWE-based PRFs of Banerjee, Peikert, and Rosen [17], and specifically on the reduction from LWE to LWR (Proposition 3.4.3). The Boneh et al. construction was subsequently generalized by Banerjee and Peikert [16], resulting in higher efficiency and tighter security reductions.

Constructions in the random oracle model. Let $\mathbb{G}$ be a finite cyclic group of prime order q and let $H\colon \{0,1\}^k \to \mathbb{G}$ be a function modeled as a random oracle. Define the function $F_s\colon \{0,1\}^k \to \mathbb{G}$, keyed by $s \in \mathbb{Z}_q$, as

$$F_s(x) = H(x)^s \in \mathbb{G}.$$

Since $F_{s_1}(x) \cdot F_{s_2}(x) = H(x)^{s_1+s_2} = F_{s_1+s_2}(x)$ then F_s is key homomorphic. Naor, Pinkas, and Reingold [103] proved that $\{F_s\}$ is a PRF family in the random oracle model, assuming DDH is hard in $\mathbb{G}$ (see Section 3.4.1 for a description of DDH).

Similarly, it is possible to construct (almost) key-homomorphic PRFs from the LWR problem in the random oracle model [40]. Let $p < q$ and let $H\colon \{0,1\}^k \to \mathbb{Z}_q$ be a function modeled as a random oracle. Define the function $F_s\colon \{0,1\}^k \to \mathbb{Z}_p$ as

$$F_s(x) = \lfloor \langle H(x), s \rangle \rceil_p, \tag{3.21}$$

where $\lfloor x \rceil_p$ equals $\lfloor (p/q) \cdot x \bmod q \rceil \bmod p$. The function can be shown to be a secure PRF in the random oracle model, assuming the LWR problem is hard (see Section 3.4.2 for a description of LWR). Because rounding is not linear, the function F_s is not actually key homomorphic. However it is *almost* key homomorphic in that

$$F_{s_1}(x) + F_{s_2}(x) - F_{s_1+s_2}(x) \in \{-1, 0, 1\}.$$

This relaxed property turns out to be sufficient for many applications.

Application I: Distributed PRFs. Distributed PRFs support splitting of the secret key among n servers so that at least t servers are needed to evaluate the PRF. Evaluating the PRF is done without reconstructing the key at a single location. This can be useful, for instance, in mitigating the risk of master key leakage, as described in Section 3.1.1 (in the context of key derivation).

Key-homomorphic PRFs give a simple, one-round solution to this problem. For instance, for n-out-of-n sharing, server i stores a random key s_i and the overall PRF key is $s = s_1 + \cdots + s_n$. To evaluate $F_s(x)$ the client sends x to all servers and each server responds with $y_i = F_{s_i}(x)$. The client combines the results to obtain $F_s(x)$ using the key-homomorphism property.

For t-out-of-n sharing, the client first homomorphically multiplies the responses from the key servers by the appropriate Lagrange coefficients and then applies key homomorphism to add the results. This still works with an almost key-homomorphic PRF as long as the PRF range is sufficiently larger than the error term. The homomorphism error is eliminated by setting the output to the high-order bits of the computed value $F_s(x)$.

Application II: Proxy re-encryption. Given a ciphertext encrypted under one symmetric key, we would like to enable a proxy to transform the ciphertext to an encryption under a different symmetric key without knowledge of either key. To this end, the proxy is provided with a short re-encryption token t. Consider a ciphertext of the form $(r, F_s(r) + m)$ where F_s is a key-homomorphic PRF. To re-encrypt from key s to key s', one sends the re-encryption token $t = -s + s'$ to the proxy, who computes $F_t(r)$ and adds it to $F_s(r) + m$ to obtain $F_{s+t}(r) + m = F_{s'}(r) + m$.

This also works with an almost key-homomorphic PRF except that here we pad each message m with a small number of zeros on the right to ensure that the small additive error term does not affect the encrypted plaintext after several re-encryptions.

Constructions without random oracles. The Boneh et al. PRF [40] is indexed by two public matrices $\mathbf{A}_0, \mathbf{A}_1 \in \{0,1\}^{n \times n}$, both sampled uniformly at random. The (secret) key for the PRF is a vector $\mathbf{s} \in \mathbb{Z}_q^n$. The PRF $F_\mathbf{s} \colon \{0,1\}^k \to \mathbb{Z}_p^n$ is defined as

$$F_\mathbf{s}(x) = \left\lfloor \mathbf{s}^\mathsf{T} \cdot \prod_{i=1}^k \mathbf{A}_{x_i} \right\rceil_p. \tag{3.22}$$

The function $F_\mathbf{s}$ satisfies $F_{\mathbf{s}_1}(x) + F_{\mathbf{s}_2}(x) - F_{\mathbf{s}_1+\mathbf{s}_2}(x) \in \{-1,0,1\}^n$. It is thus almost key homomorphic in the same sense as the function F_s from (3.21).

The Banerjee–Peikert (BP) almost key-homomorphic PRF is a generalization of the Boneh et al. construction. A basic tool underlying the construction is the *bit decomposition* operator, which allows one to control the magnitude of individual entries in a matrix. Let $\ell = \lfloor \log q \rfloor$, and for each $a \in \mathbb{Z}_q$, identify it with its unique integer residue in $\{0, \ldots, q-1\}$. Define the bit decomposition function $\mathbf{d} \colon \mathbb{Z}_q \to \{0,1\}^\ell$ as

$$\mathbf{d}(a) = (x_0, x_1, \ldots, x_{\ell-1}),$$

where $a = \sum_{i=0}^{\ell-1} x_i 2^i$ is the binary representation of a. Similarly, define the function $\mathbf{D} \colon \mathbb{Z}_q^{n \times m} \to \{0,1\}^{n\ell \times m}$ by applying $\mathbf{d}$ entry-wise.

For a full (but not necessarily complete) binary tree T, let $|T|$ denote the number of its leaves. If $|T| \geq 1$, let $T.l, T.r$ denote the left and right subtrees of T, and for a string $x \in \{0,1\}^{|T|}$ write $x = (x_l, x_r)$ for $x_l \in \{0,1\}^{|T.l|}$ and $x_r \in \{0,1\}^{|T.r|}$.

Public parameters: Moduli $q \gg p$, matrices $\mathbf{A}_0, \mathbf{A}_1 \in \mathbb{Z}_q^{n \times n\ell}$, and a binary tree T
Function key: A random $\mathbf{s} \in \mathbb{Z}_q^n$
Function evaluation: On input $x \in \{0,1\}^{|T|}$ define $F = F_\mathbf{s} \colon \{0,1\}^{|T|} \to \mathbb{Z}_p^n$ as

$$F_\mathbf{s}(x) = \left\lfloor \mathbf{s}^\mathsf{T} \cdot \mathbf{A}_T(x) \right\rceil_p,$$

where the function $\mathbf{A}_T \colon \{0,1\}^{|T|} \to \mathbb{Z}_q^{n \times n\ell}$ is defined recursively as

$$\mathbf{A}_T(x) = \begin{cases} \mathbf{A}_x, & \text{if } |T| = 1 \\ \mathbf{A}_{T.l}(x_l) \cdot \mathbf{D}(\mathbf{A}_{T.r}(x_r)), & \text{otherwise} \end{cases}$$

Size: $\operatorname{poly}(k,n)$
Depth: $O(s(T))$

Fig. 3.10: The Banerjee–Peikert key-homomorphic PRF

The BP function generalizes the function of Boneh et al. This can be seen by setting public parameters $\mathbf{B}_b = \mathbf{D}(\mathbf{A}_b)$ and a left-spine tree T (as in Figure 3.11.(a)), which (after a minor adaptation) yields the construction $F_\mathbf{s}(x) = \left\lfloor \mathbf{s}^\mathsf{T} \cdot \prod_i \mathbf{B}_{x_i} \right\rceil_p$ from (3.22).

Sequentiality and expansion.   In terms of efficiency, the cost of computing $F_\mathbf{s}(x)$ is dominated by the evaluation of $A_T(x)$. Since linear operations over $\mathbb{Z}_q$ can be computed by depth-one (unbounded fan-in) arithmetic circuits, the circuit depth of the construction is proportional to the maximum nesting depth of $\mathbf{D}(\cdot)$ terms when one unwinds A_T. This is the *sequentiality*, $s(T)$, which measures the right depth of the tree, i.e., the maximum number of right edges over all root-to-leaf paths.

For security based on the hardness of the LWE problem, the public parameters $\mathbf{A}_0, \mathbf{A}_1$ and the secret key $\mathbf{s}$ are sampled uniformly at random over $\mathbb{Z}_q$. The modulus q and underlying LWE error rate, and hence also the dimension n needed to obtain a desired level of security, are determined by the maximum number of terms of the form $\mathbf{D}(\cdot)$ that are consecutively multiplied when one unwinds the recursive definition of A_T. This is the *expansion* $e(T)$, which measures the left depth of the tree, i.e., the maximum number of left edges over all root-to-leaf paths.

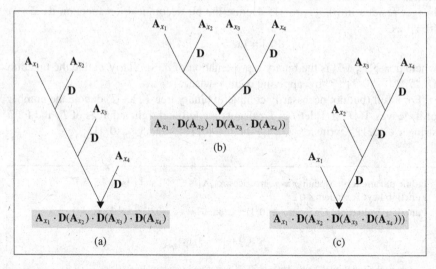

Fig. 3.11: Instantiations of the Banerjee–Peikert PRF. All functions are on four inputs with the following sequentiality (s)/expansion (e) tradeoffs: (a) $s = 1, e = 3$, (b) $s = e = 2$, (c) $s = 3, e = 1$

Theorem 3.8.2 ([16]). *If the LWE problem is* $(t, mn\ell, \varepsilon)$-*hard for some B-bounded error distribution then* $\{F_\mathbf{s}\}$ *as defined in Figure 3.10 is an almost key-homomorphic* (t', ε')-*pseudorandom function family, where*

$$t' = t - \text{poly}(n, m, k), \quad \text{and} \quad \varepsilon' = pB(n\ell)^{e(T)}/q + \text{poly}(\varepsilon).$$

The use of a left-spine tree T (as in Figure 3.11 (a)) yields a maximally parallel instantiation: Its sequentiality is $s(T) = 1$. This instantiation, however, also has maximal expansion $e(T) = |T|-1$. In Theorem 3.8.2, the modulus q and error parameter $1/p$ have to grow exponentially with $e(T)$, so using a tree with large expansion leads to a strong hardness assumption on LWE, and therefore large secret keys and public parameters. Other trees give different sequentiality/expansion tradeoffs (as in Figure 3.11 (b) and (c)).

Efficiency. The cost of computing $F_\mathbf{s}(x)$ is dominated by the evaluation of $A_T(x)$, which can be done publicly without any knowledge of the secret key s. This property can be very useful for the efficiency of certain applications, such as the homomorphic evaluation of $F_\mathbf{s}$ given an encryption of s (see Section 3.1.1).

In addition, if $A_T(x)$ has been computed and all the intermediate matrices saved, then $A_T(x)$ can be incrementally updated for an x' that differs from x in just one bit. As discussed in Sections 3.4.1 and 3.4.2, this can significantly speed up successive evaluations of $F_\mathbf{s}$ on related inputs, e.g., in a counter-like mode using a Gray code.

3.8.2 Puncturable PRFs

> *I cannot relate to emotional statements. Which of the words here is incorrect?*
> LEONID LEVIN (1989)

A function family is puncturable if it can be evaluated at all but a single point $\mathring{x}$ and its value at this point is secret [84, 43]. The GGM construction has this property, so a puncturable PRF can in principle be obtained from any one-way function.

Sahai and Waters [121] show how to build public-key encryption from any puncturable function family using an indistinguishability obfuscator. Their construction has yet to produce encryption schemes that are as practical as available alternatives. Moreover, the existence of efficient and secure indistinguishability obfuscators is currently a subject of debate. Despite these shortcomings, the methodology holds significant conceptual appeal: If indistinguishability obfuscation is possible then public-key encryption can be constructed generically from any one-way function.

Definition 3.8.3 (Puncturable function family). *A* puncturing *of a function family F_s is a pair of deterministic algorithms* Gen *and* $\mathring{F}$ *such that for all s, $\mathring{x}$, and $x \neq \mathring{x}$, $\mathring{F}_{\mathring{s}}(x) = F_s(x)$, where $\mathring{s} = $ Gen$(s, \mathring{x})$. The puncturing is (t, ε)-secure if the distributions $(\mathring{s}, F_s(\mathring{x}))$ and $(\mathring{s}, r)$ are (t, ε)-indistinguishable for every $\mathring{x}$.*

Every puncturable function family is a PRF, but the opposite may not hold. A PRF distinguisher can only make black-box queries to the function, while the adversary to a puncturable function family has a circuit that evaluates the PRF everywhere except at the challenge point. It may be interesting to study under which conditions the two notions can be formally separated. ⊘

Proposition 3.8.4. √*If F_s has a (t, ε)-secure puncturing of size at most c then it is a $(t - qc, q, q\varepsilon)$-PRF for every q.*

Proof: Assume F_s is not a $(t - qc, q, q\varepsilon)$-PRF. By a hybrid argument the following two games are $(t - qc, \varepsilon)$-distinguishable for some $i \le q$:

Answer the first $q - i$ queries randomly and the other i according to F_s.
Answer the first $q - i - 1$ queries randomly and the other $i + 1$ according to F_s.

After fixing the first $q - i - 1$ answers to maximize the distinguishing advantage we obtain that the games

F: Answer all i queries according to F_s
R: Answer the first query randomly and the other $i - 1$ according to F_s

are also $(t - qc, \varepsilon)$-distinguishable. Let $\mathring{x}$ be the first query made by the distinguisher D of size at most $t - qc$ and $\mathring{s} = \mathrm{Gen}(s, \mathring{x})$. The following circuit A of size t then breaks the assumed security of puncturing: Given a challenge $(\mathring{s}, y)$, emulate D by answering the first query by y and every subsequent query $x \ne \mathring{x}$ by $\mathring{F}_{\mathring{s}}(x)$. By the functionality of puncturing, $A(\mathring{s}, F_s(\mathring{x})) = D^F$ and $A(\mathring{s}, r) = D^R$, so the distributions $(\mathring{s}, F_s(\mathring{x}))$ and $(\mathring{s}, r)$ are (t, ε)-distinguishable.   □

A puncturable PRF.   The PRF F_s of Goldreich, Goldwasser, and Micali from Section 3.3.1 is puncturable. The puncturing is specified recursively by

$$\mathrm{Gen}(s, \mathring{a}\mathring{x}) = (\mathring{a}, G_{1-\mathring{a}}(s), \mathrm{Gen}(G_{\mathring{a}}(s), \mathring{x})),$$

$$\mathring{F}_{(\mathring{a}, y, g)}(ax) = \begin{cases} F_y(x), & \text{if } a \ne \mathring{a} \\ \mathring{F}_g(x), & \text{if } a = \mathring{a}, \end{cases}$$

where $a, \mathring{a} \in \{0, 1\}$ and $x, \mathring{x} \in \{0, 1\}^{k-1}$. In the base case $k = 0$, Gen and Eval output an empty string. The functionality requirement follows from the definition of the GGM pseudorandom function. See Figure 3.12 for an example.

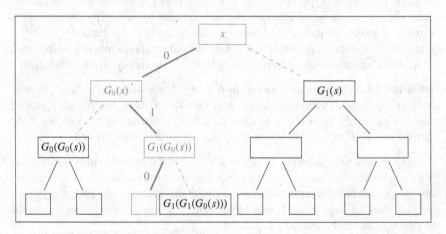

Fig. 3.12: The GGM function family punctured at $\mathring{x} = 010$. The punctured key is $\mathring{s} = (0, G_1(s), 1, G_0(G_0(s)), 0, G_1(G_1(G_0(s))))$

Proposition 3.8.5. *If G is a (t, ε)-PRG of size c then $(\text{Gen}, \mathring{F})$ is a $(t - O(ck^3), 2k\varepsilon)$-secure puncturing of F_s.*

Proof: We prove the proposition by induction on k. When $k = 0$, $(\mathring{s}, F_s(\lambda))$ and $(\mathring{s}, r)$ are both distributed like (λ, s), so the two distributions are identical. Here λ is the empty string.

Now assume $(t - O(c(k-1)^3), 2(k-1)\varepsilon)$-security holds for input length $k - 1$, namely the distributions

$$(\text{Gen}'(s, \mathring{x}), F'_s(\mathring{x})) \quad \text{and} \quad (\text{Gen}'(s, \mathring{x}), r)$$

are $(t - O(c(k-1)^3), 2(k-1)\varepsilon)$-indistinguishable for all $\mathring{x} \in \{0,1\}^{k-1}$. Here, F'_s is the GGM construction on input size $k - 1$ and Gen' is the corresponding punctured key-generation algorithm.

Claim 3.8.6. *The distributions*

$$(\text{Gen}(s, \mathring{a}\mathring{x}), F_s(\mathring{a}\mathring{x})) = (\mathring{a}, G_{1-\mathring{a}}(s), \text{Gen}'(G_{\mathring{a}}(s), \mathring{x}), F'_{G_{\mathring{a}}(s)}(\mathring{x})) \quad and$$
$$(\text{Gen}(s, \mathring{a}\mathring{x}), r) = (\mathring{a}, G_{1-\mathring{a}}(s), \text{Gen}'(G_{\mathring{a}}(s), \mathring{x}), r)$$

are $(t - O(ck^3), 2k\varepsilon)$-indistinguishable for every $\mathring{a} \in \{0,1\}$ and $\mathring{x} \in \{0,1\}^{k-1}$.

Proof: Since G is (t, ε)-pseudorandom and Gen' can be computed using $O(k^2)$ calls to G, these two distributions are $(t - O(ck^2), \varepsilon)$-indistinguishable from

$$(\mathring{a}, r_1, \text{Gen}'(r_0, \mathring{x}), F'_{r_0}(\mathring{x})) \quad \text{and} \quad (\mathring{a}, r_1, \text{Gen}'(r_0, \mathring{x}), r), \tag{3.23}$$

respectively, for random strings r_0 and r_1 of length n. The distributions (3.23) are $(t - O(c(k-1)^3), 2(k-1)\varepsilon)$-indistinguishable by inductive assumption. The claim follows by the triangle inequality.   □

This completes the inductive step.   □

From private-key to public-key encryption. Much cryptographic evidence suggests that public-key encryption needs to be based on the hardness of "structured" problems such as discrete logarithms or finding close vectors in lattices. In contrast, private-key encryption follows from the existence of one-way functions, which are seemingly abundant. This divide is explained by theoretical results that rule out a fully-black-box construction of key exchange from one-way functions [77, 75].

On the other hand, there is an appealing blueprint for upgrading encryption from private-key to public-key: Publish an obfuscation of the encryption circuit as the public key. Assuming the encryption circuit can be obfuscated in the "virtual black-box" (VBB) sense, the resulting public-key scheme can be proved secure. Unfortunately, VBB obfuscation is impossible for all but a few rudimentary classes of functions [19].

Sahai and Waters propose applying this transformation to a variant of the private-key encryption scheme (3.2) that was analyzed in Section 3.2.4. They show that the resulting public-key scheme is secure under the assumption that the obfuscator satisfies the seemingly weaker security notion of indistinguishability [19]. Garg et al. [57] give a candidate construction of an indistinguishability obfuscator. However this and related candidates were subsequently shown to be insecure. The feasibility of indistinguishability obfuscation is currently a highly active research area. Whether such obfuscation is attainable in its most general form is still uncertain.

Circuits C_0 and C_1 are *functionally equivalent* if $C_0(x) = C_1(x)$ for all x. Let **C**, **C'** denote the classes of circuits of sizes c and c', respectively.

Definition 3.8.7 (Indistinguishability obfuscation [19]). *We say that a probabilistic function* iO: **C** $\to$ **C'** *is a* (t,ε)-*indistinguishability obfuscator if, for all* $C \in$ **C**, *it holds that* iO(C) *and* C *are functionally equivalent with probability 1 (functionality), and for all pairs of functionally equivalent circuits* $C_0, C_1 \in$ **C** *the distributions* iO(C_0) *and* iO(C_1) *are* (t,ε)-*indistinguishable (indistinguishability).*

The construction of Sahai and Waters relies on the existence of a puncturable family $F_s : \{0,1\}^{2n} \to \{0,1\}^{\ell}$, a PRG $G : \{0,1\}^{n} \to \{0,1\}^{2n}$, and an indistinguishability obfuscator iO. The starting point is the following variant of the private-key encryption scheme (3.2):

$$\text{Enc}'_s(m; r) = (G(r), F_s(G(r)) \oplus m), \qquad \text{Dec}'_s(y, z) = F_s(y) \oplus z. \qquad (3.24)$$

The public-key encryption scheme of Sahai and Waters is shown in Figure 3.13. Its functionality follows from the functionality of indistinguishability obfuscation and the private-key scheme (Enc', Dec').

Private key: A key s for the scheme (Enc', Dec')
Public key: The circuit $pk = $ iO(Enc$'_s$)

Encryption/decryption: For message $m \in \{0,1\}^{\ell}$ and randomness $r \in \{0,1\}^{n}$

$$\text{Enc}_{pk}(m; r) = pk(m; r), \qquad \text{Dec}_s(y, z) = \text{Dec}'_s(y, z).$$

Fig. 3.13: The Sahai–Waters public-key encryption scheme

Proposition 3.8.8 ([121]). *Suppose that* $\{F_s\}$ *is a* (t,ε)-*puncturable family, that G is a* (t,ε)-*pseudorandom generator, and that* iO *is a* (t,ε)-*indistinguishability obfuscator, all of size at most c. Then for every two messages* $m_0, m_1 \in \{0,1\}^{\ell}$, *the following games are* $(t - O(c), 6\varepsilon + 2 \cdot 2^{-n})$-*indistinguishable:*

E_0: *Sample* pk, s, r *and output* $(pk, \text{Enc}_{pk}(m_0; r))$.
E_1: *Sample* pk, s, r *and output* $(pk, \text{Enc}_{pk}(m_1; r))$.

Proof: For $b \in \{0,1\}$ consider the following sequence of games:

E_b: Sample random s, r and $pk = \text{iO}(\text{Enc}'_s)$. Output $(pk, G(r), F_s(G(r)) \oplus m_b)$.
Y_b: Sample random $s, \mathring{y}$ and $pk = \text{iO}(\text{Enc}'_s)$. Output $(pk, \mathring{y}, F_s(\mathring{y}) \oplus m_b)$.
H_b: Sample random $s, \mathring{y} \notin \text{Im}(G)$ and $pk = \text{iO}(\text{Enc}'_s)$. Output $(pk, \mathring{y}, F_s(\mathring{y}) \oplus m_b)$.
$\mathring{F}_b$: Sample random $s, \mathring{y} \notin \text{Im}(G)$ and $\mathring{pk} = \text{iO}(\mathring{\text{Enc}}_{\mathring{s}})$. Output $(\mathring{pk}, \mathring{y}, F_s(\mathring{y}) \oplus m_b)$.
R: Sample random $s, \mathring{y} \notin \text{Im}(G), r$ and let $\mathring{pk}$ be as in $\mathring{H}_b$. Output $(\mathring{pk}, \mathring{y}, r)$.

In the game $\mathring{F}_b$, we set $\mathring{s} = \text{Gen}(s, \mathring{y})$, and $\mathring{\text{Enc}}_{\mathring{s}}(m; r) = (G(r), \mathring{F}_{\mathring{s}}(G(r)) \oplus m)$.

Claim 3.8.9. E_b and Y_b are $(t - c, \varepsilon)$-indistinguishable.

Proof: The claim follows from the pseudorandomness of G and from the fact that iO is of size at most c. □

Claim 3.8.10. Y_b and H_b are $(\infty, 2^{-n})$-indistinguishable.

Proof: The distribution H_b is Y_b conditioned on $\mathring{y}$ not landing in the image of G. By a union bound, the probability of this event is at most

$$\Pr[\mathring{y} \in \text{Im}(G)] \leq \sum_r \Pr[\mathring{y} = G(r)] \leq 2^n \cdot 2^{-2n} = 2^{-n}. \tag{3.25}$$

□

Claim 3.8.11. H_b and $\mathring{F}_b$ are (t, ε)-indistinguishable.

Proof: Fix s and $\mathring{y}$ to maximize the distinguishing advantage. After fixing, the distributions reduce to $\text{iO}(\text{Enc}'_s)$ and $\text{iO}(\mathring{\text{Enc}}_{\mathring{s}})$ (plus some fixed bits). Owing to the assumption $\mathring{y} \notin \text{Im}(G)$, the circuits Enc'_s and $\mathring{\text{Enc}}_{\mathring{s}}$ are functionally equivalent, so indistinguishability follows from the security of iO. □

Claim 3.8.12. $\mathring{F}_b$ and R are $(t - O(c), \varepsilon)$-indistinguishable.

Proof: Fix $\mathring{y}$ to maximize the distinguishing advantage. By the security of puncturing, $(\mathring{s}, F_s(\mathring{y}))$ and $(\mathring{s}, r)$ are (t, ε)-indistinguishable. Then the distributions

$$(\text{iO}(\mathring{\text{Enc}}_{\mathring{s}}), \mathring{y}, F_s(\mathring{y}) \oplus m_b) \quad \text{and} \quad (\text{iO}(\mathring{\text{Enc}}_{\mathring{s}}), \mathring{y}, r \oplus m_b)$$

are $(t - O(c), \varepsilon)$-indistinguishable. These are identical to $\mathring{F}_b$ and R, respectively. □

The proposition follows by applying the triangle inequality to the sequence of distributions $E_0, Y_0, H_0, \mathring{F}_0, R, \mathring{F}_1, H_1, Y_1, E_1$. □

The proof generalizes to the stronger adaptive security notion in which the challenge messages m_0 and m_1 are chosen after observing the public key.

Constrained PRFs and witness PRFs. *Constrained PRFs* extend puncturable PRFs in that they allow for more general constraints than mere puncturing [41, 84, 43]. A constrained PRF can be evaluated at any input x that satisfies some constraint circuit $C(x)$, but the constrained key reveals no information about the PRF values at points that do not satisfy the constraint to a computationally bounded adversary.

Brakerski and Vaikutanatan [44] construct an LWE-based function of constraint PRFs. Boneh and Waters [41] consider a more general definition in which security holds even if the adversary is given multiple constrained keys derived from different circuits. They give candidate constructions for restricted circuit classes whose security is based on strong hardness assumptions related to multilinear maps. ⑦

An even more intriguing notion is that of a *witness PRF* [132], which can be seen as a nondeterministic analogue of a constrained PRF. Here the constrained key allows for evaluation of $F_s(x)$, but only if the evaluator is also given a witness w that satisfies the constraint circuit $C(x, w)$. If no such w exists, the adversary obtains no information about the value $F_s(x)$. Witness PRFs are sufficient to realize some of the most interesting applications of indistinguishability obfuscation. What makes them intriguing is the possibility of constructing them from more standard hardness assumptions than the ones currently used to construct obfuscation. ⑦

Open Questions

> In the established physical sciences ... a rich intellectual structure has been uncovered that reveals at any time a wide range of unsolved problems or puzzles. Solutions to these provide increased understanding of the field and further enrich the structure. As long as successful problem solving continues, progress is close to being guaranteed. The possibility of almost routine progress of this nature appears to be a fundamental aspect of science. Even if it is not the most celebrated aspect, it may be the most characteristic one.
>
> LESLIE VALIANT (*Circuits of the Mind*, 1999)

Acknowledgements

This survey is dedicated to Oded Goldreich, a towering and charismatic figure, who has inspired generations of researchers through his limitless passion and devotion to intellectual inquiry. Oded has been and continues to be a dear mentor to us all, and sets a very high bar to aspire to. Without theory there would be chaos, and without Oded Goldreich there would be no theory as we know it.

We are deeply indebted to Shafi Goldwasser, Siyao Guo, Silvio Micali, Moni Naor, Chris Peikert, Omer Reingold, and Vinod Vaikuntanathan for invaluable advice. Last but not least, thanks to Yehuda Lindell for this wonderful initiative and for confidently steering the project into safe harbor.

Alon Rosen's work on this project was supported by ISF grant no. 1255/12, NSF-BSF Cyber Security and Privacy grant no. 2014/632, and by the ERC under the EU's Seventh Framework Programme (FP/2007-2013) ERC Grant Agreement no. 307952. Andrej Bogdanov's work was supported by Hong Kong RGC GRF grant CUHK14208215.

References

[1] William Aiello and Ramarathnam Venkatesan. Foiling birthday attacks in length-doubling transformations - Beneš: A non-reversible alternative to Feistel. In *Proceedings of EUROCRYPT '96*, volume 1070, pages 307–320, 1996.

[2] Adi Akavia. Solving hidden number problem with one bit oracle and advice. In *Advances in Cryptology - CRYPTO 2009: 29th Annual International Cryptology Conference*, pages 337–354, Berlin, Heidelberg, 2009. Springer Berlin Heidelberg.

[3] Adi Akavia, Andrej Bogdanov, Siyao Guo, Akshay Kamath, and Alon Rosen. Candidate weak pseudorandom functions in $AC^0 \circ MOD_2$. In *Innovations in Theoretical Computer Science, ITCS'14, Princeton, NJ, USA, January 12-14, 2014*, pages 251–260, 2014.

[4] N. Alon and J.H. Spencer. *The Probabilistic Method*. Wiley Series in Discrete Mathematics and Optimization. Wiley, 2008.

[5] Noga Alon, Oded Goldreich, Johan Hastad, and René Peralta. Simple construction of almost k-wise independent random variables. *Random Struct. Algorithms*, 3(3):289–304, 1992.

[6] Jacob Alperin-Sheriff and Daniel Apon. Dimension-preserving reductions from LWE to LWR. *IACR Cryptology ePrint Archive*, 2016:589, 2016.

[7] Joël Alwen, Stephan Krenn, Krzysztof Pietrzak, and Daniel Wichs. Learning with rounding, revisited - new reduction, properties and applications. In *Advances in Cryptology - CRYPTO 2013 - 33rd Annual Cryptology Conference, Santa Barbara, CA, USA, August 18-22, 2013. Proceedings, Part I*, pages 57–74, 2013.

[8] Prabhanjan Ananth, Zvika Brakerski, Gil Segev, and Vinod Vaikuntanathan. From selective to adaptive security in functional encryption. In *Advances*

in Cryptology - CRYPTO 2015 - 35th Annual Cryptology Conference, Santa Barbara, CA, USA, August 16-20, 2015, Proceedings, Part II, pages 657–677, 2015.

[9] Benny Applebaum. Bootstrapping obfuscators via fast pseudorandom functions. In Advances in Cryptology - ASIACRYPT 2014 - 20th International Conference on the Theory and Application of Cryptology and Information Security, Kaoshiung, Taiwan, R.O.C., December 7-11, 2014, Proceedings, Part II, pages 162–172, 2014.

[10] Benny Applebaum, David Cash, Chris Peikert, and Amit Sahai. Fast cryptographic primitives and circular-secure encryption based on hard learning problems. In CRYPTO, pages 595–618, 2009.

[11] Benny Applebaum and Shachar Lovett. Algebraic attacks against random local functions and their countermeasures. In Proceedings of the 48th Annual ACM SIGACT Symposium on Theory of Computing, STOC 2016, Cambridge, MA, USA, June 18-21, 2016, pages 1087–1100, 2016.

[12] Yuriy Arbitman, Moni Naor, and Gil Segev. Backyard cuckoo hashing: Constant worst-case operations with a succinct representation. In 51st Annual IEEE Symposium on Foundations of Computer Science, FOCS 2010, October 23-26, 2010, Las Vegas, Nevada, USA, pages 787–796, 2010.

[13] Sanjeev Arora and Rong Ge. New algorithms for learning in presence of errors. In ICALP (1), pages 403–415, 2011.

[14] László Babai, Noam Nisan, and Mario Szegedy. Multiparty protocols, pseudorandom generators for logspace, and time-space trade-offs. J. Comput. Syst. Sci., 45(2):204–232, 1992.

[15] Abhishek Banerjee, Hai Brenner, Gaëtan Leurent, Chris Peikert, and Alon Rosen. SPRING: fast pseudorandom functions from rounded ring products. In Fast Software Encryption - 21st International Workshop, FSE 2014, London, UK, March 3-5, 2014. Revised Selected Papers, pages 38–57, 2014.

[16] Abhishek Banerjee and Chris Peikert. New and improved key-homomorphic pseudorandom functions. In Advances in Cryptology - CRYPTO 2014 - 34th Annual Cryptology Conference, Santa Barbara, CA, USA, August 17-21, 2014, Proceedings, Part I, pages 353–370, 2014.

[17] Abhishek Banerjee, Chris Peikert, and Alon Rosen. Pseudorandom functions and lattices. In Advances in Cryptology - EUROCRYPT 2012 - 31st Annual International Conference on the Theory and Applications of Cryptographic Techniques, Cambridge, UK, April 15-19, 2012. Proceedings, pages 719–737, 2012.

[18] Boaz Barak, Oded Goldreich, Shafi Goldwasser, and Yehuda Lindell. Resettably-sound zero-knowledge and its applications. In 42nd Annual Symposium on Foundations of Computer Science, FOCS 2001, 14-17 October 2001, Las Vegas, Nevada, USA, pages 116–125, 2001.

[19] Boaz Barak, Oded Goldreich, Russell Impagliazzo, Steven Rudich, Amit Sahai, Salil Vadhan, and Ke Yang. On the (im)possibility of obfuscating programs. J. ACM, 59(2):6:1–6:48, May 2012.

[20] David A. Mix Barrington. Bounded-width polynomial-size branching programs recognize exactly those languages in NC^1. *J. Comput. Syst. Sci.*, 38(1):150–164, 1989.

[21] Mihir Bellare. New proofs for NMAC and HMAC: security without collision-resistance. In *Advances in Cryptology - CRYPTO 2006, 26th Annual International Cryptology Conference, Santa Barbara, California, USA, August 20-24, 2006, Proceedings*, pages 602–619, 2006.

[22] Mihir Bellare, Ran Canetti, and Hugo Krawczyk. Keying hash functions for message authentication. In *Advances in Cryptology - CRYPTO '96, 16th Annual International Cryptology Conference, Santa Barbara, California, USA, August 18-22, 1996, Proceedings*, pages 1–15, 1996.

[23] Mihir Bellare and Shafi Goldwasser. New paradigms for digital signatures and message authentication based on non-interative zero knowledge proofs. In *Advances in Cryptology - CRYPTO '89, 9th Annual International Cryptology Conference, Santa Barbara, California, USA, August 20-24, 1989, Proceedings*, pages 194–211, 1989.

[24] Mihir Bellare, Joe Kilian, and Phillip Rogaway. The security of cipher block chaining. In *Advances in Cryptology - CRYPTO '94, 14th Annual International Cryptology Conference, Santa Barbara, California, USA, August 21-25, 1994, Proceedings*, pages 341–358, 1994.

[25] Mihir Bellare and Phillip Rogaway. Random oracles are practical: A paradigm for designing efficient protocols. In *Proceedings of the 1st ACM Conference on Computer and Communications Security*, CCS '93, pages 62–73, New York, NY, USA, 1993. ACM.

[26] Avraham Ben-Aroya and Amnon Ta-Shma. Constructing small-bias sets from algebraic-geometric codes. *Theory of Computing*, 9:253–272, 2013.

[27] Michael Ben-Or and Nathan Linial. Collective coin flipping, robust voting schemes and minima of Banzhaf values. In *FOCS*, pages 408–416, 1985.

[28] Itay Berman, Iftach Haitner, Ilan Komargodski, and Moni Naor. Hardness preserving reductions via cuckoo hashing. In *TCC*, pages 40–59, 2013.

[29] Eli Biham and Adi Shamir. Differential cryptanalysis of DES-like cryptosystems. *J. Cryptology*, 4(1):3–72, 1991.

[30] Eli Biham and Adi Shamir. *Differential Cryptanalysis of the Data Encryption Standard*. Springer, 1993.

[31] Nir Bitansky, Ran Canetti, Henry Cohn, Shafi Goldwasser, Yael Tauman Kalai, Omer Paneth, and Alon Rosen. The impossibility of obfuscation with auxiliary input or a universal simulator. In *Advances in Cryptology - CRYPTO 2014 - 34th Annual Cryptology Conference, Santa Barbara, CA, USA, August 17-21, 2014, Proceedings, Part II*, pages 71–89, 2014.

[32] Nir Bitansky, Omer Paneth, and Alon Rosen. On the cryptographic hardness of finding a Nash equilibrium. *Electronic Colloquium on Computational Complexity (ECCC)*, 22:1, 2015.

[33] John Black and Phillip Rogaway. Ciphers with arbitrary finite domains. In Bart Preneel, editor, *Topics in Cryptology - CT-RSA 2002, The Cryptographer's Track at the RSA Conference, 2002, San Jose, CA, USA, February 18-*

22, 2002, Proceedings, volume 2271 of *Lecture Notes in Computer Science*, pages 114–130. Springer, 2002.

[34] A. Blum, A. Frieze, R. Kannan, and S. Vempala. A polynomial-time algorithm for learning noisy linear threshold functions. *Algorithmica*, 22(1):35–52, 1998.

[35] Avrim Blum, Merrick Furst, Michael Kearns, and Richard J. Lipton. Cryptographic primitives based on hard learning problems. In *Advances in cryptology (CRYPTO'93)*, pages 278–291. Springer, 1994.

[36] Avrim Blum, Adam Kalai, and Hal Wasserman. Noise-tolerant learning, the parity problem, and the statistical query model. *J. ACM*, 50(4):506–519, July 2003.

[37] Manuel Blum and Silvio Micali. How to generate cryptographically strong sequences of pseudo-random bits. *SIAM J. Comput.*, 13(4):850–864, 1984.

[38] Andrej Bogdanov, Siyao Guo, Daniel Masny, Silas Richelson, and Alon Rosen. On the hardness of learning with rounding over small modulus. In *Theory of Cryptography - 13th International Conference, TCC 2016-A, Tel Aviv, Israel, January 10-13, 2016, Proceedings, Part I*, pages 209–224, 2016.

[39] Andrej Bogdanov and Hoeteck Wee. A stateful implementation of a random function supporting parity queries over hypercubes. In *Proceedings of the 8th International Workshop on Randomization and Computation, RANDOM 2004*, pages 298–309, 2004.

[40] Dan Boneh, Kevin Lewi, Hart William Montgomery, and Ananth Raghunathan. Key homomorphic PRFs and their applications. In *Advances in Cryptology - CRYPTO 2013 - 33rd Annual Cryptology Conference, Santa Barbara, CA, USA, August 18-22, 2013. Proceedings, Part I*, pages 410–428, 2013.

[41] Dan Boneh and Brent Waters. Constrained pseudorandom functions and their applications. In *Advances in Cryptology - ASIACRYPT 2013 - 19th International Conference on the Theory and Application of Cryptology and Information Security, Bengaluru, India, December 1-5, 2013, Proceedings, Part II*, pages 280–300, 2013.

[42] Ravi Boppana. The average sensitivity of bounded-depth circuits. *Inf. Proc. Letters*, 63(5):257–261, 1997.

[43] Elette Boyle, Shafi Goldwasser, and Ioana Ivan. Functional signatures and pseudorandom functions. In *Public-Key Cryptography - PKC 2014 - 17th International Conference on Practice and Theory in Public-Key Cryptography, Buenos Aires, Argentina, March 26-28, 2014. Proceedings*, pages 501–519, 2014.

[44] Zvika Brakerski and Vinod Vaikuntanathan. Constrained key-homomorphic PRFs from standard lattice assumptions - or: How to secretly embed a circuit in your PRF. In *Theory of Cryptography - 12th Theory of Cryptography Conference, TCC 2015, Warsaw, Poland, March 23-25, 2015, Proceedings, Part II*, pages 1–30, 2015.

[45] Mark Braverman. Poly-logarithmic independence fools bounded-depth boolean circuits. *Communications of the ACM*, 54(4):108–115, 2011.

[46] Hai Brenner, Lubos Gaspar, Gaëtan Leurent, Alon Rosen, and François-Xavier Standaert. FPGA implementations of SPRING - and their countermeasures against side-channel attacks. In *Cryptographic Hardware and Embedded Systems - CHES 2014 - 16th International Workshop, Busan, South Korea, September 23-26, 2014. Proceedings*, pages 414–432, 2014.

[47] Nader H. Bshouty and Vitaly Feldman. On using extended statistical queries to avoid membership queries. *The Journal of Machine Learning Research*, 2:359–395, 2002.

[48] Ran Canetti, Oded Goldreich, Shafi Goldwasser, and Silvio Micali. Resettable zero-knowledge (extended abstract). In *Proceedings of the Thirty-Second Annual ACM Symposium on Theory of Computing, May 21-23, 2000, Portland, OR, USA*, pages 235–244, 2000.

[49] Marco L. Carmosino, Russell Impagliazzo, Valentine Kabanets, and Antonina Kolokolova. Learning algorithms from natural proofs. In Ran Raz, editor, *31st Conference on Computational Complexity, CCC 2016, May 29 to June 1, 2016, Tokyo, Japan*, volume 50 of *LIPIcs*, pages 10:1–10:24. Schloss Dagstuhl - Leibniz-Zentrum fuer Informatik, 2016.

[50] Fan R. K. Chung and Prasad Tetali. Communication complexity and quasi randomness. *SIAM J. Discrete Math.*, 6(1):110–123, 1993.

[51] Aloni Cohen and Saleet Klein. The GGM PRF is a weakly one-way family of functions. *IACR Cryptology ePrint Archive*, 2016:610, 2016.

[52] Yevgeniy Dodis, Jonathan Katz, John Steinberger, Aishwarya Thiruvengadam, and Zhe Zhang. Provable security of substitution-permutation networks. Cryptology ePrint Archive, Report 2017/016, 2017. http://eprint.iacr.org/2017/016.

[53] Vitaly Feldman, Parikshit Gopalan, Subhash Khot, and Ashok Kumar Ponnuswami. On agnostic learning of parities, monomials, and halfspaces. *SIAM J. Comput.*, 39(2):606–645, 2009.

[54] Amos Fiat and Adi Shamir. How to prove yourself: Practical solutions to identification and signature problems. In *Proceedings on Advances in Cryptology—CRYPTO '86*, pages 186–194, 1987. Springer-Verlag.

[55] Michael J. Freedman, Yuval Ishai, Benny Pinkas, and Omer Reingold. Keyword search and oblivious pseudorandom functions. In *Theory of Cryptography, Second Theory of Cryptography Conference, TCC 2005, Cambridge, MA, USA, February 10-12, 2005, Proceedings*, pages 303–324, 2005.

[56] Merrick L. Furst, James B. Saxe, and Michael Sipser. Parity, circuits, and the polynomial-time hierarchy. *Mathematical Systems Theory*, 17(1):13–27, 1984.

[57] Sanjam Garg, Craig Gentry, Shai Halevi, Mariana Raykova, Amit Sahai, and Brent Waters. Hiding secrets in software: a cryptographic approach to program obfuscation. *Commun. ACM*, 59(5):113–120, 2016.

[58] Sanjam Garg, Omkant Pandey, and Akshayaram Srinivasan. Revisiting the cryptographic hardness of finding a Nash equilibrium. In *Advances in Cryptology - CRYPTO 2016 - 36th Annual International Cryptology Conference,*

Santa Barbara, CA, USA, August 14-18, 2016, Proceedings, Part II, pages 579–604, 2016.

[59] Oded Goldreich. Two remarks concerning the Goldwasser-Micali-Rivest signature scheme. In *Advances in Cryptology - CRYPTO '86, Santa Barbara, California, USA, 1986, Proceedings*, pages 104–110, 1986.

[60] Oded Goldreich. Towards a theory of software protection and simulation by oblivious RAMs. In *Proceedings of the 19th Annual ACM Symposium on Theory of Computing, 1987, New York, USA*, pages 182–194, 1987.

[61] Oded Goldreich. *Foundations of Cryptography: Basic Tools.* Cambridge University Press, New York, NY, USA, 2000.

[62] Oded Goldreich. *Computational Complexity: A Conceptual Perspective.* Cambridge University Press, New York, NY, USA, 1st edition, 2008.

[63] Oded Goldreich. The GGM construction does NOT yield correlation intractable function ensembles. In *Studies in Complexity and Cryptography. Miscellanea on the Interplay between Randomness and Computation*, pages 98–108, 2011.

[64] Oded Goldreich, Shafi Goldwasser, and Silvio Micali. How to construct random functions (extended abstract). In *FOCS*, pages 464–479, 1984.

[65] Oded Goldreich, Shafi Goldwasser, and Asaf Nussboim. On the implementation of huge random objects. *SIAM J. Comput.*, 39(7):2761–2822, 2010.

[66] Oded Goldreich and Rafail Ostrovsky. Software protection and simulation on oblivious RAMs. *J. ACM*, 43(3):431–473, 1996.

[67] Shafi Goldwasser and Yael Tauman Kalai. On the impossibility of obfuscation with auxiliary input. In *46th Annual IEEE Symposium on Foundations of Computer Science (FOCS 2005), 23-25 October 2005, Pittsburgh, PA, USA, Proceedings*, pages 553–562, 2005.

[68] W. T. Gowers. A new proof of Szemerédi's theorem. *Geom. Funct. Anal.*, 11(3):465–588, 2001.

[69] Iftach Haitner, Omer Reingold, and Salil P. Vadhan. Efficiency improvements in constructing pseudorandom generators from one-way functions. *SIAM J. Comput.*, 42(3):1405–1430, 2013.

[70] Prahladh Harsha and Srikanth Srinivasan. On polynomial approximations to AC^0. *CoRR*, abs/1604.08121, 2016.

[71] Johan Hastad. *Computational limitations of small-depth circuits.* MIT Press, 1987.

[72] Johan Hastad. The shrinkage exponent of De Morgan formulas is 2. *SIAM J. Comput.*, 27(1):48–64, 1998.

[73] Johan Hastad, Russell Impagliazzo, Leonid A. Levin, and Michael Luby. A pseudorandom generator from any one-way function. *SIAM J. Comp.*, 28(4):1364–1396, 1999.

[74] Pavel Hubáček and Eylon Yogev. Hardness of continuous local search: Query complexity and cryptographic lower bounds. In *Proceedings of the Twenty-Eighth Annual ACM-SIAM Symposium on Discrete Algorithms*, pages 1352–1371, 2017.

[75] Russell Impagliazzo. A personal view of average-case complexity. In *Proceedings of the Tenth Annual Structure in Complexity Theory Conference, Minneapolis, Minnesota, USA, June 19-22, 1995*, pages 134–147. IEEE Computer Society, 1995.

[76] Russell Impagliazzo, Noam Nisan, and Avi Wigderson. Pseudorandomness for network algorithms. In Frank Thomson Leighton and Michael T. Goodrich, editors, *Proceedings of the Twenty-Sixth Annual ACM Symposium on Theory of Computing, 23-25 May 1994, Montréal, Québec, Canada*, pages 356–364. ACM, 1994.

[77] Russell Impagliazzo and Steven Rudich. Limits on the provable consequences of one-way permutations. In *Proceedings of the 21st Annual ACM Symposium on Theory of Computing, May 14-17, 1989, Seattle, Washington, USA*, pages 44–61, 1989.

[78] Yuval Ishai, Eyal Kushilevitz, Rafail Ostrovsky, and Amit Sahai. Cryptography with constant computational overhead. In Cynthia Dwork, editor, *Proceedings of the 40th Annual ACM Symposium on Theory of Computing, Victoria, British Columbia, Canada, May 17-20, 2008*, pages 433–442. ACM, 2008.

[79] Jeffrey C. Jackson. An efficient membership-query algorithm for learning DNF with respect to the uniform distribution. *Journal of Computer and System Sciences*, 55(3):414–440, 1997.

[80] Jonathan Katz and Yehuda Lindell. *Introduction to Modern Cryptography*. Chapman & Hall/CRC, 2nd edition, 2014.

[81] Michael Kearns. Efficient noise-tolerant learning from statistical queries. *Journal of the ACM (JACM)*, 45(6):983–1006, 1998.

[82] Michael J. Kearns and Umesh V. Vazirani. *An Introduction to Computational Learning Theory*. MIT Press, Cambridge, MA, USA, 1994.

[83] Michael Kharitonov. Cryptographic lower bounds for learnability of boolean functions on the uniform distribution. *J. Comput. Syst. Sci.*, 50(3):600–610, 1995.

[84] Aggelos Kiayias, Stavros Papadopoulos, Nikos Triandopoulos, and Thomas Zacharias. Delegatable pseudorandom functions and applications. In *2013 ACM SIGSAC Conference on Computer and Communications Security, CCS'13, Berlin, Germany, November 4-8, 2013*, pages 669–684, 2013.

[85] Joe Kilian and Phillip Rogaway. How to protect DES against exhaustive key search. In *Advances in Cryptology - CRYPTO '96, 16th Annual International Cryptology Conference, Santa Barbara, California, USA, August 18-22, 1996, Proceedings*, pages 252–267, 1996.

[86] Shrinivas Kudekar, Santhosh Kumar, Marco Mondelli, Henry D. Pfister, Eren Sasoglu, and Rüdiger L. Urbanke. Reed–Muller codes achieve capacity on erasure channels. In *Proceedings of the 48th Annual ACM SIGACT Symposium on Theory of Computing, STOC 2016, Cambridge, MA, USA, June 18-21, 2016*, pages 658–669, 2016.

[87] Arjen K. Lenstra, Hendrik W. Lenstra, Jr., and László Lovász. Factoring polynomials with rational coefficients. *Mathematische Annalen*, 261(4):515–534, December 1982.

[88] Leonid A. Levin. One-way functions and pseudorandom generators. *Combinatorica*, 7(4):357–363, 1987.

[89] Nathan Linial, Yishay Mansour, and Noam Nisan. Constant depth circuits, Fourier transform, and learnability. *Journal of the ACM (JACM)*, 40(3):607–620, 1993.

[90] Michael Luby and Charles Rackoff. How to construct pseudorandom permutations from pseudorandom functions. *SIAM J. Comput.*, 17(2):373–386, 1988.

[91] Anna Lysyanskaya. Unique signatures and verifiable random functions from the DH-DDH separation. In *Advances in Cryptology - CRYPTO 2002, 22nd Annual International Cryptology Conference, Santa Barbara, California, USA, August 18-22, 2002, Proceedings*, pages 597–612, 2002.

[92] Vadim Lyubashevsky. The parity problem in the presence of noise, decoding random linear codes, and the subset sum problem. In *Proceedings of the 9th International Workshop on Randomization and Computation, RANDOM 2005*, pages 378–389, 2005.

[93] Vadim Lyubashevsky, Daniele Micciancio, Chris Peikert, and Alon Rosen. SWIFFT: A modest proposal for FFT hashing. In *FSE*, pages 54–72, 2008.

[94] Vadim Lyubashevsky, Chris Peikert, and Oded Regev. On ideal lattices and learning with errors over rings. In *EUROCRYPT*, pages 1–23, 2010.

[95] Mitsuru Matsui. Linear cryptanalysis method for DES cipher. In *Workshop on the Theory and Application of Cryptographic Techniques on Advances in Cryptology*, EUROCRYPT '93, pages 386–397, Secaucus, NJ, USA, 1994. Springer-Verlag New York, Inc.

[96] Ueli M. Maurer, Krzysztof Pietrzak, and Renato Renner. Indistinguishability amplification. In Alfred Menezes, editor, *Advances in Cryptology - CRYPTO 2007, 27th Annual International Cryptology Conference, Santa Barbara, CA, USA, August 19-23, 2007, Proceedings*, volume 4622 of *Lecture Notes in Computer Science*, pages 130–149. Springer, 2007.

[97] Silvio Micali, Michael O. Rabin, and Salil P. Vadhan. Verifiable random functions. In *40th Annual Symposium on Foundations of Computer Science, FOCS '99, 17-18 October, 1999, New York, NY, USA*, pages 120–130, 1999.

[98] Eric Miles and Emanuele Viola. Substitution-permutation networks, pseudorandom functions, and natural proofs. *J. ACM*, 62(6):46:1–46:29, December 2015.

[99] Ben Morris. Improved mixing time bounds for the Thorp shuffle. *Combinatorics, Probability & Computing*, 22(1):118–132, 2013.

[100] Ben Morris, Phillip Rogaway, and Till Stegers. How to encipher messages on a small domain. In Shai Halevi, editor, *Advances in Cryptology - CRYPTO 2009, 29th Annual International Cryptology Conference, Santa Barbara, CA, USA, August 16-20, 2009. Proceedings*, volume 5677 of *Lecture Notes in Computer Science*, pages 286–302. Springer, 2009.

[101] Elchanan Mossel, Ryan O'Donnell, and Rocco P. Servedio. Learning juntas. In *Proceedings of the Thirty-fifth Annual ACM Symposium on Theory of Computing*, STOC '03, pages 206–212, New York, NY, USA, 2003. ACM.

[102] Joseph Naor and Moni Naor. Small-bias probability spaces: Efficient constructions and applications. *SIAM J. Comput*, 22:838–856, 1993.

[103] Moni Naor, Benny Pinkas, and Omer Reingold. Distributed pseudo-random functions and KDCs. In *Advances in Cryptology - EUROCRYPT '99, International Conference on the Theory and Application of Cryptographic Techniques, Prague, Czech Republic, May 2-6, 1999, Proceeding*, pages 327–346, 1999.

[104] Moni Naor and Omer Reingold. On the construction of pseudorandom permutations: Luby-Rackoff revisited. *J. Cryptology*, 12(1):29–66, 1999.

[105] Moni Naor and Omer Reingold. Synthesizers and their application to the parallel construction of pseudo-random functions. *J. Comput. Syst. Sci.*, 58(2):336–375, 1999.

[106] Moni Naor and Omer Reingold. Number-theoretic constructions of efficient pseudo-random functions. *J. ACM*, 51(2):231–262, 2004.

[107] Moni Naor, Omer Reingold, and Alon Rosen. Pseudo-random functions and factoring (extended abstract). In *Proceedings of the Thirty-Second Annual ACM Symposium on Theory of Computing, May 21-23, 2000, Portland, OR, USA*, pages 11–20, 2000.

[108] Moni Naor and Eylon Yogev. Bloom filters in adversarial environments. In *Advances in Cryptology - CRYPTO 2015 - 35th Annual Cryptology Conference, Santa Barbara, CA, USA, August 16-20, 2015, Proceedings, Part II*, pages 565–584, 2015.

[109] Noam Nisan. Pseudorandom generators for space-bounded computation. *Combinatorica*, 12(4):449–461, 1992.

[110] Ryan O'Donnell. *Analysis of Boolean Functions*. Cambridge University Press, New York, NY, USA, 2014.

[111] National Institute of Standards and Technology. Announcing request for candidate algorithm nominations for the Advanced Encryption Standard (AES). http://csrc.nist.gov/archive/aes/pre-round1/aes_9709.htm, 1997.

[112] Chris Peikert. Public-key cryptosystems from the worst-case shortest vector problem. In *STOC*, pages 333–342, 2009.

[113] L. Pitt and M. K. Warmuth. Reductions among prediction problems: On the difficulty of predicting automata. In *Structure in Complexity Theory Conference*, pages 60–69, Jun 1988.

[114] Ran Raz. The BNS-Chung criterion for multi-party communication complexity. *Computational Complexity*, 9(2):113–122, 2000.

[115] Alexander A. Razborov. Lower bounds on the size of bounded depth circuits over a complete basis with logical addition. *Matematicheskie Zametki*, 41(4):598–607, 1987.

[116] Alexander A. Razborov and Steven Rudich. Natural proofs. In *STOC*, pages 204–213, 1994.

[117] Oded Regev. On lattices, learning with errors, random linear codes, and cryptography. *J. ACM*, 56(6):1–40, 2009. Preliminary version in STOC 2005.

[118] John H. Reif and Stephen R. Tate. On threshold circuits and polynomial computation. *SIAM J. Comput.*, 21(5):896–908, 1992.

[119] Omer Reingold, Thomas Steinke, and Salil Vadhan. *Pseudorandomness for Regular Branching Programs via Fourier Analysis*, pages 655–670. Springer Berlin Heidelberg, 2013.

[120] R. L. Rivest, L. Adleman, and M. L. Dertouzos. On data banks and privacy homomorphisms. *Foundations of Secure Computation, Academia Press*, pages 169–179, 1978.

[121] Amit Sahai and Brent Waters. How to use indistinguishability obfuscation: deniable encryption, and more. In *Symposium on Theory of Computing, STOC 2014, New York, NY, USA, May 31 - June 03, 2014*, pages 475–484, 2014.

[122] Claus-Peter Schnorr. A hierarchy of polynomial time lattice basis reduction algorithms. *Theor. Comput. Sci.*, 53:201–224, 1987.

[123] Peter W. Shor. Polynomial-time algorithms for prime factorization and discrete logarithms on a quantum computer. *SIAM J. Comput.*, 26(5):1484–1509, 1997.

[124] Roman Smolensky. Algebraic methods in the theory of lower bounds for boolean circuit complexity. In *STOC*, pages 77–82, 1987.

[125] Avishay Tal. Tight bounds on the Fourier spectrum of AC^0. *Electronic Colloquium on Computational Complexity (ECCC)*, 21:174, 2014.

[126] S. Vadhan and J. Zheng. Characterizing pseudoentropy and simplifying pseudorandom generator constructions. Technical Report TR11-141, Electronic Colloquium on Computational Complexity, 2011.

[127] L. G. Valiant. A theory of the learnable. *Commun. ACM*, 27(11):1134–1142, November 1984.

[128] Emanuele Viola and Avi Wigderson. Norms, XOR lemmas, and lower bounds for polynomials and protocols. *Theory of Computing*, 4(1):137–168, 2008.

[129] Andrew C. C. Yao. Theory and applications of trapdoor functions. In *Proceedings of the 23rd Annual IEEE Symposium on Foundations of Computer Science*, pages 80–91, 1982.

[130] Andrew Chi-Chih Yao. Separating the polynomial-time hierarchy by oracles (preliminary version). In *26th Annual Symposium on Foundations of Computer Science, Portland, Oregon, USA, 21-23 October 1985*, pages 1–10, 1985.

[131] M. Zhandry. How to construct quantum random functions. In *Foundations of Computer Science (FOCS), 2012 IEEE 53rd Annual Symposium on*, pages 679–687, Oct 2012.

[132] Mark Zhandry. How to avoid obfuscation using witness PRFs. In *Theory of Cryptography - 13th International Conference, TCC 2016-A, Tel Aviv, Israel, January 10-13, 2016, Proceedings, Part II*, pages 421–448, 2016.

Chapter 4
The Many Entropies in One-Way Functions

Iftach Haitner and Salil Vadhan

Abstract Computational analogues of information-theoretic notions have given rise to some of the most interesting phenomena in the theory of computation. For example, *computational indistinguishability*, Goldwasser and Micali [9], which is the computational analogue of statistical distance, enabled the bypassing of Shannon's impossibility results on perfectly secure encryption, and provided the basis for the computational theory of pseudorandomness. *Pseudoentropy*, Håstad, Impagliazzo, Levin, and Luby [17], a computational analogue of entropy, was the key to the fundamental result establishing the equivalence of pseudorandom generators and one-way functions, and has become a basic concept in complexity theory and cryptography.

This tutorial discusses two rather recent computational notions of entropy, both of which can be easily found in any one-way function, the most basic cryptographic primitive. The first notion is *next-block pseudoentropy*, Haitner, Reingold, and Vadhan [14], a refinement of pseudoentropy that enables simpler and more efficient construction of pseudorandom generators. The second is *inaccessible entropy*, Haitner, Reingold, Vadhan, and Wee [11], which relates to *unforgeability* and is used to construct simpler and more efficient universal one-way hash functions and statistically hiding commitments.

Iftach Haitner

School of Computer Science, Tel Aviv University. E-mail: iftachh@cs.tau.ac.il, member of the Israeli Center of Research Excellence in Algorithms (ICORE) and the Check Point Institute for Information Security. Research supported by ERC starting grant 638121.

Salil Vadhan

John A. Paulson School of Engineering & Applied Sciences, Harvard University. E-mail: salil@seas.harvard.edu. Written while visiting the Shing-Tung Yau Center and the Department of Applied Mathematics at National Chiao-Tung University in Hsinchu, Taiwan. Supported by NSF grant CCF-1420938 and a Simons Investigator Award.

4.1 Introduction

One-way functions (OWFs), functions that are easy to compute and hard to invert, are the most basic, unstructured form of cryptographic hardness [22]. Yet, in a sequence of celebrated results, mostly in the 1980s and early 1990s, one-way functions were shown to imply a rich collection of cryptographic schemes and protocols, such as digital signatures and secret-key encryption schemes. At the basis of this beautiful mathematical structure are a few constructions of basic primitives: pseudorandom generators (Håstad et al. [17]), universal one-way hash functions (Naor and Yung [26], Rompel [27]), and more recently, statistically hiding commitment schemes (Haitner, Nguyen, Ong, Reingold, and Vadhan [10]). These powerful plausibility results shape our understanding of hardness, secrecy, and unforgeability in cryptography. For instance, the construction of pseudorandom generators provides strong evidence that computationally secure encryption is much richer than information-theoretically secure encryption, as it allows encrypting many more bits than the key length, in contrast to Shannon's impossibility result for information-theoretic security [28]. The construction of universal one-way hash functions yields that some "public-key" objects, such as signature schemes, can be built from "private-key" primitives, like one-way functions. A recent line of results [11, 12, 14, 29] simplified and improved all of these constructions. The crux of each new construction is defining the "right" notion of *computational entropy* and recovering this form of entropy from one-way functions.

Computational entropy. Computational analogues of information-theoretic notions have given rise to some of the most interesting phenomena in the theory of computation. For example, *computational indistinguishability*, a computational analogue of statistical indistinguishability introduced by Goldwasser and Micali [9], enabled the bypassing of Shannon's impossibility results on perfectly secure encryption [28], and provided the basis for the computational theory of pseudorandomness [2, 32]. *Pseudoentropy*, a computational analogue of entropy introduced by Håstad et al. [17], was the key to their fundamental result establishing the equivalence of pseudorandom generators and one-way functions, and has become a basic concept in complexity theory and cryptography. The above notions were further refined in [14, 29], and new computational analogues of entropy to quantify unforgeability were introduced in [11, 12]. These new abstractions have led to much simpler and more efficient constructions based on one-way functions, and to a novel equivalence between (parallelizable) constant-round statistical zero-knowledge arguments and constant-round statistically hiding commitments.

The purpose of this tutorial is to explain these computational notions of entropy and their application in constructing cryptographic primitives. The utility of the computational notions of entropy is to bridge between the very unstructured form of hardness of the primitive we start with (e.g., one-wayness) and the typically much more structured form of hardness that appears in the primitive we are trying to construct. The benefit of using such computational notions of entropy is that there exists well-developed machinery for manipulating information-theoretic entropy and making it more structured (e.g., through taking many independent copies and applying hash functions and randomness extractors); with care, analogous tools can be applied to the computational notions. For example, in each of the two constructions presented in this tutorial, the first step is to construct a "generator" with a noticeable gap between its real output entropy and its computational entropy—entropy from the point of view of a computationally bounded adversary. (For each construction, we use a different notion computational entropy.) The next step is to increase the gap between real and computational entropy and to convert them into worst-case analogues (e.g., min-entropy and max-entropy) using the standard information-theoretic tools of taking many independent samples. Finally, hashing and randomness extractors are used to obtain more structured randomness generators.

In the following, we discuss the two major types of computational entropy notions that can be found in any one-way function: *pseudoentropy*, which comes to quantify pseudorandomness and *secrecy*, and *inaccessible entropy*, which comes to quantify *unforgeability*. We do that while focusing on *next-block pseudoentropy*, a refinement of the traditional notion of pseudoentropy, and on the type of inaccessible entropy that is related to, and used as an intermediate step to construct, statistically hiding commitment schemes. In the main body of this tutorial, we discuss these two notions further, and exemplify their usability with applications to one-way function based primitives.

4.1.1 Pseudoentropy

A random variable X over $\{0, 1\}^n$ is *pseudorandom* if it is computationally indistinguishable from U_n.[1] The most natural quantitative variant of pseudorandomness is the so-called *HILL pseudoentropy* (stands for Håstad, Impagliazzo, Levin, and Luby), or just pseudoentropy.

Definition 4.1.1 ((HILL) pseudoentropy, [17], informal). *A random variable X is said to have* pseudoentropy (at least) k *if there exists a random variable Y such that:*

1. *X is computationally indistinguishable from Y.*
2. *$H(Y) \geq k$, where $H(\cdot)$ denotes Shannon entropy.*[2]

A function (i.e., a generator) $G : \{0, 1\}^n \mapsto \{0, 1\}^{m(n)}$ has pseudoentropy k if $G(U_n)$ has pseudoentropy k. An efficiently computable $G : \{0, 1\}^n \mapsto \{0, 1\}^{m(n)}$ is a pseudoentropy generator if it has pseudoentropy (at least) $H(G(U_n)) + \Delta(n)$ for some $\Delta(n) \geq 1/\operatorname{poly}(n)$. We refer to Δ as the entropy gap *of G.*[3]

---

[1] I.e., $|\Pr[D(X) = 1] = \Pr[D(U_n) = 1]| = \operatorname{neg}(n)$ for any polynomial-time distinguisher D, where U_n is uniformly distributed over $\{0, 1\}^n$, and $\operatorname{neg}(n)$ is smaller than any inverse polynomial. See Section 4.2 for the formal definitions.

[2] The *Shannon entropy* of a random variable X is defined by $H(X) = E_{x \leftarrow X}\left[\log \frac{1}{\Pr[X=x]}\right]$.

[3] Håstad et al. [17] refer to such a generator as a *false entropy generator*, and require a pseudoentropy generator to have output pseudoentropy (at least) $n + \Delta(n)$, rather than just $H(G(U_n)) + \Delta(n)$. For the sake of this exposition, however, we ignore this distinction.

Pseudoentropy plays a key role in the Håstad et al. [17] construction of pseudo-random generators from one-way functions. A pseudorandom generator (PRG) is an efficient length-extending function whose output distribution, over uniformly chosen input, is pseudorandom. Note that every pseudorandom generator $G\colon \{0,1\}^n \mapsto \{0,1\}^{m(n)}$ is a pseudoentropy generator with entropy gap at least $m(n) - n$; take $Y = U_{m(n)}$ and note that $H(Y) = m(n)$, but $H(G(U_n)) \leq H(U_n) = n$. Pseudoentropy generators are weaker in that Y may be very far from uniform, and even with $H(Y) \ll n$ (as long as $H(G(U_n))$ is even smaller). Yet, Håstad et al. [17] showed that also the converse is true, using pseudoentropy generators to construct pseudorandom generators. The first and key step of their main result (that one-way functions imply pseudorandom generators) was to show that a simple modification of any one-way function is a pseudoentropy generator with small but noticeable entropy gap, where the rest of their construction is "purifying" this generator's pseudoentropy into pseudorandomness, and thus turning it into a PRG. This shows in a sense that (a simple modification of) one-way functions have the computational notion of entropy that pseudorandom generators take to the extreme.

Constructing pseudoentropy generator from an *injective* one-way function is easy. Given such an injective function $f\colon \{0,1\}^n \mapsto \{0,1\}^*$, let $G(x) = (f(x), b(x))$, where b is an *hardcore predicate* of f.[4] G's pseudoentropy is $n + 1$, which is larger by one bit than its output (and input) entropy. Similar constructions can be applied to one-way functions that can be converted to (almost) injective one-way functions (e.g., regular one-way functions), but generalizing it to *arbitrary* one-way function is seemingly a much more challenging task. Yet, Håstad et al. [17] did manage to get a pseudoentropy generator out of an arbitrary one-way function, alas with poor parameters compared with what can easily be achieved from an injective one-way function. Specifically, while its output pseudoentropy is larger than its real output entropy, and thus it possesses a positive entropy gap, its entropy gap is tiny (i.e., $\log n/n$), and its pseudoentropy is smaller than its input length. In addition, the quantity of its pseudoentropy is not efficiently computable. These issues result in a complicated and indirect PRG construction. Constructions that followed this approach ([13, 19]), while improving and simplifying the original construction, also ended up being rather complicated and inefficient. To deal with this barrier, Haitner, Reingold, and Vadhan [14] presented a relaxation of this notion called *next-block pseudoentropy*, which can be easily obtained with strong parameters from any one-way function, yet is still strong enough for construction of PRGs.

4.1.1.1 Next-Block Pseudoentropy

Next-block pseudoentropy is similar in spirit to the Blum and Micali [3] notion of next-bit unpredictability, which was shown by Yao [32] to be equivalent to his (now-standard) definition of pseudorandomness. This equivalence says that a random variable $X = (X_1, \ldots, X_m)$ is pseudorandom iff each bit of X is *unpredictable*

---

[4] b is hardcore predicate of f if $(f(U_n), b(U_n))$ is computationally indistinguishable from $(f(U_n), U)$, for U_n and U sampled, uniformly and independently, from $\{0,1\}^n$ and $\{0,1\}$, respectively.

from the previous bits. That is, $\Pr[P(X_1, X_2, \ldots, X_{i-1}) = X_i] \leq \frac{1}{2} + \mathrm{neg}(n)$ for every i and efficient predictor (i.e., algorithm) P. Equivalently, $(X_1, X_2, \ldots, X_{i-1}, X_i)$ is computationally indistinguishable from $(X_1, X_2, \ldots, X_{i-1}, U)$ where U is a uniform bit. It is thus natural to consider what happens if we relax the pseudorandomness of X_i to *pseudoentropy* (capturing the idea that X_i is only somewhat unpredictable from the previous bits). And more generally, we can allow the X_i's to be blocks instead of bits.

Definition 4.1.2 (Next-block pseudoentropy [14], informal). *A random variable* $X = (X_1, \ldots, X_m)$ *is said to have* next-block pseudoentropy (at least) k *if there exists a sequence of random variables* $Y = (Y_1, \ldots, Y_m)$, *jointly distributed with* X, *such that:*

1. $(X_1, X_2, \ldots, X_{i-1}, X_i)$ *is computationally indistinguishable from* $(X_1, X_2, \ldots, X_{i-1}, Y_i)$, *for every* i.
2. $\sum_i \mathrm{H}(Y_i | X_1, \ldots X_{i-1}) \geq k$.

A function $G : \{0, 1\}^n \mapsto (\{0, 1\}^\ell)^m$ *is said to have* next-block pseudoentropy k *if* $(X_1, \ldots, X_m) = G(U_n)$ *has next-block pseudoentropy* k. *A* next-block pseudoentropy *generator is a polynomial-time computable function* $G : \{0, 1\}^n \mapsto (\{0, 1\}^\ell)^m$ *that has next-block pseudoentropy (at least)* $\mathrm{H}(G(U_n)) + \Delta(n)$ *for some* $\Delta(n) > 1/\mathrm{poly}(n)$, *where again* Δ *is called the* entropy gap.

That is, in total, the blocks of X "look like" they have k bits of entropy given the previous ones. Note that the case $k = m$ and blocks of size one (the X_i's are bits) amounts to the Yao [32] definition of unpredictability discussed above. The case of one block ($m = 1$) amounts to Håstad et al. [17] definition of pseudoentropy (Theorem 4.1.1), Also note that, when $m > 1$, allowing Y to be correlated with X in this definition is essential: for example, if all the blocks of X are always equal to each other (and have noticeable entropy), then there is no way to define Y that is independent of X and satisfies the first condition.

Unlike the case of (HILL) pseudoentropy, it is known how to use any one-way function to construct a next-block pseudoentropy generator with good parameters.

Constructing next-block pseudoentropy generators from one-way functions. Given a one-way function $f : \{0, 1\}^n \mapsto \{0, 1\}^n$, we construct a generator G as

$$G(x) = (f(x), x_1, \ldots, x_n). \tag{4.1}$$

The above construction was proven to achieve next-block pseudoentropy by Vadhan and Zheng [29]. The original construction of Haitner et al. [14] considered instead $G(x, h) = (f(x), h(x)_1, \ldots, h(x)_n)$, for an appropriate family of hash functions with seed length $O(n)$. In this tutorial, we will analyze the latter construction, using a family of hash functions of seed length $O(n^2)$, as it has a simpler analysis.[5]

---

[5] Interestingly, the construction we consider in this tutorial is similar to the pseudoentropy generator used by Håstad et al. [17], but here it is viewed as a next-block pseudoentropy generator.

If we consider only the original notion of pseudoentropy (Theorem 4.1.1), the above construction is problematic; the polynomial-time test $T(y, x)$ that checks whether $y = f(x)$, distinguishes $G(U_n)$ from every random variable of entropy noticeably larger than n (since T accepts only 2^n strings). However, it turns out that it does have *next-block pseudoentropy at least* $n + \log n$. This has two advantages compared with the pseudoentropy generator constructed by Håstad et al. [17]. First, the entropy gap is now $\Delta = \log n$ instead of $\Delta = \log n/n$. Second, the total amount of pseudoentropy in the output (though not the amount contributed by the individual blocks) is known. These two advantages together yield a simpler and more efficient one-way function based PRG.

4.1.2 Inaccessible Entropy

Notions of pseudoentropy as above are only useful as a *lower* bound on the "computational entropy" in a distribution. For instance, it can be shown that *every* distribution on $\{0, 1\}^n$ is computationally indistinguishable from a distribution of entropy at most polylog n. In this section we introduce another computational analogue of entropy, which we call *accessible entropy*, which is useful as an *upper* bound on computational entropy. We motivate the idea of accessible entropy with an example. Let G be the following two-block generator:

Algorithm 4.1.3 (G)

Let $m \ll n$ and let $\mathcal{H} = \{h: \{0, 1\}^n \mapsto \{0, 1\}^m\}$ be a family of collision-resistant hash functions.[6]

On public parameter $h \xleftarrow{R} \mathcal{H}$.

1. Sample $x \xleftarrow{R} \{0, 1\}^n$.
2. Output $y = h(x)$.
3. Output x.

Now, information-theoretically, G's second output block (namely x) has entropy at least $n - m \geq 1$ conditioned on h and its first output block y. This is since $(h, y = h(x))$ reveals only m bits of information about x. The collision-resistance property of h, however, implies that given the *state* of G after it outputs its first block y, there is at most one consistent value of x that can be computed in polynomial time with nonnegligible probability. (Otherwise, we would be able find two distinct messages $x \neq x'$ such that $h(x) = h(x')$.) This holds even if G is replaced by any polynomial-time cheating strategy $\widetilde{G}$. Thus, there is "real entropy" in x (conditioned on h and the first output of G), but it is "computationally inaccessible" to $\widetilde{G}$, to whom x effectively has entropy 0.

We generalize this basic idea to allow the upper bound on the "accessible entropy" to be a parameter k, and to consider both the real and accessible entropy accumulated over several blocks of a generator. In more detail, consider an *m-block*

---

[6] Given $h \xleftarrow{R} \mathcal{H}$, it is infeasible to find distinct $x, x' \in \{0, 1\}^n$ with $h(x) = h(x')$.

generator $G\colon \{0,1\}^n \mapsto (\{0,1\}^*)^m$, and let $(Y_1, \ldots, Y_m)$ be random variables denoting the m output blocks generated by applying G over randomness U_n (no public parameters are given). We define the *real entropy* of G as $\mathrm{H}(G(U_n))$, the Shannon entropy of $G(U_n)$, which is equal to

$$\sum_{i\in[m]} \mathrm{H}(Y_i \mid Y_1, \ldots, Y_{i-1}),$$

where $\mathrm{H}(X \mid Y) = \mathrm{E}_{y \xleftarrow{R} Y}[\mathrm{H}(X \mid_{Y=y})]$ is the standard notion of (Shannon) conditional entropy.

To define *accessible entropy*, consider a probabilistic polynomial-time cheating strategy $\widetilde{G}$ that before outputting the i-th block, tosses some fresh random coins r_i, and uses them to output a string y_i. We restrict out attention to G-consistent (adversarial) generators—$\widetilde{G}$'s output is always in the support of G (though it might be distributed differently). Now, let $(R_1, Y_1, \ldots, Y_m, R_m)$ be random variables corresponding to a random execution of $\widetilde{G}$. We define the *accessible entropy* achieved by $\widetilde{G}$ to be

$$\sum_{i\in[m]} \mathrm{H}(Y_i \mid R_1, \ldots, R_{i-1}).$$

The key point is that now we compute the entropy conditioned not just on the previous output blocks $Y_1, \ldots, Y_{i-1}$ (which are determined by $R_1, \ldots, R_{i-1}$), as done when computing the real entropy of G, but also on the local state of $\widetilde{G}$ prior to outputting the i-th block (which without loss of generality equal its coin tosses $R_1, \ldots, R_{i-1}$). We define the *accessible entropy* of G as the maximal accessible entropy achieved by a G-consistent, polynomial-time generator $\widetilde{G}$. We refer to the difference (real entropy) − (accessible entropy) as the *inaccessible entropy* of the generator G, and call G an *inaccessible entropy generator* if its inaccessible entropy is noticeably greater than zero.

It is important to note that if we put no computational restrictions on the computational power of a G-consistent $\widetilde{G}$, then its accessible entropy can always be as high as the real entropy of G; to generate its i-th block y_i, $\widetilde{G}$ samples x uniformly at random from the set $\{x' : G(x')_1 = y_1, \ldots, G(x')_{i-1} = y_{i-1}\}$. This strategy, however, is not always possible for a computationally bounded $\widetilde{G}$.

The collision resistance example given earlier provides evidence that when allowing public parameters, there are efficient generators whose computationally accessible entropy is much smaller than their real Shannon entropy. Indeed, the real entropy of the generator we considered above is n (namely, the total entropy in x), but its accessible entropy is at most $m + \mathrm{neg}(n) \ll n$, where m is the output length of the collision-resistant hash function.

As we shall see, we do not need collision resistance; any one-way function can be used to construct an inaccessible entropy generator (without public parameters). An application of this result is an alternative construction of statistically hiding commitment schemes from arbitrary one-way functions. This construction is significantly simpler and more efficient than the previous construction of Haitner et al. [10]. It also conceptually unifies the construction of statistically hiding commitments from

one-way functions with the construction of pseudorandom generators discussed in
the previous section: the first step of both constructions is to show that the one-
way function directly yields a generator with a gap between its real entropy and
"computational entropy" (pseudoentropy in the case of pseudorandom generators,
and accessible entropy in the case of statistically hiding commitments). This gap is
then amplified by repetitions and finally combined with various forms of hashing to
obtain the desired primitive.

Constructing an inaccessible entropy generator from one-way functions.   For
a one-way function $f\colon \{0,1\}^n \mapsto \{0,1\}^n$, consider the $(n+1)$-block generator

$$G(x) = (f(x)_1, f(x)_2, \ldots, f(x)_n, x).$$

Notice that this construction is the same as the construction of a next-block pseudoentropy generator from a one-way function (Construction 4.1), except that we
have broken $f(x)$ into one-bit blocks rather than breaking x. Again, the real entropy
of $G(U_n)$ is n. It can be shown that the accessible entropy of G is at most $n - \log n$,
so again we have an entropy gap of $\log n$ bit.

4.1.3 Rest of This Tutorial

Standard notations, definitions, and facts, are given in Section 4.2. An elaborated
discussion of next-block pseudoentropy, containing formal definitions, a construction from one-way functions, and its use in constricting pseudorandom generators,
is given in Section 4.3. An elaborated discussion of inaccessible entropy, with formal definitions, a construction from one-way functions, and its use in constructing
statistically hiding commitment schemes, is given in Section 4.4. In both sections,
we have chosen simplicity and clarity over full generality and efficiency. For details
of the latter, see the Further Reading section below.

4.1.4 Related Work and Further Reading

Pseudoentropy.   More details and improvements on the construction of pseudorandom generator from one-way functions via next-block pseudoentropy can be
found in the works of Haitner et al. [14] and Vadhan and Zheng [29]. In particular, Vadhan and Zheng [29] also show how to save a factor of n in the seed-length
blow up in the reduction from next-block pseudoentropy generator to PRG, thereby
reducing the seed length from $\tilde{O}(n^4)$ to $\tilde{O}(n^3)$ (at the price of making adaptive calls
to the one-way function). Holenstein and Sinha [20] showed that any black-box
construction of a pseudorandom generator from a one-way function on n-bit inputs
must invoke the one-way function $\Omega(n/\log n)$ times. Their lower bound also applies to regular one-way functions (of unknown regularity), and is tight in this case
(due to the constructions of [8, 13]). The constructions of Haitner et al. [14] and of
Vadhan and Zheng [29] from arbitrary one-way functions invoke the one-way function $\tilde{O}(n^3)$ times. It remains open whether the super linear number of invocations

or the super-linear seed length is necessary, or the constructions can be furthered improved.

Several other computational analogues of entropy have been studied in the literature (cf. [1, 21]), all of which serve as ways of capturing the idea that a distribution "behaves like" one of higher entropy.

Inaccessible entropy. The details of the construction of statistically hiding commitments from one-way functions via inaccessible entropy can be found in the work of Haitner et al. [16]. A preliminary version of that paper [11] uses a more general, and more complicated, notion of accessible entropy which measures the accessible entropy of *protocols* rather than generators. This latter notion is used in [11] to show that, if NP has constant-round interactive proofs that are black-box zero knowledge under parallel composition, then there exist constant-round statistically hiding commitment schemes. A subsequent work of Haitner et al. [12] uses a simplified version of accessible entropy to present a simpler and more efficient construction of *universal one-way functions* from any one-way function. One of the two inaccessible entropy generators considered in [12], for constructing universal one-way functions, is very similar to the constructionist next-block pseudoentropy and inaccessible entropy generators discussed above (in Sections 4.1.1 and 4.1.2). Hence, all of these three notions of computational entropy can be found in any one-way function using very similar constructions, all simple variants of $G(x) = (f(x), x)$, where f is an arbitrary one-way function.

The notion of inaccessible entropy, of the simpler variant appearing in [12], is in a sense implicit in the work of Rompel [27], who first showed how to base universal one-way functions on any one-way functions.

4.2 Preliminaries

4.2.1 Notation

We use calligraphic letters to denote sets, upper-case for random variables, lower-case for values, bold-face for vectors. and sanserif for algorithms (i.e., Turing machines). For $n \in \mathbb{N}$, let $[n] = \{1, \ldots, n\}$. For vector $\mathbf{y} = (y_1, \ldots, y_n)$ and $\mathcal{J} \subseteq [n]$, let $\mathbf{y}_{\mathcal{J}} = (y_{i_1}, \ldots, y_{i_{|\mathcal{J}|}})$, where $i_1 < \ldots < i_{|\mathcal{J}|}$ are the elements of $\mathcal{J}$. Let $\mathbf{y}_{<j} = \mathbf{y}_{[j-1]} = (y_1, \ldots, y_{j-1})$ and $\mathbf{y}_{\leq j} = \mathbf{y}_{[j]} = (y_1, \ldots, y_j)$. Both notations naturally extend to an ordered list of elements that is embedded in a larger vector (i.e., given $(a_1, b_1, \ldots, a_n, b_n)$, $a_{<3}$ refers to the vector (a_1, a_2)). Let poly denote the set of all positive polynomials, let $\mathsf{ppt}^{\mathsf{NU}}$ stand for a *nonuniform* probabilistic polynomial-time algorithm. A function $v \colon \mathbb{N} \mapsto [0, 1]$ is *negligible*, denoted $v(n) = \mathrm{neg}(n)$, if $v(n) < 1/p(n)$ for every $p \in$ poly and large enough n. For a function f and a set $\mathcal{S}$, let $\mathrm{Im}(f(\mathcal{S})) = \{f(x) \colon x \in \mathcal{S}\}$.

4.2.2 Random Variables

Let X and Y be random variables taking values in a discrete universe $\mathcal{U}$. We adopt the convention that, when the same random variable appears multiple times in an expression, all occurrences refer to the same instantiation. For example, $\Pr[X = X]$ is 1. For an event E, we write $X|_E$ to denote the random variable X conditioned on E. We let $\Pr_{X|Y}[x|y]$ stand for $\Pr[X = x \mid Y = y]$. The *support* of a random variable X, denoted $\mathrm{Supp}(X)$, is defined as $\{x \colon \Pr[X = x] > 0\}$. The variable X is *flat* if it is uniform on its support. Let U_n denote a random variable that is uniform over $\{0, 1\}^n$. For $t \in \mathbb{N}$, let $X^{(t)} = (X^1, \ldots, X^t)$, where $X^1, \ldots, X^t$ are independent copies of X.

We write $X \equiv Y$ to indicate that X and Y are identically distributed. We write $\Delta(X, Y)$ to denote the *statistical difference* (also known as variation distance) between X and Y, i.e.,

$$\Delta(X, Y) = \max_{T \subseteq \mathcal{U}} |\Pr[X \in T] - \Pr[Y \in T]|.$$

If $\Delta(X, Y) \leq \varepsilon$ [resp., $\Delta(X, Y) > \varepsilon$], we say that X and Y are *ε-close* [resp., *ε-far*]. Two random variables $X = X(n)$ and $Y = Y(n)$ are *statistically indistinguishable*, denoted $X \approx_{\mathsf{S}} Y$, if for any unbounded algorithm D, it holds that $|\Pr[\mathsf{D}(1^n, X(n)) = 1] - \Pr[\mathsf{D}(1^n, Y(n)) = 1]| = \mathrm{neg}(n)$.[7] Similarly, X and Y are *nonuniformly* computationally indistinguishable, denoted $X \approx_{\mathsf{nu-C}} Y$], if $|\Pr[\mathsf{D}(1^n, X(n)) = 1] - \Pr[\mathsf{D}(1^n, Y(n)) = 1]| = \mathrm{neg}(n)$ for every $\mathsf{ppt}^{\mathsf{NU}}$ D.

4.2.3 Entropy Measures

We refer to several measures of entropy. The relation and motivation of these measures is best understood by considering a notion that we will refer to as the sample-entropy: for a random variable X and $x \in \mathrm{Supp}(X)$, the *sample-entropy* of x with respect to X is the quantity

$$\mathrm{H}_X(x) := \log \tfrac{1}{\Pr[X=x]},$$

letting $\mathrm{H}_X(x) = \infty$ for $x \notin \mathrm{Supp}(X)$, and $2^{-\infty} = 0$.

The sample-entropy measures the amount of "randomness" or "surprise" in the specific sample x, assuming that x has been generated according to X. Using this notion, we can define the *Shannon entropy* $\mathrm{H}(X)$ and *min-entropy* $\mathrm{H}_\infty(X)$ as follows:

$$\mathrm{H}(X) := \mathop{\mathrm{E}}_{x \xleftarrow{R} X} [\mathrm{H}_X(x)],$$

$$\mathrm{H}_\infty(X) := \min_{x \in \mathrm{Supp}(X)} \mathrm{H}_X(x).$$

The *collision probability* of X is defined by $\mathrm{CP}(X) := \sum_{x \in \mathrm{Supp}(X)} \Pr_X[x]^2 = \Pr_{(x,x') \xleftarrow{R} X^2}[x = x']$, and its *Rényi-entropy* is defined by

$$\mathrm{H}_2(X) := -\log \mathrm{CP}(X).$$

---

[7] This is equivalent to asking that $\Delta(X(n), Y(n)) = \mathrm{neg}(n)$.

We will also discuss the *max-entropy* $H_0(X) := \log(1/|\operatorname{Supp}(X)|)$. The term "max-entropy" and its relation to the sample-entropy will be made apparent below.

It can be shown that $H_\infty(X) \le H_2(X) \le H(X) \le H_0(X)$ with each inequality being an equality if and only if X is flat. Thus, saying $H_\infty(X) \ge k$ is a strong way of saying that X has "high entropy" and $H_0(X) \le k$ a strong way of saying that X as "low entropy".

The following fact quantifies the probability that the sample-entropy is larger than the max-entropy.

Lemma 4.2.1. *For random variable X it holds that*

1. $\operatorname*{E}_{x \xleftarrow{R} X}\left[2^{H_X(x)}\right] = |\operatorname{Supp}(X)|$.
2. $\operatorname*{Pr}_{x \xleftarrow{R} X}\left[H_X(x) > \log \frac{1}{\varepsilon} + H_0(X)\right] < \varepsilon$, *for any $\varepsilon > 0$.*

Proof: For the first item, compute

$$\operatorname*{E}_{x \xleftarrow{R} X}\left[2^{H_X(x)}\right] = \sum_{x \in \operatorname{Supp}(X)} 2^{-H_X(x)} \cdot 2^{H_X(x)}$$

$$= \sum_{x \in \operatorname{Supp}(X)} 1$$

$$= |\operatorname{Supp}(X)|.$$

The second item follows by the first item and Markov inequality.

$$\operatorname*{Pr}_{x \xleftarrow{R} X}\left[H_X(x) > \log \frac{1}{\varepsilon} + H_0(X)\right] = \operatorname*{Pr}_{x \xleftarrow{R} X}\left[2^{H_X(x)} > \frac{1}{\varepsilon} \cdot |\operatorname{Supp}(X)|\right]$$

$$< \varepsilon.$$

$\square$

Conditional entropies. We will also be interested in conditional versions of entropy. For jointly distributed random variables (X, Y) and $(x, y) \in \operatorname{Supp}(X, Y)$, we define the *conditional sample-entropy* to be $H_{X|Y}(x|y) = \log \frac{1}{\Pr_{X|Y}[x|y]} = \log \frac{1}{\Pr[X=x|Y=y]}$. Then the standard *conditional Shannon entropy* can be written as

$$H(X \mid Y) = \operatorname*{E}_{(x,y) \xleftarrow{R} (X,Y)}\left[H_{X|Y}(x \mid y)\right] = \operatorname*{E}_{y \xleftarrow{R} Y}\left[H(X|_{Y=y})\right] = H(X, Y) - H(Y).$$

The following known lemma states that conditioning on a "short" variable is unlikely to change the sample-entropy by much.

Lemma 4.2.2. *Let X and Y be random variables, let $k = H_\infty(X)$, and let $\ell = H_0(Y)$. Then, for any $t > 0$, it holds that*

$$\operatorname*{Pr}_{(x,y) \xleftarrow{R} (X,Y)}\left[H_{X|Y}(x|y) < k - \ell - t\right] < 2^{-t}.$$

Proof: For $y \in \text{Supp}(Y)$, let $\mathcal{X}_y = \{x \in \text{Supp}(X): H_{X|Y}(x|y) < k - \ell - t\}$. We have $|\mathcal{X}_y| < 2^{k-\ell-t}$. Hence, $|\mathcal{X}| = \bigcup_{y \in \text{Supp}(Y)} \mathcal{X}_y| < 2^\ell \cdot 2^{k-\ell-t} = 2^{k-t}$. It follows that

$$\Pr_{(x,y) \overset{R}{\leftarrow} (X,Y)} [H_{X|Y}(x|y) < k - \ell - t] \le \Pr_{(x,y) \overset{R}{\leftarrow} (X,Y)} [x \in \mathcal{X}] < 2^{-k} \cdot 2^{k-t} = 2^{-t}.$$

$\square$

Smoothed entropies. The following lemma will allow us to think of a random variable X whose sample-entropy is high with high probability as if it has high min-entropy (i.e., as if its sample-entropy function is "smoother", with no picks).

Lemma 4.2.3. *Let X, Y be random variable and let $\varepsilon > 0$.*

1. *Suppose $\Pr_{x \overset{R}{\leftarrow} X} [H_X(x) \ge k] \ge 1 - \varepsilon$, then X is ε-close to a random variable X' with $H_\infty(X') \ge k$.*
2. *Suppose $\Pr_{(x,y) \overset{R}{\leftarrow} (X,Y)} [H_{X|Y}(x|y) \ge k] \ge 1 - \varepsilon$, then (X, Y) is ε-close to a random variable (X', Y') with $H_{X'|Y'}(x|y) \ge k$ for any $(x, y) \in \text{Supp}(X', Y')$. Further, Y' and Y are identically distributed.*

Proof Sketch. For the first item, we modify X on an ε fraction of the probability space (corresponding to when X takes on a value x such that $H_X(x) \ge k$) to bring all probabilities to be smaller than or equal to 2^{-k}.

The second item is proved via similar means, while when changing (X, Y), we do so without changing the "Y" coordinate.

Flattening Shannon entropy. It is well known that the Shannon entropy of a random variable can be converted to min-entropy (up to small statistical distance) by taking independent copies of this variable.

Lemma 4.2.4 ([31], Theorem 3.14). *Let X be a random variables taking values in a universe $\mathcal{U}$, let $t \in \mathbb{N}$, and let $0 < \varepsilon \le 1/e^2$. Then with probability at least $1 - \varepsilon$ over $x \overset{R}{\leftarrow} X^{(t)}$,*

$$H_{X^{(t)}}(x) - t \cdot H(X) \ge -O\left(\sqrt{t \cdot \log \tfrac{1}{\varepsilon}} \cdot \log(|\mathcal{U}| \cdot t)\right).$$

We will make use of the following "conditional variant" of Theorem 4.2.4:

Lemma 4.2.5. *Let X and Y be jointly distributed random variables where X takes values in a universe $\mathcal{U}$, let $t \in \mathbb{N}$, and let $0 < \varepsilon \le 1/e^2$. Then with probability at least $1 - \varepsilon$ over $(x, y) \leftarrow (X', Y') = (X, Y)^{(t)}$,*

$$H_{X'|Y'}(x \mid y) - t \cdot H(X \mid Y) \ge -O\left(\sqrt{t \cdot \log \tfrac{1}{\varepsilon}} \cdot \log(|\mathcal{U}| \cdot t)\right).$$

The proof of Theorem 4.2.5 follows the same line as the proof of Theorem 4.2.4, by considering the random variable $H_{X|Y}(X|Y)$ instead of $H_X(X)$.

Sub-additivity. The chain rule for Shannon entropy yields that

$$H(X = (X_1, \ldots, X_t)) = \sum_i H(X_i | X_1, \ldots, X_{i-1}) \le \sum_i H(X_i).$$

The following lemma shows that a variant of the above also holds for sample-entropy.

Lemma 4.2.6. *For random variables* $\mathbf{X} = (X_1, \ldots, X_t)$*, it holds that*

1. $E_{\mathbf{x} \xleftarrow{R} \mathbf{X}} \left[2^{H_{\mathbf{X}}(\mathbf{x}) - \sum_t H_{X_i}(\mathbf{x}_i)} \right] \le 1.$
2. $\Pr_{\mathbf{x} \xleftarrow{R} \mathbf{X}} \left[H_{\mathbf{X}}(\mathbf{x}) > \log \frac{1}{\varepsilon} + \sum_{i \in [t]} H_{X_i}(\mathbf{x}_i) \right] < \varepsilon,$ *for any* $\varepsilon > 0.$

Proof: As in Theorem 4.2.1, the second part follows from the first by Markov's inequality. For the first part, compute

$$E_{\mathbf{x} \xleftarrow{R} \mathbf{X}} \left[2^{H_{\mathbf{X}}(\mathbf{x}) - \sum_t H_{X_i}(\mathbf{x}_i)} \right] = \sum_{\mathbf{x} \in \text{Supp}(X)} \Pr[\mathbf{X} = \mathbf{x}] \cdot \frac{\prod_{i \in [t]} \Pr[X_i = \mathbf{x}_i]}{\Pr[\mathbf{X} = \mathbf{x}]}$$

$$= \sum_{\mathbf{x} \in \text{Supp}(X)} \prod_i \Pr[X_i = \mathbf{x}_i]$$

$$\le 1.$$

□

The following lemma generalizes Theorem 4.2.1 to settings that come up naturally when upper bounding the accessible entropy of a generator (as we do in Section 4.4):

Definition 4.2.7. *For a t-tuple random variable* $\mathbf{X} = (X_1, \ldots, X_t)$*,* $\mathbf{x} \in \text{Supp}(X)$ *and* $\mathcal{J} \subseteq [t]$*, let*

$$H_{\mathbf{X}, \mathcal{J}}(\mathbf{x}) = \sum_{i \in \mathcal{J}} H_{X_i | \mathbf{X}_{<i}}(\mathbf{x}_i | \mathbf{x}_{<i}).$$

Lemma 4.2.8. *Let* $\mathbf{X} = (X_1, \ldots, X_t)$ *be a sequence of random variables and let* $\mathcal{J} \subseteq [t]$*. Then,*

1. $E_{\mathbf{x} \xleftarrow{R} \mathbf{X}} \left[2^{H_{\mathbf{X}, \mathcal{J}}(\mathbf{x})} \right] \le |\text{Supp}(X_{\mathcal{J}})|.$
2. $\Pr_{\mathbf{x} \xleftarrow{R} \mathbf{X}} \left[H_{\mathbf{X}, \mathcal{J}}(\mathbf{x}) > \log \frac{1}{\varepsilon} + H_0(X_{\mathcal{J}}) \right] < \varepsilon,$ *for any* $\varepsilon > 0.$

Proof: The second item follows from the first one as in the proof of Theorem 4.2.1. We prove the first item by induction on t and $|J|$. The case $t = 1$ is immediate, so we assume for all $(t', \mathcal{J}')$ with $(t', |\mathcal{J}'|) < (t, |\mathcal{J}|)$ and prove it for $(t, \mathcal{J})$. Assume that $1 \in \mathcal{J}$ (the case $1 \notin \mathcal{J}$ is analogous) and let $\mathbf{X}_{-1} = (X_2, \ldots, X_t)$ and $\mathcal{J}_{-1} = \{i-1 : i \in \mathcal{J} \setminus \{1\}\}$. Compute

$$\mathop{E}_{\mathbf{x}\xleftarrow{R}\mathbf{X}}\left[2^{H_{\mathbf{x},\mathcal{J}}(\mathbf{x})}\right] = \sum_{x_1\in\mathrm{Supp}(X_1)} 2^{-H_{X_1}(x_1)}\cdot 2^{H_{X_1}(x_1)}\cdot \mathop{E}_{\mathbf{x}\xleftarrow{R}\mathbf{X}_{-1}|x_1=x_1}\left[2^{H_{\mathbf{X}_{-1}|x_1=x_1},\mathcal{J}_{-1}(\mathbf{x})}\right]$$

$$\leq \sum_{x_1\in\mathrm{Supp}(X_1)} 1\cdot\left|\mathrm{Supp}((\mathbf{X}_{-1})_{\mathcal{J}_{-1}}|x_1=x_1)\right|$$

$$= \sum_{x_1\in\mathrm{Supp}(X_1)} \left|\mathrm{Supp}(\mathbf{X}_{\mathcal{J}\setminus\{1\}}|x_1=x_1)\right|$$

$$\leq \left|\mathrm{Supp}(\mathbf{X}_{\mathcal{J}})\right|.$$

□

4.2.4 Hashing

We will use two types of (combinatorial) "hash" functions.

4.2.4.1 Two-Universal Hashing

Definition 4.2.9 (Two-universal function family). *A function family* $\mathcal{H} = \{h: \mathcal{D} \mapsto \mathcal{R}\}$ *is* two universal *if* $\forall x \neq x' \in \mathcal{D}$, *it holds that* $\Pr_{h\leftarrow\mathcal{H}}[h(x) = h(x')] \leq 1/|\mathcal{R}|$.

An example of such a function family is the set $\mathcal{H}_{s,t} = \{0,1\}^{s\times t}$ of Boolean matrices, where for $h \in \mathcal{H}_{s,t}$ and $x \in \{0,1\}^s$, we let $h(x) = h\times x$ (i.e., the matrix vector product over GF_2). Another canonical example is $\mathcal{H}_{s,t} = \{0,1\}^s$ defined by $h(x) := h\cdot x$ over $GF(2^s)$, truncated to its first t bits.

A useful application of two-universal hash functions is to convert a source of high Rényi entropy into a (close to) uniform distribution.

Lemma 4.2.10 (Leftover hash lemma [24, 23]). *Let X be a random variable over* $\{0,1\}^n$ *with* $H_2(X) \geq k$, *let* $\mathcal{H} = \{g: \{0,1\}^n \mapsto \{0,1\}^m\}$ *be two-universal, and let* $H \xleftarrow{R} \mathcal{H}$. *Then* $SD((H,H(X)),(H,\mathcal{U}_m)) \leq \frac{1}{2}\cdot 2^{(m-k)/2}$.

4.2.4.2 Many-wise Independent Hashing

Definition 4.2.11 (ℓ-Wise independent function family). *A function family* $\mathcal{H} = \{h: \mathcal{D} \mapsto \mathcal{R}\}$ *is* ℓ-wise independent *if for any distinct* $x_1,\ldots,x_\ell \in \mathcal{D}$, *it holds that* $(H(x_1),\ldots,H(x_\ell))$ *for* $H \xleftarrow{R} \mathcal{H}$ *is uniform over* $\mathcal{R}^\ell$.

The canonical example of such an ℓ-wise independent function family is $\mathcal{H}_{s,t,\ell} = (\{0,1\}^s)^\ell$ defined by $(h_0,\ldots,h_{\ell-i})(x) := \sum_{0\leq i\leq\ell-1} h_i\cdot x^i$ over $GF(2^s)$, truncated to its first t bits.

It is easy to see that, for $\ell > 1$, an ℓ-wise independent function family is two-universal, but ℓ-wise independent function families, in particular with larger value of ℓ, have stronger guarantees on their output distribution compared with two-universal hashing. We will state, and use, one such guarantee in the construction of statistically hiding commitment schemes presented in Section 4.4.

4.2.5 One-Way Functions

We recall the standard definition of one-way functions.

Definition 4.2.12 (One-way functions). *A polynomial-time computable* $f\colon \{0,1\}^n \mapsto \{0,1\}^*$ *is nonuniformly* **one way** *if for every* $\mathsf{ppt}^{\mathsf{NU}}$ A

$$\Pr_{y \leftarrow f(U_{s(n)})}\left[\mathsf{A}(1^n, y) \in f^{-1}(y)\right] = \mathrm{neg}(n). \qquad (4.2)$$

Without loss of generality, cf. [13], it can be assumed that $s(n) = n$ and f is length-preserving (i.e., $|f(x)| = |x|$).

4.3 Next-Block Entropy and Pseudorandom Generators

In this section, we formally define the notion of next-block pseudoentropy, and use it as intermediate tool to construct pseudorandom generators from one-way functions. Preferring clarity over generality, we present a simplified version of the definitions and constructions. For the full details see [14].

We start in Section 4.3.1, by presenting the formal definition of next-block pseudoentropy. In Section 4.3.2 we show that any one-way function can be used to construct a generator with a useful amount of next-block pseudoentropy. In Section 4.3.3 we develop means to manipulate next-block pseudoentropy. Finally, in Section 4.3.4, we show how to convert generators of the type constructed in Section 4.3.2 into pseudorandom generators, thus reproving the fundamental result that pseudorandom generators can be based on any one-way function.

4.3.1 Next-Block Pseudoentropy

Recall from the introduction that the next-block pseudoentropy is of a similar spirit to the Blum and Micali [3] notion of next-bit unpredictability; a random variable $X = (X_1, \ldots, X_m)$ is *next-bit unpredictable* if the bit X_i cannot be predicted with nonnegligible advantage from $X_{<i} = (X_1, X_2, \ldots, X_{i-1})$, or alternatively, X_i is pseudorandom given $X_{<i}$. Next-block pseudoentropy relaxes this notion by only requiring that X_i has some pseudoentropy given $X_{<i}$.

We now formally define the notion of next-block pseudoentropy for the cases of both Shannon entropy and min-entropy. The definition below differs from the definition of [14], in that we require the indistinguishability to hold (also) against *nonuniform adversaries*. This change simplifies the definitions and proofs (see Theorem 4.3.3), but at the price that we can only construct such pseudoentropy generators from functions that are nonuniformly one-way (i.e., ones that are hard to invert for such nonuniform adversaries). We start by recalling the more standard definitions of pseudoentropy and pseudorandomness (to be consistent with the next-block pseudoentropy definitions given below, we give the nonuniform version of these definitions).

Definition 4.3.1 (Pseudoentropy and pseudorandomness). *Let n be a security parameter and* $X = X(n)$ *be a random variable distributed over strings of length*

$\ell(n) \leq \text{poly}(n)$. *We say that* $X = X(n)$ *has* pseudoentropy *(at least)* $k = k(n)$ *if there exists a random variable* $Y = Y(n)$, *such that*

1. $H(Y) \geq k$, *and*
2. X *and* Y *are nonuniformly computationally indistinguishable. I.e., for every* ppt^{NU} D, *it holds that*

$$\Pr[D(1^n, X) = 1] - \Pr[D(1^n, Y) = 1] = \text{neg}(n).$$

If $H_\infty(Y) \geq k$, *we say that* X *has* pseudo-min-entropy *(at least)* k, *where if* $k = \ell(n)$, *we say that* X *is* pseudorandom *(which is equivalent to asking that* X *is computationally nonuniformly indistinguishable from* U_ℓ).

Finally, a polynomial-time computable function $G: \{0,1\}^n \mapsto \{0,1\}^{\ell(n)}$ *is a* pseudorandom generator *if* $\ell > n$ *and* $G(U_n)$ *is pseudorandom.*

That is, pseudoentropy is the computational analog of entropy. In construct, next-block pseudoentropy is a computational analog of unpredictability.

Definition 4.3.2. *(Next-block pseudoentropy) Let* $m = m(n)$ *be an integer function. A random variable* $X = X(n) = (X_1, \ldots, X_m)$ *is said to have* next-block (Shannon) pseudoentropy *(at least)* $k = k(n)$ *if there exists a (jointly distributed) random variable* $Y = Y(n) = (Y_1, \ldots, Y_m)$ *such that*

1. $\sum_{i=1}^m H(Y_i \mid X_{<i}) \geq k$, *and*
2. Y *is* block-wise indistinguishable from X: *for every* ppt^{NU} D *and* $i = i(n) \in [m(n)]$,

$$\Pr[D(1^n, X_{\leq i}) = 1] - \Pr[D(1^n, X_{<i}, Y_i) = 1] = \text{neg}(n).$$

Every block of X has next-block (Shannon) pseudoentropy *at least* $\alpha = \alpha(n)$ *if condition* 1 *above is replaced with*

1. $H(Y_i|_{X_{<i}=x_{<i}}) \geq \alpha$, *for every* $x \in \text{Supp}(X)$ *and* $i \in [m]$.

Every block of X has next-block pseudo-min-entropy *at least* α *if condition* 1 *above is replaced with*

1. $H_\infty(Y_i|_{X_{<i}=x_{<i}}) \geq \alpha$, *for every* $x \in \text{Supp}(X)$ *and* $i \in [m]$.

Finally, a generator G *over* $\{0,1\}^*$ *has* next-block pseudoentropy at least k *if (the random variable)* $G(U_n)$ *has. Similarly, every block of* G *has* next-block pseudoentropy [resp., pseudo-min-entropy] *at least* α *if* $G(U_n)$ *has.*

The above definitions naturally extend to generators that are only defined over some input lengths (e.g., on inputs of length $n^2 + n$ for all $n \in \mathbb{N}$). Our constructions directly yield such input-restricted generators, but since the inputs on which they are defined are the image of a polynomial (such as $n^2 + n$), they can be converted to ones defined on all inputs in a standard way.[8]

Throughout, we often omit the parameter n when its value is clear from the context.

Remark 4.3.3 (Uniform distinguishers). *When working with a random variable X with a certain guarantee about its pseudoentropy (here as a generic name for the different types of pseudoentropy), one often likes to lower-bound the amount of pseudoentropy several independent copies of X have (jointly). Such lower bounds are used, for instance, in all constructions of pseudorandom generators from one-way functions [13, 14, 17, 19, 29]. Proving such lower bounds, however, typically requires the ability to sample efficiently from X, and also from a random variable Y that realizes the pseudoentropy of X (cf. Theorem 4.3.1). While the X's in consideration are typically efficiently samplable, this is often not the case with respect to the Y's. Considering nonuniform distinguishers bypasses this issue; such distinguishers can get the samples as a nonuniform advice. An alternative approach is to alter the definition of pseudoentropy to require that the random variables in consideration (i.e., X and Y) are computationally indistinguishable by (uniform) algorithms that have access to an oracle that samples from the joint distribution of (X, Y). This is the approach taken in [14], where the construction we present here is proven to be secure in uniform settings (in order to construct pseudorandom generators secure against uniform distinguishers, from one-way functions secure against uniform inverters.*

4.3.2 Next-Block Pseudoentropy Generators from One-Way Functions

In this section, we show how to construct a next-block pseudoentropy generator G_{nb}^{f} out of a one-way function $f: \{0, 1\}^n \mapsto \{0, 1\}^n$.

Notation 4.3.4 *For $n, \ell \in \mathbb{N}$, let $\mathcal{H}_{n,\ell}$ be the family of $\ell \times n$ Boolean matrices, and let $\mathcal{H}_n = \mathcal{H}_{n,n}$. For $h \in \mathcal{H}_{n,\ell}$ and $x \in \{0, 1\}^n$, let $h(x) = hx$ (i.e., the matrix vector product over $\mathrm{GF}(2)$). Throughout, we denote by H_n the random variable that is uniformly distributed over $\mathcal{H}_n$.*

Definition 4.3.5. *On $x \in \{0, 1\}^n$, $h \in \mathcal{H}_n$, and $f: \{0, 1\}^n \mapsto \{0, 1\}^n$, define $G_{\mathrm{nb}}^{f}: \{0, 1\}^n \times \mathcal{H}_n \mapsto \{0, 1\}^n \times \mathcal{H}_n \times \{0, 1\}^n$ by*

$$G_{\mathrm{nb}}^{f}(x, h) = (f(x), h, h(x)).$$

Theorem 4.3.6. *Let $f: \{0, 1\}^n \mapsto \{0, 1\}^n$ and let $G_{\mathrm{nb}} = G_{\mathrm{nb}}^{f}$ be according to Theorem 4.3.5, viewed as a $(t(n) = n^2 + 2n)$-block generator (i.e., each output bit forms*

---

[8] I.e., on input of arbitrary length, apply the input-restricted generator on the longest prefix of the input that matches the restricted set of lengths, and append the unused suffix of the input to the output.

a separate block) over $(s(n) = n^2 + n)$-bit strings. Assuming f is nonuniformly one-way, then G_{nb}^f has next-block pseudoentropy at least $s(n) + c \cdot \log n$, for any $c > 0$.

Namely, the next-block pseudoentropy of G_{nb}^f is $\log n$ bits larger than its input entropy.

Remark 4.3.7 (Tighter reductions). *Haitner et al. [14] proved a variant of Theorem 4.3.6 in which the family H_n is replaced by a more sophisticated function family of description length $\Theta(n)$. As discussed in the introduction, Vadhan and Zheng [29] took this a step further and proved a variant of this theorem without using any function family. That is, they proved that $G_{nb}^f(x) = (f(x), x)$ has next-block pseudoentropy $n + \log n$. In both cases, the gap between the real entropy of the output and the next-block pseudoentropy is $\log n$, as in Theorem 4.3.6, but the input length is only $\Theta(n)$ (versus $\Theta(n^2)$ in Theorem 4.3.6). This better ratio between the entropy gap and the input length yields a final pseudorandom generator of much shorter seed length (see Theorem 4.3.18). Both constructions, and in particular that of [29], require a more sophisticated analysis than the one we present here (also in their nonuniform forms).*

A key step towards proving Theorem 4.3.6 is analyzing the following (possibly inefficient) function g^f:

Definition 4.3.8. *For* $f \colon \{0,1\}^n \mapsto \{0,1\}^n$, *let* $\mathsf{D_f}(y) = \lceil \log |f^{-1}(y) = \{x \in \{0,1\}^n \colon f(x) = y\}| \rceil$, *and define g^f over $\{0,1\}^n \times \mathcal{H}_n$, by*

$$g^f(x,h) = (f(x), h, h(x)_{1,\ldots,\mathsf{D_f}(f(x))}).$$

That is, $g(x,h)$ outputs a prefix of $G_{nb}(x,h)$ whose length depends on the "degeneracy" of $f(x)$. What makes g interesting is that it is both close to being injective and hard to invert. To see this, note that $\mathsf{H}_\infty(U_n|_{f(U_n)=y}) = \mathsf{H}_0(U_n|_{f(U_n)=y}) = \log |f^{-1}(y)| \approx \mathsf{D_f}(y)$. Hence, the two-universality of $\mathcal{H}$ implies that $g(U_n, H_n)$ determines U_n with constant probability. In other words, $g(U_n, H_n)$ has a single preimage with constant probability. But the two-universality of $\mathcal{H}$ also yields that, for every $k(U_n) = \mathsf{D_f}(f(U_n)) - \omega(\log n)$, it holds that $H_n(U_n)_{1,\ldots,k(U_n)}$ is statistically *close to uniform* given $(f(U_n), H_n)$. Hence, $H_n(U_n)_{1,\ldots,\mathsf{D_f}(f(U_n))}$ does not provide enough information to enable an efficient inversion of f. (The extra $O(\log n)$ bits beyond $k(U_n)$ can only increase the inversion probability by a $\mathrm{poly}(n)$ factor.)

The following claims state formally the two properties of g mentioned above. The first claim states that the collision probability of g is small,[9] yielding that g has high entropy.

Claim 4.3.9. *Let* $f \colon \{0,1\}^n \mapsto \{0,1\}^n$ *and let* $g = g^f$ *as in Theorem 4.3.8. Then* $\mathrm{CP}(g(U_n, H_n)) \leq \frac{3}{|\mathcal{H}_n \times \{0,1\}^n|}$.

---

[9] Recall that the collision probability of a random variable X is defined as $\mathrm{CP}(X) = \Pr_{(x,x') \overset{R}{\leftarrow} X^2}[x = x']$, and that its Rényi entropy defined by $\mathsf{H}_2(X) = -\log \mathrm{CP}(X)$ lower-bounds its Shannon entropy.

Definition 4.3.10 (Hard-to-invert functions). *A function* $q\colon \{0,1\}^n \mapsto \{0,1\}^*$ *is* (nonuniformly) hard to invert *if* $\Pr_{\underset{y\leftarrow q(U_n)}{R}}\left[A(1^n,y) \in q^{-1}(y)\right] = \operatorname{neg}(n)$ *for every* $\operatorname{ppt}^{\mathsf{NU}}$ A.

Namely, an hard-to-invert function is a one-way function without the efficient computability requirement.

Claim 4.3.11. *Let* $f\colon \{0,1\}^n \mapsto \{0,1\}^n$ *and let* $g = g^f$ *be according to Theorem 4.3.8. Assuming* f *is nonuniformly one-way,* g *is hard to invert.*

The proof of the above claims is given below, but first let us use it for proving Theorem 4.3.6. We will also use the Goldreich–Levin hardcore lemma.

Lemma 4.3.12 (Goldreich–Levin hardcore lemma, [7]). *Let* $q\colon \{0,1\}^n \mapsto \{0,1\}^*$ *be a hard-to-invert function and let* $\ell = \ell(n) \in O(\log n)$, *then* $(q(U_n), H_{n,\ell}, H_{n,\ell}(U_n))$ *is nonuniform computationally indistinguishable from* $(q(U_n), H_{n,\ell}, U'_\ell)$. [10]

Proving Theorem 4.3.6. Proof: [Proof of Theorem 4.3.6] Let $s(n) = n^2 + n$ be G_{nb}'s input length, and let $\mathsf{D_f}$ and $g = g^f$ be as in Theorem 4.3.8. We prove that G_{nb}'s next-block pseudoentropy is at least $s(n) + \log n - 2$, where the proof that it is larger than $s(n) + c \cdot \log n$ for any $c > 0$ follows along similar lines. Let $\ell = \ell(n) = 2\log n$ and assume for simplicity that $\log n \in \mathbb{N}$. The one-wayness of f guarantees that $\mathsf{D_f}(f(x)) \le n - \ell$ for all sufficiently large n and every $x \in \{0,1\}^n$; otherwise, the trivial inverter that returns a uniform element in $\{0,1\}^n$ inverts f with nonnegligible probability.

Define g' over $\{0,1\}^n \times \mathcal{H}_{n,n-\ell}$, by $g'(x,h) = (f(x), h, h(x)_{1,\dots,\mathsf{D_f}(f(x))})$ (i.e., we have removed the last ℓ rows from the matrix defining the hash function h). The above observation about f yields that g' is well defined, and the hardness to invert of g (Theorem 4.3.9) yields by a simple reduction that g' is also hard to invert.

Since g' is hard to invert, Theorem 4.3.12 yields that

$$(f(U_n), H_{n,n-\ell}, H_{n,n-\ell}(U_n)_{1,\dots,\mathsf{D_f}(f(U_n))}, H'_{n,\ell}, H'_{n,\ell}(U_n)) \equiv (g'(U_n, H_{n,n-\ell}), H'_{n,\ell}, H'_{n,\ell}(U'_\ell))$$

$$\approx_{\mathsf{nu\text{-}C}} (g'(U_n, H_{n,n-\ell}), H'_{n,\ell}, U'_\ell),$$

where U_n and U'_ℓ are uniformly and independently distributed over $\{0,1\}^n$ and $\{0,1\}^\ell$, respectively, and $H_{n-\ell}$ and $H'n,\ell$ are uniformly and independently distributed over $\mathcal{H}_{n,n-\ell}$ and $\mathcal{H}_{n,\ell}$, respectively. Changing the order in the above and noting that $H_n \equiv (H_{n,n-\ell}, H_{n,\ell})$, yields that

$$(f(U_n), H_n, H_n(U_n)_{1,\dots,\mathsf{D_f}(f(U_n))+\ell}) \approx_{\mathsf{nu\text{-}C}} (f(U_n), H_n, H_n(U_n)_{1,\dots,\mathsf{D_f}(f(U_n))}, U'_\ell). \quad (4.3)$$

Let $t(n) = 2n + n^2 = s(n) + n = G_{\mathrm{nb}}$'s output length. Let $X = X(n) = G_{\mathrm{nb}}(U_n, H_n)$, let $J = J(n) = s(n) + \mathsf{D_f}(f(U_n))$, and let $Y = Y(n) = (Y_1, \dots, Y_m)$ be defined by $Y_i = X_i$ if $i \notin [J+1, J+\ell]$, and Y_i is set to a uniform bit otherwise (i.e., $i \in [J+1, J+\ell]$).

---

[10] [7] states that $H_{n,\ell(n)}(U_n)$ is *computationally unpredictable* from $(v(U_n), H_{n,\ell(n)})$, but since $\left|H_{n,\ell(n)}(U_n)\right| \in O(\log n)$, the reduction to the above statement is standard.

Equation (4.3) yields that $X_{J+1,...,J+\ell}$ is computationally indistinguishable from U_ℓ given $X_{1,...,J}$ and J, yielding that

$$(J, X_{\leq J+r}) \approx_{\text{nu-C}} (J, X_{<J+r}, U) \tag{4.4}$$

for every $r \in [\ell]$, where U is a uniform bit. It follows that, for every ppt^{NU} D and $i \in [m]$, it holds that

$$\Pr\left[D(1^n, X_{\leq i}) = 1\right] - \Pr\left[D(1^n, X_{<i}, Y_i) = 1\right] \tag{4.5}$$

$$= \Pr\left[D(1^n, X_{\leq i}) = 1 \wedge i \notin [J, J+\ell]\right] - \Pr\left[D(1^n, X_{<i}, Y_i) = 1 \wedge i \notin [J, J+\ell]\right]$$

$$+ \sum_{r=1}^{\ell} \left(\Pr\left[D(1^n, X_{\leq i}) = 1 \wedge i = J+r\right] - \Pr\left[D(1^n, X_{<i}, Y_i) = 1 \wedge i = J+r\right]\right)$$

$$= 0 + \sum_{r=1}^{\ell} \left(\Pr\left[D(1^n, X_{\leq i}) = 1 \wedge i = J+r\right] - \Pr\left[D(1^n, X_{<i}, Y_i) = 1 \wedge i = J+r\right]\right)$$

$$\leq 0 + \ell \cdot \text{neg}(n)$$

$$= \text{neg}(n).$$

The second equality holds since $Y_i = X_i$ for $i \notin [J, J+\ell]$. The inequality holds since, if $\Pr\left[D(1^n, X_{\leq i}) = 1 \wedge i = J+r\right] - \Pr\left[D(1^n, X_{<i}, Y_i) = 1 \wedge i = J+r\right] > \text{neg}(n)$ for some i and r, then the nonuniform distinguisher D' that on input (j, x) returns D(x) if $j = i + r$, and a uniform bit otherwise, contradicts Equation (4.4).

It is left to prove that Y has high entropy given the blocks of X. We compute

$$\sum_{i=1}^{m} H(Y_i \mid X_{<i}) \geq \sum_{i=1}^{m} H(Y_i \mid X_{<i}, J)$$

$$= \mathop{E}_{j \leftarrow J}\left[\sum_{i=1}^{m} H(Y_i \mid X_{<i}, J = j)\right]$$

$$\geq \mathop{E}_{j \leftarrow J}\left[\sum_{i=1}^{j} H(Y_i \mid X_{<i}, J = j) + \sum_{i=j+1}^{j+\ell} H(Y_i \mid X_{<i}, J = j)\right]$$

$$= \mathop{E}_{j \leftarrow J}\left[\sum_{i=1}^{j} H(X_i \mid X_{<i}, J = j) + \sum_{i=j+1}^{j+\ell} 1\right]$$

$$= \mathop{E}_{j \leftarrow J}\left[H(X_{\leq j} \mid J = j)\right] + \ell$$

$$= H(X_{\leq J} \mid J) + \ell.$$

It follows that

$$\sum_{i=1}^{m} \mathrm{H}(Y_i \mid X_{<i}) \geq \ell + \mathrm{H}(X_{\leq J}) - \mathrm{H}(J)$$

$$\geq \ell + \mathrm{H}(X_{\leq J}) - \log n$$
$$\geq \ell + s(n) - 2 - \log n$$
$$= s(n) + \log n - 2.$$

The penultimate inequality follows by Theorem 4.3.9 (since $\mathrm{H}(X_{\leq J}) \geq \mathrm{H}_2(X_{\leq J}) = \log(1/\mathrm{CP}(X_{\leq J})) \geq s(n) - 2$). We conclude that Y realizes the claimed next-block pseudoentropy of G_{nb}. □

Proving Theorem 4.3.9. Proof: [Proof of Theorem 4.3.9] Let (U'_n, H'_n) be an independent copy of (U_n, H_n). Then

$\mathrm{CP}(g(U_n, H_n))$

$= \Pr\left[g(U'_n, H'_n) = g(U_n, H_n)\right]$

$= \Pr\left[(f(U'_n), H'_n, H'_n(U'_n)_{1,\ldots,\mathrm{D_f}(f(U'_n))}) = (f(U_n), H_n, H_n(U_n)_{1,\ldots,\mathrm{D_f}(f(U_n))})\right]$

$= \underset{y \xleftarrow{\mathrm{R}} f(U_n)}{\mathrm{E}} \left[\Pr\left[f(U'_n)=y\right]\cdot\Pr\left[H'_n=H_n\right]\cdot\Pr\left[H_n(U'_n)_{1,\ldots,\mathrm{D_f}(y)}=H_n(U_n)_{1,\ldots,\mathrm{D_f}(y)} \mid f(U'_n)=y\right]\right]$

$\leq \underset{y \xleftarrow{\mathrm{R}} f(U_n)}{\mathrm{E}} \left[\frac{2^{\mathrm{D_f}(y)}}{2^n} \cdot \frac{1}{|\mathcal{H}_n|} \cdot \left(\frac{1}{2^{\mathrm{D_f}(y)-1}} + \frac{1}{2^{\mathrm{D_f}(y)}}\right)\right]$

$\leq \dfrac{3}{|\{0,1\}^n \times \mathcal{H}_n|}.$

The first inequality holds since $\Pr\left[H_n(U'_n)_{1,\ldots,\mathrm{D_f}(y)} = H_n(U_n)_{1,\ldots,\mathrm{D_f}(y)} \mid f(U'_n) = y\right]$ is upper bounded by $\Pr\left[U'_n = U'_n \mid f(U'_n) = y\right] + \Pr\left[H_n(x)_{1,\ldots,\mathrm{D_f}(y)} = H_n(x')_{1,\ldots,\mathrm{D_f}(y)}\right]$ for some $x \neq x'$. □

Proving Theorem 4.3.11. Proof: [Proof of Theorem 4.3.11] This fact was first proven in [17] using the leftover hash lemma (Theorem 4.2.10). Here, we present a different proof that is inspired by Rackoff's proof of the Leftover Hash Lemma, and uses the high collision probability of g directly.

Let Inv_g be a nonuniform polynomial-time algorithm that inverts $g(U_n, H_n)$ with probability $\delta = \delta(n)$. We show that there exists an inverter Inv that inverts f with probability at least roughly δ^2/n, from which the claim follows.

Fix $n \in \mathbb{N}$, and let $\mathcal{L} \subseteq \mathrm{Im}(g(\{0,1\}^n \times \mathcal{H}_n))$ be the set of outputs where Inv_g inverts g correctly (without loss of generality Inv_g is deterministic). By assumption, $\Pr\left[g(U_n, H_n) \in \mathcal{L}\right] = \delta$. Since the collision probability of a distribution is at least the reciprocal of its support size, it follows that

$$CP(g(U_n, H_n)) = \Pr\left[g(U_n, H_n) = g(U'_n, H'_n)\right]$$
$$\geq \Pr\left[g(U_n, H_n), g(U'_n, H'_n) \in \mathcal{L}\right] / |\mathcal{L}|$$
$$= \delta^2 / |\mathcal{L}|.$$

By Theorem 4.3.9, $CP(g(U_n, H_n)) \leq 3 \cdot \frac{1}{|\mathcal{H}_n|} \cdot \frac{1}{2^n}$, and therefore

$$\frac{3 \cdot |\mathcal{L}|}{|\mathcal{H}_n| \cdot 2^n} \geq \delta^2. \qquad (4.6)$$

Now for $y \in \text{Im}(f(\{0, 1\}^n))$, let $\mathcal{L}_y = \{(h, z) : (y, h, z) \in \mathcal{L}\}$. It follows that

$$\Pr\left[(f(U_n), H_n, U'_{D_f(f(U_n))}) \in \mathcal{L}\right] = \mathop{E}_{y \overset{R}{\leftarrow} f(U_n)} \left[\Pr\left[(H_n, U'_{D_f(y)}) \in \mathcal{L}_y\right]\right] \qquad (4.7)$$

$$= \mathop{E}_{y \overset{R}{\leftarrow} f(U_n)} \left[\frac{|\mathcal{L}_y|}{|\mathcal{H}_n| \times 2^{D_f(y)}}\right]$$

$$= \sum_{y \in \text{Im}(f)} \frac{|f^{-1}(y)|}{2^n} \cdot \frac{|\mathcal{L}_y|}{|\mathcal{H}_n| \times 2^{D_f(y)}}$$

$$\geq \sum_{y \in \text{Im}(f)} \frac{2^{D_f(y)-1}}{2^n} \cdot \frac{|\mathcal{L}_y|}{|\mathcal{H}_n| \times 2^{D_f(y)}}$$

$$= \frac{1}{|\mathcal{H}_n| \cdot 2^{n+1}} \cdot \sum_y |\mathcal{L}_y|$$

$$= \frac{1}{|\mathcal{H}_n| \cdot 2^{n+1}} \cdot |\mathcal{L}|$$

$$\geq \delta^2 / 6.$$

Consider the following (randomized) inverter for f:

Algorithm 4.3.13 (Inv)

Oracle: Inv_g
Input: $y \in \{0, 1\}^n$

1. Let $h \overset{R}{\leftarrow} \mathcal{H}_n$, $i \overset{R}{\leftarrow} [n]$, and $z \overset{R}{\leftarrow} \{0, 1\}^i$.
2. Let $(x, h') = \text{Inv}_g(y, h, z)$.
3. Return x.

Let I be the random variable corresponding to the value of $i \overset{R}{\leftarrow} [y]$ in the execution of $\text{Inv}(y)$. Compute

$$\Pr\left[\mathrm{Inv}(f(U_n)) \in f^{-1}(f(U_n))\right]$$
$$\geq \Pr\left[I = \mathsf{D_f}(f(U_n))\right] \cdot \Pr\left[\mathrm{Inv}(f(U_n)) \in f^{-1}(f(U_n)) \mid I = \mathsf{D_f}(f(U_n))\right]$$
$$= \frac{1}{n} \cdot \Pr\left[\mathrm{Inv_g}(f(U_n), H_n, U_{\mathsf{D_f}(f(U_n))}) \in g^{-1}(f(U_n), H_n, U_{\mathsf{D_f}(f(U_n))})\right]$$
$$\geq \frac{1}{n} \cdot \delta^2/4 = \delta^2/6n.$$

The first inequality holds since I is independent of y, and the second inequality is by Equation (4.7). It follows that there exists a nonuniform polynomial-time algorithm that inverts f with probability at least $\delta(n)^2/6n$, implying that that $\delta(n) = \mathrm{neg}(n)$.

$\square$

4.3.3 Manipulating Next-Block Pseudoentropy

In this section we develop tools to manipulate next-block pseudoentropy. These tools are later used in Section 4.3.4 to convert the next-block pseudoentropy constructed in Section 4.3.2 into a pseudorandom generator.

The tools considered below are rather standard "entropy manipulations": entropy equalization (i.e., picking a random variable at random from a set of random variables to get a new random variable whose entropy is the average entropy), parallel repetition, and extraction from high-min-entropy sources, and their effect on the real entropy of random variables is clear. Fortunately, these manipulations have essentially the same effect also on the next-block pseudoentropy of a random variable. In Section 4.4.2, we show that these manipulations also have the desired effect on the *accessible entropy* of a random variable, a similarity that implies the similarity between the pseudorandom generator construction presented in this section, and the construction of statistically hiding commitment scheme, presented in Section 4.4.2.

4.3.3.1 Entropy Equalization via Truncated Sequential Repetition

This manipulation takes independent copies of an m-block random variable with next-block pseudoentropy at least k and concatenates them. It then truncates, at random, some of the first and final output blocks of the concatenated variable. The effect of this manipulation is that *each block* of the resulting variable has next-block pseudoentropy at least k/m. This per-block knowledge of the next-block pseudoentropy becomes very handy for constructing pseudorandom generators.

The price of this manipulation is that we "give away" some next-block pseudoentropy, but when taking enough copies, this loss is not significant.

Definition 4.3.14. *For* $\mathbf{z} = (z_1, \ldots, z_t)$ *and* $1 \leq j \leq m \leq t$, *let* $\mathrm{Equalizer}^m(j, \mathbf{z}) :=$
$z_j, \ldots, z_{t+j-m-1}$.

That is, $\mathrm{Equalizer}^m(j, \mathbf{z})$ removes the first $(j-1)$ and last $(m-j+1)$ elements from $\mathbf{z}$.

Lemma 4.3.15. *Let $m = m(n)$ be a power of* 2,[11] *assume* $X = X(n) = (X_1, \ldots, X_m)$ *has next-block pseudoentropy (at least)* $k = k(n)$, *and let* $w = w(n) \geq 2$ *be a polynomially bounded integer function. Let* $X^{[w]} = X^{[w]}(n)$ *be the* $(m \cdot (w-1))$*-block random variable defined by* $X^{[w]}(n) = \mathrm{Equalizer}^m(J, X^{(w)})$, *where* $J = J(n)$ *is uniformly distributed over* $[m(n)]$, *and* $X^{(w)} = X^{(w)}(n) = (X^1, \ldots, X^w)$, *for* $X^1, \ldots, X^w$ *being independent copies of* $X(n)$. *Then every block of* $X^{[w]}$ *has next-block pseudoentropy (at least)* k/m.

Namely, the next-block pseudoentropy of each block of $X^{[w]}$ is the *average* next-block pseudoentropy of the blocks of X.

Proof: Let $Y = Y(n) = (Y_1, \ldots, Y_m)$ be a random variable that realizes the next-block pseudoentropy of X, and let $Y^{(w)} = Y^{(w)}(n) = (Y^1, \ldots, Y^w)$ be jointly distributed with $X^{(w)} = (X^1, \ldots, X^w)$ in the natural way—Y^j is jointly distributed with X^j according to the joint distribution (X, Y). We prove that $Y^{[w]} = Y^{[w]}(n) = \mathrm{Equalizer}^m(J, Y^{(w)})$ realizes the claimed per-block next-block pseudoentropy of $X^{[w]}$. In the following we let $\tilde{m} = \tilde{m}(n) = (w-1) \cdot m$.

We start by proving that each block of $Y^{[w]}$ has high entropy given the previous blocks of $Y^{[w]}$. Fix $n \in \mathbb{N}$ and omit that from the notation, and fix $i \in [\tilde{m}]$. By chain rule for Shannon entropy, it holds that

$$\mathrm{H}(Y_i^{[w]} \mid X_{<i}^{[w]}) \geq \mathrm{H}(Y_{i+J-1}^{(w)} \mid X_{<i+J-1}^{(w)}, J) \tag{4.8}$$
$$= \mathrm{H}(Y_{i+J-1 \bmod m} \mid X_{<i+J-1 \bmod m}),$$

letting $m \bmod m$ be m (rather than 0). The equality follows from the fact that, for any $t \in [mw]$, $(Y_t^{(w)}, X_{t-1}^{(w)}, \ldots, X_{t'=\lfloor t/m \rfloor \cdot m+1}^{(w)})$ is independent of $X_{<t'}^{(w)}$, and is identically distributed to $(Y_{t \bmod m}, X_{<t \bmod m})$.

Since $(i + J - 1 \bmod m)$ is uniformly distributed in $[m]$, it follows that

$$\mathrm{H}(Y_{i+J-1 \bmod m} \mid X_{<i+J-1 \bmod m}, J) = \mathrm{E}_{i' \xleftarrow{\mathrm{R}} [m]}[\mathrm{H}(Y_{i'} \mid X_{<i'})] \tag{4.9}$$
$$= \frac{1}{m} \cdot \sum_{i' \xleftarrow{\mathrm{R}} [m]} \mathrm{H}(Y_{i'} \mid X_{<i'})$$
$$\geq k/m,$$

and we conclude that $\mathrm{H}(Y_i^{[w]} \mid X_{<i}^{[w]}) \geq k/m$ for every $i \in [\tilde{m}]$.

For the second part, let D be a ppt^{NU}, let $i = i(n) \in [\tilde{m}(n)]$, and let

$$\varepsilon_{\mathsf{D}}(n) := \Pr\left[\mathsf{D}(1^n, X^{[w]}(n)_{\leq i}) = 1\right] - \Pr\left[\mathsf{D}(1^n, X^{[w]}(n)_{<i}, Y^{[w]}(n)_i) = 1\right] \tag{4.10}$$

In the following we omit n whenever clear from the context. A similar argument to that used in the first part yields that

---

[11] Any other restriction that allows an efficient sampling from $[m(n)]$ will do.

$$\varepsilon_D(n) = \Pr\left[D(X_{\leq i}^{[w]}) = 1\right] - \Pr\left[D(X_{<i}^{[w]}, Y_i^{[w]}) = 1\right] \tag{4.11}$$

$$= \Pr\left[D(X_{J,...,i+J-1}^w) = 1\right] - \Pr\left[D(X_{J,...,i+J-2}^w, Y_{...,i+J-1}^w) = 1\right]$$

$$= \Pr\left[D(X_{J,...,(w-1)m}^{w-1}, X_{\leq i+J-1 \bmod m}) = 1\right] \tag{4.12}$$

$$- \Pr\left[D(X_{J,...,(w-1)m}^{w-1}, X_{<i+J-1 \bmod m}, Y_{i+J-1 \bmod m}) = 1\right]$$

$$\leq \Pr\left[D(x, X_{\leq i+j-1 \bmod m}) = 1\right] - \Pr\left[D(x, X_{<i+j-1 \bmod m}, Y_{i+j' \bmod m}) = 1\right]$$

for some fixing of $j \in [m]$ and $x \in \text{Supp}(X_{j,...,(w-1)m}^{w-1})$. Hence, there exists a ppt^{NU} D' such that

$$\varepsilon_{D'}(n) := \Pr\left[D'(X_{\leq i'}) = 1\right] - \Pr\left[D'(X_{<i'}, Y_{i'}) = 1\right] \geq \varepsilon_D(n) \tag{4.13}$$

for some $i' = i'(n) \in [m(n)]$. Since Y is block-wise indistinguishable from X, it follows that $\varepsilon_{D'}(n) = \text{neg}(n)$ and therefore $\varepsilon_D(n) = \text{neg}(n)$. Hence, $Y^{[w]}$ is block-wise indistinguishable from $X^{[w]}$.   □

4.3.3.2 Parallel Repetition

This manipulation, which simply takes parallel repetition (i.e., direct product) of a random variable, has a twofold effect. The first is that the overall next-block pseudoentropy a t-fold parallel repetition of a random variable X is t times the next-block pseudoentropy of X. Hence, if X's next-block pseudoentropy is larger than the number of bits it takes to sample it, this gap gets multiplied by t in the resulting random variable. The second effect of taking such a product is turn next-block pseudoentropy into next-block pseudo-*min-entropy*.

Lemma 4.3.16. *Let* $m = m(n)$ *and* $\ell = \ell(n)$ *be integer functions, assume every block of* $X = X(n) = (X_1,...,X_m)$ *is of length* $\ell(n)$ *and has next-block pseudoentropy (at least)* $\alpha = \alpha(n)$, *and let* $t = t(n)$ *be polynomially bounded integer function. Let* $X^{\langle t \rangle} = X^{\langle t \rangle}(n)$ *be the m-block random variable defined by* $X^{\langle t \rangle} = X^{\langle t \rangle}(n) = \left((X_1^1,...,X_1^t),...,(X_m^1,...,X_m^t)\right)$, *for* $X^1,...,X^t$ *being independent copies of X. Then every block of* $X^{\langle t \rangle}$ *has next-block pseudo-min-entropy (at least)* $\alpha'(n) = t \cdot \alpha - O(\log n \cdot (\ell + \log n) \cdot \sqrt{t})$.

Notice that the $t \cdot \alpha$ term in the above statements is the largest we could hope for the pseudoentropy—getting α bits of pseudoentropy per copy. However, since we wish to move from a pseudo-form of Shannon entropy (measuring randomness on average) to a pseudo-form of min-entropy (measuring randomness with high probability), we may have a deviation that grows like $\sqrt{t}$. By taking t large enough, this deviation becomes insignificant. For instance, consider the case that X has next-block pseudoentropy at least α and $\ell = 1$ (i.e., X is a sequence of bits), and that we would like to deduce that $X^{\langle t \rangle}$ has next-block pseudo-min-entropy $\alpha' = t \cdot (\alpha - \delta)$ for some $\delta > 0$. Theorem 4.3.16 guarantees that this happens for $t = \text{polylog}(n)/\delta^2$.

Proof: Let $Y = Y(n) = (Y_1,...,Y_m)$ be a random variable that realizes the per-block next-block pseudoentropy of X, and let $Y^{\langle t \rangle} = Y^{\langle t \rangle}(n) = $

$\left((Y_1^1, \ldots, Y_1^t), \ldots, (Y_m^1, \ldots, Y_m^t)\right)$ be jointly distributed with $X^{\langle t \rangle}$ in the natural way— Y^j is jointly distributed with X^j according to the joint distribution (X, Y). Since Y is block-wise indistinguishable from X, and since $t(n) \leq \text{poly}(n)$, a straightforward hybrid argument yields that $Y^{\langle t \rangle}$ is block-wise indistinguishable from $X^{\langle t \rangle}$.

Since $H(Y_i \mid X_{<i}) \geq \alpha$ for every $i \in [m]$, applying Theorems 4.2.3 and 4.2.5 with $\varepsilon = 2^{-\log^2 n}$ yields that there exists a random variable $W = W(n) = (W_1, \ldots, W_m)$ jointly distributed with $X^{\langle t \rangle}$, such that the following hold for every $i = i(n) \in [m(n)]$:

1. $\Delta((X_{<i}^{\langle t \rangle}, Y_i^{\langle t \rangle}), (X_{<i}^{\langle t \rangle}, W_i)) = \text{neg}(n)$, and
2. $H_\infty(W_i|_{X_{<i}^{\langle t \rangle} = x_{<i}}) \geq \alpha - O((\log n + \ell) \cdot \log n \cdot \sqrt{t})$, for every $x \in \text{Supp}(X_{<i}^{\langle t \rangle})$.

Item 1 and the previous observation yield that W is block-wise indistinguishable from $X^{\langle t \rangle}$, and by item 2 we conclude that W realizes the claimed next-block pseudo-min-entropy of $X^{\langle t \rangle}$.   □

4.3.3.3 Block-wise Extraction

The tool applies a randomness extractor separately to each of the random variable blocks, to convert per-block next-block pseudo-min-entropy into pseudorandomness. The result is a sufficiently long pseudorandom sequence. This is a computational analogue of block-source extraction in literature on randomness extractors [5, 33]. The price of this manipulation is that the length, and thus the amount of pseudorandomness, of the resulting variable is shorter than the overall pseudoentropy of the original variable, due to inherent entropy loss in randomness extraction.

Lemma 4.3.17. *Let $m = m(n)$ and $\ell = \ell(n)$ be integer functions, and assume that every block of $X = X(n) = (X_1, \ldots, X_m)$ over $(\{0, 1\}^\ell)^m$ has next-block pseudoentropy (at least) $\alpha = \alpha(n) \geq \lceil \log^2 n \rceil$. Then there exists a polynomial-time computable* $\text{Ext} \colon \{0, 1\}^\ell \times (\{0, 1\}^\ell)^m \mapsto \left(\{0, 1\}^{\lfloor \alpha \rfloor - \lceil \log^2 n \rceil}\right)^m$ *such that $(R, \text{Ext}(R, X))$, for $R = R(n) \xleftarrow{R} \{0, 1\}^\ell$, is pseudorandom.*

Proof: Let $\beta = \beta(n) = \lfloor \alpha \rfloor - \lceil \log^2 n \rceil$. For $r, x \in \{0, 1\}^\ell$, let $h_r(x) := r \cdot x$ over $\text{GF}(2^\ell)$, truncated to the first β bits. Note that $\{h_r \colon r \in \{0, 1\}^\ell\}$ is a two-universal hash family over $\{0, 1\}^\ell$. For $x = (x_1, \ldots, x_k) \in (\{0, 1\}^\ell)^k$, let $\text{Ext}(r, x) = (h_r(x_1), \ldots, h_r(x_k))$. Let D^{PRG} be ppt^{NU}, and assume that

$$\varepsilon(n) := \Pr\left[D_{\text{PRG}}(1^n, R, \text{Ext}(X, R)) = 1\right] - \Pr\left[D_{\text{PRG}}(1^n, R, U_{m \cdot \beta}) = 1\right] \neq \text{neg}(n). \tag{4.14}$$

In the following we omit n whenever clear from the context. A hybrid argument yields that there exists $i \in [m]$ and ppt^{NU} D such that

$$\Pr\left[D(R, \text{Ext}(R, X_{\leq i})) = 1\right] - \Pr\left[D(R, \text{Ext}(R, X_{<i}), U_\beta) = 1\right] \geq \varepsilon/m.$$

Let $Y = Y(n)$ be a random variable that realizes the per-block next-block **pseudo-min-entropy** of X. Since $H_\infty(Y_i|_{X_{<i}} = x_{<i}) \geq \alpha$ for every $x \in \text{Supp}(X)$, and since

$\{h_r : r \in \{0,1\}^\ell\}$ is a two-universal hash family, the leftover hash lemma (Theorem 4.2.10) yields that

$$\mathrm{SD}((R, h_R(Y_i|_{X_{<i}} = x_{<i})), (R, U_\beta)) \le 2^{-\log^2 n}$$

for every $x \in \mathrm{Supp}(X)$. It follows that

$$\mathrm{SD}(R, \mathrm{Ext}(R, X_{<i}, Y_i), (R, \mathrm{Ext}(R, X_{<i}), U_\beta)) \le 2^{-\log^2 n}$$

and therefore

$$\Pr[D(R, \mathrm{Ext}(R, X_{\le i})) = 1] - \Pr[D(R, \mathrm{Ext}(R, X_{<i}, Y_i)) = 1] \quad (4.15)$$
$$\ge \varepsilon/\ell - 2^{-\log^2 n} \ne \mathrm{neg}$$

For $n \in \mathbb{N}$, let $r_n \in \mathrm{Supp}(R)$ be the string that maximizes the above gap, and consider the distinguisher D' that on input $(1^n, z)$, returns $D(1^n, r_n, \mathrm{Ext}(r_n, z))$. Equation (4.15) yields that

$$\Pr[D'(X_{\le i}) = 1] - \Pr[D'(X_{<i}, Y_i) = 1] \ne \mathrm{neg}$$

Hence, the ppt^{NU} D' contradicts the assumed block-wise indistinguishability of Y from X. □

4.3.4 Putting It Together: One-Way Functions to Pseudorandom Generators

In this section we use the results of previous sections to construct pseudorandom generators from next-block pseudoentropy generators.

It is clear that a pseudorandom generator from n bits to $m(n) > n$ has next-block pseudoentropy $m(n)$, hence, it is a next-block entropy generator with entropy gap $(m(n)-n)$—its next-block pseudoentropy is larger than its real entropy by $(m(n)-n)$. The following theorem provides the converse direction.

Theorem 4.3.18 (Next-block pseudoentropy to pseudorandom generator). *For any polynomial-time computable and polynomially bounded integer function $s = s(n)$ and polynomial-time computable function $\Delta = \Delta(n) \le 2$, there exists a polynomial-time computable integer function $s' = s'(n) = \Theta(s \cdot \Delta^{-3} \cdot \mathrm{polylog}(n))$ such that the following holds: Assuming there exists a polynomial-time generator $G_{\mathrm{nb}} \colon \{0,1\}^s \mapsto \{0,1\}^{2s}$ with next-block pseudoentropy $s(1 + \Delta)$, then there exists a pseudorandom generator $G \colon \{0,1\}^{s'} \mapsto \{0,1\}^{s' \cdot (1 + \Theta(\Delta))}$. Furthermore, G uses G_{nb} as an oracle (i.e., black box) and on inputs of length s', all calls of G to G_{nb} are on inputs of length s.*

Proof: The proof is done by manipulating the next-block pseudoentropy of G_{nb} using the tools described in Section 4.3.3.

Let $X = X(n) = G_{nb}(U_s)$. We assume without loss of generality that, for every n, the number $m(n) = 2s(n)$ of output blocks (=bits) of G_{nb} is a power of 2 (by padding with zeros if necessary). By assumption, X has next-block pseudoentropy $s(1 + \Delta)$.

Truncated sequential repetition: pseudoentropy equalization. The first step is to use X to define a random variable $X^{[w]}$ that *each of whose blocks* has the same amount of next-block pseudoentropy— the average of the next-block pseudoentropy of the blocks of X. The entropy gap of $X^{[w]}$, in relative terms, is essentially the same as that of X.

For $w = w(n) = \lceil 8/\Delta \rceil$, let $X^{[w]} = X^{[w]}(n)$ be the truncated sequential repetition of X according to Theorem 4.3.15. Namely, $X^{[w]}$ consists of w independent copies of X, omitting the first $(J - 1)$ blocks of the first copy and the last $(m - J + 1)$ blocks of the last copy, for $J \xleftarrow{\text{R}} [m]$. Note that $X^{[w]}$ can be generated efficiently using $s' = s'(n) = \log(m) + w \cdot s$ random bits, and has $m' = m'(n) = m(w - 1)$ blocks.

By Theorem 4.3.15, each block of $X^{[w]}$ has next-block pseudoentropy $\alpha = \alpha(n) = s(1 + \Delta)/m = \frac{1}{2} + \Delta/2$.

Parallel repetition: converting Shannon pseudoentropy to pseudo-min-entropy and gap amplification. In this step $X^{[w]}$ is used to construct a random variable $(X^{[w]})^{\langle t \rangle}$ that each of whose blocks has the same amount of *pseudo-min-entropy*— about t time the per-block pseudoentropy of $X^{[w]}$.

For $t = t(n) = \lceil \log^5 n \cdot \Delta^{-2} \rceil$, let $(X^{[w]})^{\langle t \rangle} = (X^{[w]})^{\langle t \rangle}(n)$ be the t-fold parallel repetition of $X^{[w]}$ (see Theorem 4.3.16). That is, the i-th block of $(X^{[w]})^{\langle t \rangle}$, contains the i-th blocks of the t independent copies of $X^{[w]}$. Note that $(X^{[w]})^{\langle t \rangle}$ can be generated efficiently using $s'' = s''(n) = t \cdot s'$ bits, and has m' blocks.

By Theorem 4.3.16, each block of $(X^{[w]})^{\langle t \rangle}$ has next-block pseudo-min-entropy $\alpha' = \alpha'(n) = t \cdot \alpha - O(\log^2 n \cdot \sqrt{t})$, which is larger than $t \cdot (\frac{1}{2} + \Delta/4)$ for large enough n.

Randomness extraction: converting pseudo-min-entropy to pseudorandomness. In the final step, pseudorandom bits are extracted from $(X^{[w]})^{\langle t \rangle}$, by applying a randomness extractor on each of its blocks.

Theorem 4.3.17 yields that there exists an efficient Ext: $\{0, 1\}^{t(n)} \times (\{0, 1\}^t)^{m'} \mapsto \left(\{0, 1\}^{\alpha' - \lceil \log^2 n \rceil}\right)^{m'}$ such that $X^{PRG} = X^{PRG}(n) = (R, \text{Ext}(R, (X^{[w]})^{\langle t \rangle}))$, for $R = R(n) \xleftarrow{\text{R}} \{0, 1\}^t$, is pseudorandom. We remind the reader that $\text{Ext}(r, x = (x_1, \dots, x_m))$ merely applies (the same) two-universal function h_r on each of x's blocks. Note that it takes s''' bits to efficiently sample X^{PRG}, for

$$s''' = s'''(n) = t + s'' = t(\ell s + \Theta(\log n)) = \Theta(s\Delta^{-3} \cdot \text{polylog}(n)).$$

It follows that, for large enough n, the length of $X^{PRG}(n)$ is at least

$$m'(\alpha' - \lceil \log^2 n \rceil) \geq m'(t\alpha - O(\log^3 n \cdot \sqrt{t}))$$
$$> m'(t(\frac{1}{2} + \Delta/2) - O(\log^3 n \cdot \sqrt{t}))$$
$$> m't(\frac{1}{2} + \Delta/4)$$
$$= s(\ell - 1)t(1 + \Delta/2)$$
$$\geq s\ell t(1 + \Delta/4)$$
$$\geq s'''(1 + \Delta/8).$$

Hence, $|X^{\mathrm{PRG}}| = s'''(1 + \Omega(\Delta))$, and since all the above manipulations were efficient, the proof of the theorem follows. □

Remark 4.3.19 (Tighter reduction). *Vadhan and Zheng [29] noticed that, by modifying the construction used in the proof of Theorem 4.3.18, one can construct an efficient generator G and a random variable $Z = Z(n)$ such that the following hold:*

1. *It takes $s'(n) = \Theta(s(n) \cdot \Delta(n)^{-2} \cdot \mathrm{polylog}(n))$ bits to efficiently sample Z, i.e., a factor of Δ^{-1} shorter than the input length of the pseudorandom generator in Theorem 4.3.18.*
2. *$G(Z)$ is computationally indistinguishable from (Z, U), where U is a random string of length $\Omega(s(n)\Delta/n)$.*

Then, by iterating G on its output (in a similar manner to the Blum–Micali pseudorandom generator length extending approach), without investing new randomness, they get a pseudorandom generator of seed length $s(n)$.

Combining the above Theorem 4.3.18 with Theorem 4.3.6 from the previous subsection yields the following result:

Theorem 4.3.20 (One-way function to pseudorandom generator). *There exists a polynomial-time computable function $s = s(n) = \Theta(n^7 \cdot \mathrm{polylog}\, n)$ such that the following holds: Let $f : \{0,1\}^n \mapsto \{0,1\}^n$ be nonuniformly one-way function, then there exists a pseudorandom generator $G : \{0,1\}^s \mapsto \{0,1\}^{s \cdot (1 + \Omega(1/n^2))}$. Furthermore, G uses f as an oracle (i.e., black box) and on inputs of length $s(n)$, all calls of G to f are on inputs of length n.*

Proof: Pad the output of the next-block pseudoentropy generator guaranteed by Theorem 4.3.6 to make it length doubling (it is easy to see that this does not change its next-block pseudoentropy) and apply Theorem 4.3.18. □

Remark 4.3.21 (Tighter reduction, take 2). *Plugging into Theorem 4.3.18 the next-block generators of Haitner et al. [14] or of Vadhan and Zheng [29], both with $s = \Theta(n)$ and $\Delta = \Theta(\log(n)/n)$, yields a pseudorandom generator of seed length $\Theta(n^4 \cdot \mathrm{polylog}\, n)$. If the latter generators are used with the tighter reduction of Vadhan and Zheng [29] mentioned above, the resulting generator has seed length $\Theta(n^3 \cdot \mathrm{polylog}\, n)$, which is the best we know how to achieve today.*

4.4 Inaccessible Entropy and Statistically Hiding Commitment

In this section, we formally define the notion of inaccessible entropy and use it as intermediate tool to construct statistically hiding commitment from one-way functions.

We start, Section 4.4.1, by presenting the formal definition of inaccessible entropy. In Section 4.4.2, we show that any one-way function can be used to construct inaccessible entropy generator. In Section 4.4.3, we develop means to manipulate inaccessible entropy. Finally, in Section 4.4.4 we give a simplified version of the (still rather complicated) construction of statistically hiding commitments from inaccessible entropy generators.

4.4.1 Inaccessible Entropy Generators

We begin by informally recalling the definition from the introduction. Let $G: \{0,1\}^n \mapsto (\{0,1\}^*)^m$ be an m-block generator over $\{0,1\}^n$ and let $G(1^n) = (Y_1, \ldots, Y_m)$ denote the output of G over a uniformly random input. The *real entropy* of G is the (Shannon) entropy in G's output blocks, where for each block Y_i, we take its entropy conditioned on the previous blocks $Y_{<i} = (Y_1, \ldots, Y_{i-i})$. The *accessible entropy* of an arbitrary, adversarial m-block generator $\widetilde{G}$, with the same block structure as of G, is the entropy of the block of $\widetilde{G}$ conditioned not only on the previous blocks but also on the *coins used by $\widetilde{G}$ to generate the previous blocks*. The generator $\widetilde{G}$ is allowed to flip fresh random coins to generate its next block, and this is indeed the source of entropy in the block (everything else is fixed). We insist that the messages of $\widetilde{G}$ will be consistent with G: the support of $\widetilde{G}$'s messages is contained in that of G.

Moving to the formal definitions, we first define an m-block generator and then define the real and accessible entropy of such a generator.

Definition 4.4.1 (Block generators). *Let n be a security parameter, and let $m = m(n)$ and $s = s(n)$. An m-block generator is a function $G: \{0,1\}^s \mapsto (\{0,1\}^*)^m$. The generator G is* efficient *if its running time on input of length $s(n)$ is polynomial in n.*

We call parameter n the security parameter, *s the* seed length, *m the* number of blocks, *and $\ell(n) = \max_{x \in \{0,1\}^{s(n)}, i \in [m(n)]} |G(x)_i|$ the* maximal block length *of G.*

4.4.1.1 Real Entropy

Recall that we are interested in lower bounds on the real entropy of a block generator. We define two variants of real entropy: real Shannon entropy and real min-entropy. We connect these two notions through the notion of real sample-entropy. In other words, for a fixed m-tuple output of the generator, we ask how surprising were the blocks output by G in this tuple. We then get real Shannon entropy by taking the expectation of this quantity over a random execution and the min-entropy by taking the minimum (up to negligible statistical distance). An alternative approach would be to define the notions through the sum of conditional entropies (as we do in the intuitive description in the introduction). This approach would yield closely related definitions, and in fact exactly the same definition in the case of Shannon entropy (see Theorem 4.4.4).

Definition 4.4.2 (Real sample-entropy). *Let n be a security parameter, and let* G *be an m-block generator over* $\{0, 1\}^s$, *for* $m = m(n)$ *and* $s = s(n)$. *For* $i \in [m]$, *define the* real sample-entropy *of* $\mathbf{y} \in \text{Supp}((Y_1, \ldots, Y_i) = G(U_s)_{1,\ldots,i})$ *as*

$$\text{RealH}_G(\mathbf{y}) = \sum_{j \in [i]} \text{RealH}_G^j(\mathbf{y})$$

for

$$\text{RealH}_G^j(\mathbf{y}) := H_{Y_j|Y_{<j}}(\mathbf{y}_j|\mathbf{y}_{<j})$$

Definition 4.4.3 (Real entropy). *Let n be a security parameter, and let* G *be an m-block generator over* $\{0, 1\}^s$, *for* $m = m(n)$ *and* $s = s(n)$. *We say that an m-block generator* G *has* real entropy at least $k = k(n)$, *if*

$$\mathop{E}_{\mathbf{y} \overset{R}{\leftarrow} G(U_s)} [\text{RealH}_G(\mathbf{y})] \geq k$$

for every $n \in \mathbb{N}$.

    The generator G *has* real min-entropy at least k in its i-th block, *where* $i = i(n) \in [m(n)]$, *if*

$$\mathop{\text{Pr}}_{\mathbf{y} \overset{R}{\leftarrow} G(U_s)} \left[\text{RealH}_G^i(\mathbf{y}) < k \right] = \text{neg}(n).$$

We observe that the real Shannon entropy simply amounts to measuring the standard conditional Shannon entropy of G's output blocks.

Lemma 4.4.4. *For an m-block generator* G *over* $\{0, 1\}^s$, *it holds that*

$$\mathop{E}_{\mathbf{y} \overset{R}{\leftarrow} G(U_s)} [\text{RealH}_G(\mathbf{y})] = H(G(U_s)).$$

Proof: Let $(Y_1, \ldots, Y_m) = G(U_s)$, and compute

$$\mathop{E}_{\mathbf{y} \overset{R}{\leftarrow} G(U_s)} [\text{RealH}_G(\mathbf{y})] := \mathop{E}_{\mathbf{y} \overset{R}{\leftarrow} G(U_s)} \left[\sum_{i \in [m]} H_{Y_i|Y_{<i}}(\mathbf{y}_i \mid \mathbf{y}_{<i}) \right]$$

$$= \sum_{i \in [m]} \mathop{E}_{\mathbf{y} \overset{R}{\leftarrow} G(U_s)} [H_{Y_i|Y_{<i}}(\mathbf{y}_i \mid \mathbf{y}_{<i})]$$

$$= \sum_{i \in [m]} H(Y_i|Y_{<i})$$

$$= H(G(U_s)).$$

$\square$

4.4.1.2 Accessible Entropy

Recall that we are interested in *upper bounds* on the accessible entropy of a block generator. We will define two variants of accessible entropy: accessible Shannon entropy and accessible max-entropy. While the Shannon variant is in a sense more intuitive, working with the max-entropy variant, as done in Sections 4.4.2 and 4.4.4, yields simpler and more efficient applications. As in the case of real entropy, we connect these two notions through the notion of accessible sample-entropy. For a fixed execution of the adversary $\widetilde{G}$, we ask how surprising were the messages sent by $\widetilde{G}$. We then get accessible Shannon entropy by taking the expectation of this quantity over a random execution and the max-entropy by taking the maximum (up to negligible statistical distance). Here too, the definitions obtained are closely related to the definitions one would obtain by considering a sum of conditional entropies (as we did in the intuitive description earlier). For the Shannon entropy, the definitions would again be identical. (See Theorem 4.4.7.)

The definition below differs from the definition of [16], in that we require the bound on the accessible entropy to hold (also) against *nonuniform adversarial generators*. This change simplifies the definitions and proofs, but at the price that we can only construct such inaccessible entropy pseudoentropy generators from functions that are nonuniformly one-way.

Definition 4.4.5 (Online block generator). *Let n be a security parameter, and let $m = m(n)$. An m-block* online *generator is a function $\widetilde{G} \colon (\{0,1\}^v)^m \mapsto (\{0,1\}^*)^m$ for some $v = v(n)$, such that the i-th output block of $\widetilde{G}$ is a function of (only) its first i input blocks. We denote the* transcript *of $\widetilde{G}$ over random input by $T_{\widetilde{G}}(1^n) = (R_1, Y_1, \ldots, R_m, Y_m)$, for $(R_1, \ldots, R_m) \xleftarrow{R} (\{0,1\}^v)^m$ and $(Y_1, \ldots, Y_m) = \widetilde{G}(R_1, \ldots, R_i)$.*

That is, an online block generator is a special type of block generator that tosses fresh random coins before outputting each new block. In the following we let $\widetilde{G}(r_1, \ldots, r_i)_i$ stand for $\widetilde{G}(r_1, \ldots, r_i, x^*)_i$ for arbitrary $x^* \in (\{0,1\}^v)^{m-i}$ (note that the choice of x^* has no effect on the value of $\widetilde{G}(r_1, \ldots, r_i, x^*)_i$).

Definition 4.4.6 (Accessible sample-entropy). *Let n be a security parameter, let $m = m(n)$, let $i = i(n) \in [m]$, and let $\widetilde{G}$ be an online m-block online generator. The* accessible sample-entropy *of $t = (r_1, y_1, \ldots, r_i, y_i) \in \mathrm{Supp}(R_1, Y_1 \ldots, R_i, Y_i) = T_{\widetilde{G}}(1^n)_{1,\ldots,2i}$ is defined as*

$$\mathrm{AccH}_{\widetilde{G}}(t) := \sum_{j \in [i]} \mathrm{AccH}^j_{\widetilde{G}}(t)$$

for

$$\mathrm{AccH}^j_{\widetilde{G}}(t) := \mathrm{H}_{Y_j|R_{<j}}(y_j | r_{<j}).$$

The expected accessible entropy of a random transcript can be expressed in terms of the standard conditional Shannon entropy.

Lemma 4.4.7. *Let $\widetilde{G}$ be an online $m = m(n)$-block generator and let $(R_1, Y_1, \ldots, R_m, Y_m) = T_{\widetilde{G}}(1^n)$ be its transcript. Then,*

$$\underset{t \xleftarrow{R} T_{\widetilde{G}}(1^n)}{\mathrm{E}} \left[\sum_{i \in [m]} \mathrm{AccH}^i_{\widetilde{G}}(t) \right] = \sum_{i \in [m]} \mathrm{H}(Y_i | R_{<i}).$$

The proof of Theorem 4.4.7 is similar to that of Theorem 4.4.4.

The above definition is only interesting when putting restrictions on the generator's actions with respect to the underlying generator G. (Otherwise, the accessible entropy of $\widetilde{G}$ can be arbitrarily large by outputting arbitrarily long strings.) In this work, we focus on efficient generators that are consistent with respect to G. That is, the support of their output is contained in that of G.[12]

Definition 4.4.8 (Consistent generators). *Let* G *be a block generator over* $\{0, 1\}^{s(n)}$. *A block (possible online) generator* G' *over* $\{0, 1\}^{s'(n)}$ *is* G consistent *if, for every* $n \in \mathbb{N}$, *it holds that* $\mathrm{Supp}(G'(U_{s'(n)})) \subseteq \mathrm{Supp}(G(U_{s(n)}))$.

Definition 4.4.9 (Accessible entropy). *A block generator* G *has* accessible entropy *at most* $k = k(n)$ *if, for every efficient, nonuniform, G-consistent, online generator* $\widetilde{G}$ *and all large enough n,*

$$\mathop{\mathrm{E}}_{t \xleftarrow{R} T_{\widetilde{G}}(1^n)} \left[\mathrm{AccH}_{\widetilde{G}}(t) \right] \leq k.$$

The generator G *has* accessible max-entropy at most k *if*

$$\mathop{\mathrm{Pr}}_{t \xleftarrow{R} T_{\widetilde{G}}(1^n)} [\mathrm{AccH}_{\widetilde{G}}(t) > k] = \mathrm{neg}(n),$$

for every such $\widetilde{G}$.

In Section 4.4.2, we prove the existence of one-way functions implies that of an inaccessible max-entropy entropy generator: an efficient block generator whose accessible entropy is noticeably larger than its accessible entropy. The converse direction is also true.

Lemma 4.4.10. *Let* G *be an efficient block generator with real entropy* $k(n)$, *and assume that* G *has accessible entropy, or accessible max-entropy, at most* $k(n) - 1/p(n)$, *for some* $p \in \mathrm{poly}$. *Then one-way functions exist.*[13]

Proof: Omitted.   □

4.4.2 Inaccessible Entropy Generator from One-way Functions

In this section, we show how to build an inaccessible entropy generator from any one-way function. In particular, we prove the following theorem:

---

[12] In the more complicated notion of accessible entropy considered in [11], the "generator" needs to *prove* that its output blocks are in the support of G, by providing an input of G that would have generated the same blocks. It is also allowed there for a generator to fail to prove the latter with some probability, which requires a measure of accessible entropy that discounts entropy that may come from failing.

[13] Specifically, one can show that a variant of $f(x, i) = G(x)_{1,...,i}$ is a "distributional" one-way function.

Construction 4.4.11 *For $f\colon \{0,1\}^n \mapsto \{0,1\}^n$, define the $(n+1)$ block generator G^f over $\{0,1\}^n$ by*

$$\mathsf{G}^f(x) = (f(x)_1, \ldots, f(x)_n, x)$$

Namely, the first n blocks of $\mathsf{G}^f(x)$ are the bits of $f(x)$, and its final block is x.

Theorem 4.4.12 (Inaccessible entropy generators from one-way functions). *If $f\colon \{0,1\}^n \mapsto \{0,1\}^n$ is nonuniformly one-way, then the efficient block generator $\mathsf{G} = \mathsf{G}^f$ defined in Construction 4.4.11 has accessible max-entropy at most $n - \omega(\log n)$.*

Remark 4.4.13 (Tighter reduction). *[16] prove an analog theorem for the $O(n/\log n)$-block generator that groups each consecutive $\log n$ bits of $f(n)$ into a single block.*

Proof: Suppose on the contrary that there exists an efficient, nonuniform, G-consistent online block generator $\widetilde{G}$ such that

$$\Pr_{\mathsf{t} \xleftarrow{R} T_{\widetilde{G}}(1^n)} \left[\mathrm{AccH}_{\widetilde{G}}(\mathsf{t}) > n - c \cdot \log n \right] > \varepsilon(n) \tag{4.16}$$

for some constant $c > 0$, $\varepsilon(n) = 1/\mathrm{poly}(n)$, and infinitely many n's. In the following we fix $n \in \mathbb{N}$ for which the above equation holds, and omit it from the notation when its value is clear from the context. Let $m = n + 1$ and let v be abound on the number of bits used by $\widetilde{G}$ in each round. The inverter Inv for f is defined as follows:

Algorithm 4.4.14 (Inverter Inv for f from the accessible entropy generator $\widetilde{G}$)

Input: $z \in \{0,1\}^n$
Operation:

1. *For $i = 1$ to n,*

   a. *Sample $r_i \xleftarrow{R} \{0,1\}^v$ and let $y_i = \widetilde{G}(r_1, \ldots, r_i)_i$.*
   b. *If $y_i = z_i$, move to next value of i.*
   c. *Abort after n^2/ε failed attempts for sampling good r_i.*

2. *Sample $r_m \xleftarrow{R} \{0,1\}^v$ and output $\widetilde{G}(r_1, \ldots, r_m)_m$.*

Namely, Inv(y) does the only natural thing one can do with $\widetilde{G}$; it tries to make, via rewinding, $\widetilde{G}$'s first n output blocks equal to y, knowing that, if this happens then since $\widetilde{G}$ is G-consistent, $\widetilde{G}$'s m-th output block is a preimage of y.

It is clear that Inv runs in polynomial time, so we will finish the proof by showing that

$$\Pr_{y \xleftarrow{R} f(U_n)} \left[\mathrm{Inv}(y) \in f^{-1}(y) \right] \geq \varepsilon^2/16n.$$

We prove the above by relating the transcript distribution induced by the standalone execution of $\widetilde{G}(1^n)$ to that induced by the embedded execution of $\widetilde{G}$ in $\mathrm{Inv}(f(U_n))$. In more detail, we show that high-accessible-entropy transcripts with respect to the standalone execution of G, i.e., $\mathrm{AccH}_{\widetilde{G}}(\mathsf{t}) > n - c \cdot \log n$, happen with not much smaller probability also in the emulated execution. Since whenever Inv does not abort it is guaranteed to invert y, it follows that the success probability of Inv is lower bounded by the probability that $\widetilde{G}(1^n)$ outputs a high-accessible-entropy transcript, and thus is nonnegligible.

For intuition about why the above statement about high-accessible-entropy transcripts is true, consider the case of a one-way *permutation* f. By definition, high-accessible-entropy transcripts in the stand alone execution of $\widetilde{G}$ happen with probability at most $\mathrm{poly}(n)/2^n$. On the other hand, the probability that a "typical" transcript is produced by the emulated execution of $\widetilde{G}$ is about 2^{-n}—the probability that random output of f equals the transcript's first n output blocks.

Proving the above formally for arbitrary one-way functions is the subject of the following proof:

Standalone execution $\widetilde{G}(1^n)$. Let $\widetilde{T} = T_{\widetilde{G}}$, and recall that $\widetilde{T} = (\widetilde{R}_1, \widetilde{Y}_1, \ldots, \widetilde{R}_m, \widetilde{Y}_m)$ is associated with a random execution of $\widetilde{G}$ on security parameter n by

- $\widetilde{R}_i$ – the random coins of $\widetilde{G}$ in the i-th round, and
- $\widetilde{Y}_i$ – $\widetilde{G}$'s i-th output block.

Recall that, for $\mathbf{t} = (r_1, y_1, \ldots, r_m, y_m) \in \mathrm{Supp}(\widetilde{T})$, we have defined

$$\mathrm{AccH}_{\widetilde{G}}(\mathbf{t}) := \sum_{i \in [m]} \mathrm{H}_{Y_j|R_{<j}}(y_j|r_{<j}).$$

Compute

$$\Pr_{\widetilde{T}}[\mathbf{t}] = \prod_{i=1}^{m} \Pr_{\widetilde{Y}_i|\widetilde{R}_{<i}}[y_i|r_{<i}] \cdot \Pr_{\widetilde{R}_i|\widetilde{R}_{<i},\widetilde{Y}_i}[r_i|r_{<i}, y_i] \tag{4.17}$$

$$= 2^{-\sum_{i=1}^{m} \mathrm{H}_{\widetilde{Y}_i|\widetilde{R}_{<i}}(y_i|r_{<i})} \cdot \prod_{i=1}^{m} \Pr_{\widetilde{R}_i|\widetilde{R}_{<i},\widetilde{Y}_i}[r_i|r_{<i}, y_i]$$

$$= 2^{-\mathrm{AccH}_{\widetilde{G}}(\mathbf{t})} \cdot R(\mathbf{t})$$

for

$$R(\mathbf{t}) := \prod_{i=1}^{m} \Pr_{\widetilde{R}_i|\widetilde{R}_{<i},\widetilde{Y}_i}[r_i|r_{<i}, y_i]. \tag{4.18}$$

Execution embedded in $\mathrm{Inv}_g(f(U_n))$. Let $\widehat{T} = (\widehat{R}_1, \widehat{Y}_1, \ldots, \widehat{R}_m, \widehat{Y}_m)$ denote the value of $\widetilde{G}$'s coins and output blocks, of the execution done in step 2 of a random execution of the *unbounded* version of Inv (i.e., step 1.(c) is removed) on input $Z = (Z_1, \ldots, Z_{m-1}) = f(U_n)$. (This unboundedness change is only an intermediate step in the proof that does not significantly change the inversion probability of Inv, as shown below.)

Since $\widetilde{G}$ is G-consistent, it holds that $(y_1, \ldots, y_{m-1}) \in \mathrm{Supp}(f(U_n))$ for every $(r_1, y_1, \ldots, r_m, y_m) \in \mathrm{Supp}(\widetilde{T})$. It follows that every $\mathbf{t} \in \mathrm{Supp}(\widetilde{T})$ can be "produced" by the unbounded version of Inv, and therefore $\mathrm{Supp}(\widetilde{T}) \subseteq \mathrm{Supp}(\widehat{T})$. For

$\mathbf{t} \in \mathrm{Supp}(\widetilde{T})$, we compute

$$\mathrm{Pr}_{\widehat{T}}[\mathbf{t}] = \prod_{i=1}^{m} \mathrm{Pr}_{\widehat{Y}_i|\widehat{R}_{<i}}[y_i|r_{<i}] \cdot \mathrm{Pr}_{\widehat{R}_i|\widehat{R}_{<i},\widehat{Y}_i}[r_i|r_{<i}, y_i] \tag{4.19}$$

$$= \left(\prod_{i=1}^{m-1} \mathrm{Pr}_{Z_i|\widehat{Y}_{<i}}[y_i|y_{<i}] \cdot \mathrm{Pr}_{\widehat{Y}_i|\widehat{R}_{<i},Z_i}[y_i|r_{<i}, y_i] \right)$$

$$\cdot \mathrm{Pr}_{\widehat{Y}_m|\widehat{R}_{<m}}[y_m|r_{<m}] \cdot \prod_{i=1}^{m} \mathrm{Pr}_{\widehat{R}_i|\widehat{R}_{<i},\widehat{Y}_i}[r_i|r_{<i}, y_i]$$

$$= \left(\prod_{i=1}^{m-1} \mathrm{Pr}_{Z_i|\widehat{Y}_{<i}}[y_i|y_{<i}] \cdot 1 \right) \cdot \mathrm{Pr}_{\widehat{Y}_m|\widehat{R}_{<m}}[y_m|r_{<m}] \cdot \prod_{i=1}^{m} \mathrm{Pr}_{\widehat{R}_i|\widehat{R}_{<i},\widehat{Y}_i}[r_i|r_{<i}, y_i]$$

$$= \mathrm{Pr}_{f(U_n)}[y_{<m}] \cdot \mathrm{Pr}_{\widehat{Y}_m|\widehat{R}_{<m}}[y_m|r_{<m}] \cdot R(\mathbf{t})$$

$$= \mathrm{Pr}_{f(U_n)}[y_{<m}] \cdot \mathrm{Pr}_{\widetilde{Y}_m|\widetilde{R}_{<m}}[y_m|r_{<m}] \cdot R(\mathbf{t}).$$

Note that in the last line we moved from conditioning on $\widehat{R}_{<m}$ to conditioning on $\widetilde{R}_{<m}$. The third equality holds since $\mathbf{t} \in \mathrm{Supp}(\widetilde{T})$ and Inv is unbounded.

Relating the two distributions. Combining Equations (4.17) and (4.19) yields that, for $\mathbf{t} = (r_1, y_1, \ldots, r_m, y_m) \in \mathrm{Supp}(\widetilde{T})$, it holds that

$$\mathrm{Pr}_{\widehat{T}}[\mathbf{t}] = \mathrm{Pr}_{\widetilde{T}}[\mathbf{t}] \cdot \left(\mathrm{Pr}_{f(U_n)}[y_{<m}] \cdot \mathrm{Pr}_{\widetilde{Y}_m|\widetilde{R}_{<m}}[y_m|r_{<m}] \cdot 2^{\mathrm{AccH}_{\widehat{G}}(\mathbf{t})} \right). \tag{4.20}$$

In particular, if $\mathrm{AccH}_{\widehat{G}}(\mathbf{t}) \geq n - c \log n$, then

$$\mathrm{Pr}_{\widehat{T}}[\mathbf{t}] \geq \mathrm{Pr}_{\widetilde{T}}[\mathbf{t}] \cdot \frac{2^n \cdot \mathrm{Pr}_{f(U_n)}[y_{<m}]}{n^c} \cdot \mathrm{Pr}_{\widetilde{Y}_m|\widetilde{R}_{<m}}[y_m|r_{<m}] \tag{4.21}$$

$$= \mathrm{Pr}_{\widetilde{T}}[\mathbf{t}] \cdot \frac{|f^{-1}(y_{<m})|}{n^c} \cdot \mathrm{Pr}_{\widetilde{Y}_m|\widetilde{R}_{<m}}[y_m|r_{<m}].$$

If it is also the case that $\mathrm{H}_{\widetilde{Y}_m|\widetilde{R}_{<m}}(y_m|r_{<m}) \leq \log|f^{-1}(y_{<m})| + k$ for some $k > 0$, then

$$\mathrm{Pr}_{\widehat{T}}[\mathbf{t}] \geq \mathrm{Pr}_{\widetilde{T}}[\mathbf{t}] \cdot \frac{|f^{-1}(y_{<m})|}{n^c} \cdot \frac{2^{-k}}{|f^{-1}(y_{<m})|} = \frac{\mathrm{Pr}_{\widetilde{T}}[\mathbf{t}]}{2^k n^c} \tag{4.22}$$

Lower bounding the inversion probability of Inv. We conclude the proof by showing that Equation (4.22) implies the existence of a large set of transcripts that (the bounded version of) Inv performs well upon.

Let S denote the set of transcripts $\mathbf{t} = (r_1, y_1, \ldots, r_m, y_m) \in \mathrm{Supp}(\widetilde{T})$ with

1. $\mathrm{AccH}_{\widehat{G}}(\mathbf{t}) \geq n - c \log n$,
2. $\mathrm{H}_{\widetilde{Y}_m|\widetilde{R}_{<m}}(y_m|r_{<m}) \leq \log|f^{-1}(y_{<m})| + \log(4/\varepsilon)$, and
3. $\mathrm{H}_{\widetilde{Y}_i|\widetilde{Y}_{<i}}(y_i|y_{<i}) \leq \log(4n/\varepsilon)$ for all $i \in [m-1]$.

The first two properties will allow us to use Equations (4.21) and (4.22) to argue that, if S happens with significant probability with respect to $\widetilde{T}$, then this holds also with respect to $\widehat{T}$. The last property will allow us to show that this happens also with respect to the bounded version of Inv. We start by showing that S happens with significant probability with respect to $\widetilde{T}$, then show that this holds also with respect to $\widehat{T}$, and finally use it to lowerbound the success probability of Inv.

By Theorem 4.2.1,

$$\Pr_{(r_1,y_1,\ldots,r_m,y_m)\xleftarrow{R}\widetilde{T}}\left[\mathrm{H}_{\widetilde{Y}_m|\widetilde{R}_{<m}}(y_m|r_{<m}) > \log\left|f^{-1}(y_{<m})\right| + k\right] < 2^{-k} \qquad (4.23)$$

for any $k > 0$, where since $\left|\mathrm{Supp}(\widetilde{Y}_i)\right| = 1$ for all $i \in [m-1]$, it holds that

$$\Pr_{(y_1,\ldots,y_m)\xleftarrow{R}(\widetilde{Y}_1,\ldots,\widetilde{Y}_m)}\left[\exists i \in [m-1]\colon \mathrm{H}_{\widetilde{Y}_i|\widetilde{Y}_{<i}}(y_i|y_{<i}) > v\right] < (m-1)\cdot 2^{-v} \qquad (4.24)$$

for any $v > 0$.

Applying Equations (4.23) and (4.24) with $k = \log(4/\varepsilon)$ and $v = \log(4n/\varepsilon)$, respectively, and recalling that, by assumption, $\Pr_{t\xleftarrow{R}\widetilde{T}}\left[\mathrm{AccH}_{\widetilde{G}}(t) \geq n - c\log n\right] \geq \varepsilon$, yields that

$$\Pr_{\widetilde{T}}[S] \geq \varepsilon - \frac{\varepsilon}{4} - \frac{\varepsilon}{4} = \varepsilon/2 \qquad (4.25)$$

By Equation (4.22) and the first two properties of S, we have that

$$\Pr_{\widehat{T}}[S] \geq \frac{\varepsilon}{4n^c}\cdot\Pr_{\widetilde{T}}[S] \geq \frac{\varepsilon^2}{8n^c}. \qquad (4.26)$$

Finally, let $\widehat{T}'$ denote the final value of $\widehat{G}$'s coins and output blocks, induced by the *bounded* version of Inv (set to $\bot$ if Inv aborts). The third property of S yields that

$$\Pr_{\widehat{T}'}[\mathbf{t}] \geq \Pr_{\widehat{T}}[\mathbf{t}]\cdot\left(1 - (m-1)\cdot(1 - \tfrac{\varepsilon}{4n})^{n^2/\varepsilon}\right) \geq \Pr_{\widehat{T}}[\mathbf{t}]\cdot(1 - O(m\cdot 2^{-n})) \geq \Pr_{\widehat{T}}[\mathbf{t}]/2 \qquad (4.27)$$

for every $\mathbf{t} \in S$. We conclude that

$$\begin{aligned}
\Pr_{z\xleftarrow{R}f(U_n)}\left[\mathrm{Inv}(z) \in f^{-1}(z)\right] &= \Pr_{z\xleftarrow{R}f(U_n)}[\mathrm{Inv}(z)\text{ does not abort}] \\
&\geq \Pr_{\widehat{T}'}[S] \\
&\geq \frac{1}{2}\cdot\Pr_{\widehat{T}}[S] \\
&\geq \frac{\varepsilon^2}{16n^c}.
\end{aligned}$$

$\square$

4.4.3 Manipulating Real and Accessible Entropy

Following are two tools to manipulate the real and accessible entropy of a block generator. Since we are dealing with the more complex accessible entropy notion, the statements and proofs of the following lemmas are more complicated than those of Section 4.3.3 (given for the next-block entropy notion). Yet, the bottom line of the lemmas is essentially the same.

4.4.3.1 Entropy Equalization via Truncated Sequential Repetition

Similarly to what happens in Section 4.3, this tool concatenates several independent executions of an m-block generator, and then truncates, at random, some of the first and final output blocks of the concatenated string. Assuming that the (overall) real entropy of the original generator is at least k_{REAL}, then the real entropy of each block of the resulting generator is at least k_{REAL}/m. This per-block knowledge of the real entropy, is very handy when considering applications of inaccessible entropy generators, and in particular for constructions of statistically hiding commitment.

The price of this manipulation is that we "give away" some real entropy (as we do not output all blocks), while we cannot claim that the same happens to the accessible entropy. Hence, the additive gap between the real and accessible entropy of the resulting generator gets smaller. Yet, if we do enough repetition, this loss is insignificant.

Definition 4.4.15. *For security parameter n, let $m = m(n)$, let $s = s(n)$, $w = w(n)$, and let $s' = s'(n) = \log(m(n)) + w(n) \cdot s(n)$. Given an m-block generator G over $\{0,1\}^s$, define the $((w-1) \cdot m)$-block generator $G^{[w]}$ over $[m] \times (\{0,1\}^s)^w$ as follows: on input $(j,(x_1,\ldots,x_w)) \in [m] \times (\{0,1\}^s)^w$, it sets $\mathbf{y} = (y_1,\ldots,y_{wm}) = (G(x_1),\ldots,G(x_w))$, and outputs $((j,y_j), y_{j_1},\ldots,y_{(w-1)m+j-1})$.*

That is, $G^{[w]}$ truncates the first $j-1$ and last $m+1-j$ blocks of $\mathbf{y}$, and outputs the remaining $(w-1) \cdot m$ blocks one by one, while appending j to each block it outputs. (Using the terminology of Section 4.3, $G^{[w]}$ outputs $\text{Equalizer}^m(j,y_1,\ldots,y_{wm})$, where Equalizer is according to Theorem 4.3.14, while appending j to the first block.)

Lemma 4.4.16. *For security parameter n, let $m = m(n)$ be a power of 2, let $s = s(n)$ and let G be an efficient m-block generator over $\{0,1\}^s$, and let $w = w(n)$ be a polynomially computable and bounded integer function. Then, $G^{[w]}$ defined according to Theorem 4.4.15 is an efficient,[14] $((w-1) \cdot m)$-block generator that satisfies the following properties:*

Real entropy: If G has real entropy at least $k_{REAL} = k_{REAL}(n)$, then each block of $G^{[w]}$ has real entropy at least k_{REAL}/m.

---

[14] Since m is a power of 2, changing the input domain of $G^{[w]}$ to $\{0,1\}^{s'}$ for some polynomial-bounded and polynomial-time computable s', to make it an efficient block generator according to Theorem 4.4.1, can be done by standard techniques.

Accessible max-entropy: The following holds for any $d = d(n) \in \omega(\log n)$. If G has accessible max-entropy at most $k_{\text{ACC}} = k_{\text{ACC}}(n)$, then $\mathsf{G}^{[w]}$ has accessible max-entropy at most

$$k'_{\text{ACC}} := (w - 2) \cdot k_{\text{ACC}} + 2 \cdot \mathrm{H}_0(\mathsf{G}(U_s)) + \log(m) + d.$$

Roughly, each of the $(w - 2)$ non-truncated executions of G embedded in $\mathsf{G}^{[w]}$ contributes its accessible entropy to the overall accessible entropy of $\mathsf{G}^{[w]}$. In addition, we pay the max-entropy of the two truncated executions of G embedded in $\mathsf{G}^{[w]}$.
Proof: To avoid notational clutter let $\mathsf{G} = \mathsf{G}^{[w]}$.

Real entropy. The proof of this part is very similar to the proof of the first part of Theorem 4.3.15. Fix $n \in \mathbb{N}$ and omit it from the notation when clear from the context. Let $\tilde{m} = (w - 1)m$, let $\widetilde{Y} = \mathsf{G}(U_{s'} = (J, X_1, \ldots, X_w))$, let $Y^{(w)} = (\mathsf{G}(X_1), \ldots, \mathsf{G}(X_w))$, and finally for $i \in [wm]$, let $Y^{(w)\prime}_i = (J, Y^{(w)}_i)$ if $J = i$, and $Y^{(w)}_i$ otherwise. For $i \in [\tilde{m}]$, compute

$$\mathrm{H}(\widetilde{Y}_i \mid \widetilde{Y}_{<i}) = \mathrm{H}(Y^{(w)\prime}_{i+J-1} \mid Y^{(w)\prime}_{J,\ldots,i+J-2})$$
$$\geq \mathrm{H}(Y^{(w)}_{i+J-1} \mid Y^{(w)}_{J,\ldots,i+J-2}, J).$$

The proof continues as the first part of the proof of Theorem 4.3.15.

Accessible entropy. To establish the statement on the accessible entropy, let $\widetilde{\mathsf{G}}$ be an efficient G-consistent generator, and let

$$\varepsilon = \varepsilon(n) := \Pr_{\mathsf{t} \xleftarrow{R} \widetilde{\mathbb{T}}} \left[\mathrm{AccH}_{\widetilde{\mathsf{G}}}(\mathsf{t}) > k'_{\text{ACC}} \right] \tag{4.28}$$

for $\widetilde{\mathbb{T}} = T_{\widetilde{\mathsf{G}}}(1^n)$. Our goal is to show that ε is negligible in n. We do that by finding a subtranscript of $\widetilde{\mathbb{T}}$ that, with high probability, contributes more than k_{ACC} bits of accessible entropy, if the overall accessible entropy of $\widetilde{\mathbb{T}}$ is more than k'_{ACC}. We then use this observation to construct a cheating generator for G that achieves accessible entropy greater than k_{ACC} with probability that is negligibly close to ε.

Let $(R_1, Y_1, \ldots, R_{\tilde{m}}, Y_{\tilde{m}}) = \widetilde{\mathbb{T}}$ and let J be the first part of Y_1 (recall that Y_1 is of the form $(j, \cdot)$). Fix $j \in [m]$, and let $(R^j_1, Y^j_1, \ldots, R^j_{\tilde{m}}, Y^j_{\tilde{m}}) = \widetilde{\mathbb{T}}^j = \widetilde{\mathbb{T}}|_{J=j}$. Let $\mathcal{I} = \mathcal{I}(j)$ be the indices of the blocks coming from the truncated executions of G in G (i.e., $\{1, \ldots, m+1-j\} \cup \{\tilde{m}+2-j, \ldots, \tilde{m}\}$). Our first step is to show that these blocks do not contribute much more entropy than the max-entropy of $\mathsf{G}(U_n)$. Specifically, by Theorem 4.2.8, letting $\mathbf{X} = (Y^j_1, R^j_1, \ldots, Y^j_{\tilde{m}}, R^j_{\tilde{m}})$ and $\mathcal{J} = \mathcal{I}$, it holds that

$$\Pr_{\mathsf{t}=(r_1,y_1,\ldots,r_{\tilde{m}},y_{\tilde{m}}) \xleftarrow{R} \widetilde{\mathbb{T}}^j} \left[\sum_{i \in \mathcal{I}} \mathrm{H}_{Y^j_i \mid R^j_{<i}}(y_i \mid r_{<i}) > 2 \cdot \mathrm{H}_0(\mathsf{G}(U_s)) + d/2 \right] \leq 2 \cdot 2^{-d/2} = \text{neg}(n). \tag{4.29}$$

Namely, with save but negligible probability, the blocks that relate to the truncated executions of G in $\mathbb{G}$, do not contribute much more than their support size to the overall accessible entropy.

Our next step is to remove the conditioning on $J = j$ (that we have introduced to have the indices of interest fixed, which enabled us to use Theorem 4.2.8). By Theorem 4.2.1, it holds that

$$\Pr_{j \xleftarrow{R} J} \left[H_J(j) > \log(m) + d/2 \right] \leq 2^{-d/2} = \text{neg}(n). \tag{4.30}$$

Since for every $i > 1$ and $(r_1, y_1 = (j, \cdot), \ldots, r_{\tilde{m}}, y_{\tilde{m}}) \in \text{Supp}(\widetilde{\mathbb{T}})$, it holds that $H_{Y_i|R_{<i}}(y_i|r_{<i}) = H_{Y_i^j|R_{<i}^j}(y_i|r_{<i})$, and for $i = 1$, it holds that $H_{Y_1}(y_1) = H_J(j) + H_{Y_1^j}(y_1)$, the above yields that

$$\Pr_{t=(r_1,y_1,\ldots,r_{\tilde{m}},y_{\tilde{m}}) \xleftarrow{R} \widetilde{\mathbb{T}}} \left[\sum_{i \in [\tilde{m}] \setminus \mathcal{I}(J)} H_{Y_i|R_{<i}}(y_i|r_{<i}) > (w-2) \cdot k_{\text{ACC}} \right] \geq \varepsilon - \text{neg}(n). \tag{4.31}$$

Let $\mathcal{F}(j) = \{km + 2 - j : k \in [w-2]\}$, i.e., the indices of the first blocks of the non-truncated executions of G in $\mathbb{G}$, when the first block of $\mathbb{G}$ is $(j, \cdot)$. It follows that,

$$\Pr_{t=(r_1,y_1,\ldots,r_{\tilde{m}},y_{\tilde{m}}) \xleftarrow{R} \widetilde{\mathbb{T}}} \left[\exists f \in \mathcal{F}(J) : \sum_{i=f}^{f+m-1} H_{Y_i|R_{<i}}(y_i|r_{<i}) > k_{\text{ACC}} \right] \geq \varepsilon - \text{neg} \tag{4.32}$$

In particular, there exist $j^* \in [m]$, $f^* \in \mathcal{F}(j^*)$, and $\mathbf{r}^* \in \text{Supp}(R_{<f^*}|_{J=j^*})$ such that

$$\Pr_{t=(r_1,y_1,\ldots,r_{\tilde{m}},y_{\tilde{m}}) \xleftarrow{R} \widetilde{\mathbb{T}}} \left[\sum_{i=f^*}^{f^*+m-1} H_{Y_i|R_{<i}}(y_i|r_{<i}) > k_{\text{ACC}} \mid r_{<f^*} = \mathbf{r}^* \right] \geq (\varepsilon - \text{neg})/m. \tag{4.33}$$

Consider the efficient, nonuniform, G-consistent generator $\widetilde{G}$ that acts as follows: it starts a random execution of $\widetilde{\mathbb{G}}$ with its first $(f^* - 1)$ randomness blocks fixed to $\mathbf{r}^*$, and outputs the blocks indexed by $\{f^*, \ldots, f^* + m - 1\}$. Let $(R_1', Y_1', \ldots, R_m', Y_m') = T_{\widetilde{G}}$ be the transcript of $\widetilde{G}$. It is easy to verify that, for every $(r_1, y_1, \ldots, r_m, y_m) \in \text{Supp}(T_{\widetilde{G}})$ and $1 < i \leq m$, it holds that

$$H_{Y_i'|R_{<i}'}(y_i|r_{<i}) = H_{Y_{f+i}|R_{<f+i}}(y_i|(\mathbf{r}^*, r_{<i})). \tag{4.34}$$

Thus, Equation (4.33) yields that

$$\Pr_{t \xleftarrow{R} T_{\widetilde{G}}} \left[\text{AccH}_{\widetilde{G}}(\mathbf{t}) > k_{\text{ACC}} \right] > (\varepsilon - \text{neg}(n))/m.$$

Hence, the assumption about the inaccessible entropy of G yields that ε is a negligible function of n, and the proof of the lemma follows.   □

4.4.3.2 Parallel Repetition

This manipulation simply takes parallel repetition of a generator. The effect of this manipulation is twofold. The first effect is that the overall real entropy of a v-fold parallel repetition of a generator G is v times the real entropy of G. Hence, if G real entropy is larger than its accessible entropy, this gap get multiplied by v in the resulting variable. The second effect of such repetition is turning per-block real entropy into per-block *min-entropy*. The price of this manipulation is a slight decrease in the per block min-entropy of the resulting generator, compared to the sum of the per block real entropies of the independent copies of the generators used to generate it. (This loss is due to the move from Shannon entropy to min-entropy, rather than from the parallel repetition itself.) But when taking enough copies, this loss can be ignored.

Definition 4.4.17. *Let $m = m(n)$, $s = s(n)$, and $v = v(n)$. Given an m-block generator G over $\{0,1\}^s$, define the m-block generator $G^{\langle v \rangle}$ over $(\{0,1\}^s)^v$ as follows: on input $(x_1, \ldots, x_v) \in (\{0,1\}^s)^v$, the i-th block of $G^{\langle v \rangle}$ is $(G(x_1)_i, \ldots, G(x_v)_i)$.*

Lemma 4.4.18. *For security parameter n, let $m = m(n)$, let $v = v(n)$ be polynomial-time polynomially computable and bounded integer functions, and let G be an efficient,[15] m-block generator. Then $G^{\langle v \rangle}$, defined according to Theorem 4.4.17, is an efficient m-block generator that satisfies the following properties:*

Real entropy: If each block of G has real min-entropy at least $k_{\text{REAL}} = k_{\text{REAL}}(n)$, then each block of $G^{\langle v \rangle}$ has real min-entropy at least $k'_{\text{REAL}}(n) = v \cdot k_{\text{REAL}} - O((\log n + \ell) \cdot \log n \cdot \sqrt{v})$, for $\ell = \ell(n)$ being the maximal block length of G.

Accessible max-entropy: The following holds for every $d = d(n) \in \omega(\log n)$. If G has accessible max-entropy at most $k_{\text{ACC}} = k_{\text{ACC}}(n)$, then $G^{\langle v \rangle}$ has accessible max-entropy at most $k'_{\text{ACC}}(n) = v \cdot k_{\text{ACC}} + d \cdot m$.

Proof: The bound on real entropy follows readily from Theorem 4.2.5 by taking $\varepsilon = 2^{-\log^2 n}$, and noting that the support size of each block of G is at most $\ell \cdot 2^\ell$. Therefore, we focus on establishing the bound on accessible max-entropy. Let $\mathbb{G} = G^{\langle v \rangle}$, let $\widetilde{\mathbb{G}}$ be an efficient, nonuniform, $\mathbb{G}$-consistent generator, and let

$$\varepsilon = \varepsilon(n) := \Pr_{\mathbf{t} \xleftarrow{R} \widetilde{\mathbb{T}}} \left[\text{AccH}_{\widetilde{\mathbb{G}}}(\mathbf{t}) > k'_{\text{ACC}} \right] \tag{4.35}$$

for $\widetilde{\mathbb{T}} = T_{\widetilde{\mathbb{G}}}(1^n)$. Our goal is to show that ε is negligible in n.

Let $(R_1, Y_1, \ldots, R_m, Y_m) = \widetilde{\mathbb{T}}$. By definition, for $\mathbf{t} = (r_1, y_1, \ldots, r_m, y_m) \in \text{Supp}(\widetilde{\mathbb{T}})$,

$$\text{AccH}_{\widetilde{\mathbb{G}}}(\mathbf{t}) = \sum_{i \in [m]} H_{Y_i | R_{<i}}(y_i \mid r_{<i}). \tag{4.36}$$

---

[15] Changing the input domain of G to $\{0,1\}^{s'(n)}$ for some polynomial-bounded and polynomial-time computable s', to make it an efficient block generator according to Theorem 4.4.1, can be done by standard techniques.

Since $\widetilde{\mathsf{G}}$ is G-consistent, each Y_i is of the form $(Y_{i,1}, \ldots, Y_{i,v})$. Theorem 4.2.6, taking $\mathbf{X} = Y_i|_{R_{<i}=r_{<i}}$, yields that

$$\Pr_{\mathbf{t}=(r_1,y_1,\ldots,r_m,y_m)\xleftarrow{R}\widetilde{\mathbb{T}}}\left[\mathsf{H}_{Y_i|R_{<i}}(y_i|r_{<i}) > d + \sum_{j=1}^{v}\mathsf{H}_{Y_{i,j}|R_{<i}}(y_{i,j}|r_{<i})\right] \le 2^{-d} = \operatorname{neg}(n) \quad (4.37)$$

for every $i \in [m]$. Summing over all $i \in [m]$, we get that

$$\Pr_{\mathbf{t}=(r_1,y_1,\ldots,r_m,y_m)\xleftarrow{R}\widetilde{\mathbb{T}}}\left[\sum_{i\in[m]}\mathsf{H}_{Y_i|R_{<i}}(y_i|r_{<i}) > md + \sum_{i\in[m]}\sum_{j\in[v]}\mathsf{H}_{Y_{i,j}|R_{<i}}(y_{i,j}|r_{<i})\right] = \operatorname{neg}(n)$$

$$(4.38)$$

and therefore

$$\Pr_{\mathbf{t}=(r_1,y_1,\ldots,r_m,y_m)\xleftarrow{R}\widetilde{\mathbb{T}}}\left[\sum_{i\in[m]}\sum_{j\in[v]}\mathsf{H}_{Y_{i,j}|R_{<i}}(y_{i,j}|r_{<i}) \ge k'_{\mathrm{ACC}} - m \cdot d\right] \ge \varepsilon - \operatorname{neg}(n). \quad (4.39)$$

In particular, there exist $j^* \in [v]$ such that

$$\Pr_{\mathbf{t}=(r_1,y_1,\ldots,r_m,y_m)\xleftarrow{R}\widetilde{\mathbb{T}}}\left[\sum_{i\in[m]}\mathsf{H}_{Y_{i,j^*}|R_{<i}}(y_{i,j^*}|r_{<i}) > k_{\mathrm{ACC}} = (k'_{\mathrm{ACC}} - m \cdot d)/v\right] \ge \varepsilon - \operatorname{neg}(n)$$

$$(4.40)$$

Consider the following efficient, nonuniform, G-consistent generator $\widehat{G}$. This generator starts a random execution of $\widetilde{\mathsf{G}}$, and outputs y_{i,j^*} as its i-th block, for $y_i = (y_{i,1}, \ldots, y_{i,v})$ being the i-th block (locally) output by $\widetilde{\mathsf{G}}$. Let $(R'_1, Y'_1, \ldots, R'_m, Y'_m) = T_{\widehat{G}}$. It is easy to verify that, for every $(r_1, y_1, \ldots, r_m, y_m) \in \operatorname{Supp}(T_{\widehat{G}})$ and $1 < i \le m$, it holds that

$$\mathsf{H}_{Y'_i|R'_{<i}}(y_i|j, r_{<i}) = \mathsf{H}_{Y_{i,j^*}|R_{<i}}(y_i|r_{<i}). \quad (4.41)$$

Thus, Equation (4.40) yields that

$$\Pr_{\mathbf{t}\leftarrow T_{\widehat{G}}}\left[\operatorname{AccH}_{\widehat{G}}(\mathbf{t}) > k_{\mathrm{ACC}}\right] \ge \varepsilon - \operatorname{neg}(n).$$

The assumption about the inaccessible entropy of G yields that ε is negligible in n, and the proof of the lemma follows. $\square$

4.4.4 Inaccessible Entropy Generator to Statistically Hiding Commitment

In this section we prove a simplified version of the construction of statistically hiding commitments from inaccessible entropy generators. Specifically, we only prove a weaker version of Theorem 4.4.23, stated below, which is the main lemma in this reduction. But first, we recall the definition of such commitment schemes.

Statistically hiding commitment schemes. A *commitment scheme* is the cryptographic analogue of a safe. It is a two-party protocol between a *sender* S and a *receiver* R that consists of two stages. The *commit stage* corresponds to putting an object in a safe and locking it; the sender "commits" to a private message *m*. The *reveal stage* corresponds to unlocking and opening the safe; the sender "reveals" the message *m* and "proves" that it was the value committed to in the commit stage (without loss of generality by revealing coin tosses consistent with *m* and the transcript of the commit stage).

Definition 4.4.19. *A* (bit) commitment scheme[16] *is an efficient two-party protocol* Com = (S, R) *consisting of two stages. Throughout, both parties receive the security parameter* 1^n *as input.*

> COMMIT. *The sender* S *has a private input* $b \in \{0, 1\}$, *which she wishes to commit to the receiver* R, *and a sequence of coin tosses* σ. *At the end of this stage, both parties receive as common output a* commitment *z.*

> REVEAL. *Both parties receive as input a commitment* z. S *also receives the private input b and coin tosses* σ *used in the commit stage. After the interaction of* $(S(b, r), R)(z)$, R *either outputs a bit, or the reject symbol* $\perp$.

The commitment is public-coin *if the messages the receiver sends are merely the coins it flips at each round.*

For the sake of this tutorial, we focus on commitment schemes with a generic *reveal scheme: the commitment z is simply the transcript of the commit stage, and in the noninteractive reveal stage, S sends* (b, σ) *to* R, *and* R *outputs b if* S, *on input b and randomness* σ, *would have acted as the sender did in z; otherwise, it outputs* $\perp$.

Commitment schemes have two security properties. The *hiding* property informally says that, at the end of the commit stage, an adversarial receiver has learned nothing about the message *m*, except with negligible probability. The *binding* property says that, after the commit stage, an adversarial sender cannot produce valid openings for two distinct messages (i.e., to both 0 and 1), except with negligible probability. Both of these security properties come in two flavors—*statistical*, where we require security even against a computationally unbounded adversary, and *computational*, where we only require security against feasible (e.g., polynomial-time) adversaries.

Statistical security is preferable to computational security, but it is impossible to have commitment schemes that are both statistically hiding and statistically binding. In this tutorial, we focus on statistically hiding (and computationally binding) schemes, which are closely connected with the notion of inaccessible entropy generators.

---

[16] We present the definition for bit commitment. To commit to multiple bits, we may simply run a bit commitment scheme in parallel.

Definition 4.4.20. *A commitment scheme* Com $= (\mathsf{S}, \mathsf{R})$ *is* statistically hiding *if*

COMPLETENESS. *If both parties are honest, then for any bit $b \in \{0, 1\}$ that S gets as private input, R accepts and outputs b at the end of the reveal stage.*

STATISTICAL HIDING. *For every unbounded strategy $\widetilde{\mathsf{R}}$, the distributions $\mathrm{view}_{\widetilde{\mathsf{R}}}((\mathsf{S}(0), \widetilde{\mathsf{R}})(1^n))$ and $\mathrm{view}_{\widetilde{\mathsf{R}}}((\mathsf{S}(1), \widetilde{\mathsf{R}})(1^n))$ are statistically indistinguishable, where $\mathrm{view}_{\widetilde{\mathsf{R}}}(e)$ denotes the collection of all messages exchanged and the coin tosses of $\widetilde{\mathsf{R}}$ in e.*

COMPUTATIONAL BINDING. *A ppt $\widetilde{\mathsf{S}}$ succeeds in the following game (breaks the commitment) only with negligible probability in n:*

- $\widetilde{\mathsf{S}} = \widetilde{\mathsf{S}}(1^n)$ *interacts with an honest $\mathsf{R} = \mathsf{R}(1^n)$ in the commit stage, on security parameter 1^n, which yields a commitment z.*
- $\widetilde{\mathsf{S}}$ *outputs two messages τ_0, τ_1 such that $\mathsf{R}(z, \tau_b)$ outputs b, for both $b \in \{0, 1\}$.*

Com *is δ-binding if no ppt $\widetilde{\mathsf{S}}$ wins the above game with probability larger than $\delta(n) + \mathrm{neg}(n)$.*

We now discuss the intriguing connection between statistically hiding commitment and inaccessible entropy generators. Consider a statistically hiding commitment scheme in which the sender commits to a message of length k, and suppose we run the protocol with the message m chosen uniformly at random in $\{0, 1\}^k$. Then, by the statistical hiding property, the *real entropy* of the message m after the commit stage is $k - \mathrm{neg}(n)$. On the other hand, the computational binding property says that the *accessible entropy* of m after the commit stage is at most $\mathrm{neg}(n)$. This is only an intuitive connection, since we have not discussed real and accessible entropy for protocols, but only for generators. Such definitions can be found in [11], and for them it can be proven that statistical hiding commitments imply protocols in which the real entropy is much larger than the accessible entropy. Here our goal is to establish the converse, namely that a generator with a gap between its real and accessible entropy implies a statistical hiding commitment scheme. The extension of this fact for protocols can be found in [11].

Theorem 4.4.21 (Inaccessible entropy to statistically hiding commitment). *Let $k = k(n)$, $s = s(n)$, and $\delta = \delta(n)$ be polynomial-time computable functions. Let G be an efficient $m = m(n)$-block generator over $\{0, 1\}^s$. Assume that G's real Shannon entropy is at least k, that its accessible max-entropy is at most $(1 - \delta) \cdot k$, and that $k\delta \in \omega(\log n / n)$. Then for any polynomial-time computable $g = g(n) \in \omega(\log n)$ with $g \geq \mathrm{H}_0(G(U_s))$, there exists an $O(m \cdot g / \delta k)$-round, public-coin, statistically hiding and computationally binding commitment scheme. Furthermore, the construction is black box, and on security parameter 1^n, the commitment invokes G on inputs of length s.*[17]

Combining the above theorem with Theorem 4.4.12 reproves the following fundamental result:

---

[17] Given a, per n, polynomial-size advice, the commitment round complexity can be reduced to $O(m)$. See Theorem 4.4.25 for details.

Theorem 4.4.22 (One-way functions to statistically hiding commitment). *Assume there exists a nonuniformly one-way function $f \colon \{0,1\}^n \mapsto \{0,1\}^n$, then there exists an $O(n^2/\log n)$-round, public-coin statistically hiding and computationally binding commitment scheme. Furthermore, the construction is black box, and on security parameter 1^n, the commitment invokes f on inputs of length n.*[18]

The heart of the proof of Theorem 4.4.21 lies in the following lemma.

Lemma 4.4.23. *Let $k = k(n) \geq 3n$ be a polynomial-time computable function, let $m = m(n)$, $s = s(n)$, and let G be an efficient m-block generator over $\{0,1\}^s$. Then there exists a polynomial-time, $O(m)$-round, public-coin, commitment scheme Com with the following properties:*

Hiding: If each block of G has real min-entropy at least k, then Com is statistically hiding.

Binding: If the accessible max-entropy of G is at most $m(k-3n)$, then Com is computationally binding.

Furthermore, on security parameter 1^n, the protocol invokes G on inputs of length s.

We prove a weak version of Theorem 4.4.23 in Section 4.4.4.1, but we first use it for proving Theorem 4.4.21.

Proving Theorem 4.4.21. Proof: We prove Theorem 4.4.21 by manipulating the real and accessible entropy of G using the tools described in Section 4.4.3, and then applying Theorem 4.4.23 on the resulting generator.

Truncated sequential repetition: real entropy equalization. In this step we use G to define a generator $G^{[v]}$ whose *each block has the same amount* of real entropy—the average of the real entropy of the blocks of G. In relative terms, the entropy gap of $G^{[v]}$ is essentially that of G. We assume without loss of generality that $m(n)$ is a power of two.[19] We apply truncated sequential repetition (see Theorem 4.4.15) on G with parameter $w = w(n) = \max\{4, \lceil 16g/\delta k \rceil\} \leq \text{poly}(n)$. Theorem 4.4.16, taking $d = g$, yields an efficient $m' = m'(n) = (w-1) \cdot m$-block generator $G^{[w]}$ such that the following holds:

- *Each block* of $G^{[w]}$ has real entropy at least $k = k'(n) = k/m$.
- The accessible max-entropy of $G^{[w]}$ is at most

---

[18] Applying Theorem 4.4.21 with the $O(n/\log n)$-block mentioned in Theorem 4.4.13 yields an $O(n^2/\log^2 n)$-round commitment. This is the best such commitment scheme we know how to build from one-way functions and it is still far from the $(n/\log n)$ lower bound of [15], which we only know how to achieve via nonuniform protocol (see Theorem 4.4.25).

[19] Adding $2^{\lceil \log m(n) \rceil} - m(n)$ final blocks of constant value transforms a block generator to one whose block complexity is a power of two, while maintaining the same amount of real and accessible entropy.

$$a' = a'(n) = (w - 2) \cdot ((1 - \delta) \cdot k + \log m + 2g + g$$
$$\leq (w - 2) \cdot (1 - \delta) \cdot k + 4g$$
$$\leq (w - 2) \cdot (1 - \delta/2) \cdot k - (w - 2) \cdot k \cdot \delta/2 + 4g$$
$$\leq (w - 2) \cdot (1 - \delta/2) \cdot k - w \cdot k \cdot \delta/4 + 4g$$
$$\leq (w - 2) \cdot (1 - \delta/2) \cdot k$$
$$< m' \cdot (1 - \delta/2) \cdot k'.$$

Parallel repetition: converting real entropy to min-entropy and gap amplification. In this step we use $G^{[w]}$ to define a generator $(G^{[w]})^{\langle v \rangle}$ whose each block has the same amount of *min-entropy*—about v times the per-block entropy of $G^{[w]}$. The accessible entropy of $(G^{[w]})^{\langle v \rangle}$ is also about v times that of $G^{[w]}$. Let $\ell = \ell(n) \in \Omega(\log n)$ be a polynomial-time computable function that bounds the maximal block length of G. We apply the gap amplification transformation (see Theorem 4.4.17) on $G^{[w]}$ with $v = v(n) = \max\{24mn/k\delta, \lceil c \cdot (\log n \cdot \ell)/k'\delta)^2 \rceil\}$, for $c > 0$ to be determined by the analysis. Theorem 4.4.18 yields an efficient m'-block generator $(G^{[w]})^{\langle v \rangle}$ with the following properties:

- Each block of $(G^{[w]})^{\langle v \rangle}$ has real *min-entropy* at least $k'' = k''(n) = v \cdot k' - O(\log(n) \cdot \ell \cdot \sqrt{v})$.
- The accessible max-entropy of $(G^{[w]})^{\langle v \rangle}$ is at most $a'' = a''(n) = v \cdot a' + d \cdot m'$, for $d = d(n) = n/8k\delta$.

Hence for large enough n, it holds that

$$m' \cdot k'' - a'' \geq m' \cdot \left(v \cdot k' - O\left(\log(n) \cdot \ell \cdot \sqrt{v}\right)\right) - (v \cdot a' + d \cdot m')$$
$$> m' \cdot \left(v \cdot k' - O\left(\log(n) \cdot \ell \cdot \sqrt{v}\right)\right) - (v \cdot (m' \cdot (1 - \delta/2) \cdot k') + d \cdot m')$$
$$= v \cdot m' \cdot \left(k'\delta/2 - O(\log(n) \cdot \ell/\sqrt{v}) - d/v\right)$$
$$\geq v \cdot m' \cdot \left(k'\delta/2 - O(k'\delta/\sqrt{c}) - d/mn\right)$$
$$\geq v \cdot m' \cdot (k'\delta/4 - d/mn) \tag{4.42}$$
$$= v \cdot (w - 1) \cdot (k\delta/4 - d/n)$$
$$= v \cdot (w - 1) \cdot k\delta/8$$
$$\geq 3m'n.$$

Inequality (4.42) holds by taking a large enough value of c in the definition of v.

Namely, the overall real entropy of $(G^{[w]})^{\langle v \rangle}$ is larger than its accessible max-entropy by at least $3m'n$. Hence, by applying Theorem 4.4.23 with $(G^{[w]})^{\langle v \rangle}$ and $k = k''$, we get the claimed $(m' = m \cdot (w - 1) = O(m \cdot g/\delta k))$-round, public-coin, statistically hiding and computationally binding commitment. □

Remark 4.4.24 (Comparison with the construction of next-block pseudoentropy generators to pseudorandom generators). *It is interesting to see the similarity between the manipulations we apply above on the inaccessible entropy generator*

G *to construct statistically hiding commitment, and those applied in Section 4.3.4 on the next-block pseudoentropy generator to construct a pseudorandom generator. The manipulations applied in both constructions are essentially the same and achieve similar goals: from real entropy to per-block min-entropy whose overall sum is significantly larger than the accessible entropy in the above, and from next-block pseudoentropy to per-block pseudo-min-entropy whose overall sum is significantly larger than the real entropy in Section 4.3.4. Combining this fact with the similarity in the initial steps of constructing the above generators from one-way functions (inaccessible entropy generator above and next-block pseudoentropy generator in Section 4.3.4) yields that the structures of the constructions of statistically hiding commitment schemes and pseudorandom generators from one-way functions are surprisingly similar.*

Remark 4.4.25 (Constant-round and nonuniform commitments). *If the generator's number of blocks is constant, one might skip the first "entropy equalizing" step in the proof of Theorem 4.4.21 above, and rather apply parallel repetition directly on* G, *to get a generator as* $G^{[w]}$ *above, but for which we do not know the value of the (possibly different) min-entropies of each block. Since* G *and thus* $G^{[w]}$ *have constant number of blocks, applying a variant of Theorem 4.4.23 on* $G^{[w]}$ *for polynomially many possible values for the min-entropies (up to some* $1/$ poly *additive accuracy level) yields polynomially many commitments that are all binding and at least one of them is hiding. Such commitments can then be combined in a standard way to get a single scheme that is statistically hiding and computationally binding.*[20]

The equalization step can also be skipped if the amount of real entropy of each block of the m-block generator G *is efficiently computable, yielding an* $\Theta(m)$-round *commitment scheme (rather than the* $O(m \cdot \max\{\log n, g/\delta k\})$-round *we know how to achieve without this additional property). This argument also yields an* $\Theta(m)$-round, *nonuniform (the parties use a nonuniform polynomial-size advice per security parameter) commitment scheme, with no additional assumptions on the generator* G. *Combining with Theorem 4.4.12, the latter yields a* $\Theta(n/\log n)$-round *nonuniform commitment statistically hiding scheme from any one-way function, matching the lower bound of [15].*[21]

4.4.4.1 Proving a Weaker Variant of Theorem 4.4.23

We prove the following weaker variant of Theorem 4.4.23.

Lemma 4.4.26 (Weaker variant of Theorem 4.4.23). *Let* $k = k(n) \geq 3n$ *be a polynomial-time computable function, let* $m = m(n)$, $s = s(n)$, *and let* G *be an efficient m-block generator over* $\{0, 1\}^s$. *Then there exists a polynomial-time,* $O(m)$-*round, public-coin, commitment scheme* Com *with the following properties:*

---

[20] [11] used a similar approach to transform a constant-round zero-knowledge proof system for NP that remains secure under parallel composition into a constant-round statistically hiding and computationally binding commitment.

[21] The bound of [15] is stated for uniform commitment schemes, but the same bound for nonuniform commitment schemes readily follows from their proof.

Hiding (unchanged): If each block of G *has real min-entropy at least k, then* Com
is statistically hiding.

Binding: If for every efficient, G-consistent generator $\widetilde{G}$ *there exists* $i = i(n) \in [m]$
such that

$$\Pr_{t \xleftarrow{R} T_{\widetilde{G}}(1^n)} [\text{AccH}^i_{\widetilde{G}}(t) > k - 2n] = \text{neg}(n),$$

then Com *is computationally binding.*

Furthermore, on security parameter 1^n, *the protocol invokes* G *on inputs of length*
$s(n)$.

That is, rather than requiring the *overall* accessible entropy of G to be significantly smaller than its real entropy, we require that, for every efficient, G-consistent
generator $\widetilde{G}$, there exists a block in which its accessible entropy is significantly
smaller than the real entropy of this block. We do know how to construct such a
generator from one-way functions, and moreover, as we show below, such a generator implies an $\Theta(1)$-round statistically hiding commitment, which by [15] cannot be
constructed black-boxly from one-way functions. Yet, the proof of Theorem 4.4.26
given below does capture some of the main ideas of the proof of Theorem 4.4.23. In
Section 4.4.4.2, we give more ideas about the proof of Theorem 4.4.23.

To keep notation simple, we take the simplifying assumption that G's input length
on security parameter n is n, and assume without loss of generality that all its output
blocks are of the same length $\ell = \ell(n)$.[22] We omit n from the notation whenever
clear from the context.

On the very high level, to prove Theorem 4.4.26 we use a random block of G to
mask the committed bit. The guarantee about the real entropy of G yields that the
resulting commitment is hiding, where the guarantee about G's accessible entropy,
yields that the commitment is weakly (i.e., $\Theta(1/m)$) binding. This commitment is
then amplified via parallel repetition, into a full-fledged computationally binding
and statistically hiding commitment.

In more detail, the construction of the aforementioned weakly binding commitment scheme goes as follows: The receiver R sends uniformly chosen $i^* \in [m]$ to
S. The sender S starts (privately) computing a random execution of G, and sends
the first $i - 1$ output blocks to R. Then the parties interact in a (constant round)
"interactive hashing" subprotocol in which S's input is the i-th block y_i of G. This
subprotocol has the following properties:

- After seeing $y_1, \ldots, y_{i-1}$ and the hash value of y_i (i.e., the transcript of the hashing protocol), the (real) min-entropy of y_i is still high (e.g., $\Omega(n)$), and
- If the accessible max-entropy of G in the i-th block is lower than $k - 2n$ (i.e.,
  given an adversarial generator view, the support size of y_i is smaller than 2^{k-2n}),
  then y_i is *determined* from the point of view of (even a cheating) S after sending
  the hash value.

---

[22] Using the padding technique one can transform a block generator to one whose all blocks are of
the same length, without changing its real and its accessible entropy.

Next, S "commits" to its secret bit b by masking it (via XORing) with a bit extracted (via an inner product with a random string) from y_i, and the commit stage halts.

The hiding of the above scheme follows from the guarantee about the min-entropy of G's blocks. The $1/m$-binding of the scheme follows since the bound on the accessible max-entropy of G yields that the accessible entropy of at least one of G's blocks is low, and thus the sender is bounded to a single bit if the receiver has chosen this block to use for the commitment.

The aforementioned hashing protocol is defined and analyzed in Section 4.4.4.1.1, the weakly binding commitment is defined in Section 4.4.4.1.2, and in Section 4.4.4.1.3 we put it all together to prove the lemma.

4.4.4.1.1 The Interactive Hashing Protocol

The hashing protocol is the interactive hashing protocol of Ding et al. [6]. (This very protocol is used as the first step of the *computational* interactive hashing protocol used in the commitment constructed in the proof of Theorem 4.4.23.)

Let $\mathcal{H}^1 \colon \{0, 1\}^\ell \mapsto \{0, 1\}^\ell$ and $\mathcal{H}^2 \colon \{0, 1\}^\ell \mapsto \{0, 1\}^n$ be function families.

Protocol 4.4.27 (Two-round interactive hashing protocol $(\mathsf{S_{IH}}, \mathsf{R_{IH}})^{\mathcal{H}_1, \mathcal{H}_2}$)
$\mathsf{S_{IH}}$'s private input: $x \in \{0, 1\}^\ell$

1. $\mathsf{R_{IH}}$ sends $h^1 \xleftarrow{R} \mathcal{H}^1$ to $\mathsf{S_{IH}}$.
2. $\mathsf{S_{IH}}$ sends $y^1 = h^1(x)$ back to $\mathsf{R_{IH}}$.
3. $\mathsf{R_{IH}}$ sends $h^2 \xleftarrow{R} \mathcal{H}^2$ to $\mathsf{S_{IH}}$.
4. $\mathsf{S_{IH}}$ sends $y^2 = h^2(x)$ back to $\mathsf{R_{IH}}$.

We will use two properties of the above protocol. The first, which we will use for "hiding", is that $\mathsf{S_{IH}}$ sends only $\ell + n$ bits to $\mathsf{R_{IH}}$. Thus, if $\mathsf{S_{IH}}$'s input x comes from a distribution of min-entropy significantly larger than $\ell + n$, it will still have high min-entropy conditioned on $\mathsf{R_{IH}}$'s view of the protocol (with high probability). On the other hand, the following "binding" property says that, if x has max-entropy smaller than ℓ (i.e., is restricted to come from a set of size at most 2^ℓ) and $\mathcal{H}_1$ and $\mathcal{H}_2$ are "sufficiently" independent, then after the interaction ends, x will be uniquely determined, except with exponentially small probability.

The following proposition readily follows from the proof of [6, Theorem 5.6]:

Proposition 4.4.28 ([6], "statistical binding" property of $(\mathsf{S_{IH}}, \mathsf{R_{IH}})$). *Let* $\mathcal{H}^1 \colon \{0, 1\}^\ell \mapsto \{0, 1\}^\ell$ *and* $\mathcal{H}^2 \colon \{0, 1\}^\ell \mapsto \{0, 1\}^n$ *be ℓ-wise and 2-wise independent hash function families, respectively, and let $\mathcal{L} \subseteq \{0, 1\}^\ell$ be a set of size at most 2^ℓ. Let $\mathsf{S_{IH}^*}$ be an (unbounded) adversary playing the role of $\mathsf{S_{IH}}$ in $(\mathsf{S_{IH}}, \mathsf{R_{IH}})$ that, following the protocol's interaction, outputs two strings x_0 and x_1. Then, the following holds with respect to a random execution of $(\mathsf{S_{IH}}, \mathsf{R_{IH}})^{\mathcal{H}^1, \mathcal{H}^2}$:*

$$\Pr[x_0 \neq x_1 \in \mathcal{L} \ \wedge \ \forall j \in \{0, 1\} \colon h^1(x_j) = y^1 \wedge h^2(x_j) = y^2] < 2^{-\Omega(n)}.$$

4.4.4.1.2 Constructing Weakly Binding Commitment

Let $\mathcal{H}^1 = \{\mathcal{H}_n^1 = \{h^1: \{0,1\}^{\ell(n)} \mapsto \{0,1\}^{k(n)-2n}\}\}_{n\in\mathbb{N}}$ and $\mathcal{H}^2 = \{h_n^2 = \{h^2: \{0,1\}^{\ell(n)} \mapsto \{0,1\}^n\}\}_{n\in\mathbb{N}}$ be function families. Let $G: \{0,1\}^n \mapsto (\{0,1\}^{\ell(n)})^{m(n)}$ be an m-block generator. The weakly binding commitment is defined as follows:

Protocol 4.4.29 (Weakly binding commitment scheme Com = (S, R))

Common input: security parameter 1^n
S's private input: $b \in \{0,1\}$
Commit stage:

1. R sends $i^* \xleftarrow{R} [m(n)]$ to S.
2. S starts an execution of $G(r)$ for $r \xleftarrow{R} \{0,1\}^n$, and sends $(y_1,\ldots,y_{i^*-1}) = G(r)_{1,\ldots,i^*-1}$ to R.
3. The two parties interact in $(S_{IH}(y_{i^*} = G(r)_{i^*}), R_{IH})^{\mathcal{H}_n^1,\mathcal{H}_n^2}$, with S and R taking the roles of S_{IH} and R_{IH}, respectively.
4. S samples $u \xleftarrow{R} \{0,1\}^{\ell(n)}$ and sends $(\langle u, y_{i^*}\rangle_2 \oplus b, u)$ to R, for $\langle \cdot,\cdot\rangle_2$ being inner product modulo 2.

It is clear that, if $\mathcal{H}_1$, $\mathcal{H}_2$ and G are efficiently computable, then so is Com. We next prove the hiding and binding properties of Com.

Claim 4.4.30 (Hiding). *If each block of G has real min-entropy at least k, then Com is statistically hiding.*

Proof: We fix $n \in \mathbb{N}$ and omit it from the notation. For $i \in [m]$, let Y_i denote the i-th block of $G(U_n)$. By assumption, $\Pr_{y\xleftarrow{R}Y_{1,\ldots,i}}[H_{Y_{i^*}|Y_{<i}}(y_{i^*}|y_{<i}) < k] = \text{neg}(n)$. It follows (by Theorem 4.2.3) that there exists a distribution $(Y_{<i}, Y_i')$ that is statistically indistinguishable from $(Y_{<i}, Y_i)$, and $Y_i |_{Y_{<i}=y}$ has min-entropy at least k for every value $y \in \text{Supp}(Y_{<i})$.

Let $\tilde{R}$ be an arbitrary algorithm playing the role of R in Com, let $i^* \in [m]$ be its first message and let $V_{i^*}^{\tilde{R}}$ be $\tilde{R}$'s view in a random execution of $(S, \tilde{R})$, right after S sends the first $(i^* - 1)$ output blocks of G. Since $V_{i^*}^{\tilde{R}}$ is a probabilistic function of the first $(i^* - 1)$ output blocks of G, the distribution of $(V_{i^*}^{\tilde{R}}, Y_{i^*})$ is statistically indistinguishable from $(V_{i^*}^{\tilde{R}}, Y_{i^*}')$, and $Y_{i^*}' |_{V_{i^*}^{\tilde{R}}=v_{i^*}^{\tilde{R}}}$ has min-entropy at least k for every $v_{i^*}^{\tilde{R}} \in \text{Supp}(V_{i^*}^{\tilde{R}})$.

Let V be the messages sent by S in embedded execution of the interactive hashing $(S, \tilde{R})$. Since $|V| = k - 2n$, it follows (by Theorems 4.2.2 and 4.2.3) that $(V_{i^*}^{\tilde{R}}, V, Y_{i^*})$ is $(\text{neg}(n) + 2^{-\Omega(n)})$-close to a distribution $(V_{i^*}^{\tilde{R}}, V, Y_{i^*}'')$, for which $Y_{i^*}'' |_{(V_{i^*}^{\tilde{R}},H_{i^*})=(v_{i^*}^{\tilde{R}},a_{i^*})}$ has min-entropy at least n for every value $(v_{i^*}^{\tilde{R}}, a_{i^*}) \in \text{Supp}(V_{i^*}^{\tilde{R}}, V)$. Finally, by the leftover hash lemma (Theorem 4.2.10) and the two-universality of the family $\{h_u(y) = \langle u, y\rangle_2 : u \in \{0,1\}^n\}$, it holds that $\text{view}^{\tilde{R}}(S(0), \tilde{R})$ and $\text{view}^{\tilde{R}}(S(1), \tilde{R})$ are of statistical distance at most $\text{neg}(n) + 2^{-\Omega(n)}$, for $\text{view}^{\widetilde{R}}(S(b), \widetilde{R})$ stands for $\widetilde{R}$'s view at the end, the commit stage interaction $(S(b), \widetilde{R})$. □

Claim 4.4.31 (Weak binding). *Assume that $\mathcal{H}_1$, $\mathcal{H}_2$ anf G are efficiently computable,[23] that $\mathcal{H}_1$ and $\mathcal{H}_2$ are ℓ-wise and 2-wise independent, respectively, and that, for every efficient G-consistent generator $\widetilde{G}$, exists $i = i(n) \in [m(n)]$ such that $\Pr_{t \leftarrow T_{\widetilde{G}}(1^n)}^{R} \left[\text{AccH}_{\widetilde{G}}^i(t) > k(n) - 2n \right] = \text{neg}(n)$, then Com is $(1 - 1/3m(n))$-binding.*

The proof of Theorem 4.4.31 immediately follows from the next two claims.

Definition 4.4.32 (Non-failing senders). *A sender $\widetilde{S}$ is called* non-failing *with respect to a commitment scheme (S, R), if the following holds. Let Z be the transcript of the commit stage of $(\widetilde{S}, R)(1^n)$, and let Σ be the first decommitment string that $\widetilde{S}$ outputs in the (generic) reveal stage, then $\Pr[R(Z, \Sigma) = \perp] = 0$.*

That is, a non-failing sender never fails to justify its actions in the commit stage.

Claim 4.4.33 (Weak binding against non-failing senders). *Let $\mathcal{H}_1$, $\mathcal{H}_2$ and G be as in Theorem 4.4.31, then Com is $(1 - 1/2m(n))$-binding against non-failing senders.*

Claim 4.4.34. *Assume a public-coin commitment scheme is α-binding against non-failing senders, then it is $(\alpha + \text{neg})$-binding.*

Proving Theorem 4.4.33. **Proof:** Assume toward a contradiction that there exists a non-failing ppt sender $\widetilde{S}$ that breaks the $(1 - 1/2m(n))$-binding of Com. We use $\widetilde{S}$ to construct an efficient adversarial non-failing generator $\widetilde{G}$, such that, for infinitely many n's,

$$\Pr_{(r_1, y_1, w_1, \ldots) \leftarrow T_{\widetilde{G}}(1^n)}^{R} \left[H_{Y_i|R_{<i}}(y_j|r_{<i}) > k(n) - 2n \right] = \Omega(1) \qquad (4.43)$$

for every $i \in [m(n)]$.

In the following we fix $n \in \mathbb{N}$ on which $\widetilde{S}$ breaks the binding with probability at least $1 - 1/2m(n)$, and omit n from the notation when clear from the context. We assume for ease of notation that $\widetilde{S}$ is deterministic. The following generator samples $i \leftarrow^{R} [m]$, and then uses the ability of $\widetilde{S}$ for breaking the binding of the embedded hashing protocol at this round, to output a high-sample-entropy block.

---

[23] Sampling and evaluation time are polynomial in n.

Algorithm 4.4.35 ($\widetilde{G}$—Adversarial cheating generator from cheating sender)
Security parameter: 1^n
Operation:

1. Let $i \xleftarrow{R} [m]$.
2. Emulate a random execution of $(\widetilde{S}, R)(1^n)$ for the first two steps, with $i^* = i$. Let $(y_1, \ldots, y_{i-1})$ be $\widetilde{S}$'s message in this emulation.
3. Output $y_1, \ldots, y_{i-1}$ as the first $i - 1$ output block.
4. Continue the emulation of $(\widetilde{S}, R)$ till its end. Let z be the transcript of the commit stage, and let $\sigma_0 = (\cdot, r_0, \cdot)$ and $\sigma_1 = (\cdot, r_1, \cdot)$ be the two strings output by $\widetilde{S}$ at the end of this execution.
5. If $R(\sigma_1, z) \neq \perp$, let $r \xleftarrow{R} \{r_0, r_1\}$. Otherwise, set $r = r_0$.
6. Output $G(r)_i, \ldots, G(r)_m$ as the last $m + 1 - i$ output block.

The efficiency of $\widetilde{G}$ is clear, and since $\widetilde{S}$ is non-failing, it is also clear that $\widetilde{G}$ is G-consistent. In the rest of the proof we show that $\widetilde{G}$ violates the assumed bounds on the (maximal) accessible entropy of G. Specifically, that, for every $i \in [m]$, the sample-entropy of $\widetilde{G}$'s i-th output blocks is larger than $k - 2n$ with probability $\Omega(1/m)$. For ease of notation we prove it for $i = 1$.

Let $\widetilde{T} = (R_1, Y_1, \ldots, R_m, Y_m) = T_{\widetilde{G}}(1^n)$, i.e., a random transcript of $\widetilde{G}$ on security parameter n. Let $\mathcal{Y}$ be the set of all low-entropy first blocks of $\widetilde{G}$. That is,

$$\mathcal{Y} := \{y \colon H_{Y_1}(y) \leq k - 2n\}.$$

Let Z, $\Sigma_0 = (\cdot, R_0, \cdot)$, and $\Sigma_1 = (\cdot, R_1, \cdot)$, be the value of the strings z, σ_0 and σ_1, respectively, set in Step 4 of $\widetilde{G}$ in the execution described by $\widetilde{T}|_{i=1}$. For $j \in \{0, 1\}$, let $Y^j = G(R_j)_1$ if $R(Z, \Sigma_j) \neq \perp$, and $\perp$ otherwise. Since $\widetilde{S}$ (also in the emulated execution done in $\widetilde{G}$) interacts in a random execution of (S_{IH}, R_{IH}), Theorem 4.4.28 yields that

$$\Pr\left[\{Y^0, Y^1\} \subseteq \mathcal{Y} \wedge Y^0 \neq Y^1\right] < 2^{-\Omega(n)}. \tag{4.44}$$

In addition, since $\widetilde{S}$ breaks the binding with probability $1 - 1/2m$, it does so with probability at least $1/2$ when conditioning on $i^* = 1$. This yields that

$$\Pr\left[\perp \notin \{Y^0, Y^1\} \wedge Y^0 \neq Y^1\right] \geq 1/2. \tag{4.45}$$

We conclude that

$$\begin{aligned}
\Pr[Y_1 \notin \mathcal{Y}] &\geq \Pr[i = 1] \cdot 1/2 \cdot \Pr\left[\perp \notin \{Y^0, Y^1\} \wedge \{Y^0, Y^1\} \not\subseteq \mathcal{Y}\right] \\
&\geq 1/2m \cdot \Pr\left[\perp \notin \{Y^0, Y^1\} \wedge \{Y^0, Y^1\} \not\subseteq \mathcal{Y} \wedge Y^0 \neq Y^1\right] \\
&\geq 1/2m \cdot (\tfrac{1}{2} - 2^{-\Omega(n)}) \geq \Omega(1/m).
\end{aligned}$$

Namely, with probability $\Omega(1/m)$, the accessible entropy of $\widetilde{G}$'s first block is larger than $k - 2n$. Since this holds for any of the blocks, it contradicts the assumption about the accessible entropy of G. □

Proving Theorem 4.4.34. Proof: The proof follows a standard argument. Let Com $= (S, R)$ be a public-coin commitment scheme, and assume there exists an efficient cheating sender $\widetilde{S}$ that breaks the binding of Com with probability at least $\alpha(n) + 1/p(n)$, for some $p \in$ poly and infinitely many n's. We construct an efficient non-failing sender $\widehat{S}$ that breaks the binding of Com with probability $\alpha(n) + 1/2p(n)$, for infinitely many n's. It follows that if Com is $\alpha(n)$-binding for non-failing senders, then it is $(\alpha(n) + \text{neg}(n))$-binding.

We assume for simplicity that $\widetilde{S}$ is deterministic, and define the non-failing sender $\widehat{S}$ as follows: $\widehat{S}$ starts acting as $\widetilde{S}$, but before forwarding the i-th message y_i from $\widetilde{S}$ to R, it first makes sure it will be able to "justify" this message — to output an input for S that is consistent with y_i, and the message $y_1, \ldots, y_{i-i}$ it sent in the previous rounds. To find such a justification string, $\widehat{S}$ continues, in its head, the interaction between the emulated $\widetilde{S}$ and R till its end, using fresh coins for the receiver's messages. Since the receiver is public-coin, this efficient random continuation has the same distribution as a (real) random continuation of $(\widetilde{S}, R)$ has. The sender $\widehat{S}$ applies such random continuations polynomially many times, and if following one of them $\widetilde{S}$ outputs a valid decommitment string (which by definition is a valid justification string), it keeps it for future use, and outputs y_i as its i-th message. Otherwise (i.e., it failed to find a justification string for y_i), $\widehat{S}$ continues as the honest S whose coins and input bit are set to the justification string $\widehat{S}$ found in the previous round.

Since $\widehat{S}$ maintains the invariant that it can always justify its messages, it can also do that at the very end of the commitment stage, and thus outputting this string makes it a non-failing sender. In addition, note that $\widehat{S}$ only fails to find a justification string if $\widetilde{S}$ has a very low probability to open the commitment at the end of the current interaction, and thus very low probability to cheat. Hence, deviating from $\widetilde{S}$ on such transcripts will only slightly decrease the cheating probability of $\widehat{S}$ compared with that of $\widetilde{S}$.

Assume for concreteness that R sends the first message in Com. The non-failing sender $\widehat{S}$ is defined as follows:

Algorithm 4.4.36 (Non-failing sender $\widehat{S}$ from failing sender $\widetilde{S}$)
Input: 1^n
Operation:

1. Set $w = (0^{s(n)}, 0)$, for $s(n)$ being a bound on the number of coins used by S, and set Fail = false.
2. Start an execution of $\widetilde{S}(1^n)$.
3. Upon getting the i-th message q_i from R, do:

   a. If Fail = false,

     i. *Forward q_i to $\widetilde{S}$, and continue the execution of $\widetilde{S}$ till it sends its i-th message.*

     ii. // Try and get a justification string for this i-th message.

       Do the following for $3np(n)$ times:

       A. *Continue the execution of $(\widetilde{S}, R)$ till its end, using uniform random messages for R.*

       B. *Let z' and w' be the transcript and first message output by $\widetilde{S}$, respectively, at the end of this execution.*

       C. *Rewind $\widetilde{S}$ to its state right after sending its i-th message.*

       D. // Update the justification string.

       If $R(z', w') \neq \bot$. Set $w = w'$ and break the loop.

     iii. *If the maximal number of attempts has been reached, set* Fail = true.

   b. // Send the i-th message to R. If Fail = false, this will be the message sent by $\widetilde{S}$ in Step 3(a). Otherwise, the string will be computed according to the justification string found in a previous round.

   Send a_i to R, for a_i being the i-th message that $S(1^n, w)$ sends to R upon getting the first i messages sent by R.

4. *If* Fail = false, *output the same value that $\widetilde{S}$ does at the end of the execution. Otherwise, output w.*

It is clear that $\widehat{S}$ is non-failing and runs in polynomial time. It is left to argue about its success probability in breaking the binding of Com. We do that by coupling a random execution of $(\widehat{S}, R)$ with that of $(\widetilde{S}, R)$, by letting R send the same, uniformly chosen, messages in both executions. We will show that the probability that $\widetilde{S}$ breaks the binding, but $\widehat{S}$ fails to do so, is at most $1/3p(n) + m \cdot 2^{-n}$, for m being the round complexity of Com. If follows that, for infinitely many n's, $\widehat{S}$ breaks the binding of Com with probability $\alpha(n) + 1/2p(n)$.

Let δ_i denote the probability of $\widetilde{S}$ to break the binding after sending its i-th message, where the probability is over the messages to be sent by R in the next rounds. By definition of $\widehat{S}$, the probability that $\delta_i \geq 1/3p(n)$ for all $i \in [m]$, and yet $\widehat{S}$ set Fail = true, is at most $m \cdot 2^{-n}$. We conclude that the probability that $\widehat{S}$ does not break the commitment, and yet $\widetilde{S}$ does, is at most $1/2p(n) + m \cdot 2^{-n}$.   □

4.4.4.1.3 Putting It Together

Given the above, we prove Theorem 4.4.26 as follows:

Proof: [Proof of Theorem 4.4.26] Recall that we assume without loss of generality that G's blocks are all of the same length ℓ. We use efficient ℓ-wise function family $\mathcal{H}^1 = \{\mathcal{H}_n^1 = \{h^1 \colon \{0,1\}^{\ell(n)} \mapsto \{0,1\}^{k(n)-2n}\}\}_{n \in \mathbb{N}}$ and 2-wise function family $\mathcal{H}^2 = \{h_n^2 = \{h^2 \colon \{0,1\}^{\ell(n)} \mapsto \{0,1\}^n\}\}_{n \in \mathbb{N}}$ (see [4, 30] for constructions of such families).

Theorems 4.4.30 and 4.4.31 yield that the invocation of Protocol 4.4.29 with the generator G and the above function families is an $O(m)$-round, public-coin commitment scheme Com that is statistically hiding if the real entropy of G is sufficiently large, and is $(1 - \Theta(1/m))$-binding if the generator max accessible entropy in one of the blocks is sufficiently small. Let $\mathsf{Com}^{\langle m^2 \rangle} = (\mathsf{S}^{\langle m^2 \rangle}, \mathsf{R}^{\langle m^2 \rangle})$ be the m^2 parallel repetition of Com: an execution of $(\mathsf{S}^{\langle m^2 \rangle}(b), \mathsf{R}^{\langle m^2 \rangle})(1^n)$ consists of $m(n)^2$-fold parallel and independent executions of $(\mathsf{S}(b), \mathsf{R})(1^n)$. It is easy to see that $\mathsf{Com}^{\langle m^2 \rangle}$ is statistically hiding since Com is statistically hiding, and by [18] it is computationally binding since Com is $(1 - \Theta(1/m))$-binding. $\square$

4.4.4.2 About Proving Theorem 4.4.23

Recall that the weak binding of Protocol 4.4.29 is only guaranteed to hold if the underlying generator G has the following property: any non-failing cheating generator has a round in which its accessible entropy is much smaller than the real entropy G has in this round. However, as we mentioned before, building a generator with this property from one-way functions is beyond the reach of our current techniques, and is impossible to do in a black-box manner. Rather, the type of generators we do know how to build from arbitrary one-way functions are the ones assumed in the statement of the Theorem 4.4.23: the *sum* of accessible max-entropy achieved by a cheating non-failing generator is smaller than the *sum* of real entropies (of G). For the latter type of generators, a cheating generator might have high accessible entropy, i.e., as high as the real entropy of G, in *any* of the rounds (though not in all of them simultaneously). In particular, knowing i^*, the sender can put a lot of entropy in i^*'s block. To address this issue, we change the protocol so that the receiver reveals the value of i^* only *after* the interactive hashing protocol. Our hope is that, for at least one value of i, the sender must use a "low-entropy" value y_i in the interactive hashing, and thus we get a binding commitment with probability at least $1/m$. Specifically, consider the following protocol:

Protocol 4.4.37 (Commitment scheme $\mathsf{Com} = (\mathsf{S}, \mathsf{R})$, **hidden** i^***)**
Common input: security parameter 1^n
S's private input: $b \in \{0, 1\}$
Commit stage:

1. R *samples* $i^* \xleftarrow{R} [m(n)]$.
2. S *starts (internally) an execution of* $\mathsf{G}(r)$ *for* $r \xleftarrow{R} \{0, 1\}^n$.
3. *For* $i = 1$ *to* $m(n)$
   a. *The two parties interact in* $(\mathsf{S}_{\mathsf{IH}}(y_i = \mathsf{G}(r)_i), \mathsf{R}_{\mathsf{IH}})^{\mathcal{H}_n^1, \mathcal{H}_n^2}$, *with S and R taking the roles of* S_{IH} *and* R_{IH}, *respectively.*
   b. R *informs S whether* $i^* = i$.[24]
   c. *If informed that* $i \neq i^*$, *S sends* y_i *to R.*
      Otherwise,
      i. S *samples* $u \xleftarrow{R} \{0, 1\}^{\ell(n)}$ *and sends* $(\langle u, y_i \rangle_2 \oplus b, u)$ *to R.*
      ii. *The parties end the execution.*

---

[24] As defined, R is not public-coin. This, however, is easy to change, without harming the protocol's security, by letting R choose the value of i^* during the execution of the protocol using public coins. I.e., if not set before, at round i it sets i^* to be i with probability $1/(m + 1 - i)$.

Unfortunately, the basic interactive hashing protocol does not force the sender to decide whether y_i is a low-entropy string or not during the execution of the interactive hashing protocol, and a cheating sender can decide about that *after* it finds out that $i^* = i$. In more detail, given $\mathbf{y}_{<i} = (y_1, \ldots, y_{i-1})$, let $\mathcal{Y}_{\mathbf{y}_{<i}}$ be the set of low-entropy values for y_i conditioned on $\mathbf{y}_{<i}$. (This is defined with respect to a particular cheating sender strategy $\widetilde{S}$). Since there are not too many high probability distinct strings, the set $\mathcal{Y}_{\mathbf{y}_{<i}}$ is "small". Hence, the interactive hashing guarantees that the probability that the sender can produce *two* distinct elements of $\mathcal{Y}_{\mathbf{y}_{<i}}$ that are consistent with the protocol is negligible. However, it does allow the possibility that the sender can run the interactive hashing protocol consistently with some $y_i \in \mathcal{Y}_{\mathbf{y}_{<i}}$ and afterwards produce a different string y_i that is *not* in $\mathcal{Y}_{\mathbf{y}_{<i}}$, but is consistent with the interactive hashing protocol. This enables a sender to break the binding of the above as follows: consider a cheating sender that runs the generator honestly to obtain $(y_1, \ldots, y_m)$ and uses y_i in the interactive hashing in round i. (Many of these will be low-entropy strings, since the sender is not using any fresh randomness to generate each block.) Upon finding out that the y_i will be used for the commitment, the sender finds another string y_i' (not in $\mathcal{Y}_{\mathbf{y}_{<i}}$) that is consistent with the transcript of the interactive hashing protocol. With these two strings, the sender can now produce a commitment that can be opened in two ways. (Namely, choose u so that $\langle u, y_i \rangle_2 \neq \langle u, y_i' \rangle_2$, and send $(\langle u, y_i \rangle_2, u)$, which also equals $(\langle u, y_i' \rangle_2 \oplus 1, u)$ to the receiver.)

This problem can be solved by using a different interactive hashing protocol that makes it infeasible for the receiver to produce two distinct strings consistent with the protocol where even just *one* of the strings is in a small set $\mathcal{L}$. The new protocol is simply the interactive hashing protocol used above, followed by the sender sending $f(y_i)$ to the receiver, for f being a random member of a *universal one-way hash function* [26] chosen by the receiver. By Rompel [27] (see also [25, 12]) such universal one-way hash functions can be constructed, in a black-box way, from any one-way function, and thus by Theorem 4.4.10, they can be constructed from G. The binding of the new interactive hashing protocol is only computational (i.e., unbounded sender can find a collision), compared with the information-theoretic security of the previous interactive hashing protocol, but since the guarantee on the inaccessible entropy of G holds only against computationally bounded entities, this change does not matter to us. The full details of the aforementioned computationally secure interactive hashing protocol and the security proof of the resulting commitment scheme can be found in [16].

Acknowledgment

This tutorial is based on the work we did with Omer Reingold and Hoeteck Wee on inaccessible entropy [16] and with Omer on next-block pseudoentropy [14], and on the understanding developed through the numerous meetings different subsets of the four of us had through the years. We are grateful to Omer and Hoeteck for this collaboration. We also thank Caf Fixe for the excellent coffee that fueled the two of us through much of this research.

We each have individual remarks for Oded.

Iftach: I would like to thank Oded for teaching me the foundations of cryptography course in the most exciting way at the very beginning of my master's studies, and for being my very devoted and inspiring master's adviser. Without Oded, I would probably not be doing cryptography, and possibly not even doing research at all.

Salil: I am indebted to Oded for teaching me many things about research (and life in general). Most relevant to this tutorial, he guided me as I began to study the theory of pseudorandomness, and emphasized the value in seeking simpler and more intuitive proofs and expositions of important results (which motivates much of the work described in this tutorial, not to mention the tutorial itself).

References

[1] B. Barak, R. Shaltiel, and A. Wigderson. Computational analogues of entropy. In *RANDOM-APPROX*, 2003.

[2] M. Blum and S. Micali. How to generate cryptographically strong sequences of pseudo random bits. In *Proceedings of the 23rd Annual Symposium on Foundations of Computer Science (FOCS)*, pages 112–117, 1982.

[3] M. Blum and S. Micali. How to generate cryptographically strong sequences of pseudorandom bits. *SIAM Journal on Computing*, 13(4):850–864, 1984.

[4] L. J. Carter and M. N. Wegman. Universal classes of hash functions. *Journal of Computer and System Sciences*, pages 143–154, 1979.

[5] B. Chor and O. Goldreich. Unbiased bits from sources of weak randomness and probabilistic communication complexity. *SIAM J. Comput.*, 17(2):230–261, 1988.

[6] Y. Z. Ding, D. Harnik, A. Rosen, and R. Shaltiel. Constant-round oblivious transfer in the bounded storage model. In *Theory of Cryptography, First Theory of Cryptography Conference, TCC 2004*, pages 446–472, 2004.

[7] O. Goldreich and L. A. Levin. A hard-core predicate for all one-way functions. In *Proceedings of the 21st Annual ACM Symposium on Theory of Computing (STOC)*, pages 25–32, 1989.

[8] O. Goldreich, H. Krawczyk, and M. Luby. On the existence of pseudorandom generators. *SIAM Journal on Computing*, 22(6):1163–1175, 1993.

[9] S. Goldwasser and S. Micali. Probabilistic encryption. *Journal of Computer and System Sciences*, pages 270–299, 1984.

[10] I. Haitner, M. Nguyen, S. J. Ong, O. Reingold, and S. Vadhan. Statistically hiding commitments and statistical zero-knowledge arguments from any one-way function. *SIAM Journal on Computing*, 39(3):1153–1218, 2009.

[11] I. Haitner, O. Reingold, S. Vadhan, and H. Wee. Inaccessible entropy. In *Proceedings of the 41st Annual ACM Symposium on Theory of Computing (STOC)*, pages 611–620, 2009.

[12] I. Haitner, T. Holenstein, O. Reingold, S. Vadhan, and H. Wee. Universal one-way hash functions via inaccessible entropy. In *Advances in Cryptology – EUROCRYPT 2010*, pages 616–637, 2010.

[13] I. Haitner, D. Harnik, and O. Reingold. On the power of the randomized iterate. *SIAM J. Comput.*, 40(6):1486–1528, 2011. Preliminary version in *Crypto '06*.

[14] I. Haitner, O. Reingold, and S. Vadhan. Efficiency improvements in constructing pseudorandom generators from one-way functions. *SIAM Journal on Computing*, 42(3):1405–1430, 2013.

[15] I. Haitner, J. J. Hoch, O. Reingold, and G. Segev. Finding collisions in interactive protocols—tight lower bounds on the round and communication complexities of statistically hiding commitments. *SIAM Journal on Computing*, 44 (1):193–242, 2015.

[16] I. Haitner, O. Reingold, S. Vadhan, and H. Wee. Inaccessible entropy i: I.e. generators and statistically hiding commitments from one-way functions. www.cs.tau.ac.il/~iftachh/papers/AccessibleEntropy/IE1.pdf, 2016. To appear. Preliminary version, named Inaccessible Entropy, appeared at STOC 09.

[17] J. Håstad, R. Impagliazzo, L. A. Levin, and M. Luby. A pseudorandom generator from any one-way function. *SIAM Journal on Computing*, pages 1364–1396, 1999.

[18] J. Håstad, R. Pass, K. Pietrzak, and D. Wikström. An efficient parallel repetition theorem. In *Theory of Cryptography, Sixth Theory of Cryptography Conference, TCC 2010*, 2010.

[19] T. Holenstein. Pseudorandom generators from one-way functions: A simple construction for any hardness. In *Theory of Cryptography, Third Theory of Cryptography Conference, TCC 2006*, 2006.

[20] T. Holenstein and M. Sinha. Constructing a pseudorandom generator requires an almost linear number of calls. In *Proceedings of the 53rd Annual Symposium on Foundations of Computer Science (FOCS)*, pages 698–707, 2012.

[21] C.-Y. Hsiao, C.-J. Lu, and L. Reyzin. Conditional computational entropy, or toward separating pseudoentropy from compressibility. In *Advances in Cryptology – EUROCRYPT 2007*, pages 169–186, 2007.

[22] R. Impagliazzo and M. Luby. One-way functions are essential for complexity based cryptography. In *Proceedings of the 30th Annual Symposium on Foundations of Computer Science (FOCS)*, pages 230–235, 1989.

[23] R. Impagliazzo and D. Zuckerman. How to recycle random bits. In *Proceedings of the 30th Annual Symposium on Foundations of Computer Science (FOCS)*, pages 248–253, 1989.

[24] R. Impagliazzo, L. A. Levin, and M. Luby. Pseudo-random generation from one-way functions. In *Proceedings of the 21st Annual ACM Symposium on Theory of Computing (STOC)*, pages 12–24. ACM Press, 1989.

[25] J. Katz and C. Koo. On constructing universal one-way hash functions from arbitrary one-way functions. Technical Report 2005/328, Cryptology ePrint Archive, 2005.

[26] M. Naor and M. Yung. Universal one-way hash functions and their cryptographic applications. In *Proceedings of the 21st Annual ACM Symposium on Theory of Computing (STOC)*, pages 33–43, 1989.

[27] J. Rompel. One-way functions are necessary and sufficient for secure signatures. In *Proceedings of the 22nd Annual ACM Symposium on Theory of Computing (STOC)*, pages 387–394, 1990.

[28] C. Shannon. Communication theory of secrecy systems. *Bell System Technical Journal*, pages 656–715, 1949.

[29] S. Vadhan and C. J. Zheng. Characterizing pseudoentropy and simplifying pseudorandom generator constructions. In *Proceedings of the 44th Annual ACM Symposium on Theory of Computing (STOC)*, pages 817–836, 2012.

[30] M. N. Wegman and J. L. Carter. New hash functions and their use in authentication and set equality. *Journal of Computer and System Sciences*, 1981.

[31] G. Yang. *Cryptography and Randomness Extraction in the Multi-Stream Model.* PhD thesis, Tsinghua University, Beijing, China, 2015. http://eccc.hpi-web.de/static/books/Cryptography_and_Randomness_Extraction_in_the_Multi_Stream_Model.

[32] A. C. Yao. Theory and applications of trapdoor functions. In *Proceedings of the 23rd Annual Symposium on Foundations of Computer Science (FOCS)*, pages 80–91, 1982.

[33] D. Zuckerman. Simulating BPP using a general weak random source. *Algorithmica*, 16(4/5):367–391, 1996.

Chapter 5
Homomorphic Encryption

Shai Halevi

Abstract Fully homomorphic encryption (FHE) has been called the "Swiss Army knife of cryptography", since it provides a single tool that can be uniformly applied to many cryptographic applications. In this tutorial we study FHE and describe its different properties, relations with other concepts in cryptography, and constructions. We briefly discuss the three generations of FHE constructions since Gentry's breakthrough result in 2009, and cover in detail the third-generation scheme of Gentry, Sahai, and Waters (GSW).

5.1 Computing on Encrypted Data

Secure multiparty computation epitomizes the promise of cryptography, performing the seemingly impossible magic trick of processing data without having access to it. One simple example features a client holding an input x and a server holding a function f, the client wishing to learn $f(x)$ without giving away information about its input. Similarly, the server may want to hide information about the function f from the client (except, of course, the value $f(x)$). This situation arises in many practical scenarios, most notably in the context of secure cloud computing; For example, the client may want to get driving directions without revealing their location to the server.

Cryptographers have devised multiple solutions to this problem over the last 40 years, but none simpler (conceptually) than the paradigm of *computing on encrypted data*. This paradigm was suggested by Rivest et al. [81] in the very early days of public-key cryptography, under the name "privacy homomorphisms": The client simply encrypts its input x and sends the ciphertext to the server, who can "evaluate the function f on the encrypted input". The server returns the evaluated ciphertext to the client, who decrypts it and recovers the result. Of course, it takes a special encryption method to allow such processing of encrypted data; for example, Rivest

Shai Halevi
IBM T.J. Watson Research Center, Yorktown Heights, USA, e-mail: shaih@alum.mit.edu

et al. observed in [81] that "raw RSA" (where x is encrypted as $x^e \bmod N$) enables multiplication of encrypted values. They asked whether it was possible to compute more general functions on encrypted data, and what one can do with an encryption scheme that enables such computations.

Following [81], encryption schemes that support computation on encrypted data came to be known as *homomorphic encryption* (HE). In addition to the usual encryption and decryption procedures, these schemes have an *evaluation procedure* that takes ciphertexts encrypting x and a description of a function f, and returns an "evaluated ciphertext" that can be decrypted to obtain the value $f(x)$. A salient nontriviality property of such scheme is *compactness*, requiring that the complexity of decrypting an evaluated ciphertext does not depend on the function f that was used in the evaluation. Another desirable security property is *function-privacy*, requiring that the evaluated ciphertext does not reveal the function f, even to the owner of the secret key.

Many cryptosystems that support computation of *some* functions on encrypted data have been proposed over the years, but it seemed much harder to construct a compact *fully homomorphic encryption* (FHE), namely a compact scheme that can evaluate *all* (efficient) functions. It was not until 2009 that the watershed work of Gentry [47] established for the first time a blueprint for constructing such schemes and described a viable candidate. That work was followed by a sequence of rapid advancements, resulting in much more efficient FHE schemes under well established hardness assumptions, and better understanding of the relations between FHE and other branches of secure computation. The goal of this tutorial is to present an overview of that line of work.

A "paradox" and its resolution. The ability to compute on encrypted data may seem paradoxical at first glance. Consider a simple example of outsourced storage: The client stores multiple encrypted files at the server, and later wants to retrieve one of them without the server learning which one was retrieved. The client can send an encrypted index to the server, and the server will perform the computation on the encrypted index and files, resulting in an encryption of only the file that needs to be retrieved.

But the server can still see the encrypted versions of all the stored files, and now it has the encrypted version of the file that the client wants to retrieve. Can't the server just "see" which of the stored encrypted files is the one being retrieved? The resolution, of course, is that we require the encryption to be *semantically secure* [52], and in particular it must be randomized. Hence there are many different encrypted versions of each file, and the encrypted file that the server returns is different from and "seemingly unrelated" to the stored encrypted files.

5.1.1 Applications of Homomorphic Encryption

Fully homomorphic encryption has been called the "Swiss Army knife of cryptography" [6], since it provides a single tool that can be uniformly applied in a wide host of applications. Even when we have other solutions to a cryptographic problem, the

FHE-based ones are often conceptually simpler and easier to explain. Below we list a few example applications that demonstrate the power of FHE.

Outsourcing storage and computations. Perhaps the most direct application of homomorphic encryption is for outsourcing storage and computation without revealing sensitive information. Consider a small company trying to move its computing facilities to the cloud, but that is wary of the cloud provider having access to the company's confidential information. An easy solution is to encrypt the confidential information before storing it in the cloud, but how can the company use that information without shipping it back on-premises for every operation (which would defeat the purpose of outsourcing it)? Homomorphic encryption provides an elegant solution to this conundrum. The company can keep the information in the cloud in encrypted form, and the cloud provider can process the information in this form and send only the processed result back to the company to be decrypted.

PIR and other private queries. Another direct application of homomorphic encryption is to enable private queries to a database or a search engine. The simplest such example is *private information retrieval* [24], where a server is holding a large database (e.g., the US patent database), and a client wants to retrieve one record of this database without the server learning which record was retrieved. Homomorphic encryption lets the user encrypt the index of the record that it wants to retrieve. The server can evaluate the function $f_{db}(i) = db[i]$ on the encrypted index,[1] returning the encrypted result to the client, who can decrypt it and obtain the plaintext record.

The same solution applies also to the more complex settings of an SQL query to a database or a free-form query to a search engine. In both cases the server has some procedure for handling queries, which can be formalized as a function $g_{db}(\text{query}) = \text{answer}$. The client can therefore encrypt its query before sending it to the server, and the server can evaluate g_{db} on the encrypted query and return the encrypted answer.

General two-party computations. The examples above are special cases of (two-party) secure computation, where two mutually suspicious parties want to compute a common function on their joint input. Specifically we have Alice with input x and Bob with input y, and we want Alice to learn $F(x, y)$ (and nothing more), for some agreed-upon function F, and Bob should learn nothing. In the semi-honest adversarial model (where both parties are assumed to follow the prescribed protocol), this can be achieved by Alice encrypting her input x under her own key, and Bob evaluating the function $F_y(x) = F(x, y)$ on that encrypted input. By the semantic security of the encryption scheme, we know that Bob does not learn anything about Alice's input from the encryption that he sees. Also, if we use a homomorphic scheme that hides the evaluated function, then Alice does not learn anything other than the value of $F(x, y)$. (Converting this protocol to the more general malicious-adversary model can be done using standard techniques [50].)

---

[1] The function f_{db} has the database db hard wired in its description, and on input i it outputs the i-th record.

We note that all the examples so far can use *secret-key* homomorphic encryption. However, as we will see later in Section 5.2.2.6, for homomorphic encryption the distinction between public-key and secret-key encryption is immaterial.

Zero-knowledge. Homomorphic encryption can also be used in a very simple zero-knowledge proof protocol for every language L in NP. Let $R_L(x, w)$ be an NP relation defining the language $L = \{x : \exists w \text{ s.t. } R_L(x, w) = 1\}$, and we sketch a protocol (taken from [6]) by which Bob who knows w can prove to Alice that $x \in L$.

Toward a protocol, let Bob encrypt its witness w and send it to Alice, who can evaluate on the encrypted witness the function $r_x(w) = R_L(x, w)$. But Alice only has the encrypted result; she still needs Bob's help in determining the bit which is encrypted there. Of course Alice cannot just send that encryption to Bob to be decrypted, since Bob cannot be trusted to return the right answer. Instead, she chooses a random bit b, and sends the evaluated ciphertext to Bob only when $b = 1$, otherwise sending him a fresh encryption of zero. Alice finally accepts if Bob replies with the bit b; otherwise she rejects.

The soundness of this protocol follows from the fact that, for $x \notin L$, both ciphertexts will be encryptions of zero. As long as Bob cannot distinguish fresh from evaluated encryption of zero, he cannot convince Alice with probability better than 1/2. Of course we should consider what happens when the initial ciphertext sent by Bob is not a valid encryption at all, but this can be handled by simple cut-and-choose: First, Bob generates two public keys and Alice asks him to open one of them to show that it was generated correctly. Then, using the other unopened key, Bob encrypts two random strings whose XOR is the witness w, and Alice asks that he opens one set and prove that it was encrypted correctly. It is not hard to show that the resulting protocol is sound, in that for $x \notin L$ no cheating strategy can convince Alice with probability much better than 7/8.

This protocol as described is only *honest-verifier* zero knowledge, since a cheating Alice can send to Bob (say) the first bit of the encrypted witness, rather than the result of evaluating $r_x(\cdot)$. This can be fixed by using a standard commitment technique, where Bob sends to Alice not the decrypted bit itself but rather a commitment to that bit. Then Alice reveals her randomness, demonstrating to Bob that she ran the computation as needed, and only then does Bob open its commitment.

5.1.2 Beyond Homomorphic Encryption

Versatile as it is, homomorphic encryption of course does not solve every problem in cryptography. Some limitations of homomorphic encryption are listed below, and are discussed in more detail in Section 5.5.4.

- **The output is encrypted.** Although we can evaluate arbitrary functions on encrypted data, the outcome of such computation is itself a ciphertext, and no one can make sense of it without the secret key. In contrast, *obfuscation* and *functional encryption* allow some forms of encrypted computation in which the output is obtained in the clear; see Section 5.5.4.3.

- All inputs must be encrypted under the same key. To be able to compute on encrypted data, all of that data must be encrypted under the same key. Extensions of homomorphic encryption that can process together encrypted data under multiple keys are discussed in Section 5.5.4.1.
- No integrity guarantees. While homomorphic encryption enables computing on encrypted data, it does not offer any way of checking that the computation was indeed carried out as expected. Typically there is no way to tell if a given ciphertext is indeed the result of running some computation or just a fresh encryption of the same value. See Section 5.5.4.2 for more discussion.

5.1.3 Abridged History

Techniques that enable *non-compact* fully homomorphic encryption (where the size of the ciphertext grows with the complexity of the evaluated function) go back to the early 1980s. In particular, as we explain in Section 5.2.2.4, such schemes can be constructed using secure computation techniques such as Yao's garbled circuits [90]. Also known since the 1980s are compact additively homomorphic or multiplicatively homomorphic schemes, i.e., compact schemes that support only addition or only multiplication on encrypted data. Examples of such schemes include Goldwasser–Micali [52] and ElGamal [33].

Going beyond one-operation homomorphism took longer. Boneh, Goh, and Nissim described in 2005 a cryptosystem that permitted an arbitrary number of additions and one multiplication, without growing the ciphertext size [10]. The security of that scheme was based on the hardness of the subgroup-membership problem in composite-order groups that admit bilinear maps. A scheme with similar characteristics was described by Gentry et al. under the learning-with-errors assumption [47]. In 2007, Ishai and Paskin described a compact scheme that can evaluate branching programs [62], with security under the N-th residuosity assumption [77]. Also Melchor et al. [69] described a template for constructing encryption schemes that can evaluate shallow circuits, where the ciphertext size grows exponentially with the multiplication depth but additions are supported without increasing the size, and realizations of that template are known from various lattice hardness assumptions [47, 69].

5.1.3.1 Three Generations of FHE

The first plausible construction of FHE was given by Gentry in 2009 [47]. The development of FHE since that result can be roughly partitioned into three "generations". The first generation includes Gentry's original scheme using ideal lattices [47], and the somewhat simpler scheme of van Dijk et al. that uses only integer arithmetic [88]. Both these schemes suffered from a problem of rapidly growing noise, which affected both efficiency and security (see below). The second generation began in 2011 with the works of Brakerski–Vaikuntanathan [19] and Brakerski et al. [16], and was characterized by much better techniques for controlling the noise, resulting in improved efficiency while at the same time basing security on well-established hardness assumptions. These techniques were accompanied by methods for improving the plaintext-to-ciphertext expansion ratio, further improving efficiency. The third generation began with the scheme of Gentry et al. [48], exhibiting a somewhat different noise development pattern. The third-generation schemes are in general somewhat less efficient than second-generation ones, but they can be based on somewhat weaker hardness assumptions. Below we briefly sketch these three generations, and in Sections 5.3 and 5.4 we describe in detail the third-generation GSW scheme from [48].

Gentry's blueprint. In his celebrated work from 2009 [47], Gentry gave a blueprint for realizing fully homomorphic encryption and described a concrete realization of this blueprint. Gentry's realization employed ideal lattices and assumed the hardness of the "ideal coset problem" in such lattices. In his PhD thesis [37], Gentry also sketched a simpler construction (due to van Dijk) using integer arithmetic; that construction was later completed and analyzed by van Dijk, Gentry, Halevi and Vaikuntanathan in [88]. Here we use the van Dijk et al. construction (viewed as a secret-key encryption scheme) to illustrate the ideas in Gentry's blueprint.

The secret key of the integer-based scheme is a secret large odd integer p, and ciphertexts are integers that are *close to a multiple of p*. An encryption of a bit $b \in \{0, 1\}$ is an integer whose residue modulo p has the same parity as the plaintext bit b. Namely, $c = pq + 2r + b$, where the integers q, r are random and $|r| \ll p$. To decrypt such a ciphertext, first reduce it modulo p into the symmetric interval $[-p/2, p/2)$ and then output the parity of the result, $b = (c \bmod p) \bmod 2$.

Consider what happens when you add or multiply two such ciphertexts. Let $c_i = q_i p + 2r_i + b_i$ for $i = 1, 2$, and denote $c^+ = c_1 + c_2$ and $c^\times = c_1 \cdot c_2$. Then both c^+ and $c^\times$ have similar structure to the original one, namely

$$c^+ = (q_1 + q_2)p + 2(r_1 + r_2) + (b_1 + b_2) = q'p + 2r' + (b_1 \oplus b_2)$$
$$\text{and } c^\times = (q_1 c_2 + c_1 q_2)p + 2(b_1 r_2 + r_1 b_2 + 2r_1 r_2) + b_1 b_2 = q''p + 2r'' + b_1 b_2$$

for some q', q'', r', r'' (where $r' \approx r_1 + r_2$ and $r'' \approx 2r_1 r_2$). If the initial noise quantities r_1, r_2 were small enough relative to p then the new c^+ and $c^\times$ are still decryptable to the right values. More generally it is possible to compute low-degree polynomials on ciphertexts, which will be decrypted to the evaluation of the same polynomials (over $\mathbb{Z}_2$) applied to the plaintext bits. It was proved in [88] that this scheme is secure if the approximate-GCD problem is hard (which is essentially the problem of finding p), and we believe that approximate-GCD is indeed hard for appropriate parameters.

As described, the scheme above is not compact since the bit size of the ciphertext grows with the degree of the evaluated polynomial, but van Dijk et al. described in [88] a way of fixing it by publishing many near multiples of p of various sizes and using modular reduction. A more severe problem, however, is that the *homomorphic capacity* of the scheme is limited to low-degree polynomials (i.e., these are the only functions that it can evaluate). The reason is that the noise magnitude grows rapidly with the degree, until it becomes larger than $p/2$ and then decryption fails. The same noise development problem occurs also in Gentry's construction from [47], and indeed in every FHE construction since.

Bootstrapping. Gentry solved the problem of limited homomorphic capacity by introducing *bootstrapping*. He observed that any homomorphic scheme which is capable of evaluating its own decryption circuit (plus a single NAND gate) can be turned into a fully homomorphic scheme. Specifically, for every two ciphertexts c_1, c_2, consider the function

$$D^*_{c_1,c_2}(\text{sk}) \overset{def}{=} NAND(\text{Decrypt}(\text{sk}, c_1), \text{Decrypt}(\text{sk}, c_2)).$$

Namely, this function takes as input an alleged secret key, uses it to decrypt the two fixed ciphertexts c_1, c_2, and outputs the NAND of the two resulting bits. If the homomorphic capacity of the scheme suffices to evaluate the functions $D^*_{c_1,c_2}(\text{sk})$ for every two ciphertexts c_1, c_2, then the scheme is called *bootstrappable*, and it can be transformed into an FHE scheme, as follows: Publishing an encryption of the secret key sk under the public key, we can homomorphically compute the NAND of any two ciphertexts by evaluating the function $D^*_{c_1,c_2}$ on the publicly available encryption of sk.

Importantly, the homomorphic computation is only applied to the fresh encryption of sk; the ciphertexts c_1, c_2 are only used to *define the function* $D^*_{c_1,c_2}$ that we need to evaluate. We have the guarantees that, as long as c_1, c_2 are decryptable then so is the result of the homomorphic NAND, and the process can be repeated as many times as needed. Thus, we obtain a compact fully homomorphic encryption.

The first generation of FHE schemes. The first generation of FHE constructions included the schemes from [47, 88] and some variations [85, 41, 27, 40]. The main problem with those schemes was the very rapid growth of noise, which severely limited their homomorphic capacity. Specifically, starting from fresh encryptions with noise magnitude ρ, evaluating a degree-d polynomial resulted in noise magnitude of roughly ρ^d. Although these schemes feature a shallow $NC1$ decryption, still the rapid noise growth prevents them from evaluating their own decryption procedure, and additional complex transformations (involving ad hoc hardness assumptions) are needed to enable bootstrapping.

Second-generation FHE. In 2011, a sequence of works by Brakerski et al. [19, 16, 14] developed new techniques for better noise control. These techniques (some of which we describe in Section 5.3.1.4) slowed the growth of noise dramatically, roughly from linear to logarithmic in the degree of the evaluated function. This resulted in "leveled" schemes that can evaluate circuits of any *fixed* polynomial depth, as well as in bootstrappable schemes that can be made fully homomorphic. Moreover, the security of these new schemes could be based on more standard hardness assumptions such as learning with errors (which we describe in Section 5.3.1.1). Some other second-generation schemes (based on the NTRU hardness assumption) were described in [67, 13].

Other techniques were developed for improving the efficiency of homomorphic evaluation, such as "packing" many plaintext bits in a single ciphertext [86, 17, 44] and various bootstrapping optimizations [43, 2, 57]. These optimizations resulted in schemes whose asymptotic overhead (versus computing in the clear) is only poly-logarithmic in the security parameter, and with vastly improved practical performance [45, 56]. Second-generation schemes and their optimizations are not covered in detail in this tutorial, but we briefly touch on the optimizations in Section 5.5.1.

The GSW scheme and third-generation FHE. In 2013, Gentry et al. described in [48] yet another homomorphic encryption scheme, which has somewhat different flavor than the second-generation schemes above (and is arguably conceptually simpler). In particular, that scheme had *asymmetric multiplication*, in the sense that the homomorphic multiplication $c_1 \otimes c_2$ results in a different ciphertext than $c_2 \otimes c_1$ (both of which encrypt the same product $b_1 \cdot b_2$). More importantly, the noise growth is also asymmetric: the noise in the left multiplicand has greater influence on the result than the noise in the right multiplicand.

Brakerski and Vaikuntanathan observed in [20] that this asymmetry can be used to obtain even slower rates of noise growth, by designing circuits in which the left multiplicand always has small noise. This observation enabled further reduction of parameters and quantitative relaxation of the underlying hardness assumption. However, this technique is not compatible with some of the performance optimizations in second-generation schemes, and third-generation schemes have higher overhead than their second-generation counterparts.

In this tutorial we cover the GSW scheme in detail, starting in Section 5.3 from the basic leveled scheme, then showing in Section 5.4 how to use bootstrapping to turn it into a fully homomorphic scheme, and how to use the asymmetric noise development to improve parameters and relax the hardness assumption.

5.1.4 Organization of This Tutorial

In Section 5.2, we define homomorphic encryption and its properties and discuss the relations between these properties and connections with secure computation protocols. In Sections 5.3 and 5.4, we describe the GSW construction in detail, and in Section 5.5, we briefly go over many related topics, and in Section 5.6 we suggest further reading.

5.2 Defining Homomorphic Encryption

5.2.1 Notations and Basic Definitions

For an integer $q \in \mathbb{N}$, we identify the quotient group $\mathbb{Z}_q$ with its representatives in the symmetric interval $[-\frac{q}{2}, \frac{q}{2})$ (except $\mathbb{Z}_2$ which is identified with $\{0, 1\}$). For a real number $x \in \mathbb{R}$, we denote by $[x]_q$ the reduction of x modulo q into the same symmetric interval. $[x]$ is the rounding of x to the nearest integer, and $\lfloor x \rfloor, \lceil x \rceil$ are the floor and ceiling functions. All these notations extend naturally to vectors and matrices element-wise. The inner product of two vectors $\mathbf{u}, \mathbf{v}$ is denoted $\langle \mathbf{u}, \mathbf{v} \rangle$.

For a random process such as running a probabilistic Turing machine M on input x, we write $M(x)$ or $y \leftarrow M(X)$ to describe a random variable which is drawn from the output space of that process. We sometimes write $y := M(x; r)$ to separate the randomness used and the deterministic processing of that randomness. We often use the same notation for a distribution and its support set, so $y \in M(x)$ means that y is a string which is output by $M(x)$ with non-zero probability. Conversely, if S is a set, then $x \leftarrow S$ is a random variable uniformly distributed in S. The ℓ_1 statistical distance between two distributions D_1, D_2 is denoted $SD(D_1, D_2)$.

We denote the output distribution of a multistep process, or the probability of an event over that distribution, using the syntax

$$\text{Distribution} = \{\text{output} : \text{Process}\}, \text{ or } \Pr[\text{event} : \text{Process}].$$

For example, the distribution of encryptions of zero in some cryptosystem can be written as $\{c : (\mathsf{pk}, \mathsf{sk}) \leftarrow \mathsf{KeyGen}(1^\lambda), c \leftarrow \mathsf{Encrypt}(\mathsf{pk}, 0)\}$, and the probability of an adversary outputting 1 on a ciphertext from this distribution is denoted $\Pr[A(c) = 1 : (\mathsf{pk}, \mathsf{sk}) \leftarrow \mathsf{KeyGen}(1^\lambda), c \leftarrow \mathsf{Encrypt}(\mathsf{pk}, 0)]$.

5.2.1.1 Homomorphic Encryption

To define *computation* on encrypted data, we must fix some model of computation. In this tutorial we always use binary circuits with fan-in-2 gates to describe the functions that we want to compute on encrypted data.[2] For a binary circuit Π, we denote its size (i.e., number of gates) by $\mathsf{size}(\Pi)$, its depth by $\mathsf{depth}(\Pi)$ (i.e., longest input-to-output path), and the number of inputs by $\mathsf{inpLen}(\Pi)$. We briefly discuss homomorphic encryption relative to other models of computation in Section 5.5.3. On the other hand, we use somewhat informal terms such as algorithm/procedure (or adversary) when referring to computations that manipulate ciphertexts and keys. Unless stated otherwise, all the algorithms/procedures/adversaries below are (uniform) probabilistic polynomial time (PPT).

A homomorphic public-key encryption scheme (for plaintext space $\mathcal{M} = \{0, 1\}$) has four PPT procedures: the usual KeyGen, $\mathsf{Encrypt}$, and $\mathsf{Decrypt}$, and also an $\mathsf{Evaluate}$ procedure for computing on encrypted data. We slightly extend the standard syntax of key generation, allowing it to depend not only on the security parameter λ but also on a second "functionality parameter" τ. Throughout this tutorial, some schemes will make use of that parameter while others will not.

Definition 5.2.1 (Syntax). *A homomorphic encryption scheme consists of four procedures,* $\mathcal{E} = (\mathsf{KeyGen}, \mathsf{Encrypt}, \mathsf{Decrypt}, \mathsf{Evaluate})$:

- $(\mathsf{sk}, \mathsf{pk}) \leftarrow \mathsf{KeyGen}(1^\lambda, 1^\tau)$. *Takes the security parameter λ and another parameter τ and outputs a secret/public key-pair.*[3]

---

[2] Fixing circuits with binary input also means that we consider bit-encryption schemes, where the plaintext space is $\mathcal{M} = \{0, 1\}$.

[3] We assume that the size of the public and secret keys is set deterministically by λ and τ; i.e., it does not vary with the randomness of the key generation procedure.

- $c \leftarrow \mathsf{Encrypt}(\mathsf{pk}, b)$. *Given the public key and a plaintext bit, outputs a ciphertext.*
- $b \leftarrow \mathsf{Decrypt}(\mathsf{sk}, c)$. *Given the secret key and a ciphertext, outputs a plaintext bit.*
- $\mathbf{c}' \leftarrow \mathsf{Evaluate}(\mathsf{pk}, \Pi, \mathbf{c})$. *Takes a public key* pk, *a circuit* Π, *a vector of ciphertexts* $\mathbf{c} = \langle c_1, \ldots, c_t \rangle$, *one for every input bit of* Π, *and outputs another vector of ciphertexts* $\mathbf{c}'$, *one for every output bit of* Π.

The syntax from Definition 5.2.1 is naturally extended to vectors of plaintexts and ciphertexts. Namely, we write $\mathbf{c} \leftarrow \mathsf{Encrypt}(\mathsf{pk}, \mathbf{b})$, where $\mathbf{b} = (b_1, \ldots, b_t)$ and $\mathbf{c} = (c_1, \ldots, c_t)$, to denote $c_i \leftarrow \mathsf{Encrypt}(\mathsf{pk}, b_i)$ for all i. Similarly, we write $\mathbf{b} \leftarrow \mathsf{Decrypt}(\mathsf{sk}, \mathbf{c})$ to denote $b_i \leftarrow \mathsf{Decrypt}(\mathsf{sk}, c_i)$ for all i.

We sometimes refer to ciphertexts output by Encrypt as "fresh ciphertexts", and those output by Evaluate are "evaluated ciphertexts". The correctness condition below refers to both.

Definition 5.2.2 (Correctness). *Let* $\mathcal{E} = (\mathsf{KeyGen}, \mathsf{Encrypt}, \mathsf{Decrypt}, \mathsf{Evaluate})$ *be a homomorphic encryption scheme and* $\mathcal{C} = \{\mathcal{C}_\tau\}_{\tau \in \mathbb{N}}$ *be some circuit family.* $\mathcal{E}$ *is (perfectly) correct for* $\mathcal{C}$ *if it correctly decrypts both fresh and evaluated ciphertexts. Namely, for all* $\lambda, \tau \in \mathbb{N}$, *the following two conditions hold:*

- *For any* $b \in \{0, 1\}$,

$$\Pr\left[\mathsf{Decrypt}(\mathsf{sk}, c) = b : (\mathsf{sk}, \mathsf{pk}) \leftarrow \mathsf{KeyGen}(1^\lambda, 1^\tau), c \leftarrow \mathsf{Encrypt}(\mathsf{pk}, b)\right] = 1;$$

- *For every* $\Pi \in \mathcal{C}_\tau$ *and plaintext bits* $\mathbf{b} = (b_1, \ldots, b_t) \in \{0, 1\}^t$, *one for every input bit of* Π,

$$\Pr\left[\mathsf{Decrypt}(\mathsf{sk}, \mathbf{c}') = \Pi(\mathbf{b}) : \begin{array}{l} (\mathsf{sk}, \mathsf{pk}) \leftarrow \mathsf{KeyGen}(1^\lambda, 1^\tau), \\ \mathbf{c} \leftarrow \mathsf{Encrypt}(\mathsf{pk}, \mathbf{b}), \; \mathbf{c}' \leftarrow \mathsf{Evaluate}(\mathsf{pk}, \Pi, \mathbf{c}) \end{array}\right] = 1.$$

We sometimes refer informally to the largest family $\mathcal{C}$ for which $\mathcal{E}$ is correct as the *homomorphic capacity* of $\mathcal{E}$. Definition 5.2.2 can be weakened by allowing a negligible error probability, but it is more convenient to work with the stronger condition (and the constructions that we describe later can be made to meet this stronger condition). Some examples of homomorphism relative to interesting circuit families include the following:

Fully homomorphic encryption. We say that $\mathcal{E}$ is *fully homomorphic* if it is correct for a family $\mathcal{C}$ such that $\mathcal{C}_1$ by itself already contains all Boolean circuits. In this case we can ignore the parameter τ in KeyGen; i.e., we can always run it with $\tau = 1$. (Note that the size of the circuit does not figure into the security requirement, and Evaluate always runs in time polynomial in the circuit description, so considering circuits of superpolynomial size in λ does not cause any problems.)

Leveled/somewhat homomorphic encryption. We say that $\mathcal{E}$ is a *leveled* homomorphic encryption scheme if it is correct for a family $\mathcal{C}$ such that, for all τ, $\mathcal{C}_\tau$ contains all Boolean circuits of depth up to τ.

More generally, we may refer to a scheme informally as *somewhat homomor-phic* if it is correct for a family C where the complexity of the circuits in C_τ grows with τ. A common example that was used in the first-generation schemes starting with Gentry's original blueprint (e.g., [47, 88, 85, 41]) is when C_τ contains circuits computing multivariate polynomials of total degree up to τ and up to 2^τ monomials.

Additively homomorphic encryption. $\mathcal{E}$ is *additively homomorphic* if it is correct for a family C such that C_1 contains all Boolean circuits made up of only XOR gates. Here too we ignore the parameter τ in KeyGen. One example of additive homomorphism is the Goldwasser–Micali scheme [52].

A weaker version of additive homomorphism (which is realized by most lattice-based encryption schemes) does not support unlimited number of addition operations, but only (say) at most exponential in τ. Namely, $\mathcal{E}$ is *almost additively homomorphic* if it is correct for a family C where, for all τ, C_τ contains all the sums (mod 2) of up to 2^τ variables.

The semantic security of a homomorphic encryption scheme is defined in the usual way [52], without reference to the Evaluate algorithm; indeed Evaluate is a public algorithm with no secrets. Namely, we require that a PPT adversary cannot distinguish between encryptions of 0 and encryptions of 1, even if it knows the public key. Definition 5.2.3 below handles the "functionality parameter" τ by considering it an adversarial quantity (that the adversary must output in unary to ensure that it is polynomially bounded).

Definition 5.2.3 (Semantic security). *Let $\mathcal{E} = $ (KeyGen, Encrypt, Decrypt, Evaluate) be a homomorphic encryption scheme, and let A be an adversary. The advantage of A w.r.t. $\mathcal{E}$ is defined as*

$$Adv_A^{\mathcal{E}}(\lambda) \stackrel{def}{=} \left| \Pr\left[A(\mathsf{pk}, c) = 1 : \begin{array}{l} 1^\tau \leftarrow A(1^\lambda), \ (\mathsf{sk}, \mathsf{pk}) \leftarrow \mathsf{KeyGen}(1^\lambda, 1^\tau), \\ c \leftarrow \mathsf{Encrypt}(\mathsf{pk}, 1) \end{array}\right] \right.$$
$$\left. - \Pr\left[A(\mathsf{pk}, c) = 1 : \begin{array}{l} 1^\tau \leftarrow A(1^\lambda), \ (\mathsf{sk}, \mathsf{pk}) \leftarrow \mathsf{KeyGen}(1^\lambda, 1^\tau), \\ c \leftarrow \mathsf{Encrypt}(\mathsf{pk}, 0) \end{array}\right] \right|.$$

The scheme $\mathcal{E}$ is semantically secure if, for every PPT adversary A, the advantage $Adv_A^{\mathcal{E}}(\lambda)$ is negligible in λ.

In the rest of this tutorial we only consider semantically secure schemes, often without mentioning this requirement.

5.2.1.2 Secret-Key Homomorphic Encryption

It is sometimes convenient to consider secret-key variants of the definitions above, especially since it was shown by Rothblum [82] that these notions are essentially equivalent for homomorphic encryption (see Theorem 5.2.19). The syntax and correctness conditions for secret-key homomorphic encryption are similar to those in Definitions 5.2.1 and 5.2.2 except that KeyGen only outputs the secret key sk rather than the pair (sk, pk), the Encrypt procedure uses sk rather than pk for encryption, and the Evaluate procedure gets as input only Π and $\mathbf{c}$ but not pk.

The security definition is also similar, except that, in lieu of the public key, the adversary is given a sequence of ciphertexts (rather than just one), encrypting bits of one of two sequences of its choosing, and it needs to guess which of the two sequences was encrypted.

Definition 5.2.4 (Semantic security, secret-key encryption). *Let* $\mathcal{E}$ = (KeyGen, Encrypt, Decrypt, Evaluate) *be a secret-key homomorphic encryption scheme, and let A be an adversary. The* advantage *of A w.r.t.* $\mathcal{E}$ *is defined as*

$$
SKAdv_A^{\mathcal{E}}(\lambda) \overset{def}{=} \left| \Pr\left[\begin{array}{l} |\mathbf{b_0}| = |\mathbf{b_1}| \ \& \\ A(\mathsf{pk}, \mathbf{c}) = 1 \end{array} : \begin{array}{l} (1^\tau, \mathbf{b_0}, \mathbf{b_1}) \leftarrow A(1^\lambda), \ \mathsf{sk} \leftarrow \mathsf{KeyGen}(1^\lambda, 1^\tau), \\ \mathbf{c} \leftarrow \mathsf{Encrypt}(\mathsf{sk}, \mathbf{b_1}) \end{array} \right] \right.
$$
$$
\left. - \Pr\left[\begin{array}{l} |\mathbf{b_0}| = |\mathbf{b_1}| \ \& \\ A(\mathsf{pk}, \mathbf{c}) = 1 \end{array} : \begin{array}{l} (1^\tau, \mathbf{b_0}, \mathbf{b_1}) \leftarrow A(1^\lambda), \ \mathsf{sk} \leftarrow \mathsf{KeyGen}(1^\lambda, 1^\tau), \\ \mathbf{c} \leftarrow \mathsf{Encrypt}(\mathsf{sk}, \mathbf{b_0}) \end{array} \right] \right|.
$$

The scheme $\mathcal{E}$ *is semantically secure if, for every PPT adversary A, the advantage* $SKAdv_A^{\mathcal{E}}(\lambda)$ *is negligible in* λ.

5.2.2 Properties of Homomorphic Encryption Schemes

Property	Description	Defined in	Comments
Secret-key variant	Same key to encrypt, decrypt	Def. 5.2.4	Equivalent to public key variant, Theorem 5.2.19
Strong homomorphism	Evaluated ctxts $\tilde{=}$ fresh ctxts	Defs. 5.2.5,5.2.6	Implies strong compactness, function privacy, and multi-hop
Compactness	Evaluated ctxts are short	Defs. 5.2.8,5.2.9	Strong & weak variants
Function privacy	Evaluated ctxts hide function	Def. 5.2.10	Implied by secure 2PC, Theorem 5.2.13
Multi-hop	Can reprocess evaluated ctxts	Def. 5.2.14	Orthogonal to compactness and function privacy

Table 5.1: Properties of homomorphic encryption

By themselves, the correctness and security properties from above are not enough to rule out uninteresting realizations. Specifically, any secure encryption scheme can be made "homomorphic" by an Evaluate procedure that simply attaches a description of the circuit Π to the ciphertext tuple $\mathbf{c}$, and a Decrypt procedure that first decrypts all the ciphertexts and then evaluates Π on the corresponding plaintext bits.

Such uninteresting realizations are ruled out by the additional requirements that we define below. We begin with the simplest and strongest condition, which we call *strong homomorphism*, as well as three weaker (but still useful) conditions, namely *compactness*, *circuit hiding*, and *multi-hop homomorphism*. We also state and prove some lemmas about the relations between these notions. A summary of the definitions and results in this section is given in Table 5.1.

5.2.2.1 Strong Homomorphism

Strong homomorphism requires evaluated ciphertexts to look the same (i.e., have the same distribution) as fresh ciphertexts.

Definition 5.2.5 (Strong homomorphism). *Scheme* $\mathcal{E} = ($KeyGen, Encrypt, Decrypt, Evaluate$)$ *is* strongly homomorphic *for a circuit family* $\mathcal{C} = \{\mathcal{C}_\tau\}_{\tau \in \mathbb{N}}$ *if, for all* $\tau \in \mathbb{N}$ *and every* $\Pi \in \mathcal{C}_\tau$ *and plaintext bits* $\mathbf{b} = (b_1, \ldots, b_t) \in \{0, 1\}^t$, *one for every input bit of* Π, *the two distribution ensembles below are statistically close up to a distance negligible in* λ:

$$\text{Fresh}_{\Pi, \mathbf{b}}(\lambda) \stackrel{def}{=} \{(\text{pk}, \mathbf{c}, \mathbf{c}') \ : \ (\text{sk}, \text{pk}) \leftarrow \text{KeyGen}(1^\lambda, 1^\tau),$$
$$\mathbf{c} \leftarrow \text{Encrypt}(\text{pk}, \mathbf{b}), \ \mathbf{c}' \leftarrow \text{Encrypt}(\text{pk}, \Pi(\mathbf{b}))\},$$
$$\text{Eval}_{\Pi, \mathbf{b}}(\lambda) \stackrel{def}{=} \{(\text{pk}, \mathbf{c}, \mathbf{c}') \ : \ (\text{sk}, \text{pk}) \leftarrow \text{KeyGen}(1^\lambda, 1^\tau),$$
$$\mathbf{c} \leftarrow \text{Encrypt}(\text{pk}, \mathbf{b}), \ \mathbf{c}' \leftarrow \text{Evaluate}(\text{pk}, \Pi, \mathbf{c})\}.$$

Definition 5.2.5 can be relaxed to require only computational indistinguishability rather than statistical closeness, but some care must be taken when defining it. Specifically, for some applications we require that even the party that generated the keys cannot distinguish between these two distributions, hence we need them to be indistinguishable *even given the randomness that was used by* KeyGen.

Definition 5.2.6 (Computationally strong homomorphism). *Scheme* $\mathcal{E} = ($KeyGen, Encrypt, Decrypt, Evaluate$)$ *is* computationally strongly homomorphic *for a circuit family* $\mathcal{C} = \{\mathcal{C}_\tau\}_{\tau \in \mathbb{N}}$ *if, for all* $\tau \in \mathbb{N}$ *and every* $\Pi \in \mathcal{C}_\tau$ *and plaintext bits* $\mathbf{b} = (b_1, \ldots, b_t) \in \{0, 1\}^t$, *one for every input bit of* Π, *the two distribution ensembles below are computationally indistinguishable:*

$$\text{Fresh}^*_{\Pi, \mathbf{b}}(\lambda) \stackrel{def}{=} \{(r, \mathbf{c}, \mathbf{c}') \ : \ r \leftarrow \$, \ (\text{sk}, \text{pk}) := \text{KeyGen}(1^\lambda, 1^\tau; r),$$
$$\mathbf{c} \leftarrow \text{Encrypt}(\text{pk}, \mathbf{b}), \ \mathbf{c}' \leftarrow \text{Encrypt}(\text{pk}, \Pi(\mathbf{b}))\},$$
$$\text{Eval}^*_{\Pi, \mathbf{b}}(\lambda) \stackrel{def}{=} \{(r, \mathbf{c}, \mathbf{c}') \ : \ r \leftarrow \$, \ (\text{sk}, \text{pk}) := \text{KeyGen}(1^\lambda, 1^\tau; r),$$
$$\mathbf{c} \leftarrow \text{Encrypt}(\text{pk}, \mathbf{b}), \ \mathbf{c}' \leftarrow \text{Evaluate}(\text{pk}, \Pi, \mathbf{c})\}.$$

Definitions 5.2.5 and 5.2.6 can be modified in the obvious way to handle secret-key homomorphic encryption. Although these definitions are stated relative to a fixed circuit family $\mathcal{C}$, one readily sees that this dependence (as well as the dependence on τ) is immaterial: If some $\mathcal{C}_{\tau^*}$ contains AND and XOR gates (or any other functionally complete set of gates) then we can extend the Evaluate procedure to evaluate any circuit, by repeatedly evaluating each gate on the outputs of the preceding gates. Moreover, the output distribution when evaluating a circuit Π is at most $\text{negl}(\lambda) \cdot \text{size}(\Pi)$ away from that of fresh encryption of the outputs. A similar statement applies also in the computational setting, using the fact that these distributions are indistinguishable even given the secret key (since the correctness condition involved the secret key). Hence we have:

Proposition 5.2.7. *Any encryption scheme which is (computationally) strongly homomorphic relative to a circuit family C, where some C_{τ^*} contains AND and XOR gates, can be transformed to a (computationally) strongly fully homomorphic scheme (i.e. strongly homomorphic relative to a circuit family C' with C'_1 containing all circuits).*

Given Proposition 5.2.7, we always assume below that any strongly homomorphic scheme is strongly *fully* homomorphic, and we suppress the irrelevant parameter τ when describing such schemes.

5.2.2.2 Compactness

The main deficiency in the uninteresting realization in which Evaluate just appends the description of Π to the ciphertexts is that we expect the decryption work to be the same whether the decrypted ciphertext is fresh or evaluated. This is clearly the case if the scheme is strongly homomorphic, but being strongly homomorphic is often overkill. A weaker notion that captures a lot of the power of homomorphic computation is *compactness*, which only requires that the *size* of the ciphertext does not grow with the complexity of the evaluated circuit.

Definition 5.2.8 (Compactness). *A homomorphic encryption scheme $\mathcal{E}$ = (KeyGen, Encrypt, Decrypt, Evaluate) is compact if there exists a fixed polynomial bound $B(\cdot)$ so that, for all $\lambda, \tau \in \mathbb{N}$, any circuit Π with t inputs and a single output, and plaintext bits $\mathbf{b} = (b_1, \ldots, b_t) \in \{0, 1\}^t$, it holds that*

$$\Pr\left[|c'| \le B(\lambda) : \begin{array}{l} (\mathsf{sk}, \mathsf{pk}) \leftarrow \mathsf{KeyGen}(1^\lambda, 1^\tau), \\ \mathbf{c} \leftarrow \mathsf{Encrypt}(\mathsf{pk}, \mathbf{b}), \ c' \leftarrow \mathsf{Evaluate}(\mathsf{pk}, \Pi, \mathbf{c}) \end{array}\right] = 1.$$

We note that the bound $B(\cdot)$ above depends only on λ but not on τ. This means that, even if we allow some aspects of the scheme (such as the public-key size) to depend on the parameter τ, the size of the evaluated ciphertexts must not grow with τ.

In some settings it is useful to consider a weaker condition, where we allow the ciphertext size to grow with τ so long as it remains smaller then the size of circuits in C_τ. We use $\log |C_\tau|$ as our measure of the size of circuits in C_τ, since you need at least as many bits to describe these circuits (and note that we only count single-output circuits). This yields the following definition:

Definition 5.2.9 (Weak compactness). *A homomorphic encryption scheme $\mathcal{E}$ = (KeyGen, Encrypt, Decrypt, Evaluate) is weakly compact if there exists a fixed polynomial bound $B(\cdot, \cdot)$ so that (i) for all $\lambda, \tau \in \mathbb{N}$, any circuit Π with t inputs and a single output, and plaintext bits $\mathbf{b} = (b_1, \ldots, b_t) \in \{0, 1\}^t$, it holds that*

$$\Pr\left[|c'| \le B(\lambda, \tau) : \begin{array}{l} (\mathsf{sk}, \mathsf{pk}) \leftarrow \mathsf{KeyGen}(1^\lambda, 1^\tau), \\ \mathbf{c} \leftarrow \mathsf{Encrypt}(\mathsf{pk}, \mathbf{b}), \ c' \leftarrow \mathsf{Evaluate}(\mathsf{pk}, \Pi, \mathbf{c}) \end{array}\right] = 1,$$

and (ii) $B(\lambda, \tau) = poly(\lambda) \cdot o(\log |\mathcal{C}_\tau|)$.

5.2.2.3 Circuit Privacy

Circuit privacy roughly means that the ciphertext generated by Evaluate does not reveal anything about the circuit that it evaluates, beyond the output value of that circuit, even to the party who generated the public and secret keys. To define it, we view the operation of Evaluate as a protocol between a client who generates the keys and encrypts its input, and a server who evaluates some function on that input and returns the result to the client. We then formalize circuit privacy as the usual input privacy property for the server, namely we require that the client can be simulated given only the output value that it learns.

Definition 5.2.10 (Circuit privacy, semi-honest). *A homomorphic encryption scheme* $\mathcal{E} = $ (KeyGen, Encrypt, Decrypt, Evaluate), *correct for the circuit family* $\mathcal{C}$, *is circuit private for* $\mathcal{C}$, *if there exists an efficient simulator* Sim *such that, for every* $\tau \in \mathbb{N}$, $\Pi \in \mathcal{C}_\tau$, *and plaintext bits* $\mathbf{b} = (b_1, \ldots, b_t) \in \{0, 1\}^t$, *one for every input bit of* Π, *we have*

$$\mathsf{Real}_{\Pi, \mathbf{b}}(\lambda) \stackrel{(c)}{\approx} \mathsf{Sim}(1^\lambda, 1^\tau, \mathbf{b}, \Pi(\mathbf{b})), \ where$$
$$\mathsf{Real}_{\Pi, \mathbf{b}}(\lambda) \stackrel{def}{=} \{(r, r', c') \ : r, r' \leftarrow \$, \ (\mathsf{sk}, \mathsf{pk}) := \mathsf{KeyGen}(1^\lambda, 1^\tau; r),$$
$$\mathbf{c} := \mathsf{Encrypt}(\mathsf{pk}, \mathbf{b}; \ r'), \ c' \leftarrow \mathsf{Evaluate}(\mathsf{pk}, \Pi, \mathbf{c})\}.$$

It is important to note that the simulator Sim is given the output $\Pi(\mathbf{b})$ *but not the description of* Π *itself*, and it needs to simulate the view that includes the randomness for both key generation and encryption, as well as the evaluated ciphertext.

Circuit privacy against malicious adversaries. Definition 5.2.10 above applies only to the semi-honest case in which the client uses the prescribed KeyGen and Encrypt procedures. The more general case was considered by Ostrovsky et al. [76]. Roughly, they defined circuit privacy against malicious adversaries by requiring that, for every (pk^*, c^*) (even ones that are not generated honestly), there exists an "implied plaintext" b^* such that $\mathsf{Evaluate}(\mathsf{pk}^*, \Pi, c^*)$ can be simulated knowing only pk^*, c^*, and $\Pi(b^*)$ (but without knowing Π itself).

Building on techniques of Gentry et al. [46] (see Theorem 5.2.13 below), they show how to get a compact scheme which is circuit private against malicious adversary, by combining a compact scheme which is not circuit private with a circuit private scheme which is not compact.

5.2.2.4 Circuit Private Homomorphic Encryption Versus Two-Message SFE

As we discussed in the introduction, circuit private homomorphic encryption implies a two-message (semi-honest) secure function evaluation (SFE) protocol for any function. We now show these two notions are essentially equivalent. Namely we show how to realize (non-compact) circuit private fully homomorphic encryption from any two-message semi-honest SFE protocol for general functions.

Recall the structure of a two-message SFE protocol for a function $F(x, y)$, where one party (the client) holds x, the other party (the server) holds y, and the client needs to learn $F(x, y)$.

Definition 5.2.11 (Two-message SFE protocol). *A two-message two-party SFE protocol for a function $F(\cdot, \cdot)$ consists of three procedures, $\mathcal{P}_F = (\mathsf{SFE1}_F, \mathsf{SFE2}_F, \mathsf{SFE3}_F)$ as follows:*

- *The client computes $(s, m_1) \leftarrow \mathsf{SFE1}_F(1^\lambda, x)$, sending m_1 to the server and keeping the state s to itself;*
- *The server responds with $m_2 \leftarrow \mathsf{SFE2}_F(1^\lambda, y, m_1)$;*
- *The client recovers the result as $z \leftarrow \mathsf{SFE3}_F(s, m_2)$.*

The (perfect) correctness of the protocol means that we have $z = F(x, y)$ with probability 1.

Definition 5.2.12 (Semi-honest security). *The security of the protocol $\mathcal{P}_F$ is defined by means of two simulators, Sim_1 and Sim_2, that simulate the view of the two parties. Specifically for all inputs x, y for F, we have*

$$\mathsf{Sim}_1(1^\lambda) \overset{(c)}{\approx} \mathsf{SFE1}_F(1^\lambda, x) \quad and \quad \mathsf{Sim}_2(1^\lambda, F(x, y)) \overset{(c)}{\approx} \mathsf{cView}_{x,y}(\lambda), \ where$$

$$\mathsf{cView}_{x,y}(\lambda) \overset{def}{=} \{(r, m_2) : r \leftarrow \$, \ (s, m_1) := \mathsf{SFE1}_F(1^\lambda, x; r), \ m_2 \leftarrow \mathsf{SFE2}_F(1^\lambda, y)\}.$$

Intuitively, a two-message SFE protocol can be thought of as the encryption of x via SFE1 followed by evaluation via SFE2 and decryption via SFE3, but is not quite homomorphic encryption yet. In particular, there is no public key involved, and the same party (the client) is doing both the encryption and the decryption.[4] In contrast, a public key homomorphic encryption should be thought of as a three-player game: first a recipient publishes a public key, then a sender (client) encrypts the data **b** under that public key, next an evaluator (server) evaluates a circuit Π on the encrypted data, and finally the recipient decrypts the result and recovers $\Pi(\mathbf{b})$. Another issue is that, as described above, the client's SFE1 function handles the entire input x at once, whereas we need the client processing to be "decomposable" (cf. [61]), i.e., encrypting each bit of x separately.

If the underlying SFE protocol already happened to be decomposable (such as Yao's garbled circuit protocol that uses bit-by-bit oblivious transfer), then it is straightforward to turn it into homomorphic encryption using an auxiliary (standard) public-key encryption scheme. The recipient chooses a public/secret key pair for the encryption scheme, the sender sends the first SFE message and in addition also the encryption of the client's SFE-state s under the public key, and the evaluator forwards the encrypted state to the recipient together with the second SFE message.

---

[4] We cannot use here the equivalence between public- and secret-key homomorphic encryption from Theorem 5.2.19, since it only applies to *compact schemes*.

The recipient uses its secret key to decrypt and recover the SFE state s, and then uses the procedure SFE3 with this state to recover $F(x, y)$.

Since two-message SFE implies both semantically secure encryption (cf. [49]) and two-message SFE with decomposable client processing (e.g., via Yao's protocol), we get a non-compact circuit private HE from any two-message protocol for secure evaluation of all functions. A more direct proof of this implication, using techniques similar to Gentry's bootstrapping [47], is described in the next theorem.

Theorem 5.2.13. *A circuit private fully homomorphic encryption scheme can be constructed from public-key encryption and a two-message semi-honest SFE protocol for all circuits.*

Proof: Let $\mathcal{E} = (\mathsf{KeyGen}, \mathsf{Encrypt}, \mathsf{Decrypt})$ be a public-key encryption scheme, consider the universal function $U(\mathbf{b}, \Pi) = \Pi(\mathbf{b})$, and define the related function $U'(\cdot, \cdot)$ as

$$U'(\mathsf{sk}, (\mathbf{c}, \Pi)) \overset{def}{=} U(\mathsf{Decrypt}(\mathsf{sk}, \mathbf{c}), \Pi) \; (= \Pi(\mathsf{Decrypt}(\mathsf{sk}, \mathbf{c})).$$

Let $\mathcal{P}_{U'} = (\mathsf{SFE1}_{U'}, \mathsf{SFE2}_{U'}, \mathsf{SFE3}_{U'})$ be a two-message SFE protocol for U', and use $\mathcal{E}$ and $\mathcal{P}_{U'}$ to construct a fully homomorphic public-key encryption scheme $\mathcal{E}' = (\mathsf{KeyGen}', \mathsf{Encrypt}', \mathsf{Decrypt}', \mathsf{Evaluate}')$, as follows:

- $\mathsf{KeyGen}'(1^\lambda)$ runs the underlying key generation $(\mathsf{sk}, \mathsf{pk}) \leftarrow \mathsf{KeyGen}(1^\lambda)$, and then the first-message procedure of the SFE protocol $(s, m_1) \leftarrow \mathsf{SFE1}_{U'}(1^\lambda, \mathsf{sk})$. It outputs $(\mathsf{sk}' = s, \mathsf{pk}' = (\mathsf{pk}, m_1))$ (where pk is used for encryption and m_1 is used for evaluation).
- $\mathsf{Encrypt}'(\mathsf{pk}' = (\mathsf{pk}, m_1), b)$ just uses the $\mathsf{Encrypt}$ procedure of the underlying scheme, outputting $c = \mathsf{Encrypt}(\mathsf{pk}, b)$.
- $\mathsf{Evaluate}'(\mathsf{pk}' = (\mathsf{pk}, m_1), \Pi, \mathbf{c})$ runs the second-message procedure of the SFE protocol for U', outputting $\mathbf{c}' \leftarrow \mathsf{SFE2}_{U'}(1^\lambda, m_1, (\mathbf{c}, \Pi))$.
- $\mathsf{Decrypt}(\mathsf{sk}' = s, \mathbf{c}')$ runs the last procedure of the SFE protocol for U', outputting $z \leftarrow \mathsf{SFE3}_{U'}(s, c')$.

Correctness of $\mathcal{E}'$ follows from that of $\mathcal{E}$ and $\mathcal{P}_{U'}$: If $\mathbf{c} = \mathsf{Encrypt}(\mathsf{pk}, \mathbf{b})$ then by correctness of $\mathcal{E}$ we have $\mathbf{b} = \mathsf{Decrypt}(\mathsf{sk}, \mathbf{c})$, and by correctness of $\mathcal{P}_{U'}$ we have $z = U'(\mathsf{sk}, (\mathbf{c}, \Pi)) = \Pi(\mathsf{Decrypt}(\mathsf{sk}, \mathbf{c})) = \Pi(\mathbf{b})$.

Semantic security follows from the semantic security of the underlying $\mathcal{E}$ and from client security of $\mathcal{P}_{U'}$. To show that $\mathsf{Encrypt}(\mathsf{pk}, 0)$ is indistinguishable from $\mathsf{Encrypt}(\mathsf{pk}, 1)$ even given pk and m_1, consider a hybrid experiment in which m_1 is generated by the simulator $m_1 \leftarrow \mathsf{Sim}_1(1^\lambda)$ instead of being a part of the output of $\mathsf{SFE1}(1^\lambda, \mathsf{sk})$. The client security of $\mathcal{P}_{U'}$ implies that this hybrid experiment is indistinguishable from the real encryption scheme. But in this hybrid, m_1 no longer depends on the secret key sk, and therefore by semantic security of $\mathcal{E}$ we get that $\mathsf{Encrypt}(\mathsf{pk}, 0)$ is indistinguishable from $\mathsf{Encrypt}(\mathsf{pk}, 1)$.

Finally, the circuit privacy of $\mathcal{E}'$ follows from the server security of $\mathcal{P}_{U'}$: The simulator $\mathsf{Sim}_{\mathcal{E}'}$ that we need for circuit privacy is constructed from the client view simulator Sim_2 above: $\mathsf{Sim}_{\mathcal{E}'}(1^\lambda, b, z)$ first chooses randomness r, r' for the

key generation and encryption of the underlying encryption scheme, then sets
$(\mathsf{sk}, \mathsf{pk}) := \mathsf{KeyGen}(1^\lambda; \; r)$ and $\mathbf{c} := \mathsf{Encrypt}(\mathsf{pk}, \mathbf{b}; \; r')$. Next it runs Sim_2 to get
$(r'', \mathbf{c}') \leftarrow \mathsf{Sim}_2(1^\lambda, z)$. Then $\mathsf{Sim}_{\mathcal{E}'}$ outputs (r, r'') as the randomness for KeyGen',
r' as the randomness for $\mathsf{Encrypt}'$, and $\mathbf{c}'$ as the evaluated ciphertext. Indistinguisha-
bility between the simulated and real views follows directly from that of Sim_2. ∎

5.2.2.5 Multi-hop Homomorphic Encryption

In settings where we do not have strong homomorphism, the evaluated ciphertexts
produced by Evaluate may differ from freshly encrypted ones, bringing up the question of whether one can keep computing on evaluated ciphertexts. An *i-hop* homomorphic encryption scheme is one where Evaluate can be called on its own output
up to i times (while still being able to decrypt the result), and a *multi-hop* homomorphic encryption scheme is one which is i-hop for all i. Note that the number of
hops supported by a scheme is somewhat orthogonal to its homomorphic capacity.
For example the Goldwasser–Micali cryptosystem is only additively homomorphic
but is multi-hop, while the scheme constructed from a two-message SFE protocol
in Theorem 5.2.13 above is fully homomorphic but supports only a single hop. Also
it is clear that strong homomorphism implies multi-hop homomorphism. Gentry et
al. studied multi-hop homomorphism in [46]. They extended the notion of circuit
privacy to the multi-hop case and described how it can be realized (with or without
compactness); their definitions and results are summarized below:

Let $\mathcal{E} = (\mathsf{KeyGen}, \mathsf{Encrypt}, \mathsf{Decrypt}, \mathsf{Evaluate})$ be a homomorphic encryption
scheme. The syntax of Evaluate is extended in the natural way to a sequence of
circuits: An ordered sequence of circuits $\overrightarrow{\Pi} = (\Pi_1, \ldots, \Pi_t)$ is *compatible* if the
output length of Π_j is the same as the input length of Π_{j+1} for all j. The composed
function $\Pi_t(\cdots \Pi_2(\Pi_1(\cdot)) \cdots)$ is denoted $(\Pi_t \circ \cdots \circ \Pi_1)$. The extended procedure
Evaluate* takes as input the public key, a compatible sequence $\overrightarrow{\Pi} = (\Pi_1, \ldots, \Pi_t)$,
and ciphertexts $\mathbf{c}_0$. For $i = 1, 2, \ldots, t$ it sets $\mathbf{c}_i \leftarrow \mathsf{Evaluate}(\mathsf{pk}, \Pi_i, \mathbf{c}_{i-1})$, outputting
the last $\mathbf{c}_t$.

Definition 5.2.14 (Multi-hop homomorphic encryption). *For a circuit family $\mathcal{C}$*
and $i \in \mathbb{N}$, we say that $\mathcal{E}$ is i-hop homomorphic for $\mathcal{C}$ if, for all $\lambda, \tau \in \mathbb{N}$ and
every compatible sequence $\overrightarrow{\Pi} = (\Pi_1, \ldots, \Pi_t)$ with $t \le i$ functions such that $\tilde{\Pi} =$
$\Pi_t \circ \cdots \circ \Pi_1 \in \mathcal{C}_\tau$, we have

$$\Pr\left[\mathsf{Decrypt}(\mathsf{sk}, \mathbf{c}') = \tilde{\Pi}(\mathbf{b}) : \begin{array}{l} (\mathsf{sk}, \mathsf{pk}) \leftarrow \mathsf{KeyGen}(1^\lambda, 1^\tau), \\ \mathbf{c} \leftarrow \mathsf{Encrypt}(\mathsf{pk}, \mathbf{b}), \; \mathbf{c}' \leftarrow \mathsf{Evaluate}^*(\mathsf{pk}, \overrightarrow{\Pi}, \mathbf{c}) \end{array}\right] = 1.$$

We say that $\mathcal{E}$ is a multi-hop *homomorphic encryption scheme if it is i-hop for all $i \in$*
$\mathbb{N}$.

Theorem 5.2.15 (Multi-hop homomorphism [46]).

- *If a 1-hop circuit private, fully homomorphic encryption scheme exists, then for*
  any constant i there exists an i-hop circuit private, fully homomorphic encryp-
  tion scheme.

- *If both 1-hop circuit private fully homomorphic encryption scheme and 1-hop compact fully homomorphic encryption scheme exist, then there exists a multi-hop circuit private, compact, fully homomorphic encryption scheme.*
- *Under the decision Diffie–Hellman assumption, there exists a (non-compact) multi-hop circuit-private fully homomorphic encryption scheme.*

In the rest of this tutorial we only consider multi-hop schemes.

5.2.2.6 From Secret-Key to Public-Key Homomorphic Encryption

One demonstration of the power of compact homomorphic encryption is a result of Rothblum [82] showing that it enables a transformation from secret-key to public-key encryption. As a warm-up, we demonstrate this result for strongly homomorphic encryption. Let $\mathcal{E}$ = (KeyGen, Encrypt, Decrypt, Evaluate) be a *secret-key scheme* which is strongly fully homomorphic. We transform $\mathcal{E}$ to a public-key strongly fully homomorphic scheme $\mathcal{E}'$ = (KeyGen′, Encrypt′, Decrypt, Evaluate) with the same Decrypt and Evaluate procedures, but modified KeyGen′ and Encrypt′:

- KeyGen′(1^λ) first runs the underlying KeyGen to get sk $\leftarrow$ KeyGen(1^λ). Then it runs the underlying encryption to encrypt 0 and 1, getting $c_0 \leftarrow$ Encrypt(sk, 0) and $c_1 \leftarrow$ Encrypt(sk, 1). It outputs (sk, pk = (c_0, c_1)).
- Encrypt′(pk = $(c_0, c_1), b$) uses the Evaluate procedure for the underlying scheme. Specifically let Π_{id} be a circuit computing the identity function, then it outputs $c \leftarrow$ Evaluate(Π_{id}, c_b).

The strong homomorphism condition implies that the output of Encrypt′ is statistically close to (resp. computationally indistinguishable from) Encrypt(sk, b), even conditioned on the public key (resp. the secret key). Hence the modified scheme maintains the semantic security and strong homomorphism of the underlying scheme, and we have:

Proposition 5.2.16. *Any secret-key strongly homomorphic encryption scheme can be transformed to a public-key strongly homomorphic scheme.*

When the secret-key scheme that we are given is not strongly homomorphic, the transformation above may fail to provide semantic security. Rothblum observed in [82] that semantic security can be obtained by capitalizing on the fact that a compact homomorphic encryption scheme must lose some information in the course of homomorphic evaluation, since the evaluation output is short. Using this loss of information to provide security is done by means of (a special case of) the leftover hash lemma [58], which is stated below.

Lemma 5.2.17 (Linear-hashing extractor). *Fix some $n, q, m \in \mathbb{N}$, and for every matrix $\mathbf{A} \in \mathbb{Z}_q^{n \times m}$ consider the multiply-by-$\mathbf{A}$ function $h_\mathbf{A}(\mathbf{s}) \stackrel{def}{=} [\mathbf{A} \times \mathbf{s}]_q$.*
Then for every subset $S \subseteq \mathbb{Z}_q^m$ and every linear subspace $L \subseteq \mathbb{Z}_q^n$, the distribution $\{(\mathbf{A}, h_\mathbf{A}(\mathbf{s})) : \mathbf{A} \leftarrow L^m, \mathbf{s} \leftarrow S\}$ is statistically close up to $|L| \cdot \sqrt{2/|S|}$ to the uniform distribution over L^{m+1}.

The special case $q = 2, n = 1$, and $L = \mathbb{Z}_2$ is summarized in the following corollary:

Corollary 5.2.18. *For $m \in \mathbb{N}$ and a bit-string $r \in \{0, 1\}^m$, denote the inner-product-with-r function by $h_r(s) \overset{def}{=} [\langle r, s \rangle]_2$. Then for every subset $S \subseteq \{0, 1\}^m$, the distribution $\{(r, h_r(s)) : r \leftarrow \{0, 1\}^m, s \leftarrow S\}$ is statistically close up to $\sqrt{8/|S|}$ to the uniform distribution over $\{0, 1\}^{m+1}$.*

We are now ready to describe the transformation from private-key to a public-key encryption.

Theorem 5.2.19 (Secret-key to public-key [82]). *Any compact, multi-hop, secret-key fully homomorphic scheme can be transformed into a compact, multi-hop, public-key fully homomorphic scheme.*

Proof: Let $\mathcal{E}$ = (KeyGen, Encrypt, Decrypt, Evaluate) be a compact, multi-hop, *secret-key* fully homomorphic scheme, and let $B(\lambda)$ be a bound on the size of evaluated circuits under $\mathcal{E}$. We transform $\mathcal{E}$ to a public-key scheme $\mathcal{E}'$ = (KeyGen', Encrypt', Decrypt, Evaluate) with the same Decrypt and Evaluate procedures, but modified KeyGen' and Encrypt':

- KeyGen'$(1^\lambda, 1^\tau)$ first runs the underlying KeyGen to get sk $\leftarrow$ KeyGen$(1^\lambda, 1^\tau)$. Letting $m = 2(B(\lambda) + \lambda)$, it next chooses a random string $r \leftarrow \{0, 1\}^m$ and for each bit r_i in r it computes $c_i \leftarrow$ Encrypt(pk, r_i) and denotes $\mathbf{c}^* = (c_1, \ldots, c_m)$. Finally it outputs the secret key sk and the public key pk $= (r, \mathbf{c}^*)$.
- Encrypt'(pk $= (r, \mathbf{c}), b$) chooses at random $s \leftarrow \{0, 1\}^m$ subject to the condition $\langle r, s \rangle = b$ (mod 2). Denoting by Π_s an m-input circuit made of XOR gates that computes the function $h_s(\cdot)$, it outputs the ciphertext $c \leftarrow$ Evaluate$(\Pi_s, \mathbf{c}^*)$.

Correctness follows from that of the underlying scheme: Since $\mathbf{c}^* =$ Encrypt(sk, r) then for freshly encrypted ciphertexts we have Decrypt(sk, c) $= \Pi_s(r) = h_s(r) = b$. Similarly for evaluated ciphertexts, for $\mathbf{c} =$ Encrypt'(pk, $\mathbf{b}$) $=$ Evaluate$(\Pi_s, \mathbf{c}^*)$, where each input bit b_i in $\mathbf{b}$ is encrypted using some s_i such that $circuit_{s_i}(r) = b_i$. Then for any Π' such that $\Pi' \circ \Pi_s \in \mathcal{C}_\tau$, we have

$$\text{Evaluate}(\Pi', \mathbf{c}) = \text{Evaluate}^*(\Pi' \circ \Pi_s, \mathbf{c}^*) = \Pi'(\Pi_s(r)) = \Pi'(\mathbf{b}).$$

To prove semantic security, consider a hybrid experiment in which the ciphertexts $\mathbf{c}^*$ in the public key are generated not as encryption of r but rather encryption of 0, $\mathbf{c}^* \leftarrow$ Encrypt(sk, 0). By semantic security of the underlying scheme $\mathcal{E}$, no adversary can distinguish between the public key in the real scheme and that in the hybrid experiment, except with negligible probability. It remains to show that, in this hybrid game, the ciphertext is nearly independent of the encrypted bit.

Note that, with this setting for $\mathbf{c}^*$, the evaluated ciphertext $c \leftarrow$ Evaluate$(\Pi_s, \mathbf{c}^*)$ is independent of the random string r, and it carries at most $B = B(\lambda)$ bits of information about s (since it is only B-bits long). It is therefore sufficient to show that, given $r \in \{0, 1\}^m$ and B bits of information about s, one can have at most a negligible advantage in guessing the inner product $b = \mathbf{r}, \mathbf{s}$ (mod 2).

We denote $E_{\mathbf{c}^*}(s) \stackrel{def}{=} \mathsf{Evaluate}(\Pi_s(\mathbf{c}^*))$, and for any B-bit ciphertext c consider the pre image $E_{\mathbf{c}^*}^{-1}(c) \stackrel{def}{=} \{s \in \{0,1\}^m : E_{\mathbf{c}^*}(s) = c\}$. By Corollary 5.2.18, for any fixed c, the conditional distribution $D_{\mathbf{c}^*,c} \stackrel{def}{=} \{(r, \langle r, s\rangle)|E_{\mathbf{c}^*}(s) = c\}$ is statistically close up to $\sqrt{8/\left|E_{\mathbf{c}^*}^{-1}(c)\right|}$ to the uniform distribution over $\{0,1\}^{m+1}$. Hence for every adversary algorithm A, we have

$$\Pr\left[A(r, E_{\mathbf{c}^*}(s)) = \langle r, s\rangle : r, s \leftarrow \{0,1\}^m\right]$$

$$= \sum_{c \in \{0,1\}^B} \Pr[E_{\mathbf{c}^*}(s) = c : s \leftarrow \{0,1\}^m] \cdot \Pr\left[A(r,c) = \langle r, s\rangle : r \leftarrow \{0,1\}^m, s \leftarrow E_{\mathbf{c}^*}^{-1}(c)\right]$$

$$\leq \sum_{c \in \{0,1\}^B} \frac{\left|E_{\mathbf{c}^*}^{-1}(c)\right|}{2^m} \cdot \left(\underbrace{\Pr\left[A(r,c) = b : r \leftarrow \{0,1\}^m, b \leftarrow \{0,1\}\right]}_{=1/2} + \sqrt{8/\left|E_{\mathbf{c}^*}^{-1}(c)\right|}\right)$$

$$= \frac{1}{2} + \sum_{c \in \{0,1\}^B} \frac{\sqrt{8\left|E_{\mathbf{c}^*}^{-1}(c)\right|}}{2^m} < \frac{1}{2} + \frac{2^B \cdot \sqrt{8 \cdot 2^m}}{2^m} < \frac{1}{2} + 3 \cdot 2^{B-m/2} = \frac{1}{2} + 3 \cdot 2^{-\lambda}.$$

∎

Remark 5.2.20. *For the transformation above, the secret-key scheme $\mathcal{E}$ need not be fully homomorphic (nor multi-hop); for example, it is sufficient for it to be additively homomorphic since the circuits Π_s are all linear. The result $\mathcal{E}'$ would still be a public-key encryption scheme, but it may not be homomorphic since the new encryption procedure used up some of the homomorphic capacity of $\mathcal{E}$. Specifically, if the secret-key scheme $\mathcal{E}$ is i-hop homomorphic relative to some circuit family $\mathcal{C}$, then $\mathcal{E}'$ is $(i-1)$-hop homomorphic relative to the family $\mathcal{C}' = \{\Pi' : (\Pi' \circ \Pi_s) \in \mathcal{C} \,\forall s\}$.*

This transformation applies also to weakly compact schemes; all we need is for the size of evaluated inner-product ciphertexts to grow slower than the dimension of the vectors used for the inner product.

5.3 Realizing Leveled Homomorphic Encryption

In this section, we show how to implement *leveled* homomorphic encryption, i.e., where the complexity of the encryption scheme grows with the depth of the circuits that it can evaluate. Specifically below we describe the GSW construction due to Gentry, Sahai, and Waters [48] in its most basic form, getting a leveled homomorphic encryption, with semantic security under the (sub exponential) decision-LWE assumption. Later in Section 5.4, we show how to use Gentry's bootstrapping technique to get fully homomorphic encryption (under the additional assumption of circular security), and also quantitatively improve the hardness assumption to quasipolynomial (or even polynomial) decision-LWE.

5.3.1 Tools

We begin by describing the basic tools that underlie the construction. We describe the learning-with-errors problem, and a *flattening gadget* and some other useful tricks for reducing the norm of vectors.

5.3.1.1 Learning with Errors (LWE)

The learning-with-errors (LWE) problem, first formulated and studied by Regev [80], underlies much of lattice-based cryptography. At a very high level, this average-case computational problem considers noisy modular linear equations, and the hardness assumption states that it is hard to solve such systems (or even decide if a solution exists).

The LWE problem is parametrized by integers q, n, m and a distribution χ over $\mathbb{Z}_q$. The parameter n is related to the security parameter, and we consider a modulus q which is at least polynomially larger than n (or even as large as $q = 2^{n^\epsilon}$) and $m = \Theta(n \log q)$. The distribution χ is concentrated on "small integers", namely we assume $\Pr[x \leftarrow \chi : |x| > \alpha q] < \mathsf{negl}(n)$ for some small $\alpha \ll 1$ (to be determined later).[5] The LWE distribution with these parameters is defined as

$$LWE[n, m, q, \chi] \stackrel{def}{=} \{(\mathbf{A}, \mathbf{b}) : \mathbf{A} \leftarrow \mathbb{Z}_q^{n \times m}, \mathbf{s} \leftarrow \mathbb{Z}_q^n, \boldsymbol{\eta} \leftarrow \chi^m, \mathbf{b} := [\mathbf{s}\mathbf{A} + \boldsymbol{\eta}]_q\}.$$

In words, we choose a uniformly random n-by-m matrix $\mathbf{A}$ and a row n-vector $\mathbf{s}$ over $\mathbb{Z}_q$, and an m-vector $\boldsymbol{\eta}$ whose entries are drawn from χ, and compute $\mathbf{b} := [\mathbf{s}\mathbf{A} + \boldsymbol{\eta}]_q$. The vector $\mathbf{s}$ is called *the secret* and $\boldsymbol{\eta}$ is called *the noise* (or the error).

Remark 5.3.1. *Applebaum et al. proved in [4] that a variant in which $\mathbf{s}$ is drawn from χ^n (rather than being uniformly random) is equally hard. Hence we formalize the hardness assumption below using a uniform secret $\mathbf{s}$, but we can use it with a small secret when needed. For most of this tutorial we get by with a uniform $\mathbf{s}$, but on occasion also consider variants that need the secret to be small.*

Since m is significantly larger than n, the row-span of $\mathbf{A}$ is a rather low-dimension random linear subspace of $\mathbb{Z}_q^m$. It follows that with high probability, the row span of $\mathbf{A}$ has large minimum distance (in l_∞ norm), roughly $q^{1-n/m}$. Hence for $\alpha \ll q^{-n/m}$, it holds with high probability (over $\mathcal{A}$) that there is a unique point in the row span of $\mathbf{A}$ within distance αq of $\mathbf{b}$ (call that point $\mathbf{b}'$), and the secret $\mathbf{s}$ is the unique solution to $\mathbf{s}\mathbf{A} = \mathbf{b}' \pmod{q}$.

The argument above shows that with high probability the secret $\mathbf{s}$ is uniquely defined, but computing it from $\mathbf{A}$ and $\mathbf{b}$ seems to be hard. Indeed, Regev described in [80] a worst-case to average-case quantum reduction from approximating the

---

[5] Often χ is taken to be a discrete Gaussian distribution with parameter $\alpha' \approx \alpha$ [71].

shortest-vector search problem in an arbitrary dimension-n lattice to solving a random instance of LWE, where the approximation factor is essentially n/α. Follow-up work [78, 18] described classical reductions of some other worst-case problems to LWE with similar dependence on α. These reductions provide ample evidence of the hardness of the search problem of computing s from A and b. Moreover, for many parameter regimes, the search problem of computing s can be further reduced to the problem of distinguishing the pair (A, b) from uniform [8, 80, 70]. It is the hardness of this decision problem which is most convenient for use in cryptography.

We often think of the pair (A, b) as an $(n + 1)$-by-m matrix with b being the last row. Denoting this matrix by A', it satisfies the equation $(s, -1) \times A' = \eta \pmod{q}$ with η having low norm, yet our hardness assumption says that A' is pseudorandom in $\mathbb{Z}^{(n+1) \times m}$. Thinking of $n' = n + 1$ as the security parameter, we can therefore state our hardness assumption as follows:

Definition 5.3.2 (Decision-LWE). *For parameters n, m, q, α (that depend on the security parameter λ), the decision-LWE hardness assumption ($DLWE[n, m, q, \alpha]$) states that there exists an efficiently sampleable ensemble $\{\psi_\lambda\}_\lambda$ over pairs ($s \in \mathbb{Z}_q^n, A \in \mathbb{Z}_q^{n \times m}$), for which the following conditions hold:*

- *The induced distribution ensemble over A is pseudorandom over $\mathbb{Z}_q^{n \times m}$.*
- *The l_∞-norm of $\eta \overset{def}{=} [sA]_q \in \mathbb{Z}_q^m$ is bounded by αq with overwhelming probability, and $s_n = -1$.*

(Note that above we use the notations n, s, A rather than n', s', A' from before; this will be more convenient in the sequel.)

Remark 5.3.3. *The DLWE assumption becomes stronger as α gets smaller. We have strong evidence that it holds for any polynomial fraction $\alpha(n) = 1/poly(n)$, and distinguishing A from random seems hard also for quasipolynomial or even nearly exponential fractions such as 2^{-n^ϵ}. On the other hand, for an exponentially small fraction, $\alpha = 2^{-O(n)}$, lattice-reduction tools allow us to find the secret s in polynomial time (so in particular we can distinguish A from random).*

Also we clearly need $\alpha q \geq 1$ (else the only integer vector satisfying $\|\eta\|_\infty \leq \alpha q$ is the all-zero vector), and there are attacks due to Arora and Ge [5] that apply when $\alpha q = O(1)$. Below we always use settings where $\alpha q = n$ (which is nearly the smallest possible). Hence in our setting the DLWE hardness assumption becomes stronger as q increases, and for $q = 2^{\Omega(n)}$ we know that it no longer holds. In this section we will need to assume that DLWE holds for $q = 2^{n^\epsilon}$, but later in the text we can relax this to $q = 2^{polylog(n)}$ and even $q = poly(n)$.

Finally note that the assumption becomes stronger as m increases, but all evidence points to this assumption holding for every polynomial $m = m(n)$. Below we will use $m \approx 2n \log q$.

5.3.1.2 Public-Key Encryption from LWE

Regev described in [80] a simple public-key encryption whose security is based on the DLWE assumption. That construction, which is naturally additively homomorphic, plays an important role in many homomorphic encryption schemes, including the GSW scheme that we describe later in this section.

The salient features of the Regev encryption scheme is that the secret key is a vector $\mathbf{s} \in \mathbb{Z}_q^n$ with $s_n = -1$, and an encryption of a bit b is a vector $\mathbf{u} \in \mathbb{Z}_q^n$ such that $\langle \mathbf{s}, \mathbf{u} \rangle = b \cdot \lfloor q/2 \rfloor + \delta \pmod{q}$ where δ is a small noise. Clearly adding/subtracting two ciphertexts yields an encryption of the XOR of the two encrypted bits, with noise which is the sum of the two noise elements for the individual ciphertext. It is easy to see how to construct a secret-key encryption scheme with ciphertexts as above, and since that scheme is additively homomorphic then one can use Theorem 5.2.19 to turn it into a public-key scheme. A more direct way of getting a public-key scheme is described below. Security of this scheme is reduced to the DLWE assumption; the proof is nearly identical to Lemma 5.3.6 later in this section.

Key generation: KeyGen(1^λ). given the parameters n, m, q and the distribution ψ_n for the DLWE assumption, draw a pair $(\mathbf{s}, \mathbf{A}) \leftarrow \psi_n$, outputting the secret key $\mathbf{s} \in \mathbb{Z}_q^n$ and public key $\mathbf{A} \in \mathbb{Z}_q^{n \times m}$.

Encryption: Encrypt($\mathbf{A}, \mathbf{b}$). For a public key $\mathbf{A} \in \mathbb{Z}_q^{n \times m}$ and plaintext bit $b \in \{0, 1\}$, choose a uniform $\{0, 1\}$ vector $\mathbf{r} \leftarrow \{0, 1\}^m$ and output the ciphertext vector $\mathbf{u} := [b \cdot \lfloor q/2 \rfloor \cdot (0, \dots, 0, -1) + \mathbf{A} \times \mathbf{r}]_q \in \mathbb{Z}_q^n$.

Observe that indeed $\langle \mathbf{s}, \mathbf{u} \rangle = [b \cdot \lfloor q/2 \rfloor + \mathbf{s}\mathbf{A}\mathbf{r} = b \cdot \lfloor q/2 \rfloor + \langle \boldsymbol{\eta}, \mathbf{r} \rangle$, and $|\langle \boldsymbol{\eta}, \mathbf{r} \rangle|$ is small as needed.

Decryption: Decrypt($\mathbf{s}, \mathbf{u}$). Compute $z := [\langle \mathbf{s}, \mathbf{u} \rangle]_q$, outputting 0 if $|z| < q/4$ and 1 otherwise.

5.3.1.3 The Flattening Gadget

A very useful technical tool in many lattice-based cryptosystems (including GSW encryption) is a "flattening gadget" that allows one to take a high-norm vector and represent it by a low-norm vector of higher dimension, while maintaining some linear-algebraic properties. We want a "representation function" $f : \mathbb{Z}_q \to \mathbb{Z}_q^\ell$ (for some not-too-large ℓ) with the properties:

- For any $z \in \mathbb{Z}_q$, the l_∞-norm of $f(z)$ is much smaller than q; and
- Recovering z from $f(z)$ is a linear operation. That is, there exists a "gadget vector" $\mathbf{g} \in \mathbb{Z}_q^\ell$ such that for every $z \in \mathbb{Z}_q$ we have $\langle \mathbf{g}, f(z) \rangle = z \pmod{q}$.

Note that the function f itself need not be linear, but its inverse is linear. A simple function with these properties is obtained by breaking z into its binary representation: Let $\ell = \lceil \log q \rceil$ and $f(z) = (z_0, z_1, \dots, z_{\ell-1})$ be the vector of bits in the binary (2's-complement) representation of $z \in [-q/2, q/2)$, with z_0 the least-significant bit and $z_{\ell-1} \in \{0, -1\}$ representing the most-significant bit. Then $\|f(z)\|_\infty \leq 1$ and setting $\mathbf{g} = (1, 2, \dots, 2^{\ell-1})$ we have $\langle \mathbf{g}, f(z) \rangle = \sum_{i=1}^{\ell-1} 2^i z_i = z$.

To stress the fact that our representation function is an inverse of a linear function, we denote it below by $g^{-1}(\cdot)$. Note again that $\mathbf{g}$ is a vector (representing a linear function), but g^{-1} is a non-linear function.

The same representation extends naturally to vectors and matrices. For an n-vector $\mathbf{z} = (z_1, \ldots, z_n) \in \mathbb{Z}^n$, we let $G^{-1}(\mathbf{z})$ be the concatenation of all the vectors $g^{-1}(z_i)$, namely $G^{-1}(\mathbf{z}) \overset{def}{=} (g^{-1}(z_1)|g^{-1}(z_2)| \ldots |g^{-1}(z_n)) \in \mathbb{Z}_q^{n\ell}$. If we think of $\mathbf{z}$ and $G^{-1}(\mathbf{z})$ as column vectors and consider the "gadget matrix"

$$\mathbf{G} \overset{def}{=} \begin{pmatrix} 1\ 2\ \ldots\ 2^{\ell-1} & & & \\ & 1\ 2\ \ldots\ 2^{\ell-1} & & \\ & & \ddots & \\ & & & 1\ 2\ \ldots\ 2^{\ell-1} \end{pmatrix} \in \mathbb{Z}_q^{n\times n\ell},$$

then for any vector $\mathbf{z} \in \mathbb{Z}_q^n$ we have $\|G^{-1}(\mathbf{z})\|_\infty \leq 1$ and $\mathbf{G} \times G^{-1}(\mathbf{z}) = \mathbf{z}$. Similarly for an $n \times m$ matrix $\mathbf{A} = (\mathbf{a}_1| \ldots |\mathbf{a}_m)$ with columns $\mathbf{a}_i \in \mathbb{Z}_q^n$, we let

$$G^{-1}(\mathbf{A}) \overset{def}{=} (G^{-1}(\mathbf{a}_1)| \ldots |G^{-1}(\mathbf{a}_m)) \in \mathbb{Z}_q^{n\ell\times m}.$$

Then for any matrix $\mathbf{A} \in \mathbb{Z}_q^{n\times m}$ we have $\|G^{-1}(\mathbf{A})\|_\infty \leq 1$ and $\mathbf{G} \times G^{-1}(\mathbf{A}) = \mathbf{A}$.

5.3.1.4 Modulus and Key Switching

Below we describe the two tricks of modulus switching and key switching, due to Brakerski et al. [19, 17], which can be used in some cases to reduce the size of the modulus and the dimension of the LWE secret vectors. These tricks are not strictly needed to obtain fully homomorphic encryption, but they can be used to improve its parameters and efficiency and to quantitatively weaken the hardness assumptions that are needed for its security.

Modulus switching. Modulus switching lets one convert approximate linear relations modulo one integer into relations modulo another.

Lemma 5.3.4. *Fix the dimension $n \in \mathbb{N}$ and moduli $p, q \in \mathbb{N}$, and let $\mathbf{s}, \mathbf{u} \in \mathbb{Z}_q^n$, such that their mod-$q$ inner product is bounded away from $q/4$, specifically $[\langle \mathbf{s}, \mathbf{u} \rangle]_q = b \cdot \lfloor q/2 \rfloor + \delta$ where $|\delta| < q(\frac{1}{4} - \frac{\|\mathbf{s}\|_1}{2p})$.*

Let $\mathbf{u}' = \lceil \mathbf{u} \cdot p/q \rfloor$, then $[\langle \mathbf{s}, \mathbf{u} \rangle]_p = b \cdot \lfloor p/2 \rfloor + \delta'$ where $|\delta'| \leq \frac{p}{q}|\delta| + \frac{\|\mathbf{s}\|_1}{2} < p/4$.

Proof: Let ϵ denote the rounding error in the computation of $\mathbf{u}'$, i.e., $\mathbf{u}' = p/q \cdot \mathbf{u} + \epsilon$, note that $\|\epsilon\|_\infty \leq 1/2$. Since over the integers we have the equality $\langle \mathbf{s}, \mathbf{u} \rangle = b \cdot \lfloor q/2 \rfloor + \delta + kq$ for some $k \in \mathbb{N}$, then we get

$$\langle \mathbf{s}, \mathbf{u}' \rangle = (p/q)\langle \mathbf{s}, \mathbf{u} \rangle + \langle \mathbf{s}, \epsilon \rangle = b \cdot \lfloor p/2 \rfloor + \underbrace{\frac{p}{q}\delta + \langle \mathbf{s}, \epsilon \rangle}_{=\delta'} + kp,$$

with $|\delta'| < \frac{p}{q}|\delta| + \frac{\|\mathbf{s}\|_1}{2} < q/4$, as needed. ∎

We can use this lemma in settings where we have a low-norm secret LWE vector $\mathbf{s}$ (such as when it is drawn from the error distribution χ, as described by Applebaum et al. [4]). In this situation we can switch from a mod-q vector $\mathbf{u}$ to a mod-p vector $\mathbf{u}'$ for $p \ll q$, with only a small penalty in terms of increased added noise. As $p \ll q$, then mod-p arithmetic has smaller complexity than mod-q arithmetic.

Key switching. Key switching let us publish a public pseudorandom gadget for converting approximate linear relations relative to a secret vector $\mathbf{t}$ into relations relative to another vector $\mathbf{s}$.

Specifically, fix the DLWE parameters n, m, q, α, where $m = n'\lceil \log q \rceil$ for some n'. Let $(\mathbf{s}, \mathbf{A}) \leftarrow \psi$ be drawn according to the distribution from Definition 5.3.2, so $\mathbf{A} \in \mathbb{Z}_q^{n \times m}$ is pseudorandom, $s_n = -1$, and $\boldsymbol{\eta} = [\mathbf{s}\mathbf{A}]_q$ has low norm $\|\boldsymbol{\eta}\|_\infty < \alpha q$.

Fix any vector $\mathbf{t} \in \mathbb{Z}_q^{n'}$ and let $\mathbf{A}'_{s:t} \in \mathbb{Z}_q^{n \times m}$ be the matrix obtained by subtracting $\mathbf{t}\mathbf{G}$ modulo q from the last row of $\mathbf{A}$, where $\mathbf{G} \in \mathbb{Z}_q^{n' \times m}$ is the matrix from the flattening gadget above. (Recall that $m = n'\lceil \log q \rceil$, as needed for this gadget.) Clearly, since $\mathbf{A}$ is pseudorandom then so is $\mathbf{A}'_{s:t}$ for any fixed $\mathbf{t}$ independent of $\mathbf{s}$. Also since $s_n = -1$ then
$$\mathbf{s}\mathbf{A}'_{s:t} = \mathbf{s}\mathbf{A} + \mathbf{t}\mathbf{G} = \mathbf{t}\mathbf{G} + \boldsymbol{\eta} \quad (\bmod\ q).$$

The use of the key-switching gadget $\mathbf{A}'_{s:t}$ is summarized in the following lemma:

Lemma 5.3.5. *Fix the parameters $n', n, m, q \in \mathbb{N}$ as above, and let $\mathbf{s} \in \mathbb{Z}_q^n$, $\mathbf{t} \in \mathbb{Z}_q^{n'}$, and $\mathbf{A}'_{s:t} \in \mathbb{Z}_q^{n \times m}$ such that $\mathbf{s}\mathbf{A}'_{s:t} = \mathbf{t}\mathbf{G} + \boldsymbol{\eta} \pmod q$.*

Let $\mathbf{u}' \in \mathbb{Z}_q^{n'}$ be a vector whose mod-q inner product with $\mathbf{t}$ is bounded away from $q/4$, specifically $[\langle \mathbf{t}, \mathbf{u}' \rangle]_q = b \cdot \lfloor q/2 \rfloor + \delta'$ where $|\delta'| < q/4 - \|\boldsymbol{\eta}\|_1$. Computing $\mathbf{u} := [\mathbf{A}'_{s:t} \times G^{-1}(\mathbf{u}')]_q$, we have
$$[\langle \mathbf{s}, \mathbf{u} \rangle]_p = b \cdot \lfloor q/2 \rfloor + \delta,$$

where $|\delta| \le |\delta'| + \|\boldsymbol{\eta}\|_1 < p/4$.

Proof:
$$\langle \mathbf{s}, \mathbf{u} \rangle = \mathbf{s} \times \mathbf{A}'_{s:t} \times G^{-1}(\mathbf{u}') = (\mathbf{t}\mathbf{G} + \boldsymbol{\eta}) \times G^{-1}(\mathbf{u}') = \mathbf{t}\mathbf{G} \times G^{-1}(\mathbf{u}') + \langle \boldsymbol{\eta}, G^{-1}(\mathbf{u}') \rangle$$
$$= \langle \mathbf{t}, \mathbf{u}' \rangle + \langle \boldsymbol{\eta}, G^{-1}(\mathbf{u}') \rangle = b \cdot \lfloor q/2 \rfloor + \underbrace{\delta' + \langle \boldsymbol{\eta}, G^{-1}(\mathbf{u}') \rangle}_{=\delta},$$

and since $G^{-1}(\mathbf{u}')$ is a dimension-m 0/1 vector then $|\langle \boldsymbol{\eta}, G^{-1}(\mathbf{u}') \rangle| < \|\boldsymbol{\eta}\|_1$, hence $|\delta| \le |\delta'| + \|\boldsymbol{\eta}\|_1 < p/4$. ∎

One use of Lemma 5.3.5 is to reduce the dimension of an LWE secret from n' to $n < n'$, which we can do as long as n is large enough so that the $DLWE[n, m, q, \alpha]$ hardness assumption still holds. As with modulus-switching, this can be used to get lower-complexity arithmetic operations.

5.3.2 The GSW Encryption Scheme

5.3.2.1 First Try

The high-level intuition for the GSW scheme [48] comes from the concepts of *eigenvectors and eigenvalues* in linear algebra. Let $\mathbb{F}$ be some field and let $\mathbf{C} \in \mathbb{F}^{n \times n}$ be a square matrix over $\mathbb{F}$. Recall that $\mathbf{s} \in \mathbb{F}^n$ is a (left-) eigenvector of $\mathbf{C}$ with corresponding eigenvalue $u \in \mathbb{F}$ if we have $\mathbf{s} \times \mathbf{C} = \mathbf{s} \cdot u$ (with operations in $\mathbb{F}$). It is easy to see that, if $\mathbf{C}_1, \mathbf{C}_2$ are two n-by-n matrices that share the same eigenvector $\mathbf{s}$ with corresponding eigenvalues u_1, u_2, then

$$\mathbf{s} \times (\mathbf{C}_1 \pm \mathbf{C}_2) = \mathbf{s} \cdot (u_1 \pm u_2) \text{ and } \mathbf{s} \times (\mathbf{C}_1 \times \mathbf{C}_2) = \mathbf{s} \cdot (u_1 \cdot u_2).$$

In words, the scalar $u_1 \pm u_2$ is the eigenvalue of $\mathbf{C}_1 \pm \mathbf{C}_2$ corresponding to the eigenvector $\mathbf{s}$, and similarly $u_1 \cdot u_2$ is the eigenvalue of $\mathbf{C}_1 \times \mathbf{C}_2$ corresponding to $\mathbf{s}$.

It is therefore tempting to construct a cryptosystem where $\mathbf{s}$ is the secret key and an encryption of a value u is a matrix that has $\mathbf{s}$ as an eigenvector with u the corresponding eigenvalue. Then we could use matrix addition and multiplication to implement homomorphic addition and multiplication over $\mathbb{F}$, getting a fully homomorphic scheme. The problem, of course, is that this scheme is insecure: Given the ciphertext matrix $\mathbf{C}$ it is easy to compute the eigenvectors of $\mathbf{C}$, and one of these eigenvectors is the secret key.

5.3.2.2 Second Try

Attempting to improve security, we may try adding some noise, making $\mathbf{s}$ an *approximate* rather than an exact eigenvector of the ciphertext matrices, and relying on the hardness of LWE to get security. Specifically, we would like to work over $\mathbb{Z}_q$ and maintain the invariant that a plaintext scalar u is encrypted relative to a secret key $\mathbf{s}$ by a matrix $\mathbf{C}$ such that $\mathbf{s} \times \mathbf{C} \approx \mathbf{s} \cdot u = \mathbf{s} \times \mathbf{C} + \boldsymbol{\eta}$ for a small noise vector $\boldsymbol{\eta}$. We note that adding noise over the real field would have very little effect, since the algorithm for computing eigenvectors over the reals is very geometric in spirit, and is robust to inaccuracies or noise. On the other hand, computing eigenvectors over discrete fields is done using Gaussian elimination, which is algebraic and very brittle in the presence of small noise.

Adding some noise may help security, but does it hurt the homomorphic operations? At least for addition things still seem to work: If we have $\mathbf{s} \times \mathbf{C}_i = \mathbf{s} \cdot u_i + \boldsymbol{\eta}_i$ for $i = 1, 2$ then also $\mathbf{s} \times (\mathbf{C}_1 \pm \mathbf{C}_2) = \mathbf{s} \cdot (u_1 \pm u_2) + (\boldsymbol{\eta}_1 \pm \boldsymbol{\eta}_2)$ so $\mathbf{s}$ is still an approximate eigenvector of the matrix $(\mathbf{C}_1 \pm \mathbf{C}_2)$, corresponding to the eigenvalue $(u_1 \pm u_2)$ with the (still small) noise vector $(\boldsymbol{\eta}_1 \pm \boldsymbol{\eta}_2)$. For multiplication, however, we have

$$\begin{aligned} \mathbf{s} \times (\mathbf{C}_1 \times \mathbf{C}_2) &= (\mathbf{s} \cdot u_1 + \boldsymbol{\eta}_1) \times \mathbf{C}_2 = \mathbf{s} \times \mathbf{C}_2 \cdot u_1 + \boldsymbol{\eta}_1 \times \mathbf{C}_2 \\ &= (\mathbf{s} \cdot u_2 + \boldsymbol{\eta}_2) \cdot u_1 + \boldsymbol{\eta}_1 \times \mathbf{C}_2 \\ &= \mathbf{s} \cdot u_1 u_2 + (u_1 \cdot \boldsymbol{\eta}_2 + \boldsymbol{\eta}_1 \times \mathbf{C}_2) \pmod{q}. \end{aligned} \quad (5.1)$$

We would like to think of $\mathbf{s}$ as an approximate eigenvector of $\mathbf{C}_1 \times \mathbf{C}_2$ corresponding to the eigenvalue $(u_1 \cdot u_2)$ with noise vector $\boldsymbol{\eta}^* = (u_1 \cdot \boldsymbol{\eta}_2 + \boldsymbol{\eta}_1 \times \mathbf{C}_2)$, but $\boldsymbol{\eta}^*$ may not be small anymore: If the ciphertext matrix $\mathbf{C}_2$ has large entries, then so would the vector $\boldsymbol{\eta}^*$, no matter how small $\boldsymbol{\eta}_1$ is. Similarly, if the plaintext scalar u_1 is large then $u_1 \cdot \boldsymbol{\eta}_2$ will be large.

5.3.2.3 Final Try

To recover functionality, we want to ensure that both the plaintext scalars and ciphertext matrices are kept small. Keeping the plaintext small can be done by encrypting only 0's and 1's and using only NAND gates, which are implemented over $\mathbb{Z}_q$ as $NAND(x, y) = 1 - xy$.

To ensure that the ciphertext matrices have small entries we use the flattening gadget from Section 5.3.1.3. Recalling the form of the noise from Equation (5.1), we would like to use the low-norm $G^{-1}(\mathbf{C}_2)$ instead of $\mathbf{C}_2$ itself in the multiplication procedure. Namely, we want the homomorphic multiplication procedure to be $\mathbf{C}_1 \times G^{-1}(\mathbf{C}_2)$. To make the dimensions match, we need the ciphertext matrices $\mathbf{C}$ to be n-by-N matrices with $N = n\ell$ (recall that $\ell = \lceil \log q \rceil$).

To maintain correctness we need to introduce the gadget $\mathbf{G}$ into the invariant that we maintain: A plaintext scalar u is now encrypted relative to a secret key $\mathbf{s}$ by a matrix $\mathbf{C}$ such that $\mathbf{s} \times \mathbf{C} \approx \mathbf{s}' \cdot u$, where $\mathbf{s}' = \mathbf{s} \times \mathbf{G}$. With this modification, let $\mathbf{C}_i \in \mathbb{Z}_q^{n \times N}$ (for $i = 1, 2$) be two matrices that encrypt two bits $b_i \in \{0, 1\}$ relative to the secret key $\mathbf{s}$, i.e., $\mathbf{s} \times \mathbf{C}_i = b_i \cdot (\mathbf{s} \times \mathbf{G}) + \boldsymbol{\eta}_i$ for small noise vectors $\boldsymbol{\eta}_i$. Then we have

$$\mathbf{s} \times (\mathbf{C}_1 \times G^{-1}(\mathbf{C}_2)) = (b_1 \cdot \mathbf{s} \times \mathbf{G} + \boldsymbol{\eta}_1) \times G^{-1}(\mathbf{C}_2)$$
$$= b_1 \cdot \mathbf{s} \times \mathbf{G} \times G^{-1}(\mathbf{C}_2) + \boldsymbol{\eta}_1 \times G^{-1}(\mathbf{C}_2)$$
$$= b_1 \cdot \mathbf{s} \times \mathbf{C}_2 + \boldsymbol{\eta}_1 \times G^{-1}(\mathbf{C}_2) = b_1(b_2 \cdot \mathbf{s} \times \mathbf{G} + \boldsymbol{\eta}_2) + \boldsymbol{\eta}_1 \times G^{-1}(\mathbf{C}_2)$$
$$= b_1 b_2 \cdot (\mathbf{s} \times \mathbf{G}) + (b_1 \cdot \boldsymbol{\eta}_2 + \boldsymbol{\eta}_1 \times G^{-1}(\mathbf{C}_2)) \pmod{q}$$

Let us define the homomorphic NAND operation as

$$\mathsf{homNAND}(\mathbf{C}_1, \mathbf{C}_2) \stackrel{def}{=} [\mathbf{G} - (\mathbf{C}_1 \times G^{-1}(\mathbf{C}_2))]_q, \tag{5.2}$$

so we get

$$\mathbf{s} \times \mathsf{homNAND}(\mathbf{C}_1, \mathbf{C}_2) = \mathbf{s} \times \mathbf{G} - \mathbf{s} \times \mathbf{C}_1 \times G^{-1}(\mathbf{C}_2) \tag{5.3}$$
$$= \underbrace{(1 - b_1 b_2)}_{NAND(b_1, b_2)} \cdot (\mathbf{s} \times \mathbf{G}) - \underbrace{(b_1 \cdot \boldsymbol{\eta}_2 + \boldsymbol{\eta}_1 \times G^{-1}(\mathbf{C}_2))}_{\boldsymbol{\eta}'} \pmod{q}.$$

As $b_1 \in \{0, 1\}$ and $G^{-1}(\mathbf{C}_2) \in \{-1, 0, 1\}^{N \times N}$, the l_∞ norm of $\boldsymbol{\eta}'$ is bounded by

$$\|\boldsymbol{\eta}'\|_\infty \leq \|\boldsymbol{\eta}_2\|_\infty + N \cdot \|\boldsymbol{\eta}_1\|_\infty \leq (N + 1) \cdot \max\{\|\boldsymbol{\eta}_1\|, \|\boldsymbol{\eta}_2\|\}.$$

Consider now a depth-d circuit made of NAND gates, and assume that the inputs to the circuit are encrypted with noise vectors with norm below some bound B (below we use $B = n \cdot m$). Then the noise vectors at level i of the circuit have norm bounded by $B \cdot (N + 1)^i$, and in particular the output has noise bounded by $B \cdot (N + 1)^d$.

5.3.2.4 The GSW Leveled Scheme

We are now ready to describe the complete construction. We already established that the secret key is a vector $\mathbf{s} \in \mathbb{Z}_q^n$ and ciphertexts are matrices $\mathbf{C} \in \mathbb{Z}_q^{n \times N}$, and that we maintain the invariant that an encryption of a bit $b \in \{0, 1\}$ at level i of the circuit satisfies $\mathbf{s} \times \mathbf{C} = b \cdot (\mathbf{s} \times \mathbf{G}) + \boldsymbol{\eta}$ where $\|\boldsymbol{\eta}\|_\infty \leq n \cdot m \cdot (N + 1)^i$. It remains to explain how to encrypt and decrypt, set the parameters, and argue security.

KeyGen($1^\lambda, 1^\tau$). We first select the DLWE parameters n, m, q, ψ_n (with $\alpha q = n$) so as to enable homomorphic evaluation of circuits of depth up to τ. This is described later in this section. Denoting $N = n \cdot \lceil \log q \rceil$, we remark that the parameters are chosen so that $n \cdot m \cdot (N + 1)^{\tau+1} < q/4$.

The KeyGen procedure draws a pair $(\mathbf{s}, \mathbf{A}) \leftarrow \psi_n$, outputting the secret key $\mathbf{s} \in \mathbb{Z}_q^n$ and public key $\mathbf{A} \in \mathbb{Z}_q^{n \times m}$, after ensuring that $\mathbf{s} \neq 0$ and that the l_∞-norm of $\boldsymbol{\eta} = [\mathbf{sA}]_q$ is bounded by n (else it draws another pair).

Encrypt($\mathbf{A}, b$). For a public key $\mathbf{A} \in \mathbb{Z}_q^{n \times m}$ and plaintext bit $b \in \{0, 1\}$, the Encrypt procedure chooses a uniform $\{0, 1\}$ matrix $\mathbf{R} \leftarrow \{0, 1\}^{m \times N}$ and outputs the ciphertext matrix $\mathbf{C} := [b \cdot \mathbf{G} + \mathbf{A} \times \mathbf{R}]_q \in \mathbb{Z}_q^{n \times N}$.

We observe that $\mathbf{sC} = b \cdot \mathbf{sG} + \mathbf{sAR} = b \cdot \mathbf{sG} + \boldsymbol{\eta}\mathbf{R}$, and $\|\boldsymbol{\eta}\mathbf{R}\|_\infty \leq n \cdot m$, so $\mathbf{C}$ satisfies our invariant for fresh ciphertexts.

Evaluate($\Pi, \vec{\mathbf{C}}$). For a circuit of NAND gates of depth up to τ, go over the circuit in topological order from inputs to outputs; for every gate with inputs encrypted by $\mathbf{C}_1, \mathbf{C}_2$, compute the output encryption as $\mathbf{C}_{out} := \mathbf{G} - \mathbf{C}_1 \times \mathbf{G}^{-1}(\mathbf{C}_2)$.

By the analysis from above, a ciphertext $\mathbf{C}$ at level i of the circuit satisfies $\mathbf{sC} = b \cdot \mathbf{sG} + \boldsymbol{\eta}$, where b is the plaintext bit on the corresponding wire and $\|\boldsymbol{\eta}\|_\infty \leq n \cdot m \cdot (N + 1)^i$.

Decrypt($\mathbf{s}, \mathbf{C}$). Let $\mathbf{w} = -\lfloor q/2 \rfloor \cdot (0, \ldots, 0, 1) \in \mathbb{Z}_q^n$ be a scaled version of the n-th unit vector, and note that $\langle \mathbf{s}, \mathbf{w} \rangle = \lfloor q/2 \rfloor$ (since $s_n = -1$). The Decrypt procedure computes $z := [\mathbf{s} \times \mathbf{C} \times \mathbf{G}^{-1}(\mathbf{w})]_q$, outputting 0 if $|z| < q/4$ and 1 otherwise.

Correctness. To see that correctness holds, consider a ciphertext $\mathbf{C}$ at a level τ or below, so we have $\mathbf{sC} = b \cdot \mathbf{sG} + \boldsymbol{\eta}$ with $\|\boldsymbol{\eta}\|_\infty \leq n \cdot m \cdot (N + 1)^\tau$. Hence

$$z = \mathbf{s} \times \mathbf{C} \times \mathbf{G}^{-1}(\mathbf{w}) = (b \cdot \mathbf{sG} + \boldsymbol{\eta})\mathbf{G}^{-1}(\mathbf{w}) = b \cdot \langle \mathbf{s}, \mathbf{w} \rangle + \langle \boldsymbol{\eta}, \mathbf{G}^{-1}(\mathbf{w}) \rangle = b \cdot \lfloor q/2 \rfloor + v;$$

since $\|\boldsymbol{\eta}\|_\infty \leq n \cdot m \cdot (N + 1)^\tau$ and $\mathbf{G}^{-1}(\mathbf{w})$ is a 0/1 vector then $|v| < n \cdot m \cdot (N + 1)^{\tau+1} < q/4$, and therefore $|z| < q/4$ if $b = 0$ and $|z| > q/4$ if $b = 1$.

Lemma 5.3.6 (Semantic security). *The GSW scheme above is semantically secure under the DLWE$[n, m, q, \alpha]$ hardness assumption with $\alpha = n/q$ and $m \geq 1 + 2n(2 + \log q)$.*

Proof: Under the DLWE$[n, m, q, \alpha]$ hardness assumption, the public-key matrix $\mathbf{A}$ is pseudorandom in $\mathbb{Z}_q^{n \times m}$. It is sufficient therefore to prove that, if $\mathbf{A}$ was truly random, then the distribution of fresh encryption matrices would be statistically close to uniform in $\mathbb{Z}_q^{n \times N}$, regardless of the plaintext bit b.

Let $S = \{0, 1\}^m$ and $L = \mathbb{Z}_q^n$; by Lemma 5.2.17 the distribution over $(\mathbf{A}, [\mathbf{Ar}]_q)$ for uniform $\mathbf{A} \leftarrow \mathbb{Z}_q^{n \times m}$ and $\mathbf{r} \leftarrow S$ is close to uniform over $\mathbb{Z}_q^{n \times (m+1)}$ up to statistical distance of

$$q^n \cdot \sqrt{2/|S|} \leq 2^{n \log q} \cdot 2^{(1-m)/2} \leq 2^{n \log q - n(2 + \log q)} = 2^{-2n}.$$

It follows that, except for probability 2^{-n} over the choice of $\mathbf{A}$, the distribution of $[\mathbf{Ar}]_q$ conditioned on $\mathbf{A}$ (defined over the random choice $\mathbf{r} \leftarrow \{0, 1\}^m$) is 2^{-n}-close to uniform over $\mathbb{Z}_q^n$. Hence, the distribution of $[\mathbf{AR}]_q$ conditioned on $\mathbf{A}$ is $N2^{-n}$-close to uniform over $\mathbb{Z}_q^{n \times N}$, and therefore so is the distribution of the ciphertext matrix $\mathbf{C} = [b \cdot \mathbf{G} + \mathbf{AR}]_q$. ∎

Parameters for the basic GSW scheme. The security and correctness arguments above rely on the conditions $m \geq 1 + 2n(2 + \log q)$ and $n \cdot m \cdot (N + 1)^{\tau+1} < q/4$, respectively, where $N = n \cdot \lceil \log q \rceil$. Substituting, we get the condition $q > 4n \cdot (1 + 2n(2 + \log q)) \cdot (1 + n\lceil \log q \rceil)^{\tau+1}$, which we can simplify as $q > (2n \log q)^{\tau+3}$.

On the other hand, we need to keep $q \leq 2^{n^\epsilon}$ for some $\epsilon < 1$ (else DLWE is no longer hard). This yields the condition $n^\epsilon > (\tau + 3)(\log n + \log \log q + 1)$, which we can again simplify (for large enough τ, n) as $n^\epsilon > 2\tau \log n$. One could check that these conditions are all satisfied by the following setting:

- $n = \max\{\lambda, \lceil (\frac{4}{\epsilon}\tau \log \tau)^{1/\epsilon} \rceil\}$
- $q = \lceil 2^{n^\epsilon} \rceil$,
- $m = 1 + \lceil 2n(2 + \log q) \rceil = O(n^{1+\epsilon})$, and
- $\alpha = n/q = n \cdot 2^{-n^\epsilon}$.

We note that, with this setting, the size of ciphertexts (fresh or evaluated) is polynomial in λ and τ, while the number of circuits in $\mathcal{C}_\tau$ is doubly exponential in τ, so the scheme is weakly compact as per Definition 5.2.9. Hence we have proved the following theorem:

Theorem 5.3.7. *Under the DLWE$[n, m, q, \alpha]$ hardness assumption with $q = 2^{n^\epsilon}$, $\alpha = n \cdot 2^{-n^\epsilon}$, and $m = O(n^{1+\epsilon})$, there exists a semantically-secure weakly-compact leveled homomorphic encryption scheme, where the complexity of evaluating each gate in a depth-d circuit is poly$(\lambda, d^{1/\epsilon})$.*

5.4 Realizing Fully Homomorphic Encryption

Above we described the basic GSW construction from [48], obtaining a leveled homomorphic encryption with security under the subexponential decision-LWE hardness assumption. In Section 5.4.1 below, we describe Gentry's *bootstrapping* technique [47] for transforming some leveled schemes into fully homomorphic ones, and then explain in Section 5.4.2 how to apply it to the GSW scheme. This yields either a leveled homomorphic encryption with security under the quasipolynomial (or even polynomial) decision-LWE hardness assumption, or alternatively a fully homomorphic scheme whose security depends on the same (quasi)polynomial DLWE in conjunction with a circular-security assumption.

5.4.1 Bootstrapping

So far we have a scheme $\mathcal{E}$ such that, for any bounded depth d, we can evaluate depth-d circuits by setting the parameters of $\mathcal{E}$ to size poly(d). To increase the homomorphic capacity of the scheme, however, we need to choose larger parameters, so also the complexity of encryption/evaluation/decryption increases. Gentry's insight in [47] was that this dependence can be broken if we manage to find a setting in which the homomorphic capacity is just slightly bigger than the decryption complexity.

We start by setting some notations. Fix some homomorphic encryption scheme $\mathcal{E} = (\mathsf{KeyGen}, \mathsf{Encrypt}, \mathsf{Decrypt}, \mathsf{Evaluate})$ and a class $\mathcal{C} = \{\mathcal{C}_\tau\}$ of circuits with one output bit. Throughout this section we assume that all ciphertexts for parameters (λ, τ) have the same length (and hence the decryption procedure can be described by a single circuit).

- For $\lambda, \tau \in \mathbb{N}$, let $\mathcal{CT}_\mathcal{E}(\lambda, \tau)$ denote the set of all the fresh and evaluated ciphertexts that can result from evaluating circuits in $\mathcal{C}_\tau$:

$$\mathcal{CT}_\mathcal{E}(\lambda, \tau) \stackrel{def}{=} \left\{ \mathsf{Encrypt}(\mathsf{pk}, b) : (\mathsf{pk}, \mathsf{sk}) \in \mathsf{KeyGen}(1^\lambda, 1^\tau), \ b \in \{0, 1\} \right\}$$
$$\cup \left\{ \mathsf{Evaluate}(\mathsf{pk}, \Pi, \mathbf{c}) : \begin{array}{l} (\mathsf{pk}, \mathsf{sk}) \in \mathsf{KeyGen}(1^\lambda, 1^\tau), \\ \Pi \in \mathcal{C}_\tau, \ \mathbf{b} \in \{0, 1\}^{\mathsf{inpLen}(\Pi)}, \\ \mathbf{c} \in \mathsf{Encrypt}(\mathsf{pk}, \mathbf{b}) \end{array} \right\}.$$

- Consider the decryption procedure for parameters λ, τ, and for any ciphertext $c \in \mathcal{CT}_\mathcal{E}(\lambda, \tau)$ denote by $D_c(\mathsf{sk}) \stackrel{def}{=} \mathsf{Decrypt}(\mathsf{sk}, c)$ the decryption circuit with c hardwired in. For any two ciphertexts $c_1, c_2 \in \mathcal{C}_\mathcal{E}(\lambda, \tau)$ let the *augmented decryption circuit* for these two ciphertexts be

$$D^*_{c_1, c_2}(\mathsf{sk}) \stackrel{def}{=} NAND(D_{c_1}(\mathsf{sk}), D_{c_2}(\mathsf{sk})).$$

Definition 5.4.1 (Bootstrappable encryption). *A homomorphic encryption scheme* $\mathcal{E} = (\mathsf{KeyGen}, \mathsf{Encrypt}, \mathsf{Decrypt}, \mathsf{Evaluate})$ *is bootstrappable if its homomorphic capacity includes all the augmented decryption circuits. Specifically, there exists an (efficiently computable) polynomially bounded function* $\tau(\cdot)$ *such that, for every* $\lambda \in \mathbb{N}$ *and any* $c_1, c_2 \in \mathcal{CT}_\mathcal{E}(\lambda, \tau(\lambda))$, *we have* $D^*_{c_1, c_2} \in \mathcal{C}_{\tau(\lambda)}$.

Theorem 5.4.2 (Bootstrapping [47]). *Any bootstrappable homomorphic encryption scheme can be transformed into a compact leveled homomorphic encryption scheme.*

Proof: Let $\mathcal{E}$ = (KeyGen, Encrypt, Decrypt, Evaluate) be a bootstrappable homomorphic encryption scheme; we describe how to transform it into a compact leveled scheme $\mathcal{E}'$ = (KeyGen', Encrypt', Decrypt', Evaluate').

- KeyGen'$(1^\lambda, 1^d)$. Let $\tau = \tau(\lambda)$ (which is unrelated to the input parameter d). For $i = 0, 1, \ldots, d$ run the underlying key generation to get $(\mathsf{sk}_i, \mathsf{pk}_i) \leftarrow$ KeyGen$(1^\lambda, 1^\tau)$, and for $i < d$ encrypt all the bits of the i-th secret key under the $i + 1$-st public key, $\mathbf{c}_i^* \leftarrow$ Encrypt$(\mathsf{pk}_{i+1}, \mathsf{sk}_i)$. The secret key of $\mathcal{E}'$ consists of all the sk_i's, and the public key consists of all the pk_i's and $\mathbf{c}_i^*$'s,

$$\mathsf{sk}' = (\mathsf{sk}_0, \ldots, \mathsf{sk}_d), \quad \mathsf{pk}' = (\mathsf{pk}_0, \mathbf{c}_1^*, \mathsf{pk}_1, \mathbf{c}_2^*, \ldots, \mathbf{c}_{d-1}^*, \mathsf{pk}_d).$$

- Encrypt'$(\mathsf{pk}', \mathbf{b})$. Encryption uses the first underlying public key, setting $c \leftarrow$ Encrypt(pk_0, b) and outputting $(0, c)$ (with the tag 0 signifying that this is a fresh ciphertext).

- Evaluate'$(\mathsf{pk}', \Pi, \mathbf{c})$. We assume w.l.o.g. that Π is made of NAND gates and is *leveled*; i.e., the two inputs to any gate at level i come from gates at level $i - 1$. The Evaluate' procedure goes over the circuit in topological order from inputs to outputs; for every gate at level i with inputs $(i - 1, c_1)$ and $(i - 1, c_2)$, compute the description of the circuit $D_{c_1,c_2}(\cdot)$. Then use the underlying evaluation procedure to set $c' \leftarrow$ Evaluate$(\mathsf{pk}_i, D_{c_1,c_2}, \mathbf{c}_{i-1}^*)$ and use (i, c') as the output ciphertext of this gate. The Evaluate' procedure outputs the ciphertexts at the output gate of Π.

- Decrypt'(sk', c'). On $c' = (i, c)$, use the i-th secret key with the underlying decryption procedure to output $b \leftarrow$ Decrypt(sk_i, c).

Correctness is shown by induction over Π; the fresh ciphertexts $\mathbf{c}_i^*$ are correct (relative to secret key sk_0) because the underlying scheme is correct for fresh ciphertexts, and similarly the ciphertexts encrypting the inputs to Π (relative to sk_0).

Consider now any gate at level i in Π, and assume by induction that the two ciphertexts at the input satisfy $c_1, c_2 \in \mathcal{CT}_\mathcal{E}(\lambda, \tau)$, and that both these ciphertexts are correct. Namely setting $pt_j \leftarrow$ Decrypt(sk_{i-1}, c_j) (for $j = 1, 2$), b_1, b_2 are indeed the input bits to this gate when Π is evaluated on $\mathbf{b}$.

Let $c' \leftarrow$ Evaluate$(\mathsf{pk}_i, D_{c_1,c_2}^*, \mathbf{c}_{i-1}^*)$. Since $c_1, c_2 \in \mathcal{CT}_\mathcal{E}(\lambda, \tau)$ then $D_{c_1,c_2}^* \in \mathcal{C}_\tau$ (since $\mathcal{E}$ is bootstrappable). As $\mathbf{c}_i^*$ is a fresh encryption of sk_{i-1} under pk_i, then by definition also $c' \in \mathcal{CT}_\mathcal{E}(\lambda, \tau)$, and moreover by correctness of $\mathcal{E}$ we have

$$\text{Decrypt}(\mathsf{sk}_i, c') = D_{c_1,c_2}^*(\mathsf{sk}_{i-1}) = NAND(D_{c_1}(\mathsf{sk}_{i-1}), D_{c_2}(\mathsf{sk}_{i-1})) = NAND(b_1, b_2),$$

as needed. This completes the proof of correctness.

To see that $\mathcal{E}'$ is semantically secure we consider a sequence of hybrid experiments: For $k = 0, 1, \ldots, d$, let $\mathcal{H}_k$ be an experiment that proceeds just like the semantic security experiment of $\mathcal{E}'$ except for key generation: In $\mathcal{H}_k$, we use $\mathbf{c}_i^* \leftarrow$ Encrypt$(\mathsf{pk}_{i+1}, \mathsf{sk}_i)$ as in the scheme for $i = 0, \ldots, k-1$, but for $i = k, \ldots, d-1$ we encrypt the all-zero string instead, setting $\mathbf{c}_i^* \leftarrow$ Encrypt$(\mathsf{pk}_{i+1}, \mathbf{0})$.

We observe that $\mathcal{H}_d$ is the actual semantic security experiment, for which we need to prove that the advantage of the adversary is negligible in λ. For all k the only difference between $\mathcal{H}_k$ and $\mathcal{H}_{k-1}$ is in some ciphertexts that are encrypted under pk_k, and the corresponding sk_k is never used anywhere in the experiment (in particular it is not encrypted under pk_{k+1}), then by semantic security of the underlying $\mathcal{E}$ we know that the adversary's advantage in $\mathcal{H}_{k-1}$ is close to that of $\mathcal{H}_k$ up to a negligible difference. Taken together, this means that the advantage in $\mathcal{H}_0$ is close to that of $\mathcal{H}_d$ up to a negligible difference. But since sk_0 is not used anywhere in $\mathcal{H}_0$, then by semantic security of the underlying $\mathcal{E}$ the adversary in $\mathcal{H}_0$ only has advantage negligible in λ. We conclude that also in $\mathcal{H}_d$ the adversary only has negligible advantage, as needed. ∎

Below we sometimes refers to homomorphic evaluation of decryption as the *recryption* procedure.

Remark 5.4.3. *In many homomorphic encryption schemes, the* Decrypt *procedure can be partitioned into a public post-evaluation processing phase that depends only on the public key, followed by the "actual decryption" that uses the secret key. We note that in this case the circuits D_c and $D^*_{c_1,c_2}$ can be thought of as having the postprocessed ciphertext hardwired and consisting of only the "actual decryption" phase. Alternatively we could think of the postprocessing phase as belonging to the* Evaluate *procedure.*

Also, the secret key can be preprocessed, independently of the ciphertext to be decrypted, in order to decrease the complexity of the "actual encryption"; this preprocessing can be thought of as part of KeyGen.

5.4.1.1 Fully Homomorphic Encryption

The above transformation yields a compact scheme, but not a fully homomorphic one, since we need a new secret/public key-pair for every level in Π. A natural variant of this transformation uses a single pair, and includes in the public key for $\mathcal{E}'$ also an encryption of the secret key of $\mathcal{E}$ under its own public key. It is clear that correctness still holds, but the security of the result can no longer be reduced to just semantic security of the underlying scheme $\mathcal{E}$. Rather, we now need to assume that $\mathcal{E}$ enjoys also *circular security*. Circular security can be defined in different ways; for our purposes we only need a weak version (taken from [23]) that requires semantic security to hold even given Encrypt(pk, sk).

Definition 5.4.4 (Weak circular security [23]). *Let $\mathcal{E}$ = (KeyGen, Encrypt, Decrypt) be an encryption scheme (homomorphic or not), and let A be an adversary. The (weak) circular-security advantage of A w.r.t. $\mathcal{E}$ is defined as*

$$CircAdv_A^{\mathcal{E}}(\lambda) \stackrel{def}{=} \left| \Pr\left[A(\mathsf{pk}, \mathbf{c}^*, c) = 1 : \begin{array}{l} 1^\tau \leftarrow A(1^\lambda),\ (\mathsf{sk}, \mathsf{pk}) \leftarrow \mathsf{KeyGen}(1^\lambda, 1^\tau), \\ \mathbf{c}^* \leftarrow \mathsf{Encrypt}(\mathsf{pk}, \mathsf{sk}), c \leftarrow \mathsf{Encrypt}(\mathsf{pk}, 1) \end{array} \right] \right.$$
$$\left. - \Pr\left[A(\mathsf{pk}, \mathbf{c}^*, c) = 1 : \begin{array}{l} 1^\tau \leftarrow A(1^\lambda),\ (\mathsf{sk}, \mathsf{pk}) \leftarrow \mathsf{KeyGen}(1^\lambda, 1^\tau), \\ \mathbf{c}^* \leftarrow \mathsf{Encrypt}(\mathsf{pk}, \mathsf{sk}), c \leftarrow \mathsf{Encrypt}(\mathsf{pk}, 0) \end{array} \right] \right|.$$

$\mathcal{E}$ *is weakly circular secure if, for every PPT adversary A, the advantage $CircAdv_A^{\mathcal{E}}(\lambda)$ is negligible in λ.*

Theorem 5.4.5. *Any weakly circular-secure bootstrappable homomorphic encryption scheme can be transformed into a compact fully homomorphic encryption scheme.*

The proof of Theorem 5.4.5 is very similar to Theorem 5.4.2, except that security follows directly from Definition 5.4.4.

5.4.2 The GSW Scheme Is Bootstrappable

Below we show that the GSW scheme from Section 5.3 above can be made bootstrappable. To this end, we need to analyze the complexity of the decryption procedure, and establish that it is within the homomorphic capacity of the scheme.

5.4.2.1 Decryption Complexity

Recall that the decryption formula for the GSW scheme is

$$\text{Decrypt}(\mathbf{s}, \mathbf{C}) = \begin{cases} 0 & \text{if } |[\mathbf{s} \times \mathbf{C} \times \mathbf{w}^T]_q| < q/4 \\ 1 & \text{otherwise} \end{cases},$$

where $\mathbf{w}$ is some fixed vector that does not depend on the secret key. We think of the multiplication by $\mathbf{w}$ as a post-evaluation processing step (as mentioned in Remark 5.4.3), computing the vector $\mathbf{u} := [\mathbf{C} \times \mathbf{w}]_q$. The vector $\mathbf{u}$ is a Regev ciphertext (cf. Section 5.3.1.2) relative to the secret key $\mathbf{s}$, and the actual decryption consists of computing the integer inner product $z := \langle \mathbf{s}, \mathbf{u} \rangle$ and checking if $|[z]_q| < q/4$. It is well known that computing modular inner product is in $NC1$ (e.g., [63]). Hence, the actual decryption can be done using a circuit of depth logarithmic in the bitsize of $\mathbf{s}$ (which is $n \log q$), namely in depth $\Theta(\log n + \log \log q)$. Below we illustrate one such circuit. Denoting $k = \lceil z/q \rfloor$ (so $[z]_q = z - kq$), we observe that

$$[z]_{q/2} = \begin{cases} [z]_q & = z - 2k \cdot (q/2) & \text{if } |[z_q]| < q/4, \\ [z]_q \pm (q/2) = z - (2k \pm 1) \cdot (q/2) & \text{if } |[z_q]| > q/4. \end{cases}$$

Since $[z]_{q/2} = z - \lceil z/(q/2) \rfloor \cdot (q/2)$, it follows that comparing $|[z]_q|$ with $q/4$ can be done by checking if $\lceil z/(q/2) \rfloor$ is even or odd, namely by computing the bit $\lceil z/(q/2) \rfloor \bmod 2$.

To slightly simplify things, when setting the parameters for any depth-d homomorphism, we make the modulus q one bit larger than it strictly needs to be, thus ensuring that the eventual noise is bounded below $q/8$ (rather than $q/4$). This means that we have the guarantee that $|[z]_q|$ is either smaller than $q/8$ or larger than $3q/8$, so we can afford some error in the calculations without affecting the result of comparing with $q/4$. In particular, we have the guarantee that the value $z/(q/2)$ is within $1/4$ of an integer, so an error of less than $1/4$ in computing that value will not affect the way that it is rounded.

Let $\hat{q}$ be an approximation of the rational number $1/2q$ up to $t = 3 + \lceil \log n + 2 \log q \rceil$ bits of precision. Since $|\hat{q} - (1/2q)| < 2^{-t}$ and $|z| < nq^2$, then $|z\hat{q} - (z/2q)| < nq^2 \cdot 2^{-t} <$

$1/8$, and therefore $\lceil z/(q/2) \rfloor = \lceil z\hat{q} \rfloor$. Our decryption circuit is therefore constructed as follows:

- Still in the post-evaluation processing phase, after setting $\mathbf{u} = \lceil [\mathbf{Cw}]_q$, we compute the rational vector $\mathbf{r} = [\hat{q} \cdot \mathbf{u}]_2$, whose entries have t bits of precision.
- The actual decryption consists of computing the inner product $\langle \mathbf{s}, \mathbf{r} \rangle$ (over the rationals) and outputting the first bit to the left of the binary point (i.e., the most-significant bit of $[\langle \mathbf{s}, \mathbf{r} \rangle]_2$).

Each of the multiplications involved in the inner product $\langle \mathbf{s}, \mathbf{r} \rangle$ requires adding $\log q$ numbers, each of up to t bits. Summing up n such products, we therefore need to add $n \log q$ numbers, each of up to t bits.

To add these numbers, we use the 3-for-2 addition method (cf. [63]),[6] where the sum of three ℓ-bit numbers can be replaced by the sum of two numbers of up to $\ell + 1$ bits: Let x, y, z be three ℓ-bit numbers and consider the i-th bit position. The sum $x_i + y_i + z_i < 3$ can be represented by only two bits: the lower bit is the XOR of the three and the upper bit is their majority; i.e., we replace the three numbers x, y, z by the two numbers u, v, such that $u_i = XOR(x_i, y_i, z_i)$ and $v_{i+1} = MAJ(x_i, y_i, z_i)$.

Repeating this process recursively, after $\Theta(\log(n \log q))$ levels, we are left with only two t-bit numbers (since we can ignore all but the first bit to the left of the binary point). Adding these last two numbers can be done in logarithmic depth in the bit length t, using carry look-ahead. Here we are only interested in the carry bit into the first position to the right of the binary point, which can be expressed as $r := \bigvee_{i=0}^{t-1} \left(x_i \wedge y_i \bigwedge_{j=i+1}^{t-1} (x_j \vee y_j) \right)$. This expression has constant depth and fan-in $\Theta(t^2)$, so it can be computed by a fan-in-2 circuit of depth $\Theta(\log t)$. Hence we get total depth of $d = \Theta(\log t + \log(n \log q)) = \Theta(\log n + \log \log q)$.

Parameters for bootstrappable homomorphic encryption. To obtain a bootstrappable construction we need to set the parameters so that the complexity of (augmented) decryption stays within the homomorphic capacity of the scheme. By the analysis above, this means that we need to support evaluation of circuits of depth $\tau \le \rho(\log n + \log \log q)$ for some constant ρ.

Recall from Section 5.3.2 that to support depth-τ homomorphism we need $q \ge (2n \log q)^{\tau+3}$, and substituting the value τ from above we get the sufficient condition $q \ge (n \log q)^{\rho'(\log n + \log \log q)}$ for some other constant $\rho' < 2\rho$. For $n/\log n > 4\rho'$, we can meet all the conditions with the following setting:

- $n = \lambda$,
- $q = \lceil n^{4\rho' \log n} \rceil = 2^{\Theta(\log^2 n)}$,
- $m = 1 + \lceil 2n(2 + \log q) \rceil = \Theta(n \log^2 n)$, and
- $\alpha = n/q = 2^{-\Theta(\log^2 n)}$.

These parameters yield a bootstrappable scheme under the quasipolynomial DLWE assumption, and by Theorem 5.4.2 also a compact leveled scheme under the same

---

[6] As described in Remark 5.4.7 below, we can use modulus-switching and key-switching techniques to decrease the vector dimension and the size of q prior to decryption. Doing so we could get a bootstrappable scheme even when using less efficient addition methods.

assumption. If we also assume circular security, then using Theorem 5.4.5 we get a compact fully homomorphic scheme.

Theorem 5.4.6. *Under the DLWE$[n, m, q, \alpha]$ hardness assumption with $q = 2^{polylog(n)}$, $\alpha = 2^{-polylog(n)}$, and $m = n \cdot polylog(n)$, there exists a semantically secure compact leveled homomorphic encryption scheme. The public-key size needed for evaluating level-d circuits is linear in d, but the ciphertext size and the complexity of evaluating each gate is only poly(λ), independent of d.*

Further assuming circular security of the basic GSW scheme with these parameters, there exists a semantically secure compact fully homomorphic encryption scheme.

Remark 5.4.7. *The parameters above can be improved slightly using the modulus-switching and key-switching tricks from Section 5.3.1.4. To use modulus-switching we choose the secret key from the error distribution χ^n rather than uniformly at random from $\mathbb{Z}_q^n$, and use the result of Applebaum et al. [4] to argue that security is unaffected. We also include a key-switching gadget $\mathbf{A}'_{s_n:s^*}$ in the public key, where $\mathbf{s}^* \in \mathbb{Z}_q^{n'}$ with $n' \ll n$.*

Then during post-evaluation processing we switch the Regev ciphertext $\mathbf{u}$ relative to $\mathbf{s}_n$ to a lower-dimension ciphertext relative to $\mathbf{s}^*$, and then modulus-switch it to a smaller modulus $q' \ll q$. Then decryption needs to implement $[\langle \mathbf{s}^*, \mathbf{u}^* \rangle]_{q'} \overset{?}{<} q'/4$, which has lower complexity than the previous test $[\langle \mathbf{s}, \mathbf{u} \rangle]_q \overset{?}{<} q/4$.

Used judiciously, this technique lets us set $q' = poly(n)$ (whereas $q = quasipoly(n)$). This yields significant improvement in the recryption complexity, but by itself does not allow us to relax the necessary hardness assumption from quasipolynomial to polynomial DLWE. The reason is that, although decryption is evaluated relative to the smaller q', the public encryption key and fresh ciphertexts must still use the larger q. Relaxing the hardness assumption requires other techniques, as described next.

5.4.3 Homomorphic Encryption Under Polynomial DLWE

Is it possible to weaken the quasipolynomial DLWE assumption from above and get FHE under polynomial DLWE? At first glance, the answer seems to be negative: recryption seems to require circuit depth of at least $\log n$, and each level increases the noise by at least some small polynomial factor, so the accumulated noise (and hence the size of the modulus q and the resulting LWE approximation factor) is at least $poly(n)^{\log n}$.

Brakerski and Vaikuntanathan, however, observed in [20] that the asymmetric noise growth from Equations 5.1 and 5.4 provides a way out. Recall that, for two ciphertext matrices $\mathbf{C}_1, \mathbf{C}_2$ with associated plaintext bits b_1, b_2 and noise vectors η_1, η_2, the noise vector when multiplying $\mathbf{C}_1 \times G^{-1}(\mathbf{C}_2)$ has the form $\eta' = b_1 \cdot \eta 2 + \eta_1 \times G^{-1}(\mathbf{C}_2)$, so η_1 has much greater influence on η' than η_2. If we can ensure that we always keep η_1 small, even if η_2 is much bigger, then we can slow down the noise growth considerably.

As an illustrating example, consider multiplying a sequence of n ciphertexts, $\mathbf{C}_i$, $i = 1, \ldots n$, with associated plaintext bits b_i and noise vectors $\boldsymbol{\eta}_i$ of similar magnitude (say $\|\boldsymbol{\eta}_i\|_\infty \le n$ for all i). This n-wise product can be implemented in a balanced binary tree, or using left- or right-associative trees (or any form in between), and these different strategies exhibit very different noise behavior. The balanced strategy is

$$\mathbf{C}_{\text{bal}} = \mathbf{C}_1 \times G^{-1}(\mathbf{C}_2) \times G^{-1}(\mathbf{C}_3 \times G^{-1}(\mathbf{C}_4))$$
$$\times G^{-1}(\mathbf{C}_5 \times G^{-1}(\mathbf{C}_6) \times G^{-1}(\mathbf{C}_7 \times G^{-1}(\mathbf{C}_8))) \cdots$$

and its noise behavior is exactly what we analyzed above: We have a $\log(n)$-high binary tree of multiplications, and the noise magnitude at level i up the tree is roughly $m^i \cdot n$. Hence, the resulting matrix $\mathbf{C}_{bal}$ has a quasipolynomial noise magnitude of about $m^{\log n}$. The left-associative strategy is

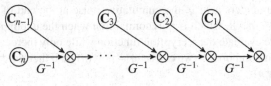

$$\mathbf{C}_{\text{left}} = (\cdots((\mathbf{C}_1 \times G^{-1}(\mathbf{C}_2)) \times G^{-1}(\mathbf{C}_3)) \cdots) \times G^{-1}(\mathbf{C}_n),$$

and its noise is much bigger. Specifically, let us denote by $\mathbf{C}_i^*, b_i^*, \boldsymbol{\eta}_i^*$ the ciphertext, plaintext, and noise after multiplying the leftmost i matrices. After the multiplication $\mathbf{C}_i^* \times G^{-1}(C_{i+1})$, the noise vector is $\boldsymbol{\eta}_{i+1}^* = b_i^* \boldsymbol{\eta}_{i+1} + \boldsymbol{\eta}_i^* G^{-1}(\mathbf{C}_i)$, which has magnitude of roughly $\|\boldsymbol{\eta}_{i+1}^*\|_\infty \approx \|\boldsymbol{\eta}_{i+1}\|_\infty + m \cdot \|\boldsymbol{\eta}_i^*\|_\infty \approx (1 + m + \cdots + m^i) \cdot n$. Hence, the overall noise magnitude is roughly $m^n \cdot n$, which is fully exponential in n.

On the other hand, the right-associative strategy is

$$\mathbf{C}_{\text{rght}} = \mathbf{C}_1 \times G^{-1}(\mathbf{C}_2 \times G^{-1}(\cdots \mathbf{C}_{n-1} \times G^{-1}(\mathbf{C}_n) \cdots)),$$

and this strategy has a much smaller noise than even the balanced one. Again let us denote by $\mathbf{C}_i^*, b_i^*, \boldsymbol{\eta}_i^*$ the ciphertext, plaintext, and noise after multiplying the matrices i through n. After incorporating also the $i - 1$-st matrix, $\mathbf{C}_{i-1} \times G^{-1}(C_i^*)$, the noise vector is $\boldsymbol{\eta}_{i-1}^* = b_i \boldsymbol{\eta}_i^* + \boldsymbol{\eta}_{i-1} G^{-1}(\mathbf{C}_i^*)$, which has magnitude at most $\|\boldsymbol{\eta}_{i-1}^*\|_\infty \le \|\boldsymbol{\eta}_i^*\|_\infty + m \cdot \|\boldsymbol{\eta}_{i-1}\|_\infty \le n(m + m + \ldots + m)$. Hence, the overall noise magnitude is at most mn^2, which is only polynomial in n.

"Asymmetric circuits" and branching programs. To take advantage of the noise asymmetry, we need to design "asymmetric circuits" in which all the multiplications have the form $\mathbf{C} \times G^{-1}(\mathbf{C}^*)$, where $\mathbf{C}_1$ is a fresh encryption of an input bit (and hence has small noise) while $\mathbf{C}^*$ can be an evaluated ciphertext. One approach that naturally yields such circuits uses Barrington's theorem [7] and permutation branching programs.

Definition 5.4.8 (Permutation branching programs). *A width-w, length-ℓ permutation branching-program over inputs in $\{0, 1\}^n$ consists of a sequence of ℓ tuples, $BP = ((\text{inpLen}(i), \mathbf{A}_{i,0}, , \mathbf{A}_{i,1}) : i = 1 \ldots, \ell)$ where the $\mathbf{A}_{i,b}$'s are permutation matrices in $\{0, 1\}^{w \times w}$, and $\text{inpLen} : [\ell] \to [n]$ specifies the order in which input bits are examined (i.e., step i in the branching program examines the input bit $x_{\text{inpLen}(i)}$). The function computed by this branching program is*

$$f_{BP}(x) \overset{def}{=} (\prod_{i=1}^{\ell} A_{i, x_{\text{inpLen}(i)}})[1, 1].$$

In words, $f_{BP}(x) = 1$ if composing all the permutations chosen by the bits of x in the different steps yields a permutation that maps 1 to itself, and otherwise $f_{BP}(x) = 0$.

Theorem 5.4.9 (Barrington's Theorem [7]). *If the function $f : \{0, 1\}^n \to \{0, 1\}$ can be computed by a depth-d fan-in-2 binary circuit, then f can also be computed by a width-5, length-4^d permutation branching program.*

Barrington's theorem directly yields a polynomial-size asymmetric circuit for computing any $NC1$ circuit: We keep an "evaluated state" consisting of the current cumulative product $\prod_{i=j+1}^{\ell} A_{i, x_{\text{inpLen}(i)}}$, then multiply this state on the left by the "fresh matrix" $\mathbf{A}'_j = x_k \mathbf{A}_{j,1} + (1 - x_k)\mathbf{A}_{j,0}$, with $k = \text{inpLen}(j)$. Since the $\mathbf{A}_{i,b}$'s are all permutation matrices then all the intermediate values in this computation are always in $\{0, 1\}$ (and moreover every sum computed during this computation always has exactly one term equaling 1 and all other terms equaling 0).

When evaluating this circuit on encrypted data, we get an encryption of $\mathbf{A}'_j$ that depends linearly on the fresh encryption of $x_{\text{inpLen}(j)}$, and we multiply it (on the left) by the evaluated encryption of the cumulative product so far. When using the GSW scheme with parameters n, m, q, the cumulative noise at the end of the calculation is bounded by $4^d \cdot m \cdot n$, which is polynomial in n when the depth d is logarithmic. We can therefore evaluate the recryption function while only increasing the noise to magnitude polynomial in n, so we can set $q = \text{poly}(n)$ (and therefore $\alpha = 1/\text{poly}(n)$) and $m = O(n \log n)$.

Theorem 5.4.10. *Under the DLWE$[n, m, q, \alpha]$ hardness assumption with $q = \text{poly}(n)$, $\alpha = 1/\text{poly}(n)$, and $m = O(n \log n)$, there exists a semantically secure compact leveled homomorphic encryption scheme. The public-key size needed for evaluating level-d circuits is linear in d, but the complexity of evaluating each gate is only $\text{poly}(\lambda)$, independent of d.*

Further assuming circular security of the basic GSW scheme with these parameters, there exists a semantically secure compact fully homomorphic encryption scheme.

Remark 5.4.11. *The key- and modulus-switching tricks from Remark 5.4.7 can be used here too, to reduce both the recryption complexity and the constant in the exponent of the polynomial-DLWE assumption. Brakerski and Vaikuntanathan describe in [20] how iterated application of these two tricks can be used to reduce the hardness assumption to DLWE with $\alpha = 1/n^{1/2+\epsilon}$ for any constant $\epsilon > 0$, which nearly* matches the best setting $\alpha = 1/\tilde{O}(\sqrt{n})$ for any known lattice-based public-key encryption.

The concrete efficiency of recryption was significantly improved by Alperin-Sheriff and Peikert [3], while still relying on the same DLWE with $\alpha = 1/n^{1/2+\epsilon}$. See Section 5.5.1 for more discussion of efficiency considerations.

5.4.4 Realizing Strong Homomorphism

The fully homomorphic scheme from above may still fail to provide strong homomorphism or even circuit privacy. Following Gentry [47], we can achieve statistical strong homomorphism using a Refresh procedure based on noise-flooding. A naive use of this technique would require increasing the parameters and using a stronger DLWE variant, but Ducas and Stehlé showed in [31] that iterated use of Refresh can avoid these limitations.

For the rest of this section, it will be convenient to assume that, the recryption procedure of the fully homomorphic encryption returns not the GSW ciphertext matrix $\mathbf{C}$ but rather the post-processed "Regev ciphertext" $\mathbf{u} = [\mathbf{Cw}]_q$, which is decrypted by computing $z := [\langle \mathbf{s}, \mathbf{u} \rangle]_q$ and comparing $|z|$ with $q/4$. (The distinction between these two forms of ciphertexts is only a matter of convenience, as we can always get back a GSW ciphertext by running the recryption procedure again without post-processing.) We denote running the recryption process on the post-processed $\mathbf{u}$ and returning the post-processed result by $\mathbf{u}' \leftarrow \mathsf{Recrypt}_{\mathsf{pk}}(\mathbf{u})$.

Rerandomizing a ciphertext. For a vector $\mathbf{s} \in \mathbb{Z}_q^n$, denote the linear subspace orthogonal to $\mathbf{s}$ by

$$L_{\mathbf{s}}^{\perp} \stackrel{def}{=} \{\mathbf{v} \in \mathbb{Z}_q : \langle \mathbf{s}, \mathbf{v} \rangle = 0 \pmod{q}\}.$$

Also denote the scaled unit vector by $\mathbf{w} \stackrel{def}{=} \lfloor q/2 \rfloor \cdot (0, \ldots, 0, -1)$, and the "radius-$\rho$ 1-dimensional ball" by

$$\mathcal{B}_\rho \stackrel{def}{=} \{x \cdot (0, \ldots, 0, 1) : x \in \mathbb{Z}, |x| \le \rho\}.$$

An easy-to-verify property that we use below is that, for $\rho', \rho \in \mathbb{N}$ and any $\mathbf{u} \in \mathcal{B}_{\rho'}$, the statistical distance between the uniform distributions on $\mathcal{B}_\rho$ and on $\mathbf{u} + \mathcal{B}_\rho$ is bounded by $\rho'/(2\rho + 1)$.

Since the last entry in a GSW secret key $\mathbf{s}$ is $s_n = -1$, then for $\rho < \lfloor q/4 \rfloor$ any vector $\mathbf{u} \in L_{\mathbf{s}}^{\perp} + \mathcal{B}_\rho$ is decrypted to zero and any vector $\mathbf{u} \in L_{\mathbf{s}}^{\perp} + \mathcal{B}_\rho + \mathbf{w}$ is decrypted to one.

Let $\mathbf{u}$ be some fixed vector in either $L_{\mathbf{s}}^{\perp} + \mathcal{B}_{\rho'}$ or $L_{\mathbf{s}}^{\perp} + \mathcal{B}_{\rho'} + \mathbf{w}$. We rerandomize $\mathbf{u}$ by adding to it a random element in $L_{\mathbf{s}}^{\perp} + \mathcal{B}_\rho$ for some $\rho > \rho'$ such that $\rho + \rho' < \lfloor q/4 \rfloor$. The resulting vector $\mathbf{u}'$ still decrypts to the same bit as $\mathbf{u}$, and the statistical distance between the distribution of $\mathbf{u}'$ and the uniform distribution over $L_{\mathbf{s}}^{\perp} + \mathcal{B}_\rho$ (or over $L_{\mathbf{s}}^{\perp} + \mathcal{B}_\rho + \mathbf{w}$) is bounded by $\rho'/(2\rho + 1)$. If $\rho \gg \rho'$ then the distribution of $\mathbf{u}'$ is almost independent of the original vector $\mathbf{u}$, except for the plaintext bit that it decrypts to. To perform rerandomization, it is therefore sufficient to be able to choose a nearly uniform vector in $L_{\mathbf{s}}^{\perp} + \mathcal{B}_{\rho}$. It turns out that the public-key matrix $\mathbf{A}$ is all we need for that purpose.

Lemma 5.4.12. *For any fixed vector* $\mathbf{s} \in \mathbb{Z}_q^n$ *with* $s_n = -1$, *denote by* $\mathcal{D}_{\mathbf{s}}$ *the distribution over public keys corresponding to the secret key* $\mathbf{s}$; *namely choosing the top* $n - 1$ *rows at random* $\mathbf{A}' \leftarrow \mathbb{Z}_q^{(n-1) \times m}$ *and the last row as* $\mathbf{s}'\mathbf{A}' + \boldsymbol{\eta}$, *where* $\mathbf{s}'$ *are the first* $n - 1$ *entries in* $\mathbf{s}$ *and* $\boldsymbol{\eta} \leftarrow \chi^m$.

Then with probability at least $1 - 2^{-n}$ *over the choice of* $\mathbf{A} \leftarrow \mathcal{D}_{\mathbf{s}}$ *and for all* $\rho \in \mathbb{N}$, *the distribution*

$$\mathcal{R}_{\mathbf{A},\rho} \stackrel{def}{=} \{\mathbf{A}\mathbf{r} + \mathbf{v} \; : \; \mathbf{r} \leftarrow \{0,1\}^m, \; \mathbf{v} \leftarrow \mathcal{B}_{\rho}\}$$

is close to the uniform distribution over $L_{\mathbf{s}}^{\perp} + \mathcal{B}_{\rho}$, *up to statistical distance at most* $\frac{nm}{2\rho+1} + 2^{-n}$.

Proof: Let $\mathbf{s}'$ be the first $n - 1$ entries of $\mathbf{s}$, $\mathbf{A}'$ be the first $n - 1$ rows of $\mathbf{A}$, and $\tilde{\mathbf{A}}$ be the matrix $\mathbf{A}$ with the last row replaced by $\mathbf{s}'\mathbf{A}'$ (i.e., the last row of $\mathbf{A}$ with the error $\boldsymbol{\eta}$ removed). Then $\mathbf{s}\tilde{\mathbf{A}} = 0$, and moreover the columns of $\tilde{\mathbf{A}} \in \mathbb{Z}_q^{n \times m}$ are uniform and independent in $L_{\mathbf{s}}^{\perp}$. By Lemma 5.2.17, with probability $1 - 2^{-n}$ over $\tilde{\mathbf{A}}$, the distribution of $[\tilde{\mathbf{A}}\mathbf{r}]_q$ conditioned on $\tilde{\mathbf{A}}$ is 2^{-n} away from uniform over $L_{\mathbf{s}}^{\perp}$.

Next observe that $\mathbf{A}\mathbf{r} = \tilde{\mathbf{A}}\mathbf{r} + \boldsymbol{\delta}$, where $\boldsymbol{\delta} = \langle \boldsymbol{\eta}, \mathbf{r} \rangle \cdot (0, \ldots, 0, 1)^t \in \mathcal{B}_{nm}$. We therefore have $\mathbf{A}\mathbf{r} + \mathbf{v} = \tilde{\mathbf{A}}\mathbf{r} + \boldsymbol{\delta} + \mathbf{v}$, where $\tilde{\mathbf{A}}\mathbf{r}$ is 2^{-n}-close to uniform over $L_{\mathbf{s}}^{\perp}$, and regardless of the value of $\boldsymbol{\delta}$ we have that $\boldsymbol{\delta} + \mathbf{v}$ is $\frac{nm}{2\rho+1}$-close to uniform over $\mathcal{B}_{\rho}$. Hence $\mathbf{A}\mathbf{r} + \mathbf{v}$ is close to uniform in $L_{\mathbf{s}}^{\perp} + \mathcal{B}_{\rho}$, up to $\frac{nm}{2\rho+1} + 2^{-n}$. ∎

Corollary 5.4.13. *Let* $\rho, \rho' \in \mathbb{N}$, *and fix the two vectors* $\mathbf{s} \in \mathbb{Z}_q^n$ *with* $s_n = -1$ *and* $\mathbf{u} \in (L_{\mathbf{s}}^{\perp} + \mathcal{B}_{\rho'}) \cup (L_{\mathbf{s}}^{\perp} + \mathcal{B}_{\rho'} + \mathbf{w})$. *Then with probability at least* $1 - 2^{-n}$ *over the choice of* $\mathbf{A} \leftarrow \mathcal{D}_{\mathbf{s}}$, *the distribution* $\mathbf{u} + \mathcal{R}_{\mathbf{A},\rho}$ *is within statistical distance* $\frac{nm+\rho'}{2\rho+1} + 2^{-n}$ *of:*

- *The uniform distribution over* $L_{\mathbf{s}}^{\perp} + \mathcal{B}_{\rho}$ *if* $\mathbf{u} \in L_{\mathbf{s}}^{\perp} + \mathcal{B}_{\rho'}'$, *or*
- *The uniform distribution over* $L_{\mathbf{s}}^{\perp} + \mathcal{B}_{\rho} + \mathbf{w}$ *if* $\mathbf{u} \in L_{\mathbf{s}}^{\perp} + \mathcal{B}_{\rho'}' + \mathbf{w}$.

Strong homomorphic encryption. To obtain strong homomorphic encryption, we begin with the fully homomorphic scheme from above but modify the parameters, making q larger by some factor β (to be determined later) than what is needed to get full homomorphism. Specifically, we make q large enough to ensure that after recryption (and post-evaluation processing) the noise is bounded by some $\rho' < q/8 - \beta$; i.e., we always get a vector $\mathbf{u} \in (L_{\mathbf{s}}^{\perp} + \mathcal{B}_{\rho'}) \cup (L_{\mathbf{s}}^{\perp} + \mathcal{B}_{\rho'} + \mathbf{w})$. We then define a refresh procedure as

$$\mathsf{Refresh}_{\mathsf{pk}}(\mathbf{u}) = [\mathsf{Recrypt}_{\mathsf{pk}}(\mathbf{u}) + \mathcal{R}_{\mathbf{A},\beta}]_q.$$

We then modify both the encryption and evaluation procedures, making them output $\mathbf{u}' \leftarrow \mathsf{Refresh}_{\mathsf{pk}}(\mathbf{u})$ rather than the vector $\mathbf{u}$ as before. By Corollary 5.4.13 the output distribution of the new Encrypt and Evaluate is close to uniform over $L_{\mathbf{s}}^{\perp} + \mathcal{B}_{\rho}$ or $L_{\mathbf{s}}^{\perp} + \mathcal{B}_{\rho} + \mathbf{w}$ (depending on the encrypted bit), where $\rho = \rho' + \beta < q/8$. Correctness is not affected since the parameters are set so that the noise after Refresh is still bounded below $q/8$.

The statistical distance from uniform is at most $\frac{nm+\rho'}{2\beta+1} + 2^{-n}$, so to get negligible distance we need $\beta > (nm + \rho') \cdot 2^{\omega(\log n)}$. This means that β (and therefore q) must be superpolynomial in n, so to get strong homomorphism in this way we need to assume hardness of superpolynomial DLWE.

Strong homomorphism from polynomial DLWE. It was observed by Ducas and Stehlé [31] that iterating Refresh can be used to go beyond superpolynomial DLWE. To show this, we use the following general lemma:

Lemma 5.4.14 (Iterated refresh [31]). *Let D be an arbitrary domain and let f : $D \to D$ be a randomized function. If for some $\delta < 1$ it holds that $SD(f(x_1), f(x_2)) < \delta$ for any $x_1, x_2 \in D$, then for every $k \in \mathbb{N}$ and $x_1, x_2 \in D$ we have $SD(f^k(x_1), f^k(x_2)) < \delta^k$.*

Proof: The proof is by induction on k. The basis $k = 0$ holds vacuously, so assume that it holds for k and we prove for $k + 1$. Let $x_1, x_2 \in D$, so by the induction hypothesis we have $SD(f^k(x_1), f^k(x_2)) < \delta^k$.

The distributions $f^k(x_1), f^k(x_2)$ can therefore be expressed as convex combinations $f^k(x_1) = (1 - \delta^k) \cdot \mathcal{D} + \delta^k \cdot \mathcal{D}'_1$ and $f^k(x_2) = (1 - \delta^k) \cdot \mathcal{D} + \delta^k \cdot \mathcal{D}'_2$ for the same $\mathcal{D}$ and different $\mathcal{D}'_i$'s. Namely for $i = 1, 2$, $y_i \leftarrow f^k(x_i)$ is obtained by choosing a bit $b \in \{0, 1\}$ with $\Pr[b = 1] = \delta^k$, then drawing $y_i \leftarrow \mathcal{D}$ if $b = 0$ and $y_i \leftarrow \mathcal{D}'_i$ if $b = 1$. It follows that

$$SD(f^{k+1}(x_1), f^{k+1}(x_2)) \le (1 - \delta^k) \cdot \underbrace{SD(f(\mathcal{D}), f(\mathcal{D}))}_{=0} + \delta^k \cdot \underbrace{SD(f(\mathcal{D}'_1), f(\mathcal{D}'_2))}_{\le \delta} \le \delta^{k+1},$$

as needed.   ∎

Applying Lemma 5.4.14 to the Refresh procedure from above, we can now set the parameters so that $\beta = 2nm \cdot \rho'$. With this setting, for every $\mathbf{u}, \mathbf{u}' \in CT$ that encrypt the same bit, we get $SD(\text{Refresh}_{\text{pk}}(\mathbf{u}_1), \text{Refresh}_{\text{pk}}(\mathbf{u}_2)) < 1/2$, so after $\omega(\log n)$ iterations we get negligible statistical distance. Since ρ' can be set to poly(n) as per Section 5.4.3 above, then we get $q = \rho' + \beta = \rho' \cdot (1 + 2nm) = \text{poly}(n)$, so we can rely on the hardness of polynomial DLWE.

Theorem 5.4.15. *Under the DLWE$[n, m, q, \alpha]$ hardness assumption with $q = poly(n)$, $\alpha = 1/poly(n)$, and $m = O(n \log n)$, in conjunction with circular security of the basic GSW scheme with these parameters, there exists a semantically secure strong fully homomorphic encryption scheme.*

5.5 Advanced Topics

In this section we briefly discuss other aspects of homomorphic encryption. We begin in Section 5.5.1 by describing the active research for devising more practical homomorphic encryption, reducing the overhead of computing on encrypted data as compared with computing on plaintext data. In Section 5.5.2, we touch on some (mostly failed) attempts at realizing homomorphic encryption by means other than lattice-based cryptography. In Section 5.5.3, we discuss carrying out computation on encrypted data using models of computation other than circuits. Finally, in Section 5.5.4, we describe uses of techniques similar to the GSW homomorphic encryption scheme to obtain other functionalities, such as multikey homomorphism, homomorphic commitment and signatures, multilinear maps, and obfuscation.

5.5.1 Faster Homomorphic Encryption

The GSW cryptosystem from above is capable of evaluating arbitrary circuits, but at a steep price: Letting the *overhead* of a homomorphic scheme be the ratio of encrypted computation complexity to unencrypted computation complexity (using a circuit model of computation), it is not hard to see that as described above this scheme has a very large polynomial overhead: Each plaintext bit is encrypted by a matrix of dimensions at least $\tilde{\Omega}(\lambda) \times \tilde{\Omega}(\lambda)$ (and entries of size polylog(λ) bits). Each NAND operation in the basic GSW scheme requires the multiplication of two such matrices, which takes $\tilde{\omega}(\lambda^{2.3})$ even using the most asymptotically efficient algorithm. (Of course, to use bootstrapping we would need to implement full homomorphic description for every gate, which would drive the overhead much higher.)

A lot of work over the last few years was devoted to improving this overhead, both asymptotically and practically. Perhaps the most significant improvement comes from working over large extension rings rather than over the integers, relying on the ring-LWE hardness assumption (RLWE) [68].[7] Working over a large ring of extension degree d allows one to reduce the degree of the matrices involved to as little as $n = \lambda/d$ while maintaining hardness, so in particular when setting $d = \lambda$ we can get $n = 1$ and $m = O(\log q) = \tilde{O}(\lambda)$. This yields ciphertexts of bit-size $O(\log^2 q) = \tilde{O}(\lambda)$, and the complexity of implementing basic NAND (without bootstrapping) is similarly reduced to $\tilde{O}(\lambda)$. Hence we get a variant of the basic weakly compact scheme with overhead quasilinear in λ.

A second major improvement comes from packing multiple plaintext bits in every ciphertext. Specifically, Smart and Vercauteren observed in [86] that, since our "scalars" now live in some polynomial ring, the Chinese remainder theorem in that ring can be used to encode many bits in each scalar, yielding multiple "plaintext slots" where additions and multiplications are applied to each slot separately. Careful choice of parameters lets one get as many as $\ell = \tilde{\Omega}(\lambda)$ such plaintext slots, making the plaintext-to-ciphertext expansion ration polylogarithmic in λ, and allowing one to compute the same function on ℓ different inputs at the price of a single computation.

We note, however, that packing many bits in each plaintext scalar is in general incompatible with the Brakerski–Vaikuntanathan method of exploiting the asymmetric noise growth: Packed scalars typically have norm polynomial in d (the extension degree of the ring), even if only 0's and 1's are packed in the slots. Since the

---

[7] Specifically we use cyclotomic rings, since they have many desirable algebraic properties.

GSW noise depends also on the plaintext size, we have to content ourselves with multiplicative growth of noise for every multiplication operation. In fact, using the packing technique yields better results for the "second-generation schemes" such as those in [17, 14, 67, 13] than for the "third-generation" GSW scheme [48].

But we can go even beyond batching. It was observed in [68, 17, 86] that the automorphisms in the polynomial ring can be used to "rotate" the contents of the plaintext slots, and Gentry et al. show in [44] how to use these "rotations" to perform efficient routing of plaintext slots between successive levels of any arbitrary circuit. This technique is then used in [44] to perform an entire computation on "packed" ciphertexts, resulting in a scheme with only poly-logarithmic overhead even when computing a single function on a single input. This can be extended to bootstrapping, yielding a fully homomorphic scheme with polylogarithmic overhead. (Further optimizations for bootstrapping were described in [43, 2, 57].)

There has also been much work devoted to practical efficiency and implementing of homomorphic encryption. For example Gentry et al. reported in [45] on an implementation of the "second-generation" Brakerski–Gentry–Vaikuntanathan scheme (BGV) and its use for evaluating "real-world circuits" such as the AES encryption/decryption circuits, and that implementation was further optimized in the HElib library of Halevi and Shoup [56], who also implemented practical bootstrapping for packed ciphertexts in a matter of minutes [57]. Also, building on techniques from [20, 3], Ducas and Micciancio implemented bootstrapping for a (non-packed) GSW-like scheme in less than a second [30].

5.5.2 Other Attempts at Realizing Homomorphic Encryption

Attempts to realize homomorphic encryption go back to the dawn of public-key cryptography, when the concept was first proposed by Rivest, Adleman, and Dertouzos [81]. Below we sketch some directions that were explored over the years, even though as of yet none of these directions have panned out.

5.5.2.1 The Hidden-Ideal Paradigm

One natural approach is to construct a scheme that uses an algebraic ring R and an ideal $I \subset R$, and relies for security on the hardness of distinguishing random elements in I from random elements in R. The plaintext space of such a scheme is the quotient ring R/I, ciphertexts are (representations of) elements in R, and homomorphic addition and multiplication are just the '+' and '×' operations in R.

This approach was implicit in many additive homomorphic schemes; it was made explicit by Fellows and Koblitz [32], who also suggested a concrete realization that they called Polly Cracker. That scheme uses the ring of multivariate polynomials over some field, $R = F[X_1, \ldots, X_n]$, and the ideal I is a set of polynomials that have common root, $p(s_1, \ldots, s_n) = 0$. Ciphertexts are polynomials $p \in R$, the root itself $\mathbf{s} = (s_1, \ldots, s_n)$ is the secret key, and decryption corresponds to evaluating $p(\mathbf{s})$.

There is a lot of freedom in choosing the concrete representation of elements and their probability distributions (note that these R, I are infinite). The challenge in designing such a scheme is to find a succinct representation that allows efficient sampling and computation of '+' and '×', but where (at least) recovering s is hard. Many attempts to find such representations has been made, so far with no success; see [66] for a survey. We note that, even though no candidate construction so far have survived cryptanalysis, there is also no reason to think that no such candidate exists.

5.5.2.2 Homomorphic Encryption from Binary Codes

Following Gentry's blueprint for constructing homomorphic encryption schemes, some attempts were made to instantiate this blueprint using binary codes as opposed to integer lattices. The hope was, that since the problem of learning-parity-with-noise (LPN) is similar in some ways to the learning-with-errors (LWE) problem, then the techniques for constructing LWE-based homomorphic encryption would extend also to LPN. The main challenge is that LPN with its notion of Hamming distance provides a very narrow range for noise manipulation. Specifically, while in LWE-based constructions we can handle noise with Euclidean norm polynomial in the dimension, when it comes to Hamming distance the noise must be strictly smaller then the dimension.

A notable attempt to port Gentry's blueprint to the LPN-based setting was made by Bogdanov and Lee [9]. They described a construction that has noticeable de-cryption error probability, which is carefully controlled via evaluation of majority gates in conjunction with the linear decryption function. That construction was later broken by Gauthier et al. [36], and moreover Brakerski proved in [15] that the ap-proach from [9] cannot work as-is. Specifically, he proved that a scheme which is capable of computing majority cannot have a learnable decryption function (such as a linear function), even if it has a significant decryption error probability. Al-though Brakerski's result does not rule out basing homomorphic encryption on LPN, it does say that the decryption procedure of that scheme must be at least "some-what complicated", rather than the simple inner product of some LPN-based (non-homomorphic) schemes such as [1].

5.5.2.3 Homomorphic Encryption from Group Theory

An alternative approach, using concepts from group theory, was proposed by Nuida in [73]: For a group G (written multiplicatively), a subgroup $H \subset G$ is *normal* in G if $g^{-1}hg \in H$ for any $h \in H$ and $g \in G$. A simple scheme with plaintext space $\{0, 1\}$ that uses such G, H represents 0 by a random $h \in H$ and 1 by a random $g \in G$. Homomorphic OR is implemented by the group operation $\text{homOR}(g_1, g_2) := g_1g_2$, and homomorphic AND is implemented by the commutator $\text{homAND}(g_1, g_2) = g_1g_2g_1^{-1}g_2^{-1}$. This can be used to compute arbitrary functions by using deMorgan's laws to push negations to the inputs, and encrypting a bit b as a pair $(Enc(b), Enc(1-b))$.

Such a scheme would need to provide methods for choosing random elements in G and H, rely on the indistinguishability of H from G for security, and provide a trapdoor that enables distinguishing H from G as a secret key. Some candidate implementations of this approach are discussed in [73], and some earlier proposals were shown to be insecure. As for the hidden-ideal paradigm, here too we currently neither have a viable candidate nor know of a reason to think that such candidates are impossible.

5.5.3 Homomorphic Encryption for Other Models of Computation

Although circuits are a convenient and universal model of (classical) computation, other models have been considered as well, both weaker and stronger. Weaker models of computation were considered before Gentry's result, and they sometimes allow schemes based on different (non-lattice) hardness assumptions. Stronger models are also considered, as they could provide better efficiency for applications. Below we list a few such models, and what is known about them.

Truth-tables. Homomorphic encryption for truth-tables allows an encryptor to encrypt the index into a table, and an evaluator to compute from it an encryption of the content of the corresponding entry in the table. This is closely related to the notion of *single-server private information retrieval* (PIR) [65]. Indeed, a two-round single-server PIR protocol immediately yields a weakly compact *secret-key* encryption scheme which is homomorphic for truth-tables (cf. [62]).

Moreover, a PIR protocol can be transformed to a public-key scheme using an auxiliary public-key encryption scheme: The recipient chooses a public/secret key pair for the encryption scheme, the sender sends the PIR-client message and in addition also an encryption of the client's PIR-state s under the public key, and the evaluator forwards the encrypted state to the recipient together with the PIR reply. The recipient uses its secret key to decrypt and recover the SFE state s, and then uses the procedure SFE3 with this state to recover $F(x, y)$. The result is a public-key encryption scheme capable of "evaluating" any table-lookup, and it is compact as long as the client's PIR state is short. We note that all PIR constructions have small client state, and this can be enforced generically by having the client use a pseudorandom generator (PRG) to derive its randomness, and using the PRG seed as the client state.

Since two-message PIR implies also public-key encryption [29, 49], we have that compact public-key homomorphic encryption for truth-tables can be realized from any two-message PIR protocol. For example, this yields realizations with security based on various factoring-related assumptions such as quadratic residuosity [52], N-th residuosity [77], and phi-hiding [22]. See [75] for a survey of single-server PIR.

Branching programs. Polynomial-size branching programs are a fairly strong model of computation, being able to evaluate at least the complexity class $NC1$. Ishai and Paskin described in [62] a weakly compact encryption scheme which is homomorphic for branching programs, using the Damgård–Jurik cryptosystem [28] whose security relies on the N-th residuosity assumption.

Turing machines and RAM. Although circuits are universal, and hence fully-homomorphic encryption for circuits can evaluate any function on encrypted data, other models of computation such as Turing machines or RAM computation can provide faster processing. It is therefore desirable to make the complexity of homomorphic evaluation as low as the Turing-machine complexity or the RAM-complexity of the evaluated function, as opposed to its circuit complexity. Unfortunately this is often not possible, for example it is clear that the table lookup function $f_T(i) = T[i]$ cannot be evaluated for an encrypted index in its RAM complexity of $O(1)$. Nonetheless, a significant body of recent work (such as [51] and [42]) has been devoted to finding cases where processing encrypted data with better than circuit complexity is possible.

Homomorphic quantum computations. Going beyond classical computations, one may wish to be able to apply quantum computations to an encrypted quantum state. Note that we are asking for more than simply a classical homomorphic-encryption scheme which is resistant to quantum attacks.[8] Instead, imagine trying to run Shor's algorithm [84] for factoring an encrypted integer. Being able to evaluate classical circuits on encrypted data is not enough here; we need to be able to evaluate also quantum gates.

A first step toward homomorphic quantum computation was recently taken by Broadbent and Jeffery [21], who described a quantum homomorphic encryption scheme for a restricted class of quantum circuits, assuming classical fully homomorphic encryption. Specifically, their scheme can handle circuits with unbounded number of Clifford-group gates but only a constant non-Clifford depth. (This is somewhat analogous to classical arithmetic circuits with unlimited additions but constant multiplication depth.)

5.5.4 Beyond Homomorphic Encryption

Powerful as it is, homomorphic encryption is just one of a number of new cryptographic primitives that were developed in the last decade using tools from lattice-based cryptography. Below we describe some other primitives that use similar tools.

5.5.4.1 Multikey Homomorphic Encryption

One limitation of homomorphic encryption is that it can only process encrypted data relative to one key. Many times, however, we want to be ale to process data that was encrypted relative to several different keys. For example, multiple parties, each with its own key, may upload their encrypted data to the cloud, and we want the cloud to aggregate this data and compute useful statistics on it. Of course, recovering the plaintext result would then depend on all the parties cooperating, each bringing its corresponding secret key. A homomorphic scheme that supports such processing is called *multikey homomorphic*.

---

[8] Since the learning-with-errors problem is assumed to be hard even for quantum computers, then so are all LWE-based homomorphic encryption schemes.

The concept of multikey homomorphic encryption, along with a concrete realization based on the NTRU cryptosystem [68], was first described by López-Alt et al. in [67]. One drawback of that scheme is that an upper bound on the number of parties must be known at key-generation time, since the parameters grow with the number of parties. (A similar realization is possible under LWE, but it only supports a constant number of parties.)

A different realization under LWE (or RLWE) was recently described by Clear and McGoldrick [25], and later significantly simplified by Mukherjee and Wichs [72]. These schemes can support an arbitrary number of parties, but they rely on a common reference string that must be known at key-generation time.

5.5.4.2 Homomorphic Commitments and Signatures

Although homomorphic encryption allows computing on encrypted data, it does not provide any integrity guarantees for the computed values. For example, in the client-server application in which the client encrypts its input x and the server evaluates on it a function f, the client has no guarantees that the alleged evaluated ciphertext was indeed produced by evaluating f on the encrypted x.

Verifying the integrity of remote computation is generally known as *verifiable computation*, and it is the subject of a very active research effort. See, e.g., [89] for a survey (focusing on the practical-oriented side of that work). Some useful tools in this area are homomorphic commitments and signatures, which can be constructed using techniques similar to those used in the GSW cryptosystem, as noted by Gorbunov et al. [55].

Homomorphic commitments are similar to homomorphic encryption, except that, in addition to the ciphertext-evaluation procedure Evaluate, there is also a decommitment-evaluation procedure deEvaluate for computing on the corresponding randomness, which is used by the committer. The property of deEvaluate is that, whenever we have $\mathbf{c} = \mathsf{Encrypt}(\mathsf{pk}, \mathbf{b}; \mathbf{r})$ (where $\mathbf{r}$ is the randomness used for encryption) and $c' \leftarrow \mathsf{Evaluate}(\mathsf{pk}, \Pi, \mathbf{c})$, then computing $r' \leftarrow \mathsf{deEvaluate}(\mathsf{pk}, \Pi, \mathbf{c}, \mathbf{b}, \mathbf{r})$ we get $\mathsf{Encrypt}(\mathsf{pk}, \Pi(\mathbf{b}); r') = c'$. Thinking of the randomness $\mathbf{r}$ as being a decommitment string, this means that the committer can compute the randomness r' that would open the evaluated ciphertext c' to the plaintext $b' = \Pi(\mathbf{b})$. It is easy to see that the basic GSW scheme as described in Section 5.3.2.4 supports such a decommitment-evaluation routine, since whenever we have two ciphertexts $\mathbf{C}_i$ such that $\mathbf{s} \times \mathbf{C}_i = b_i \cdot (\mathbf{s} \times \mathbf{G}) + \boldsymbol{\eta}_i$, then their sum and product satisfy

$$\mathbf{s} \times (\mathbf{C}_1 \pm \mathbf{C}_2) = (b_1 \pm b_2) \cdot (\mathbf{s} \times \mathbf{G}) + (\boldsymbol{\eta}_1 \pm \boldsymbol{\eta}_2)$$
$$\text{and } \mathbf{s} \times (\mathbf{C}_1 \times G^{-1}(\mathbf{C}_2)) = (b_1 \cdot b_2) \cdot (\mathbf{s} \times \mathbf{G}) + (b_1 \cdot \boldsymbol{\eta}_2 + \boldsymbol{\eta}_1 \times G^{-1}(\mathbf{C}_2)),$$

and these noise terms can be computed efficiently by the committer.

In homomorphic signatures, a data originator uses its secret key to sign messages, and it publishes the vector of messages $\mathbf{b} = (b_1, \ldots, b_n)$ and the corresponding vector of signatures $\boldsymbol{\sigma} = (\sigma_1, \ldots, \sigma_n)$. A data processor, knowing $\mathbf{b}, \boldsymbol{\sigma}$, and the public key, can efficiently generate a short evaluated signature $\sigma_{\Pi, b'}$ on the pair

$(\Pi, \Pi(\mathbf{b}))$, and that signature can be verified using the public key (even without knowing the original data $\mathbf{b}$). Gorbunov et al. described in [55] a construction of homomorphic signatures from homomorphic commitments, in which verifying an evaluated signature $\sigma_{\Pi,b'}$ can be partitioned to an offline phase that depends only on Π and an online phase that depends also on b' and $\sigma_{\Pi,b'}$, such that the complexity of the online phase is independent of Π.

5.5.4.3 Functional Encryption, Obfuscation, and Multilinear Maps

Homomorphic encryption is in particular a secure encryption scheme. So while it is possible to compute on encrypted data (or with encrypted programs), the result is still encrypted and it takes the secret key to make sense of it. In many applications, however, we would like to process encrypted data or programs, and get (only) the result of the computation in the clear. For example, consider applying a spam filter to encrypted email: Although the content of the email messages should remain secret, we may want the mail server to learn the spam/no-spam bit *in the clear* so that it can forward to us only the non-spam messages.

For another example, imagine that we have a good model for predicting the risk of heart attack based on various indicators, and we want to release this model for use by the public. At the same time, we want to withhold the inner workings of this model, either due to intellectual property concerns, or because we need to protect the privacy of patient data that was used to devise this model. Here too, we may want the model itself to be encrypted, but anyone should be able to evaluate the model on their own indicators and get the result in the clear.

These examples illustrate typical uses of *functional encryption* (the first example) and *code obfuscation* (the second example), and a large body of research is devoted to studying these concepts. Functional encryption for simple functions can be constructed from pairing-based cryptography (e.g., [64, 83, 11, 74]), and some variants that support all functions but offer weaker security can be based on the hardness of LWE (e.g., [53, 54]). However, more is required to obtain fully secure functional encryption for all functions, or code obfuscation for any expressive class of functions. As of now, the only viable tool that we have for realizing these concepts are the so-called *cryptographic multilinear maps*.

Cryptographic multilinear maps were envisioned by Boneh and Silverberg [12], but were constructed for the first time only a decade later by Garg et al. [34]. On a high level, they enable evaluation of arithmetic circuits over a large field on "encrypted" data, getting in the clear the bit saying whether or not the result is equal to zero, without being able to "decrypt" any of the intermediate values. We currently have three candidate constructions for multilinear maps [34, 26, 39] (with some variations on each), all following the same high-level approach: Very roughly, they all begin with some homomorphic encryption scheme, and then publish a *defective secret key*, which allows testing for zero but not decryption.

To use such multilinear maps for obfuscation or functional encryption, one needs to randomize the computation so that no two intermediate values will ever be equal to each other, but where all the randomness can be canceled on the output wire so that the zero-test can be used to determine the output value. Such randomization techniques were found for $NC1$ circuits, and a bootstrapping technique using homomorphic encryption is used to extend these constructions to any polynomial-size circuits. Following Garg et al. [35], this approach was used in very many works; see, e.g., [60] for a survey.

5.6 Suggested Reading

Below are pointers to additional reading on related topics that are not covered in detail in this tutorial.

Multi-hop and circuit-private FHE. The connections with secure computation protocols with emphasis on multihop and function privacy (without compactness) were studied by Gentry et al. [47] in the semi-honest model. Their treatment was extended to the malicious adversary model by Ostrovsky et al. [76].

Second-generation FHE. A good survey that covers the basics of the second-generation FHE schemes was written by Vaikuntanathan [87], with more details given in the work of Brakerski et al. [17]. The techniques for reducing the plaintext-to-ciphertext overhead to polylogarithmic are described in the work of Gentry et al. [44], and many practical optimizations are described in the work of Halevi and Shoup [56]. The *scale-invariant* flavor of second-generation schemes was introduced by Brakerski [14] and used also in the work of Bos et al. [13].

Third-generation FHE. The GSW cryptosystem was presented by Gentry et al. in [48], together with some extensions such as identity-based FHE. The use of asymmetric circuits was proposed by Brakerski and Vaikuntanathan [20], and additional bootstrapping optimizations using this approach were described by Alperin-Sheriff and Peikert [3] and by Ducas and Micciancio [30].

Multikey FHE. The concept of a multikey FHE was introduced by López-Alt et al. in [67], along with a solution based on NTRU. A construction based on LWE was first described by Clear and McGoldrick [25], and later significantly simplified by Mukherjee and Wichs [72] and improved further by Peikert and Shiehian [79].

Homomorphic commitments and signatures. An interesting usage of techniques very similar to those described in this tutorial for the purpose of homomorphic commitments and signatures was described by Gorbunov et al. in [55].

Acknowledgements I drew on many sources for this tutorial, most extensively on Craig Gentry's PhD thesis [37], a survey by Vinod Vaikuntanathan [87], and a blog by Boaz Barak and Zvika Brakerski [6]. I would like to thank Craig Gentry for teaching me most of what I know about FHE, and also the many other people with whom I collaborated on work in this area. Special thanks is due to Yehuda Lindell for the initiative to write this book.

References

[1] M. Alekhnovich. More on average case vs approximation complexity. *Computational Complexity*, 20(4):755–786, 2011. Extended abstract in FOCS 2003.

[2] J. Alperin-Sheriff and C. Peikert. Practical bootstrapping in quasilinear time. In R. Canetti and J. A. Garay, editors, *Advances in Cryptology - CRYPTO 2013 - 33rd Annual Cryptology Conference, Santa Barbara, CA, USA, August 18-22, 2013. Proceedings, Part I*, volume 8042 of *Lecture Notes in Computer Science*, pages 1–20. Springer, 2013.

[3] J. Alperin-Sheriff and C. Peikert. Faster bootstrapping with polynomial error. In J. A. Garay and R. Gennaro, editors, *Advances in Cryptology - CRYPTO 2014 - 34th Annual Cryptology Conference, Santa Barbara, CA, USA, August 17-21, 2014, Proceedings, Part I*, volume 8616 of *Lecture Notes in Computer Science*, pages 297–314. Springer, 2014.

[4] B. Applebaum, D. Cash, C. Peikert, and A. Sahai. Fast cryptographic primitives and circular-secure encryption based on hard learning problems. In S. Halevi, editor, *Advances in Cryptology - CRYPTO 2009, 29th Annual International Cryptology Conference, Santa Barbara, CA, USA, August 16-20, 2009. Proceedings*, volume 5677 of *Lecture Notes in Computer Science*, pages 595–618. Springer, 2009.

[5] S. Arora and R. Ge. New algorithms for learning in presence of errors. In L. Aceto, M. Henzinger, and J. Sgall, editors, *Automata, Languages and Programming - 38th International Colloquium, ICALP 2011, Zurich, Switzerland, July 4-8, 2011, Proceedings, Part I*, volume 6755 of *Lecture Notes in Computer Science*, pages 403–415. Springer, 2011.

[6] B. Barak and Z. Brakerski. The Swiss Army knife of cryptography. Blog document, accessed January 2016, http://windowsontheory.org/2012/05/01/the-swiss-army-knife-of-cryptography/, 2012.

[7] D. A. M. Barrington. Bounded-width polynomial-size branching programs recognize exactly those languages in NC1. *J. Comput. Syst. Sci.*, 38(1):150–164, 1989.

[8] A. Blum, M. L. Furst, M. J. Kearns, and R. J. Lipton. Cryptographic primitives based on hard learning problems. In D. R. Stinson, editor, *Advances in Cryptology - CRYPTO '93, 13th Annual International Cryptology Conference, Santa Barbara, California, USA, August 22-26, 1993, Proceedings*, volume 773 of *Lecture Notes in Computer Science*, pages 278–291. Springer, 1993.

[9] A. Bogdanov and C. H. Lee. Homomorphic encryption from codes. IACR Cryptology ePrint Archive, Report 2011/622, 2011. http://eprint.iacr.org/2011/622.

[10] D. Boneh, E. Goh, and K. Nissim. Evaluating 2-DNF formulas on ciphertexts. In J. Kilian, editor, *Theory of Cryptography, Second Theory of Cryptography Conference, TCC 2005, Cambridge, MA, USA, February 10-12, 2005, Proceedings*, volume 3378 of *Lecture Notes in Computer Science*, pages 325–341. Springer, 2005.

[11] D. Boneh, A. Sahai, and B. Waters. Functional encryption: Definitions and challenges. In Y. Ishai, editor, *Theory of Cryptography - 8th Theory of Cryptography Conference, TCC 2011, Providence, RI, USA, March 28-30, 2011. Proceedings*, volume 6597 of *Lecture Notes in Computer Science*, pages 253–273. Springer, 2011.

[12] D. Boneh and A. Silverberg. Applications of multilinear forms to cryptography. Cryptology ePrint Archive, Report 2002/080, 2002. http://eprint.iacr.org/2002/080.

[13] J. W. Bos, K. E. Lauter, J. Loftus, and M. Naehrig. Improved security for a ring-based fully homomorphic encryption scheme. In M. Stam, editor, *Cryptography and Coding - 14th IMA International Conference, IMACC 2013, Oxford, UK, December 17-19, 2013. Proceedings*, volume 8308 of *Lecture Notes in Computer Science*, pages 45–64. Springer, 2013.

[14] Z. Brakerski. Fully homomorphic encryption without modulus switching from classical GapSVP. In R. Safavi-Naini and R. Canetti, editors, *Advances in Cryptology - CRYPTO 2012 - 32nd Annual Cryptology Conference, Santa Barbara, CA, USA, August 19-23, 2012. Proceedings*, volume 7417 of *Lecture Notes in Computer Science*, pages 868–886. Springer, 2012.

[15] Z. Brakerski. When homomorphism becomes a liability. In *TCC*, pages 143–161, 2013.

[16] Z. Brakerski, C. Gentry, and V. Vaikuntanathan. Fully homomorphic encryption without bootstrapping. In *Innovations in Theoretical Computer Science (ITCS'12)*, 2012. Available at http://eprint.iacr.org/2011/277.

[17] Z. Brakerski, C. Gentry, and V. Vaikuntanathan. (Leveled) fully homomorphic encryption without bootstrapping. *ACM Transactions on Computation Theory*, 6(3):13, 2014.

[18] Z. Brakerski, A. Langlois, C. Peikert, O. Regev, and D. Stehlé. Classical hardness of learning with errors. In *Proceedings of the Forty-fifth Annual ACM Symposium on Theory of Computing*, STOC '13, pages 575–584, New York, NY, USA, 2013. ACM.

[19] Z. Brakerski and V. Vaikuntanathan. Efficient fully homomorphic encryption from (standard) LWE. *SIAM J. Comput.*, 43(2):831–871, 2014.

[20] Z. Brakerski and V. Vaikuntanathan. Lattice-based FHE as secure as PKE. In M. Naor, editor, *Innovations in Theoretical Computer Science, ITCS'14, Princeton, NJ, USA, January 12-14, 2014*, pages 1–12. ACM, 2014.

[21] A. Broadbent and S. Jeffery. Quantum homomorphic encryption for circuits of low T-gate complexity. In R. Gennaro and M. Robshaw, editors, *Advances in Cryptology - CRYPTO 2015 - 35th Annual Cryptology Conference, Santa Barbara, CA, USA, August 16-20, 2015, Proceedings, Part II*, volume 9216 of *Lecture Notes in Computer Science*, pages 609–629. Springer, 2015.

[22] C. Cachin, S. Micali, and M. Stadler. Computationally private information retrieval with polylogarithmic communication. In J. Stern, editor, *Advances in Cryptology - EUROCRYPT '99, International Conference on the Theory and Application of Cryptographic Techniques, Prague, Czech Republic, May 2-6,*

1999, Proceeding, volume 1592 of *Lecture Notes in Computer Science*, pages 402–414. Springer, 1999.

[23] D. Cash, M. Green, and S. Hohenberger. New definitions and separations for circular security. In M. Fischlin, J. Buchmann, and M. Manulis, editors, *Public Key Cryptography - PKC 2012*, volume 7293 of *Lecture Notes in Computer Science*, pages 540–557. Springer Berlin Heidelberg, 2012.

[24] B. Chor, E. Kushilevitz, O. Goldreich, and M. Sudan. Private information retrieval. *J. ACM*, 45(6):965–981, 1998.

[25] M. Clear and C. McGoldrick. Multi-identity and multi-key leveled FHE from learning with errors. In R. Gennaro and M. Robshaw, editors, *Advances in Cryptology - CRYPTO 2015 - 35th Annual Cryptology Conference, Santa Barbara, CA, USA, August 16-20, 2015, Proceedings, Part II*, volume 9216 of *Lecture Notes in Computer Science*, pages 630–656. Springer, 2015.

[26] J. Coron, T. Lepoint, and M. Tibouchi. Practical multilinear maps over the integers. In R. Canetti and J. A. Garay, editors, *Advances in Cryptology - CRYPTO 2013 - 33rd Annual Cryptology Conference, Santa Barbara, CA, USA, August 18-22, 2013. Proceedings, Part I*, volume 8042 of *Lecture Notes in Computer Science*, pages 476–493. Springer, 2013.

[27] J. Coron, A. Mandal, D. Naccache, and M. Tibouchi. Fully homomorphic encryption over the integers with shorter public keys. In P. Rogaway, editor, *Advances in Cryptology - CRYPTO 2011 - 31st Annual Cryptology Conference, Santa Barbara, CA, USA, August 14-18, 2011. Proceedings*, volume 6841 of *Lecture Notes in Computer Science*, pages 487–504. Springer, 2011.

[28] I. Damgård, M. Jurik, and J. B. Nielsen. A generalization of Paillier's public-key system with applications to electronic voting. *Int. J. Inf. Sec.*, 9(6):371–385, 2010.

[29] G. DiCrescenzo, T. Malkin, and R. Ostrovsky. Single database private information retrieval implies oblivious transfer. In B. Preneel, editor, *Advances in Cryptology - EUROCRYPT 2000, International Conference on the Theory and Application of Cryptographic Techniques, Bruges, Belgium, May 14-18, 2000, Proceeding*, volume 1807 of *Lecture Notes in Computer Science*, pages 122–138. Springer, 2000.

[30] L. Ducas and D. Micciancio. FHEW: bootstrapping homomorphic encryption in less than a second. In E. Oswald and M. Fischlin, editors, *Advances in Cryptology - EUROCRYPT 2015 - 34th Annual International Conference on the Theory and Applications of Cryptographic Techniques, Sofia, Bulgaria, April 26-30, 2015, Proceedings, Part I*, volume 9056 of *Lecture Notes in Computer Science*, pages 617–640. Springer, 2015.

[31] L. Ducas and D. Stehlé. Sanitization of FHE ciphertexts. Manuscript, Available from https://heat-project.eu/School/Damien%20Stehle/HEAT_FHE_Stehle.pdf, 2016.

[32] M. Fellows and N. Koblitz. Combinatorial cryptosystems galore! *Contemporary Mathematics*, 168:51–51, 1994.

[33] T. El Gamal. A public key cryptosystem and a signature scheme based on discrete logarithms. *IEEE Transactions on Information Theory*, 31(4):469–472, 1985.

[34] S. Garg, C. Gentry, and S. Halevi. Candidate multilinear maps from ideal lattices. In T. Johansson and P. Q. Nguyen, editors, *Advances in Cryptology - EUROCRYPT 2013, 32nd Annual International Conference on the Theory and Applications of Cryptographic Techniques, Athens, Greece, May 26-30, 2013. Proceedings*, volume 7881 of *Lecture Notes in Computer Science*, pages 1–17. Springer, 2013.

[35] S. Garg, C. Gentry, S. Halevi, M. Raykova, A. Sahai, and B. Waters. Candidate indistinguishability obfuscation and functional encryption for all circuits. In *54th Annual IEEE Symposium on Foundations of Computer Science, FOCS 2013, 26-29 October, 2013, Berkeley, CA, USA*, pages 40–49. IEEE Computer Society, 2013.

[36] V. Gauthier, A. Otmani, and J.-P. Tillich. A distinguisher-based attack of a homomorphic encryption scheme relying on Reed-Solomon codes. Cryptology ePrint Archive, Report 2012/168, 2012. http://eprint.iacr.org/2012/168.

[37] C. Gentry. *A Fully Homomorphic Encryption Scheme*. PhD thesis, Stanford University, Stanford, CA, USA, 2009. AAI3382729.

[38] C. Gentry. Fully homomorphic encryption using ideal lattices. In M. Mitzenmacher, editor, *Proceedings of the 41st Annual ACM Symposium on Theory of Computing, STOC 2009, Bethesda, MD, USA, May 31 - June 2, 2009*, pages 169–178. ACM, 2009.

[39] C. Gentry, S. Gorbunov, and S. Halevi. Graph-induced multilinear maps from lattices. In Y. Dodis and J. B. Nielsen, editors, *Theory of Cryptography - 12th Theory of Cryptography Conference, TCC 2015, Warsaw, Poland, March 23-25, 2015, Proceedings, Part II*, volume 9015 of *Lecture Notes in Computer Science*, pages 498–527. Springer, 2015.

[40] C. Gentry and S. Halevi. Fully homomorphic encryption without squashing using depth-3 arithmetic circuits. In R. Ostrovsky, editor, *IEEE 52nd Annual Symposium on Foundations of Computer Science, FOCS 2011, Palm Springs, CA, USA, October 22-25, 2011*, pages 107–109. IEEE Computer Society, 2011.

[41] C. Gentry and S. Halevi. Implementing Gentry's fully-homomorphic encryption scheme. In *Advances in Cryptology - EUROCRYPT'11*, volume 6632 of *Lecture Notes in Computer Science*, pages 129–148. Springer, 2011.

[42] C. Gentry, S. Halevi, M. Raykova, and D. Wichs. Outsourcing private RAM computation. In *55th IEEE Annual Symposium on Foundations of Computer Science, FOCS 2014, Philadelphia, PA, USA, October 18-21, 2014*, pages 404–413. IEEE Computer Society, 2014.

[43] C. Gentry, S. Halevi, and N. P. Smart. Better bootstrapping in fully homomorphic encryption. In M. Fischlin, J. A. Buchmann, and M. Manulis, editors, *Public Key Cryptography - PKC 2012 - 15th International Conference on Practice and Theory in Public Key Cryptography, Darmstadt, Germany,*

May 21-23, 2012. Proceedings, volume 7293 of *Lecture Notes in Computer Science*, pages 1–16. Springer, 2012.

[44] C. Gentry, S. Halevi, and N. P. Smart. Fully homomorphic encryption with polylog overhead. In D. Pointcheval and T. Johansson, editors, *Advances in Cryptology - EUROCRYPT 2012 - 31st Annual International Conference on the Theory and Applications of Cryptographic Techniques, Cambridge, UK, April 15-19, 2012. Proceedings*, volume 7237 of *Lecture Notes in Computer Science*, pages 465–482. Springer, 2012. Available from http://eprint.iacr.org/2011/566.

[45] C. Gentry, S. Halevi, and N. P. Smart. Homomorphic evaluation of the AES circuit. In R. Safavi-Naini and R. Canetti, editors, *Advances in Cryptology - CRYPTO 2012 - 32nd Annual Cryptology Conference, Santa Barbara, CA, USA, August 19-23, 2012. Proceedings*, volume 7417 of *Lecture Notes in Computer Science*, pages 850–867. Springer, 2012.

[46] C. Gentry, S. Halevi, and V. Vaikuntanathan. i-hop homomorphic encryption and rerandomizable Yao circuits. In T. Rabin, editor, *Advances in Cryptology - CRYPTO 2010, 30th Annual Cryptology Conference, Santa Barbara, CA, USA, August 15-19, 2010. Proceedings*, volume 6223 of *Lecture Notes in Computer Science*, pages 155–172. Springer, 2010. http://eprint.iacr.org/2010/145.

[47] C. Gentry, S. Halevi, and V. Vaikuntanathan. A simple BGN-type cryptosystem from LWE. In H. Gilbert, editor, *Advances in Cryptology - EUROCRYPT 2010, 29th Annual International Conference on the Theory and Applications of Cryptographic Techniques, French Riviera, May 30 - June 3, 2010. Proceedings*, volume 6110 of *Lecture Notes in Computer Science*, pages 506–522. Springer, 2010.

[48] C. Gentry, A. Sahai, and B. Waters. Homomorphic encryption from learning with errors: Conceptually-simpler, asymptotically-faster, attribute-based. In R. Canetti and J. A. Garay, editors, *Advances in Cryptology - CRYPTO 2013, Part I*, pages 75–92. Springer, 2013.

[49] Y. Gertner, S. Kannan, T. Malkin, O. Reingold, and M. Viswanathan. The relationship between public key encryption and oblivious transfer. In *41st Annual Symposium on Foundations of Computer Science, FOCS 2000, 12-14 November 2000, Redondo Beach, California, USA*, pages 325–335. IEEE Computer Society, 2000.

[50] O. Goldreich, S. Micali, and A. Wigderson. How to play any mental game or a completeness theorem for protocols with honest majority. In A. V. Aho, editor, *Proceedings of the 19th Annual ACM Symposium on Theory of Computing, 1987, New York, New York, USA*, pages 218–229. ACM, 1987.

[51] S. Goldwasser, Y. T. Kalai, R. A. Popa, V. Vaikuntanathan, and N. Zeldovich. How to run Turing machines on encrypted data. In R. Canetti and J. A. Garay, editors, *Advances in Cryptology - CRYPTO 2013 - 33rd Annual Cryptology Conference, Santa Barbara, CA, USA, August 18-22, 2013. Proceedings, Part II*, volume 8043 of *Lecture Notes in Computer Science*, pages 536–553. Springer, 2013.

[52] S. Goldwasser and S. Micali. Probabilistic Encryption. *J. Comput. Syst. Sci.*, 28(2):270–299, 1984.

[53] S. Gorbunov, V. Vaikuntanathan, and H. Wee. Functional encryption with bounded collusions via multi-party computation. In R. Safavi-Naini and R. Canetti, editors, *Advances in Cryptology - CRYPTO 2012 - 32nd Annual Cryptology Conference, Santa Barbara, CA, USA, August 19-23, 2012. Proceedings*, volume 7417 of *Lecture Notes in Computer Science*, pages 162–179. Springer, 2012.

[54] S. Gorbunov, V. Vaikuntanathan, and H. Wee. Predicate encryption for circuits from LWE. In R. Gennaro and M. Robshaw, editors, *Advances in Cryptology - CRYPTO 2015 - 35th Annual Cryptology Conference, Santa Barbara, CA, USA, August 16-20, 2015, Proceedings, Part II*, volume 9216 of *Lecture Notes in Computer Science*, pages 503–523. Springer, 2015.

[55] S. Gorbunov, V. Vaikuntanathan, and D. Wichs. Leveled fully homomorphic signatures from standard lattices. In R. A. Servedio and R. Rubinfeld, editors, *Proceedings of the Forty-Seventh Annual ACM on Symposium on Theory of Computing, STOC 2015, Portland, OR, USA, June 14-17, 2015*, pages 469–477. ACM, 2015.

[56] S. Halevi and V. Shoup. Algorithms in HElib. In J. A. Garay and R. Gennaro, editors, *Advances in Cryptology - CRYPTO 2014 - 34th Annual Cryptology Conference, Santa Barbara, CA, USA, August 17-21, 2014, Proceedings, Part I*, volume 8616 of *Lecture Notes in Computer Science*, pages 554–571. Springer, 2014.

[57] S. Halevi and V. Shoup. Bootstrapping for HElib. In E. Oswald and M. Fischlin, editors, *Advances in Cryptology - EUROCRYPT 2015 - 34th Annual International Conference on the Theory and Applications of Cryptographic Techniques, Sofia, Bulgaria, April 26-30, 2015, Proceedings, Part I*, volume 9056 of *Lecture Notes in Computer Science*, pages 641–670. Springer, 2015.

[58] J. Håstad, R. Impagliazzo, L. A. Levin, and M. Luby. A pseudorandom generator from any one-way function. *SIAM J. Comput.*, 28(4):1364–1396, Mar. 1999.

[59] J. Hoffstein, J. Pipher, and J. H. Silverman. NTRU: A ring-based public key cryptosystem. In J. Buhler, editor, *Algorithmic Number Theory, Third International Symposium, ANTS-III, Portland, Oregon, USA, June 21-25, 1998, Proceedings*, volume 1423 of *Lecture Notes in Computer Science*, pages 267–288. Springer, 1998.

[60] M. Horváth. Survey on cryptographic obfuscation. Cryptology ePrint Archive, Report 2015/412, 2015. http://eprint.iacr.org/2015/412.

[61] Y. Ishai, E. Kushilevitz, R. Ostrovsky, and A. Sahai. Cryptography with constant computational overhead. In C. Dwork, editor, *Proceedings of the 40th Annual ACM Symposium on Theory of Computing, Victoria, British Columbia, Canada, May 17-20, 2008*, pages 433–442. ACM, 2008.

[62] Y. Ishai and A. Paskin. Evaluating branching programs on encrypted data. In *Theory of Cryptography - TCC'07*, volume 4392 of *Lecture Notes in Computer Science*, pages 575–594. Springer, 2007.

[63] R. M. Karp and V. Ramachandran. Parallel algorithms for shared-memory machines. In J. van Leeuwen, editor, *Handbook of Theoretical Computer Science (Vol. A)*, pages 869–941. MIT Press, Cambridge, MA, USA, 1990.

[64] J. Katz, A. Sahai, and B. Waters. Predicate encryption supporting disjunctions, polynomial equations, and inner products. *J. Cryptology*, 26(2):191–224, 2013.

[65] E. Kushilevitz and R. Ostrovsky. Replication is NOT needed: SINGLE database, computationally-private information retrieval. In *38th Annual Symposium on Foundations of Computer Science, FOCS '97, Miami Beach, Florida, USA, October 19-22, 1997*, pages 364–373. IEEE Computer Society, 1997.

[66] F. Levy-dit-Vehel, M. G. Marinari, L. Perret, and C. Traverso. A survey on Polly Cracker systems. In *Gröbner Bases, Coding, and Cryptography*, pages 285–305. Springer, 2009.

[67] A. López-Alt, E. Tromer, and V. Vaikuntanathan. On-the-fly multiparty computation on the cloud via multikey fully homomorphic encryption. In H. J. Karloff and T. Pitassi, editors, *Proceedings of the 44th Symposium on Theory of Computing Conference, STOC 2012, New York, NY, USA, May 19 - 22, 2012*, pages 1219–1234. ACM, 2012.

[68] V. Lyubashevsky, C. Peikert, and O. Regev. On ideal lattices and learning with errors over rings. *J. ACM*, 60(6):43, 2013.

[69] C. A. Melchor, P. Gaborit, and J. Herranz. Additively homomorphic encryption with d-operand multiplications. In T. Rabin, editor, *Advances in Cryptology - CRYPTO 2010, 30th Annual Cryptology Conference, Santa Barbara, CA, USA, August 15-19, 2010. Proceedings*, volume 6223 of *Lecture Notes in Computer Science*, pages 138–154. Springer, 2010.

[70] D. Micciancio and C. Peikert. Trapdoors for lattices: Simpler, tighter, faster, smaller. In D. Pointcheval and T. Johansson, editors, *Advances in Cryptology - EUROCRYPT 2012 - 31st Annual International Conference on the Theory and Applications of Cryptographic Techniques, Cambridge, UK, April 15-19, 2012. Proceedings*, volume 7237 of *Lecture Notes in Computer Science*, pages 700–718. Springer, 2012.

[71] D. Micciancio and O. Regev. Worst-case to average-case reductions based on Gaussian measures. *SIAM J. Comput.*, 37(1):267–302, 2007.

[72] P. Mukherjee and D. Wichs. Two round mutliparty computation via multi-key FHE. Cryptology ePrint Archive, Report 2015/345, 2015. http://eprint.iacr.org/2015/345, accessed Jan, 2016.

[73] K. Nuida. Candidate constructions of fully homomorphic encryption on finite simple groups without ciphertext noise. Cryptology ePrint Archive, Report 2014/097, 2014. http://eprint.iacr.org/2014/097, accessed Jan 2016.

[74] A. O'Neill. Definitional issues in functional encryption. Cryptology ePrint Archive, Report 2010/556, 2010. http://eprint.iacr.org/2010/556.

[75] R. Ostrovsky and W. E. Skeith III. A survey of single-database private information retrieval: Techniques and applications. In T. Okamoto and X. Wang, editors, *Public Key Cryptography - PKC 2007, 10th International Conference*

on Practice and Theory in Public-Key Cryptography, Beijing, China, April 16-20, 2007, Proceedings, volume 4450 of Lecture Notes in Computer Science, pages 393–411. Springer, 2007. Available at http://eprint.iacr.org/2007/059.

[76] R. Ostrovsky, A. Paskin-Cherniavsky, and B. Paskin-Cherniavsky. Maliciously circuit-private FHE. In J. A. Garay and R. Gennaro, editors, Advances in Cryptology - CRYPTO 2014 - 34th Annual Cryptology Conference, Santa Barbara, CA, USA, August 17-21, 2014, Proceedings, Part I, volume 8616 of Lecture Notes in Computer Science, pages 536–553. Springer, 2014. Available from https://eprint.iacr.org/2013/307.

[77] P. Paillier. Public-key cryptosystems based on composite degree residuosity classes. In J. Stern, editor, Advances in Cryptology - EUROCRYPT '99, International Conference on the Theory and Application of Cryptographic Techniques, Prague, Czech Republic, May 2-6, 1999, Proceeding, volume 1592 of Lecture Notes in Computer Science, pages 223–238. Springer, 1999.

[78] C. Peikert. Public-key cryptosystems from the worst-case shortest vector problem: extended abstract. In M. Mitzenmacher, editor, Proceedings of the 41st Annual ACM Symposium on Theory of Computing, STOC 2009, Bethesda, MD, USA, May 31 - June 2, 2009, pages 333–342. ACM, 2009.

[79] C. Peikert and S. Shiehian. Multi-key FHE from LWE, revisited. Cryptology ePrint Archive, Report 2016/196, 2016. http://eprint.iacr.org/.

[80] O. Regev. On lattices, learning with errors, random linear codes, and cryptography. J. ACM, 56(6), 2009.

[81] R. Rivest, L. Adleman, and M. Dertouzos. On data banks and privacy homomorphisms. In Foundations of Secure Computation, pages 169–177. Academic Press, 1978.

[82] R. Rothblum. Homomorphic encryption: From private-key to public-key. In Y. Ishai, editor, Theory of Cryptography - 8th Theory of Cryptography Conference, TCC 2011, Providence, RI, USA, March 28-30, 2011. Proceedings, volume 6597 of Lecture Notes in Computer Science, pages 219–234. Springer, 2011.

[83] A. Sahai and B. Waters. Slides on functional encryption. PowerPoint presentation, 2008. http://www.cs.utexas.edu/~bwaters/presentations/files/functional.ppt.

[84] P. W. Shor. Polynomial-time algorithms for prime factorization and discrete logarithms on a quantum computer. SIAM Review, 41(2):303–332, 1999.

[85] N. P. Smart and F. Vercauteren. Fully homomorphic encryption with relatively small key and ciphertext sizes. In P. Q. Nguyen and D. Pointcheval, editors, Public Key Cryptography - PKC 2010, 13th International Conference on Practice and Theory in Public Key Cryptography, Paris, France, May 26-28, 2010. Proceedings, volume 6056 of Lecture Notes in Computer Science, pages 420–443. Springer, 2010.

[86] N. P. Smart and F. Vercauteren. Fully homomorphic SIMD operations. Des. Codes Cryptography, 71(1):57–81, 2014.

[87] V. Vaikuntanathan. Computing blindfolded: New developments in fully homo-
      morphic encryption. In R. Ostrovsky, editor, *IEEE 52nd Annual Symposium
      on Foundations of Computer Science, FOCS 2011, Palm Springs, CA, USA,
      October 22-25, 2011*, pages 5–16. IEEE Computer Society, 2011.
[88] M. van Dijk, C. Gentry, S. Halevi, and V. Vaikuntanathan. Fully homomor-
      phic encryption over the integers. In *Advances in Cryptology - EUROCRYPT
      2010, 29th Annual International Conference on the Theory and Applications
      of Cryptographic Techniques, French Riviera, May 30 - June 3, 2010. Proceed-
      ings*, pages 24–43, 2010.
[89] M. Walfish and A. J. Blumberg. Verifying computations without reexecuting
      them. *Commun. ACM*, 58(2):74–84, 2015.
[90] A. C. Yao. Protocols for secure computations (extended abstract). In *23rd
      Annual Symposium on Foundations of Computer Science – FOCS '82*, pages
      160–164. IEEE, 1982.

Chapter 6
How to Simulate It – A Tutorial on the Simulation Proof Technique

Yehuda Lindell

Abstract One of the most fundamental notions of cryptography is that of *simulation*. It stands behind the concepts of semantic security, zero knowledge, and security for multiparty computation. However, writing a simulator and proving security via the use of simulation is a nontrivial task, and one that many newcomers to the field often find difficult. In this tutorial, we provide a guide to how to write simulators and prove security via the simulation paradigm. Although we have tried to make this tutorial as stand-alone as possible, we assume some familiarity with the notions of secure encryption, zero-knowledge, and secure computation.

6.1 Introduction

What is simulation? Although it means different things in different settings, there is a clear common denominator. Simulation is a way of comparing what happens in the "real world" with what happens in an "ideal world" where the primitive in question is *secure by definition*. For example, the definition of semantic security for encryption compares what can be learned by an adversary who receives a real ciphertext with what can be learned by an adversary who receives nothing. The definition states that an encryption scheme is secure if they can both learn approximately the same amount of information. This is very strange. Clearly, the latter adversary who receives nothing can learn nothing about the plaintext since it receives no information. However, this is exactly the point. Since the adversary who receives nothing can learn nothing by triviality (this is an "ideal world" that is secure by definition), this implies that in the real world, where the adversary receives the ciphertext, nothing is learned as well.

At first, this seems to be a really complicated way of saying something simple. Why not just define encryption to be secure if nothing is learned? The problem is that it is not at all clear how to formalize the notion that "nothing is learned". If we try to

Yehuda Lindell
Dept. of Computer Science, Bar-Ilan University, Israel, e-mail: lindell@biu.ac.il

say that an adversary who receives a ciphertext cannot output any information about the plaintext, then what happens if the adversary already has information about the plaintext? For example, the adversary may know that it is English text. Of course, this has nothing to do with the security of the scheme since the adversary knew this beforehand and independently of the ciphertext. The simulation-based formulation of security enables us to exactly formalize this. We say that an encryption scheme is secure if the only information derived (or output by the adversary) is that which is based on a priori knowledge. If the adversary receiving no ciphertext is able to output the same information as the adversary receiving the ciphertext, then this is indeed the case.

It is unclear at this point why this is called "simulation"; what we have described is a comparison between two worlds. This will be explained throughout the tutorial (first in Section 6.3). For now, it suffices to say that security proofs for definitions formulated in this way work by constructing a simulator that resides in the alternative world that is secure by definition, and generates a view for the adversary in the real world that is computationally indistinguishable from its real view. In fact, as we will show, there are three distinct but intertwined tasks that a simulator must fulfill:

1. it must generate a view for the real adversary that is indistinguishable from its real view;
2. it must extract the effective inputs used by the adversary in the execution; and
3. it must make the view generated be consistent with the output that is based on this input.

We will not elaborate on these points here, since it is hard to explain them clearly out of context. However, they will become clear by the end of the tutorial.

Organization. In this tutorial, we will demonstrate the simulation paradigm in a number of different settings, together with explanations about what is required from the simulator and proof. We demonstrate the aforementioned three different tasks of the simulator in simulation-based proofs via a gradual progression. Specifically, in Section 6.3, we provide some more background to the simulation paradigm and how it expresses itself in the context of encryption. Then, in Section 6.4, we show how to simulate secure computation protocols for the case of semihonest adversaries (who follow the protocol specification, but try to learn more than allowed by inspecting the protocol transcript). We begin with this case since semihonest simulation is considerably easier than in the malicious case. Next, we demonstrate the three elements of simulation through the following progression: In Section 6.5, we show how to simulate in the context of zero-knowledge proofs. In this context, the corrupted party (who is the verifier) has no private input or output. Thus, the simulation consists of the first task only: *generating a view* that is indistinguishable from the potentially malicious verifier's view in an execution with a real prover. Next, we proceed to secure computation with security in the presence of (static) malicious adversaries. After presenting the definitions in Section 6.6, we proceed to the problem of secure coin tossing in Section 6.7. In this task, the parties receive output and the simulator must generate a view that is *consistent with this output*. Thus, an additional element of the simulator's role is added. (In this section, we also demonstrate the hybrid model and the technique of how to write simulation-based proofs in this model.) Then, in Section 6.8, we consider the oblivious transfer functionality and show how the simulator *extracts the inputs* of the adversary. This completes the three elements of simulation-based proofs. Finally, in Section 6.9, we show how to simulate in the common reference string model, and in Section 6.10, we briefly discuss some advanced topics related to simulation: concurrent composition, the random oracle model, and adaptive corruptions.

6.2 Preliminaries and Notation

For a finite set $S \subseteq \{0, 1\}^*$, we write $x \in_R S$ to say that x is distributed uniformly over the set S. We denote by U_n the uniform distribution over the set $\{0, 1\}^n$. A function $\mu(\cdot)$ is negligible, if for every positive polynomial $p(\cdot)$ and all sufficiently large n's, it holds that $\mu(n) < 1/p(n)$. Finally, we denote the empty string by λ.

Computational indistinguishability. A probability ensemble $X = \{X(a, n)\}_{a \in \{0,1\}^*; n \in \mathbb{N}}$ is an infinite sequence of random variables indexed by $a \in \{0, 1\}^*$ and $n \in \mathbb{N}$. In the context of secure computation, the value a will represent the parties' inputs and n will represent the security parameter. Two probability ensembles $X = \{X(a, n)\}_{a \in \{0,1\}^*; n \in \mathbb{N}}$ and $Y = \{Y(a, n)\}_{a \in \{0,1\}^*; n \in \mathbb{N}}$ are said to be computationally indistinguishable, denoted by $X \stackrel{c}{\equiv} Y$, if for every nonuniform polynomial-time algorithm D there exists a negligible function $\mu(\cdot)$ such that for every $a \in \{0, 1\}^*$ and every $n \in \mathbb{N}$,

$$|\Pr[D(X(a, n)) = 1] - \Pr[D(Y(a, n)) = 1]| \leq \mu(n).$$

All parties are assumed to run in time that is polynomial in the security parameter. (Formally, every party considered has a security parameter tape upon which the value 1^n is written. Then the party is polynomial in the input on this tape. We note that this means that a party may not even be able to read its entire input, as would occur in the case where its input is longer than its overall running time.)

Nonuniformity. The above notion of computational indistinguishability is inherently nonuniform, and this is not merely because we allow D to be nonuniform. In order to see why this is the case, we show what it means if two ensembles are *not* computationally indistinguishable. We first write out the requirement of computational indistinguishability in full (not using the notion "negligible function"). That is, $X \stackrel{c}{\equiv} Y$ if for every nonuniform polynomial-time algorithm D and every polynomial $p(\cdot)$ there exists an $N \in \mathbb{N}$ such that for every $n > N$ and every $a \in \{0, 1\}^*$,

$$|\Pr[D(X(a, n)) = 1] - \Pr[D(Y(a, n)) = 1]| < \frac{1}{p(n)}.$$

Now, the contradiction of this is that there exists a D and a polynomial $p(\cdot)$ such that, for every $N \in \mathbb{N}$, there exists an $n > N$ and an $a \in \{0, 1\}^*$ for which

$$|\Pr[D(X(a, n)) = 1] - \Pr[D(Y(a, n)) = 1]| \geq \frac{1}{p(n)}.$$

Stated in short, there exists a D and a polynomial $p(\cdot)$ such that, for an infinite number of n's, there exists an $a \in \{0, 1\}^*$ for which

$$|\Pr[D(X(a,n)) = 1] - \Pr[D(Y(a,n)) = 1]| \geq \frac{1}{p(n)}.$$

In particular, this means that for every such n there can be a different a. Now, in order to carry out a reduction that breaks some cryptographic primitive or assumption if the ensembles are *not* computationally indistinguishable, it is necessary for the reduction to know the value of a associated with its given n. The value a associated with n must therefore be written on the advice tape of the reduction algorithm, making it inherently nonuniform.

Order of quantifiers for computational indistinguishability. We observe that the definition of computational indistinguishability above is *not* the same as saying that for every $a \in \{0, 1\}^*$ it holds that $\{X(a,n)\}_{n\in\mathbb{N}} \overset{c}{\equiv} \{Y(a,n)\}_{n\in\mathbb{N}}$. In order to see why, observe that this formulation here guarantees that for every a and every nonuniform probabilistic polynomial-time D, there exists a negligible function μ such that for every n, D distinguishes $X(a,n)$ from $Y(a,n)$ with probability at most $\mu(n)$. This means that there can be a different negligible function for every a, and this function can even depend on a. In particular, consider the negligible function μ_a that equals 1 for every $n < 2^{|a|}$ and equals 2^{-n} for every $n \geq 2^{|a|}$, and assume that for every $a \in \{0, 1\}^*$ the function μ_a is taken. Such a function meets the definition requirements. However, this notion is too weak to be of use. For example, zero knowledge would become trivial for all languages in $\mathcal{NP}$ since the simulator could output $\perp$ if $n < 2^{|x|}$ where x is the statement being proven, and can just find the witness in the case that $n \geq 2^{|x|}$. This problem does not arise with the actual definition because it requires that there exists a single negligible function for *all* values of $a \in \{0, 1\}^*$.

6.3 The Basic Paradigm – Semantic Security

The birth of complexity-based cryptography (or "provable security") began with the first rigorous definition of the security of encryption [24]. The formulation captures the notion that *nothing* is learned about the plaintext from the ciphertext. As we discussed in the Introduction, this is actually very nontrivial to formalize. Since we have motivated this definition in the Introduction, we proceed directly to present it.

The definition allows the length of the plaintext to depend on the security parameter, and allows for arbitrary distributions over plaintexts (as long as the plaintexts sampled are of polynomial length). The definition also takes into account an arbitrary auxiliary information function h of the plaintext that may be leaked to the adversary through other means (e.g., because the same message x is used for some other purpose as well). The aim of the adversary is to learn some function f of the plaintext, from the ciphertext and the provided auxiliary information. According to the definition, it should be possible to learn the same information from the auxiliary information alone (and from the length of the plaintext), and without the ciphertext.

Definition 6.3.1 (Def. 5.2.1 in [18]). *A private-key encryption scheme* (G, E, D) *is* semantically secure *(in the private-key model) if for every nonuniform probabilistic polynomial-time algorithm* $\mathcal{A}$ *there exists a nonuniform probabilistic polynomial-time algorithm* $\mathcal{A}'$ *such that for every probability ensemble* $\{X_n\}_{n \in \mathbb{N}}$ *with* $|X_n| \leq$ poly(n), *every pair of polynomially-bounded functions* $f, h : \{0, 1\}^* \rightarrow \{0, 1\}^*$, *every positive polynomial* $p(\cdot)$ *and all sufficiently large* n:

$$\Pr_{k \leftarrow G(1^n)} \left[\mathcal{A}(1^n, E_k(X_n), 1^{|X_n|}, h(1^n, X_n)) = f(1^n, X_n) \right]$$

$$< \Pr \left[\mathcal{A}'(1^n, 1^{|X_n|}, h(1^n, X_n)) = f(1^n, X_n) \right] + \frac{1}{p(n)}.$$

(The probability in the above terms is taken over X_n *as well as over the internal coin tosses of the algorithms* G, E, *and* $\mathcal{A}$ *or* $\mathcal{A}'$.)

Observe that the adversary $\mathcal{A}$ is given the ciphertext $E_k(X_n)$ as well as auxiliary information $h(1^n, X_n)$, and attempts to guess the value of $f(1^n, X_n)$. Algorithm $\mathcal{A}'$ also attempts to guess the value of $f(1^n, X_n)$, but is given *only* $h(1^n, X_n)$ and the length of X_n. The security requirement states that $\mathcal{A}'$ can correctly guess $f(1^n, X_n)$ with almost the same probability as $\mathcal{A}$. Intuitively, then, the ciphertext $E_k(X_n)$ does not reveal any information about $f(1^n, X_n)$, for any f, since whatever can be learned by $\mathcal{A}$ (given the ciphertext) can be learned by $\mathcal{A}'$ (without the ciphertext).

Semantic security as simulation. Although the definition does not explicitly mention "simulation" or an ideal world, the definition follows this exact paradigm. In the world in which $\mathcal{A}'$ resides, it is given only the auxiliary information and plaintext length, and not the ciphertext. Thus, $\mathcal{A}'$ resides in an ideal world where, trivially, anything that it learns is from the auxiliary information and plaintext length only. The proof that $\mathcal{A}'$ can learn as much as $\mathcal{A}$ can learn is exactly the comparison between the real world and the ideal world, as discussed in the Introduction.

It is now possible to explain why this ideal/real world comparison is called *simulation*. The reason is that the *proof technique* used to show that a scheme meets a definition formalized in this way is simulation. Let us examine how one would go about proving that an encryption scheme meets Definition 6.3.1. The main question is how can one construct a machine $\mathcal{A}'$ that outputs $f(1^n, X_n)$ with almost the same probability as $\mathcal{A}$? How can $\mathcal{A}'$ even know what $\mathcal{A}$ does? The answer is that $\mathcal{A}'$ *simulates* an execution of $\mathcal{A}$ and outputs what $\mathcal{A}$ does. If $\mathcal{A}'$ could *perfectly simulate* such an execution—by providing $\mathcal{A}$ with its expected inputs—then $\mathcal{A}'$ would output $f(1^n, X_n)$ with exactly the same probability as $\mathcal{A}$ would. However, clearly $\mathcal{A}'$ cannot do this since it does not receive $E_k(X_n)$ for input. This is solved by having $\mathcal{A}'$ give $\mathcal{A}$ an encryption of garbage instead, as follows:

Simulator $\mathcal{A}'$: Upon input $1^n, 1^{|X_n|}, h = h(1^n, X_n)$, algorithm $\mathcal{A}'$ works as follows:

1. $\mathcal{A}'$ runs the key generation algorithm $G(1^n)$ in order to receive k (note that $\mathcal{A}'$ indeed needs to be given 1^n in order to do this).

2. $\mathcal{A}'$ computes $c = E_k\left(0^{|X_n|}\right)$ as an encryption of "garbage" (note that $\mathcal{A}'$ indeed needs to be given $1^{|X_n|}$ in order to do this).

3. $\mathcal{A}'$ runs $\mathcal{A}(1^n, c, 1^{|X_n|}, h)$ and outputs whatever $\mathcal{A}$ outputs.

The simulation that $\mathcal{A}'$ runs is clearly flawed; instead of giving $\mathcal{A}$ an encryption of X_n it gives $\mathcal{A}$ an encryption of zeroes. However, if encryptions are *indistinguishable*, then $\mathcal{A}$ should output $f(1^n, X_n)$ with approximately the same probability when given $E_k(X_n)$ as when given $E_k\left(0^{|X_n|}\right)$. Otherwise, it would be possible to distinguish such encryptions by seeing whether $\mathcal{A}$ succeeds in outputting $f(1^n, X_n)$ or not. Therefore, such a proof proceeds by showing that $\mathcal{A}$ indeed cannot distinguish between two such encryptions. For example, if the encryption works by XORing the plaintext with the output of a pseudorandom generator, then the reduction works by showing that any nonnegligible difference between the probability that $\mathcal{A}$ correctly outputs $f(1^n, X_n)$ in the two cases can be converted into a distinguisher that distinguishes the output of the pseudorandom generator from random with nonnegligible probability.

This modus operandi is actually typical of all simulation-based proofs. The simulator somehow simulates an execution for the adversary while handing it "garbage" that looks indistinguishable. Then, the proof proceeds by showing that the simulation is "good", or else the given assumption can be broken.

6.4 Secure Computation – Simulation for Semi-honest Adversaries

6.4.1 Background

The model that we consider here is that of two-party computation in the presence of *static semi-honest* adversaries. Such an adversary controls one of the parties (statically, and so at the onset of the computation) and follows the protocol specification exactly. However, it may try to learn more information than allowed by looking at the transcript of messages that it received and its internal state. Note that this is a very weak adversary model; if the adversary does anything not according to specification—even just choosing its random tape in a non-random way—then it may be able to completely break the protocol (and there are actual examples of natural protocols with this property). Nevertheless, a protocol that is secure in the presence of semi-honest adversaries does guarantee that there is no *inadvertent leakage* of information; when the parties involved essentially trust each other but want to make sure that no record of their input is found elsewhere, then this can suffice. Beyond this, protocols that are secure for semi-honest adversaries are often designed as the first step towards achieving stronger notions of security.

We note that it is much easier to define and prove security for semi-honest adversaries than for malicious adversaries, since we know exactly what the adversary will do (it just follows the protocol specification).

6.4.2 Defining Security for Semi-honest Adversaries

Two-party computation. A two-party protocol problem is cast by specifying a possibly random process that maps pairs of inputs to pairs of outputs (one for each party). We refer to such a process as a functionality and denote it $f : \{0,1\}^* \times \{0,1\}^* \to \{0,1\}^* \times \{0,1\}^*$, where $f = (f_1, f_2)$. That is, for every pair of inputs $x, y \in \{0,1\}^n$, the output pair is a random variable $(f_1(x,y), f_2(x,y))$ ranging over pairs of strings. The first party (with input x) wishes to obtain $f_1(x,y)$, and the second party (with input y) wishes to obtain $f_2(x,y)$.

Privacy by simulation. As expected, we wish to formalize the idea that a protocol is secure if whatever can be computed by a party participating in the protocol can be computed based on its input and output only. This is formalized according to the simulation paradigm by requiring the existence of a simulator who generates the view of a party in the execution. However, since the parties here have input and output, the simulator must be given a party's input and output in order to generate the view. Thus, security here is formalized by saying that a party's view in a protocol execution be simulatable given its *input* and *output*. This formulation implies that the parties learn nothing from the protocol *execution* beyond what they can derive from their input and prescribed output.

One important point to note is that, since the parties are semi-honest, it is guaranteed that they use the actual inputs written on their input tapes. This is important since it means that the output is well defined, and not dependent on the adversary. Specifically, for inputs x, y, the output is defined to be $f(x,y)$, and so the simulator can be given this value. As we will see, this is very different in the case of malicious adversaries, for the simple reason that a malicious adversary can ignore the input written on the input tape and can take any other input. (This is similar to the fact that a malicious verifier in zero knowledge can ignore its random tape and use internal hardcoded randomness instead.)

Definition of security. We begin with the following notation:

- Let $f = (f_1, f_2)$ be a probabilistic polynomial-time functionality and let π be a two-party protocol for computing f. (Throughout, whenever we consider a functionality, we always assume that it is polynomially time computable.)
- The view of the i-th party ($i \in \{1, 2\}$) during an execution of π on (x, y) and security parameter n is denoted by $\mathsf{view}_i^\pi(x, y, n)$ and equals $(w, r^i; m_1^i, ..., m_t^i)$, where $w \in \{x, y\}$ (its input depending on the value of i), r^i equals the contents of the i-th party's *internal* random tape, and m_j^i represents the j-th message that it received.
- The output of the i-th party during an execution of π on (x, y) and security parameter n is denoted by $\mathsf{output}_i^\pi(x, y, n)$ and can be computed from its own view of the execution. We denote the joint output of both parties by $\mathsf{output}^\pi(x, y, n) = (\mathsf{output}_1^\pi(x, y, n), \mathsf{output}_2^\pi(x, y, n))$.

Definition 6.4.1. *Let* $f = (f_1, f_2)$ *be a functionality. We say that* π *securely computes* f *in the presence of static semi-honest adversaries if there exist probabilistic polynomial-time algorithms* S_1 *and* S_2 *such that*

$$\left\{ (S_1(1^n, x, f_1(x,y)), f(x,y)) \right\}_{x,y,n} \stackrel{c}{\equiv} \left\{ (\mathsf{view}_1^\pi(x, y, n), \mathsf{output}^\pi(x, y, n)) \right\}_{x,y,n}, \text{ and}$$

$$\left\{ (S_2(1^n, y, f_2(x,y)), f(x,y)) \right\}_{x,y,n} \stackrel{c}{\equiv} \left\{ (\mathsf{view}_2^\pi(x, y, n), \mathsf{output}^\pi(x, y, n)) \right\}_{x,y,n},$$

where $x, y \in \{0, 1\}^*$ such that $|x| = |y|$, and $n \in \mathbb{N}$.

Observe that according to the definition, it is not enough for the simulator S_i to generate a string indistinguishable from $\text{view}_i^\pi(x, y)$. Rather, the *joint distribution* of the simulator's output and the functionality output $f(x, y) = (f_1(x, y), f_2(x, y))$ must be indistinguishable from $(\text{view}_i^\pi(x, y), \text{output}^\pi(x, y))$. This is necessary for probabilistic functionalities. In particular, consider the case that the parties wish to securely compute some randomized functionality $f(x, y)$, where the parties receive different output. For example, let x and y be lists of data elements, and let f be a functionality that outputs an *independent* random sample of $x \cup y$ of some predetermined size to each party. Now, consider a protocol that securely outputs the *same* random sample to both parties (and where each party's view can be simulated). Clearly, this protocol should *not* be secure. In particular, party P_1 should have no information about the sample received by P_2, and vice versa. Now, consider a simpler definition of security which compares the distribution generated by the simulator only with the view of the adversary (and not the joint distribution). Specifically, the definition requires that

$$\left\{ S_1(1^n, x, f_1(x, y)) \right\}_{x,y,n} \stackrel{c}{\equiv} \left\{ \text{view}_1^\pi(x, y, n) \right\}_{x,y,n}, \text{ and}$$

$$\left\{ S_2(1^n, y, f_2(x, y)) \right\}_{x,y,n} \stackrel{c}{\equiv} \left\{ \text{view}_2^\pi(x, y, n) \right\}_{x,y,n}.$$

It is not difficult to see that the aforementioned protocol that securely computes the same output to both *is* secure under this definition. This is due to the fact that each party's view consists of a random sample of $x \cup y$, as required, and this view can be simulated. The requirement that each sample be independent cannot be expressed by looking at each output separately. This therefore demonstrates that the definition is not satisfactory (since a clearly insecure protocol is "secure by definition"). For this reason, Definition 6.4.1 is formulated by looking at the *joint distribution*.

A simpler formulation for deterministic functionalities. In the case where the functionality f is deterministic, the aforementioned simpler definition can be used (along with an additional correctness requirement) since the problem described above does not arise. We first present the definition, and then explain why it suffices.

The definition has two requirements **(a)** correctness, meaning that the output of the parties is correct, and **(b)** privacy, meaning that the view of each party can be (separately) simulated. Formally, correctness is the requirement that there exists a negligible function μ such that for every $x, y \in \{0, 1\}^*$ and every n,

$$\Pr\left[\text{output}^\pi(x, y, n) \neq f(x, y)\right] \leq \mu(n),$$

and privacy is the requirement that there exist probabilistic polynomial-time S_1 and S_2 such that

$$\left\{\mathcal{S}_1(1^n, x, f_1(x,y))\right\}_{x,y\in\{0,1\}^*; n\in\mathbb{N}} \stackrel{c}{\equiv} \left\{\text{view}_1^\pi(x,y,n)\right\}_{x,y\in\{0,1\}^*; n\in\mathbb{N}}, \qquad (6.1)$$

$$\left\{\mathcal{S}_2(1^n, y, f_2(x,y))\right\}_{x,y\in\{0,1\}^*; n\in\mathbb{N}} \stackrel{c}{\equiv} \left\{\text{view}_2^\pi(x,y,n)\right\}_{x,y\in\{0,1\}^*; n\in\mathbb{N}}. \qquad (6.2)$$

For the case of deterministic functionalities f, any protocol that meets the correctness and privacy requirements is secure by Definition 6.4.1. In order to see this, observe that the distinguisher is given the indices x, y of the ensemble and so can compute $f(x, y)$ by itself. Thus,

$$\left\{\mathcal{S}_1(1^n, x, f_1(x,y))\right\}_{x,y\in\{0,1\}^*; n\in\mathbb{N}} \stackrel{c}{\equiv} \left\{\text{view}_1^\pi(x,y,n)\right\}_{x,y\in\{0,1\}^*; n\in\mathbb{N}} \qquad (6.3)$$

implies that

$$\left\{(\mathcal{S}_1(1^n, x, f_1(x,y)), f(x,y))\right\}_{x,y,n} \stackrel{c}{\equiv} \left\{(\text{view}_1^\pi(x,y,n), f(x,y))\right\}_{x,y,n}. \qquad (6.4)$$

In addition, the correctness requirement guarantees that $\text{output}^\pi(x, y, n)$ is computationally indistinguishable from $f(x, y)$, implying that

$$\left\{(\text{view}_1^\pi(x,y,n), f(x,y))\right\}_{x,y,nN} \stackrel{\text{'}c}{\equiv} \left\{(\text{view}_1^\pi(x,y,n), \text{output}^\pi(x,y,n))\right\}_{x,y,n}. \qquad (6.5)$$

Combining Equations (6.4) and (6.5), we have that

$$\left\{(\mathcal{S}_1(1^n, x, f_1(x,y)), f(x,y))\right\}_{x,y,n} \stackrel{c}{\equiv} \left\{(\text{view}_1^\pi(x,y,n), \text{output}^\pi(x,y,n))\right\}_{x,y,n},$$

and so the protocol meets Definition 6.4.1. This argument works for deterministic functionalities, but does not work for probabilistic ones. The reason is that Eq. (6.4) needs to be read as the *same* sample of $f(x, y) = (f_1(x,y), f_2(x,y))$ given to $\mathcal{S}_1$ and appearing in the random variable next to it in the ensemble. However, when we say that the distinguisher can compute $f(x, y)$ by itself, it is *not* true that it can sample $f(x, y)$ so that $f_1(x, y)$ is the same input given to the simulator. This problem does not arise for deterministic functionalities, since $f(x, y)$ is a single well-defined value. Thus, the claim that Eq. (6.3) implies Eq. (6.4) holds only for deterministic functionalities. See [18, Section 7.2.2] for more discussion on these definitions.

The fact that Definition 6.4.1 implies privacy and correctness is immediate. Thus, for deterministic functionalities, these formulations are equivalent.

Triviality for semi-honest adversaries. We remark that many problems become trivial in the case of semi-honest adversaries. For example, zero knowledge is trivial since the "prover" can just say this is correct. Since all parties are semi-honest, including the prover, this guarantees that the statement is indeed correct. Another example is commitments: in order to "commit" to a value x, the committer can simply store it locally without sending anything. Then, in order to "decommit", the committer can just send the value. This protocol is perfectly hiding. In addition, it is perfectly binding since a semi-honest adversary follows the specification and so will always send the correct value. Finally, if a number of parties wish to toss an unbiased coin, then one of them can simply locally toss a coin and send the result to all the others. Since the party tossing the coin is semi-honest, this guarantees that the coin is unbiased. Having said this, we stress that standard secure computation tasks—where multiple parties with inputs wish to compute a joint function of their inputs—are certainly not trivial.

Auxiliary information. In Section 6.3, and in the definition of security for malicious adversaries in Section 6.6, auxiliary information is explicitly provided to the adversary. In contrast, here it appears that there is no auxiliary information. However, auxiliary input is implicit in the definition since computational indistinguishability with respect to *nonuniform* adversaries is required. Thus, the distinguisher *is* given auxiliary input. Note that there is no need to provide any auxiliary information to the adversary running the protocol, since it is semi-honest and thus follows the exact same instructions irrespective of any auxiliary input.

6.4.3 Oblivious Transfer for Semi-honest Adversaries

In this section, we consider a standard two-party functionality, where both parties have private inputs and wish to compute an output. We will show how to securely compute the bit oblivious transfer functionality, defined by $f((b_0, b_1), \sigma) = (\lambda, b_\sigma)$, where $b_0, b_1, \sigma \in \{0, 1\}$ [36, 16]. Stated in words, P_1 has a pair of input bits (b_0, b_1) and P_2 has a choice bit σ. The function is such that P_1 receives no output (denoted by the empty string λ), and in particular learns nothing about σ. In contrast, P_2 receives the bit of its choice b_σ and learns nothing about the other bit $b_{1-\sigma}$. This is called "oblivious transfer" since the first party has two inputs and sends exactly one of the inputs to the receiver, according to the receiver's choice, without knowing which is sent. We present the protocol of [16] in Protocol 6.4.2, which relies on *enhanced trapdoor permutations*.

Background – enhanced trapdoor permutations [18, Appendix C.1]. Informally, a family of trapdoor permutations is a family of bijective functions with the property that randomly sampled functions are hard to invert on randomly sampled values (in its range). However, there exists a trapdoor so that given the trapdoor, the function *can* be efficiently inverted. *Enhanced* trapdoor permutations have the additional property that it is possible to sample values from the range, so that it is hard to invert the function on these values even when given the coins used for sampling. Formally, a collection of trapdoor permutations is a collection of functions $\{f_\alpha\}_\alpha$ accompanied by four probabilistic polynomial-time algorithms I, S, F, F^{-1} such that:

1. $I(1^n)$ selects a random n-bit index α of a permutation f_α along with a corresponding trapdoor τ. Denote by $I_1(1^n)$ the α-part of the output.
2. $S(\alpha)$ samples an (almost uniform) element in the domain (equivalently, the range) of f_α. We denote by $S(\alpha; r)$ the output of $S(\alpha)$ with random tape r; for simplicity we assume that $r \in \{0, 1\}^n$.
3. $F(\alpha, x) = f_\alpha(x)$, for α in the range of I_1 and x in the range of $S(\alpha)$.
4. $F^{-1}(\tau, y) = f_\alpha^{-1}(y)$ for y in the range of f_α and (α, τ) in the range of I.

Then, the family is a collection of enhanced trapdoor permutations if for every nonuniform probabilistic polynomial-time adversary $\mathcal{A}$ there exists a negligible function μ such that for every n,

$$\Pr\left[\mathcal{A}(1^n,\alpha,r) = f_\alpha^{-1}(S(\alpha;r))\right] \le \mu(n),$$

where $\alpha \leftarrow I_1(1^n)$ and $r \in_R \{0,1\}^n$ is random. Observe that given α and r, $\mathcal{A}$ can compute $y = S(\alpha;r)$. Thus, $\mathcal{A}$'s task is to invert y, when it is also given the random coins used by S to sample y. See [18, Appendix C.1] for more discussion on the definition and for constructions of enhanced trapdoor permutations.

We will also refer to a hard-core predicate B of a family of enhanced trapdoor permutations [17, Section 2.5]. We say that B is a hard-core predicate of (I, S, F, F^{-1}) if for every nonuniform probabilistic polynomial-time adversary $\mathcal{A}$ there exists a negligible function μ such that for every n,

$$\Pr\left[\mathcal{A}(1^n,\alpha,r) = B\left(\alpha, f_\alpha^{-1}(S(\alpha;r))\right)\right] \le \frac{1}{2} + \mu(n).$$

The protocol idea. The idea behind the protocol is that P_1 chooses an enhanced trapdoor permutation, and sends the permutation description (without the trapdoor) to P_2. Then, P_2 samples two elements y_0, y_1 where it knows the preimage of y_σ but does *not* know the preimage of $y_{1-\sigma}$. Party P_2 sends y_0, y_1 to P_1, who inverts them both using the trapdoor, and sends b_0 masked by the hard-core bit of $f^{-1}(y_0)$, and b_1 masked by the hard-core bit of $f^{-1}(y_1)$. Party P_2 is able to obtain b_σ since it knows $f^{-1}(y_\sigma)$, but is unable to obtain $b_{1-\sigma}$ since it does not know $f^{-1}(y_{1-\sigma})$ and so cannot guess its hard-core bit with probability nonnegligibly greater than $1/2$. In addition, P_1 sees only y_0, y_1 which are identically distributed (even though P_2 generates them differently), and so learns nothing about P_2's bit σ. See Protocol 6.4.2 for the protocol description.

PROTOCOL 6.4.2 (Oblivious transfer [16])

- **Inputs:** P_1 has $b_0, b_1 \in \{0,1\}$ and P_2 has $\sigma \in \{0,1\}$. (Both parties have (I, S, F, F^{-1}) defining a collection of enhanced trapdoor permutations and a hard-core predicate B.)
- **The protocol:**
  1. P_1 runs $I(1^n)$ to obtain a permutation–trapdoor pair (α, τ). P_1 sends α to P_2.
  2. P_2 runs $S(\alpha)$ twice; denote the first value obtained by x_σ and the second by $y_{1-\sigma}$. Then, P_2 computes $y_\sigma = F(\alpha, x_\sigma) = f_\alpha(x_\sigma)$, and sends y_0, y_1 to P_1.
  3. P_1 uses the trapdoor τ and computes $x_0 = F^{-1}(\alpha, y_0) = f_\alpha^{-1}(y_0)$ and $x_1 = F^{-1}(\alpha, y_1) = f_\alpha^{-1}(y_1)$. Then, it computes $\beta_0 = B(\alpha, x_0) \oplus b_0$ and $\beta_1 = B(\alpha, x_1) \oplus b_1$, where B is a hard-core predicate of f. Finally, P_1 sends (β_0, β_1) to P_2.
  4. P_2 computes $b_\sigma = B(\alpha, x_\sigma) \oplus \beta_\sigma$ and outputs the result.

We prove the following theorem:

Theorem 6.4.3. *Assume that (I, S, F, F^{-1}) constitutes a family of enhanced trapdoor permutations with a hard-core predicate B. Then, Protocol 6.4.2 securely computes the functionality $f((b_0, b_1), \sigma) = (\lambda, b_\sigma)$ in the presence of static semi-honest adversaries.*

Proof: Since this is the first proof in this tutorial, we prove it in excruciating detail; in later proofs we will not necessarily work through all the fine details. The oblivious transfer functionality is deterministic, and thus it suffices to use the simpler formulation of security. Correctness is immediate, and we therefore proceed to the simulation. We construct a separate simulator for each party ($\mathcal{S}_1$ for P_1's view and $\mathcal{S}_2$ for P_2's view, as in Definition 6.4.1).

Consider first the case that P_1 is corrupted. Observe that P_1 receives no output. Thus, we merely need to show that a simulator can generate the view of the incoming messages received by P_1. In the protocol, P_1 receives a single message consisting of a pair of values y_0, y_1 in the domain of f_α. Formally, $\mathcal{S}_1$ is given (b_0, b_1) and 1^n and works as follows:

1. $\mathcal{S}_1$ chooses a uniformly distributed random tape r for P_1 (of the length required, which is what is needed to run I).
2. $\mathcal{S}_1$ computes $(\alpha, \tau) \leftarrow I(1^n; r)$, using the r from above.
3. $\mathcal{S}_1$ runs $S(\alpha)$ twice with independent randomness to sample values y_0, y_1.
4. Finally, $\mathcal{S}_1$ outputs $((b_0, b_1), r; (y_0, y_1))$; the pair (y_0, y_1) simulates the incoming message from P_2 to P_1 in the protocol.

Note that $\mathcal{S}_1$ cannot sample y_0, y_1 in the same way as the honest P_2 since it does not know P_2's input σ. Nevertheless, the definition of a collection of trapdoor permutations states that $S(\alpha)$ outputs a value that is almost uniformly distributed in the domain of f_α (and the domain equals the range, since it is a permutation). Thus, it follows that the distribution over $F(\alpha, S(\alpha))$ is statistically close to the distribution over $S(\alpha)$. This implies that

$$\{(F(\alpha, x_0), y_1)\} \overset{s}{\equiv} \{(y_0, y_1)\} \overset{s}{\equiv} \{(y_0, F(\alpha, x_1))\},$$

where α is in the range of I, and x_0, x_1, y_0, y_1 are all samples of $S(\alpha)$. The view of P_1 includes a pair as above, along with a uniformly generated tape. Note that the pair $(F(\alpha, x_0), y_1)$ is exactly what P_1 sees when P_2 has input $\sigma = 0$, that the pair (y_0, y_1) is the simulator-generated view, and that the pair $(y_0, F(\alpha, x_1))$ is exactly what P_1 sees when P_2 has input $\sigma = 1$. Thus, we conclude that for every $\sigma \in \{0, 1\}$,

$$\{\mathcal{S}_1(1^n, (b_0, b_1))\} \overset{s}{\equiv} \{\mathsf{view}_1^\pi((b_0, b_1), \sigma)\}$$

as required.

Next, we proceed to the case that P_2 is corrupted, and construct a simulator $\mathcal{S}_2$. In this case, we need to do something very different in the simulation. In particular, we need to construct a view so that the output defined by that view equals the real output of the protocol. (Observe that a party's view includes its input, random tape, and all incoming messages. Thus, by running the protocol instructions on this view, an output is obtained. This output has to be the "correct" one, or the distinguisher can easily see that it is not the view of a real execution.) Recall that $\mathcal{S}_2$ receives P_2's input *and output*, and thus is able to achieve the above. In this protocol, this is achieved by having $\mathcal{S}_2$ set $\beta_\sigma = B(\alpha, x_\sigma) \oplus b_\sigma$, like the real P_1. In contrast, $\mathcal{S}_2$ is unable to compute $\beta_{1-\sigma}$ correctly, since it does not know $b_{1-\sigma}$.

Simulator S_2 receives for input 1^n plus P_2's input and output bits (σ, b_σ). Then:

1. S_2 chooses a uniform random tape for P_2. Since P_2's randomness is for running $S(\alpha)$ twice, we denote the random tape by r_0, r_1.[1]
2. S_2 runs $I(1^n)$ and obtains (α, τ).
3. S_2 computes $x_\sigma = S(\alpha; r_\sigma)$ and $y_{1-\sigma} = S(\alpha; r_{1-\sigma})$, and sets $x_{1-\sigma} = F^{-1}(\tau, y_{1-\sigma})$.
4. S_2 sets $\beta_\sigma = B(\alpha, x_\sigma) \oplus b_\sigma$, where b_σ is P_2's output received by S_2.
5. S_2 sets $\beta_{1-\sigma} = B(\alpha, x_{1-\sigma})$.
6. S_2 outputs $(\sigma, r_0, r_1; \alpha, (\beta_0, \beta_1))$.

First, note that by putting the "σ-value" first, the real view of P_2 in an execution can be written as

$$\text{view}_2^\pi((b_0, b_1), \sigma) = \left(\sigma, r_0, r_1; \alpha, (B(\alpha, x_\sigma) \oplus b_\sigma, B(\alpha, x_{1-\sigma}) \oplus b_{1-\sigma})\right),$$

where $x_0 = S(\alpha; r_0)$ and $x_1 = S(\alpha; r_1)$. In contrast, the output of the simulator written in this way is

$$S_2(1^n, \sigma, b_\sigma) = \left(\sigma, r_0, r_1; \alpha, (B(\alpha, x_\sigma) \oplus b_\sigma, B(\alpha, x_{1-\sigma}))\right),$$

where $x_0 = S(\alpha; r_0)$ and $x_1 = S(\alpha; r_1)$. Thus, these are *identical* when $b_{1-\sigma} = 0$. Formally, when $b_{1-\sigma} = 0$, for every $\sigma, b_\sigma \in \{0, 1\}$ and every n

$$\left\{ S_2(1^n, \sigma, b_\sigma) \right\} \equiv \left\{ \text{view}_1^\pi((b_0, b_1), \sigma) \right\}.$$

It therefore remains to show that the view is *indistinguishable* in the case that $b_{1-\sigma} = 1$. The only difference between the two is whether $\beta_{1-\sigma} = B(\alpha, x_{1-\sigma})$ or $\beta_{1-\sigma} = B(\alpha, x_{1-\sigma}) \oplus 1$. Thus, we need to show that for every $\sigma, b_\sigma \in \{0, 1\}$,

$$\left\{ \left(\sigma, r_0, r_1; \alpha, (B(\alpha, x_\sigma) \oplus b_\sigma, B(\alpha, x_{1-\sigma})) \right) \right\}$$
$$\stackrel{c}{\equiv} \left\{ \left(\sigma, r_0, r_1; \alpha, (B(\alpha, x_\sigma) \oplus b_\sigma, B(\alpha, x_{1-\sigma}) \oplus 1) \right) \right\},$$

where the distribution on the left is that generated by S_2 and the distribution on the right is the real one when $b_{1-\sigma} = 1$. Assume by contradiction that there exists a nonuniform probabilistic polynomial-time distinguisher D, a polynomial $p(\cdot)$ and an infinite series of tuples (σ, b_σ, n) such that

$$\Pr[D(\sigma, r_0, r_1; \alpha, (B(\alpha, x_\sigma) \oplus b_\sigma, B(\alpha, x_{1-\sigma}))) = 1]$$
$$- \Pr[D(\sigma, r_0, r_1; \alpha, (B(\alpha, x_\sigma) \oplus b_\sigma, B(\alpha, x_{1-\sigma}) \oplus 1)) = 1] \geq \frac{1}{p(n)}. \quad (6.6)$$

(Without loss of generality, we assume that for infinitely many n's, D outputs 1 with greater or equal probability when receiving $B(\alpha, x_{1-\sigma})$ than when receiving $B(\alpha, x_{1-\sigma}) \oplus 1$.) We construct a nonuniform probabilistic polynomial-time guessing algorithm A that uses D to guess the hard-core predicate.

---

[1] In almost all cases, the simulation begins by the simulator choosing a uniform random tape for the party.

Algorithm $\mathcal{A}$ is given σ, b_σ on its advice tape, and receives $(1^n, \alpha, r)$ for input. $\mathcal{A}$'s aim is to guess $B(\alpha, S(\alpha; r))$. Algorithm $\mathcal{A}$ sets $r_{1-\sigma} = r$ (from its input), chooses a random r_σ, and computes $x_\sigma = S(\alpha; r_\sigma)$ and $\beta_\sigma = B(\alpha, x_\sigma) \oplus b_\sigma$. Finally, $\mathcal{A}$ chooses a random $\beta_{1-\sigma}$, invokes D on input $(\sigma, r_0, r_1; \alpha, (\beta_\sigma, \beta_{1-\sigma}))$ and outputs $\beta_{1-\sigma}$ if D outputs 1, and $1 - \beta_{1-\sigma}$ otherwise. Observe that if $\mathcal{A}$ guesses $\beta_{1-\sigma}$ correctly then it invokes D on $(\sigma, r_0, r_1; \alpha, (B(\alpha, x_\sigma) \oplus b_\sigma, B(\alpha, x_{1-\sigma})))$, and otherwise it invokes D on $(\sigma, r_0, r_1; \alpha, (B(\alpha, x_\sigma) \oplus b_\sigma, B(\alpha, x_{1-\sigma}) \oplus 1))$. Thus, if D outputs 1, then $\mathcal{A}$ assumes that it guessed $\beta_{1-\sigma}$ correctly (since D outputs 1 with higher probability when given $B(\alpha, x_{1-\sigma})$ than when given $B(\alpha, x_{1-\sigma}) \oplus 1$). Otherwise, it assumes that it guessed $\beta_{1-\sigma}$ incorrectly and so outputs $1 - \beta_{1-\sigma}$. It therefore follows that

$$\Pr[\mathcal{A}(1^n, \alpha, r) = B(\alpha, x)]$$

$$= \frac{1}{2} \cdot \Pr[\mathcal{A}(1^n, \alpha, r) = B(\alpha, x) \mid \beta_{1-\sigma} = B(\alpha, x)]$$

$$+ \frac{1}{2} \cdot \Pr[\mathcal{A}(1^n, \alpha, r) = B(\alpha, x) \mid \beta_{1-\sigma} \neq B(\alpha, x)]$$

$$= \frac{1}{2} \cdot \Pr[D(\sigma, r_0, r_1; \alpha, (B(\alpha, x_\sigma) \oplus b_\sigma, B(\alpha, x_{1-\sigma}))) = 1]$$

$$+ \frac{1}{2} \cdot \Pr[D(\sigma, r_0, r_1; \alpha, (B(\alpha, x_\sigma) \oplus b_\sigma, B(\alpha, x_{1-\sigma}) \oplus 1)) = 0]$$

$$= \frac{1}{2} \cdot \Pr[D(\sigma, r_0, r_1; \alpha, (B(\alpha, x_\sigma) \oplus b_\sigma, B(\alpha, x_{1-\sigma}))) = 1]$$

$$+ \frac{1}{2} \cdot (1 - \Pr[D(\sigma, r_0, r_1; \alpha, (B(\alpha, x_\sigma) \oplus b_\sigma, B(\alpha, x_{1-\sigma}) \oplus 1)) = 1])$$

$$= \frac{1}{2} + \frac{1}{2} \cdot \Pr[D(\sigma, r_0, r_1; \alpha, (B(\alpha, x_\sigma) \oplus b_\sigma, B(\alpha, x_{1-\sigma}))) = 1]$$

$$- \frac{1}{2} \cdot \Pr[D(\sigma, r_0, r_1; \alpha, (B(\alpha, x_\sigma) \oplus b_\sigma, B(\alpha, x_{1-\sigma}) \oplus 1)) = 1].$$

By the contradicting assumption in Eq. (6.6), we have that

$$\Pr[\mathcal{A}(1^n, \alpha, r) = B(\alpha, x)] \geq \frac{1}{2} + \frac{1}{2p(n)},$$

in contradiction to the assumption that B is a hard-core predicate of f. We conclude that $\mathcal{S}_2$'s output is computationally indistinguishable from the view of P_2 in a real execution. ∎

Discussion. We remark that this protocol is a good example of the fact that security in the presence of semi-honest adversaries guarantees nothing if the corrupted party does not behave completely honestly. In particular, if P_2 generates *both* y_0 and y_1 by choosing x_0, x_1 and computing $y_0 = F(\alpha, x_0)$ and $y_1 = F(\alpha, x_1)$, then it will learn both b_0 and b_1. Furthermore, P_1 has no way of detecting this at all.

This concludes our treatment of semi-honest adversaries. As we have seen, proving security for semi-honest adversaries requires constructing a simulator that generates the entire view itself. This view must be a function of the input and output, since the view fully defines the output. Unlike in the case of malicious adversaries, who may behave in an arbitrary way, semi-honest adversaries follow the protocol specification exactly. Thus, there is no need to "rewind" them or "interact" with them, in contrast to what we will see in the sequel below.

6.5 Simulating the View of Malicious Adversaries – Zero Knowledge

In this section we will consider simulation in the context of zero-knowledge proof systems. Unlike what we have seen until now, simulation for zero knowledge considers malicious adversaries (in particular, malicious verifiers) who may behave arbitrarily and not necessarily according to the protocol specification. However, as we have mentioned in the Introduction, in zero knowledge there are no private inputs or output. Thus, the simulator needs to generate the view of the verifier in a proof, without the additional complexity of considering inputs and outputs. As we will see below, this can already be challenging.

We will begin by defining zero knowledge and commitments in Sections 6.5.1 and 6.5.2, respectively. Then, in Section 6.5.3, we present a non-constant round zero-knowledge proof for any language in $\mathcal{NP}$. Additional proof techniques are needed to achieve constant-round zero knowledge, as we show in Section 6.5.4. Finally, we highlight the difference between semi-honest and malicious adversaries by comparing with honest-verifier zero knowledge (which considers semi-honest verifiers) in Section 6.5.5.

6.5.1 Defining Zero Knowledge

Notation. Let A be a probabilistic polynomial-time machine. We denote by $A(x, y, r)$ the output of the machine A on input x, auxiliary input y and random tape r. In contrast to the rest of this tutorial where the parties are assumed to be polynomial time in a *separate security parameter* n (see Section 6.2), in this section we set $n = |x|$ and so A runs in time that is polynomial in the length of the statement x. We do this in order to be consistent with the standard definitions of zero knowledge.

Let A and B be interactive machines. We denote by $\mathsf{output}_B(A(x, y, r_A), B(x, z, r_B))$ the output of party B in an interactive execution with party A, on public input x, where A has auxiliary input y and random tape r_A, and B has auxiliary input z and random tape r_B. We will sometimes drop r_A or r_B from this notation, which will mean that the random tape is not fixed but rather chosen at random. For example we denote by $\mathsf{output}_B(A(x, y), B(x, z))$ the random variable $\mathsf{output}_B(A(x, y, U_m), B(x, z, U'_{m'}))$ where m (resp., m') is the number of random bits that A (resp., B) uses on input of size $|x|$.

The definition. Loosely speaking, an interactive proof system for a language L involves a prover P and a verifier V, where upon common input x, the prover P attempts to convince V that $x \in L$. We note that the prover is often given some private auxiliary input that "helps" it to prove the statement in question to V. Such a proof system has the following two properties:

1. *Completeness:* this states that when honest P and V interact on common input $x \in L$, then V is convinced of the correctness of the statement that $x \in L$ (except with at most negligible probability).
2. *Soundness:* this states that when V interacts with any (cheating) prover P^* on common input $x \notin L$, then V will be convinced *with at most negligible probability*. (Thus V cannot be tricked into accepting a false statement.)

A formal definition of interactive proofs can be found in [17, Section 4.2].

We now recall the definition of zero knowledge [25]. Informally speaking, a proof is zero knowledge if there exists a simulator that can generate the view of the verifier from the statement alone. We remark that the corrupted verifier may output anything it wishes, including its view. Thus, one may equivalently consider the view of the verifier and its output. For the sake of this tutorial, we will only consider black-box zero knowledge [23, 17], where the simulator receives only oracle access to the verifier. In addition, we will consider only $\mathcal{NP}$ languages. We therefore present this definition only.

Definition 6.5.1. *Let (P, V) be an interactive proof system for an $\mathcal{NP}$ language L, and let R_L be the associated $\mathcal{NP}$-relation. We say that (P, V) is* black-box *computational* zero knowledge *if there exists a probabilistic polynomial-time oracle machine S such that for every nonuniform probabilistic polynomial-time algorithm V^* it holds that*

$$\left\{ \mathrm{output}_{V^*}(P(x, w), V^*(x, z)) \right\}_{(x,w) \in R_L, z \in \{0,1\}^*} \stackrel{c}{\equiv} \left\{ S^{V^*(x,z,r,\cdot)}(x) \right\}_{x \in L, z \in \{0,1\}^*},$$

where r is uniformly distributed, and where $V^*(x, z, r, \cdot)$ denotes the next-message function *of the interactive machine V^* when the common input x, auxiliary input z and random tape r are fixed (i.e., the next message function of V^* receives a message history $\mathbf{m}$ and outputs $V^*(x, z, r, \mathbf{m})$).*

In some cases, the simulator (and verifier) are allowed to run in *expected* polynomial-time and not strict polynomial time. We will refer to this later.

We remark that in our definition above, we fix the random tape of the verifier. With very few exceptions (e.g., the non-black box uniform zero-knowledge protocol of [1]), the ability to set the random tape of the adversary does not help. This is due to the fact that the adversary can completely ignore its random tape, and can use a pseudorandom function applied to its history with an internally hardcoded key. Thus, in most cases of simulation, one can just ignore the random tape. Note that if the definition is not black box, then it is necessary to choose a random tape for the adversary. However, in most cases, this can just be chosen to be uniformly distributed of the appropriate length, and then ignored.

6.5.2 Preliminaries – Commitment Schemes

We will use commitment schemes in a number of places throughout the tutorial. We denote by Com a noninteractive perfectly binding commitment scheme. Let $c = \mathsf{Com}_n(x; r)$ denote a commitment to x using random string r and with security parameter n. We will typically omit the explicit reference to n and will write $c = \mathsf{Com}(x; r)$. Let $\mathsf{Com}(x)$ denote a commitment to x using uniform randomness. Let $\mathsf{decom}(c)$ denote the decommitment value of c; to be specific, if $c = \mathsf{Com}(x; r)$, then $\mathsf{decom}(c) = (x, r)$.

A formal definition of commitment schemes can be found in [17, Section 4.4.1]. Informally, perfect binding is formalized by saying that the sets of all commitments to different values are disjoint; that is, for all $x_1 \neq x_2$ it holds that $C_{x_1} \cap C_{x_2} = \emptyset$, where $C_{x_1} = \{c \mid \exists r : c = \mathsf{Com}(x_1; r)\}$ and $C_{x_2} = \{c \mid \exists r : c = \mathsf{Com}(x_2; r)\}$. Computational hiding can be formalized in multiple ways, and basically states that commitments to different strings are computationally indistinguishable. For bit commitments, this can easily be stated by requiring that $C_0 \overset{c}{\equiv} C_1$, where $C_b = \{\mathsf{Com}(b; U_n)\}_{n \in \mathbb{N}}$ is the ensemble of commitments to bit b.

LR-security of commitments. One of the proofs below is made significantly easier by using a definition of security of commitments that is both adaptive and already includes security for multiple commitments. We present a definition that is based on the LR-oracle definition of encryption [4]. The LR-oracle (left or right oracle) definition is formulated by providing the adversary with an oracle that receives two equal-length inputs, and either always returns a commitment to the first (left) input or always returns a commitment to the second (right) input. The task of the adversary is to determine whether it is receiving left or right commitments. This definition is much easier to work with, as we will see below, partly because the hybrid argument relating to multiple commitments is already built in. We first define the oracle as

$$LR^b_{\mathsf{Com}}(x_0, x_1) = \begin{cases} \mathsf{Com}(x_b) & \text{if } |x_0| = |x_1| \\ \bot & \text{otherwise} \end{cases}, \text{ where } \mathsf{Com}(x) \text{ denotes a (noninteractive)}$$

commitment to x. We define the LR experiment with a noninteractive perfectly binding commitment scheme Com and an adversary $\mathcal{A}$ who is given LR^0_{Com} or LR^1_{Com} and attempts to distinguish between these cases. The experiment is as follows:

Experiment LR-commit$_{\mathsf{Com},\mathcal{A}}(1^n)$:

1. Choose a random $b \leftarrow \{0, 1\}$.
2. Set $b' \leftarrow \mathcal{A}^{LR^b_{\mathsf{Com}}(\cdot,\cdot)}(1^n)$.
3. Output 1 if and only if $b' = b$.

The following can be proven via a standard hybrid argument:

Theorem 6.5.2. *If Com is a noninteractive perfectly binding commitment scheme with security for nonuniform adversaries, then for every nonuniform probabilistic polynomial-time adversary $\mathcal{A}$, there exists a negligible function μ such that*

$$\Pr\left[\text{LR-commit}_{\mathsf{Com},\mathcal{A}}(1^n) = 1\right] \leq \frac{1}{2} + \mu(n).$$

We remark that *nonuniform* security is needed, as we will see below.

6.5.3 Non-constant-Round Zero Knowledge

Consider the zero-knowledge proofs for $\mathcal{NP}$ of 3-coloring [22] and Hamiltonic-ity [6]. Both of these protocols work by the prover first sending commitments. Next, the verifier sends a "challenge" asking the prover to open some of the commitments. Finally, the prover sends the appropriate decommitments, and the verifier checks that the results are as expected. In the case of 3-coloring, the prover commits to a random valid coloring, and the verifier asks to open the colors associated with a single edge. In the case of Hamiltonicity, the prover commits to the adjacency matrix of a random permutation of the graph, and the verifier asks to either open the entire graph or to open a simple cycle. In both of these cases, if the prover knows the challenge of the verifier ahead of time, then it can easily prove without knowing the required $\mathcal{NP}$ witness. Let us focus on the 3-coloring case. If the prover does not know a 3-coloring, then it cannot commit to a valid coloring. Thus, there must be at least one edge in the graph which assigns the same color to both endpoints of the edge in the committed coloring by the prover. If the verifier asks to open the colors of this edge, then the prover will be caught cheating. Thus, the prover can cheat with probability at most $1/|E|$ (where E is the set of edges). By repeating the proof $n \cdot |E|$ times (where n is the number of nodes in the graph), we have that the prover can get away with cheating with probability at most $\left(1 - \frac{1}{|E|}\right)^{n \cdot |E|} < e^{-n}$, which is negligible. Thus, this proof is *sound*.

PROTOCOL 6.5.3 (Zero-knowledge proof for 3-coloring)

- *Common input:* a graph $G = (V, E)$ with $V = \{v_1, \ldots, v_n\}$
- *Auxiliary input for the prover:* a coloring of the graph $\psi : V \rightarrow \{1, 2, 3\}$ such that for every $(v_i, v_j) \in E$ it holds that $\psi(v_i) \neq \psi(v_j)$
- *The proof system:* Repeat the following $n \cdot |E|$ times (using independent randomness each time):

  1. The prover selects a random permutation π over $\{1, 2, 3\}$, defines $\phi(v) = \pi(\psi(v))$ for all $v \in V$, and computes $c_i = \mathsf{Com}(\phi(v_i))$ for all i. The prover sends the verifier the commitments $(c_1, \ldots, c_n)$.
  2. The verifier chooses a random edge $e \in_R E$ and sends e to the prover.
  3. Let $e = (v_i, v_j)$ be the edge received by the prover. The prover sends $\mathsf{decom}(c_i), \mathsf{decom}(c_j)$ to the verifier.
  4. Let $\phi(v_i)$ and $\phi(v_j)$ denote the respective decommitment values from c_i and c_j. The verifier checks that the decommitments are valid, that $\phi(v_i), \phi(v_j) \in \{1, 2, 3\}$, and that $\phi(v_i) \neq \phi(v_j)$. If not, it halts and outputs 0.

  If the checks pass in all iterations, then the verifier outputs 1.

Regarding *zero knowledge*, observe that in each execution a new random coloring of the edges is committed to by the prover, and the verifier only sees the colors of a single edge. Thus, the verifier simply sees two (different) random colors for the endpoints of the edges each time. This clearly reveals nothing about the coloring of the graph. We stress that such an argument is insufficient, and we must prove this intuition by constructing a simulator. The idea behind the simulation here is that if the simulator knows the edge to be queried ahead of time, then it can commit to random different colors on the endpoints of that edge and to garbage elsewhere. By the hiding property of the commitment scheme, this will be indistinguishable. As we will see, the simulator will simply repeatedly guess the edge that is to be queried ahead of time until it is correct.

The rewinding technique (with commitments as envelopes). We begin by describing how to construct a simulator when we model the commitments as perfect envelopes that reveal nothing until opened. The key tool for constructing a simulator is that of *rewinding*. Specifically, the simulator invokes the verifier, and guesses a random edge $e = (v_i, v_j) \in_R E$ with the hope that the verifier will query that edge. The simulator then sends the verifier (its oracle in the black-box case) commitments to a coloring whereby v_i and v_j are given two different random colors in $\{1, 2, 3\}$ and zeroes for the rest. If the verifier replies with the edge $e' = e$, then the simulator opens the envelopes for the nodes in e, and the simulation of this iteration is complete. Otherwise, the simulator rewinds the verifier to the beginning of the iteration and tries again, this time choosing a new random edge. This is repeated until $e' = e$ and so the simulator succeeds. (In order to get negligible soundness error, many sequential executions of the protocol are run, and so after it succeeds the simulator proceeds to the next iteration. This essentially means fixing the transcript of incoming messages to this point, and continuing with the residual verifier that is defined by the fixed transcript prefix.) Since the verifier has no way of knowing which edge e the simulator chose (since this fact is hidden inside unopened envelopes), the expected number of repetitions required is $|E|$, and the probability that more than $n \cdot |E|$ repetitions are needed is negligible. Note that the distribution over the view of the verifier in the simulation is identical to its view in a real execution. This is due to the fact that in both a real proof and in a simulation the verifier sees a set of "envelopes" and an opening to two different random colors. The difference between the two is that in a real proof no rewinding took place, in contrast to the simulation. However, this fact is not evident in the verifier's final view, and so they both look the same.

This concept of rewinding is often confusing at first sight. We therefore add two remarks. First, one may wonder how it is possible to "technically" rewind the verifier. In fact, when considering black-box zero knowledge, this is trivial. Specifically, the simulator is given oracle access to the *next-message function* $V^*(x, z, r, \cdot)$ of the verifier. This means that it provides a transcript $\mathbf{m} = (m_1, m_2, \ldots)$ of incoming messages and receives back the next message sent when V^* has input x, auxiliary input z, random tape r and incoming messages $\mathbf{m}$. Now, rewinding is essentially S calling its oracle with $(r, (m_1, m_2, m_3))$ and then with $(r, (m_1, m_2, m_3'))$, and so on. It is worthwhile also translating this notion of rewinding into modern computing terms. Virtual machines (VMs) are now very common. Snapshots of a VM can be taken at any time, and it is possible to rewind a VM by simply restoring the snapshot. The VM then continues from exactly the same state as before, and it has no way of knowing that this "rewinding" took place. This is exactly what a simulator does with the verifier.

A second point that is sometimes confusing is why the zero-knowledge property, and in particular the existence of a simulator, does not contradict soundness. If the simulator can prove the theorem without knowing the witness (and possibly even if the theorem is not true), then what prevents a cheating prover from doing the same? The answer is that the simulator has additional power that the prover does not have. In our example above, this power is the ability to rewind the verifier; a real prover *cannot* rewind the verifier, in contrast to the simulator. Conceptually, this makes a lot of sense. The motivation behind the simulation paradigm is that whatever the verifier can learn in a real interaction with the prover it can learn *by itself*. The verifier can indeed generate its view by applying the simulator to itself and rewinding, as described above. The prover, who is an external entity to the verifier, cannot do this.

The above analysis and explanation relate to the case that commitments are modeled as ideal envelopes. It is important to stress that this modeling of commitments is an oversimplification that bypasses the main technical difficulties involved when proving that the simulation works. First, it is necessary to show that the view of the verifier is indistinguishable in the simulation and real execution. This requires a reduction to the hiding property of commitments, since the actual distribution is *very* different. In particular, the real prover commits to a valid coloring of the graph, whereas the commitment in the simulation is to zeroes except for the nodes on the opened edge. A second, more subtle, issue is that it is required to prove that the simulation halts successfully within $n \cdot |E|$ attempts, except with negligible probability. In the "envelopes" case, this is immediate. However, when using actual commitments that are just computationally hiding, this needs a proof (perfectly hiding commitments could be used, but then the protocol would only be computationally sound, and a reduction to the computationally binding property of the commitment would anyway be needed in order to prove soundness). In order to see the issue that arises here, consider the case of a verifier who can break the commitments. Such a verifier could work as follows: if the committed values constitute a valid coloring then send a random edge; otherwise, if they are all zeroes except for two nodes, then send any edge apart from the one connecting those two nodes. Clearly, when the simulator works with this verifier, it never succeeds. Now, by the hiding property of commitments, this should not happen. However, it shows that the success of the simulator also depends on the computational hiding of the commitments, and thus a reduction to this property is needed as well. Formally, this can be solved by proving—via a reduction to the hiding property of commitments—that the probability that any given edge is queried by the verifier when it receives valid-prover commitments in the first message is negligibly close to the probability that the edge is queried when it receives (garbage) simulator-generated commitments. Our actual proof will work differently, since we will first show that there exists a hypothetical simulator who receives the correct coloring and generates a distribution identical to a real proof, and then we will show that the actual simulator generates a distribution that is computationally indistinguishable from the hypothetical one. In addition, we prove that the hypothetical simulator halts successfully within $n \cdot |E|$ attempts except with negligible probability. Thus, the fact that the actual simulator generates a distribution that is computationally indistinguishable from the hypothetical one also implies that it halts successfully within $n \cdot |E|$ attempts, except with negligible probability.

On dealing with aborts. At some point in the simulation, it is possible that V^* does not reply with a valid edge. In this case, we have to specify what the simulator should do. In fact, the protocol itself must specify to the honest prover what to do in such a case. One strategy is to state that if the verify returns an illegal value, then the honest prover halts the execution. This certainly works and will be necessary in later cases (e.g., constant-round zero knowledge), where the prover is unable to proceed if the verifier does not respond with a valid value. However, in this specific case, the easiest thing to do is to have the real prover interpret any invalid reply as a default edge. In this case, the simulator will deal with an invalid message in the same way. According to this strategy, there are actually no invalid messages from V^*, and this somewhat simplifies the simulation.

A formal proof of security. We are now ready to prove the zero-knowledge property of the 3-coloring protocol (we do not prove soundness since the focus of this tutorial is on *simulation*).

Theorem 6.5.4. *Let* Com *be a perfectly binding commitment scheme with security for nonuniform adversaries. Then, the 3-coloring protocol of [22] is black-box computational zero knowledge.*

Proof: We begin by describing the simulator. S is given a graph $G = (V, E)$ with $V = \{v_1, \ldots, v_n\}$ and oracle access to some probabilistic polynomial-time $V^*(x, z, r, \cdot)$, and works as follows:

1. S initializes the message history transcript $\mathbf{m}$ to be the empty string λ.
2. Repeat $n \cdot |E|$ times:
   a. S sets $j = 1$.
   b. S chooses a random edge $(v_k, v_\ell) \in_R E$ and chooses two random different colors for v_k and v_ℓ. Formally, S chooses $\phi(v_k) \in_R \{1, 2, 3\}$ and $\phi(v_\ell) \in_R \{1, 2, 3\} \setminus \{\phi(v_k)\}$. For all other $v_i \in V \setminus \{v_k, v_\ell\}$, S sets $\phi(v_i) = 0$.
   c. For every $i = 1, \ldots, n$, S computes $c_i = \mathsf{Com}(\phi(v_i))$.
   d. S "sends" the vector $(c_1, \ldots, c_n)$ to V^*. Formally, S queries $\mathbf{m}$ concatenated with this vector to its oracle (indeed S does not interact with V^* and so cannot actually "send" it any message). Let $e \in E$ be the reply back from the oracle.
   e. If $e = (v_k, v_\ell)$, then S completes this iteration by concatenating the commitments $(c_1, \ldots, c_n)$ and $(\mathsf{decom}(c_k), \mathsf{decom}(c_\ell))$ to $\mathbf{m}$. Formally, S updates the history string $\mathbf{m} \leftarrow (\mathbf{m}, (c_1, \ldots, c_n), (\mathsf{decom}(c_k), \mathsf{decom}(c_\ell)))$.
   f. If $e \neq (v_k, v_\ell)$ then S sets $j \leftarrow j + 1$. If $j = n \cdot |E|$, then S outputs a fail symbol $\perp$. Else (when $j \neq n \cdot |E|$), S returns to step 2b (i.e., S tries again for this i). This return to step 2b is the *rewinding* of V^* by the simulator.

3. S outputs whatever V^* outputs on the final transcript $\mathbf{m}$.

It is clear that S runs in polynomial time, since each repetition runs for at most $n \cdot |E|$ iterations, and there are $n \cdot |E|$ repetitions.

   In order to prove that S generates a transcript that is indistinguishable from a real transcript, we need to prove a reduction to the security of the commitment scheme.

We begin by constructing an alternative simulator S' who is given a valid coloring ψ as auxiliary input. We stress that S' is *not* a valid simulator, since it is given ψ. Rather, it is a thought experiment used in the proof. Now, S' works in exactly the same way as S (choosing e at random, rewinding, and so on) except that in every iteration it chooses a random permutation π over $\{1, 2, 3\}$, sets $\phi(v) = \pi(\psi(v))$, and computes $c_i = \mathsf{Com}(\phi(v_i))$ for *all* i, exactly like the real prover.

We begin by proving that, conditioned on S' not outputting $\bot$, it generates output that is identically distributed to V^*'s output in a real proof. That is, for every V^*, every $(G, \psi) \in R_L$, and every $z \in \{0, 1\}^*$,

$$\left\{ \mathsf{output}_{V^*}(P(G, \psi), V^*(G, z)) \right\} \equiv \left\{ S'^{V^*(G,z,r,\cdot)}(G, \psi) \mid S'^{V^*(G,r,\cdot)}(G, \psi) \neq \bot \right\}. \quad (6.7)$$

In order to see this, observe that the distribution over the commitments viewed by V^* is identical to a real proof (since they are commitments to a random permutation of a valid coloring). The only difference is that S' chooses an edge e ahead of time and only concludes an iteration if the query sent by V^* equals e. However, since e is chosen uniformly every time, and since V^* is rewound to the beginning of each iteration until it succeeds (and we condition on it indeed succeeding), these have identical distributions.

Next, we prove that S' outputs $\bot$ with at most negligible probability. Observe that the commitments provided by S' reveal no information whatsoever about the choice of e in that iteration (this is due to the fact that the commitments are the same for *every* choice of e). Thus, the probability that a single iteration succeeds is exactly $1/|E|$, implying that S' outputs $\bot$ for one of the i's in the simulation with probability $\left(1 - \frac{1}{|E|}\right)^{n \cdot |E|} < e^{-n}$. There are $n \cdot |E|$ iterations, and so by the union bound, S' outputs $\bot$ somewhere in the simulation with probability less than $n \cdot |E| \cdot e^{-n}$, which is negligible. This implies that[2]

$$\left\{ S'^{V^*(G,z,r,\cdot)}(G, \psi) \mid S'^{V^*(G,z,r,\cdot)}(G, \psi) \neq \bot \right\} \overset{c}{\equiv} \left\{ S'^{V^*(G,z,r,\cdot)}(G, \psi) \right\}. \quad (6.8)$$

Finally, we prove that the outputs of S and S' are computationally indistinguishable:

$$\left\{ S'^{V^*(G,z,r,\cdot)}(G, \psi) \right\} \overset{c}{\equiv} \left\{ S^{V^*(G,z,r,\cdot)}(G) \right\}. \quad (6.9)$$

Intuitively, we prove this via a reduction to the security of the commitment scheme. Specifically, assume by contradiction, that there exists a probabilistic polynomial-time verifier V^*, a probabilistic polynomial-time distinguisher D, and a polynomial $p(\cdot)$ such that for an infinite sequence (G, ψ, z) where $(G, \psi) \in R$ and $z \in \{0, 1\}^*$,

$$\left| \Pr\left[D\left(G, \psi, z, S'^{V^*(G,z,r,\cdot)}(G, \psi)\right) = 1 \right] - \Pr\left[D\left(G, \psi, z, S^{V^*(G,z,r,\cdot)}(G)\right) = 1 \right] \right| \geq \frac{1}{p(n)},$$

where n denotes the number of nodes in G, and R denotes the 3-coloring relation. Without loss of generality, assume that D outputs 1 with higher probability when

---

[2] Observe that for all events A and F, $\Pr[A] = \Pr[A \wedge F] + \Pr[A \wedge \neg F] \leq \Pr[F] + \Pr[A \mid \neg F]$. Thus, if F occurs with negligible probability, then $|\Pr[A] - \Pr[A|\neg F]|$ is negligible.

it receives the output of S' than when it receives the output of S. We construct a nonuniform probabilistic polynomial-time adversary A for the commitment experiment LR-commit as defined in Section 6.5.2. Adversary A receives (G, ψ, z) on its advice tape (for n, where G has n nodes), and works as follows:

1. A initializes V^* with input graph G, auxiliary input z, and a uniform random tape r.
2. Then, A runs the instructions of S' with input (G, ψ) and oracle $V^*(x, z, r; \cdot)$, with some changes. First, note that A knows ψ and so can compute $\phi(v) = \pi(\psi(v))$ just like S'. Next, A does not generate the commitments by computing $c_i = \text{Com}(\phi(v_i))$ for all i, as S' does. Rather, A works as follows. For every iteration of the simulation:

   a. For the randomly chosen edge $e = (v_k, v_\ell)$, adversary A generates commitments $c_k = \text{Com}(\phi(v_k))$ and $c_\ell = \text{Com}(\phi(v_\ell))$ by itself.
   b. For all other i (i.e., for all $i \in \{1, \ldots, n\} \setminus \{k, \ell\}$), adversary A queries its LR-oracle with the pair $(0, \phi(i))$. Denote by c_i the commitment received back.

   A simulates S' querying V^* with the commitments $(c_1, \ldots, c_n)$ as a result of the above. Observe that A can decommit to v_k, v_ℓ as needed by S', since it computed the commitments itself.
3. When S' concludes, then A invokes D on the output generated by S', and outputs whatever D outputs.

Observe that when $b = 1$ in the LR-oracle experiment, the commitments $c_1, \ldots, c_n$ are generated as valid commitments to a random coloring, and the distribution over V^*'s view is identical to an execution of S'. Thus (conditioning on the b chosen in LR-commit),

$$\Pr\left[\text{LR-commit}_{\text{Com}, A}(1^n) = 1 \mid b = 1\right] = \Pr\left[D\left(G, z, S'^{V^*(G,z,r;\cdot)}(G, \psi)\right) = 1\right].$$

Likewise, when $b = 0$ in the LR-oracle experiment, then the commitments $c_1, \ldots, c_n$ are all 0 except for the commitments c_j, c_k, which are to two random different colors. Thus, this is exactly the distribution generated by S, and

$$\Pr\left[\text{LR-commit}_{\text{Com}, A}(1^n) = 1 \mid b = 0\right] = \Pr\left[D\left(G, z, S^{V^*(G,z,r;\cdot)}(G)\right) = 0\right].$$

We have

$$\Pr\left[\text{LR-commit}_{\text{Com}, A}(1^n) = 1\right]$$

$$= \frac{1}{2} \cdot \Pr\left[\text{LR-commit}_{\text{Com}, A}(1^n) = 1 \mid b = 1\right]$$

$$\quad + \frac{1}{2} \cdot \Pr\left[\text{LR-commit}_{\text{Com}, A}(1^n) = 1 \mid b = 0\right]$$

$$= \frac{1}{2} \cdot \Pr\left[D\left(G, z, S'^{V^*(G,z,r;\cdot)}(G, \psi)\right) = 1\right] + \frac{1}{2} \cdot \Pr\left[D\left(G, z, S^{V^*(G,z,r;\cdot)}(G)\right) = 0\right]$$

$$= \frac{1}{2} \cdot \Pr\left[D\left(G, z, \mathcal{S}'^{V^*(G,z,r,\cdot)}(G, \psi)\right) = 1\right] + \frac{1}{2} \cdot \left(1 - \Pr\left[D\left(G, z, \mathcal{S}^{V^*(G,z,r,\cdot)}(G)\right) = 1\right]\right)$$

$$= \frac{1}{2} + \frac{1}{2} \cdot \left(\Pr\left[D\left(G, z, \mathcal{S}'^{V^*(G,z,r,\cdot)}(G, \psi)\right) = 1\right] - \Pr\left[D\left(G, z, \mathcal{S}^{V^*(G,z,r,\cdot)}(G)\right) = 1\right]\right)$$

$$\geq \frac{1}{2} + \frac{1}{2p(n)}.$$

This contradicts the security of Com, as stated in Theorem 6.5.2. Combining Equations (6.7)–(6.9), we conclude that

$$\left\{\text{output}_{V^*}(P(G, \psi), V^*(G, z))\right\} \stackrel{c}{\equiv} \left\{\mathcal{S}^{V^*(G,z,r,\cdot)}(G)\right\},$$

thereby completing the proof. ∎

Discussion on the proof technique. The main technique used in the above proof is to construct an alternative, hypothetical simulator $\mathcal{S}'$ who is given the actual coloring. Of course, $\mathcal{S}'$ could work by just playing the real prover. However, this would not help us prove the indistinguishability of $\mathcal{S}$. Thus, we design $\mathcal{S}'$ to work in exactly the same way as $\mathcal{S}$, except that it generates commitments that are the same as the real prover. In this way, we *separate* the two differences between $\mathcal{S}$ and a real prover: (a) the flow of $\mathcal{S}$ that involves choosing e and rewinding, and (b) the commitments that are incorrectly generated. The only difference between the real prover and $\mathcal{S}'$ is the flow, and the first part of the proof shows that this results in at most a negligible difference. Then, the second part of the proof, showing that the outputs of $\mathcal{S}'$ and $\mathcal{S}$ are computationally indistinguishable, works via reduction to the commitments. This technique is often used in simulation-based proofs, and in some cases there are series of simulators that bridge the differences between the real execution and the simulation. This is similar to sequences of hybrids in game-based proofs, with the only difference being that the sequence here is from the simulation to the real execution (or vice versa). We recommend reading more about this technique in the tutorial on sequences of games by Shoup [38].

6.5.4 Constant-Round Zero Knowledge

Constant-round zero-knowledge introduces a number of difficulties regarding simulation. The protocol itself, as described in [20], is actually very simple and straightforward. However, its proof is far more involved than it seems, and requires new techniques that are important in general. In addition, it highlights difficulties that arise in many places when carrying out simulation.

Background. Before proceeding, we first consider simply running the $n \cdot |E|$ executions of the 3-coloring protocol in parallel, instead of sequentially. At first sight, this does not seem to make a difference to the zero-knowledge property, since the order of execution does not change what is revealed. Despite this, all known simulation attempts fail, and so we simply have no way of proving that this is still zero knowledge. In order to see why, in the suggested parallel protocol, the prover sends $N \stackrel{\text{def}}{=} n \cdot |E|$ vectors of commitments to random colorings, the verifier responds with N edges, and the prover opens the commitments of the two nodes of the edge. The only way that we know to simulate this protocol is for the simulator to *guess the query edges* ahead of time. However, the probability of correctly guessing N random edges before the verifier sends them is just $|E|^{-n|E|}$, which is exponentially small. It is important to understand that rewinding does *not* solve the problem, since the verifier can choose different random edges each time, even if it has a fixed random tape. For example, the verifier could have a key to a pseudorandom function hardwired, and can choose its randomness in every execution as a function of the (entire) first message that it receives. As a result, when rewinding, effectively new randomness is used each time and the simulator would have to try an exponential number of rewinding attempts. Indeed, Goldreich and Krawczyk showed that this parallel protocol is not *black-box* zero knowledge, and in fact that no constant-round public-coin proof for a language not in $\mathcal{BPP}$ is black-box zero knowledge [21] (where public coin means that the verifier's queries are just random coin tosses). Despite this, we have no proof that it is not zero knowledge in general. We stress again that the lack of a known attack on a protocol is not sufficient to conclude that it is secure. Thus, an alternative protocol is needed.

The solution presented by Goldreich and Kahan to this problem is to simply have the verifier commit to its query *before* the prover sends its commitments. This prevents a malicious verifier from changing its query during rewinding. Details appear in Protocol 6.5.5.

PROTOCOL 6.5.5 (The Goldreich–Kahan proof system [20])

The proof system of [20] works as follows (we provide a clear, yet rather informal description here):

1. The prover sends the first message of a (two-round) perfectly hiding commitment scheme, denoted $\mathrm{Com_h}$. See [17, Section 4.9.1] for a definition of such commitments.
2. The verifier chooses $N \stackrel{\text{def}}{=} n \cdot |E|$ random edges $e_1, \ldots, e_N \in_R E$. Let $q = (e_1, \ldots, e_N)$ be the query string; the verifier commits to q using the perfectly hiding commitment $\mathrm{Com_h}$.
3. The prover prepares the first message in N parallel executions of the basic three-round proof system in Protocol 6.5.3 (i.e., commitments to N independent random colorings of the graph), and sends commitments to all using the perfectly binding commitment scheme Com.
4. The verifier decommits to the string q.
5. If the verifier's decommitment is invalid, then the prover aborts. Otherwise, the prover sends the appropriate decommitments in every execution. Specifically, if e_i is the edge in the i-th execution, then the prover decommits to the nodes of that edge in the i-th set of commitments to colorings.
6. The verifier outputs 1 if and only if all checks pass (as in the original proof system).

Before discussing zero knowledge, we remark that the commitments from the verifier are perfectly hiding, whereas the commitments from the prover are perfectly binding. This is necessary for proving soundness, but since our focus here is on simulation, we will not refer to this issue from here on; see [20] or [17, Section 4.9] for a proof of soundness.

The main difference between this protocol and the simple parallel repetition of the basic 3-coloring protocol is the fact that the verifier is committed ahead of time to its queries. Thus, the simulator can first receive the verifier's commitments, and can then send garbage commitments and receive back the decommitments. After receiving the decommitments the simulator knows all of the queries, and can *rewind* the verifier back to the point after it sent the commitments and give new prover commitments like in the simulation of a single execution. This works because the verifier is committed to its edge queries before it receives the prover commitments, and so cannot change them. Thus, the simulator can learn the edges (by giving garbage commitments first) and can then provide "good" commitments for which it is able to decommit and complete the proof.

Despite its simplicity, there are a number of issues that must be dealt with when translating this into a formal proof. First, we have to deal with the fact that the verifier may not decommit correctly in step 4. This may seem simple—if this happens, then just have the simulator abort as well. This makes sense since in a real proof the prover would abort in such a case. However, the problem is that the verifier may sometimes decommit correctly and sometimes not decommit correctly, and this decision may be taken as a result of the messages it receives (specifically, the commitments sent by the prover). If this is the case, and the verifier aborts with some probability p, then the simulator will abort with probability approximately $2p$.[3] Note that this problem is not solved by interpreting an invalid decommit as default edges, as in Protocol 6.5.3, since the simulator will prepare commitments to default edges if the verifier aborted the first time and will not be able to answer if the verifier does not abort the second time, or vice versa.

The following strategy for the simulator S addresses this problem:

1. S invokes V^* and internally hands it an honestly generated first (receiver) message of the perfectly hiding commitment protocol.
2. S receives V^*'s reply consisting of a commitment c.
3. S sends V^* garbage commitments and receives its decommitment. If the decommitment is not valid, it aborts. Otherwise, denote the decommitted string by $q = (e_1, \ldots, e_N)$.
4. S rewinds V^* to the beginning (sending the same first message of the perfectly hiding commitment protocol) and receives its commitment c. (Since V^* has a fixed random tape and this is the first step of the protocol, it always sends the same commitment c.) Then, S hands simulated prover commitments to V^* that can be answered according to q; i.e., send commitments to random distinct colors on the nodes of the edge committed by the verifier and to 0 elsewhere. If V^* aborts on these commitments, then S repeats this step with fresh randomness. When V^* provides correct decommitments, S proceeds to the next step.

---

[3] This holds since the probability of abort when the simulator sends the first garbage commitments equals p, and the probability of abort when the simulator sends the good commitments the second time (if a first abort did not occur) is also p. Thus, we have that the simulator aborts with probability $p + (1 - p) \cdot p = 2p - p^2$.

5. S sends V^* decommitments to the nodes on the committed edge, and outputs whatever V^* outputs.

One issue that arises when trying to prove that this simulation strategy works is that the commitment to q is perfectly hiding and thus only *computationally binding*. This means that it is possible that V^* decommits to a valid $q' \neq q$, but in such a case the simulation will fail. This possibility is ruled out by showing that if this occurs with nonnegligible probability, then V^* can be used to break the computational binding of the commitments.

More importantly, it turns out that this strategy is overly simplistic, for a very important reason. Specifically, it is not necessarily the case that the simulator runs in expected polynomial time.[4] This may seem surprising. In particular, let ϵ denote the probability that V^* does not abort ($\epsilon = 1-p$ from above). Then, supposedly, we have that the expected running time of the simulator is $1-\epsilon+\epsilon\cdot\frac{1}{\epsilon}$ times a fixed polynomial for computing all the commitments and so on. This is the case since with probability $1 - \epsilon$ the verifier V^* aborts and the simulation ends, and with probability ϵ the simulation proceeds to step 4. However, since each attempt to receive a decommitment from V^* in this step succeeds with probability ϵ only, we expect to have to repeat $1/\epsilon$ times. Thus, the overall expected cost is $\text{poly}(n)\cdot(1-\epsilon+\epsilon\cdot\frac{1}{\epsilon}) = \text{poly}(n)\cdot(2-\epsilon)$. Despite being appealing, and true when commitments are modeled as "perfect envelopes", the above analysis is simply false. In particular, the probability that the verifier decommits correctly when receiving the first prover commitments to pure garbage is not necessarily the same as the probability that it decommits correctly when receiving the simulator-generated commitments. In order to see this, if the verifier was all powerful, it could break open the commitments and purposefully make the simulation fail by decommitting when it receives pure garbage (or fully valid commitments) and not decommitting when it receives commitments that can be opened only to its query string. This means that we can only argue that this does not happen by a reduction to the commitments, and this also means that there may be a negligible difference. Thus, we actually have that the expected running time of the simulator is

$$\text{poly}(n) \cdot \left(1 - \epsilon(n) + \epsilon(n) \cdot \frac{1}{\epsilon(n) - \mu(n)}\right)$$

for some negligible function μ. Now, it is once again tempting to conclude that the above is polynomial because $\mu(n)$ is negligible, and so $\epsilon(n) - \mu(n)$ is almost the same as $\epsilon(n)$. This is indeed true for "large" values of $\epsilon(n)$. For example, if $\epsilon(n) > 2\mu(n)$ then $\epsilon(n)-\mu(n) > \epsilon(n)/2$. This then implies that $\epsilon(n)/(\epsilon(n)-\mu(n)) < 2$. Unfortunately, however, this is *not* true in general. For example, consider the case that $\mu(n) = 2^{-n}$ and $\epsilon(n) = \mu(n) + 2^{-n/2} = 2^{-n} + 2^{-n/2}$. Then,

$$\frac{\epsilon(n)}{\epsilon(n) - \mu(n)} = \frac{2^{-n} + 2^{-n/2}}{2^{-n/2}} = 2^{n/2} + 1,$$

---

[4] Note that the simulator, as is, certainly does not run in strict polynomial time. However, this is inherent for black-box constant-round protocols [2], and we show only that it runs in expected polynomial time.

which is exponential in n. We therefore have that the simulation does not run in expected polynomial time. This technical problem was observed and solved by [20]. This problem arises in other places, and essentially in any place that rewinding is used where a different (but indistinguishable) distribution is used between rewindings, and some success criteria must be reached in order to proceed (e.g., the party must decommit correctly). For just one example of where this arises in the context of general secure computation, see [31, Section 4.2]. We remark that in the specific case of constant-round zero-knowledge proofs, it is possible to bypass this problem by changing the protocol [37]. However, in other cases—for example, efficient secure two-party computation—it is not necessarily possible without incurring additional cost.

We show how to deal with this problem in the proof of the theorem below.

Theorem 6.5.6. *Let* $\mathsf{Com_h}$ *and* Com *be perfectly hiding and perfectly binding commitment schemes, respectively, with security in the presence of nonuniform probabilistic polynomial-time adversaries. Then, Protocol 6.5.5 is black-box computational zero knowledge with an expected polynomial-time simulator.*

Proof: We first present the simplified strategy above for a black-box simulator S given oracle access to a verifier V^* (with a fixed input, auxiliary input, and random tape), and then explain how to modify it. The simplified simulator S works as follows:

1. S hands V^* the first message of $\mathsf{Com_h}$ (formally, this is via the oracle, but we write it this way for conciseness).
2. S receives from V^* its perfectly hiding commitment c to some query string $q = (e_1, \ldots, e_N)$, where $N = n \cdot |E|$.
3. S generates N vectors of n commitments to 0, hands them to V^*, and receives back its reply.
4. If V^* aborts by not replying with a valid decommitment to c (and the decommitment is to a vector of N edges), then S aborts and outputs whatever V^* outputs. Otherwise, let $q = (e_1, \ldots, e_N)$ be the decommitted value. S proceeds to the next step.
5. *Rewinding phase – S repeatedly rewinds V^* back to the point where it receives the prover commitments, until it decommits to q from above:*
   a. S generates N vectors of commitments $\mathbf{c}_1, \ldots, \mathbf{c}_N$, as follows: Let $e_i = (v_j, v_k)$ in q. Then, the j-th and k-th commitments in $\mathbf{c}_i$ are to random distinct colors in $\{1, 2, 3\}$ and all other commitments are to 0. Simulator S hands all vectors to V^*, and receives back its reply.
   b. If V^* does not generate a valid decommitment, then S returns to the previous step (using fresh randomness).
   c. If V^* generates a valid decommitment to some $q' \neq q$, then S outputs ambiguous and halts.
   d. Otherwise, V^* exits the loop and proceeds to the next step.
6. S completes the proof by handing V^* decommitments to the appropriate nodes in all of $\mathbf{c}_1, \ldots, \mathbf{c}_N$, and outputs whatever V^* outputs.

The intuition behind the simulation is clear. S repeatedly rewinds until the string q is the one that it initially chose. In this case, it can decommit appropriately and conclude the proof. Intuitively, the fact that the result is computationally indistinguishable from a real proof by an honest prover follows from the hiding property of the perfectly binding commitments, as in the proof of Theorem 6.5.4 in Section 6.5.3.

As we have already demonstrated, this simplified strategy suffers from the problem that S actually may not run in expected polynomial time. This is solved by ensuring that the simulator S never runs "too long". Specifically, if S proceeds to the rewinding phase of the simulation, then it first estimates the value of $\epsilon(n)$, which is the probability that V^* does not abort given garbage commitments. This is done by repeating Step 3 of the simulation (sending fresh random commitments to all zeroes) until $m = O(n)$ successful decommits occurs (for a polynomial $m(n)$; to be exact $m = 12n$ suffices), where a successful decommit is where V^* decommits to q, the string it first decommitted to. We remark that as in the original strategy, if V^* correctly decommits to a different $q' \neq q$ then S outputs ambiguous. Then, an estimate $\tilde{\epsilon}$ of ϵ is taken to be m/T, where T is the overall number of attempts until m successful decommits occurred. As shown in [20], this suffices to ensure that the probability that $\tilde{\epsilon}$ is not within a constant factor of $\epsilon(n)$ is at most 2^{-n}. (An exact computation of how to achieve this exact bound using Chernoff can be found in [26, Section 6.5.3].)

Next, S runs the rewinding phase in step 5 of the simulation up to n times. Each time, S limits the number of rewinding attempts in the rewinding phase to $n/\tilde{\epsilon}$ iterations. We have the following cases:

1. If within $n/\tilde{\epsilon}$ rewinding iterations, S obtains a successful decommitment from V^* to q, then it completes the proof as described. It can do so in this case because the prover commitments enable it to answer the query q.
2. If S obtains a valid decommitment to some $q' \neq q$ then it outputs ambiguous.
3. If S does not obtain any correct decommitment within $n/\tilde{\epsilon}$ attempts, then S aborts this attempted rewinding phase.

As mentioned, the above phase is repeated up to n times, each time using independent coins. If the simulator S does not successfully conclude in any of the n attempts, then it halts and outputs fail. We will show that this strategy ensures that the probability that S outputs fail is negligible.

In addition to the above, S keeps a count of its overall running time and if it reaches 2^n steps, then it halts, outputting fail. (This additional time-out is needed to ensure that S does not run too long in the case that the estimate $\tilde{\epsilon}$ is not within a constant factor of $\epsilon(n)$. Recall that this "bad event" can only happen with probability 2^{-n}.)

We first claim that S runs in expected polynomial time.

Claim 6.5.7. *Simulator S runs in expected time that is polynomial in n.*

Proof: Observe that in the first and all later iterations, all of S's work takes a strict polynomial-time number of steps. We therefore need to bound only the number of rewinding iterations. Before proceeding, however, we stress that rewinding iterations only take place if V^* provides a valid decommitment in the first place. Thus, all rewinding only occurs with probability $\epsilon(n)$.

Now, S first rewinds in order to obtain an estimate $\tilde{\epsilon}$ of $\epsilon(n)$. This involves repeating until $m(n) = 12n$ successful decommitments are obtained. Therefore, the expected number of repetitions in order to obtain $\tilde{\epsilon}$ equals exactly $12n/\epsilon(n)$ (since the expected number of trials for a single success is $1/\epsilon(n)$; observe that in all of these repetitions the commitments are to all zeroes). After the estimate $\tilde{\epsilon}$ has been obtained, S runs the rewinding phase of step 5 for a maximum of n times, in each phase limiting the number of rewinding attempts to $n/\tilde{\epsilon}$.

Given the above, we are ready to compute the expected running time of S. In order to do this, we differentiate between two cases. In the first case, we consider what happens if $\tilde{\epsilon}$ is *not* within a constant factor of $\epsilon(n)$. The only thing we can say about S's running time in this case is that it is bound by 2^n (since this is an overall bound on its running time). However, since this event happens with probability at most 2^{-n}, this case adds only a polynomial number of steps to the overall expected running time. We now consider the second case, where $\tilde{\epsilon}$ *is* within a constant factor of $\epsilon(n)$ and thus $\epsilon(n)/\tilde{\epsilon} = O(1)$. In this case, we can bound the expected running time of S by

$$\text{poly}(n) \cdot \epsilon(n) \cdot \left(\frac{12n}{\epsilon(n)} + n \cdot \frac{n}{\tilde{\epsilon}} \right) = \text{poly}(n) \cdot \frac{\epsilon(n)}{\tilde{\epsilon}} = \text{poly}(n),$$

and this concludes the analysis.   ∎

Next, we prove that the probability that S outputs fail is negligible.

Claim 6.5.8. *The probability that S outputs* fail *is negligible in n.*

Proof: Notice that the probability that S outputs fail is less than or equal to the probability that it does not obtain a successful decommitment in any of the n rewinding phase attempts *plus* the probability that it runs for 2^n steps.

We first claim that the probability that S runs for 2^n steps is negligible. We have already shown in Claim 6.5.7 that S runs in expected polynomial time. Therefore, the probability that an execution will deviate so far from its expectation and run for 2^n steps is negligible. (It is enough to use Markov's inequality to establish this fact.)

We now continue by considering the probability that in all n rewinding phase attempts, S does not obtain a successful decommitment within $n/\tilde{\epsilon}$ steps. First, recall that $\epsilon(n)$ equals the probability that V^* decommits when given commitments to all zeroes. Next, observe that there exists a negligible function μ such that the probability that V^* decommits when given commitments as in step 5a is at least $\epsilon(n) - \mu(n)$. If $\epsilon(n)$ is a negligible function then this is immediate (since it just means that V^* decommits with probability at least 0, which is always correct). In contrast, if $\epsilon(n)$ is nonnegligible, then this can be proven by a direct reduction to the hiding property of the commitment scheme. In particular, if V^* decommits with probability that is non-negligibly different in both cases, then this in itself can be used to distinguish commitments of one type from another. Having established this, consider the following two possible cases:

1. *Case 1:* $\epsilon(n) \le 2\mu(n)$: In this case, V^* decommits to its query string with only negligible probability. This means that the probability that S even reaches the rewinding phase is negligible. Thus, S only outputs fail with negligible probability.

2. *Case 2:* $\epsilon(n) > 2\mu(n)$: Recall that V^* successfully decommits in any iteration with probability at least $\epsilon(n) - \mu(n)$. Now, since in this case $\epsilon(n) > 2\mu(n)$, we have that $\epsilon(n) - \mu(n) > \frac{\epsilon(n)}{2}$. Thus, the expected number of iterations needed until V^* successfully decommits is $\frac{1}{\epsilon(n)-\mu(n)} < \frac{2}{\epsilon(n)}$. Assuming that $\tilde{\epsilon}$ is within a constant factor of $\epsilon(n)$, we have that $2/\epsilon(n) = O(1/\tilde{\epsilon})$ and so the expected number of rewindings in any given rewinding attempt is bound by $O(1/\tilde{\epsilon})$. Therefore, by Markov's inequality, the probability that S tries more than $n/\tilde{\epsilon}$ iterations in any given rewinding phase attempt is at most $O(1/n)$. It follows that the probability that S tries more than this number of iterations in n independent rewinding phases is negligible in n (specifically, it is bound by $O(1/n)^n$).

   This holds under the assumption that $\tilde{\epsilon}$ is within a constant factor of $\epsilon(n)$. However, the probability that $\tilde{\epsilon}$ is *not* within a constant factor of $\epsilon(n)$ is also negligible.

Putting the above together, we have that S outputs fail with negligible probability only.   ∎

Next, we prove the following:

Claim 6.5.9. *The probability that S outputs* ambiguous *is negligible in n.*

Proof sketch: Intuitively, if there exists an infinite series of inputs for which S outputs ambiguous with nonnegligible probability, then this can be used to break the computational binding of the $\mathsf{Com_h}$ commitment scheme. The only subtlety is that S runs in expected polynomial time, whereas an attacker for the binding of the commitment scheme must run in strict polynomial time. Nevertheless, this can be overcome by simply truncating S to twice its expected running time. By Markov's inequality, this reduces the success probability of the binding attack by at most $1/2$, and so this is still nonnegligible.   ∎

It remains to prove that the output distribution generated by S is computationally indistinguishable from the output of V^* in a real proof with an honest prover. We have already shown that S outputs fail or ambiguous with only negligible probability. Thus, the only difference between the output distribution generated by S and the output distribution generated in a real proof is the perfectly binding commitments to the colors. As in the proof of Theorem 6.5.4, this can be formally proven by constructing an alternative simulator who is given the coloring and works in the same way as S except that it generates the commitments via its oracle. Then, the LR-commit experiment can be used to show indistinguishability between this and a real proof for nonuniform distinguishers. We omit the details due to the similarity to Theorem 6.5.4. This completes the proof.   ∎

Discussion. Beyond the Goldreich–Kahan technique itself, which is of importance and arises in multiple situations where rewinding-based simulation is used, there are two important lessons to be taken away from this proof. First, negligible differences can make a difference, and care must be taken wherever they appear. The intuition that a negligible event does not happen, and that computationally indistinguishable distributions behave the same, is correct only up to a point. The case shown here is an excellent example of this. Second, great care must be taken to prove every claim made via a reduction to the primitive that guarantees it. In the constant-round protocol for zero knowledge, it is clear to everyone that in order to prove indistinguishability of the simulation, a reduction to the security of the commitment scheme is necessary. (Although, without doing it carefully, the need for security in the presence of nonuniform adversaries can be missed.) However, it is far less clear that it is necessary to prove that the simulation runs in polynomial time, that the perfectly hiding commitment remains computationally binding, and so on. In general, any property that does not hold when the cryptographic primitive is completely broken requires a reduction. Thus, when proving security, a good mental experiment to carry out is to consider what happens to the simulation and proof when the adversary is *all powerful*. If some important property needed in the proof no longer holds, then a reduction is needed to prove it. Furthermore, if there is a property of a cryptographic primitive that is not used anywhere in the proof, then one should reconsider whether it is actually needed.

We also remark that the simulator presented here runs in *expected polynomial time* and not strict polynomial time. This is inherent for constant-round black-box zero knowledge, as proven in [2] (perhaps surprisingly, it is not possible to somehow truncate the simulator's execution and obtain only a negligible difference). Thus, in some cases—and in particular when considering constant-round protocols—simulators are relaxed to be allowed to run in expected polynomial time.

Soundness. We reiterate that, in order to prove security for zero knowledge, it is necessary to separately prove that soundness holds. We have omitted this here since it is not the focus of the tutorial.

6.5.5 Honest-Verifier Zero Knowledge

A proof system is honest-verifier zero knowledge if the zero-knowledge property holds for *semi-honest* verifiers. We stress that the proof system must be sound for malicious provers. Otherwise, as we have mentioned above, it is meaningless (the prover can just say "trust me").

It is instructional to consider honest-verifier zero knowledge as well, since this enables a comparison with the simulation technique above for arbitrary malicious verifiers, and serves as a good contrast between semi-honest simulation as in Section 6.4 and the remainder of this tutorial that considers malicious adversaries. As we will see, simulation for semi-honest adversaries is very different than for malicious adversaries.

Parallel 3-coloring. Consider the basic 3-coloring protocol described in Protocol 6.5.3 run $n \cdot |E|$ times in parallel. Specifically, the prover generates $n \cdot |E|$ sets of commitments to random colorings and sends them to the verifier. The verifier chooses $q = (e_1, \ldots, e_N)$ at random and sends q to the prover. Finally, the prover decommits as in the protocol.

The simulator S for honest-verifier zero knowledge. We proceed directly to describe the simulator for this protocol. Given a graph $G = (V, E)$ with $|V| = n$ and auxiliary input z, the simulator S works as follows:

1. Let $N = n \cdot |E|$. Then, for $i = 1, \ldots, N$, S chooses a random edge $e_i \in E$, and sets $q = (e_1, \ldots, e_N)$. Let r_q be the random coin tosses that define q.
2. For every $i = 1, \ldots, N$:

   a. Let $e_i = (v_j, v_k)$.
   b. S chooses random $\phi(v_j) \in_R \{1, 2, 3\}$ and $\phi(v_k) \in_R \{1, 2, 3\} \setminus \{\phi(v_j)\}$. For all other $v_\ell \in V \setminus \{v_j, v_k\}$, S sets $\phi(v_\ell) = 0$.
   c. S sets the commit vector $\mathbf{c}_i = (c_i^1, \ldots, c_i^n) = (\mathrm{Com}(\phi(v_1)), \ldots, \mathrm{Com}(\phi(v_n)))$.
   d. S sets the decommit vector $\mathbf{d}_i = (\mathrm{decom}(c_i^j), \mathrm{decom}(c_i^k))$.

3. S outputs the view of the (semi-honest) verifier, defined by

$$\langle G, z, r_q; (\mathbf{c}_1, \ldots, \mathbf{c}_N), (\mathbf{d}_1, \ldots, \mathbf{d}_N) \rangle.$$

Before proving that this is indeed indistinguishable from a real view in a real interaction, observe that there is no rewinding here and the simulator S just chooses the query string of the verifier. This is allowed since a semi-honest verifier chooses its query string by reading it directly from its random tape. Since S chose r_q randomly, and writes r_q on the verifier's random tape, it is given that the verifier's query is q. The reason why S need not rewind at all is because it already knows the query string (indeed, it chose it). In fact, S here does not "interact" with the verifier at all, unlike the simulator for regular (malicious) zero knowledge that interacts with V^*. Rather, S just generates the transcript of messages, independently of the adversary. This is allowed since the verifier is semi-honest, and so we know exactly what it will do already.

Restating the above, it is not necessary to interact with the adversary or rewind it to somehow guess the query string, since we know exactly how the verifier chooses that string in the semi-honest case. Thus, the problem that the verifier can choose its query in an arbitrary way, and in particular possibly based on the first message, does not arise. This means that a simpler protocol suffices, and it is much easier to prove security. Recall that this parallel 3-coloring protocol is *not* black-box zero knowledge for malicious verifiers [21]. Thus, honest-verifier zero knowledge is strictly easier to achieve than black-box zero knowledge.

Theorem 6.5.10. *If* Com *is a perfectly binding commitment scheme, then the parallel 3-coloring protocol is honest-verifier zero knowledge.*

Proof sketch: Assume by contradiction that there exists an infinite series of (G, z) and a distinguisher D, such that D distinguishes the output of S from a real execution transcript with nonnegligible probability. Then, a nonuniform polynomial-time distinguisher $\mathcal{A}$, given a valid coloring ψ of G on its advice tape, can be constructed for the commitment scheme, as follows: $\mathcal{A}$ works exactly like $\mathcal{S}$, but uses its LR-oracle (as in Section 6.5.3) to generate pairs of commitments to either a real random coloring or to simulator-generated commitment values (the two random colors for the query edge and zeroes otherwise). The distinguisher $\mathcal{A}$ works in a very similar way to in the proof of Theorem 6.5.4. As with the proof of Theorem 6.5.4, the distribution generated when the commitments are to the real colorings is exactly that of a real execution, and otherwise it is the simulation. Thus, the distributions are indistinguishable, as required.   ∎

6.6 Defining Security for Malicious Adversaries

6.6.1 Motivation

In this section, we present the definition of security for the case of malicious adversaries who may use any efficient attack strategy and thus may arbitrarily deviate from the protocol specification. In this case, it does not suffice to require the existence of a simulator that can generate the view of the corrupted party, based on its prescribed input and output as is sufficient for the case of semi-honest adversaries. First and foremost, the generation of such a view depends on the actual input used by the adversary, and this input affects the actual output received. Furthermore, in contrast to the case of semi-honest adversaries, the adversary may not use the input that it is provided. Thus, for example, a simulator for the case where P_1 is corrupted cannot just take x and $f(x, y)$ and generate a view (in order to prove that nothing more than the output is learned), because the adversary may not use x at all. Furthermore, beyond the possibility that a corrupted party may learn more than it should, we require that a corrupted party should not be able to cause the output to be incorrectly distributed. This is not captured by considering the view of the adversary alone.

In order to capture these threats, and others, the security of a protocol is analyzed by comparing what an adversary can do in the protocol with what it can do in an ideal scenario that is secure by definition. In this context, the ideal model consists of an *ideal* computation involving an incorruptible *trusted third party* to whom the parties send their inputs. The trusted party computes the functionality on the inputs and returns to each party its respective output. Loosely speaking, a protocol is secure if any adversary interacting in the real protocol (where no trusted third party exists) can do no more harm than if it were involved in the ideal computation. See [8, 18] for detailed motivation and discussion on this definitional paradigm.

We remark that in defining security for two parties it is possible to consider only the setting where one of the parties is corrupted, or to also consider the setting where neither of the parties are corrupted, in which case the adversary seeing the transcript between the parties should learn nothing. Since this latter case can easily be achieved by using encryption between the parties, we present the simpler formulation of security that assumes that exactly one party is always corrupted.[5]

Before proceeding, it is worth contrasting the above to the case of zero knowledge (where malicious verifiers were considered). Recall that in the context of zero knowledge, simulation is used to show that the adversary learns *nothing*. Specifically, the adversary is able to generate its view by itself, without receiving any external information, and thus it learns nothing from the real interaction. This works for zero knowledge where the adversarial party has no private input and is supposed to learn nothing. In fact, in the case of zero knowledge, the adversarial verifier does learn that the statement is correct. However, the definition of zero knowledge only states that the adversarial verifier may learn nothing when the statement is in the language, and so is "correct". This makes sense since zero-knowledge proofs are typically used to ensure that parties behave "correctly". Thus, when the verifier is corrupted, the prover is honest and so the statement is supposed to be true. (The case of a corrupted prover who wishes to prove an incorrect statement to an honest verifier is covered separately by soundness.) In the coming sections, we will consider the more general case where parties are supposed to learn output, and also possibly have input. As we will see, this considerably changes the way simulators work, although the techniques shown so far are also needed.

6.6.2 The Definition

Execution in the ideal model. In the case of no honest majority (and in particular in the two-party case that we consider here), it is in general impossible to achieve guaranteed output delivery and fairness [15]. This "weakness" is therefore incorporated into the ideal model by allowing the adversary in an ideal execution to abort the execution or obtain output without the honest party obtaining its output. Denote the participating parties by P_1 and P_2 and let $i \in \{1, 2\}$ denote the index of the corrupted party, controlled by an adversary $\mathcal{A}$. An ideal execution for a function $f : \{0, 1\}^* \times \{0, 1\}^* \rightarrow \{0, 1\}^* \times \{0, 1\}^*$ proceeds as follows:

Inputs: Let x denote the input of party P_1, and let y denote the input of party P_2. The adversary $\mathcal{A}$ also has an auxiliary input denoted by z. All parties are initialized with the same value 1^n on their security parameter tape (including the trusted party).

Send inputs to trusted party: The honest party P_j sends its prescribed input to the trusted party. The corrupted party P_i controlled by $\mathcal{A}$ may either abort (by replacing the input with a special abort$_i$ message), send its prescribed input, or send some other input of the same length to the trusted party. This decision is made by $\mathcal{A}$ and may depend on the input value of P_i and the auxiliary input z. Denote the pair of inputs sent to the trusted party by (x', y') (note that if $i = 2$ then $x' = x$ but y' does not necessarily equal y, and vice versa if $i = 1$).

---

[5] There is no need to consider the case of both parties corrupted, since in such a case there is nothing to protect. In the case of adaptive corruptions (see Section 6.10.3), there is reason to consider corrupting both. However, this is beyond the scope of this tutorial.

Early abort option: If the trusted party receives an input of the form abort$_i$ for some $i \in \{1,2\}$, it sends abort$_i$ to the honest party P_j and the ideal execution terminates. Otherwise, the execution proceeds to the next step.

Trusted party sends output to adversary: At this point the trusted party computes $f_1(x',y')$ and $f_2(x',y')$ and sends $f_i(x',y')$ to party P_i (i.e., it sends the corrupted party its output).

Adversary instructs trusted party to continue or halt: $\mathcal{A}$ sends either continue or abort$_i$ to the trusted party. If it sends continue, the trusted party sends $f_j(x',y')$ to the honest party P_j. Otherwise, if $\mathcal{A}$ sends abort$_i$, the trusted party sends abort$_i$ to party P_j.

Outputs: The honest party always outputs the output value it obtained from the trusted party. The corrupted party outputs nothing. The adversary $\mathcal{A}$ outputs any arbitrary (probabilistic polynomial-time computable) function of the prescribed input of the corrupted party, the auxiliary input z, and the value $f_i(x',y')$ obtained from the trusted party.

Let $f : \{0,1\}^* \times \{0,1\}^* \to \{0,1\}^* \times \{0,1\}^*$ be a two-party functionality, where $f = (f_1, f_2)$, let $\mathcal{A}$ be a nonuniform probabilistic polynomial-time machine, and let $i \in \{1,2\}$ be the index of the corrupted party. Then, the ideal execution of f on inputs (x,y), auxiliary input z to $\mathcal{A}$, and security parameter n, denoted by IDEAL$_{f,\mathcal{A}(z),i}(x,y,n)$, is defined as the output pair of the honest party and the adversary $\mathcal{A}$ from the above ideal execution.

Execution in the real model. We next consider the real model in which a real two-party protocol π is executed (and there exists no trusted third party). In this case, the adversary $\mathcal{A}$ sends all messages in place of the corrupted party, and may follow an arbitrary polynomial-time strategy. In contrast, the honest party follows the instructions of π. We consider a simple network setting where the protocol proceeds in rounds, where in each round one party sends a message to the other party. (In the multiparty setting, this is an unsatisfactory model and one must allow all parties to send messages at the same time. However, in this case, it is standard to assume a *rushing* adversary, meaning that it receives the messages sent by the honest parties before it sends its own.)

Let f be as above and let π be a two-party protocol for computing f, meaning that when P_1 and P_2 are both honest, then the parties output $f_1(x,y)$ and $f_2(x,y)$, respectively, after an execution of π with respective inputs x and y. Furthermore, let $\mathcal{A}$ be a nonuniform probabilistic polynomial-time machine and let $i \in \{1,2\}$ be the index of the corrupted party. Then, the real execution of π on inputs (x,y), auxiliary input z to $\mathcal{A}$, and security parameter n, denoted by REAL$_{\pi,\mathcal{A}(z),i}(x,y,n)$, is defined as the output pair of the honest party and the adversary $\mathcal{A}$ from the real execution of π.

Security as emulation of a real execution in the ideal model. Having defined the ideal and real models, we can now define security of protocols. Loosely speaking, the definition asserts that a secure protocol (in the real model) emulates the ideal model (in which a trusted party exists). This is formulated by saying that adversaries in the ideal model are able to simulate executions of the real-model protocol.

Definition 6.6.1. *Let f be a two-party functionality and let π be a two-party protocol that computes f.[6] Protocol π is said to* securely compute f with abort in the presence of static malicious adversaries *if for every nonuniform probabilistic polynomial-time adversary $\mathcal{A}$ for the real model, there exists a nonuniform probabilistic polynomial-time adversary $\mathcal{S}$ for the ideal model, such that for every $i \in \{1, 2\}$,*

$$\left\{ \mathrm{IDEAL}_{f, \mathcal{S}(z), i}(x, y, n) \right\}_{x, y, z, n} \stackrel{c}{\equiv} \left\{ \mathrm{REAL}_{\pi, \mathcal{A}(z), i}(x, y, n) \right\}_{x, y, z, n},$$

where $x, y \in \{0, 1\}^*$ under the constraint that $|x| = |y|$, $z \in \{0, 1\}^*$, and $n \in \mathbb{N}$.

The above definition assumes that the parties (and adversary) know the input lengths (this can be seen from the requirement that $|x| = |y|$ is balanced and so all the inputs in the vector of inputs are of the same length). We remark that some restriction on the input lengths is unavoidable because, as in the case of encryption, to some extent such information is always leaked. We will ignore this throughout, and just assume that the functionality is such that the parties know the lengths of all inputs.

In this tutorial we only consider security with abort. Therefore, in the latter when we say "securely computes" the intention is always *with abort*.

Discussion. Observe that Definition 6.6.1 implies *privacy* (meaning that nothing but the output is learned), *corrrectness* (meaning that the output is correctly computed), and more. This holds because the IDEAL and REAL distributions include both the corrupted and honest parties' outputs. Specifically, in the ideal model, the adversary cannot learn anything about the honest party's input beyond what is revealed in the output. Now, since the IDEAL and REAL distributions must be indistinguishable, this in particular implies that the output of the adversary in the IDEAL and REAL executions is indistinguishable. Thus, whatever the adversary learns in a real execution can be learned in the ideal model. Regarding correctness, if the adversary can cause the honest party's output to diverge from a correct value in a real execution, then this will result in a nonnegligible difference between the distribution over the honest party's output in the real and ideal executions. Observe that correctness in the real model only is rather tricky to define. Is a computation correct if there *exists* some input for the corrupted party such that the output of the honest party is the correct result on that input and its own? This is a very unsatisfactory definition. First, it is possible that such an input exists, but it may be computationally hard to find. Second, it is possible that it is easy to find such an input, but only if the honest party's input is already known.[7] The ideal/real definition solves all of these problems at once. This is because in the ideal model, the adversary has to send its input explicitly to the trusted party, and correctness is judged relative to the actual input

---

[6] A prerequisite of any secure protocol is that it computes the functionality, meaning that two honest parties receive correct output. As we show at the end of Section 6.8, this is a *necessary* requirement.

[7] This relates to an additional property that is guaranteed by the definition, called *independence of inputs*, meaning that the corrupted party is unable to make its input depend on the honest party's input. For example, in a closed-bid auction, it should not be possible for a corrupted party to make its bid be exactly $1 greater than the honest party's bid.

sent. This also means that parties actually "know" their inputs in protocols that are secure. See [18, Section 7.2.3] for more discussion.

Remark 6.6.2. (Deterministic versus probabilistic adversaries): *In all of the proofs in this tutorial —and in most proofs in general—the real-world adversary $\mathcal{A}$ is used in a black-box manner. Thus, the simulator $\mathcal{S}$, who is given input x and auxiliary input z for the corrupted party, can begin by choosing a random string r and defining the residual adversary $\mathcal{A}'(\cdot) \stackrel{\text{def}}{=} \mathcal{A}(x, z, r; \cdot)$, with security parameter 1^n (as on its own security parameter tape). From then on, $\mathcal{S}$ works with $\mathcal{A}'$ and simulates for $\mathcal{A}'$. Due to the above, it suffices to consider a deterministic adversary, with a fixed input, auxiliary input, and random tape. This simplifies the treatment throughout.*

Expected polynomial-time simulation. It is sometimes necessary to relax the requirement on the simulator and allow it to run in *expected* polynomial time. As we have mentioned, this is the case for constant-round zero knowledge and thus when using constant-round zero-knowledge proofs inside other protocols. However, it is also necessary when constructing constant-round protocols for *general* secure computation (where a protocol for general secure computation can be used to securely compute any polynomial-time computable function). This is due to the fact that such a general protocol can be used to securely compute the "zero-knowledge proof of knowledge" functionality. Thus, if the simulator is black box, it must run in expected polynomial time [2].

6.6.3 Modular Sequential Composition

A protocol that is secure under *sequential* composition maintains its security when run multiple times, as long as the executions are run sequentially (meaning that each execution concludes before the next execution begins). Sequential composition theorems are theorems that state "if a protocol is secure in the stand-alone model under definition X, then it remains secure under X under sequential composition". Thus, we are interested in proving protocols secure under Definitions 6.4.1 and 6.6.1 (for semi-honest, and malicious adversaries), and immediately deriving their security under sequential composition. This is important for two reasons. First, sequential composition constitutes a security goal within itself, as security is guaranteed even when parties run many executions, albeit sequentially. Second, sequential composition theorems are useful tools that help in writing proofs of security. Specifically, it enables one to design a protocol using calls to ideal functionalities (as subprotocols), and to analyze its security in this partially ideal setting. This makes protocol design and analysis significantly more simple. Thus, the use of composition theorems in order to help in proving simulation-based proofs of security is one of the most important techniques.

We do not present proofs of the sequential composition theorems for the semi-honest and malicious cases, and we recommend reading these proofs in [18]; see Sections 7.3.1 and 7.4.2, respectively. However, we do present a formal *statement* of the theorem for malicious adversaries, as we will use it in the tutorial.

Modular sequential composition. The basic idea behind the formulation of the modular sequential composition theorems is to show that it is possible to design a protocol that uses an ideal functionality as a subroutine, and then analyze the security of the protocol when a trusted party computes this functionality. For example, assume that a protocol is constructed using oblivious transfer as a subroutine. Then, first we construct a protocol for oblivious transfer and prove its security. Next, we prove the security of the protocol that uses oblivious transfer as a subroutine, in a model where the parties have access to a trusted party computing the oblivious transfer functionality. The composition theorem then states that when the "ideal calls" to the trusted party for the oblivious transfer functionality are replaced with real executions of a secure protocol computing this functionality, the protocol remains secure. We begin by presenting the "hybrid model" where parties communicate by sending regular messages to each other (as in the real model) but also have access to a trusted party (as in the ideal model).

The hybrid model. We consider a *hybrid model* where parties both interact with each other (as in the real model) and use trusted help (as in the ideal model). Specifically, the parties run a protocol π that contains "ideal calls" to a trusted party computing some functionalities $f_1, \ldots, f_{p(n)}$. These ideal calls are just instructions to send an input to the trusted party. Upon receiving the output back from the trusted party, the protocol π continues. The protocol π is such that f_i is called before f_{i+1} for every i (this just determines the "naming" of the calls as $f_1, \ldots, f_{p(n)}$ in that order). In addition, if a functionality f_i is *reactive* (meaning that it contains multiple stages), then no messages are sent by the parties directly to each other from the time that the first message is sent to f_i to the time that all stages of f_i have concluded. We stress that the honest party sends its input to the trusted party in the same round and does not send other messages until it receives its output (this is because we consider *sequential composition* here). The trusted party may be used a number of times throughout the execution of π. However, each use is independent (i.e., the trusted party does not maintain any state between these calls). We call the regular messages of π that are sent amongst the parties standard messages and the messages that are sent between parties and the trusted party ideal messages.

Sequential composition – malicious adversaries. Let $f_1, \ldots, f_{p(n)}$ be probabilistic polynomial-time functionalities and let π be a two-party hybrid-model protocol that uses ideal calls to a trusted party computing $f_1, \ldots, f_{p(n)}$. Furthermore, let $\mathcal{A}$ be a nonuniform probabilistic polynomial-time machine and let i be the index of the corrupted party. Then, the $f_1, \ldots, f_{p(n)}$-hybrid execution of π on inputs (x, y), auxiliary input z to $\mathcal{A}$, and security parameter n, denoted $\text{HYBRID}_{\pi, \mathcal{A}(z), i}^{f_1, \ldots, f_{p(n)}}(x, y, n)$, is defined as the output of the honest party and the adversary $\mathcal{A}$ from the hybrid execution of π with a trusted party computing $f_1, \ldots, f_{p(n)}$.

Let $\rho_1, \ldots, \rho_{p(n)}$ be protocols (as we will see, ρ_i takes the place of f_i in π). Consider the real protocol $\pi^{\rho_1, \ldots, \rho_{p(n)}}$ that is defined as follows: All standard messages of π are unchanged. When a party is instructed to send an ideal message α to the trusted party to compute f_j, it begins a real execution of ρ_j with input α instead. When this execution of ρ_j concludes with output y, the party continues with π as if y were the output received from the trusted party for f_j (i.e., as if it were running in the hybrid model).

The composition theorem states that, if $\rho_1, \ldots, \rho_{p(n)}$ securely compute $f_1, \ldots, f_{p(n)}$ respectively, and π securely computes some functionality g in the $f_1, \ldots, f_{p(n)}$-hybrid model, then $\pi^{\rho_1, \ldots, \rho_{p(n)}}$ securely computes g in the real model. As discussed above, the hybrid model that we consider here is where the protocols are run sequentially. Thus, the fact that sequential composition only is considered is implicit in the theorem, via the reference to the hybrid model.

Theorem 6.6.3. *Let $p(n)$ be a polynomial, let $f_1, \ldots, f_{p(n)}$ be two-party probabilistic polynomial-time functionalities, and let $\rho_1, \ldots, \rho_{p(n)}$ be protocols such that each ρ_i securely computes f_i in the presence of malicious adversaries. Let g be a two-party functionality and let π be a protocol that securely computes g in the $f_1, \ldots, f_{p(n)}$-hybrid model in the presence of malicious adversaries. Then, $\pi^{\rho_1, \ldots, \rho_{p(n)}}$ securely computes g in the presence of malicious adversaries.*

Composition with expected polynomial-time simulation. The composition theorem proven by [8, 18] holds for strict polynomial-time adversaries, and certain difficulties arise when considering expected polynomial-time simulation. This issue was considered by [28], and a far simpler solution was later provided in [19]. Although of importance, we will ignore this issue in this tutorial.

Sequential composition – semi-honest adversaries. A composition theorem that is analogous to Theorem 6.6.3 also holds for semi-honest adversaries; see [18, Section 7.4.2].

6.7 Determining Output – Coin Tossing

Previously, we considered the simulation of malicious adversaries in the context of zero knowledge. However, as we have mentioned, zero knowledge is an easier case since the verifier receives no output (if the prover is honest, then the verifier already knows that the statement is true). In this section, we consider the problem of coin tossing. The coin-tossing functionality has no input, but the parties must receive the same uniformly distributed output. Thus, in this section, we demonstrate simulation in this more difficult scenario, where the view must be generated and correlated to the actual output.

6.7.1 Coin Tossing a Single Bit

In this section, we present the protocol by Blum for tossing a single coin securely [5]. The protocol securely computes the functionality $f_{ct}(\lambda, \lambda) = (U_1, U_1)$, where U_1 is a random variable that is uniformly distributed over $\{0, 1\}$. We stress that we only consider security with abort here, and thus it is possible for one party to see the output and then abort before the other receives it (e.g., in the case that it is not a favorable outcome for that party). Indeed, it is impossible for two parties to toss a coin fairly so that neither party can cause a premature abort or bias the outcome [15].

Tossing a single coin. The idea behind the protocol is very simple: both parties locally choose a random bit, and the result is the XOR of the two bits. The problem that arises is that if P_1 sends its random bit to P_2 first, then P_2 can cheat and send a bit that forces the output to be the result that it desires. One possible way to solve this problem is to have P_1 and P_2 *simultaneously* send their bits to each other. However, we do not have simultaneous channels that force independence. (Formally, we defined a real model where protocols proceed in rounds and in each round one message is sent from one party to the other.) This is solved by having P_1 send a *commitment* to its bit b_1, rather than b_1 itself. From the hiding property of the commitment scheme, when P_2 sends b_2 it must send it independently of b_1 (since it only receives a commitment). Likewise, from the binding property of the commitment scheme, P_1 cannot change b_1 after it is committed. Therefore, even though P_1 sees b_2 before decommitting, it cannot change the value. See Protocol 6.7.1 for a description of the protocol.

PROTOCOL 6.7.1 (Blum's coin tossing of a single bit)

- **Security parameter:** Both parties have security parameter 1^n
- **The protocol:**

  1. P_1 chooses a random $b_1 \in \{0, 1\}$ and a random $r \in \{0, 1\}^n$ and sends $c = \mathsf{Com}(b_1; r)$ to P_2.
  2. Upon receiving c, party P_2 chooses a random $b_2 \in \{0, 1\}$ and sends b_2 to P_1.
  3. Upon receiving b_2, party P_1 sends (b_1, r) to P_2 and outputs $b = b_1 \oplus b_2$. (If P_2 does not reply, or replies with an invalid value, then P_2 sets $b_2 = 0$.)
  4. Upon receiving (b_1, r) from P_1, party P_2 checks that $c = \mathsf{Com}(b_1; r)$. If yes, it outputs $b = b_1 \oplus b_2$; else it outputs $\perp$.

Before we proceed to proving the security of Protocol 6.7.1, we discuss the main challenges in carrying out the simulation. This is our first example of a "standard" secure computation. The simulator here is the ideal-model adversary. As such, it *externally interacts* with the trusted party computing the functionality (in this case, $f_{\mathsf{ct}}(\lambda, \lambda) = (U_1, U_1)$), and *internally interacts* with the real-model adversary as part of the simulation. Throughout simulation-based proofs, it is very important to emphasize the difference between such interactions. (Of course, internal interaction is not real, and is just the simulator internally feeding messages to $\mathcal{A}$ that it runs as a subroutine, as in Section 6.5.) In general, the simulator needs to send the trusted party the corrupted party's input and receive back its output. In this specific case of coin tossing, the parties have no input, and so the adversary just receives the output from the trusted party (formally, the parties send an empty string λ as input so that the trusted party knows to compute the functionality). The challenge of the simulator is to make the output of the execution that it simulates equal the output that it received from the trusted party.

We elaborate on this challenge: in the simulation, the simulator receives the output bit b from the trusted party and needs to make the result of the execution equal b. Thus, it has to be able to *completely bias* the outcome to be a specific value. This contradicts the basic security of a coin-tossing protocol! However, like zero knowledge versus soundness in the case of zero-knowledge proofs, this contradiction is overcome by the fact that the simulator has some *additional power* that a real adversary does not have. As before, the additional power it has here is the ability to rewind the adversary. Intuitively, since we are tossing a single bit, and in each execution the probability that the result equals b is $1/2$, it follows that the simulator can just run the protocol numerous times from scratch, until the result is b. Since we expect to need to rewind only twice, we are guaranteed that the simulator will succeed within n attempts, except with negligible probability. However, another concern arises here. Specifically, a corrupted P_1 may abort and refuse to decommit to its first commitment. Observe that P_1 already knows the output at this point, and so this decision may be a function of what the output will be. Fortunately, in the ideal model, the definition of security allows the corrupted party to obtain the input, and not necessarily provide the output to the honest party. However, the simulation must take great care to not skew the probability of this happening (if in a real execution P_2 receives output with probability p when the output will be 0, and receives output with probability q when the output will be 1, then these probabilities must be negligibly close to p and q in the simulation as well). We now proceed to the actual proof (this proof is based heavily on [18, Section 7.4.3.1]).

Theorem 6.7.2. *Assume that* Com *is a perfectly binding commitment scheme. Then, Protocol 6.7.1 securely computes the bit coin-tossing functionality defined by* $f_{ct}(\lambda, \lambda) = (U_1, U_1)$.

Proof: It is clear that Protocol 6.7.1 computes f_{ct}, since when both parties are honest they output $b_1 \oplus b_2$, which is uniformly distributed. We now proceed to prove that the protocol is secure.

Let $\mathcal{A}$ be a nonuniform probabilistic polynomial-time adversary. As discussed in Remark 6.6.2, we may consider a deterministic $\mathcal{A}$. We first consider the case that P_2 is corrupted. We describe the simulator $\mathcal{S}$:

1. $\mathcal{S}$ sends λ externally to the trusted party computing f_{ct} and receives back a bit b.
2. $\mathcal{S}$ initializes a counter $i = 1$.
3. $\mathcal{S}$ invokes $\mathcal{A}$, chooses a random $b_1 \in_R \{0, 1\}$ and $r \in_R \{0, 1\}^n$, and internally hands $\mathcal{A}$ the value $c = \text{Com}(b_1; r)$ as if it was sent by P_2.
4. If $\mathcal{A}$ replies with $b_2 = b \oplus b_1$, then $\mathcal{S}$ internally hands $\mathcal{A}$ the pair (b_1, r) and outputs whatever $\mathcal{A}$ outputs. (As in the protocol, if $\mathcal{A}$ does not reply or replies with an invalid value, then this is interpreted as $b_2 = 0$.)
5. If $\mathcal{A}$ replies with $b_2 \neq b \oplus b_1$ and $i < n$, then $\mathcal{S}$ sets $i = i + 1$ and returns back to step 3.
6. If $i = n$, then $\mathcal{S}$ outputs fail.

We first prove that $\mathcal{S}$ outputs fail with negligible probability. Intuitively, this is the case since $\mathcal{A}$'s response bit b_2 is (computationally) independent of b_1. In order to see this, observe that an iteration succeeds if and only if $b_1 \oplus b_2 = b$, where b_2 is $\mathcal{A}$'s response to $\mathsf{Com}(b_1)$. We have

$$\Pr[\mathcal{A}(\mathsf{Com}(b_1)) = b_1 \oplus b] = \frac{1}{2} \cdot \Pr[\mathcal{A}(\mathsf{Com}(0)) = b] + \frac{1}{2} \cdot \Pr[\mathcal{A}(\mathsf{Com}(1)) = 1 \oplus b]$$

$$= \frac{1}{2} \cdot \Pr[\mathcal{A}(\mathsf{Com}(0)) = b] + \frac{1}{2} \cdot (1 - \Pr[\mathcal{A}(\mathsf{Com}(1)) = b])$$

$$= \frac{1}{2} + \frac{1}{2} \cdot (\Pr[\mathcal{A}(\mathsf{Com}(0)) = b] - \Pr[\mathcal{A}(\mathsf{Com}(1)) = b]),$$

where the probability is taken over the choice of b_1 and the randomness used to generate the commitment. By the assumption that Com is a perfectly binding commitment scheme, and thus is computationally hiding, we have that there exists a negligible function μ such that for every $b \in \{0, 1\}$

$$\left| \Pr[\mathcal{A}(\mathsf{Com}(0)) = b] - \Pr[\mathcal{A}(\mathsf{Com}(1)) = b] \right| \leq \mu(n),$$

and so

$$\frac{1}{2} \cdot (1 - \mu(n)) \leq \Pr[\mathcal{A}(\mathsf{Com}(b_1)) = b_1 \oplus b] \leq \frac{1}{2} \cdot (1 + \mu(n)). \tag{6.10}$$

(We stress that, in Eq. (6.10), the probability is taken over the choice of b_1 and the randomness used to generate $\mathsf{Com}(b_1)$.) Since $\mathcal{S}$ outputs fail if and only if $\mathcal{A}(\mathsf{Com}(b_1)) \neq b_1 \oplus b$ in *all* n iterations, we have that $\mathcal{S}$ outputs fail with probability at most

$$\left(\frac{1}{2} \cdot (1 + \mu(n)) \right)^n < \left(\frac{2}{3} \right)^n,$$

which is negligible (the inequality holds for all large enough n's).

Next, we show that, conditioned on the fact that $\mathcal{S}$ does not output fail, the output distributions IDEAL and REAL are statistically close. Observe that in both the real and ideal (i.e., simulated) executions, the bit b_2 sent by $\mathcal{A}$ is fully determined by b_1, r. Specifically, we can write $b_2 = \mathcal{A}(\mathsf{Com}(b_1; r))$. We therefore have that both distributions are of the form $(b, \mathcal{A}(\mathsf{Com}(b_1; r), b_1, r))$, where $b = b_1 \oplus \mathcal{A}(\mathsf{Com}(b_1; r))$. The difference between the distributions is as follows:

- **Real:** In a real execution, b_1 and r are uniformly distributed.
- **Ideal:** In an ideal execution, a random b is chosen, and then random b_1 and r are chosen under the constraint that $b_1 \oplus \mathcal{A}(\mathsf{Com}(b_1; r)) = b$.

In order to see that these distributions are statistically close, we calculate the probability that every (b_1, r) is chosen according to the distributions. Fix $\hat{b}_1, \hat{r}$. Then, in the real execution it is immediate that $(\hat{b}_1, \hat{r})$ appears with probability exactly $2^{-(n+1)}$.

Regarding the ideal execution, denote by $S_b = \{(b_1, r) \mid b_1 \oplus \mathcal{A}(\mathsf{Com}(b_1; r)) = b\}$. Observe that S_b contains all the pairs (b_1, r) that can lead to an output of b in the ideal execution (since $\mathcal{S}$ concludes when $b_1 \oplus \mathcal{A}(\mathsf{Com}(b_1; r)) = b$). We claim that the fixed $(\hat{b}_1, \hat{r})$ appears in the ideal execution with probability

$$\frac{1}{2} \cdot \frac{1}{|S_b|}. \tag{6.11}$$

This holds because b is uniformly chosen by the trusted party, and *conditioned on not outputting* fail, simulator S samples a uniformly distributed element from S_b. (This can be seen by the fact that S concludes as soon as it obtains an element of S_b, and in every iteration it chooses a random b_1, r with the "hope" that it is in S_b.)

It remains to show that for every $b \in \{0, 1\}$, the set S_b has close to 2^n elements. However, this follows directly from Eq. (6.10). Specifically, Eq. (6.10) states that for every b, the probability that $A(\text{Com}(b_1; r)) = b_1 \oplus b$ is $\frac{1}{2} \cdot (1 \pm \mu(n))$. However, this probability is exactly the probability that $(b_1, r) \in S_b$. This implies that

$$\frac{1}{2} \cdot (1 - \mu(n)) \leq \frac{|S_b|}{2^{n+1}} \leq \frac{1}{2} \cdot (1 + \mu(n)),$$

and so

$$2^n \cdot (1 - \mu(n)) \leq |S_b| \leq 2^n \cdot (1 + \mu(n)).$$

Combining this with Eq. (6.11), we have that the pair $(\hat{b}_1, \hat{r})$ appears with probability between $2^{-(n+1)} \cdot (1 - \mu(n))$ and $2^{-(n+1)} \cdot (1 + \mu(n))$. This is therefore statistically close to the probability that $(\hat{b}_1, \hat{r})$ appears in a real execution. The real and ideal output distributions are therefore statistically close.[8]

We now turn to the case that P_1 is corrupted. The simulation here needs to take into account the case that A does not reply with a valid message and so aborts. The simulator S works as follows:

1. S sends λ externally to the trusted party computing f_{ct} and receives back a bit b.
2. S invokes A and internally receives the message c that A sends to P_1.
3. S internally hands A the bit $b_2 = 0$ as if coming from P_2, and receives back its reply. Then, S internally hands A the bit $b_2 = 1$ as if coming from P_2, and receives back its reply. We have the following cases:

   a. If A replies with a valid decommitment (b_1, r) such that $\text{Com}(b_1; r) = c$ in both iterations, then S externally sends continue to the trusted party. In addition, S defines $b_2 = b_1 \oplus b$, internally hands A the bit b_2, and outputs whatever A outputs.

   b. If A does not reply with a valid decommitment in either iteration, then S externally sends abort$_1$ to the trusted party. Then, S internally hands A a random bit b_2 and outputs whatever A outputs.

   c. If A replies with a valid decommitment (b_1, r) such that $\text{Com}(b_1; r) = c$ only when given b_2 where $b_1 \oplus b_2 = b$, then S externally sends continue to

---

[8] It may seem surprising that we obtain statistical closeness, even though we are relying on the computational hiding of the commitment scheme. However, the computational hiding is used only to ensure that S outputs fail with negligible probability, and holds when considering any polynomial-time A.

the trusted party. Then, S internally hands A the bit $b_2 = b_1 \oplus b$ and outputs whatever A outputs.

d. If A replies with a valid decommitment (b_1, r) such that $\mathsf{Com}(b_1; r) = c$ only when given b_2 where $b_1 \oplus b_2 \neq b$, then S externally sends abort_1 to the trusted party. Then, S internally hands A the bit $b_2 = b_1 \oplus b \oplus 1$ and outputs whatever A outputs.

We prove that the output distribution is identical. We consider three cases:

1. *Case 3a – A always replies with a valid decommitment:* In this case, A's view in a real execution consists of a random bit b_2, and the honest P_2's output equals $b = b_1 \oplus b_2$, where b_1 is the committed value in c. Since b_1 is fully determined by the commitment c before b_2 is chosen by P_1, it follows that b is uniformly distributed.

   In contrast, in an ideal execution, the bit b is uniformly chosen. Then, A's view consists of $b_2 = b_1 \oplus b$, and the honest P_2's output equals b. Since b_1 is fully determined by the commitment c before any information about b is given to A, it follows that $b_2 = b_1 \oplus b$ is uniformly distributed.

   In both cases, the bits b and b_2 are uniformly distributed under the constraint that $b \oplus b_2 = b_1$. Thus, the joint distributions over A's output and the honest party's output are identical in the real and ideal executions.

2. *Case 3b – A never replies with a valid decommitment:* In this case, A's view consists of a uniformly distributed bit, exactly like in a real execution. In addition, the honest P_2 outputs $\perp$ in both the real and ideal executions (with probability 1). Thus, the joint distributions over A's output and the honest party's output are identical in the real and ideal executions.

3. *Case 3c and 3d – A replies with a valid decommitment for exactly one value $\hat{b}_2 \in \{0, 1\}$:* Let b_1 be the value committed in the commitment c sent by A (since A is deterministic and this is the first message, this is a fixed value). Then, in the real execution, if P_2 sends $\hat{b}_2$ then A replies with a valid decommitment and the honest P_2 outputs $b = b_1 \oplus \hat{b}_2$. In contrast, if P_2 sends $\hat{b}_2 \oplus 1$, then A does not reply with a valid decommitment and P_2 outputs $\perp$.

   Consider now the ideal execution. If $b \oplus b_1 = \hat{b}_2$, then S hands A the bit $\hat{b}_2$. In this case, A replies with a valid decommitment and the honest party P_2 outputs $b = b_1 \oplus \hat{b}_2$. In contrast, if $b \oplus b_1 = \hat{b}_2 \oplus 1$, then S hands A the bit $\hat{b} \oplus 1$. In this case, A does not reply with a valid decommitment and P_2 outputs $\perp$.

   We therefore see that the distribution over the view of A and the output of P_2 is identical in both cases.

This completes the proof of the theorem.   ∎

Discussion. The proof of Theorem 6.7.2 is surprising in its complexity. The intuition behind the security of Protocol 6.7.1 is very straightforward. Nevertheless, formally justifying this fact is very difficult.[9] Some specific observations are worth

---

[9] I would like to add a personal anecdote here. The first proof of security that I read that followed the ideal/real simulation paradigm with security for malicious adversaries was this proof by Oded

making. First, as in the zero-knowledge proofs, the mere fact that the simulator (for the case of P_2 corrupted) runs in polynomial time is not straightforward and requires a reduction to the security of the commitment scheme. Second, in the malicious setting, many additional issues needed to be dealt with:

1. The adversary can send any message and so the simulator must "interact" with it.
2. The adversary may abort in some cases and this must be carefully simulated so that the distribution is not skewed when aborts can happen.
3. The adversary may abort after it receives the output and before the honest party receives the output. This must be correlated with the abort and continue instructions sent to the trusted party, in order to ensure that the honest party aborts with the same probability in the real and ideal executions, and that this behavior matches the view of the adversary.

Third, it is worth comparing this proof with those of zero knowledge in Section 6.5. In both cases, we deal with a malicious adversary. However, in zero knowledge, there is no "joint distribution" over the output, since there is no output. Thus, it suffices to simulate the view of the verifier V^* alone. Although this is not so easy, it is far less delicate than this proof here. The need to consider the joint distribution over the outputs, and to simulate for the output received from the trusted party (whatever it may be), adds considerable complexity.

Technique discussion. It is worthwhile observing that S essentially plays the role of the honest party, in that it generates the messages from the honest party that the adversary expects to see. This is true in all simulations. Of course, S does not actually send the messages that the honest party sends, since S has to make the output received by $\mathcal{A}$ equal the output sent by the trusted party computing the functionality. This is something that cannot be possible in a real execution, or else a corrupted party could fully determine the output.

Interaction with the trusted party or ideal functionality. As we have seen, the simulator externally interacts with the trusted party computing the functionality. In many papers, the simulator is described as interacting directly with the functionality itself (and not a trusted party computing it). This is merely an issue of terminology, and the intention is exactly the same.

6.7.2 Securely Tossing Many Coins and the Hybrid Model

In this section, we will show how to toss many coins. Of course, we could apply the sequential composition theorem and obtain that, in order to toss some $\ell = \text{poly}(n)$ coins, the parties can carry out ℓ sequential executions of Protocol 6.7.1. However,

---

Goldreich (it appeared in a very early draft on Secure Multiparty Computation that can be found at www.wisdom.weizmann.ac.il/~oded/pp.html). I remember reading it multiple times until I understood why all the complications were necessary. Thus, for me, this proof brings back fond memories of my first steps in secure computation.

we wish to toss many coins in a *constant number of rounds*. Formally, the functionality is parameterized by a polynomial ℓ and is defined by $f_{ct}^\ell(\lambda, \lambda) = (U_{\ell(n)}, U_{\ell(n)})$. Note that the security parameter n is also given to the trusted party, and thus it can compute the length $\ell(n)$ itself.

Our main aim in this section is to introduce simulation-based proofs in the hybrid model. As such, we will assume that we are given a constant-round protocol that securely computes the zero-knowledge proof of knowledge functionality for any $\mathcal{NP}$ relation. This functionality is parameterized by a relation $R \in \mathcal{NP}$ and is defined by $f_{zk}^R((x, w), x) = (\lambda, R(x, w))$. Note that f_{zk} receives x from both parties; if different values of x are received then the output is 0. Formally, we define

$$f_{zk}^R((x, w), x') = \begin{cases} (\lambda, R(x, w)) & \text{if } x = x' \\ (\lambda, 0) & \text{otherwise} \end{cases}.$$

We remark that any zero-knowledge proof of knowledge for R, as defined in [17, Section 4.7], securely computes the functionality f_{zk}^R. This folklore fact was formally proven in [27]. The existence of a constant-round zero-knowledge proof of knowledge was proven in [30]. Thus, we conclude that f_{zk}^R can be securely computed in a constant number of rounds.

As we will see here, working in the hybrid model *greatly simplifies* things. In fact, the proof of security in this section—for a far more complex protocol than for tossing a single coin—is far simpler.

Protocol idea. As in Protocol 6.7.1, the idea behind the protocol is to have P_1 commit to a random string ρ_1 of length $\ell(n)$, and then for P_2 to reply with another random string ρ_2 of length $\ell(n)$. The result is the XOR $\rho_1 \oplus \rho_2$ of these two strings. Unfortunately, we do not know how to simulate such a protocol. This is due to the fact that when P_2 is corrupted, S would need to rewind the adversary $\mathcal{A}$ an exponential number of times in order to make $\rho_1 \oplus \rho_2$ equal a specific string ρ provided by the trusted party. This is similar to the problem with simulating the basic three-round zero-knowledge protocol when running it many times in parallel. We solve this problem by not having P_1 decommit to ρ_1 at all. Rather, it sends ρ_1 and proves in zero knowledge that this is the value in the commitment. In the real world, this is the same as decommitting (up to the negligible probability that P_1 can cheat in the proof). However, in the ideal simulation, the simulator can cheat in the zero-knowledge proof and send $\rho_1 = \rho \oplus \rho_2$, where ρ is the value received from the trusted party, even though the value committed to is completely different.

In the case that P_1 is corrupted, there is another problem that arises. Specifically, in order to simulate, the simulator first needs to learn the value ρ_1 committed before it can set $\rho_2 = \rho \oplus \rho_1$. Thus, it first needs to hand $\mathcal{A}$ a random ρ_2 with the hope that it will decommit ρ_1 and correctly prove the proof. If it does not, then the simulator can just abort. If it does send ρ_1 and correctly proves the zero-knowledge proof, then the simulator can now rewind and hand it $\rho_2 = \rho \oplus \rho_1$. However, what happens if $\mathcal{A}$ aborts given this ρ_2? If the simulator aborts now then the probability of abort is much higher in the ideal execution than in a real execution (because it aborts with the probability that $\mathcal{A}$ aborts when given a random ρ_2 *plus* the probability that $\mathcal{A}$ aborts when receiving $\rho_2 = \rho_1 \oplus \rho$). But, the simulator cannot do anything else since there is only one ρ_2 that can be used at this point. We solve this problem by adding a zero-knowledge proof of knowledge that P_1 proves as soon as it commits to ρ_1. The simulator can then extract ρ_1 and set $\rho_2 = \rho_1 \oplus \rho$ without any rewinding (of course, beyond the internal rewinding needed to prove the security of f_{zk}^R; nevertheless, thanks to the composition theorem we can ignore this here). If $\mathcal{A}$ aborts on this ρ_2 then the simulator aborts; otherwise it does not. This gives the required probability of abort, as we will see. See Protocol 6.7.3 for the full specification.

PROTOCOL 6.7.3 (Multiple coin tossing)

- **Input:** Both parties have input 1^n (where $\ell(n)$ is the number of coins to be tossed).
- **Security parameter:** Both parties have security parameter 1^n.
- **Hybrid functionalities:** Let $L_1 = \{c \mid \exists (x, r) : c = \mathsf{Com}(x; r)\}$ be the language of all valid commitments, and let R_1 be its associated $\mathcal{NP}$ relation (for statement c the witness is x, r such that $c = \mathsf{Com}(x; r)$). Let $L_2 = \{(c, x) \mid \exists r : c = \mathsf{Com}(x; r)\}$ be the language of all pairs of commitments and committed values, and let R_2 be its associated $\mathcal{NP}$ relation (for statement (c, x) the witness is r such that $c = \mathsf{Com}(x; r)$). The parties have access to a trusted party that computes the zero-knowledge proof of knowledge functionalities $f_{\mathsf{zk}}^{R_1}$ and $f_{\mathsf{zk}}^{R_2}$ for relations R_1 and R_2, respectively.
- **The protocol (for tossing $\ell(n)$ coins):**
  1. P_1 chooses a random $\rho_1 \in \{0, 1\}^{\ell(n)}$ and a random $r \in \{0, 1\}^{\mathrm{poly}(n)}$ of length sufficient to commit to $\ell(n)$ bits, and sends $c = \mathsf{Com}(\rho_1; r)$ to P_2.
  2. P_1 sends $(c, (\rho_1, r))$ to $f_{\mathsf{zk}}^{R_1}$.
  3. Upon receiving c, party P_2 sends c to $f_{\mathsf{zk}}^{R_1}$ and receives back a bit b. If $b = 0$ then P_2 outputs $\perp$ and halts. Otherwise, it proceeds.
  4. P_2 chooses a random $\rho_2 \in \{0, 1\}^{\ell(n)}$ and sends ρ_2 to P_1.
  5. Upon receiving ρ_2, party P_1 sends ρ_1 to P_2 and sends $((c, \rho_1), r)$ to $f_{\mathsf{zk}}^{R_2}$. (If P_2 does not reply, or replies with an invalid value, then P_1 sets $\rho_2 = 0^{\ell(n)}$.)
  6. Upon receiving ρ_1, party P_2 sends (c, ρ_1) to $f_{\mathsf{zk}}^{R_2}$ and receives back a bit b. If $b = 0$ then P_2 outputs $\perp$ and halts. Otherwise, it outputs $\rho = \rho_1 \oplus \rho_2$.
  7. P_1 outputs $\rho = \rho_1 \oplus \rho_2$.

Technique discussion – proving in the hybrid model. Before proceeding to prove the security of Protocol 6.7.3, we explain how a proof of security in the hybrid model works. Recall that the sequential composition theorem states that if a protocol securely computes a functionality f in the g-hybrid model for some functionality g, then it remains secure when using a secure subprotocol that securely computes g. An important observation here is that in the hybrid model with g, there is no "negligible error" or "computational indistinguishability" when computing g. Rather, g is secure by definition, and an incorruptible trusted party computes it. Thus, there is no need to prove a reduction that if an adversary can break the protocol for securely computing f, then there exists an adversary that breaks the subprotocol that securely computes g. As we have seen above, such reductions are often a major effort in the proof, and thus working in a hybrid model saves this effort.

A second important observation is that a protocol that is designed in the g-hybrid model for some g contains instructions for sending inputs to the trusted party computing f. Furthermore, parties receive outputs from the computation of g from the trusted party. This means that an *adversary* for the protocol also sends its inputs to the computation of g in the clear, and expects to receive its outputs back. In the specific example of Protocol 6.7.3, the functionality used is a zero-knowledge proof of knowledge functionality. Thus, if the adversary controls the party running the prover, then it directly sends the *input and witness* pair (x, w) to f_{zk}. This means that a simulator who internally runs the adversary will receive (x, w) from the adversary and so immediately has the input and witness. Observe that there is no need to run the proof's knowledge extractor and deal with negligible error and polynomial-time issues. The simulator obtains these for free. Likewise, if the adversary controls the party running the verifier, then it expects to receive 1 as output from f_{zk} (in the typical case that an honest party never tries to prove an incorrect statement in the protocol). Thus, the simulator can just hand it 1 as the output from the trusted party, and there is no need for it to run the zero-knowledge simulator and prove a reduction that computational indistinguishability holds. In addition, this "simulation" that works by sending 1 is *perfect*.

   In summary, in the simulation, the simulator *plays the trusted party that computes the functionality used in the hybrid model* that interacts with the adversary. The simulator directly receives the input that the adversary sends and can write any output that it likes. (We stress that this should not be confused with the trusted party that the simulator externally interacts with in the ideal model. This interaction is unchanged.) As a result, S has many types of interactions and it is very helpful to the reader to explicitly differentiate between them within the proof:

1. *External interaction with the trusted party:* this is real interaction where S sends and receives messages externally.
2. *Internal simulated interaction with the real adversary $\mathcal{A}$:* this is simulated interaction and involves internally invoking $\mathcal{A}$ as a subroutine on incoming messages. This interaction is of two subtypes:

   a. *Internal simulation of real messages between $\mathcal{A}$ and the honest party.*
   b. *Internal simulation of ideal messages between $\mathcal{A}$ and the trusted party computing the functionality used as a subprotocol in the hybrid model.*

We attempt to differentiate between these types of interactions in the simulator description.

Theorem 6.7.4. *Assume that* Com *is a perfectly binding commitment scheme and let ℓ be a polynomial. Then, Protocol 6.7.3 securely computes the functionality $f_{ct}^{\ell}(\lambda, \lambda) = (U_{\ell(n)}, U_{\ell(n)})$ in the $\left(f_{zk}^{R_1}, f_{zk}^{R_2}\right)$-hybrid model.*

Proof: As with Protocol 6.7.1, it is clear that Protocol 6.7.3 computes f_{ct}^{ℓ} and two honest parties output a uniformly distributed string of length $\ell(n)$. We therefore proceed to prove that the protocol is secure. We construct a simulator who is given an output string ρ and generates a transcript that results in ρ being the output. The simulator utilizes the calls to $f_{zk}^{R_1}$ and $f_{zk}^{R_2}$ in order to do this. We first consider the case that P_1 is corrupted, and then the case that P_2 is corrupted.

P_1 **corrupted:** Simulator S works as follows:

1. S invokes A, and receives the message c that A sends to P_2, and the message $(c', (\rho_1, r))$ that A sends to $f_{zk}^{R_1}$.

2. If $c' \neq c$ or $c \neq \text{Com}(\rho_1; r)$, then S sends abort_1 to the trusted party computing f_{ct}^{ℓ}, simulates P_2 aborting, and outputs whatever A outputs. Otherwise, it proceeds to the next step.

3. S sends 1^n to the external trusted party computing f_{ct}^{ℓ} and receives back a string $\rho \in \{0, 1\}^{\ell(n)}$.

4. S sets $\rho_2 = \rho \oplus \rho_1$ (where ρ is as received from f_{ct}^{ℓ} and ρ_1 is as received from A as part of its message to $f_{zk}^{R_1}$), and internally hands ρ_2 to A.

5. S receives the message ρ_1' that A sends to P_2, and the message $((c'', \rho_1''), r'')$ that A sends to $f_{zk}^{R_2}$. If $c'' \neq c$ or $\rho_1' \neq \rho_1''$ or $c \neq \text{Com}(\rho_1''; r'')$ then S sends abort_1 to the trusted party computing f_{ct}^{ℓ}, simulates P_2 aborting, and outputs whatever A outputs.

   Otherwise, S externally sends continue to the trusted party, and outputs whatever A outputs.

We show that the simulation in this case is *perfect*; that is, the joint output distribution in the ideal model with S is identically distributed to the joint output distribution in an execution of Protocol 6.7.3 in the f_{zk}-hybrid model with A. In order to show this, we consider three phases of the execution: (1) A, controlling P_1, sends c to P_2 and $(c, (\rho_1, r))$ to $f_{zk}^{R_1}$; (2) P_2 sends ρ_2 to P_1; and (3) A sends ρ_2 to P_2 and $((c, \rho_1), r)$ to $f_{zk}^{R_2}$.

1. *Phase 1:* Since A is deterministic (see Remark 6.6.2) and there is no rewinding, the distribution over the first phase is identical in the real and ideal executions. (If these messages cause P_2 to output $\bot$, then this is the entire distribution and so is identical.)

2. *Phase 2:* Assume that the phase 1 messages do not result in P_2 outputting $\bot$. Then, we claim that for *every* triple (c, ρ_1, r) making up the phase 1 messages, the distribution over ρ_2 received by A is identical in the real and ideal executions. In a real execution, the honest P_2 chooses $\rho_2 \in_R \{0, 1\}^{\ell(n)}$ uniformly and independently of (c, ρ_1, r). In contrast, in an ideal execution, $\rho \in_R \{0, 1\}^{\ell(n)}$ is chosen uniformly and then ρ_2 is set to equal $\rho \oplus \rho_1$ (where ρ_1 is previously *fixed* since it is committed in a perfectly binding commitment). Since ρ is chosen independently of ρ_1, we have that $\rho_1 \oplus \rho$ is also uniformly distributed in $\{0, 1\}^{\ell(n)}$ and independent of (c, ρ_1, r).

3. *Phase 3:* Assume again that the phase 1 messages do not result in P_2 outputting $\bot$. Then, we claim that for *every* (c, ρ_1, r, ρ_2) making up the phase 1 and 2 messages, it holds that the honest P_2 outputs the exact same value in a real execution with A and in an ideal execution with S. In order to see this, observe that this phase consists only of A sending ρ_1' to P_2 and $((c'', \rho_1''), r'')$ to $f_{zk}^{R_2}$. There are two cases:

   a. *Case 1 –* $c'' = c$ and $\rho_1' = \rho_1''$ and $c = \text{Com}(\rho''; r'')$): In this case, in a real execution the trusted party computing $f_{zk}^{R_2}$ will send 1 to P_2 and in an ideal execution S will send continue to the trusted party. This holds because both $\mathcal{A}$ and P_2 send the same public statement (c, ρ_1') to $f_{zk}^{R_2}$ and it holds that $c = \mathsf{Com}(\rho_1'; r'')$. Now, in a real execution, P_2 outputs $\rho_1' \oplus \rho_2$, whereas in an ideal execution P_2 outputs $\rho = \rho_1 \oplus \rho_2$. However, since c is a *perfectly binding* commitment scheme, we have that $\rho_1' = \rho_1$. This implies that in this case the honest P_2 outputs the same $\rho = \rho_1 \oplus \rho_2$ in the real and ideal executions.

b. *Case 2 – $c'' \neq c$ or $\rho_1' \neq \rho_1''$ or $c \neq \mathsf{Com}(\rho''; r'')$):* In this case, in an ideal execution $\mathcal{S}$ will send abort_1 to the trusted party (by its specification), and the honest P_2 will output $\bot$. In a real execution, in this case, the trusted party computing $f_{zk}^{R_2}$ will send 0 to P_2. This is because either $\mathcal{A}$ and P_2 send different statements to the trusted party ((c, ρ_1') versus (c'', ρ_1'')) or the witness is incorrect and $c \neq \mathsf{Com}(\rho''; r'')$. Thus, the honest P_2 in a real protocol execution will also output $\bot$.

We have shown that the distributions in each phase are identical, conditioned on the previous phases. This therefore proves that the overall joint distribution over $\mathcal{A}$'s view and P_2's output is identical in the real and ideal executions. (Although the simulation is perfect, this does not mean that the real protocol is perfectly secure, since this analysis is in the hybrid model only.)

P_2 is corrupted. Simulator $\mathcal{S}$ works as follows:

1. $\mathcal{S}$ sends 1^n to the external trusted party computing f_{ct}^{ℓ} and receives back a string $\rho \in \{0, 1\}^{\ell(n)}$. $\mathcal{S}$ externally sends continue to the trusted party (P_1 always receives output).
2. $\mathcal{S}$ chooses a random $r \in \{0, 1\}^{\mathrm{poly}(n)}$ of sufficient length to commit to $\ell(n)$ bits, and computes $c = \mathsf{Com}(0^{\ell(n)}; r)$.
3. $\mathcal{S}$ internally invokes $\mathcal{A}$ and hands it c.
4. $\mathcal{S}$ receives back some ρ_2 from $\mathcal{A}$ (if $\mathcal{A}$ does not send a valid ρ_2 then $\mathcal{S}$ sets $\rho_2 = 0^{\ell(n)}$ as in the real protocol).
5. $\mathcal{S}$ sets $\rho_1 = \rho_2 \oplus \rho$ and internally hands $\mathcal{A}$ the message ρ_1 as if coming from P_1.
6. $\mathcal{S}$ receives some pair (c', ρ_1') from $\mathcal{A}$ as it sends to $f_{zk}^{R_2}$ (as the "verifier"). If $(c', \rho_1') \neq (c, \rho_1)$ then $\mathcal{S}$ internally simulates $f_{zk}^{R_2}$ sending 0 to $\mathcal{A}$. Otherwise, $\mathcal{S}$ internally simulates $f_{zk}^{R_2}$ sending 1 to $\mathcal{A}$.
7. $\mathcal{S}$ outputs whatever $\mathcal{A}$ outputs.

The *only* difference between a real execution of the protocol (in the f_{zk}-hybrid model) and an ideal execution with the simulator is the commitment c received by $\mathcal{A}$. In a real execution it is a commitment to ρ_1, whereas in the simulation it is a commitment to $0^{\ell(n)}$. It may be tempting to simply say that these distributions are therefore indistinguishable, by the hiding property of the commitment scheme. However, as we have stressed before, a reduction must be given in order to prove this formally. In this specific case, such a reduction is not as straightforward as it may seem. In order to see this, observe that in a reduction, the distinguisher would ask for a commitment to either ρ_1 or to $0^{\ell(n)}$ and then would run the simulator $\mathcal{S}$ with the only difference being that it uses the commitment c received instead of generating itself. Since $\mathcal{S}$ simulates $f_{zk}^{R_1}$ and $f_{zk}^{R_2}$, it need not know the randomness used (or even whether it is a commitment to ρ_1 or to $0^{\ell(n)}$). Thus, it can seemingly carry out the reduction. The problem with this is that S receives ρ externally and sets $\rho_1 = \rho_2 \oplus \rho$. Since ρ_2 is received from $\mathcal{A}$ (controlling P_2) *after* $\mathcal{A}$ receives c, the distinguisher for the commitment scheme only knows the value of ρ_1 *after* it obtains the commitment c in the distinguishing game. Thus, the reduction fails because in the commitment experiment, the pair of values are of course determined ahead of time (it is not possible to commit to either x_1 or x_2 when x_2 is chosen after the commitment is given and may be a function of the commitment value c).

We therefore begin by first showing an alternative way to generate the joint output distribution of S and the honest P_1 in the ideal model. Let S' work in the same way as S except that instead of receiving ρ externally from the trusted party, S' chooses ρ by itself (uniformly at random) after receiving ρ_2 from $\mathcal{A}$. In addition, the output of the honest party is set to be ρ. Stated differently, S' outputs the pair $(\rho, \text{output}(\mathcal{A}))$, where $\text{output}(\mathcal{A})$ is the output of $\mathcal{A}$ after the simulation. It is immediate that the output of S' is *identically distributed* to an ideal execution. That is

$$\left\{ S'(1^n) \right\}_{n \in \mathbb{N}} \equiv \left\{ \text{IDEAL}_{f_{ct}^\ell, S}(1^n, 1^n, n) \right\}_{n \in \mathbb{N}}. \tag{6.12}$$

This is due to the fact that the only difference is the point at which ρ is chosen. However, since it is chosen independently in both cases, the output distribution is the same. (Note that S' is not a valid simulator since the trusted party does not choose the output ρ. Nevertheless, we present S' as a way of proving the indistinguishability of two distributions, and not as a valid simulator.)

We now wish to show that the output of S' is computationally indistinguishable from the real output $\text{REAL}_{\pi, \mathcal{A}}(1^n, 1^n, n)$. Since we have already shown that its output is identical to the ideal output distribution, this completes the proof. In order to prove this, we construct an adversary D for the commitment scheme. We use a definition that a commitment to $0^{\ell(n)}$ is computationally indistinguishable from a commitment to a random string R of length $\ell(n)$, even given the random string R. (This follows easily from the standard definition of hiding for commitments, and in particular, from the LR-oracle formulation in Section 6.5.2.)

The adversary D is given a commitment c and (random) string R and runs the code of S' with the following differences: First, instead of computing $c = \text{Com}(0^{\ell(n)}; r)$ by itself, it uses c that it received as input. In addition, instead of choosing ρ uniformly and setting $\rho_1 = \rho \oplus \rho_2$, distinguisher D sets $\rho_1 = R$ and $\rho = \rho_1 \oplus \rho_2$. Apart from that, D follows the instructions of S'. We have:

- If D receives the commitment $c = \text{Com}(0^{\ell(n)})$, then its output is identical to the output of S'. In order to see this, observe that the only difference is that D sets $\rho = \rho_2 \oplus \rho_1$ where $\rho_1 = R$ is uniformly distributed (ρ_1 does not appear elsewhere in the execution since c is a commitment to 0). Since ρ_1 is random and independent of everything else, ρ is uniformly distributed, exactly as in an execution of S'. The commitment c is also exactly as generated by S'. Thus, the output distribution is identical.
- If D receives the commitment $c = \text{Com}(\rho_1)$, then its output is identical to the joint output distribution from a real execution. This holds because the commit-

ment from P_1 is a commitment to a random ρ_1, and the same ρ_1 is sent to $\mathcal{A}$ in the last message of the protocol. In addition, the output of the honest party is $\rho_1 \oplus \rho_2$ exactly like in a real execution. Thus, this is just a real execution between an honest P_1 and the adversary $\mathcal{A}$.

It follows from the hiding property of the commitment scheme that the output distributions generated by D are computationally indistinguishable. Therefore, the output of $\mathcal{S}'$—which is identical to the output in a real execution—is computationally indistinguishable from the joint output of a real execution. That is,

$$\left\{ \mathcal{S}'(1^n) \right\}_{n \in \mathbb{N}} \overset{c}{\equiv} \left\{ \text{REAL}_{\pi, \mathcal{A}}(1^n, 1^n, n) \right\}_{n \in \mathbb{N}}. \tag{6.13}$$

The proof is completed by combining Equations (6.12) and (6.13). ∎

Discussion – the power of proving in the hybrid model. We remark that the proof for Protocol 6.7.3 is considerably more simple than the proof for Protocol 6.7.1. This may seem somewhat surprising since the protocol is far more complex. However, it is actually not at all surprising since the proof of security is carried out in the f_{zk}-hybrid model. This is a very powerful tool, and it makes proving security much easier. For one thing, in this specific case, no rewinding is necessary. Thus, it is not necessary to justify that the simulation is polynomial time, and it is also not necessary to justify that the output distribution is not skewed by the rewinding procedure.

6.8 Extracting Inputs – Oblivious Transfer

In the coin-tossing functionality, the parties have no input. Thus, the simulator's challenge is to receive the output from the trusted party and to generate a view of a real execution for the adversary that corresponds to the received output. However, in general, functionalities *do* have input, and in this case the output from the trusted party is only defined after the parties provide input. Thus, the simulator must *extract* the input from the adversary, send it to the trusted party, and receive back the output. The view generated by the simulator must then correspond to this input and output. As we will see below, this introduces additional challenges.

In this section, we will study the oblivious transfer functionality defined by $f_{\text{ot}}((x_0, x_1), \sigma) = (\lambda, x_\sigma)$ where x_0, x_1 are from a fixed domain and σ is a bit [16, 36]. We present a version of the oblivious transfer protocol of [35] (the original protocol of [35] is in the common reference string model and will be presented in Section 6.9).

Preliminaries – the RAND procedure. Before presenting the protocol, we will describe and prove an important property of a probabilistic procedure, called *RAND*, that is used in the protocol. Let $\mathbb{G}$ be a multiplicative group of prime order q. Define the probabilistic procedure

$$RAND(g, x, y, z) = (u, v) = \left(g^s \cdot y^t, \ x^s \cdot z^t \right),$$

where $s, t \in_R \mathbb{Z}_q$ are uniformly random.

Claim 6.8.1. *Let g be a generator of* $\mathbb{G}$ *and let* $x, y, z \in \mathbb{G}$. *If* (g, x, y, z) *do not form a Diffie–Hellman tuple (i.e., there does not exist* $a \in \mathbb{Z}_q$ *such that* $y = g^a$ *and* $z = x^a$), *then* $RAND(g, x, y, z)$ *is uniformly distributed in* $\mathbb{G}^2$.

Proof: We prove that for every $(a, b) \in \mathbb{G} \times \mathbb{G}$,

$$\Pr[u = a \wedge v = b] = \frac{1}{|\mathbb{G}|^2}, \tag{6.14}$$

where $(u, v) = RAND(g, x, y, z)$ and the probability is taken over the random choices of $s, t \in \mathbb{Z}_q$ (this implies that (u, v) is uniformly distributed). Let $\alpha, \beta, \gamma \in \mathbb{Z}_q$ be values such that $x = g^\alpha$, $y = g^\beta$, and $z = g^\gamma$ and $\gamma \neq \alpha \cdot \beta \bmod q$. (Note that if $\gamma = \alpha \cdot \beta \bmod q$ then this implies that $z = g^\gamma = (g^\alpha)^\beta = x^\beta$ and so $y = g^\beta$ and $z = x^\beta$, in contradiction to the assumption in the claim.) Then,

$$u = g^s \cdot y^t = g^s \cdot (g^\beta)^t = g^{s+\beta \cdot t} \quad \text{and} \quad v = x^s \cdot z^t = (g^\alpha)^s \cdot (g^\gamma)^t = g^{\alpha \cdot s + \gamma \cdot t}.$$

Now, let $\delta, \epsilon \in \mathbb{Z}_q$ such that $a = g^\delta$ and $b = g^\epsilon$. Then, since s, t are uniformly distributed in $\mathbb{Z}_q$, it follows that Eq. (6.14) holds if and only if there is a single solution to the equations

$$s + \beta \cdot t = \delta \quad \text{and} \quad \alpha \cdot s + \gamma \cdot t = \epsilon.$$

(Observe that g, x, y, z and a, b are fixed. Thus, $\alpha, \beta, \gamma, \delta, \epsilon$ are fixed and s, t are uniformly chosen.) Now, there exists a single solution to these equations if and only if the matrix

$$\begin{pmatrix} 1 & \beta \\ \alpha & \gamma \end{pmatrix}$$

is invertible, which is the case here because its determinant is $\alpha \cdot \beta - \gamma$ and by the assumption $\alpha \cdot \beta \neq \gamma \bmod q$ and so $\alpha \cdot \beta - \gamma \neq 0 \bmod q$. This completes the proof. ∎

The protocol idea. We are now ready to present the protocol. The idea behind the protocol is as follows: The receiving party P_2 generates a tuple (g_0, g_1, h_0, h_1) that is not a Diffie–Hellman tuple and sends it to P_1 (along with a proof that it is indeed not a Diffie–Hellman tuple).[10] Next, P_2 computes $g = (g_\sigma)^r$ and $h = (h_\sigma)^r$ and sends the pair to P_1. Then, P_1 computes $(u_0, v_0) = RAND(g_0, g, h_0, h)$ and $(u_1, v_1) = RAND(g_1, g, h_1, h)$. Finally, P_1 uses v_0 to mask the input x_0 and uses v_1 to mask x_1. We will prove that if (g_0, g_1, h_0, h_1) is not a Diffie–Hellman tuple, then for every g, h it holds that at least one of $(g_0, g, h_0, h), (g_1, g, h_1, h)$ is not a Diffie–Hellman tuple. Thus, at least one of the values v_0, v_1 is *uniformly distributed* as proven in Claim 6.8.1, and so a corrupted P_2 can only learn at most one of x_0, x_1.

---

[10] The protocol is actually a bit different in that P_2 generates a tuple (g_0, g_1, h_0, h_1) so that $(g_0, g_1, h_0, \frac{h_1}{g_1})$ *is* a Diffie–Hellman tuple. Of course, this implies that (g_0, g_1, h_0, h_1) is *not* a Diffie–Hellman tuple. This method is used since it enables P_2 to prove that (g_0, g_1, h_0, h_1) is not a Diffie–Hellman tuple very efficiently by proving that $(g_0, g_1, h_0, \frac{h_1}{g_1})$ *is* a Diffie–Hellman tuple.

Regarding the case that P_1 is corrupted, we must argue that it cannot learn P_2's input bit σ. However, P_1 only sees $(g_\sigma)^r$, $(h_\sigma)^r$ and this hides σ by the Decisional Diffie–Hellman assumption. We *stress* that the above "explanation" regarding security explains why P_1 cannot learn P_2's input and why P_2 can learn at most one of x_0, x_1. However, it does *not* show how to simulate, and this requires additional ideas, as we will show. The full description appears in Protocol 6.8.2.

PROTOCOL 6.8.2 (Oblivious transfer)

- **Inputs:** Party P_1's input is a pair (x_0, x_1), and party P_2's input is a bit σ. We assume for simplicity that $x_0, x_1 \in \mathbb{G}$ where $\mathbb{G}$ is defined in the auxiliary input.
- **Auxiliary input:** Both parties hold a security parameter 1^n and $(\mathbb{G}, q, g_0)$, where $\mathbb{G}$ is an efficient representation of a group of prime order q with a generator g_0, and q is of length n. (It is possible to generate this group in the protocol, if needed.)
- **Hybrid functionality:** Let $L = \{(\mathbb{G}, q, g_0, x, y, z) \mid \exists a \in \mathbb{Z}_q : y = (g_0)^a \wedge z = x^a\}$ be the language of all Diffie–Hellman tuples (where $(\mathbb{G}, q, g_0)$ are as above), and let R_L be its associated $\mathcal{NP}$-relation. The parties have access to a trusted party that computes the zero-knowledge proof of knowledge functionality $f_{zk}^{R_L}$ associated with relation R_L.
- **The protocol:**
    1. Party P_2 chooses random values $y, \alpha \in_R \mathbb{Z}_q$ and computes $g_1 = (g_0)^y$, $h_0 = (g_0)^\alpha$, and $h_1 = (g_1)^{\alpha+1}$ and sends (g_1, h_0, h_1) to party P_1.
    2. P_2 sends statement $\left(\mathbb{G}, q, g_0, g_1, h_0, \frac{h_1}{g_1}\right)$ and witness α to $f_{zk}^{R_L}$.
    3. P_1 sends statement $\left(\mathbb{G}, q, g_0, g_1, h_0, \frac{h_1}{g_1}\right)$ to $f_{zk}^{R_L}$ and receives back a bit. If the bit equals 0, then it halts and outputs $\perp$. Otherwise, it proceeds to the next step.
    4. P_2 chooses a random value $r \in_R \mathbb{Z}_q$, computes $g = (g_\sigma)^r$ and $h = (h_\sigma)^r$, and sends (g, h) to P_1.
    5. P_1 computes $(u_0, v_0) = RAND(g_0, g, h_0, h)$ and $(u_1, v_1) = RAND(g_1, g, h_1, h)$. P_1 sends P_2 the values (u_0, w_0) where $w_0 = v_0 \cdot x_0$, and (u_1, w_1) where $w_1 = v_1 \cdot x_1$.
    6. P_2 computes $x_\sigma = w_\sigma/(u_\sigma)^r$.
    7. P_1 outputs λ, and P_2 outputs x_σ.

Theorem 6.8.3. *Assume that the Decisional Diffie–Hellman problem is hard in the auxiliary input group $\mathbb{G}$. Then, Protocol 6.8.2 securely computes f_{ot} in the presence of malicious adversaries.*

Proof: We begin by showing that Protocol 6.8.2 computes f_{ot} (meaning that two honest parties running the protocol compute the correct output). This holds since when both parties are honest, we have:

$$\frac{w_\sigma}{(u_\sigma)^r} = \frac{v_\sigma \cdot x_\sigma}{(u_\sigma)^r} = \frac{g^s \cdot h^t \cdot x_\sigma}{((g_\sigma)^s \cdot (h_\sigma)^t)^r} = \frac{((g_\sigma)^r)^s \cdot ((h_\sigma)^r)^t \cdot x_\sigma}{((g_\sigma)^s \cdot (h_\sigma)^t)^r} = \frac{(g_\sigma)^{r \cdot s} \cdot (h_\sigma)^{r \cdot t} \cdot x_\sigma}{(g_\sigma)^{r \cdot s} \cdot (h_\sigma)^{r \cdot t}} = x_\sigma.$$

We now proceed to prove security, and separately consider the case that P_1 is corrupted and the case that P_2 is corrupted.

P_1 **is corrupted.** Recall that in general the simulator S needs to extract the corrupted party's input in order to send it to the trusted party, and needs to simulate its view so that its output corresponds to the output received back from the trusted party. However, in this case, P_1 receives no output, and so S's task is somewhat simpler; it needs to extract $\mathcal{A}$'s input while generating a view of an interaction with an honest P_2. Since a corrupted P_1 is not supposed to learn anything about P_2's input, it seems that the following strategy should work:

1. Internally invoke $\mathcal{A}$ and run a complete execution between $\mathcal{A}$ and an honest P_2 with input $\sigma = 0$. Let x_0 be the output that P_2 receives as output from the protocol execution.
2. Rewind and internally invoke $\mathcal{A}$ from scratch and run a complete execution between $\mathcal{A}$ and an honest P_2 with input $\sigma = 1$. Let x_1 be the output that P_2 receives as output from the protocol execution.
3. Send (x_0, x_1) to the external trusted party computing f_{ot}.
4. Output whatever $\mathcal{A}$ outputs on either one of the two executions above.

Intuitively, this works since S obtains the output that P_2 would have obtained upon either input. In addition, the view of P_2 does not reveal its input bit (as we have described above), and thus either view can be taken. Unfortunately, this intuition is completely wrong. In order to see why, consider an adversary $\mathcal{A}$ who chooses x_0, x_1 randomly by applying a pseudorandom function to its view until the last step of the protocol (but otherwise works honestly). Furthermore, assume that $\mathcal{A}$ outputs the inputs it chose. Now, S does not know if the honest P_2 in the ideal model has input $\sigma = 0$ or $\sigma = 1$. If the honest P_2 has input $\sigma = 0$ and S outputs what $\mathcal{A}$ outputs on the second execution above, then the output that P_2 has in the ideal model will not match either x_0 or x_1 output by $\mathcal{A}$ (except with negligible probability). The same will occur if P_2 has input $\sigma = 1$ and S outputs what $\mathcal{A}$ outputs on the first execution above. In contrast, in a real execution, P_2 always outputs one of x_0 or x_1 output by $\mathcal{A}$ (depending on its value σ). Thus this strategy completely fails and it is easy to distinguish between a real and ideal execution.

We therefore use a completely different strategy for extracting $\mathcal{A}$'s input that does not involve rewinding. The idea behind the strategy is as follows: As we have mentioned above, if (g_0, g_1, h_0, h_1) is not a Diffie–Hellman tuple, then one of x_0, x_1 is hidden information-theoretically. However, if (g_0, g_1, h_0, h_1) *is* a Diffie–Hellman tuple, then it is actually possible to efficiently recover *both* x_0 and x_1 from P_1's message. Therefore, S will provide (g_0, g_1, h_0, h_1) that is a Diffie–Hellman tuple and will simply "cheat" by simulating $f_{zk}^{R_L}$'s response to be 1 even though the statement is false. By the Decisional Diffie–Hellman assumption, this will be indistinguishable, but will enable S to extract both inputs. S works as follows:

1. S internally invokes $\mathcal{A}$ controlling P_1 (we assume that $\mathcal{A}$ is deterministic; see Remark 6.6.2).
2. S chooses $y, \alpha \in_R \mathbb{Z}_q$ and computes $g_1 = (g_0)^y$, $h_0 = (g_0)^\alpha$, and $h_1 = (g_1)^\alpha$. (Note that $h_1 = (g_1)^\alpha$ and not $(g_1)^{\alpha+1}$ as an honest P_2 would compute it.)
3. S internally hands (g_1, h_0, h_1) to $\mathcal{A}$.

4. When $\mathcal{A}$ sends a message intended for $f_{zk}^{R_L}$: If the message is $\left(\mathbb{G}, q, g_0, g_1, h_0, \frac{h_1}{g_1}\right)$ then $\mathcal{S}$ internally hands $\mathcal{A}$ the bit 1 as if it came from $f_{zk}^{R_L}$. If the message equals anything else, then $\mathcal{S}$ simulates $\mathcal{A}$ receiving 0 from $f_{zk}^{R_L}$.

5. $\mathcal{S}$ chooses a random value $r \in_R \mathbb{Z}_q$, computes $g = (g_0)^r$ and $h = (h_0)^r$, and internally sends (g, h) to $\mathcal{A}$. (This is exactly like an honest P_2 with input $\sigma = 0$.)

6. When $\mathcal{A}$ sends messages $(u_0, w_0), (u_1, w_1)$ then simulator $\mathcal{S}$ computes $x_0 = w_0/(u_0)^r$ and $x_1 = w_1/(u_1)^{r \cdot y^{-1} \bmod q}$. (If the message is not formed correctly, then $\mathcal{S}$ sends abort$_1$ to the trusted party and outputs whatever $\mathcal{A}$ outputs. Otherwise, it proceeds.)

7. $\mathcal{S}$ sends (x_0, x_1) to the trusted party computing f_{ot}. (Formally, $\mathcal{S}$ receives back output λ and then sends continue to the trusted party. This is not really necessary since only P_2 receives output. Nevertheless, formally, $\mathcal{S}$ must send continue in order for P_2 to receive output.)

8. $\mathcal{S}$ outputs whatever $\mathcal{A}$ outputs, and halts.

In order to show that the simulation achieves indistinguishability, we first change the protocol. Denote Protocol 6.8.2 by π, and denote by π' a protocol that is the same as π except for the two following differences:

1. P_2 chooses $y, \alpha \in_R \mathbb{Z}_q$ and computes $g_1 = (g_0)^y$, $h_0 = (g_0)^\alpha$, and $h_1 = (g_1)^\alpha$, instead of computing $h_1 = (g_1)^{\alpha+1}$.

2. $f_{zk}^{R_L}$ is modified so that it sends 1 to P_1 if and only if P_1 and P_2 sends the same statement (and irrespective of the witness sent by P_2).

We claim that for every probabilistic polynomial-time nonuniform adversary $\mathcal{A}$ controlling P_1,

$$\left\{\text{REAL}_{\pi,\mathcal{A}(z)}((x_0, x_1), \sigma, n)\right\}_{x_0,x_1,\sigma,z,n} \overset{c}{\equiv} \left\{\text{REAL}_{\pi',\mathcal{A}(z)}((x_0, x_1), \sigma, n)\right\}_{x_0,x_1,\sigma,z,n} . \quad (6.15)$$

We stress that we *only* claim that the output distributions of π and π' are indistinguishable when P_1 is corrupted. We make no claim when P_2 is corrupted, and indeed it is not true in that case. This suffices since we are currently proving the case that P_1 is corrupted. There is one difference between π and π' and this is how g_1, h_0, h_1 are chosen. (The change to $f_{zk}^{R_L}$ is just to ensure that the output is always 1 unless $\mathcal{A}$ sends a different statement. Since P_2 is honest, this makes no difference.) However, in order to prove Eq. (6.15), we have to show both that the *joint distribution over* $\mathcal{A}$'s view and P_2's output is indistinguishable in π and π'. Note that the joint distribution including P_2's output must be considered since P_2 computes its output as a function of (u_σ, w_σ), which is computed using (g_1, h_0, h_1) that is generated differently in π'.

We prove this via a straightforward reduction to the DDH assumption in $\mathbb{G}$. We use a variant that states that for every probabilistic polynomial-time nonuniform distinguisher D there exists a negligible function μ such that

$$\left|\Pr[D(\mathbb{G}, q, g_0, g_1, (g_0)^r, (g_1)^r) = 1] - \Pr[D(\mathbb{G}, q, g_0, g_1, (g_0)^r, (g_1)^{r+1}) = 1]\right| \leq \mu(n) \quad (6.16)$$

where $\mathbb{G}$ is a group of prime order q with generator g_0, $g_1 \in \mathbb{G}$ is a random group element, and $r \in \mathbb{Z}_q$ is randomly chosen. This assumption can be proven to be true if the standard DDH assumption holds. In order to see this, observe that by the standard DDH assumption,

$$|\Pr[D(\mathbb{G}, q, g_0, g_1, (g_0)^r, (g_1)^r) = 1] - \Pr[D(\mathbb{G}, q, g_0, g_1, (g_0)^r, (g_1)^s) = 1]| \le \mu(n),$$
(6.17)

where $g_1 \in \mathbb{G}$ and $r, s \in \mathbb{Z}_q$ are randomly chosen. In addition, the distribution over $(g_0, g_1, (g_0)^r, (g_1)^s)$ is *identical* to the distribution over $(g_0, g_1, (g_0)^r, (g_1)^{s+1})$. Thus, a straightforward reduction to the standard DDH assumption gives that

$$\left|\Pr[D(\mathbb{G}, q, g_0, g_1, (g_0)^r, (g_1)^s) = 1] - \Pr[D(\mathbb{G}, q, g_0, g_1, (g_0)^r, (g_1)^{r+1}) = 1]\right| \le \mu(n).$$
(6.18)

In order to see this, a distinguisher D' receiving (g_0, g_1, h_0, h_1) can run D on $(g_0, g_1, h_0, h_1 \cdot g_1)$. If D' received $(g_0, g_1, (g_0)^r, (g_1)^r)$ then it generates a tuple of the form $(g_0, g_1, (g_0)^r, (g_1)^{r+1})$, and if D' received $(g_0, g_1, (g_0)^r, (g_1)^s)$ then it generates a tuple of the form $(g_0, g_1, (g_0)^r, (g_1)^{s+1})$, which as we have mentioned is identical to $(g_0, g_1, (g_0)^r, (g_1)^s)$. Thus, if D can distinguish with nonnegligible probability in Eq. (6.18), then D' can use D to solve the standard DDH problem. Combining Equations (6.17) and (6.18), we obtain that Eq. (6.16) holds.

We now proceed to prove Eq. (6.15) based on the above DDH variant. Assume, by contradiction, that there exists an adversary $\mathcal{A}$ controlling P_1, a distinguisher D_π, a polynomial $p(\cdot)$, and an infinite series of tuples $(\mathbb{G}, q, g, x_0, x_1, \sigma, z, n)$ with $|q| = n$ such that

$$\left|\Pr\left[D_\pi(\text{REAL}_{\pi, \mathcal{A}(z)}((x_0, x_1), \sigma, n)) = 1\right] - \Pr\left[D_\pi(\text{REAL}_{\pi', \mathcal{A}(z)}((x_0, x_1), \sigma, n)) = 1\right]\right| \ge \frac{1}{p(n)}.$$

We construct a nonuniform probabilistic polynomial-time distinguisher D who receives input $(\mathbb{G}, q, g_0, g_1, h_0, h_1)$, and a tuple (x_0, x_1, σ, z, n) on its advice tape (where n equals the security parameter used for the DDH instance generation), and works as follows:

1. D invokes $\mathcal{A}$ and an honest P_2 with security parameter 1^n, respective inputs x_0, x_1, and σ, and auxiliary input z for $\mathcal{A}$.
2. D runs the execution between $\mathcal{A}$ and P_2 following the instructions of π' with one change. Instead of P_2 choosing $y, \alpha \in \mathbb{Z}_q$ and generating g_1, h_0, h_1, distinguisher D takes these values from its input. Everything else is the same; observe that P_2 does not use y, α anywhere else inside π' and thus D can carry out the simulation of π' in this way.
3. D invokes D_π on the joint output of $\mathcal{A}$ and the honest P_2 from this execution, and outputs whatever D_π outputs.

Since the only difference between π and π' is how the values g_1, h_0, h_1 are chosen, we have that

$$\Pr[D(\mathbb{G}, q, g_0, g_1, (g_0)^r, (g_1)^r) = 1] = \Pr\left[D_\pi(\text{REAL}_{\pi', \mathcal{A}(z)}((x_0, x_1), \sigma, n)) = 1\right]$$

and

$$\Pr[D(\mathbb{G}, q, g_0, g_1, (g_0)^r, (g_1)^{r+1}) = 1] = \Pr\left[D_\pi(\text{REAL}_{\pi, \mathcal{A}(z)}((x_0, x_1), \sigma, n)) = 1\right].$$

Thus,

$$\left| \Pr[D(\mathbb{G}, q, g_0, g_1, (g_0)^r, (g_1)^r) = 1] - \Pr[D(\mathbb{G}, q, g_0, g_1, (g_0)^r, (g_1)^{r+1}) = 1] \right| \geq \frac{1}{p(n)},$$

in contradiction to the assumption that the DDH problem is hard in $\mathbb{G}$. Thus, Eq. (6.15) holds.

Next, we prove that for every $\mathcal{A}$ controlling P_1,

$$\left\{ \text{REAL}_{\pi', \mathcal{A}}((x_0, x_1), \sigma, n) \right\}_{x_0, x_1, \sigma \in \{0,1\}^*; n \in \mathbb{N}} \equiv \left\{ \text{IDEAL}_{f_{\text{ot}}, \mathcal{S}}((x_0, x_1), \sigma, n) \right\}_{x_0, x_1, \sigma \in \{0,1\}^*; n \in \mathbb{N}} \tag{6.19}$$

(i.e., the distributions are *identical*). There are two differences between the description of π' and an ideal execution with $\mathcal{S}$:

1. In an ideal execution, the pair (g, h) in the view of $\mathcal{A}$ is generated by computing $(g_0)^r$ and $(h_0)^r$. In contrast, in π', these values are generated by P_2 computing $(g_\sigma)^r$ and $(h_\sigma)^r$.
2. In an ideal execution, the honest P_2's outputs are determined by the trusted party, based on (x_0, x_1) sent by $\mathcal{S}$ and its input σ (unknown to $\mathcal{S}$). In contrast, in π', the honest P_2's output is determined by the protocol instructions.

Regarding the first difference, we claim that the view of $\mathcal{A}$ in both cases is *identical*. When $\sigma = 0$ then this is immediate. However, when $\sigma = 1$ it also holds. This is because $g_1 = (g_0)^y$ and $h_1 = (h_0)^y$ (where the latter is because $h_1 = (g_1)^\alpha = ((g_0)^y)^\alpha = ((g_0)^\alpha)^y = (h_0)^y$). Thus, $(g_0)^r = (g_1)^{r \cdot y^{-1} \bmod q}$ and $(h_0)^r = (h_1)^{r \cdot y^{-1} \bmod q}$. Since r is uniformly distributed in $\mathbb{Z}_q$, the values r and $r \cdot y^{-1} \bmod q$ are both uniformly distributed. Therefore, $((g_\sigma)^r, (h_\sigma)^r)$ as generated in π' is identically distributed to $((g_0)^r, (h_0)^r)$ as generated by $\mathcal{S}$ in an ideal execution.

Regarding the second difference, it suffices to show that the values (x_0, x_1) sent by $\mathcal{S}$ to the trusted party computing f_{ot} are the exact outputs that P_2 receives in π' on that transcript. There are two cases:

- *Case 1 – P_2 in π' has input $\sigma = 0$:* In this case, in both π' and the ideal execution with $\mathcal{S}$, we have that $g = (g_0)^r$ and $h = (h_0)^r$. Furthermore, in π', party P_2 outputs $x_0 = w_0/(u_0)^r$. Likewise, in an ideal execution with $\mathcal{S}$, the value x_0 is defined by $\mathcal{S}$ to be $w_0/(u_0)^r$. Thus, the value is identical.
- *Case 2 – P_2 in π' has input $\sigma = 1$:* In this case, in π', the pair (g, h) is generated by computing $g = (g_1)^r$ and $h = (h_1)^r$ for a random r, and P_2's output is obtained by computing $x_1 = w_1/(u_1)^r$. In contrast, in an ideal execution with $\mathcal{S}$, the pair (g, h) is generated by computing $g = (g_0)^r$ and $h = (h_0)^r$ for a random r, and P_2's output is defined by $\mathcal{S}$ to be $w_1/(u_1)^{r \cdot y^{-1} \bmod q}$.
  Fix the messages (g_1, h_0, h_1) and (g, h) sent by P_2 to $\mathcal{A}$ in either π' or in an ideal execution with $\mathcal{S}$. In both cases, there exists a unique y such that $g_1 = (g_0)^y$ and $h_1 = (h_0)^y$ (from P_2's instructions in π' and from $\mathcal{S}$'s specification). Let k be the unique value such that $g = (g_1)^k$ and $h = (h_1)^k$. In an execution of π' the value k is set to equal r as chosen by P_2. In contrast, in an ideal execution with $\mathcal{S}$, the value k is set to equal $r \cdot y^{-1} \bmod q$ where r is the value chosen by $\mathcal{S}$.

(The fact that this is the correct value of k is justified above.) Now, in *both* a real execution of π' and an ideal execution with $\mathcal{S}$, party P_2's output is determined by $w_1/(u_1)^k$. Thus, the output is the same in both cases.

This completes the proof of Eq. (6.19). The computational indistinguishability for the simulation in the case that P_1 is corrupted is obtained by combining Equations (6.15) and (6.19).

Before proceeding to prove the case where P_2 is corrupted, we remark that our proof of indistinguishability of the ideal and real executions does not work in a single step. This is due to the fact that $\mathcal{S}$ needs to have y where $g_1 = (g_0)^y$ in order to extract x_1. However, in the DDH reduction, y is not given to the distinguisher (indeed, the DDH problem is easy if y is given). Thus, the proof is carried out in two separate steps.

P_2 is corrupted. We now proceed to the case where P_2 is corrupted. First, $\mathcal{S}$ needs to extract P_2's input bit σ in order to send it to the trusted party and receive back x_σ. As we will show, this is made possible by the fact that in the $f_{\mathsf{zk}}^{R_L}$-hybrid model $\mathcal{S}$ receives the witness α from $\mathcal{A}$ (recall that in this model, $\mathcal{A}$ controlling P_2 must send the valid witness directly to $f_{\mathsf{zk}}^{R_L}$ or P_1 will abort). $\mathcal{S}$ will use α to determine whether $\mathcal{A}$ "used" input $\sigma = 0$ or $\sigma = 1$. Next, $\mathcal{S}$ needs to generate a view for $\mathcal{A}$ that is indistinguishable from a real view. The problem is that $\mathcal{S}$ is given x_σ but *not* $x_{1-\sigma}$. However, Claim 6.8.1 guarantees that $RAND$ completely hides $x_{1-\sigma}$ (since, as we will show, the tuple input to $RAND$ in this case is not a Diffie–Hellman tuple). Thus, $\mathcal{S}$ can use any fixed value in place of $x_{1-\sigma}$ and the result is identically distributed. Indeed, in this case we will show that the simulation is *perfect*. We now describe the simulator $\mathcal{S}$:

1. $\mathcal{S}$ internally invokes $\mathcal{A}$ controlling P_2.
2. $\mathcal{S}$ internally obtains (g_1, h_0, h_1) from $\mathcal{A}$, as it intends to send to P_1.
3. $\mathcal{S}$ internally obtains an input tuple and α from $\mathcal{A}$, as it intends to send to $f_{\mathsf{zk}}^{R_L}$.
4. $\mathcal{S}$ checks that the input tuple equals $(\mathbb{G}, q, g_0, g_1, h_0, \frac{h_1}{g_1})$, that $h_0 = (g_0)^\alpha$ and $\frac{h_1}{g_1} = (g_1)^\alpha$. If not, $\mathcal{S}$ externally sends abort_2 to the trusted party computing f_{ot}, outputs whatever $\mathcal{A}$ outputs, and halts. Else, it proceeds.
5. $\mathcal{S}$ internally obtains a pair (g, h) from P_2. If $h = g^\alpha$ then $\mathcal{S}$ sets $\sigma = 0$. Otherwise, it sets $\sigma = 1$.
6. $\mathcal{S}$ externally sends σ to the trusted party computing f_{ot} and receives back x_σ. ($\mathcal{S}$ sends continue to the trusted party; this is not really needed since P_1 has only an empty output. Nevertheless, formally it needs to be sent.)
7. $\mathcal{S}$ computes $(u_\sigma, v_\sigma) = RAND(g_\sigma, g, h_\sigma, h)$ and $w_\sigma = v_\sigma \cdot x_\sigma$. In addition, $\mathcal{S}$ sets $(u_{1-\sigma}, w_{1-\sigma})$ to be independently uniformly distributed in $\mathbb{G}^2$.
8. $\mathcal{S}$ internally hands $(u_0, w_0), (u_1, w_1)$ to $\mathcal{A}$.
9. $\mathcal{S}$ outputs whatever $\mathcal{A}$ outputs and halts.

We construct an alternative simulator $\mathcal{S}'$ in an alternative ideal model with a trusted party who sends *both* of P_1's inputs x_0, x_1 to $\mathcal{S}'$ upon receiving σ. Simulator $\mathcal{S}'$ works in exactly the same way as $\mathcal{S}$ with the exception that it computes $(u_{1-\sigma}, w_{1-\sigma})$

by first computing $(u_{1-\sigma}, v_{1-\sigma}) = RAND(g_{1-\sigma}, g, h_{1-\sigma}, h)$ and $w_{1-\sigma} = v_{1-\sigma} \cdot x_{1-\sigma}$, instead of choosing them uniformly.

First, we claim that the output distribution of the adversary $\mathcal{S}'$ in the alternative ideal model is *identical* to the output of the adversary $\mathcal{A}$ in a real execution with an honest P_1 (it is not necessary to consider P_1's output since it has none in f_{ot}). This follows because $\mathcal{S}'$ generates (u_0, w_0) and (u_1, w_1) exactly like an honest P_1, using the correct inputs (x_0, x_1). In addition, $\mathcal{S}'$ verifies the validity of (g_1, h_0, h_1) using witness α, exactly like $f_{\text{zk}}^{R_L}$. Thus, the result is just a real execution of the protocol. (Observe that the determination of σ by $\mathcal{S}'$ is actually meaningless since it is not used in the generation of (u_0, w_0) and (u_1, w_1).)

We now claim that the output distribution of the adversary $\mathcal{S}'$ in the alternative ideal model is *identical* to the output of the adversary $\mathcal{S}$ in an ideal execution with f_{ot}. Since the only difference is in how $(u_{1-\sigma}, w_{1-\sigma})$ are computed, we need to show that the values $u_{1-\sigma}, w_{1-\sigma}$ generated by $\mathcal{S}'$ are independent uniformly distributed values in $\mathbb{G}$. We stress that the value σ here is the one determined by $\mathcal{S}$ in the simulation in step 5.

First, consider the case that $\sigma = 0$. By step 5, this implies that $h = g^\alpha$. We first claim that in this case (g_1, g, h_1, h) is *not* a Diffie–Hellman tuple. This follows from the fact that by Step 4 we have that $\frac{h_1}{g_1} = (g_1)^\alpha$ and so $h_1 = g_1^{\alpha+1}$. This implies that $(g_1, g, h_1, h) = (g_1, g, (g_1)^{\alpha+1}, g^\alpha)$, which is *not* a Diffie–Hellman tuple. Now, by Claim 6.8.1, since (g_1, g, h_1, h) is not a Diffie–Hellman tuple, it follows that $(u_1, v_1) = RAND(g_1, g, h_1, h)$ is uniformly distributed in $\mathbb{G}^2$, so $(u_1, w_1) = (u_1, v_1 \cdot x_1)$ is uniformly distributed. Thus, (u_1, w_1) are identically distributed in the executions with $\mathcal{S}$ and $\mathcal{S}'$.

Next, consider the case that $\sigma = 1$. By step 5, this implies that $h \neq g^\alpha$; let $\alpha' \neq \alpha \bmod q$ such that $h = g^{\alpha'}$. As above, we first show that (g_0, g, h_0, h) is *not* a Diffie–Hellman tuple. By step 4 we have that $h_0 = (g_0)^\alpha$ and so $(g_0, g, h_0, h) = (g_0, g, (g_0)^\alpha, g^{\alpha'})$ where $\alpha \neq \alpha' \bmod q$. Thus, it is not a Diffie–Hellman tuple. As in the previous claim, using Claim 6.8.1 we have that in this case (u_0, w_0) as generated by $\mathcal{S}'$ is uniformly distributed and so has the same distribution as (u_0, w_0) generated by $\mathcal{S}$. This completes the proof. ∎

Correctness in the case of two honest parties. Recall that Definition 6.6.1 includes a separate requirement that π computes f, meaning that two honest parties obtain correct output, and indeed our proof of Protocol 6.8.2 begins by showing that π computes f. In order to see that this separate requirement is necessary, consider the oblivious transfer functionality $f((x_0, x_1), \sigma) = (\lambda, x_\sigma)$ and consider the following protocol π:

1. P_1 sends x_0 to P_2.
2. P_2 outputs x_0.

We will now show that without the requirement that π computes f, this protocol is secure. Let $\mathcal{A}$ be an adversary. In the case that P_1 is corrupted, we construct an ideal simulator that invokes $\mathcal{A}$ and receives the string x_0 that $\mathcal{A}$ intends to send to P_2. Simulator $\mathcal{S}$ then sends (x_0, x_0) to the trusted party. Clearly, $\mathcal{A}$'s view is identical in both cases, and likewise the output of the honest P_2 is x_0 in both the real and ideal executions. In the case that P_2 is corrupted, the simulator S sends $\sigma = 0$ to the trusted party and receives back x_0. Simulator S then internally simulates P_1 sending x_0 to $\mathcal{A}$. Here too, the view of $\mathcal{A}$ is identical in the real and ideal executions. This demonstrates why it is necessary to separately require that π computes f.

6.9 The Common Reference String Model – Oblivious Transfer

Until now, we have considered the *plain model* with no trusted setup. However, in some cases, a trusted setup is used to obtain additional properties; for example, a common reference string can be used to achieve noninteractive zero knowledge [7], which is impossible in the plain model. In addition, this is used to achieve security under composition, as will be discussed briefly in Section 6.10.1.

The common reference string model. Let M be a probabilistic polynomial-time machine that generates a common reference string that is given to both parties. We remark that in the common *random* string model, $M(1^n)$ outputs a uniformly-distributed string of length poly(n), whereas in the common *reference* string model, the distribution can be arbitrary. Let CRS denote "common reference string".

In the CRS model, in the real model the parties are provided the same string generated by M, whereas in the ideal model the simulator chooses the string. Since the real and ideal models must be indistinguishable, this means that the CRS chosen by the simulator must be indistinguishable from the CRS chosen by M. However, this still provides considerable power to the simulator. For example, assume that the CRS contains an encryption key pk to a CCA-secure public-key encryption scheme. Then, in the real model, neither party knows the associated secret key. In contrast, since the simulator chooses the CRS, it can know the associated secret key and so can decrypt any ciphertext generated by the adversary.

The motivation behind this definition is that if an adversary can attack the protocol in the real model, then it can also attack the protocol in the ideal model with the simulator. The fact that the simulator can choose the CRS does not change anything in this respect. Indeed, as we have discussed previously, the simulator *must* have additional power beyond that of a legitimate party. (Recall that in the context of zero knowledge, if there is no additional power then the zero-knowledge property will contradict the soundness property, since a cheating prover could run the simulator strategy.) Until now, we have considered a simulator that can rewind the adversary. In the CRS model, it is possible to construct a simulator that does *not* rewind the adversary, since its additional power is in choosing the CRS itself.

There are two ways to define security in the CRS model. The first is to include the CRS in the output distributions. Specifically, one can modify the REAL output distribution to include the CRS generated by M, the output of the adversary $\mathcal{A}$, and the output of the honest party. Then, the IDEAL output distribution includes the output of S (which include two parts—the CRS generated by S and the output of the adversary) and the output of the honest party. Alternatively, it is possible to define an ideal CRS functionality $f_{crs}(1^n, 1^n) = (M(1^n), M(1^n))$. Then, one constructs a protocol and proves its security in the f_{crs}-hybrid model. As we have already seen, in the f-hybrid model, the simulator S plays the role of f in the simulation of the protocol. Thus, this means that S can choose the CRS in the f_{crs}-hybrid model, as we have discussed.

Before proceeding to demonstrate the simulation technique in this model, we remark that the sequential composition theorem of Section 6.6.3 only holds when each execution of the protocol is independent. Thus, it is *not* possible to generate a single CRS and then run many sequential executions of the protocol using the same CRS, while relying on the composition theorem. Rather, it is necessary either to use a different CRS for each execution (not recommended) or to explicitly prove that security holds for many executions. This can be done by defining a *multi-execution functionality* and then proving its security in the f_{crs}-hybrid model. For example, a multi-execution functionality for oblivious transfer could be defined as follows:

> **The multi-execution oblivious transfer $f_{\text{m-ot}}$ works as follows:** Until one of the parties sends end, repeat the following:
>
> 1. Wait to receive (x_0, x_1) from P_1, and σ from P_2.
> 2. Send x_σ to P_2.

Typically, such functionalities are not defined in this way, since the CRS model is usually used in the context of *concurrent composition*, where executions are run concurrently and not sequentially. In the concurrent setting, parties can send inputs whenever they wish. In order to match executions, a session identifier *sid* is used; specifically, P_1 sends (sid, x_0, x_1), P_2 sends (sid, σ), and then the functionality sends (sid, x_σ) to P_2. We discuss concurrent composition briefly in Section 6.10.1.

Oblivious transfer in the CRS model. In Section 6.8, we described an oblivious transfer protocol that was based on the protocol of Peikert et al. [35]. The original protocol in [35] was designed in the CRS model, and achieves universal composability (see Section 6.10.1). We can modify Protocol 6.8.2 to a *two-round protocol* in the CRS model by simply defining the CRS to be $(\mathbb{G}, q, g_0, g_1, h_0, h_1)$ where (g_0, g_1, h_0, h_1) is *not* a Diffie–Hellman tuple; see Protocol 6.9.1. We will prove that Protocol 6.9.1 is secure for a single oblivious transfer (we do not prove security under multiple executions since our aim is to demonstrate the use of the CRS and not to show the full power of the protocol).

Theorem 6.9.2. *Assume that the Decisional Diffie–Hellman problem is hard relative to the group sampling algorithm used by f_{crs}. Then, Protocol 6.9.1 securely computes f_{ot} in the presence of malicious adversaries in the f_{crs}-model.*

Proof sketch: The proof here is very similar to that of Theorem 6.8.2. In particular, the fact that Protocol 6.9.1 computes f_{ot} follows from exactly the same computation.

In the case that P_1 is corrupted, the simulator S in the proof of Theorem 6.8.2 chose (g_1, h_0, h_1) so that (g_0, g_1, h_0, h_1) *is* a Diffie–Hellman tuple. Given this fact, and given that it knows y such that $g_1 = (g_0)^y$, simulator S was able to extract both x_0, x_1 from $\mathcal{A}$. Now, in this case, S chooses the CRS so that (g_0, g_1, h_0, h_1) *is*

PROTOCOL 6.9.1 (Oblivious transfer [35])

- **Inputs:** Party P_1's input is a pair (x_0, x_1), and party P_2's input is a bit σ. We assume for simplicity that $x_0, x_1 \in \mathbb{G}$ where $\mathbb{G}$ is defined in the CRS.
- **Auxiliary input:** Both parties hold a security parameter 1^n.
- **Hybrid functionality f_{crs}:** A group $\mathbb{G}$ of order q (of length n) with generator g_0 is sampled, along with three random elements $g_1, h_0, h_1 \in_R \mathbb{G}$ of the group. f_{crs} sends $(\mathbb{G}, q, g_0, g_1, h_0, h_1)$ to P_1 and P_2.
- **The protocol:**

    1. P_2 chooses a random value $r \in_R \mathbb{Z}_q$, computes $g = (g_\sigma)^r$ and $h = (h_\sigma)^r$, and sends (g, h) to P_1.
    2. P_1 computes $(u_0, v_0) = RAND(g_0, g, h_0, h)$ and $(u_1, v_1) = RAND(g_1, g, h_1, h)$. P_1 sends P_2 the values (u_0, w_0) where $w_0 = v_0 \cdot x_0$, and (u_1, w_1) where $w_1 = v_1 \cdot x_1$.
    3. P_2 computes $x_\sigma = w_\sigma / (u_\sigma)^r$.
    4. P_1 outputs λ, and P_2 outputs x_σ.

---

a Diffie–Hellman tuple. Also, since it chooses g_1, it knows y such that $g_1 = (g_0)^y$. Thus, $\mathcal{S}$ internally hands this (g_0, g_1, h_0, h_1) to $\mathcal{A}$ when $\mathcal{A}$ calls f_{crs}, as if it was generated by f_{crs}. From then on, $\mathcal{S}$ uses the exact same strategy as the simulator in the proof of Theorem 6.8.3. The proof of indistinguishability works in exactly the same way.

In the case that P_2 is corrupted, the simulator $\mathcal{S}$ in the proof of Theorem 6.8.2 was able to extract $\mathcal{A}$'s input σ using the witness α (where $h_0 = (g_0)^\alpha$). Simulator $\mathcal{S}$ obtained α from $\mathcal{A}$'s message to $f_{\mathrm{zk}}^{R_L}$. In this case, $\mathcal{S}$ chooses the CRS. Thus, it generates (g_0, g_1, h_0, h_1) as in the protocol specification and takes α where $h_0 = (g_0)^\alpha$. $\mathcal{S}$ then uses α exactly as the simulator in the proof of Theorem 6.8.2 in order to extract σ. (Observe that in Protocol 6.8.2, $h_1 = (g_0)^{\alpha+1}$. This makes the tuple not a Diffie–Hellman tuple, but not a random one either. In contrast, here the tuple is random. Nevertheless, any non-Diffie–Hellman tuple suffices, and the simulator in the proof of Theorem 6.8.2 only needs the discrete log α of h_0 to base g_0 in order to extract. Specifically, if $h = g^\alpha$ then it determines that the input is $\sigma = 0$, and otherwise it is $\sigma = 1$. This remains the same when h_1 is taken to be a random element.) Based on the above, $\mathcal{S}$ chooses (g_0, g_1, h_0, h_1) as described above, and hands it to $\mathcal{A}$ when it calls f_{crs}. Beyond that, $\mathcal{S}$ works in exactly the same way as $\mathcal{S}$ in the proof of Theorem 6.8.3. ∎

6.10 Advanced Topics

In this section, we briefly mention some advanced topics, and include pointers for additional reading.

6.10.1 Composition and Universal Composability

In this tutorial, we focused on the stand-alone model. As discussed in Section 6.6.3, this implies security under sequential composition. However, in the real-world setting, many secure and insecure protocols are run concurrently, and it is desirable to have security in this setting. The definition of security presented in Section 6.6 does *not* guarantee security under concurrent composition. There are a number of definitions that have been proposed to achieve this level of security. The most popular is that of universal composability (UC) [9]. This definition expands upon the definition of Section 6.6 by adding an *environment machine*, which is essentially an interactive distinguisher. The environment writes the inputs to the parties' input tapes and reads their outputs. In addition, it externally interacts with the adversary throughout the execution. The environment's "goal" is to distinguish between a real protocol execution and an ideal execution. One very important artifact of this definition is that the simulator can no longer rewind the adversary in the simulation. This is because the real adversary can actually do nothing but fulfill the instructions of the environment. Now, since the environment is an *external* machine that the real and ideal adversaries interact with, this means that the simulator has to simulate for an external adversary. Due to this, rewinding is not possible, and it actually follows that without an honest majority it is impossible to securely compute a large class of functionalities in the UC framework in the plain model without any trusted setup [13]. However, given a trusted setup, e.g., a common reference string as in Section 6.9, it is possible to securely compute any functionality for any number of corrupted parties under the UC definition [14]. Indeed, the oblivious transfer protocol described in Section 6.9 has been proven secure in the UC framework [35].

The general UC framework is rather complex, as it enables one to model almost any task and any setting. In case one is interested in standard secure computation tasks, without guaranteeing fairness, it is possible to use the simpler equivalent formalization described in [10].

6.10.2 Proofs in the Random Oracle Model

In many cases, the random oracle model is used to gain higher efficiency or other properties otherwise unobtainable. The setting of secure computation is no exception. However, beyond its inherent heuristic nature [12], there are some very subtle definitional issues here that must be considered. One issue that arises is whether or not the distinguisher obtains access to the random oracle, and if so, how. If the distinguisher does not have any access, then this is a very weak definition, and sequential composition will not be guaranteed. If we provide the distinguisher with the same randomly chosen oracle as the parties and the (real and ideal) adversary, then we obtain a *nonprogrammable* random oracle [33], which may not be strong enough. A third alternative is to provide the distinguisher with the random oracle, but in the ideal world to allow the simulator to still control the oracle. This is a somewhat strange formulation, but something of this type seems necessary in some cases.

In the UC framework, the random oracle can be modeled as an ideal functionality computing a random function. This matches the third alternative in some sense, since the simulator controls the oracle in the case of an ideal execution. It is somewhat different, however, since the environment—who plays the distinguisher—cannot directly access the oracle.

We will not do more in this tutorial than point out that these issues exist and need to be dealt with carefully if the random oracle is to be used in the context of secure computation. We recommend reading [33] for a basic treatment of modeling random oracles in secure computation, and [39, 40] for a treatment of the issue of oracle-dependent auxiliary input (and more). We conclude by remarking that in [34] it is pointed out that other properties that are sometimes expected (such as deniability) are not necessarily obtained in the random oracle model. In many cases of standard secure computation, this is not needed. However, this is another example of why the random oracle model needs to be treated with great care in these settings.

6.10.3 Adaptive Security

In this tutorial we have considered only the case of *static adversaries*, where the subset of corrupted parties is fixed before the protocol execution begins. In contrast, an *adaptive adversary* can choose which parties to corrupt throughout the protocol, based on the messages viewed. A classic example of a protocol that is secure for static adversaries but not for adaptive adversaries is as follows: Consider a very large number of parties (say, linear in the security parameter n), and consider a protocol which begins by securely choosing a random subset of the parties who then carry out the computation for the rest. Assume that the adversary is limited to corrupting a constant fraction of the parties, and assume that $\sqrt{n}$ parties are chosen to compute the result. Then, except with negligible probability, there will be at least one honest party in the chosen $\sqrt{n}$. Thus, as long as a protocol that is secure for any number of corrupted parties is used, we have that security is preserved. This is true for the case of static adversaries. However, an adaptive adversary can wait until the $\sqrt{n}$ parties are chosen, and then adaptively corrupt all of them. Since it only corrupts a constant fraction (less than half for $n > 6$), this is allowed. Clearly, such an adversary completely breaks the protocol, since it controls all the parties who carry out the actual computation.

In order to provide security for such adversaries, it is necessary to be able to simulate even when an adversary corrupts a party midway. The challenge that this raises is that when an adversary corrupts a real party in the middle of an execution, then it obtains its current state. Thus, the simulator must be able to generate a transcript—without knowing a party's input—and later be able to "explain" that transcript as a function of an honest party's instructions on its input, where the input is provided later (upon corruption).

There are two main models that have been considered for the case of adaptive adversaries. In the first, it is assumed that parties cannot securely erase data; this is called the no erasures model. Thus, the adversary obtains the party's entire view—its input, random tape, and incoming messages—upon corruption. This forces the simulator to generate such a view, *after* having generated (at least part of) the protocol transcript. Amongst other things, this means that a transcript has to match all possible inputs, and so it must be *noncommitting*. See [11] for a basic treatment and constructions in the case of an honest majority, see [8] for a definitional treatment in the stand-alone model, and see [14] for constructions in the case of no honest majority.

A weaker model of adaptive security is one which assumes that parties *can* securely erase data; this is called the erasures model. In this case, it is possible for parties to erase some of their data. This makes simulation easier since it is not necessary to generate the entire view, but only the current state. See [3] for a very efficient solution for the case of an honest majority, and see [29] for an example of a two-party protocol that is adaptively secure with erasures. These examples demonstrate why the erasures model is easier to work with.[11]

Acknowledgements

First and foremost, I would like to express my deepest gratitude to Oded Goldreich, for years of guidance, education and inspiration. I feel honored and privileged to have been Oded's student, and to have gained from his extraordinary dedication and personal example. I have learned important lessons from Oded's high moral standards in science, and in general, and these continue to motivate me. Finally, I would like to thank Oded for his sincere caring, from the time that I first met him and until today.

I thank Ben Riva for suggesting that such a tutorial would be very useful, and my students Ran Cohen, Omer Shlomovits and Avishay Yanay, who provided helpful comments on the write-up.

References

[1] B. Barak. How to Go Beyond the Black-Box Simulation Barrier. In 42*nd* *FOCS*, pages 106–115, 2001.

[2] B. Barak and Y. Lindell. Strict Polynomial-Time in Simulation and Extraction. *SIAM Journal on Computing,* 33(4):783–818, 2004. (Extended abstract in the 34-*th STOC*, 2002.)

---

[11] In my personal subjective opinion, there has been too much focus on the *no erasures* model. Since achieving security without erasures is so difficult, this has unnecessarily dissuaded people from working in the adaptive model at all, especially when considering efficient protocols. The community would be better served by constructing protocols that are secure with erasures than just those that are secure under static adversaries, since the former captures a very realistic attack threat. Unfortunately, however, it seems that such work is doomed since most people seem to either not care about adaptive security at all, or if they do care then they consider the erasures model to be too weak.

[3] D. Beaver and S. Haber. Cryptographic Protocols Provably Secure Against Dynamic Adversaries. In *EUROCRYPT'92,* Springer-Verlag (LNCS 658), pages 307–323, 1992.

[4] M. Bellare, A. Desai, E. Jokipii, and P. Rogaway. A Concrete Security Treatment of Symmetric Encryption: Analysis of the DES Modes of Operation. In the *38th Symposium on Foundations of Computer Science* (FOCS), 1997.

[5] M. Blum. Coin Flipping by Phone. *IEEE Spring COMPCOM*, pages 133–137, 1982.

[6] M. Blum. How to Prove a Theorem So No One Else Can Claim It. *Proceedings of the International Congress of Mathematicians*, pages 1444–1451, 1986.

[7] M. Blum, P. Feldman and S. Micali. Non-Interactive Zero-Knowledge and its Applications. In 20-*th STOC,* pages 103–112, 1988.

[8] R. Canetti. Security and Composition of Multiparty Cryptographic Protocols. *Journal of Cryptology*, 13(1):143–202, 2000.

[9] R. Canetti. Universally Composable Security: A New Paradigm for Cryptographic Protocols. In the *42nd FOCS*, pages 136–145, 2001. Full version available at http://eprint.iacr.org/2000/067.

[10] R. Canetti, A. Cohen and Y. Lindell. A Simpler Variant of Universally Composable Security for Standard Multiparty Computation. In *CRYPTO 2015,* Springer (LNCS 9216), pages 3–22, 2015.

[11] R. Canetti, U. Feige, O. Goldreich and M. Naor. Adaptively Secure Multi-Party Computation. In 28-*th STOC*, pages 639–648, 1996.

[12] R. Canetti, O. Goldreich, and S. Halevi. The Random Oracle Methodology, Revisited. In the *Journal of the ACM*, 51(4):557–594, 2004. (An extended abstract appeared in the 30-*th STOC*, 1998.)

[13] R. Canetti, E. Kushilevitz and Y. Lindell. On the Limitations of Universal Composable Two-Party Computation Without Set-Up Assumptions. *Journal of Cryptology,* 19(2):135-167, 2006. (Extended abstract appeared at *EUROCRYPT 2003.*)

[14] R. Canetti, Y. Lindell, R. Ostrovsky and A. Sahai. Universally Composable Two-Party and Multi-Party Computation. In 34-*th STOC*, pages 494–503, 2002. Full version available at http://eprint.iacr.org/2002/140.

[15] R. Cleve. Limits on the Security of Coin Flips when Half the Processors are Faulty. In 18-*th STOC,* pages 364–369, 1986.

[16] S. Even, O. Goldreich and A. Lempel. A Randomized Protocol for Signing Contracts. In *Communications of the ACM,* 28(6):637–647, 1985.

[17] O. Goldreich. *Foundations of Cryptography Vol. I – Basic Tools*. Cambridge University Press, 2001.

[18] O. Goldreich. *Foundations of Cryptography Vol. II – Basic Applications.* Cambridge University Press, 2004.

[19] O. Goldreich. On Expected Probabilistic Polynomial-Time Adversaries: A Suggestion for Restricted Definitions and Their Benefits. In the *Journal of Cryptology*, 23(1):1–36, 2010. (Extended abstract appeared in TCC 2007.)

[20] O. Goldreich and A. Kahan. How To Construct Constant-Round Zero-Knowledge Proof Systems for NP. *Journal of Cryptology*, 9(3):167–190, 1996.

[21] O. Goldreich and H. Krawczyk. On the Composition of Zero-Knowledge Proof Systems. *SIAM Journal on Computing*, 25(1):169–192, 1996.

[22] O. Goldreich, S. Micali and A. Wigderson. Proofs that Yield Nothing but their Validity or All Languages in NP Have Zero-Knowledge Proof Systems. *Journal of the ACM*, 38(1):691–729, 1991.

[23] O. Goldreich and Y. Oren. Definitions and Properties of Zero-Knowledge Proof Systems. *Journal of Cryptology*, 7(1):1–32, 1994.

[24] S. Goldwasser and S. Micali. Probabilistic Encryption. *Journal of Computer and System Sciences*, 28(2):270–299, 1984.

[25] S. Goldwasser, S. Micali and C. Rackoff The Knowledge Complexity of Interactive Proof Systems. *SIAM Journal on Computing*, 18(1):186–208, 1989.

[26] C. Hazay and Y. Lindell. *Efficient Secure Two-Party Protocols: Techniques and Constructions.* Springer, 2010.

[27] C. Hazay and Y. Lindell. A Note on Zero-Knowledge Proofs of Knowledge and the ZKPOK Ideal Functionality. *Cryptology ePrint Archive: Report 2010/552*, 2010.

[28] J. Katz and Y. Lindell. Handling Expected Polynomial-Time Strategies in Simulation-Based Security Proofs. In the *Journal of Cryptology*, 21(3):303–349, 2008. (An extended abstract appeared in TCC 2005.)

[29] Y. Lindell. Adaptively Secure Two-Party Computation with Erasures. In *CT-RSA*, Springer (LNCS 5473), pages 117–132, 2009. Full version in the *Cryptology ePrint Archive*, Report 2009/031.

[30] Y. Lindell. A Note on Constant-Round Zero-Knowledge Proofs of Knowledge. In the *Journal of Cryptology*, 26(4):638-654, 2013.

[31] Y. Lindell and B. Pinkas. An Efficient Protocol for Secure Two-Party Computation in the Presence of Malicious Adversaries. *Journal of Cryptology*, 28(2):312350, 2015. (Extended abstract in *EUROCRYPT 2007*.)

[32] M. Naor and O. Reingold. Number-Theoretic Constructions Of Efficient Pseudo-Random Functions. In *Journal of ACM*, 51(2):231–262, 2004.

[33] J.B. Nielsen. Separating Random Oracle Proofs from Complexity Theoretic Proofs: The Non-committing Encryption Case. In *CRYPTO 2002*, Springer (LNCS 2442), pages 111–126, 2002.

[34] R. Pass. On Deniability in the Common Reference String and Random Oracle Model. In *CRYPTO 2003*, Springer (LNCS 2729), pages 316–337, 2003.

[35] C. Peikert, V. Vaikuntanathan and B. Waters. A Framework for Efficient and Composable Oblivious Transfer. In *CRYPTO 2008*, Springer (LNCS 5157), pages 554–571, 2008.

[36] M. Rabin. How to Exchange Secrets by Oblivious Transfer. Tech. Memo TR-81, Aiken Computation Laboratory, Harvard University, 1981. (See *Cryptology ePrint Archive: Report 2005/187*.)

[37] A. Rosen. A Note on Constant-Round Zero-Knowledge Proofs for NP. In *TCC 2004*, Springer (LNCS 2951), pages 191–202, 2004.

[38] V. Shoup. Sequences of Games: A Tool for Taming Complexity in Security Proofs. *Cryptology ePrint Archive, Report 2004/332*, 2004.

[39] D. Unruh. Random Oracles and Auxiliary Input. In *CRYPTO 2007*, Springer (LNCS 4622), pages 205-223, 2007.

[40] H. Wee. Zero Knowledge in the Random Oracle Model, Revisited. In *ASIACRYPT 2009*, Springer (LNCS 5912), pages 417–434, 2009.

Chapter 7
The Complexity of Differential Privacy

Salil Vadhan

Abstract Differential privacy is a theoretical framework for ensuring the privacy of individual-level data when performing statistical analysis of privacy-sensitive datasets. This tutorial provides an introduction to and overview of differential privacy, with the goal of conveying its deep connections to a variety of other topics in computational complexity, cryptography, and theoretical computer science at large. This tutorial is written in celebration of Oded Goldreich's 60th birthday, starting from notes taken during a minicourse given by the author and Kunal Talwar at the 26th McGill Invitational Workshop on Computational Complexity [1].

To Oded, my mentor, role model, collaborator, and friend.
Your example gives me a sense of purpose as a researcher.

Salil Vadhan
Center for Research on Computation & Society, School of Engineering & Applied Sciences, Harvard University, Cambridge, Massachusetts, USA, e-mail: salil@seas.harvard.edu. webpage: http://seas.harvard.edu/~salil.
Written in part while visiting the Shing-Tung Yau Center and the Department of Applied Mathematics at National Chiao-Tung University in Hsinchu, Taiwan. Supported by NSF grant CNS-1237235, a grant from the Sloan Foundation, and a Simons Investigator Award.

7.1 Introduction and Definition

7.1.1 Motivation

Suppose you are a researcher in the health or social sciences who has collected a rich dataset on the subjects you have studied, and want to make the data available to others to analyze as well. However, the dataset has sensitive information about your subjects (such as disease diagnoses, financial information, or political affiliations), and you have an obligation to protect their privacy. What can you do?

The traditional approach to such privacy problems is to try to "anonymize" the dataset by removing obvious identifiers, such as name, address, and date of birth, and then share the anonymized dataset. However, it is now well understood that this approach is ineffective, because the data that remains is often still sufficient to determine who is who in the dataset, given appropriate auxiliary information. This threat is not hypothetical; there have now been many high-visibility demonstrations that such "re-identification" attacks are often quite easy to carry out in practice, using publicly available datasets as sources of auxiliary information [84].

A more promising approach is to mediate access to the data through a trusted interface, which will only answer queries posed by data analysts. However, ensuring that such a system protects privacy is nontrivial. Which queries should be permitted? Clearly, we do not want to allow queries that target a particular individual (such as "Does Sonny Rollins have sensitive trait X?"), even if they are couched as aggregate queries (e.g., "How many people in the dataset are 84-year-old jazz saxophonists with trait X?"). Even if a single query does not seem to target an individual, a combination of results from multiple queries can do so (e.g., "How many people in the dataset have trait X?" and "How many people in the dataset have trait X and are *not* 84-year-old jazz saxophonists?"). These attacks can sometimes be foiled by only releasing *approximate* statistics, but Dinur and Nissim [31] exhibited powerful "reconstruction attacks" which showed that, given sufficiently many approximate statistics, one can reconstruct almost the entire dataset. Thus, there are fundamental limits to what can be achieved in terms of privacy protection while providing useful statistical information, and we need a theory that can assure us that a given release of statistical information is safe.

Cryptographic tools such as secure function evaluation and functional encryption do not address these issues. The kind of security guarantee such tools provide is that nothing is leaked *other than the outputs of the functions being computed*. Here we are concerned about the possibility that the outputs of the functions (i.e., queries) already leak too much information. Indeed, addressing these privacy issues is already nontrivial in a setting with a trusted data curator, whereas the presence of a trusted third party trivializes most of cryptography.

Differential privacy is a robust definition of privacy protection for data-analysis interfaces that:

- ensures meaningful protection against adversaries with arbitrary auxiliary information (including ones that are intimately familiar with the individuals they are targeting),

- does not restrict the computational strategy used by the adversary (in the spirit of modern cryptography), and
- provides a quantitative theory that allows us to reason about how much statistical information is safe to release and with what accuracy.

Following the aforementioned reconstruction attacks of Dinur and Nissim [31], the concept of differential privacy emerged through a series of papers by Dwork and Nissim [35], Blum, Dwork, McSherry, and Nissim [13], and Dwork, McSherry, Nissim, and Smith [48], with the latter providing the elegant indistinguishability-based definition that we will see in the next section.

In the decade since differential privacy was introduced, a large algorithmic literature has developed showing that differential privacy is compatible with a wide variety of data-analysis tasks. It also has attracted significant attention from researchers and practitioners outside theoretical computer science, many of whom are interested in bringing differential privacy to bear on real-life data-sharing problems. At the same time, it has turned out to be extremely rich from a theoretical perspective, with deep connections to many other topics in theoretical computer science and mathematics. The latter connections are the focus of this tutorial, with an emphasis on connections to topics in computational complexity and cryptography. For a more in-depth treatment of the algorithmic aspects of differential privacy, we recommend the monograph of Dwork and Roth [36].

7.1.2 The Setting

The basic setting we consider is where a trusted curator holds a dataset x about n individuals, which we model as a tuple $x \in \mathcal{X}^n$, for a *data universe* $\mathcal{X}$. The interface to the data is given by a (randomized) *mechanism* $\mathcal{M} : \mathcal{X}^n \times \mathcal{Q} \to \mathcal{Y}$, where $\mathcal{Q}$ is the *query space* and $\mathcal{Y}$ is the *output space* of $\mathcal{M}$. To avoid introducing continuous probability formalism (and to be able to discuss algorithmic issues), we will assume that $\mathcal{X}$, $\mathcal{Q}$, and $\mathcal{Y}$ are discrete.

The picture we have in mind is as follows:

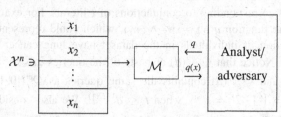

for a dataset $x = (x_1, \ldots, x_n)$.

7.1.3 Counting Queries

A basic type of query that we will examine extensively is a *counting query*, which is specified by a predicate on rows $q \colon \mathcal{X} \to \{0, 1\}$, and is extended to datasets $x \in \mathcal{X}^n$ by counting the fraction of people in the dataset satisfying the predicate:

$$q(x) = \frac{1}{n} \sum_{i=1}^{n} q(x_i),$$

(Note that we abuse notation and use q for both the predicate on rows and the function that averages q over a dataset.) The examples mentioned above in Section 7.1.1 demonstrate that it is nontrivial to ensure privacy even when answering counting queries, because answers to several counting queries can be combined to reveal information about individual rows.

There are several specific families of counting queries that are important for statistical analysis and will come up many times in this tutorial:

Point Functions (Histograms): Here $\mathcal{X}$ is an arbitrary set and for each $y \in \mathcal{X}$ we consider the predicate $q_y : \mathcal{X} \rightarrow \{0, 1\}$ that evaluates to 1 only on input y. The family $\mathcal{Q}^{\mathrm{pt}} = \mathcal{Q}^{\mathrm{pt}}(\mathcal{X})$ consists of the counting queries corresponding to all point functions on data universe $\mathcal{X}$. (Approximately) answering all of the counting queries in $\mathcal{Q}^{\mathrm{pt}}$ amounts to (approximately) computing the *histogram* of the dataset.

Threshold Functions (CDFs): Here $\mathcal{X}$ is a totally ordered set, and we consider the set $\mathcal{Q}^{\mathrm{thr}} = \mathcal{Q}^{\mathrm{thr}}(\mathcal{X})$ of threshold functions. That is, for each $y \in \mathcal{X}$, $\mathcal{Q}^{\mathrm{thr}}$ contains counting query corresponding to the function $q_y(z)$ that outputs 1 iff $z \leq y$. (Approximately) answering all of the counting queries in $\mathcal{Q}^{\mathrm{thr}}$ is tantamount to (approximating) the *cumulative distribution function* of the dataset.

Attribute Means (1-way Marginals): Here $\mathcal{X} = \{0, 1\}^d$, so each individual has d Boolean attributes, and $\mathcal{Q}^{\mathrm{means}} = \mathcal{Q}^{\mathrm{means}}(d)$ contains the counting queries corresponding to the d coordinate functions $q_j : \{0, 1\}^d \rightarrow \{0, 1\}$ defined by $q_j(w) = w_j$ for $j = 1, \ldots, d$. Thus, (approximately) answering all of the queries in $\mathcal{Q}^{\mathrm{means}} = \mathcal{Q}^{\mathrm{means}}(d)$ amounts to (approximately) computing the fraction of the dataset possessing each of the d attributes. These are also referred to as the *(1-way) marginal statistics* of the dataset.

Conjunctions (Contingency Tables): Here again $\mathcal{X} = \{0, 1\}^d$, and for an integer $t \in \{0, 1, 2, \ldots, d\}$, we consider the family $\mathcal{Q}_t^{\mathrm{conj}} = \mathcal{Q}_t^{\mathrm{conj}}(d)$ of counting queries corresponding to conjunctions of t literals. For example, $\mathcal{Q}_2^{\mathrm{conj}}(5)$ contains the function $q(w) = w_2 \wedge \neg w_4$, which could represent a query like "what fraction of individuals in the dataset have lung cancer and are nonsmokers?". Notice that $\mathcal{Q}_1^{\mathrm{conj}}(d)$ consists of the queries in $\mathcal{Q}^{\mathrm{means}}(d)$ and their negations, and $\mathcal{Q}_d^{\mathrm{conj}}(d)$ contains the same queries as $\mathcal{Q}^{\mathrm{pt}}(\{0, 1\}^d)$. We have $|\mathcal{Q}_t^{\mathrm{conj}}(d)| = \binom{d}{t} \cdot 2^t = d^{\Theta(t)}$ when $t \leq d^{1-\Omega(1)}$. We also consider the family $\mathcal{Q}^{\mathrm{conj}} = \mathcal{Q}^{\mathrm{conj}}(d) = \cup_{t=0}^{d} \mathcal{Q}_t^{\mathrm{conj}}(d)$, which is of size 3^d. The counting queries in $\mathcal{Q}_t^{\mathrm{conj}}$ are also called *t-way marginals* and answering all of them amounts to computing the *t-way contingency table* of the dataset. These are important queries for statistical analysis, and indeed the answers to all queries in $\mathcal{Q}^{\mathrm{conj}}$ is known to be a "sufficient statistic" for "logit models."

Arbitrary Queries: Sometimes we will not impose any structure on the data universe $\mathcal{X}$ or query family $\mathcal{Q}$ except possibly to restrict attention to families of efficiently computable queries. For the latter, we encode elements of both $\mathcal{X}$ and $\mathcal{Q}$ as strings, so $\mathcal{X} = \{0, 1\}^d$, $\mathcal{Q} = \{q_y : \mathcal{X} \to \{0, 1\}\}_{y \in \{0,1\}^s}$ for some $s, d \in \mathbb{N}$, where $q_y(w) = \mathsf{Eval}(y, w)$ for some polynomial-time evaluation function $\mathsf{Eval} : \{0, 1\}^s \times \{0, 1\}^d \to \{0, 1\}$.

7.1.4 Differential Privacy

The definition of differential privacy requires that no individual's data has much effect on what an adversary sees. That is, if we consider any two datasets x and x' that differ on one row (which we will denote $x \sim x'$), the output distribution of $\mathcal{M}$ on x should be "similar" to that of $\mathcal{M}$ on x'. Specifically, we require that

$$\forall T \subseteq \mathcal{Y}, \ \Pr[\mathcal{M}(x, q) \in T] \leq (1 + \varepsilon) \cdot \Pr[\mathcal{M}(x, q) \in T].$$

The reverse relationship ($\Pr[\mathcal{M}(x', q) \in T] \leq (1 + \varepsilon) \cdot \Pr[\mathcal{M}(x, q) \in T]$) follows by symmetry, swapping x and x'. The choice of a multiplicative measure of closeness between distributions is important, and we will discuss the reasons for it later. It is technically more convenient to use e^ε instead of $(1 + \varepsilon)$, because the former behaves more nicely under multiplication ($e^{\varepsilon_1} \cdot e^{\varepsilon_2} = e^{\varepsilon_1 + \varepsilon_2}$). This gives the following formal definition:

Definition 7.1.1 ((Pure) differential privacy [48]). *For $\varepsilon \geq 0$, we say that a randomized mechanism $\mathcal{M} : \mathcal{X}^n \times \mathcal{Q} \to \mathcal{Y}$ is ε-differentially private if, for every pair of neighboring datasets $x \sim x' \in \mathcal{X}^n$ (i.e., x and x' differ in one row) and every query $q \in \mathcal{Q}$, we have*

$$\forall T \subseteq \mathcal{Y}, \ \Pr[\mathcal{M}(x, q) \in T] \leq e^\varepsilon \cdot \Pr[\mathcal{M}(x', q) \in T].$$

Equivalently,

$$\forall y \in \mathcal{Y}, \ \Pr[\mathcal{M}(x, q) = y] \leq e^\varepsilon \cdot \Pr[\mathcal{M}(x', q) = y].$$

Here we typically take ε as small, but nonnegligible (not cryptographically small), for example, a small constant, such as $\varepsilon = 0.1$. Smaller ε provides better privacy, but as we will see, the definition is no longer useful when $\varepsilon < 1/n$. We will also think of n as known and public information, and we will study asymptotic behavior as $n \to \infty$.

We will often think of the query as fixed, and remove q from notation. In this section, we consider answering only one query; a major focus of subsequent sections will be the problem of answering many queries.

7.1.5 Basic Mechanisms

Before discussing the definition further, let us see some basic constructions of differentially private mechanisms.

Randomized response. Let $q : \mathcal{X} \to \{0, 1\}$ be a counting query, and $x \in \mathcal{X}^n$ be a dataset. For each row x_i, let

$$y_i = \begin{cases} q(x_i) & \text{with prob. } (1 + \varepsilon)/2, \\ \neg q(x_i) & \text{with prob. } (1 - \varepsilon)/2 \end{cases}$$

and

$$\mathcal{M}(x_1, \ldots, x_n) = (y_1, \ldots, y_n).$$

If $x \sim x'$ are datasets that differ on the i-th row, their output distributions differ only if $q(x_i) \neq q(x_i')$, in which case the outputs differ only in the i-th components, denoted y_i and y_i', respectively. We have

$$\frac{\Pr[y_i = q(x_i)]}{\Pr[y_i' = q(x_i)]} = \frac{(1 + \varepsilon)/2}{(1 - \varepsilon)/2} = e^{O(\varepsilon)}.$$

And $\Pr[y_i = q(x_i')] \leq \Pr[y_i' = q(x_i')]$. Thus, randomized response is $O(\varepsilon)$-differentially private.

We can use the result of randomized response to estimate the value of the counting query $q(x)$ as follows. Note that $E[y_i] = \varepsilon \cdot q(x_i) + (1 - \varepsilon)/2$. Thus, by the Chernoff bound, with high probability we have

$$\left| \frac{1}{n} \sum_i \frac{1}{\varepsilon} \cdot \left(y_i - \frac{(1 - \varepsilon)}{2} \right) - q(x) \right| \leq O\left(\frac{1}{\sqrt{n} \cdot \varepsilon} \right).$$

As $n \to \infty$, we get an increasingly accurate estimate of the average.

An advantage of randomized response is that it does not require a trusted, centralized data curator; each subject can carry out the randomization on her own and publicly announce her noisy bit y_i. Indeed, this method was introduced in the 1960s by Warner [108] for carrying out sensitive surveys in the social sciences, where participants may not feel comfortable revealing information to the surveyor. In Section 7.9, we will discuss the "local model" for differential privacy, which encompasses general mechanisms and interactive protocols where subjects ensure their own privacy and need not trust anyone else.

The Laplace mechanism [48]. Let q be a counting query; it is natural to try to protect privacy by simply adding noise. That is, $\mathcal{M}(x) = q(x) + \text{noise}$. But how much noise do we need to add, and according to what distribution?

Note that, if $x \sim x'$, we have $|q(x) - q(x')| \leq 1/n$. This suggests "noise" of magnitude $1/(\varepsilon n)$ should be enough to make $\mathcal{M}(x)$ and $\mathcal{M}(x')$ "ε-indistinguishable" in the sense required by differential privacy.

Which distribution will satisfy the multiplicative definition of differential privacy? Recall that, at every output y, the density of the output distribution should be the same under x and x' up to a factor of e^{ε}. The density of $\mathcal{M}(x)$ at y is the density of the noise distribution at $z = y - q(x)$, and the density of $\mathcal{M}(x')$ at y is the density of the noise distribution at $z' = y - q(x')$; again $|z - z'| \leq 1/n$. So we see that it suffices for the density of the noise distribution to change by a factor of at most e^ε over intervals of length $1/n$.

This leads us to the *Laplace distribution* $\mathrm{Lap}(\sigma)$:

$$\text{the density of } \mathrm{Lap}(\sigma) \text{ at } z \propto e^{-|z|/\sigma}.$$

If we set $\sigma = 1/\varepsilon n$, then we see that the ratio of densities is as we want: for $z \geq 0$, we have

$$\frac{\text{density of } \mathrm{Lap}(1/\varepsilon n) \text{ at } z + 1/n}{\text{density of } \mathrm{Lap}(1/\varepsilon n) \text{ at } z} = e^{1/(n\sigma)} = e^{-\varepsilon}.$$

(For $z \leq -1/n$, the ratio of densities is e^ε, and for $z \in (-1/n, 0)$, it is between $e^{-\varepsilon}$ and e^ε.)

It may seem more natural to use Gaussian noise, but it does not quite achieve the definition of differential privacy that we have given: in the tail of a Gaussian, the density changes by an unbounded multiplicative factor over intervals of fixed width. Later, we will see a relaxation of differential privacy (called (ε, δ)-differential privacy) that is achieved by adding Gaussian noise of appropriate variance.

$\mathrm{Lap}(\sigma)$ has mean 0 and standard deviation $\sqrt{2} \cdot \sigma$, and has exponentially vanishing tails:

$$\Pr[|\mathrm{Lap}(\sigma)| > \sigma t] \leq e^{-t}.$$

The Laplace mechanism is not specific to counting queries; all we used was that $|q(x) - q(x')| \leq 1/n$ for $x \sim x'$. For an arbitrary query $q : \mathcal{X}^n \to \mathbb{R}$, we need to scale the noise to its *global sensitivity*:

$$GS_q = \max_{x \sim x'} |q(x) - q(x')|.$$

Then we have:

Definition 7.1.2 (The Laplace mechanism). *For a query* $q : \mathcal{X}^n \to \mathbb{R}$, *a bound* B, *and* $\varepsilon > 0$, *the* Laplace mechanism $\mathcal{M}_{q,B}$ *over data universe* $\mathcal{X}$ *takes a dataset* $x \in \mathcal{X}^n$ *and outputs*

$$\mathcal{M}_{q,B}(x) = q(x) + \mathrm{Lap}(B/\varepsilon).$$

From the discussion above, we have:

Theorem 7.1.3 (Properties of the Laplace mechanism).

1. *If* $B \geq GS_q$, *the Laplace mechanism* $\mathcal{M}_{q,B}$ *is* ε-*differentially private.*
2. *For every* $x \in \mathcal{X}^n$ *and* $\beta > 0$,

$$\Pr[|\mathcal{M}_{q,B}(x) - q(x)| > (B/\varepsilon) \cdot \ln(1/\beta)] \leq \beta.$$

As noted above, for a counting query q, we can take $B = 1/n$, and thus with high probability we get error $O(1/(\varepsilon n))$, which is significantly better than the bound of $O(1/\varepsilon \sqrt{n})$ given by randomized response.

Global sensitivity is also small for a variety of other queries of interest:

1. For $q(x) = \max\{q_1(x), q_2(x), \ldots, q_t(x)\}$, we have $\mathrm{GS}_q \leq \max_i\{\mathrm{GS}_{q_i}\}$.
2. For $q(x) = d(x, H)$ where $H \subseteq \mathcal{X}^n$ and d is Hamming distance,[1] we have $\mathrm{GS}_q \leq 1$. ("Is my data set close to one that satisfies my hypothesis H?").
3. A *statistical query* (sometimes called a *linear query* in the differential privacy literature) is a generalization of a counting query to averaging a real-valued function on the dataset. That is, we are given a bounded function $q : \mathcal{X} \to [0, 1]$, and are interested in the query:

$$q(x) = \frac{1}{n} \sum_{i=1}^{n} q(x_i).$$

Then $\mathrm{GS}_q \leq 1/n$.

We promised that we would only work with discrete probability, but the Laplace distribution is continuous. However, one can discretize both the query values $q(x)$ and the Laplace distribution to integer multiples of B (yielding a scaled version of a geometric distribution) and Theorem 7.1.3 will still hold. We ignore this issue in the rest of the tutorial for the sake of simplicity (and consistency with the literature, which typically refers to the continuous Laplace distribution).

7.1.6 Discussion of the Definition

We now discuss why differential privacy utilizes a multiplicative measure of similarity between the probability distributions $\mathcal{M}(x)$ and $\mathcal{M}(x')$.

Why not statistical distance? The first choice that one might try is to use statistical difference (total variation distance). That is, we require that, for every $x \sim x'$, we have

$$\mathrm{SD}(\mathcal{M}(x), \mathcal{M}(x')) \overset{\mathrm{def}}{=} \max_{T \subseteq \mathcal{Y}} \big| \Pr[\mathcal{M}(x) \in T] - \Pr[\mathcal{M}(x') \in T] \big| \leq \delta.$$

ε-Differential privacy implies the above definition with $\delta = 1 - e^{-\varepsilon} \leq \varepsilon$, but not conversely.

We claim that, depending on the setting of δ, such a definition either does not allow for any useful computations or does not provide sufficient privacy protection.

$\delta \leq 1/2n$: Then by a hybrid argument, for all pairs of datasets $x, x' \in \mathcal{X}^n$ (even nonneighbors), we have $\mathrm{SD}(\mathcal{M}(x), \mathcal{M}(x')) \leq n\delta \leq 1/2$. Taking x' to be a fixed (e.g., all-zeroes) dataset, this means that, with probability $1/2$ on $\mathcal{M}(x)$, we get an answer independent of the dataset x and the mechanism is useless.

$\delta \geq 1/2n$: In this case, the mechanism "with probability $1/2$, output a random row of the dataset" satisfies the definition. We do not consider a mechanism that outputs an individual's data in the clear to be protecting privacy.

---

[1] The *Hamming distance* $d(x, x')$ between two datasets $x, x' \in \mathcal{X}^n$ is the number of rows on which x and x' differ.

However, it turns out to be quite useful to consider the following relaxation of differential privacy, which incorporates a negligible statistical distance term δ in addition to the multiplicative ε:

Definition 7.1.4 ((Approximate) differential privacy). *For $\varepsilon \geq 0, \delta \in [0,1]$, we say that a randomized mechanism $\mathcal{M} \colon \mathcal{X}^n \times \mathcal{Q} \to \mathcal{Y}$ is (ε,δ)-differentially private if, for every two neighboring datasets $x \sim x' \in \mathcal{X}^n$ (x and x' differ in one row) and every query $q \in \mathcal{Q}$, we have*

$$\forall T \subseteq \mathcal{Y}, \ \Pr[\mathcal{M}(x,q) \in T] \leq e^{\varepsilon} \cdot \Pr[\mathcal{M}(x',q) \in T] + \delta. \tag{7.1}$$

Here, we will insist that δ is cryptographically negligible (in particular, $\delta \leq n^{-\omega(1)}$); it can be interpreted as an upper bound on the probability of catastrophic failure (e.g., the entire dataset being published in the clear). This notion is often called *approximate differential privacy*, in contrast with *pure differential privacy* as given by Definition 7.1.1. Note that, unlike pure differential privacy, with approximate differential privacy it is *not* sufficient to verify Inequality (7.1) for sets T of size 1. (Consider a mechanism that outputs the entire dataset along with a random number from $\{1, \ldots, \lceil 1/\delta \rceil\}$; then $\Pr[\mathcal{M}(x,q) = y] \leq \delta \leq e^{\varepsilon} \cdot \Pr[\mathcal{M}(x',q) = y] + \delta$ for all y, but clearly does not provide any kind of privacy or satisfy Definition 7.1.4.)

More generally, we will call two random variables Y and Y' taking values in $\mathcal{Y}$ (ε,δ)-*indistinguishable* if:

$$\forall T \subseteq \mathcal{Y}, \ \Pr[Y \in T] \leq e^{\varepsilon} \cdot \Pr[Y' \in T] + \delta, \text{ and}$$
$$\Pr[Y' \in T] \leq e^{\varepsilon} \cdot \Pr[Y \in T] + \delta$$

Setting $\varepsilon = 0$ is equivalent to requiring that $\mathrm{SD}(Y, Y') \leq \delta$. (ε,δ)-Indistinguishability has the following nice characterization, which allows us to interpret (ε,δ)-differential privacy as "ε-differential privacy with probability at least $1 - \delta$":

Lemma 7.1.5 (Approximate DP as smoothed[2] DP [19]). *Two random variables Y and Y' are (ε,δ)-indistinguishable if and only if there are events $E = E(Y)$ and $E' = E'(Y')$ such that:*
 1. $\Pr[E], \Pr[E'] \geq 1 - \delta$, and
 2. $Y|_E$ and $Y'|_{E'}$ are $(\varepsilon,0)$-indistinguishable.

Proof: We prove the "if" direction, and omit the converse (which is rather technical). For every set T, we have

$$\Pr[Y \in T] \leq \Pr[Y \in T|E] \cdot \Pr[E] + \Pr[\overline{E}]$$
$$\leq \Pr[Y \in T|E] \cdot (1 - \delta) + \delta$$
$$\leq e^{\varepsilon} \cdot \Pr[Y' \in T|E'] \cdot (1 - \delta) + \delta$$
$$\leq e^{\varepsilon} \cdot \Pr[Y' \in T|E'] \cdot \Pr[E'] + \delta$$
$$\leq e^{\varepsilon} \cdot \Pr[Y' \in T] + \delta$$

∎

---

[2] The terminology "smoothed" was coined by [91] for similar variants of entropy measures.

A Bayesian interpretation. Although statistical distance is not a good choice (on its own), there are many other choices of distance measures, and we still have not justified why a multiplicative measure is a particularly good choice. One justification comes from a Bayesian interpretation of the definition of differential privacy [48, 33, 65]. Consider a prior distribution (X, X') on neighboring datasets, modeling an adversary's prior on a real dataset X and a dataset X' that would have been obtained if a particular individual had not participated. Given an output $y \leftarrow \mathcal{M}(X)$, the adversary will have a posterior belief on the dataset, given by the conditional distribution $X|_{\mathcal{M}(X)=y}$. We will argue that differential privacy implies that this posterior is close to the posterior that would have been obtained if the mechanism had been run on X' instead, which we think of as capturing "ideal" privacy for the individual.

Proposition 7.1.6 (DP implies Bayesian privacy). *Let* $\mathcal{M} : \mathcal{X}^n \to \mathcal{Y}$ *be any* ε-*differentially private mechanism and let* (X, X') *be any joint distribution on* $\mathcal{X}^n \times \mathcal{X}^n$ *such that* $\Pr[X \sim X'] = 1$. *Then for every dataset* $x \in \mathcal{X}^n$ *and output* $y \in \mathrm{Supp}(\mathcal{M}(X)) = \mathrm{Supp}(\mathcal{M}(X'))$,[3]

$$\mathrm{SD}(X|_{\mathcal{M}(X)=y}, X|_{\mathcal{M}(X')=y}) \le 2\varepsilon.$$

A special case of the proposition is when we fix $X' = x'$ to be constant (so that there is nothing to learn from X') and $X = (X_i, x'_{-i})$ is varying only in the data of one individual. Then the proposition says that in such a case (where the adversary knows all but the i-th row of the dataset), the adversary's posterior on X_i is close to its prior. Indeed,

$$\mathrm{SD}(X_i|_{\mathcal{M}(X)=y}, X_i) = \mathrm{SD}(X_i|_{\mathcal{M}(X)=y}, X_i|_{\mathcal{M}(X')=y'}) = \mathrm{SD}(X|_{\mathcal{M}(X)=y}, X|_{\mathcal{M}(X')=y'}) \le 2\varepsilon.$$

That is, whatever an adversary could have learned about an individual, it could have learned from the rest of the dataset.

Proof: By Bayes' rule,

$$\Pr[X = x|\mathcal{M}(X) = y] = \frac{\Pr[\mathcal{M}(X) = y|X = x] \cdot \Pr[X = x]}{\Pr[\mathcal{M}(X) = y]}$$
$$\le \frac{e^\varepsilon \cdot \Pr[\mathcal{M}(X') = y|X = x] \cdot \Pr[X = x]}{e^{-\varepsilon} \cdot \Pr[\mathcal{M}(X') = y]}$$
$$= e^{2\varepsilon} \cdot \Pr[X = x|\mathcal{M}(X') = y].$$

By symmetry (swapping X and X'), we also have $\Pr[X = x|\mathcal{M}(X') = y] \le e^{2\varepsilon} \cdot \Pr[X = x|\mathcal{M}(X) = y]$. Having all probability masses equal up to a multiplicative factor of $e^{2\varepsilon}$ implies that the statistical distance is at most $1 - e^{-2\varepsilon} \le 2\varepsilon$. ∎

There is also a converse to the proposition: if $\mathcal{M}$ guarantees that the two posterior distributions are close to each other (even in statistical difference), then $\mathcal{M}$ must be differentially private. In fact, this will hold even for the special case mentioned above where X' is constant.

Proposition 7.1.7 (Bayesian privacy implies DP). *Let* $\mathcal{M} : \mathcal{X}^n \to \mathcal{Y}$ *be any randomized mechanism, and let* $x_0 \sim x_1 \in \mathcal{X}^n$ *be two neighboring datasets. Define the*

---

[3] $\mathrm{Supp}(Z)$ is defined to be the *support* of random variable Z, i.e., $\{z : \Pr[Z = z] > 0\}$.

joint distribution (X, X') *to equal* (x_0, x_0) *with probability 1/2 and to equal* (x_1, x_0) *with probability 1/2. Suppose that, for some* $y \in \text{Supp}(\mathcal{M}(x_0) \cap \text{Supp}(\mathcal{M}(x_1))$,

$$\text{SD}(X|_{\mathcal{M}(X)=y}, X|_{\mathcal{M}(X')=y}) \le \varepsilon \le 1/4. \tag{7.2}$$

Then

$$e^{-O(\varepsilon)} \cdot \Pr[\mathcal{M}(x_1) = y] \le \Pr[\mathcal{M}(x_0) = y] \le e^{O(\varepsilon)} \cdot \Pr[\mathcal{M}(x_1) = y].$$

In particular, if for all pairs $x_0 \sim x_1$ *of neighboring datasets, we have that* $\text{Supp}(\mathcal{M}(x_0)) = \text{Supp}(\mathcal{M}(x_1))$ *and (7.2) holds for all outputs* $y \in \text{Supp}(\mathcal{M}(x_0))$, *then* $\mathcal{M}$ *is* $O(\varepsilon)$-*differentially private.*

Note that, for the joint distributions (X, X') in Proposition 7.1.7, we have $\Pr[X \sim X'] = 1$, so this is indeed a converse to Proposition 7.1.7.

Proof: Since X' is constant, $X|_{\mathcal{M}(X')=y}$ is the same as the prior X (namely, uniformly random from $\{x_0, x_1\}$). Thus, by hypothesis, for $b = 0, 1$, we have

$$\frac{1}{2} - \varepsilon \le \Pr[X = x_b | \mathcal{M}(X) = y] \le \frac{1}{2} + \varepsilon.$$

On the other hand, by Bayes' rule,

$$\begin{aligned} \Pr[\mathcal{M}(x_b) = y] &= \Pr[\mathcal{M}(X) = y | X = x_b] \\ &= \frac{\Pr[X = x_b | \mathcal{M}(X) = y] \cdot \Pr[\mathcal{M}(X) = y]}{\Pr[X = x_b]} \\ &\in \left[\frac{(1/2) - \varepsilon}{1/2} \cdot \Pr[\mathcal{M}(X) = y], \frac{(1/2) + \varepsilon}{1/2} \cdot \Pr[\mathcal{M}(X) = y] \right]. \end{aligned}$$

Thus, $\Pr[\mathcal{M}(x_0) = y] / \Pr[\mathcal{M}(x_1) = y]$ is between $(1/2 - \varepsilon)/(1/2 + \varepsilon) = e^{-O(\varepsilon)}$ and $(1/2 + \varepsilon)/(1/2 - \varepsilon) = e^{O(\varepsilon)}$. ∎

There are also (ε, δ) analogues of the above propositions, where we require that, with all but negligible probability (related to δ), the posterior probability distributions should be close to each other [65].

Interpretations of the Definition. We can now provide some more intuitive interpretations of (and cautions about) the definition of differential privacy:

- Whatever an adversary learns about you, she could have learned from the rest of the dataset (in particular, even if you did not participate). Note that this does *not* say that the adversary does not learn anything about you; indeed, learning about the population implies learning about individuals. For example, if an adversary learns that smoking correlates with lung cancer (the kind of fact that differential privacy is meant to allow learning) and knows that you smoke, it can deduce that you are more likely to get lung cancer. However, such a deduction is not because of the use of your data in the differentially private mechanism, and thus may not be considered a privacy violation.

- The mechanism will not leak a significant amount of information specific to an individual (or a small group, as we will see in the next section). Consequently, differential privacy is not an achievable privacy notion if the goal of the analysis is to take an action on a specific individual in the dataset (e.g., to identify a candidate for a drug trial, a potential terrorist, or a promising customer).

The above interpretations hold regardless of what auxiliary information or computational strategy the adversary uses. Indeed, the definition provides an information-theoretic form of security. In Section 7.10, we will consider a computational analogue of differential privacy, where we restrict to polynomial-time adversaries.

Variants of the definition and notation. In our treatment, the dataset is an *ordered* n-tuple $x \in \mathcal{X}^n$, where n is known and public (not sensitive information).

A common alternative treatment is to consider datasets x that are *multisets* of elements of $\mathcal{X}$, without a necessarily known or public size. Then, a convenient notation is to represent x as a histogram – that is, as an element of $\mathbb{N}^{\mathcal{X}}$. In the multiset definition, the distance between two datasets is the symmetric difference $|x \Delta x'|$, which corresponds to ℓ_1 distance in histogram notation. Thus, neighboring datasets (at distance 1) are ones that differ by addition or removal of one item. Differential privacy under this definition has a nice interpretation as hiding whether you participated in a dataset at all (without having to replace you by an alternate row to keep the dataset size the same).

There is not a big difference between the two notions, as one can estimate $n = |x|$ with differential privacy (it is just a counting query), the distance between two unordered datasets of the same size under addition/removal versus substitution differ by at most a factor of 2, and one can apply a differentially private mechanism designed for ordered tuples to an unordered dataset by randomly ordering the elements of the dataset.

7.1.7 Preview of the Later Sections

The primary goal of this tutorial is to illustrate connections of differential privacy to computational complexity and cryptography. Consequently, our treatment of the algorithmic foundations of differentially private is very incomplete, and we recommend the monograph of Dwork and Roth [36] for a thorough treatment, including more proofs and examples for the background material that is only sketched here. We also focus heavily on counting queries in this tutorial, because they suffice to bring out most of the connections we wish to illustrate. However, the algorithmic literature on differential privacy now covers a vast range of data-analysis tasks, and obtaining a thorough complexity-theoretic understanding of such tasks is an important direction for future work.

The topics that will be covered in the later sections are as follows:

Section 7.2: We will describe composition theorems that allow us to reason about the level of differential privacy provided when many differentially private algorithms are executed independently. In particular, this will give us algorithms to answer nearly n^2 counting queries accurately while satisfying differential privacy.

Section 7.3: We will briefly survey some alternatives to using global sensitivity to calibrate the level of noise added for differentially private estimates; sometimes we can get away with adding noise that is proportional to the sensitivity of the query in a local neighborhood of our dataset x (but we need to be careful in doing so).

Section 7.4: We will present some remarkable algorithms that can answer many more than n^2 counting queries with differential privacy. These algorithms are inspired by ideas from computational learning theory, such as Occam's razor and the multiplicative weights method. Unfortunately, these algorithms are computationally quite expensive, requiring time that is polynomial in the size of the data universe $\mathcal{X}$ (which in turn is exponential in the bit-length of row elements).

Section 7.5: We will prove a number of information-theoretic lower bounds on differential privacy, showing that it is impossible to answer too many queries with too much accuracy. Some of the lower bounds will be based on combinatorial and geometric ideas (such as "discrepancy"), and others will be on fingerprinting codes, which were developed as a tool in cryptography (for secure digital content distribution).

Section 7.6: We will turn to computational hardness results for differential privacy, giving evidence that there is no way in general to make the algorithms of Section 7.4 computationally efficient. These hardness results will be based on cryptographic constructs (such as traitor-tracing schemes and digital signatures), and one result will also use probabilistically checkable proofs.

Section 7.7: Next, we will turn to some additional algorithms that bypass the hardness results of Section 7.6 by focusing on specific, structured families of counting queries (and use alternative output representations). The methods employed include low-degree approximations of Boolean functions (via Chebychev polynomials) and convex geometry and optimization (semidefinite programming, Gaussian width, Grothendieck's inequality).

Section 7.8: We will then look at PAC learning with differential privacy, showing both some very general but computationally inefficient positive results, as well as some efficient algorithms. We will then see how methods from communication complexity have been used to show that the sample complexity of differentially private PAC learning (with pure differential privacy) is inherently higher than that of nonprivate PAC learning.

Section 7.9: In this section, we will explore generalizations of differential privacy to the case where the data is distributed among multiple parties, rather than all being held by a single trusted curator. We will show, using connections to randomness extractors and to information complexity, that sometimes distributed differential privacy cannot achieve the same level of accuracy attained in the centralized model.

Section 7.10: The aforementioned limitations of multiparty differential privacy can be avoided by using cryptography (namely, secure multiparty computation) to implement the trusted curator. However, this requires a relaxation of differential

privacy to computationally bounded adversaries. We will present the definition
of computational differential privacy, and point out its connection to the notion
of "pseudodensity" studied in the theory of pseudorandomness.

7.2 Composition Theorems for Differential Privacy

7.2.1 Postprocessing and Group Privacy

One central property of differential privacy, which we will use throughout the tutorial, is that it is preserved under "postprocessing":

Lemma 7.2.1 (Postprocessing). *If* $\mathcal{M} : \mathcal{X}^n \to \mathcal{Y}$ *is* (ε, δ)*-differentially private
and* $\mathcal{F} : \mathcal{Y} \to \mathcal{Z}$ *is any randomized function, then* $\mathcal{F} \circ \mathcal{M} : \mathcal{X}^n \to \mathcal{Z}$ *is* (ε, δ)*-
differentially private.*

Proof: Consider $\mathcal{F}$ to be a distribution on deterministic functions $f : \mathcal{Y} \to \mathcal{Z}$.
Then, for every $x \sim x' \in \mathcal{X}^n$ and every subset $T \subseteq \mathcal{Z}$, we have

$$\Pr[(\mathcal{F} \circ \mathcal{M})(x) \in T] = \operatorname*{E}_{f \leftarrow \mathcal{F}}[\Pr[\mathcal{M}(x) \in f^{-1}(T)]]$$

$$\leq \operatorname*{E}_{f \leftarrow \mathcal{F}}[e^{\varepsilon} \cdot \Pr[\mathcal{M}(x') \in f^{-1}(T)] + \delta]$$

$$= e^{\varepsilon} \cdot \Pr[(\mathcal{F} \circ \mathcal{M})(x') \in T] + \delta.$$

∎

Another useful property, alluded to in Section 7.1.6, is that differential privacy
provides protection for small groups of individuals. For $x, x' \in \mathcal{X}^n$, let $d(x, x')$ denote the Hamming distance between x and x', or in other words the number of rows
that need to be changed to go from x to x' (so $x \sim x'$ iff $d(x, x') \leq 1$).

Then the "group privacy" lemma for differential privacy is as follows:

Lemma 7.2.2 (Group privacy). *If* $\mathcal{M}$ *is an* (ε, δ)*-differentially private mechanism,
then for all pairs of datasets* $x, x' \in \mathcal{X}^n$, $\mathcal{M}(x)$ *and* $\mathcal{M}(x')$ *are* $(k\varepsilon, k \cdot e^{k\varepsilon} \cdot \delta)$*-
indistinguishable for* $k = d(x, x')$.

Proof: We use a hybrid argument. Let $x_0, x_1, x_2, \ldots, x_k$ be such that $x_0 = x$ and
$x_k = x'$ and for each i such that $0 \leq i \leq k - 1$, x_{i+1} is obtained from x_i by changing
one row. Then, for all $T \subseteq \mathcal{Y}$, since $\mathcal{M}$ is (ε, δ)-differentially private,

$$\Pr[\mathcal{M}(x_0) \in T] \leq e^{\varepsilon} \Pr[\mathcal{M}(x_1) \in T] + \delta$$

$$\leq e^{\varepsilon} (e^{\varepsilon} \Pr[\mathcal{M}(x_2) \in T] + \delta) + \delta$$

$$\vdots$$

$$\leq e^{k\varepsilon} \cdot \Pr[\mathcal{M}(x_k) \in T] + (1 + e^{\varepsilon} + e^{2\varepsilon} + \cdots + e^{(k-1)\cdot\varepsilon}) \cdot \delta$$

$$\leq e^{k\varepsilon} \cdot \Pr[\mathcal{M}(x_k) \in T] + k \cdot e^{k\varepsilon} \cdot \delta.$$

∎

Note that, when $\delta = 0$, ε-differential privacy provides nontrivial guarantees for datasets x, x' even at distance n, namely $(n\varepsilon, 0)$-indistinguishability, which in particular implies that $\mathcal{M}(x)$ and $\mathcal{M}(x')$ have the same support. In contrast, when $\delta > 0$, we only get nontrivial guarantees for datasets at distance $k \leq \ln(1/\delta)/\varepsilon$; when k is larger, $k \cdot e^{k\varepsilon} \cdot \delta$ is larger than 1. This gap is a source of the additional power of (ε, δ)-differential privacy (as we will see).

7.2.2 Answering Many Queries

Now we consider a different form of composition, where we independently execute several differentially private mechanisms. Let $\mathcal{M}_1, \mathcal{M}_2, \dots, \mathcal{M}_k$ be differentially private mechanisms. Let

$$\mathcal{M}(x) = (\mathcal{M}_1(x), \mathcal{M}_2(x), \dots, \mathcal{M}_k(x)),$$

where each $\mathcal{M}_i$ is run with independent coin tosses; for example, this is how we might obtain a mechanism answering a k-tuple of queries.

The basic composition lemma says that the privacy degrades at most linearly with the number of mechanisms executed.

Lemma 7.2.3 (Basic composition). *If $\mathcal{M}_1, \dots, \mathcal{M}_k$ are each (ε, δ)-differentially private, then $\mathcal{M}$ is $(k\varepsilon, k\delta)$-differentially private.*

However, if we are willing to tolerate an increase in the δ term, the privacy parameter ε only needs to degrade proportionally to $\sqrt{k}$:

Lemma 7.2.4 (Advanced composition [42]). *If $\mathcal{M}_1, \dots, \mathcal{M}_k$ are each (ε, δ)-differentially private and $k < 1/\varepsilon^2$, then for all $\delta' > 0$, $\mathcal{M}$ is $(O(\sqrt{k \log(1/\delta')}) \cdot \varepsilon, k\delta + \delta')$-differentially private.*

We now prove the above lemmas, starting with basic composition.
Proof of Lemma 7.2.3: We start with the case $\delta = 0$. Fix datasets x, x' such that $x \sim x'$. For an output $y \in \mathcal{Y}$, define the *privacy loss* to be

$$L_{\mathcal{M}}^{x \to x'}(y) = \ln\left(\frac{\Pr[\mathcal{M}(x) = y]}{\Pr[\mathcal{M}(x') = y]}\right) = -L_{\mathcal{M}}^{x' \to x}(y).$$

When $L_{\mathcal{M}}^{x \to x'}(y)$ is positive, the output y is "evidence" that the dataset is x rather than x'; and conversely when it is negative.

Notice that ε^*-differential privacy of $\mathcal{M}$ is equivalent to the statement that, for all $x \sim x'$ and all $y \in \text{Supp}(\mathcal{M}(x)) \cup \text{Supp}(\mathcal{M}(x'))$,

$$|L_{\mathcal{M}}^{x \to x'}(y)| \leq \varepsilon^*.$$

Now, for $\mathcal{M} = (\mathcal{M}_1, \mathcal{M}_2, \dots, \mathcal{M}_k)$ and $y = (y_1, y_2, \dots, y_k)$, we have

$$L_{\mathcal{M}}^{x \to x'}(y) = \ln\left(\frac{\Pr[\mathcal{M}_1(x) = y_1 \wedge \mathcal{M}_2(x) = y_2 \wedge \cdots \wedge \mathcal{M}_k(x) = y_k]}{\Pr[\mathcal{M}_1(x') = y_1 \wedge \mathcal{M}_2(x') = y_2 \wedge \cdots \wedge \mathcal{M}_k(x') = y_k]}\right)$$

$$= \ln\left(\frac{\prod_{i=1}^{k} \Pr[\mathcal{M}_i(x) = y_i]}{\prod_{i=1}^{k} \Pr[\mathcal{M}_i(x') = y_i]}\right)$$

$$= \sum_{i=1}^{k} L_{\mathcal{M}_i}^{x \to x'}(y_i),$$

so

$$\left|L_{\mathcal{M}}^{x \to x'}(y)\right| \le \sum_{i=1}^{k} \left|L_{\mathcal{M}_i}^{x \to x'}(y_i)\right| \le k \cdot \varepsilon.$$

For the case that $\delta > 0$, we use Lemma 7.1.5. Specifically, since $\mathcal{M}_i(x_i)$ and $\mathcal{M}_i(x_i')$ are (ε, δ)-indistinguishable, there are events E_i and E_i' of probability at least $1 - \delta$ such that, for all y_i, we have

$$\left|\ln\left(\frac{\Pr[\mathcal{M}(x_i) = y_i | E_i]}{\Pr[\mathcal{M}(x_i') = y_i | E_i']}\right)\right| \le \varepsilon.$$

Thus, in the above analysis, we instead condition on the events $E = E_1 \wedge E_2 \wedge \cdots \wedge E_k$ and $E' = E_1' \wedge E_2' \wedge \cdots \wedge E_k'$, redefining our privacy losses as

$$L_{\mathcal{M}_i}^{x_i \to x_i'}(y_i) = \ln\left(\frac{\Pr[\mathcal{M}_i(x_i) = y_i | E_i]}{\Pr[\mathcal{M}(x_i') = y_i | E_i']}\right),$$

$$L_{\mathcal{M}}^{x \to x'}(y) = \ln\left(\frac{\Pr[\mathcal{M}(x) = y | E]}{\Pr[\mathcal{M}(x') = y | E']}\right).$$

Then we still have

$$\left|L_{\mathcal{M}}^{x \to x'}(y)\right| \le \sum_{i=1}^{k} \left|L_{\mathcal{M}_i}^{x \to x'}(y_i)\right| \le k \cdot \varepsilon.$$

By a union bound, the probability of the events E and E' are at least $1 - k \cdot \delta$, so by Lemma 7.1.5, $\mathcal{M}(x)$ and $\mathcal{M}(x')$ are $(k\varepsilon, k\delta)$-indistinguishable, as required. ∎

We now move on to advanced composition.

Proof sketch of Lemma 7.2.4:   We again focus on the $\delta = 0$ case; the extension to $\delta > 0$ is handled similarly to the proof of Lemma 7.2.3. The intuition for how we can do better than the linear growth in ε is that some of the y_i's will have positive privacy loss (i.e., give evidence for dataset x) while some will have negative privacy loss (i.e., give evidence for dataset x'), and the cancellations between these will lead to a smaller overall privacy loss.

To show this, we consider the *expected* privacy loss

$$\mathop{\mathrm{E}}_{y_i \leftarrow \mathcal{M}_i(x)}[L_{\mathcal{M}_i}^{x \to x'}(y_i)].$$

By definition, this equals the Kullback–Leibler divergence (a.k.a. relative entropy)

$$D(\mathcal{M}_i(x) \| \mathcal{M}_i(x')),$$

which is known to always be nonnegative.

We first prove the following claim, which shows that the expected privacy loss of a differentially private mechanism is quite a bit smaller than the upper bound on the maximum privacy loss of ε:

Claim 7.2.5. *If* $\mathcal{M}_i$ *is* ε-*differentially private, where* $\varepsilon \leq 1$, *then*

$$\underset{y_i \leftarrow \mathcal{M}_i(x)}{\mathrm{E}} [L_{\mathcal{M}_i}^{x \rightarrow x'}(y_i)] \leq 2\varepsilon^2.$$

Proof of claim: We will show that

$$D(\mathcal{M}_i(x) \| \mathcal{M}_i(x')) + D(\mathcal{M}_i(x') \| \mathcal{M}_i(x)) \leq 2\varepsilon^2,$$

and then the result follows by the nonnegativity of divergence. Now,

$$D(\mathcal{M}_i(x) \| \mathcal{M}_i(x')) + D(\mathcal{M}_i(x') \| \mathcal{M}_i(x)) = \underset{y_i \leftarrow \mathcal{M}_i(x)}{\mathrm{E}} [L_{\mathcal{M}_i}^{x \rightarrow x'}(y_i)] + \underset{y_i \leftarrow \mathcal{M}_i(x')}{\mathrm{E}} [L_{\mathcal{M}_i}^{x' \rightarrow x}(y_i)]$$

$$= \underset{y_i \leftarrow \mathcal{M}_i(x)}{\mathrm{E}} [L_{\mathcal{M}_i}^{x \rightarrow x'}(y_i)] - \underset{y_i \leftarrow \mathcal{M}_i(x')}{\mathrm{E}} [L_{\mathcal{M}_i}^{x \rightarrow x'}(y_i)],$$

and using the upper bound of ε on privacy loss we get that

$$\underset{y_i \leftarrow \mathcal{M}_i(x)}{\mathrm{E}} [L_{\mathcal{M}_i}^{x \rightarrow x'}(y_i)] - \underset{y_i \leftarrow \mathcal{M}_i(x')}{\mathrm{E}} [L_{\mathcal{M}_i}^{x \rightarrow x'}(y_i)]$$

$$\leq 2 \cdot \left(\underset{y_i \in \mathrm{Supp}(\mathcal{M}_i(x)) \cup \mathrm{Supp}(\mathcal{M}_i(x'))}{\max} \left| L_{\mathcal{M}_i}^{x \rightarrow x'}(y_i) \right| \right) \cdot \mathrm{SD}(\mathcal{M}_i(x), \mathcal{M}_i(x'))$$

$$\leq 2\varepsilon \cdot (1 - e^{-\varepsilon})$$

$$\leq 2\varepsilon^2,$$

where SD is statistical distance, and we use the fact that $(\varepsilon, 0)$-indistinguishability implies a statistical distance of at most $1 - e^{-\varepsilon}$. ∎

Thus by linearity of expectation, for the overall expected privacy loss, we have

$$\underset{y \leftarrow \mathcal{M}(x)}{\mathrm{E}} [L_{\mathcal{M}}^{x \rightarrow x'}(y)] = k \cdot O(\varepsilon^2) \overset{\mathrm{def}}{=} \mu.$$

Applying the Hoeffding bound for random variables whose absolute value is bounded by ε, we get that, with probability at least $1 - \delta'$ over $y \leftarrow \mathcal{M}(x)$,

$$L_{\mathcal{M}}^{x \rightarrow x'}(y) \leq \mu + O\left(\sqrt{k \log(1/\delta')} \right) \cdot \varepsilon \leq O\left(\sqrt{k \log(1/\delta')} \right) \cdot \varepsilon \overset{\mathrm{def}}{=} \varepsilon',$$

where the second inequality uses the assumption that $k < 1/\varepsilon^2$ (so $k\varepsilon^2 \leq \sqrt{k\varepsilon^2}$ and hence $\mu \leq O(\sqrt{k}) \cdot \varepsilon$).

Now for any set T, we have

$$\Pr[\mathcal{M}(x) \in T] \le \Pr_{y \leftarrow \mathcal{M}(x)}\left[L_{\mathcal{M}}^{x \to x'}(y) > \varepsilon'\right] + \sum_{y \in T: L_{\mathcal{M}}^{x \to x'}(y) \le \varepsilon'} \Pr[\mathcal{M}(x) = y]$$

$$\le \delta' + \sum_{y \in T: L_{\mathcal{M}}^{x \to x'}(y) \le \varepsilon'} e^{\varepsilon'} \cdot \Pr[\mathcal{M}(x') = y]$$

$$\le \delta' + e^{\varepsilon'} \cdot \Pr[\mathcal{M}(x') \in T],$$

so $\mathcal{M}$ is indeed (ε', δ')-differentially private. ∎

It should be noted that, although Lemma 7.2.4 is stated in terms of queries being asked *simultaneously* (in particular, *nonadaptively*), a nearly identical proof (appealing to Azuma's inequality, instead of Hoeffding) shows that an analogous conclusion holds even when the queries (i.e., mechanisms) are chosen *adaptively* (i.e., the choice of $\mathcal{M}_{i+1}$ depends on the outputs of $\mathcal{M}_1(x), \dots, \mathcal{M}_i(x)$).

Observe that, if we have a set $\mathcal{Q}$ of $k = |\mathcal{Q}|$ counting queries and we wish to obtain a final privacy of (ε, δ'), then we can achieve this by first adding Laplace noise to achieve an initial privacy guarantee of ε_0 for each query and then use the composition theorems. To use the basic composition lemma, we would have to set

$$\varepsilon_0 = \frac{\varepsilon}{k},$$

so the Laplace noise added per query has scale

$$O\left(\frac{1}{\varepsilon_0 n}\right) = O\left(\frac{k}{\varepsilon n}\right).$$

To obtain a bound on the *maximum* noise added to any of the queries, we can do a union bound over the k queries. Setting $\beta = 1/O(k)$ in Theorem 7.1.3, with high probability, the maximum noise will be at most

$$\alpha = O\left(\frac{k \cdot \log k}{\varepsilon n}\right).$$

Steinke and Ullman [99] showed how to save the $\log k$ factor by carefully correlating the noise used for the k queries, and thus showed:

Theorem 7.2.6 (Arbitrary counting queries with pure differential privacy [99]).
For every set $\mathcal{Q}$ of counting queries and $\varepsilon > 0$, there is an ε-differentially private mechanism $\mathcal{M} : \mathcal{X}^n \to \mathbb{R}^{\mathcal{Q}}$ such that, on every dataset $x \in \mathcal{X}^n$, with high probability $\mathcal{M}(x)$ answers all the queries in $\mathcal{Q}$ to within additive error

$$\alpha = O\left(\frac{|\mathcal{Q}|}{\varepsilon n}\right).$$

Thus, taking ε to be constant, we can answer any $|\mathcal{Q}| = o(n)$ counting queries with vanishingly small error, which we will see is optimal for pure differential privacy (in Section 7.5.2).

Similarly, to use the advanced composition theorem, we would have to set

$$\varepsilon_0 = \frac{\varepsilon}{c \cdot \sqrt{k \cdot \log(1/\delta)}},$$

yielding a maximum error of

$$\alpha = O\left(\frac{\log k}{\varepsilon_0 n}\right) = O\left(\frac{\sqrt{k \cdot \log(1/\delta)} \cdot \log k}{\varepsilon n}\right).$$

Again, it is known how to (mostly) remove the $\log k$ factor:

Theorem 7.2.7 (Arbitrary counting queries with approximate differential privacy [99]). *For every set $\mathcal{Q}$ of counting queries over data universe $\mathcal{X}$, and $\varepsilon, \delta > 0$, there is an (ε, δ)-differentially private mechanism $\mathcal{M} : \mathcal{X}^n \to \mathbb{R}^k$ such that, on every dataset $x \in \mathcal{X}^n$, with high probability $\mathcal{M}(x)$ answers all the queries to within error*

$$\alpha = O\left(\frac{\sqrt{|\mathcal{Q}|} \cdot \log(1/\delta) \cdot \log \log |\mathcal{Q}|}{\varepsilon n}\right).$$

Again taking ε to be constant and δ to be negligible (e.g., $\delta = 2^{-\log^2(n)}$), we can take $k = |\mathcal{Q}| = \tilde{\Omega}(n)$ and obtain error $o(1/\sqrt{n})$ (smaller than the sampling error!), which we will see is essentially optimal for any reasonable notion of privacy (in Section 7.5.1). If we want error $o(1)$, we can take $k = \tilde{\Omega}(n^2)$, which is known to be optimal for differential privacy if the answers are not coordinated based on the queries [43] or if the data universe is large (as we will see in Section 7.5). However, in Section 7.4, we will see some beautiful algorithms that can answer many more than n^2 queries if the data universe is not too large (forcing the queries to have some implicit relationships) by carefully coordinating the noise between the queries.

Optimal composition. Remarkably, Kairouz, Oh, and Viswanath [64] have given an *optimal* composition theorem for differential privacy, which provides an exact characterization of the best privacy parameters that can be guaranteed when composing a number of (ε, δ)-differentially private mechanisms. The key to the proof is showing that an (ε, δ) generalization of randomized response (as defined in Section 7.1.5) is the worst mechanism for composition. Unfortunately, the resulting optimal composition bound is quite complex, and indeed is even #P-complete to compute exactly when composing mechanisms with different $(\varepsilon_i, \delta_i)$ parameters [82]. Thus, for theoretical purposes, it is still most convenient to use Lemmas 7.2.3 and 7.2.4, which give the right asymptotic behavior for most settings of parameters that tend to arise in theoretical applications.

7.2.3 Histograms

The bounds of Theorems 7.2.6 and 7.2.7 are for arbitrary, worst-case families of counting queries. For specific families of counting queries, one may be able to do much better. A trivial example is when the same query is asked many times; then we can compute just one noisy answer, adding noise $\mathrm{Lap}(1/\varepsilon)$, and give the same answer for all the queries. A more interesting example is the family $\mathcal{Q}^{\mathrm{pt}}$ of point functions on a data universe $\mathcal{X}$, as defined in Section 7.1.3. Answering all $|\mathcal{X}|$ queries in Q^{pt} (i.e., estimating the histogram of the dataset) using the above theorems would incur error at least $\sqrt{|\mathcal{X}|}/\varepsilon n$. However, it turns out that we can achieve error $O(\log|\mathcal{X}|)/\varepsilon n$.

Proposition 7.2.8 (Laplace histograms). *For every finite data universe $\mathcal{X}$, $n \in \mathbb{N}$, and $\varepsilon > 0$, there is an ε-differentially private mechanism $\mathcal{M} : \mathcal{X}^n \to \mathbb{R}^{\mathcal{X}}$ such that, on every dataset $x \in \mathcal{X}^n$, with high probability $\mathcal{M}(x)$ answers all of the counting queries in $Q^{pt}(\mathcal{X})$ to within error*

$$O\left(\frac{\log|\mathcal{X}|}{\varepsilon n}\right).$$

Proof sketch: Recall that $Q^{pt}(\mathcal{X})$ contains a query q_y for each $y \in \mathcal{X}$, where on a row $w \in \mathcal{X}$, $q_y(w)$ is 1 iff $w = y$. The mechanism $\mathcal{M}$ adds independent noise distributed according to $\text{Lap}(2/\varepsilon n)$ to the result of each query $q_y \in Q^{pt}$. This ensures that each individual noisy answer is $\varepsilon/2$-differentially private. To show that we obtain ε-differential privacy overall, the key observation is that, for two neighboring datasets x, x', there are only two queries $q_y, q_{y'} \in Q^{pt}$ on which x and x' differ (corresponding to the values that x and x' have in the row where they differ). Thus, the proof of basic composition lemma (Lemma 7.2.3) implies that $\mathcal{M}(x)$ and $\mathcal{M}(x')$ are $(2 \cdot (\varepsilon/2), 0)$-indistinguishable, as desired. ∎

We can also use the output of this mechanism to answer an arbitrary counting query $q : \mathcal{X} \to \{0, 1\}$, noting that $q(x) = \sum_{y\in\mathcal{X}} q_y(x) \cdot q(y)$. The above mechanism gives us $a_y = q_y(x) + \text{Lap}(2/\varepsilon n)$ for every $y \in \mathcal{X}$, from which we can compute the quantity $a = \sum_{y\in\mathcal{X}} a_y \cdot q(y)$, which has expectation $q(x)$ and standard deviation $O(\sqrt{|\mathcal{X}|}/\varepsilon n)$. For answering multiple queries, we can apply Chernoff/Hoeffding and union bounds,[4] yielding the following:

Theorem 7.2.9 (Arbitrary counting queries via the Laplace histogram). *For every set Q of counting queries on data universe $\mathcal{X}$, $n \in \mathbb{N}$, and $\varepsilon > 0$, there is an ε-differentially private mechanism $\mathcal{M} : \mathcal{X}^n \to \mathbb{R}^{Q}$ such that on every dataset $x \in \mathcal{X}^n$, with high probability $\mathcal{M}(x)$ answers all the queries to within error*

$$O\left(\frac{\sqrt{|\mathcal{X}| \cdot \log|Q|}}{\varepsilon n}\right).$$

Note that the dependence on $k = |Q|$ has improved from $\sqrt{k}$ obtained by advanced composition or Theorem 7.2.7 to $\sqrt{\log k}$, at the price of introducing a (rather large) dependence on $|\mathcal{X}|$. Thus, for a family Q of counting queries on data universe $\mathcal{X}$, it is

---

[4] A bit of care is needed since the $\text{Lap}(2/\varepsilon n)$ noise random variables are not bounded. This can be handled by first arguing that, with high probability, at most a $2^{-\Theta(t)}$ fraction of the noise random variables have magnitude in the range $[t/\varepsilon n, 2t/\varepsilon n)$. Then, conditioned on the magnitudes of the noise random variables (but not their signs), we can group the random variables according to their magnitudes (up to a factor of 2) and apply Hoeffding to each group separately.

better to use the Laplace histogram when $|\mathcal{X}| \ll |\mathcal{Q}|$ and it is better to use advanced composition or Theorem 7.2.7 when $|\mathcal{X}| > |\mathcal{Q}|$.

Let us summarize the best error bounds we have seen so far for the example families of counting queries given in Section 7.1.3.

Table 7.1: Error bounds for specific query families on a data universe $\mathcal{X}$ of size $D = 2^d$ (e.g., $\mathcal{X} = \{0, 1\}^d$ or $\mathcal{X} = \{1, 2, \ldots, D\}$).

Query family $\mathcal{Q}$	$|\mathcal{Q}|$	$(\varepsilon, 0)$-dp	Ref.	(ε, δ)-dp	Ref.
$\mathcal{Q}^{\text{pt}}$	D	$O\left(\frac{d}{\varepsilon n}\right)$	Prop. 7.2.8	$O\left(\frac{d}{\varepsilon n}\right)$	Prop. 7.2.8
$\mathcal{Q}^{\text{thr}}$	D	$\frac{\tilde{O}(\sqrt{D})}{\varepsilon n}$	Thm. 7.2.9	$\frac{\tilde{O}(\sqrt{D})}{\varepsilon n}$	Thm. 7.2.9
$\mathcal{Q}^{\text{conj}}$	3^d	$\frac{\tilde{O}(\sqrt{D})}{\varepsilon n}$	Thm. 7.2.9	$\frac{\tilde{O}(\sqrt{D})}{\varepsilon n}$	Thm. 7.2.9
$\mathcal{Q}^{\text{means}}$	d	$O\left(\frac{d}{\varepsilon n}\right)$	Thm. 7.2.6	$O\left(\frac{\sqrt{d \log(1/\delta)} \cdot \log \log d}{\varepsilon n}\right)$	Thm. 7.2.7
$\mathcal{Q}^{\text{conj}}_t$ for $t \ll d$	$O(d^t)$	$O\left(\frac{d^t}{\varepsilon n}\right)$	Thm. 7.2.6	$O\left(\frac{d^{t/2} \cdot \sqrt{\log(1/\delta)} \cdot \log \log d}{\varepsilon n}\right)$	Thm. 7.2.7

We will see substantial improvements to most of these bounds in later sections.

7.3 Alternatives to Global Sensitivity

In this section, we consider the question of whether we can do better than adding noise $\text{Lap}(\text{GS}_q / \varepsilon)$, where GS_q denotes the global sensitivity of query q (cf. Theorem 7.1.3).

As a first attempt, let us define a notion of "local sensitivity" at x:

$$\text{LS}_q(x) = \max \left\{ q(x) - q(x') \mid : x' \sim x \right\}.$$

The difference from global sensitivity is that we only take the maximum over datasets x' that are neighbors to our input dataset x, rather than taking the maximum over all neighboring pairs $x' \tilde{x}''$.

Naively, we might hope that $\mathcal{M}(x) = q(x) + \textit{Noise}(O(\text{LS}_q(x)))$ might provide differential privacy. Indeed, the local sensitivity provides a lower bound on the error we need to introduce:

Proposition 7.3.1 (Local sensitivity lower bound). *Let* $q : \mathcal{X}^n \to \mathbb{R}$ *be a real-valued query and* $\mathcal{M} : \mathcal{X}^n \to \mathcal{Y}$ *be an* (ε, δ)-*differentially private mechanism. Then*

1. For every $x_0 \sim x_1 \in \mathcal{X}^n$, *there is a* $b \in \{0, 1\}$ *such that*

$$\Pr\left[|\mathcal{M}(x_b) - q(x_b)| < \frac{|q(x_0) - q(x_1)|}{2}\right] \leq \frac{1 + \delta}{1 + e^{-\varepsilon}} = \frac{1}{2} + O(\delta + \varepsilon).$$

2. *For every $x \in \mathcal{X}^n$, there is some x' at Hamming distance at most 1 from x such that*

$$\Pr\left[|\mathcal{M}(x') - q(x')| < \frac{\mathrm{LS}_q(x)}{2}\right] \leq \frac{1 + \delta}{1 + e^{-\varepsilon}} = \frac{1}{2} + O(\delta + \varepsilon).$$

Proof:

1. Let $\mathcal{G}_b = \left\{ y \in \mathbb{R} : |y - q(x_b)| < \frac{|q(x_0) - q(x_1)|}{2} \right\}$ and $p = \min\{\Pr[\mathcal{M}(x_0) \in \mathcal{G}_0], \Pr[\mathcal{M}(x_1) \in \mathcal{G}_1]\}$. Then:

$$\begin{aligned}
1 - p &\geq \Pr[\mathcal{M}(x_0) \notin \mathcal{G}_0] \\
&\geq \Pr[\mathcal{M}(x_0) \in \mathcal{G}_1] \\
&\geq e^{-\varepsilon} \cdot \Pr[\mathcal{M}(x_1) \in \mathcal{G}_1] - \delta \\
&\geq e^{-\varepsilon} \cdot p - \delta.
\end{aligned}$$

Solving, we deduce that $p \leq (1 + \delta)/(1 + e^{-\varepsilon})$.

2. Follows from part 1 by taking $x_0 = x$ and $x_1 \sim x$ such that $\mathrm{LS}_q(x) = |q(x) - q(x_1)|$. ∎

The problem with trying to use the local sensitivity to calibrate the noise is that we do not want the amount of noise to itself distinguish between neighboring x and x'. For instance, let x be such that $q(x) = q(x') = 0$ for all $x' \sim x$, but where there is one such neighbor $x' \sim x$ where x' has a neighbor x'' such that $q(x'') = 10^9$. $\mathrm{LS}_q(x) = 0$, but $\mathrm{LS}_q(x')$ is large, and answering queries noisily based on LS_q would violate privacy because it distinguishes between x and x'.

Still, perhaps one could hope to provide only a small amount of noise if LS_q is small everywhere "near" x. For example, consider the query that asks for the *median* of n points $\{x_1, x_2, \ldots x_n\} \subseteq [0, 1]$. The global sensitivity for this query is high. Indeed, consider the instance x where $(n + 1)/2$ entries are 1 and $(n - 1)/2$ entries are 0 (and thus the median is 1), as compared with the neighboring instance x' where one entry is changed from 1 to 0 (and thus the median is 0).

On the other hand, if there are *many* data points near the median, then it would follow that the local sensitivity is small, not only at x but also at all datasets close to x. For such instances x, we could indeed get away with adding only a small amount of noise, while maintaining privacy. This is the type of situation that we will investigate. There are several related approaches that have been taken along these lines, which we will discuss:

1. Smooth sensitivity [86]
2. Propose–test–release [34]
3. Releasing stable values [96]
4. Privately bounding local sensitivity [68]

We remark that yet another approach, called *restricted sensitivity*, aims to add even *less* noise than the local sensitivity [12, 68, 27, 89]. The observation is that Proposition 7.3.1 does *not* say that the error on x must be at least $\mathrm{LS}_q(x)/2$; rather it says that the error must be at least $\mathrm{LS}_q(x)/2$ on x *or one of its neighbors*. Thus if we have a hypothesis that our dataset belongs to some set $H \subseteq \mathcal{X}^n$ (e.g. in the case of a social network, we might believe that the graph is of bounded degree), it might suffice to add noise proportional to the *restricted sensitivity*, where we maximize $|q(x) - q(x')|$ over $x \sim x' \in H$, which can be much smaller than even the local sensitivity. The noise will still need to be at least $\mathrm{LS}_q(x)/2$ on some neighbors x' of x, but these can be neighbors outside of H.

7.3.1 Smooth Sensitivity

Define *smooth sensitivity* of query $q : \mathcal{X}^n \to \mathbb{R}$ at x as follows:

$$\mathrm{SS}_q^\varepsilon(x) = \max\{\mathrm{LS}_q(x') \cdot e^{-\varepsilon d(x,x')} : x' \in \mathcal{X}^n\},$$

where $d(x, x')$ denotes Hamming distance. Intuitively, we are smoothing out the local sensitivity, so that it does not change much between neighboring datasets.

Nissim, Raskhodnikova, and Smith [86] introduced the notion of smooth sensitivity and showed that:

- Adding noise $O(\mathrm{SS}_q^\varepsilon(x)/\varepsilon)$ (according to a Cauchy distribution) is sufficient for ε-differential privacy.
- SS_q can be computed efficiently when q is the median query (despite the fact that it is defined as the maximum over a set of size $|\mathcal{X}|^n$), as well as for a variety of graph statistics (under edge-level differential privacy, cf. Section 7.3.4).

Zhang et al. [111] gave an alternative approach to "smoothing out" local sensitivity, which empirically provides improvements in accuracy.

7.3.2 Propose–Test–Release

A different way to provide less noise is to simply not allow certain queries. That is: rather than using Laplace noise at a level that is high enough no matter what possible dataset might be queried, an alternative is to initially *propose* an amount of noise that seems tolerable, and then *test* whether answering a query with this amount of noise would violate privacy (namely, if the noise magnitude is less than the local sensitivity in a neighborhood of the current dataset). If the test passes, then we *release* a noisy answer. But perhaps we detect that adding this (small) amount of noise *would* violate privacy. In that case, we simply refuse to answer. Of course, we should carry out the test in a differentially private manner.

More precisely, propose–test–release consists of the following three steps (parameterized by a query $q : \mathcal{X}^n \to \mathbb{R}$ and $\varepsilon, \delta, \beta \geq 0$), yielding a mechanism $\mathcal{M} : \mathcal{X}^n \to \mathbb{R} \cup \{\bot\}$ that does the following on a dataset $x \in \mathcal{X}^n$:

1. Propose a target bound β on local sensitivity.
2. Let $\hat{d} = d(x, \{x' : \mathrm{LS}_q(x') > \beta\}) + \mathrm{Lap}(1/\varepsilon)$, where d denotes Hamming distance.
3. If $\hat{d} \leq \ln(1/\delta)/\varepsilon$, output $\bot$.
4. If $\hat{d} > \ln(1/\delta)/\varepsilon$, output $q(x) + \mathrm{Lap}(\beta/\varepsilon)$.

Proposition 7.3.2 (Propose–test–release [34]). *For every query* $q : \mathcal{X}^n \to \mathbb{R}$ *and* $\varepsilon, \delta, \beta \geq 0$, *the above algorithm is* $(2\varepsilon, \delta)$-*differentially private.*

Proof: Consider any two neighboring datasets $x \sim x'$. Because of the Laplacian noise in the definition of $\hat{d}$ and the fact that Hamming distance has global sensitivity at most 1, it follows that

$$\Pr[\mathcal{M}(x) = \perp] \in [e^{-\varepsilon} \cdot \Pr[\mathcal{M}(x') = \perp], e^{\varepsilon} \cdot \Pr[\mathcal{M}(x') = \perp]]. \tag{7.3}$$

Also, for those outputs that are not $\perp$, we have two cases:

Case 1: $\mathrm{LS}_q(x) > \beta$. In this case, $d(x, \{x'' : \mathrm{LS}_q(x'') > \beta\}) = 0$, so the probability that $\hat{d}$ will exceed $\ln(1/\delta)/\varepsilon$ is at most δ. Thus, for every set $T \subseteq \mathbb{R} \cup \{\perp\}$, we have

$$\begin{aligned}
\Pr[\mathcal{M}(x) \in T] &\leq \Pr[\mathcal{M}(x) \in T \cap \{\perp\}] + \Pr[\mathcal{M}(x) \neq \perp] \\
&\leq e^{\varepsilon} \cdot \Pr[\mathcal{M}(x') \in T \cap \{\perp\}] + \delta \\
&\leq e^{\varepsilon} \cdot \Pr[\mathcal{M}(x') \in T] + \delta,
\end{aligned}$$

where the second inequality follows from (7.3), noting that $T \cap \{\perp\}$ equals either $\{\perp\}$ or $\emptyset$.

Case 2: $\mathrm{LS}_q(x) \leq \beta$. In this case, $|q(x) - q(x')| \leq \beta$, which in turn implies the $(\varepsilon, 0)$-indistinguishability of $q(x)+\mathrm{Lap}(\beta/\varepsilon)$ and $q(x')+\mathrm{Lap}(\beta/\varepsilon)$. Thus, by (7.3) and basic composition, we have $(2\varepsilon, 0)$-indistinguishability overall. ∎

Notice that, like smooth sensitivity, the naive algorithm for computing $d(x, \{x' : \mathrm{LS}_q(x') > \beta\})$ enumerates over all datasets $x' \in \mathcal{X}^n$. Nevertheless, for the median function, it can again be computed efficiently.

7.3.3 Releasing Stable Values

A special case of interest in propose–test–release is when $\beta = 0$. Then it can be verified that $d(x, \{x' : \mathrm{LS}_q(x') > \beta\}) = d(x, \{x' : q(x') \neq q(x)\}) - 1$, so the algorithm is testing whether the function q is constant in a neighborhood of x (of radius roughly $\ln(1/\delta)/\varepsilon$), and if so, it outputs q with no noise; that is, if q is stable around x, then we can safely release the value $q(x)$ (*exactly*, with no noise!), provided our test of stability is differentially private. This also applies to, and indeed makes the most sense for, discrete-valued functions $q : \mathcal{X}^n \to \mathcal{Y}$. In more detail, the mechanism works as follows on $x \in \mathcal{X}^n$:

1. Let $\hat{d} = d(x, \{x' : q(x') \neq q(x)\})+\mathrm{Lap}(1/\varepsilon)$, where d denotes Hamming distance.
2. If $\hat{d} \leq 1 + \ln(1/\delta)/\varepsilon$, output $\perp$.
3. Otherwise output $q(x)$.

Similarly to Proposition 7.3.2, we have:

Proposition 7.3.3 (Releasing stable values). *For every query* $q : \mathcal{X}^n \to \mathcal{Y}$ *and* $\varepsilon, \delta > 0$, *the above algorithm is* (ε, δ)-*differentially private.*

Consider, for example, the *mode* function $q : \mathcal{X}^n \to \mathcal{X}$, where $q(x)$ is defined to be the most frequently occurring data item in x (breaking ties arbitrarily). Then $d(x, \{x' : q(x') \neq q(x)\})$ equals half of the gap in the number of occurrences between the mode and the second most frequently occurring item (rounded up). So we have:

Proposition 7.3.4 (Stability-based mode). *For every data universe* $\mathcal{X}$, $n \in \mathbb{N}$, *and* $\varepsilon, \delta \geq 0$, *there is an* (ε, δ)-*differentially private algorithm* $\mathcal{M} : \mathcal{X}^n \rightarrow \mathcal{X}$ *such that, for every dataset* $x \in \mathcal{X}^n$ *where the difference between the number of occurrences of the mode and the second most frequently occurring item is larger than* $4\lceil \ln(1/\delta)/\varepsilon \rceil$, $\mathcal{M}(x)$ *outputs the mode of* x *with probability at least* $1 - \delta$.

If instead we had used the Laplace Histogram of Proposition 7.2.8 (outputting the bin $y \in \mathcal{X}$ with the largest noisy count), we would require a gap of $\Theta(\log|\mathcal{X}|)/\varepsilon$ in the worst case, so the stability-based method is better when $|\mathcal{X}|$ is large compared with $1/\delta$. Indeed, let us now show how stability-based ideas can in fact produce noisy histograms with an error bound of $O(\log(1/\delta))/\varepsilon n$.

Theorem 7.3.5 (Stability-based histograms [24]). *For every finite data universe* $\mathcal{X}$, $n \in \mathbb{N}$, $\varepsilon \in (0, \ln n)$, *and* $\delta \in (0, 1/n)$, *there is an* (ε, δ)-*differentially private mechanism* $\mathcal{M} : \mathcal{X}^n \rightarrow \mathbb{R}^{\mathcal{X}}$ *such that, on every dataset* $x \in \mathcal{X}^n$, *with high probability* $\mathcal{M}(x)$ *answers all of the counting queries in* $\mathcal{Q}^{pt}(\mathcal{X})$ *to within error*

$$O\left(\frac{\log(1/\delta)}{\varepsilon n}\right).$$

The intuition for the algorithm is that, if we only released noisy answers for point functions q_y that are nonzero on the dataset x, the error bound in Proposition 7.2.8 would improve from $O(\log|\mathcal{X}|)/\varepsilon n$ to $O(\log n)/\varepsilon n \leq O(\log(1/\delta))/\varepsilon n$, since at most n point functions can be nonzero on any dataset (namely those corresponding to the rows of the dataset). However, revealing which point functions are nonzero would not be differentially private. Thus, we only release the point functions that are *far* from being zero (i.e., ones where the query is nonzero on all datasets at noisy distance at most $O(\log(1/\delta)/\varepsilon)$ from the given dataset, analogously to Proposition 7.3.3).

Proof: The algorithm is the same as the Laplace histogram of Proposition 7.2.8, except that we do not add noise to counts that are zero, and reduce all noisy counts that are smaller than $O(\log(1/\delta)/\varepsilon n$ to zero.

Specifically, given a dataset $x \in \mathcal{X}^n$, the algorithm works as follows:

1. For every point $y \in \mathcal{X}$:

   a. If $q_y(x) = 0$, then set $a_y = 0$.
   b. If $q_y(x) > 0$, then:
      i. Set $a_y \leftarrow q_y(x) + \text{Lap}(2/\varepsilon n)$.
      ii. If $a_y < 2\ln(2/\delta)/\varepsilon n + 1/n$, then set $a_y \leftarrow 0$.

2. Output $(a_y)_{y \in \mathcal{X}}$.

Now let us analyze this algorithm.

Utility: The algorithm gives exact answers for queries q_y where $q_y(x) = 0$. There are at most n queries q_y with $q_y(x) > 0$ (namely, ones where $y \in \{x_1, \ldots, x_n\}$). By the tails of the Laplace distribution and a union bound, with high probability, all of the noisy answers $q_y(x) + \text{Lap}(2/\varepsilon n)$ computed in step 1(b)i have error at most

$O((\log n)/\varepsilon n) \le O(\log(1/\delta)/\varepsilon n)$. Truncating the small values to zero in step 1(b)ii introduces an additional error of up to $2\ln(1/\delta)/\varepsilon n + 1/n = O(\log(1/\delta)/\varepsilon n)$.

Privacy: Consider two neighboring datasets $x \sim x'$, where dataset x' is obtained by replacing row x_i with x_i'. Then the only point queries that differ on x and x' are q_{x_i} and $q_{x_i'}$. Since the answers to different queries q_y are independent, we can analyze the answer to each query separately and then apply composition. Consider the answers $a_{x_i}(x)$ and $a_{x_i}(x')$ to query q_{x_i} on datasets x and x', respectively. We know that $q_{x_i}(x) > 0$ (since row x_i is in x). If we also have $q_{x_i}(x') > 0$, then $a_{x_i}(x)$ and $a_{x_i}(x')$ are $(\varepsilon/2, 0)$-indistinguishable by the differential privacy of the Laplace mechanism. (We can view the truncation step as postprocessing.) If $q_{x_i}(x') = 0$, then $a_{x_i}(x')$ is always 0, and $q_{x_i}(x) = 1/n$ (since x and x' agree on all other rows), which means that $\Pr[a_{x_i}(x) \ne 0] = \Pr[\mathrm{Lap}(2/\varepsilon n) \ge 2\ln(2/\delta)/\varepsilon n] \le \delta/2$ and we have $(0, \delta/2)$-indistinguishability. Thus, in all cases, $a_{x_i}(x)$ and $a_{x_i}(x')$ are $(\varepsilon/2, \delta/2)$-indistinguishable. By symmetry the same holds for the answers $a_{x_i'}(x)$ and $a_{x_i'}(x')$. On all other queries y, $a_y(x)$ and $a_y(x')$ are identically distributed. By basic composition, the joint distributions of all answers are (ε, δ)-indistinguishable. ∎

7.3.4 Privately Bounding Local Sensitivity

Rather than *proposing* (arbitrarily) a threshold β as in propose–test–release, more generally we might try to *compute* a differentially private upper bound on the local sensitivity. That is, we will try to compute a differentially private estimate $\hat{\beta} = \hat{\beta}(x)$ such that, with probability at least $1-\delta$, $\mathrm{LS}_q(x) \le \hat{\beta}$. If we can do this, then outputting $q(x) + \mathrm{Lap}(\hat{\beta}/\varepsilon)$ will give an (ε, δ)-differentially private algorithm, by an analysis as in the previous section.

The setting in which we will explore this possibility is where our dataset is a graph and we want to estimate the number of triangles in the graph.

There are (at least) two notions of privacy that one might wish to consider for graph algorithms:

- *Edge-level privacy.* In this setting, we say that $G \sim G'$ if the graphs G and G' differ on one edge. This is a special case of the setting we have been studying, where we think of an n-vertex graph as a dataset consisting of $\binom{n}{2}$ rows from universe $\mathcal{X} = \{0, 1\}$.
- *Node-level privacy.* In this setting, we say that $G \sim G'$ if the graphs G and G' differ only on edges that are adjacent to one vertex. This does not quite fit in the tuple-dataset setting we have been studying, but the concept of differential privacy naturally generalizes to this (as well as any other family of "datasets" with some notion of "neighbors").

In applications (e.g., to social networks), node-level privacy is a preferable notion of privacy, since it simultaneously protects all of the relationships associated with a vertex (which typically represents an individual person), rather than just a single relationship at a time. However, since our goal is only to illustrate the method of privately bounding local sensitivity, we will consider only edge-level privacy. Let

$q_\Delta(G)$ be the number of triangles in G (where the Δ is meant to be evocative of a triangle). It can be verified that

$$\mathrm{LS}_{q_\Delta}(G) = \max\{j : \exists u \exists v\ u \text{ and } v \text{ have } j \text{ common neighbors}\}.$$

This, in turn, is no more than the maximum degree of G. In contrast the global sensitivity is $\mathrm{GS}_{q_\Delta} = n - 2$. However, if we consider the global sensitivity of the local sensitivity, we have $\mathrm{GS}_{\mathrm{LS}_{q_\Delta}} = 1$. (If we think of the local sensitivity as a discrete analogue of a derivative, then this is the analogue of having a bounded second derivative, despite the derivative sometimes being large.)

Consider the following mechanism $\mathcal{M}(G)$:

- Compute $\hat{\beta} = \mathrm{LS}_{q_\Delta}(G) + \mathrm{Lap}(1/\varepsilon) + \ln(1/\delta)/\varepsilon.$
- Output $q_\Delta(G) + \mathrm{Lap}(\hat{\beta}/\varepsilon).$

This mechanism can be shown to be $(2\varepsilon, \delta)$-differentially private, and the total noise is of magnitude

$$O\left(\frac{\mathrm{LS}_{q_\Delta}(G) + (1 + \log(1/\delta))/\varepsilon}{\varepsilon}\right).$$

Note that this approach is computationally efficient if we can efficiently evaluate the query q, can efficiently calculate LS_q (which can be done using $m \cdot (|\mathcal{X}| - 1)$ evaluations of q when the dataset is in $\mathcal{X}^m$), and have an upper bound on $\mathrm{GS}_{\mathrm{LS}_q}$.

7.4 Releasing Many Counting Queries with Correlated Noise

We have seen (in Theorems 7.2.6, 7.2.7, and 7.2.9) that any set $\mathcal{Q}$ of counting queries over data universe $\mathcal{X}$ can be answered with differential privacy and an error of at most

$$\alpha \le O\left(\min\left\{\frac{|\mathcal{Q}|}{\varepsilon n}, \frac{\sqrt{|\mathcal{Q}| \cdot \log(1/\delta)} \cdot \log\log|\mathcal{Q}|}{\varepsilon n}, \frac{\sqrt{|\mathcal{X}| \cdot \log|\mathcal{Q}|}}{\varepsilon n}\right\}\right)$$

on each of the queries (with high probability). When both $|\mathcal{Q}|$ and $|\mathcal{X}|$ are larger than n^2, the amount of error is larger than 1, and hence these approaches provide nothing useful (recall that the true answers lie in $[0, 1]$).

In this section, we will see two methods that can answer many more than n^2 counting queries on a data universe of size much larger than n^2. Both use ideas from learning theory.

7.4.1 The SmallDB Algorithm

Theorem 7.4.1 (The smallDB algorithm, Blum et al. [14]). *For every set $\mathcal{Q}$ of counting queries on a data universe $\mathcal{X}$ and every $\varepsilon > 0$, there exists an ε-*

differentially private mechanism $\mathcal{M}$ such that, for all datasets $x \in \mathcal{X}^n$, with high probability $\mathcal{M}(x)$ answers all queries in $\mathcal{Q}$ to within error at most

$$\alpha = O\left(\frac{\log|\mathcal{Q}|\log|\mathcal{X}|}{\varepsilon n}\right)^{1/3}.$$

Moreover, $M(x)$ outputs a "synthetic dataset" $y \in \mathcal{X}^m$ with $m = O(\log|\mathcal{Q}|/\alpha^2)$ such that, with high probability, we have $|q(y) - q(x)| \le \alpha$ for all $q \in \mathcal{Q}$, i.e., we can calculate all the answers using the (smaller) synthetic dataset.

In fact, the bounds can be improved to $\alpha = \tilde{O}(\mathrm{VC}(\mathcal{Q}) \cdot \log|\mathcal{X}|/\varepsilon n)^{1/3}$ and $m = \mathrm{VC}(\mathcal{Q}) \cdot \tilde{O}(1/\alpha^2)$, where $\mathrm{VC}(\mathcal{Q})$ is the Vapnik–Chervonenkis dimension of the class $\mathcal{Q}$.[5]

The key point is that the error grows (less than) logarithmically with the number $|\mathcal{Q}|$ of queries and the size $|\mathcal{X}|$ of the data universe; this allows us to handle even exponentially many queries. (On the other hand, the error vanishes more slowly with n than the earlier results we have seen — like $1/n^{1/3}$ rather than $1/n$.) Let us compare the implications of the smallDB algorithm for concrete query families with the bounds we saw in Section 7.2 for pure differential privacy (Table 7.1):

Table 7.2: Error bounds for specific query families under $(\varepsilon, 0)$-differential privacy on a data universe $\mathcal{X}$ of size $D = 2^d$ (e.g. $\mathcal{X} = \{0, 1\}^d$ or $\mathcal{X} = \{1, 2, \ldots, D\}$). Highlighted cells indicate the best bounds in the regime where $n \le D^{o(1)}$ or $n \le d^{o(t)}$.

Query family $\mathcal{Q}$	$|\mathcal{Q}|$	$\mathrm{VC}(\mathcal{Q})$	Previous bound	Ref.	Theorem 7.4.1
$\mathcal{Q}^{\mathrm{pt}}$	D	1	$O\left(\frac{d}{\varepsilon n}\right)$	Prop. 7.2.8	$\tilde{O}\left(\frac{d}{\varepsilon n}\right)^{1/3}$
$\mathcal{Q}^{\mathrm{thr}}$	D	1	$\frac{\tilde{O}(\sqrt{D})}{\varepsilon n}$	Thm. 7.2.9	$\tilde{O}\left(\frac{d}{\varepsilon n}\right)^{1/3}$
$\mathcal{Q}^{\mathrm{conj}}$	3^d	d	$\frac{\tilde{O}(\sqrt{D})}{\varepsilon n}$	Thm. 7.2.9	$O\left(\frac{d^2}{\varepsilon n}\right)^{1/3}$
$\mathcal{Q}^{\mathrm{means}}$	d	$\lfloor \log_2 d \rfloor$	$O\left(\frac{d}{\varepsilon n}\right)$	Thm. 7.2.6	$O\left(\frac{d\log d}{\varepsilon n}\right)^{1/3}$
$\mathcal{Q}_t^{\mathrm{conj}}$ for $t \ll d$	$O(d^t)$	$O(t\log d)$	$O\left(\frac{d}{\varepsilon n}\right)$	Thm. 7.2.6	$O\left(\frac{t\cdot d\log d}{\varepsilon n}\right)^{1/3}$

We see that there is an exponential improvement in the dependence on $D = 2^d = |\mathcal{X}|$ for the case of threshold functions and conjunctions (and similarly in the dependence on t for t-way conjunctions). In particular, we only need n to be polynomially large in the bit-length d of the rows to have vanishingly small error; in such a case, we can produce and publish a differentially private synthetic dataset that accurately summarizes exponentially many ($2^{\Theta(d)}$) statistics about the original dataset (e.g., the fractions of individuals with every combination of attributes, as in $\mathcal{Q}^{\mathrm{conj}}(d)$). It is amazing that such a rich release of statistics is compatible with strong privacy protections.

---

[5] $\mathrm{VC}(\mathcal{Q})$ is defined to be the largest number k such that there exist $x_1, \ldots, x_k \in \mathcal{X}$ for which $\{(q(x_1), \ldots, q(x_k)) : q \in \mathcal{Q}\} = \{0, 1\}^k$. Clearly, $\mathrm{VC}(\mathcal{Q}) \le \log|\mathcal{Q}|$.

These improvements also hold compared with the bounds we had for (ε, δ)-differential privacy (where the dependence on $|\mathcal{Q}|$ was only quadratically better than for pure differential privacy). On the other hand, for point functions and attribute means, our earlier bounds (even for pure differential privacy) are better than what is given by Theorem 7.4.1.

Proof of Theorem 7.4.1:   We begin by establishing the existence of at least one accurate m-row synthetic dataset y^*: Let y^* be a random sample of m rows from x, say with replacement for simplicity. By the Chernoff bound,

$$\Pr[\; \exists q \in \mathcal{Q} \text{ s.t. } |q(y^*) - q(x)| > \alpha \;)] \;\leq\; 2^{-\Omega(m\alpha^2)} \cdot |\mathcal{Q}| \;<\; 1,$$

for an appropriate choice of $m = O(\log |\mathcal{Q}|/\alpha^2)$. This is similar to "Occam's razor" arguments in computational learning theory (cf. [70]). In fact, it is known that $m = O(\text{VC}(\mathcal{Q}) \cdot \log(1/\alpha)/\alpha^2)$ suffices.

Of course, outputting a random subsample of the dataset will not be differentially private. Instead, we use (a special case of) the *exponential mechanism* of McSherry and Talwar [79]. Specifically, consider the following mechanism $\mathcal{M}(x)$:

1. For each $y \in \mathcal{X}^m$, define $\text{weight}_x(y) = \exp\left(-\varepsilon n \cdot \max_{q \in Q} |q(y) - q(x)|\right)$.
2. Output y with probability proportional to $\text{weight}_x(y)$. That is,

$$\Pr[\mathcal{M}(x) = y] = \frac{\text{weight}_x(y)}{\sum_{z \in \mathcal{X}^m} \text{weight}_x(z)}.$$

Notice that, if $x \sim x'$, then $\text{weight}_x(y)$ and $\text{weight}_{x'}(y)$ differ by a multiplicative factor of at most e^ε. That is, we smoothly vary the weight put on different synthetic datasets according to the amount of error they will give us, with low-error synthetic datasets receiving the highest weight.

Let us now formally analyze this algorithm.

Privacy: Fix $x \sim x' \in \mathcal{X}^n$, $y \in \mathcal{X}^m$. Then,

$$\Pr[\mathcal{M}(x) = y] = \frac{\text{weight}_x(y)}{\sum_{y'} \text{weight}_x(y')} \leq \frac{e^\varepsilon \cdot \text{weight}_{x'}(y)}{\sum_{y'} e^{-\varepsilon} \cdot \text{weight}_{x'}(y')} \leq e^{2\varepsilon} \cdot \Pr[M(x') = y].$$

Thus, we have 2ε-differential privacy.

Accuracy: Define an output $y \in \mathcal{X}^m$ to be β-*accurate* if $\max_{q \in \mathcal{Q}} |q(y) - q(x)| \leq \beta$. Our goal is to show that, with high probability, $\mathcal{M}(x)$ is 2α-accurate. Recall that earlier we showed that there *exists* an α-accurate output y^*. We have

$$\Pr[\mathcal{M}(x) \text{ is not } 2\alpha\text{-accurate}] = \sum_{\substack{y \in \mathcal{X}^m, \\ y \text{ not } 2\alpha\text{-accurate}}} \frac{\text{weight}_x(y)}{\sum_z \text{weight}_x(z)}$$

$$\leq \sum_{\substack{y \in \mathcal{X}^m, \\ y \text{ not } 2\alpha\text{-accurate}}} \frac{\text{weight}_x(y)}{\text{weight}_x(y^*)}$$

$$\leq |\mathcal{X}|^m \cdot \frac{\exp(-\varepsilon n \cdot 2\alpha)}{\exp(-\varepsilon n \cdot \alpha)}$$

$$\ll 1 \qquad (\text{if } \alpha\varepsilon n > 2m\log|\mathcal{X}|).$$

Recall that $m = O(\log|\mathcal{Q}|)/\alpha^2$. Solving for α gives the theorem. ∎

The exponential mechanism is quite general and powerful, and can be used to design differentially private mechanisms for sampling "good" outputs from any output space $\mathcal{Y}$. Specifically, we can replace the expression

$$-\max_{q \in Q} |q(y) - q(x)|$$

with an arbitrary "score function" $\text{score}(x, y)$ indicating how good y is as an output on dataset x, and replace the factor of n in the exponent with a bound B on the reciprocal of $\max_z \text{GS}_{\text{score}(\cdot, z)}$. That is, we obtain the following mechanism $\mathcal{M}_{\text{score},B}(x)$:

1. For each $y \in \mathcal{Y}$, define $\text{weight}_x(y) = \exp(\varepsilon \cdot \text{score}(x, y)/B)$.
2. Output y with probability proportional to $\text{weight}_x(y)$. That is,

$$\Pr[\mathcal{M}(x) = y] = \frac{\text{weight}_x(y)}{\sum_{z \in \mathcal{Y}} \text{weight}_x(z)}.$$

Similarly to the proof of Theorem 7.4.1, it can be shown that:

Proposition 7.4.2 (The exponential mechanism, McSherry and Talwar [79]).
For every function $\text{score} : \mathcal{X}^n \times \mathcal{Y} \to \mathbb{R}$ *such that* $\mathcal{Y}$ *is finite,* $\varepsilon \geq 0$, *and* $B > 0$,

1. *If* $B \geq \max_z \text{GS}_{\text{score}(\cdot, z)}$, *then the mechanism* $\mathcal{M}_{\text{score},B}$ *is* 2ε-*differentially private,* *and*
2. *For every dataset* $x \in \mathcal{X}^n$, *with high probability,* $\mathcal{M}_{\text{score},B}(x)$ *outputs* y *such that*

$$\text{score}(x, y) \geq \text{argmax}_{y^*} \text{score}(x, y^*) - O(\log|\mathcal{Y}|) \cdot B/\varepsilon.$$

The downside. While the exponential mechanism is very powerful, it can be computationally very expensive, as a direct implementation requires enumerating over all $y \in \mathcal{Y}$. Indeed, in the application of Theorem 7.4.1, the computation time is roughly

$$|\mathcal{Y}| = |\mathcal{X}|^m = \exp\left(\frac{\log|\mathcal{Q}|\log|\mathcal{X}|}{\alpha^2}\right),$$

so it is very slow. For example, we get runtime $\exp(d^2/\alpha^2)$ for the query family $\mathcal{Q}^{\text{conj}}$ of conjunctions on $\{0, 1\}^d$.

7.4.2 Private Multiplicative Weights

We now present a state-of-the-art algorithm for general queries:

Theorem 7.4.3 (Private multiplicative weights, Hardt and Rothblum [58]). *For every set Q of counting queries on a data universe $\mathcal{X}$ and every $\varepsilon, \delta > 0$, there exists an (ε, δ)-differentially private mechanism $\mathcal{M}$ such that, for all datasets $x \in \mathcal{X}^n$, with high probability $\mathcal{M}(x)$ answers all queries in Q to within error at most*

$$\alpha = O\left(\frac{\sqrt{\log |\mathcal{X}| \cdot \log(1/\delta)} \cdot \log |Q|}{\varepsilon n} \right)^{1/2}.$$

Moreover, $\mathcal{M}(x)$ can answer the queries in an online fashion (answering each query as it arrives) and runs in time $\mathrm{poly}(n, |\mathcal{X}|)$ *per query.*

The algorithm can also be modified to produce a synthetic dataset, though we will not show this here.

Note that the error vanishes more quickly with n than in Theorem 7.4.1 (as $1/n^{1/2}$ rather than $1/n^{1/3}$), and the $\log |\mathcal{X}|$ has been replaced by $\sqrt{\log |\mathcal{X}| \cdot \log(1/\delta)}$. Comparing with the results we have seen for our example query families, we have

Table 7.3: Error bounds for specific query families under (ε, δ)-differential privacy on a data universe $\mathcal{X}$ of size $D = 2^d$ (e.g., $\mathcal{X} = \{0, 1\}^d$ or $\mathcal{X} = \{1, 2, \ldots, D\}$). Highlighted cells indicate the best bounds in the regime where $n \leq D^{o(1)}$ or $n \leq d^{o(t)}$ and $\delta \geq 2^{-\mathrm{polylog}(n)}$. In the case of incomparable bounds, both are highlighted.

Query family Q	Sect. 7.2	Ref.	Thm. 7.4.1	Thm. 7.4.3
Q^{pt}	$O\left(\frac{d}{\varepsilon n}\right)$	Prop. 7.2.8		$O\left(\frac{d^{3/2} \cdot \sqrt{\log(1/\delta)}}{\varepsilon n}\right)^{1/2}$
Q^{thr}	$\frac{\tilde{O}(\sqrt{D})}{\varepsilon n}$	Thm. 7.2.9	$\tilde{O}\left(\frac{d}{\varepsilon n}\right)^{1/3}$	$O\left(\frac{d^{3/2} \cdot \sqrt{\log(1/\delta)}}{\varepsilon n}\right)^{1/2}$
Q^{conj}	$\frac{\tilde{O}(2^{d/2})}{\varepsilon n}$	Thm. 7.2.9	$O\left(\frac{d^2}{\varepsilon n}\right)^{1/3}$	$O\left(\frac{d^{3/2} \cdot \sqrt{\log(1/\delta)}}{\varepsilon n}\right)^{1/2}$
Q^{means}	$O\left(\frac{\sqrt{d \log(1/\delta)} \cdot \log \log d}{\varepsilon n}\right)$	Thm. 7.2.7		$O\left(\frac{\sqrt{d \log(1/\delta)} \cdot \log \log d}{\varepsilon n}\right)^{1/2}$
Q^{conj}_t for $t \ll d$	$O\left(\frac{d^{t/2} \cdot \sqrt{\log(1/\delta)} \cdot \log \log d}{\varepsilon n}\right)$	Thm. 7.2.7	$O\left(\frac{t \cdot d \log d}{\varepsilon n}\right)^{1/3}$	$O\left(\frac{t \log d \sqrt{d \log(1/\delta)}}{\varepsilon n}\right)^{1/2}$

For Q^{conj} and Q^{conj}_t, we obtain a saving in the dependence on $|\mathcal{X}| = 2^d$. In particular, for answering all conjunctions on $\{0, 1\}^d$ with error tending to zero, we only need $n = \omega(d^{3/2} \cdot \sqrt{\log(1/\delta)}/\varepsilon)$ rather than $n = \omega(d^2/\varepsilon)$ as in Theorem 7.4.1. The running time has improved too, but is still at least $|\mathcal{X}| \cdot |Q|$, which is exponential in d. (Of course, in this generality, one needs $|\mathcal{X}| \cdot |Q|$ bits to specify an arbitrary set of counting queries on $\{0, 1\}^d$.)

Proof: The algorithm views the dataset x as a distribution on types $r \in \mathcal{X}$:

$$x(r) = \frac{\#\{i \in [n] : x_i = r\}}{n}.$$

Then,

$$q(x) = \mathop{E}_{r \leftarrow x} [q(r)].$$

The algorithm will maintain a distribution h on $\mathcal{X}$, some hypothesis for what the data distribution is. It will try to answer queries with h, and update h when it leads to too much error. It will turn out that only a small number of updates are needed, and this will imply that the overall privacy loss is small. Here are the details:

1. INITIALIZE the hypothesis h to the uniform distribution on $\mathcal{X}$.
2. REPEAT at most $O(\log |\mathcal{X}|)/\alpha^2$ times (outer loop)
   a. RANDOMIZE the accuracy threshold: $\hat{\alpha} = \alpha/2 + \mathrm{Lap}(1/\varepsilon_0 n)$, where ε_0 is a parameter that will be set later in the proof.
   b. REPEAT (inner loop)
      i. Receive next query q.
      ii. If $|q(x) - q(h)| + \mathrm{Lap}(1/\varepsilon_0 n) < \hat{\alpha}$, then output $a = q(h)$ and CONTINUE inner loop. Otherwise, output $a = q(x) + \mathrm{Lap}(1/\varepsilon_0 n)$ (with fresh noise) and EXIT inner loop.
   c. UPDATE the hypothesis h:
      i. Reweight using query q: $\forall w \in \mathcal{X} \ g(w) = \begin{cases} h(w)\mathrm{e}^{(\alpha/8)\cdot q(w)} & \text{if } a > q(h), \\ h(w)\mathrm{e}^{-(\alpha/8)\cdot q(w)} & \text{if } a < q(h). \end{cases}$
      ii. Renormalize: $\forall w \in \mathcal{X} \ h(w) = \dfrac{g(w)}{\sum_{v \in \mathcal{X}} g(v)}.$
   d. CONTINUE outer loop.

Utility analysis: By the exponentially vanishing tails of the Laplace distribution, with high probability none of the (at most $3|\mathcal{Q}|$) samples from $\mathrm{Lap}(1/\varepsilon_0 n)$ used in steps 2a and 2(b)ii has magnitude larger than

$$O\left(\frac{\log |\mathcal{Q}|}{\varepsilon_0 n}\right) \leq \frac{\alpha}{8},$$

provided we set $\varepsilon_0 \geq c \log |\mathcal{Q}|/\alpha n$ for a sufficiently large constant c. By the triangle inequality, this implies that all answers that we provide are within $\pm 3\alpha/4$ of $q(x)$.

Now, we must show that the mechanism will not stop early.

Claim 7.4.4. *Assuming all the samples from* $\mathrm{Lap}(1/\varepsilon_0 n)$ *have magnitude at most* $\alpha/8$, *the outer loop cannot exceed its budget of* $O(\log |\mathcal{X}|)/\alpha^2$ *iterations.*

Proof sketch: We use the Kullback–Leibler divergence $D(x\|h)$ as a potential function. At the start, h is the uniform distribution on $|\mathcal{X}|$, so

$$D(x\|h) = \log |\mathcal{X}| - H(x) \leq \log |\mathcal{X}|,$$

where $H(x)$ is the Shannon entropy of the distribution x. Suppose that, in some iteration, we do an update (i.e., reweight and renormalize) to go from hypothesis h

to hypothesis h'. Since all the noise samples have magnitude at most $\alpha/8$, we must have $|q(x) - q(h)| \geq \alpha/4$ in order to do an update, and in this case $b - q(h)$ has the same sign as $q(x) - q(h)$. By a tedious but standard calculation (used in typical analyses of the multiplicative weights method), this implies that

$$D(x\|h') \leq D(x\|h) - \Omega(\alpha^2).$$

Since divergence is always nonnegative, we can have at most $\log|\mathcal{X}|/\Omega(\alpha^2)$ updates. ∎

Privacy analysis: The mechanism takes a dataset x and outputs a sequence $(a_1,\ldots,a_k)$ of noisy answers to a sequence of queries $(q_1,\ldots,q_k)$ (which we will treat as fixed in this analysis). Note that the output $(a_1,\ldots,a_k)$ is determined by the sequence $(b_1,\ldots,b_k)$ where $b_i = \perp$ if there is no update on query q_i and $b_i = a_i$ otherwise. (This information suffices to maintain the hypothesis h used by the algorithm, as the update to h done in step 2c depends only on the current query q_i and the noisy answer $a_i = b_i$.) Thus, by closure under postprocessing (Lemma 7.2.1), it suffices to show that the mechanism that outputs the sequence $(b_1,\ldots,b_k)$ is (ε,δ)-differentially private. This mechanism, in turn, is obtained by (adaptively) composing $O(\log|\mathcal{X}|)/\alpha^2$ submechanisms, each corresponding to one execution of the outer loop. Specifically, each such submechanism is parameterized by the output of the previous submechanisms, which is of the form $(b_1,\ldots,b_{i-1})$ with $b_{i-1} \neq \perp$, and produces the output $(b_i,\ldots,b_j)$ corresponding to one more execution of the outer loop — so $b_i = b_{i+1} = \cdots = b_{j-1} = \perp$ and $b_j \neq \perp$ (unless $j = k$, in which case we may also have $b_j = \perp$).

We will argue below that each such submechanism is $4\varepsilon_0$-differentially private (even though the number of queries it answers can be unbounded). Given this claim, we can apply advanced composition to deduce that the overall mechanism satisfies (ε,δ)-differential privacy for

$$\varepsilon = O\left(\sqrt{\frac{\log|\mathcal{X}|\log(1/\delta)}{\alpha^2}} \cdot \varepsilon_0\right).$$

Substituting $\varepsilon_0 = c\log|\mathcal{Q}|/\alpha n$ (as needed in the utility analysis above) and solving for α yields the theorem.

So now we turn to analyzing a submechanism $\mathcal{M}$ corresponding to a single execution of the outer loop (after a fixed prior history $(b_1,\ldots,b_{i-1})$). Since it suffices to verify pure differential privacy with respect to singleton outputs, it suffices to show that, for every hypothesis h (determined by the prior history $(b_1,\ldots,b_{i-1})$) and every possible output sequence $b = (b_i,\ldots,b_j)$ with $b_i = b_{i+1} = \cdots = b_{j-1} = \perp$, the following mechanism $\mathcal{M}_{h,b}(x)$, which tests whether the output of the next iteration of the outer loop is b, is $4\varepsilon_0$-differentially private:

1. SAMPLE $v_\alpha, v_i, v_{i+1}, \ldots, v_j, v_a \leftarrow \mathrm{Lap}(1/\varepsilon_0 n)$. (Making all random choices at start.)
2. RANDOMIZE the accuracy threshold: $\hat{\alpha} = \alpha/2 + v_\alpha$.

3. REPEAT for $t = i$ to j (inner loop)

    a. Receive next query q_t.

    b. If $b_t = \perp$ and $|q_t(x) - q_t(h)| + v_t \geq \hat{\alpha}$, then HALT and OUTPUT 0.

    c. If $b_t \neq \perp$ (which implies $t = j$), then:

        i. If $|q_t(x) - q_t(h)| + v_t < \hat{\alpha}$, HALT and OUTPUT 0.

        ii. If $q_t(x) + v_a \neq b_j$, HALT and OUTPUT 0.

4. OUTPUT 1 (if we have not halted with output 0 so far).

Let us consider the case when $b_j \neq \perp$; the case when $b_j = \perp$ is similar but simpler. We will argue $4\varepsilon_0$-differential privacy even when $v_i, v_{i+1}, \ldots, v_{j-1}$ are fixed to arbitrary values (so the only randomness is from v_α, v_j, v_a); averaging over these independent random variables will preserve differential privacy.

To show this, we will show that we can compute the output of $\mathcal{M}_{h,b}$ from the composition of three algorithms, which are ε_0-, $2\varepsilon_0$-, and ε_0-differentially private, respectively.

To determine whether we ever halt and output 0 in step 3b it suffices to calculate

$$\beta = \hat{\alpha} - \max_{i \leq t < j}(|q_t(x) - q_t(h)| + v_t) = \alpha/2 + v_\alpha - \max_{i \leq t < j}(|q_t(x) - q_t(h)| + v_t).$$

We halt and output 0 in one of the executions of step 3b iff $\beta \leq 0$. The calculation of β is ε_0-differentially private by the Laplace mechanism because $\alpha/2 - \max_{i \leq t < j}(|q_t(x) - q_t(h)| + v_t)$ has sensitivity at most $1/n$ as a function of the dataset x (recalling that h and the v_t's for $i \leq t < j$ are all fixed) and v_α is distributed according to $\mathrm{Lap}(1/\varepsilon_0 n)$. This argument is the key to why the private multiplicative weights can answer so many queries—we are only paying once for privacy despite the fact that this condition involves an unbounded number of queries.

Given β, to determine whether or not we halt and output 0 in step 3(c)i, it suffices to test whether $|q_j(x) - q_j(h)| + v_j \geq \hat{\alpha} = \beta + \max_{i \leq t < j}(|q_t(x) - q_t(h)| + v_t)$. This is $2\varepsilon_0$-differentially private by the Laplace mechanism because $|q_j(x) - q_j(h)| - \beta - \max_{i \leq t < j}(|q_t(x) - q_t(h)| + v_t)$ has sensitivity at most $2/n$ as a function of x and v_j is independently distributed according to $\mathrm{Lap}(1/\varepsilon_0 n)$.

Finally, step 3(c)ii is ε_0-differentially private by the Laplace mechanism (with fresh randomness v_a). ∎

Remark 7.4.5.

- *The hypothesis h maintained by the private multiplicative weights algorithm can be thought of as a fractional version of a synthetic dataset. Indeed, with a bit more work it can be ensured that at the end of the algorithm, we have $|q(h) - q(x)| \leq \alpha$ for all $q \in \mathcal{Q}$. Finally, random sampling from the distribution h can be used to obtain a true, integral synthetic dataset $y \in \mathcal{X}^m$ of size $m = O(\log |\mathcal{Q}|/\alpha^2)$ just like in Theorem 7.4.1.*

- *The algorithm works in an online fashion, meaning that it can answer query q_i without knowing the future queries $q_{i+1}, q_{i+2}, \ldots$. However, if all queries are given simultaneously, the algorithm can be sped up by using the exponential* *mechanism (Proposition 7.4.2) to identify queries that will generate an update (rather than wasting time on queries that do not generate an update) [61].*

7.5 Information-Theoretic Lower Bounds

In the previous section, we have seen differentially private algorithms that can answer many counting queries with good accuracy. Now we turn to lower bounds, with the goal of showing that these algorithms are nearly optimal in terms of the number of queries and accuracy they can achieve. These lower bounds will be information-theoretic, meaning that they apply regardless of the computational resources of the mechanism $\mathcal{M}$.

7.5.1 Reconstruction Attacks and Discrepancy

7.5.1.1 Reconstruction

We begin by defining a very weak standard for privacy, namely, avoiding an attack that reconstructs almost all of the dataset:

Definition 7.5.1 (Blatant nonprivacy, Dinur and Nissim [31]). *A mechanism $\mathcal{M} : \mathcal{X}^n \to \mathcal{Y}$ is called* blatantly nonprivate *if, for every $x \in \mathcal{X}^n$, one can use $\mathcal{M}(x)$ to compute an $x' \in \mathcal{X}^n$, such that x' and x differ in at most $n/10$ coordinates (with high probability over the randomness of $\mathcal{M}$).*

It can be shown that a mechanism that is $(1, 0.1)$-differentially private cannot be blatantly nonprivate (if $|\mathcal{X}| > 1$). Indeed, if we run an (ε, δ)-differentially private mechanism $\mathcal{M}$ on a uniformly random dataset $X \leftarrow \mathcal{X}^n$, then the expected fraction of rows that any adversary can reconstruct is at most $e^{\varepsilon}/|\mathcal{X}| + \delta$ (since if we replace any row X_i with an independent row X'_i, $\mathcal{M}(X_{-i}, X'_i)$ reveals no information about X_i and thus does not allow for reconstructing X_i with probability larger than $1/|\mathcal{X}|$).

We now give some fundamental lower bounds, due to Dinur and Nissim [31], on the tradeoff between the error and the number of counting queries that can be answered while avoiding blatant nonprivacy. These lower bounds predate, and indeed inspired, the development of differential privacy.

Let $\mathcal{X} = \{0, 1\}$. Then a dataset of n people is simply a vector $x \in \{0, 1\}^n$. We will consider (normalized) *inner-product queries* specified by a vector $q \in \{0, 1\}^n$: the intended answer to the query q is $\langle q, x \rangle / n \in [0, 1]$. Think of the bits in x as specifying a sensitive attribute of the n members of the dataset and q as specifying a subset of the population according to some publicly known demographics. Then $\langle q, x \rangle / n$ measures the correlation between the specified demographic traits and the sensitive attribute.

These are not exactly counting queries, but they can be transformed into counting queries as follows: Let $\tilde{\mathcal{X}} = [n] \times \{0, 1\}$ be our data universe, map an inner-product query $q \in \{0, 1\}^n$ to the counting query $\tilde{q}((i, b)) = q_i \cdot b$, and consider datasets of the form $\tilde{x} = ((1, x_1), (2, x_2), \ldots, (n, x_n))$, $\tilde{q}((i, b)) = q_i \cdot b$. Then $\tilde{q}(\tilde{x}) = \langle q, x \rangle / n$, and reconstructing x is equivalent to reconstructing $\tilde{x}$, which again contradicts $(1, 0.1)$-differential privacy.

Theorem 7.5.2 (Reconstruction from many queries with large error [31]). *Let* $x \in \{0, 1\}^n$. *If we are given, for each* $q \in \{0, 1\}^n$, *a value* $y_q \in \mathbb{R}$ *such that*

$$\left| y_q - \frac{\langle q, x \rangle}{n} \right| \le \alpha,$$

then one can use the y_q's *to compute* $x' \in \{0, 1\}^n$ *such that* x *and* x' *differ in at most* 4α *fraction of coordinates.*

Corollary 7.5.3. *If* $\mathcal{M}(x)$ *is a mechanism that outputs values* y_q *as above with* $\alpha \le 1/40$, *then* $\mathcal{M}$ *is blatantly nonprivate.*

Thus at least $\Omega(1)$ additive error is needed for privately answering all 2^n normalized inner-product queries, which as noted correspond to 2^n counting queries on a data universe of size $2n$.

The smallDB mechanism (Theorem 7.4.1) can answer $\exp(\tilde{\Omega}(n))$ counting queries over a data universe $\mathcal{X}$ with ε-differential privacy and error α provided $|\mathcal{X}| \le \exp(\text{polylog}(n))$ and $\varepsilon, \alpha \ge 1/\text{polylog}(n)$. Corollary 7.5.3 says that we cannot push this further to answer 2^n queries.

Proof of Theorem 7.5.2: Pick any $x' \in \{0, 1\}^n$ such that, for all $q \in \{0, 1\}^n$,

$$\left| y_q - \frac{\langle q, x' \rangle}{n} \right| \le \alpha.$$

(We know that at least one such x' exists, namely x.)

We need to prove that x and x' differ on at most a 4α fraction of coordinates. Let $q_1 = x$ and let q_0 be the bitwise complement of x. Then, the relative Hamming distance between x and x' equals

$$
\begin{aligned}
\frac{d(x, x')}{n} &= \frac{|\langle q_0, x \rangle - \langle q_0, x' \rangle| + |\langle q_1, x \rangle - \langle q_1, x' \rangle|}{n} \\
&\le \left| \frac{\langle q_0, x \rangle}{n} - y_{q_0} \right| + \left| y_{q_0} - \frac{\langle q_0, x' \rangle}{n} \right| + \left| \frac{\langle q_1, x \rangle}{n} - y_{q_1} \right| + \left| y_{q_1} - \frac{\langle q_1, x' \rangle}{n} \right| \\
&\le 4 \cdot \alpha.
\end{aligned}
$$

∎

Of course we can avoid the above attack by restricting the adversary to fewer than 2^n queries. The next theorem will say that, even for much fewer queries (indeed $O(n)$ queries), we must incur a significant amount of error, $\alpha \ge \Omega(1/\sqrt{n})$. This is tight, matching Theorem 7.2.7 up to a factor of $O(\sqrt{\log(1/\delta)} \cdot \log\log n)$. We will in fact study the more general question of what additive error is needed for privately answering any set $\mathcal{Q}$ of counting queries.

Let $q_1, \ldots, q_k \in \{0, 1\}^n$ be a collection of vectors, which we view as specifying inner-product queries $\langle q, x \rangle / n$ as above. Suppose we have a mechanism $\mathcal{M}$

that answers these queries to within error α, i.e., with high probability outputs $y_1, \ldots, y_k \in [0, 1]$ with

$$\left| y_j - \frac{\langle q_j, x \rangle}{n} \right| \leq \alpha.$$

Let us try to show that $\mathcal{M}$ is blatantly nonprivate. Our privacy-breaking strategy is the same: take any $x' \in \{0, 1\}^n$ with

$$\left| y_j - \frac{\langle q_j, x' \rangle}{n} \right| \leq \alpha$$

for each j.

Then, by the triangle inequality, we have $|\langle q_j, x - x' \rangle|/n \leq 2\alpha$ for all $j = 1, \ldots, k$. For blatant nonprivacy, we want to use this to deduce that x and x' have Hamming distance at most $n/10$, i.e., $\|x - x'\|_1 \leq n/10$. Suppose not. Let $z = x - x'$. Let $\mathcal{Q}$ denote the $k \times n$ matrix whose rows are the q_j. Thus, we have

1. z is a $\{0, +1, -1\}$ vector with $\|z\|_1 > n/10$,
2. $\|\mathcal{Q}z\|_\infty \leq 2\alpha n$.

Thus, we have a contradiction (and hence can conclude that $\mathcal{M}$ is blatantly nonprivate) if the partial discrepancy of $\mathcal{Q}$, defined as follows, is larger than $2\alpha n$:

Definition 7.5.4 ((Partial) discrepancy). *For a $k \times n$ matrix $\mathcal{Q}$, we define its* discrepancy $\mathsf{Disc}(\mathcal{Q})$ *and its partial discrepancy* $\mathsf{PDisc}(\mathcal{Q})$ *as*

$$\mathsf{Disc}(\mathcal{Q}) = \min_{z \in \{\pm 1\}^n} \|\mathcal{Q}z\|_\infty, \text{ and}$$
$$\mathsf{PDisc}(\mathcal{Q}) = \min_{\substack{z \in \{0, +1, -1\}^n, \\ \|z\|_1 > n/10}} \|\mathcal{Q}z\|_\infty.$$

The qualifier "partial" refers to the fact that we allow up to 90% of z's coordinates to be zero, in contrast to ordinary discrepancy which only considers vectors $z \in \{\pm 1\}^n$. A more combinatorial perspective comes if we think of the rows of $\mathcal{Q}$ as characteristic vectors of subsets of $\mathcal{X}$, and z as a partial ± 1-coloring of the elements of $\mathcal{X}$. Then $\|\mathcal{Q}z\|_\infty$ measures the largest imbalance in coloring over all the sets in $\mathcal{Q}$, and $\mathsf{PDisc}(\mathcal{Q})$ refers to minimizing this maximum imbalance over all partial colorings z.

Summarizing the discussion before Definition 7.5.4, we have:

Theorem 7.5.5 (Reconstruction via partial discrepancy). *Let $q_1, \ldots, q_k \in \{0, 1\}^n$ and $\mathcal{Q}$ be the $k \times n$ matrix whose rows are the q_j's. Then any mechanism $\mathcal{M}$: $\{0, 1\}^n \to \mathbb{R}^k$ that answers all of the normalized inner-product queries specified by $q_1, \ldots, q_k$ to within additive error α smaller than $\mathsf{PDisc}(\mathcal{Q})/2n$ is blatantly nonprivate.*

We note that Theorem 7.5.5 is a generalization of Theorem 7.5.2. Indeed, if $\mathcal{Q}$ is the $2^n \times n$ matrix whose rows are all bitstrings of length n (i.e., the family of all subsets of $[n]$), then the partial discrepancy of $\mathcal{Q}$ is greater than $n/20$. (For a partial coloring z with greater than $n/10$ nonzero entries, either the set of coordinates on which z is 1 or the set of coordinates on which z is -1 will have imbalance greater than $n/20$.)

Let us now use Theorem 7.5.5 to deduce the second theorem of Dinur and Nissim [31].

Theorem 7.5.6 (Reconstruction from few queries with small error [31]). *There exists $c > 0$ and $q_1, \ldots, q_n \in \{0, 1\}^n$ such that any mechanism that answers the normalized inner-product queries specified by $q_1, \ldots, q_n$ to within error at most $c/\sqrt{n}$ is blatantly nonprivate.*

In fact, the theorem holds for a random set of queries, as follows from combining the following lemma (setting $k = s = n$) with Theorem 7.5.5:

Lemma 7.5.7 (Discrepancy of a random matrix). *For all integers $k \geq s \geq 0$, with high probability, a $k \times s$ matrix Q with uniform and independent entries from $\{0, 1\}$ has partial discrepancy at least*

$$\Omega\left(\min\left\{\sqrt{s \cdot (1 + \log(k/s))}, s\right\}\right).$$

Up to the hidden constant, this is the largest possible discrepancy for a $k \times s$ matrix. Indeed, a random coloring achieves discrepancy at most $O(\sqrt{s} \cdot \log k)$ (by a Chernoff bound and union bound). The celebrated "six standard deviations suffice" result of Spencer [97] improves the $\log k$ to $\log(k/s)$.

Proof sketch: Pick the rows $q_1, \ldots, q_k \in \{0, 1\}^s$ uniformly at random. Fix $z \in \{0, +1, -1\}^s$ with $\|z\|_1 > s/10$. Then for each j, $\langle q_j, z \rangle$ is a difference of two binomial distributions, at least one of which is the sum of more than $s/20$ independent, unbiased $\{0, 1\}$ random variables (since z has more than $s/20$ coordinates that are all 1 or all -1). By anticoncentration of the binomial distribution (cf. [76, Prop. 7.3.2]), we have for every $t \geq 0$

$$\Pr_{q_j}\left[|\langle q_j, z \rangle| \geq \min\{t\sqrt{s}, s/20\}\right] \geq \max\left\{1 - O(t), \Omega\left(e^{-O(t^2)}\right)\right\}.$$

Thus, for each z we have

$$\Pr\left[\forall j \in [k], |\langle q_j, z \rangle| < \min\{t\sqrt{s}, s/20\}\right] \leq \min\left\{O(t), 1 - \Omega\left(e^{-O(t^2)}\right)\right\}^k.$$

By a union bound, we have

$$\Pr\left[\exists z \in \{-1, 0, +1\}^s : \|z\|_1 > s/10 \text{ and } \forall j \in [k], |\langle q_j, z \rangle| < \min\{t\sqrt{s}, s/20\}\right]$$
$$< 3^s \cdot \min\left\{O(t), 1 - \Omega\left(e^{-O(t^2)}\right)\right\}^k.$$

We now choose t to ensure that this probability is small. For every $k \geq s$, taking t to be a small enough constant suffices to ensure that $3^s \cdot O(t)^k \ll 1$. However, once k/s is sufficiently large, we can take a larger value of t (corresponding to higher discrepancy) if we use the other term in the min. Specifically, we can take $t = c\sqrt{\log(ck/s)}$ for a sufficiently small constant c, and obtain

$$3^s \cdot \left(1 - \Omega\left(e^{-O(t^2)}\right)\right)^k \le 3^s \cdot \left(1 - \Omega\left(\frac{s}{ck}\right)\right)^k = 3^s \cdot e^{-\Omega(s/c)} \ll 1.$$

In all cases, we can take $t = \Omega\left(\sqrt{1 + \log(k/s)}\right)$, as needed for the lemma. ∎

The reconstruction attacks we gave in the proof of the above theorems take time more than 2^n, because they require searching for a vector $x' \in \{0,1\}^n$ such that

$$\forall j \left| y_j - \frac{\langle q_j, x' \rangle}{n} \right| \le \alpha. \tag{7.4}$$

However, it is known how to obtain a polynomial-time reconstruction attack for certain query families. In particular, a polynomial-time analogue of Theorem 7.5.6 can be obtained by using a linear program to efficiently find a *fractional* vector $x' \in [0,1]^n$ satisfying Condition (7.4) and then rounding x' to an integer vector. To show that this attack works, we need to lower-bound the fractional analogue of partial discrepancy, namely

$$\inf_{\substack{z \in [-1,1]^n, \\ \|z\|_1 > n/10}} \|Qz\|_\infty,$$

which again can be shown to be $\Omega(\sqrt{n})$ for a random $n \times n$ matrix Q, as well as for some explicit constructions [37].

One can consider a relaxed notion of accuracy, where the mechanism is only required to give answers with at most $c/\sqrt{n}$ additive error for 51% of the queries, and for the remaining 49% it is free to make arbitrary error. Even such a mechanism can be shown to be blatantly nonprivate. If one wants this theorem with a polynomial-time privacy-breaking algorithm, then this can also be done with the 51% replaced by about 77%. (This is a theorem of Dwork, McSherry, and Talwar [39], and is based on connections to compressed sensing.)

7.5.1.2 Discrepancy Characterizations of Error for Counting Queries

We now work towards characterizing the error required for differential privacy for answering a given set of counting queries. Let $q_1, \ldots, q_k \in \{0,1\}^{\mathcal{X}}$ be a given set of *counting queries* over a data universe $\mathcal{X}$ (viewed as vectors of length $|\mathcal{X}|$). We will abuse notation and use Q to denote both the set $\{q_1, \ldots, q_k\}$ of counting queries as well as the $k \times |\mathcal{X}|$ matrix whose rows are the q_j. For a set $S \subseteq \mathcal{X}$, we let Q_S denote the restriction of Q to the columns of S.

Then we have:

Theorem 7.5.8 (Partial discrepancy lower bound). *Let $Q = \{q : \mathcal{X} \to \{0,1\}\}$ be a set of counting queries over data universe $\mathcal{X}$, and let $\mathcal{M} : \mathcal{X}^n \to \mathbb{R}^Q$ be a $(1, 0.1)$-differentially private mechanism that with high probability answers every query in Q with error at most α. Then*

$$\alpha \ge \max_{\substack{S \subseteq \mathcal{X}, |S| \le 2n \\ |S| \text{ even}}} \mathrm{PDisc}(Q_S)/2n.$$

Proof sketch: Suppose for contradiction that $\alpha < \mathsf{PDisc}(\mathcal{Q}_S)/2n$ for some set S of size at most $2n$. Let us restrict attention to datasets x of the following form: the first $|S|/2$ rows of x, denoted y, consist of $|S|/2$ distinct elements of S, and the rest are fixed to an arbitrary value $w \in \mathcal{X}$. Then for a counting query $q : \mathcal{X} \to \{0, 1\}$, we have

$$q(x) = \frac{\langle q_S, \chi(y) \rangle + (n - |S|/2) \cdot q(w)}{n},$$

where $q_S \in \{0, 1\}^S$ is the vector $(q(s))_{s \in S}$ (one of the rows in $\mathcal{Q}_S$) and $\chi(y) \in \{0, 1\}^S$ is the characteristic vector of y (i.e., the indicator of which elements of S are in y). Thus, an estimate of $q(x)$ to within additive error at most α yields an estimate of the normalized inner product $\langle q_S, \chi(y) \rangle / |S|$ to within additive error $\alpha n/|S| < \mathsf{PDisc}(\mathcal{Q}_S)/2$. If we have such estimates for every query $q \in \mathcal{Q}$, then by Theorem 7.5.5, we can reconstruct at least 90% of the coordinates of the characteristic vector $\chi(y)$, which can be shown to contradict $(1, 0.1)$-differential privacy. ∎

If we do not fix n but require the error to scale linearly with n, then this lower bound can be phrased in terms of *hereditary partial discrepancy*, which is defined to be

$$\mathsf{HerPDisc}(\mathcal{Q}) \stackrel{\text{def}}{=} \max_{S \subseteq \mathcal{X}} \mathsf{PDisc}(\mathcal{Q}_S).$$

In this language, we have the theorem of Muthukrishnan and Nikolov [83]:

Theorem 7.5.9 (Hereditary discrepancy lower bound [83]). *For every set $\mathcal{Q} = \{q : \mathcal{X} \to \{0, 1\}\}$ of counting queries over data universe $\mathcal{X}$, the following holds for all sufficiently large n (in particular for all $n \geq |\mathcal{X}|/2$): Let $\mathcal{M} : \mathcal{X}^n \to \mathbb{R}^{\mathcal{Q}}$ be a $(1, 0.1)$-differentially private mechanism that with high probability answers every query in $\mathcal{Q}$ with error at most α. Then*

$$\alpha \geq (\mathsf{HerPDisc}(\mathcal{Q}) - 1)/2n.$$

(We subtract 1 from the hereditary partial discrepancy to compensate for the fact it removes the constraint that $|S|$ is even from Theorem 7.5.8.) Put differently, the hereditary partial discrepancy is a lower bound on the non-normalized error (αn) needed to answer the queries with differential privacy (for sufficiently large n). Remarkably, Nikolov, Talwar, and Zhang [85] showed that this bound is nearly tight:

Theorem 7.5.10 (Hereditary discrepancy upper bound [85]). *For every set $\mathcal{Q} = \{q : \mathcal{X} \to \{0, 1\}\}$ of counting queries over data universe $\mathcal{X}$, every $\varepsilon, \delta > 0$, and $n \in \mathbb{N}$, there is an (ε, δ)-differentially private mechanism $\mathcal{M} : \mathcal{X}^n \to \mathbb{R}^{\mathcal{Q}}$ that answers every query in $\mathcal{Q}$ with error*

$$\alpha \leq \frac{\mathsf{HerPDisc}(\mathcal{Q}) \cdot \mathrm{polylog}(|\mathcal{Q}|) \cdot \sqrt{\log(1/\delta)}}{\varepsilon n}$$

with high probability.

We will not prove the latter theorem, but will get a taste of its techniques in Section 7.7.3. We note that the distinction between partial discrepancy and ordinary discrepancy becomes less significant once we move to the hereditary versions. Indeed, if we define $\mathsf{HerDisc}(Q) \stackrel{\text{def}}{=} \max_{S \subseteq \mathcal{X}} \mathsf{Disc}(Q_S)$, then it is known that

$$\mathsf{HerPDisc}(Q) \leq \mathsf{HerDisc}(Q) \leq \mathsf{HerPDisc}(Q) \cdot O(\min\{\log|\mathcal{X}|, \log|Q|\}). \quad (7.5)$$

(See the book by Matoušek [75] for proofs.) Hereditary discrepancy is a well-studied concept in combinatorics, and a remarkable byproduct of the aforementioned work on differential privacy was a polylogarithmic approximation algorithm for hereditary discrepancy, solving a long-standing open problem [85].

7.5.1.3 Discrepancy Lower Bounds for Specific Query Families

Note that Theorems 7.5.9 and 7.5.10 only provide a nearly tight characterization in case we look for error bounds of the form $f(Q)/n$, which scale linearly with n (ignoring the dependence on ε and $\log(1/\delta)$ for this discussion). In particular, the lower bound of Theorem 7.5.9 only says that $\mathsf{HerPDisc}(Q)$ is a lower bound on the function $f(Q)$ *for sufficiently large n*. If our dataset size n is below the point at which this lower bound kicks in, we may be able to achieve significantly smaller error.

For finite dataset sizes n, we can use the lower bound of Theorem 7.5.8:

$$\alpha \geq \max_{\substack{S \subseteq \mathcal{X}, |S| \leq 2n \\ |S| \text{ even}}} \mathsf{PDisc}(Q_S)/2n.$$

Unfortunately, partial discrepancy is a combinatorially complex quantity, and can be hard to estimate. Fortunately, there are several relaxations of it that can be easier to estimate and thereby prove lower bounds:

Proposition 7.5.11. *Let Q be a $k \times |\mathcal{X}|$ query matrix (with $\{0, 1\}$ entries). Then:*

1. For every $S \subseteq \mathcal{X}$ and $T \subseteq [k]$, we have

$$\mathsf{PDisc}(Q_S)) > \frac{1}{10}\sqrt{\frac{|S|}{|T|}} \cdot \sigma_{\min}(Q_S^T),$$

where Q_S^T denotes the $|T| \times |S|$ submatrix of Q_S with rows indexed by T, and $\sigma_{\min}(Q_S^T)$ denotes the smallest singular value of Q_S^T.

2.

$$\max_{\substack{S \subseteq \mathcal{X}, |S| \leq 2n \\ |S| \text{ even}}} \mathsf{PDisc}(Q_S) > \frac{\min\{VC(Q) - 1, 2n\}}{20}.$$

Proof:

1. We have

$$\mathrm{PDisc}(\mathcal{Q}_S) \geq \mathrm{PDisc}(\mathcal{Q}_S^T)$$

$$= \min_{\substack{z \in \{-1,1\}^{|S|}, \\ \|z\|_1 > |S|/10}} \|\mathcal{Q}_S^T z\|_\infty$$

$$> \inf_{z \neq 0} \frac{\|\mathcal{Q}_S^T z\|_\infty}{\|z\|_1 \cdot 10/|S|}$$

$$\geq \inf_{z \neq 0} \frac{\|\mathcal{Q}_S^T z\|_2 / \sqrt{|T|}}{(\|z\|_2 \cdot \sqrt{|S|}) \cdot 10/|S|}$$

$$= \frac{1}{10} \sqrt{\frac{|S|}{|T|}} \cdot \sigma_{\min}(\mathcal{Q}_S^T).$$

2. By definition of VC dimension, there is an even-sized set S of at least $\min\{(\mathrm{VC}(\mathcal{Q}) - 1, 2n\}$ columns for which the rows of $\mathcal{Q}_S$ contain all 2^k binary strings of length k. The partial discrepancy of this set of vectors is thus greater than $k/20$.

∎

Combining Proposition 7.5.11 with Theorem 7.5.8, we obtain lower bounds on the error α needed by differentially private mechanisms in terms of least singular values of submatrices $\mathcal{Q}_S^T$ and in terms of the VC dimension $\mathrm{VC}(\mathcal{Q})$. The lower bound on error in terms of least singular values is due to Kasiviswanathan et al. [66], and the lower bound on error in terms of VC dimension is due to Blum et al. [14]. An advantage of using the singular-value relaxation in place of partial discrepancy is that it allows for a polynomial-time reconstruction attack, similarly to the discussion after the proof of Theorem 7.5.6. The attack based on VC dimension is based on brute-force enumeration, just like Theorem 7.5.2, but the search space is of size $2^{\mathrm{VC}(\mathcal{Q})} \leq |\mathcal{Q}|$.

Recall that the largest possible discrepancy among $k \times s$ matrices (with $k \geq s$) is achieved (up to constant factors) by a random matrix, with the bound stated in Lemma 7.5.7. To apply this for lower bounds on differentially private release of counting queries, we can take $\mathcal{Q}$ to be a family of k random counting queries over a data universe $\mathcal{X}$, and $S \subseteq \mathcal{X}$ to be an arbitrary subset of size $s = \min\{|\mathcal{Q}|, |\mathcal{X}|, n\}$. Then $\mathcal{Q}_S$ is a random matrix, and combining Lemma 7.5.7 and Theorem 7.5.8, we obtain:

Theorem 7.5.12 (Largest possible discrepancy lower bound). *For every data universe $\mathcal{X}$ and $n, k \in \mathbb{N}$, there is a family of k counting queries $\mathcal{Q}$ over $\mathcal{X}$ such that, if $\mathcal{M} : \mathcal{X}^n \to \mathbb{R}^{\mathcal{Q}}$ is a $(1, 0.1)$-differentially private mechanism that with high probability answers every query in $\mathcal{Q}$ with error at most α, we have*

$$\alpha \geq \Omega \left(\min \left\{ \frac{\sqrt{|\mathcal{Q}|}}{n}, \frac{\sqrt{|\mathcal{X}| \cdot (1 + \log(|\mathcal{Q}|/|\mathcal{X}|))}}{n}, \sqrt{\frac{\log(|\mathcal{Q}|/n)}{n}}, 1 \right\} \right).$$

Let us compare this with the upper bounds that we have for (ε, δ)-differential privacy given by Theorems 7.2.7, 7.2.9, and 7.4.3. For every family of counting queries, choosing the best of these algorithms will give an error bound of

$$\alpha \leq O\left(\min\left\{\frac{\sqrt{|\mathcal{Q}| \cdot \log(1/\delta)} \cdot \log\log|\mathcal{Q}|}{\varepsilon n}, \frac{\sqrt{|\mathcal{X}|} \cdot \log|\mathcal{Q}|}{\varepsilon n}, \sqrt{\frac{\sqrt{\log|\mathcal{X}|} \cdot \log(1/\delta)} \cdot \log|\mathcal{Q}|}{\varepsilon n}}, 1\right\}\right).$$

Ignoring factors of $\log(1/\delta)$ and $1/\varepsilon$, the first two bounds nearly match the first two lower bounds of Theorem 7.5.12. The third bound, however, differs by the $\sqrt{\log|\mathcal{X}|}$ factor that appears in the error bound of private multiplicative weights but does not appear in the lower bound (which leaves open the possibility of having vanishingly small error whenever $|\mathcal{Q}| \leq f(n)$ for some $f(n) = \exp(\tilde{\Omega}(n))$, independent of the size of the data universe). In Section 7.5.3, we will see different lower-bound techniques that can yield this $\sqrt{\log|\mathcal{X}|}$ factor.

Let us now turn to the concrete families of counting queries from Section 7.1.3:

- **Point functions** ($\mathcal{Q}^{\mathrm{pt}}$): Here $\mathsf{PDisc}(\mathcal{Q}_S) = 1$ for every S (since all the sets are of size 1), so we do not obtain any interesting lower bound.
- **Threshold functions** ($\mathcal{Q}^{\mathrm{thr}}$): Here also $\mathsf{PDisc}(\mathcal{Q}_S) = 1$ for every S, because if we write $S = \{s_1 < s_2 < \cdots < s_t\}$ and color s_j according to the parity of j, every subset of S defined by a threshold function (i.e., every prefix of S) has imbalance at most 1.
- **Attribute means on** $\{0,1\}^d$ ($\mathcal{Q}^{\mathrm{means}}(d)$): Here we can analyze $\mathsf{PDisc}(\mathcal{Q}_S)$ for a uniformly random subset $S \subseteq \{0,1\}^d$ of size $s = \min\{n, d\}$. Then $\mathcal{Q}_S$ is statistically close to a uniformly random $\{0,1\}$ matrix of size $d \times s$, which by Lemma 7.5.7, has partial discrepancy $\Omega\left(\sqrt{s \cdot (1 + \log(d/s))}\right)$ with high probability. So when $d < n$, we have an error lower bound of $\Omega\left(\sqrt{d}/n\right)$, which is nearly tight, matching the upper bound of Theorem 7.2.7 up to a factor of $\sqrt{\log(1/\delta)} \cdot \log\log d/\varepsilon$. But when $d > n$, the lower bound is no better than $\Omega\left(\sqrt{(\log d)/n}\right)$, which leaves quite a large gap from the upper bound, which remains $O\left(\sqrt{d \cdot \log(1/\delta) \log\log d}/\varepsilon\right)$. In particular, the upper bound is useless when $d = \omega(n^2)$, but the lower bound leaves open the possibility of having vanishingly small error for any $d = 2^{o(n)}$.
- **t-way conjunctions on** $\{0,1\}^d$ ($\mathcal{Q}_t^{\mathrm{conj}}(d)$): The VC dimension of this class is at least $t \cdot \lfloor \log(d/t) \rfloor$, so we have an error lower bound of $\Omega(\min\{t\log(d/t)/n, 1\})$. For $t = O(1)$, Kasiviswanathan et al. [66] showed that, for the subset $T \subset \mathcal{Q}_t^{\mathrm{conj}}(d)$ consisting of the $\binom{d}{t}$ monotone conjunctions (without negations), if we pick a random set S of size $\min\{n, d^t/\operatorname{polylog}(d)\}$, we have $\sigma_{\min}(\mathcal{Q}_S^T) \geq \Omega(d^{t/2}/\operatorname{polylog}(n))$ with high probability. Consequently, we have

$$\mathsf{PDisc}(\mathcal{Q}_S) \geq \frac{1}{10} \cdot \sqrt{\frac{|S|}{\binom{d}{t}}} \cdot \Omega\left(\frac{d^{t/2}}{\operatorname{polylog}(n)}\right) = \tilde{\Omega}\left(\sqrt{\min\{n, d^t\}}\right).$$

When $n > d^t$, we get an error bound of $\alpha \geq \tilde{\Omega}(d^{t/2})/n$, which is tight up to polylogarithmic factors, but when $n = o(d^t)$, we are again quite far from the upper bounds of Theorem 7.2.7.

- **All conjunctions on** $\{0, 1\}^d$ ($\mathcal{Q}^{\text{conj}}(d)$): The VC dimension of this class is at least d, yielding an error lower bound of $\Omega(\min\{d/n, 1\})$. Matoušek et al. [77] showed that the hereditary discrepancy of $\mathcal{Q} = \mathcal{Q}^{\text{conj}}(d)$ is $\tilde{\Theta}((2/\sqrt{3})^d)$ and thus the same is also true for the partial hereditary discrepancy (by Inequality (7.5)). To use Theorem 7.5.8 when $n < 2^{d-1}$, we can restrict attention to the first $d' = \lfloor \log_2 n \rfloor$ variables, and obtain

$$\max_{\substack{S \subseteq \mathcal{X}, |S| \leq 2n \\ |S| \text{ even}}} \text{PDisc}(\mathcal{Q}_S) \geq \tilde{\Omega}\left(\min\left\{\left(\frac{2}{\sqrt{3}}\right)^d, \left(\frac{2}{\sqrt{3}}\right)^{d'}\right\}\right) \geq \tilde{\Omega}\left(\min\left\{2^{0.21d}, n^{0.21}\right\}\right).$$

This yields an error lower bound of

$$\alpha \geq \tilde{\Omega}\left(\min\left\{\frac{2^{0.21d}}{n}, \frac{1}{n^{0.79}}\right\}\right).$$

By the hereditary discrepancy upper bound (Theorem 7.5.10), there is an algorithm that achieves error $\alpha \leq \frac{\tilde{O}((2/\sqrt{3})^d) \cdot \sqrt{\log(1/\delta)}}{\varepsilon n} \approx \frac{2^{0.21d} \cdot \sqrt{\log(1/\delta)}}{\varepsilon n}$, so the bounds are nearly matching when $n \gg 2^{0.21d}$. But when $n = 2^{o(d)}$, the lower bound of $1/n^{0.79}$ is quite far from the upper bound of $O(d^{3/2} \sqrt{\log(1/\delta)}/\varepsilon n)^{1/2}$ given by private multiplicative weights (Theorem 7.4.3).

Table 7.4 summarizes these lower bounds and compares them with the upper bounds we have seen.

Table 7.4: Error bounds for specific query families under (ε, δ)-differential privacy on a data universe $\mathcal{X}$ of size $D = 2^d$ (e.g., $\mathcal{X} = \{0, 1\}^d$ or $\mathcal{X} = \{1, 2, \ldots, D\}$). Lower bounds apply for $(1, 0.1)$-differential privacy.

Query family $\mathcal{Q}$	Upper bounds	Ref.	Lower bounds from Thm. 7.5.8
$\mathcal{Q}^{\text{means}}$	$O\left(\frac{\sqrt{d\log(1/\delta)} \cdot \log\log d}{\varepsilon n}\right)$	Thm. 7.2.7	$\Omega\left(\frac{\sqrt{d}}{n}\right)$ if $d \leq n$
			$\Omega\left(\sqrt{\frac{1+\log(d/n)}{n}}\right)$ if $d > n$
$\mathcal{Q}_t^{\text{conj}}, t \ll d$	$O\left(\frac{d^{t/2} \cdot \sqrt{\log(1/\delta)} \cdot \log\log d}{\varepsilon n}\right)$	Thm. 7.2.7	$\min\left\{\frac{\tilde{\Omega}(d^{t/2})}{n}, \tilde{\Omega}\left(\frac{1}{\sqrt{n}}\right)\right\}$ if $t = O(1)$
	$O\left(\frac{t\log d \sqrt{d\log(1/\delta)}}{\varepsilon n}\right)^{1/2}$	Thm. 7.4.3	$\Omega\left(\min\left\{\frac{t\log(d/t)}{n}, 1\right\}\right)$
$\mathcal{Q}^{\text{conj}}$	$\frac{\tilde{O}(2^{0.21d})}{n}$	Thm. 7.5.10	$\min\left\{\frac{\tilde{\Omega}(2^{0.21d})}{\varepsilon n}, \tilde{\Omega}\left(\frac{1}{n^{0.79}}\right)\right\}$
	$O\left(\frac{d^{3/2} \cdot \sqrt{\log(1/\delta)}}{\varepsilon n}\right)^{1/2}$	Thm. 7.4.3	$\Omega\left(\min\left\{\frac{d}{n}, 1\right\}\right)$

7.5.2 Packing Lower Bounds

We will now see a geometric approach to lower bounds that often gives tight lower bounds on $(\varepsilon, 0)$-differential privacy, and can separate it from (ε, δ)-differential privacy. In particular, we will prove that answering k arbitrary counting queries with $(\varepsilon, 0)$-differential privacy requires an error of $\alpha \geq \Omega(k/\varepsilon n)$, whereas we saw in Theorem 7.2.7 that we can achieve error $O(\sqrt{k} \cdot \log(1/\delta)/\varepsilon n)$ with (ε, δ)-differential privacy.

The approach is not specific to counting queries, and can be applied to virtually any computational problem that we might try to solve with differential privacy. Suppose that, for every dataset $x \in \mathcal{X}^n$, we have a set $\mathcal{G}_x \subseteq \mathcal{Y}$ of outputs that are "good" for x. Then the lower bound says that, if we have a "large" collection of datasets x such that the sets $\mathcal{G}_x$ are disjoint, then any $(\varepsilon, 0)$-differentially private mechanism must fail to produce a good output with high probability on at least one of the datasets in this collection.

Theorem 7.5.13 (Packing lower bound [59, 10]). *Let $C \subseteq \mathcal{X}^n$ be a collection of datasets all at Hamming distance at most m from some fixed dataset $x_0 \in \mathcal{X}^n$, and let $\{\mathcal{G}_x\}_{x \in C}$ be a collection of* disjoint *subsets of $\mathcal{Y}$. If there is an (ε, δ)-differentially private mechanism $\mathcal{M} : \mathcal{X}^n \rightarrow \mathcal{Y}$ such that $\Pr[\mathcal{M}(x) \in \mathcal{G}_x] \geq p$ for every $x \in C$, then*

$$\frac{1}{|C|} \geq p \cdot e^{-m \cdot \varepsilon} - \delta.$$

In particular, when $p = 1/2$ and $\delta = 0$, we have $|C| \leq 2 \cdot e^{m\varepsilon}$.

Proof: By group privacy (Lemma 7.2.2), for every $x \in C$, we have

$$\Pr[\mathcal{M}(x_0) \in \mathcal{G}_x] \geq p \cdot e^{-m\varepsilon} - m\delta.$$

Since the sets $\mathcal{G}_x$ are disjoint, we have

$$1 \geq \Pr\left[\mathcal{M}(x_0) \in \bigcup_{x \in C} \mathcal{G}_x\right]$$

$$= \sum_{x \in C} \Pr[\mathcal{M}(x_0) \in \mathcal{G}_x]$$

$$\geq |C| \cdot (p \cdot e^{-m\varepsilon} - m\delta).$$

$\blacksquare$

Note that, when $\delta = 0$, the theorem (setting $m = n$) says that we can only have roughly $e^{\varepsilon n} \ll |\mathcal{X}|^n$ datasets on which a differentially private mechanism's behavior is really distinct.

But for $\delta > 0$, the theorem says nothing when $m > \ln(1/\delta)/\varepsilon$ (because $p \cdot e^{-m\varepsilon} - m\delta < 0$). The reason is the use of group privacy (Lemma 7.2.2), which tells us nothing when considering datasets that are at distance larger than $\ln(1/\delta)/\varepsilon$.

Let us now see how packing implies a lower bound of $\Omega(\min\{\log|\mathcal{X}|, \log(1/\delta)\}/\varepsilon n)$ for nonredundant classes of counting queries, namely ones where all elements of the data universe are distinguishable by the queries.

Theorem 7.5.14 (Packing lower bound for nonredundant queries). *Let* $\mathcal{Q} = \{q : \mathcal{X} \to \{0,1\}\}$ *be any class of counting queries that distinguish all the elements of* $\mathcal{X}$. *That is, for all* $w \neq w' \in \mathcal{X}$, *there is a query* $q \in \mathcal{Q}$ *such that* $q(w) \neq q(w')$. *Suppose* $\mathcal{M} : \mathcal{X}^n \to \mathbb{R}^{\mathcal{Q}}$ *is an* (ε, δ)-differentially private mechanism that with high probability answers every query in $\mathcal{Q}$ with error at most α. Then*

$$\alpha \geq \min\left\{\Omega\left(\frac{\log|\mathcal{X}|}{\varepsilon n}\right), \Omega\left(\frac{\log(1/\delta)}{\varepsilon n}\right), \frac{1}{2}\right\}.$$

Note that an error bound of $1/2$ is achievable by the trivial $(0,0)$-differentially private algorithm that answers $1/2$ for all queries.

The hypothesis holds for all of the concrete query families we have considered (point functions, threshold functions, attribute means, and t-way conjunctions). In particular, for the class of point functions $\mathcal{Q}^{\text{pt}}(\{0,1\}^d)$, the lower bound of $\alpha \geq \Omega(\min\{d/\varepsilon n, \log(1/\delta)/\varepsilon n\})$ is tight, matched by Proposition 7.2.8 and Theorem 7.3.5 (which algorithm is better depends on whether d or $\log(1/\delta)$ is larger). In particular, this shows that approximate differential privacy can achieve smaller error (namely $\tilde{O}(\sqrt{d}) \cdot \sqrt{\log(1/\delta)}/\varepsilon n$) than is possible with pure differential privacy when $\log(1/\delta) < d/\text{polylog}(d)$.

For attribute means over $\{0,1\}^d$ (i.e., $\mathcal{Q}^{\text{means}}(d)$), we obtain a tight lower bound of $\Omega(d/\varepsilon n)$ when $\delta = 0$, which matches the upper bound for arbitrary sets of $k = d$ counting queries given by Theorem 7.2.6. By Theorem 7.2.7, approximate differential privacy can achieve asymptotically smaller error when $k > \log(1/\delta)$.

Proof: For a dataset $x \in \mathcal{X}^n$, let $\mathcal{G}_x$ be the closed ℓ_∞ ball of radius α around the vector $(q(x))_{q \in \mathcal{Q}}$. The assumption about $\mathcal{M}$ implies that, for every dataset $x \in \mathcal{X}^n$, we have $\Pr[\mathcal{M}(x) \in \mathcal{G}_x] \geq 1/2$.

We will now construct a set $\mathcal{C}$ of $|\mathcal{X}|$ datasets for which the $\mathcal{G}_x$'s are disjoint. Specifically, for each $w \in \mathcal{X}$, let $x(w) \in \mathcal{X}^n$ be the dataset whose first $m = \lfloor 2\alpha n + 1 \rfloor$ rows are all equal to w, and whose remaining $n - m$ rows are all equal to w_0 for a fixed element $w_0 \in \mathcal{X}$. We will take $\mathcal{C} = \{x(w) : w \in \mathcal{X}\}$. To see that $\mathcal{G}_{x(w)}$ and $\mathcal{G}_{x(w')}$ are disjoint for every $w \neq w'$, let q be a query such that $q(w) \neq q(w')$ (which exists by hypothesis). Then $|q(x(w)) - q(x(w'))| = m/n > 2\alpha$. The datasets in $\mathcal{C}$ are all at distance at most m from the dataset $x(w_0)$. Thus by Theorem 7.5.13, we deduce that

$$\frac{1}{|\mathcal{X}|} \geq e^{-\varepsilon m}/2 - \delta,$$

which implies that either $\delta \geq e^{-\varepsilon m}/4$, in which case $\alpha \geq \Omega(\ln(1/\delta)/\varepsilon n)$, or $1/|\mathcal{X}| \geq e^{-\varepsilon m}/4$, in which case $\alpha \geq \Omega(\log|\mathcal{X}|/\varepsilon n)$.   ∎

Now, let us see how the packing lower bound can be applied to arbitrary sets $\mathcal{Q}$ of counting queries to obtain tight bounds on the *sample complexity*—how large n

needs to be to achieve an arbitrarily small, but constant error α—with the matching upper bound coming from an instantiation of the exponential mechanism.

To formalize this, let $\mathcal{X}$ be our data universe, and consider the $|\mathcal{X}|$ vectors in $\mathbb{R}^{\mathcal{Q}}$ corresponding to the tuples of answers that can be achieved on individual elements on $\mathcal{X}$; that is, for each $w \in \mathcal{X}$, let $a_w = (q(w))_{q \in \mathcal{Q}}$. Now, following Hardt and Talwar [59], we consider the convex body $K = \text{ConvexHull}(\{a_w : w \in \mathcal{X}\})$ that is the convex hull of all of these vectors. Notice that, for any dataset $x \in \mathcal{X}$, the tuple of answers on x is $a_x = (1/n) \sum_{i=1}^{n} a_{x_i} \in K$.

Define the *packing number* $P_\alpha(K)$ to be the largest number of points we can fit in K such that all the pairwise ℓ_∞ distances are greater than α. (That is, the closed ℓ_∞ balls of radius $\alpha/2$ centered at the points are disjoint. But we do not require that the balls themselves are entirely contained within K; this notion of packing is sometimes referred to as *metric entropy*.)

Theorem 7.5.15 (Packing characterization of sample complexity).

1. *For all sufficiently small $\beta > 0$, there is an $\alpha > 0$ such that the following holds for all sets $\mathcal{Q} = \{q : \mathcal{X} \to \{0, 1\}\}$ of counting queries, $n \in \mathbb{N}$, and $\varepsilon \in (0, 1)$: If $\mathcal{M} : \mathcal{X}^n \to \mathbb{R}^{\mathcal{Q}}$ is an $(\varepsilon, 0)$-differentially private mechanism that, on every dataset $x \in \mathcal{X}^n$, answers all of the queries in $\mathcal{Q}$ to within error at most α with high probability, then*

$$n \geq \frac{\log(P_\beta(K))}{\beta \varepsilon},$$

   where K is the convex body corresponding to $\mathcal{Q}$ as defined above.

2. *For every $\alpha > 0$, there is a $\beta > 0$ such that the following holds for all sets $\mathcal{Q} = \{q : \mathcal{X} \to \{0, 1\}\}$ of counting queries, $n \in \mathbb{N}$, and $\varepsilon \in (0, 1)$: If*

$$n \geq \frac{\log(P_\beta(K))}{\beta \varepsilon},$$

   where K is the convex body corresponding to $\mathcal{Q}$, then there is an $(\varepsilon, 0)$-differentially private mechanism that, on every dataset $x \in \mathcal{X}^n$, answers all of the queries in $\mathcal{Q}$ to within error at most α with high probability.

Thus, to achieve error $\alpha = o(1)$, it is necessary and sufficient to have $n = \omega(P_{o(1)}(K))$. The above theorem is based on ideas from [93, Lecture 6].[6]

Proof:

1. Let $M = P_\beta(K)$ and let $a_1, \ldots, a_M$ be the corresponding points in K, all at pairwise ℓ_∞ distance greater than β.

   Our first step will be to approximate the points a_j by points $a_{y^{(j)}}$ for datasets of size $m = \beta n/2$, so that $\|a_j - a_{y^{(j)}}\|_\infty \leq \beta/3$. The definition of K tells us that, for

---

[6] In [93, Lecture 6], the bounds are stated in terms of the discrete set of points $K_n = \{a_x : x \in \mathcal{X}^n\}$ rather than the convex body K. An advantage of Theorem 7.5.15 is that the set K does not depend on n (since we are trying to characterize n in terms of it), but the formulation in [93] has the advantage of applying even to arbitrary low-sensitivity families (rather than just counting or statistical queries).

each point a_j there is a distribution D_j on $\mathcal{X}$ such that $a_j = \mathbb{E}_{w \leftarrow D_j}[a_w]$, where $a_w = (q(w))_{q \in \mathcal{Q}}$ is the vertex of K corresponding to the answers on $w \in \mathcal{X}$. We will probabilistically construct the dataset $y^{(j)} \in \mathcal{X}^m$ by randomly sampling m rows according to D_j. As mentioned in the proof of Theorem 7.4.1, if $m \geq O(\mathrm{VC}(\mathcal{Q}) \cdot \log(1/\beta)/\beta^2)$, then standard results in learning theory show that with high probability we have $\|a_j - a_{y^{(j)}}\|_\infty \leq \beta/3$, as desired. By Proposition 7.5.11 and Theorem 7.5.8, we know that $n \geq \Omega(\mathrm{VC}(\mathcal{Q})/\alpha)$ (for sufficiently small α), and thus $m = \beta n/2 \geq \Omega(\beta \mathrm{VC}(\mathcal{Q})/\alpha)$. Thus we can take α small enough (depending on β), to ensure that we have $m \geq O(\mathrm{VC}(\mathcal{Q}) \cdot \log(1/\beta)/\beta^2)$ as needed.

Given the datasets $y^{(j)} \in \mathcal{X}^m$, observe that the points $a_{y^{(j)}}$ are at pairwise distance greater than $\beta - 2\beta/3 = \beta/3$ (by the triangle inequality). Now we construct datasets $x^{(j)} \in \mathcal{X}^n$ of size n by padding the $y^{(j)}$'s with $n - m$ copies of a fixed row w from $\mathcal{X}$; the points $a_{x^{(j)}}$ are now at pairwise distance greater than $(m/n) \cdot (\beta/3) = \beta^2/6$. So if for every $x \in \mathcal{X}^n$, we take the set $\mathcal{G}_x$ to be a closed ℓ_∞ ball of radius $\beta^2/12$, then the sets $\{\mathcal{G}_{x^{(j)}}\}_{1 \leq j \leq M}$ are disjoint. Moreover we can take $\alpha \leq \beta^2/12$, and then the α-accuracy hypothesis on $\mathcal{M}$ says that, for every $x \in \mathcal{X}^n$, $\Pr[\mathcal{M}(x) \in \mathcal{G}_x] \geq 1/2$.

So all the conditions of Theorem 7.5.13 are satisfied (with $p = 1/2$, $\delta = 0$) and we obtain

$$2^{(\log e) \cdot (\beta n/2) \cdot \varepsilon} = e^{m \cdot \varepsilon} \geq \frac{M}{2} \geq M^{(\log e)/2},$$

where the latter inequality uses $M \geq 1/(2\beta) \geq 2^{3.6} \geq 2^{1/(1 - (\log e)/2)}$ for any $\mathcal{Q}$ containing a nonconstant query and sufficiently small β. This implies that $n \geq \log(P_\beta(K)/\beta\varepsilon$, as desired.

2. Let $M = P_\beta(K)$, and let $a_1, \ldots, a_M$ be the corresponding points in K all at pairwise distance greater than β from each other. By the maximality of the packing, every point in K is at ℓ_∞ distance at most β from at least one of the a_i's (otherwise we could add the point to obtain a larger packing).[7] On a dataset $x \in \mathcal{X}^n$, we will use the exponential mechanism (Proposition 7.4.2) to sample a point a_j that is close to a_x in ℓ_∞ distance, in a manner similar to Theorem 7.4.1. Specifically,

$$\mathcal{M}(x) : \text{output } a_j \text{ with probability} \propto e^{-\varepsilon n \cdot \|a_j - a_x\|_\infty}.$$

Indeed, Theorem 7.4.1 is a special case of this mechanism where we take the a_j's to be the answer vectors a_y that we get from small datasets $y \in \mathcal{X}^m$. By Proposition 7.4.2 (with $\mathrm{score}(x, a_j) = -\|a_j - a_x\|_\infty$), this mechanism is 2ε-differentially private, and achieves error at most $\beta + O(\log M)/\varepsilon n$ with high probability. Thus, if $n \geq (\log M)/\beta(2\varepsilon)$ and β is sufficiently small (depending on α), we obtain error at most α with high probability.

∎

Note that there is a significant loss in the dependence on the error α in the proofs, so this theorem does not determine the rate at which we can get the error to decay

---

[7] In other words $\{a_1, \ldots, a_M\}$ form a β-net of K with respect to ℓ_∞ norm.

as a function of the other parameters (for example, whether we can get it to decay linearly in n or $\sqrt{n}$). If we work with ℓ_2 rather than ℓ_∞ error, then tighter characterizations of the rate of error decay are known (up to factors $\text{polylog}(|\mathcal{Q}|,|\mathcal{X}|)$), by applying more sophisticated geometric methods to the convex body K [59, 11, 85].

7.5.3 Fingerprinting Lower Bounds

The lower bounds from Sections 7.5.1 and 7.5.2 above address two extreme ranges of δ. Reconstruction attacks prove lower bounds even for constant δ (e.g., $\delta = .1$), and packing (mainly) proves lower bounds for $\delta = 0$. Recall that, for satisfactory privacy guarantees, the desired range of δ is that it should be cryptographically negligible, i.e., $\delta = n^{-\omega(1)}$, as (ε, δ)-differential privacy allows for leaking each row with probability δ. In particular, when $\delta \geq 1/n$, we can output a subsample consisting of a δ fraction of the rows of the dataset, which in turns allows for answering any family $\mathcal{Q}$ of counting queries to within accuracy $\alpha = O\left(\sqrt{(\log|\mathcal{Q}|)/\delta n}\right)$ (by a Chernoff Bound). (When δ is constant, this matches the best lower bound we can get from discrepancy in the regime where $n \ll \min\{|\mathcal{Q}|, |\mathcal{X}|\}$, cf. Theorem 7.5.12.) Thus, to prove lower bounds of the form $\alpha = \Omega(1)$, we need to focus on the regime $\delta \leq O(\log|\mathcal{Q}|)/n$.

It turns out that a very well-suited tool for this task is *fingerprinting codes*, which were developed in the cryptography literature by Boneh and Shaw [15] for a completely different task. Specifically, they were designed for preventing piracy of digital content. Imagine a digital movie distribution company that wants to deliver copies of a movie to n different customers, and the company wants to mark each copy so that, if one of the customers or a coalition S of the customers released a pirated copy of the movie created from their own copies, the distribution company would be able to point a finger at one of the pirates in S. There are d scenes in the movie, and each of them can be watermarked by either 0 or 1 (say by choosing one of two slightly different angles from which the movie was shot). The colluding pirates may splice their copies to evade detection. The fingerprinting code should help protect the movie by specifying for each scene and each customer whether it should be watermarked by 0 or 1. An associated tracing algorithm should determine one of the colluding pirates with high probability from the code and a pirated copy.

Definition 7.5.16 (Fingerprinting codes, syntax). *A fingerprinting code of length $d = d(n)$ for n users consists of two randomized algorithms:*

1. *A generating algorithm* Gen *that takes the number n of users and produces an $n \times d$ binary fingerprinting matrix C where $C_{i,j} \in \{0, 1\}$ determines the watermark of customer i in scene j along with a tracing key tk. (It turns out that without loss of generality we can take tk = C.)*

2. *A tracing algorithm* Trace *that takes as input the tracing key tk and watermarks $w \in \{0, 1\}^d$ from a potentially pirated movie and outputs an element of $[n] \cup \{\bot\}$ (which we interpret as an accused customer or "fail").*

For a generating matrix C and a coalition $S \subseteq \{1,\ldots,n\}$, we say that $w \in \{0, 1\}^d$ is *feasible for S* if, for every $j \in \{1,\ldots,d\}$, w_j equals to $c_{i,j}$ for some $i \in S$. Put differently, if C_S, the submatrix of C consisting of the rows in S, is constant on value b_j on some column j, then we require that $w_j = b_j$. This captures the constraint that the coalition produces its pirated movie by splicing its copies together.

That is, a coalition S can deploy an arbitrary (randomized) pirating algorithm $\mathcal{P}$: $\{0, 1\}^{|S| \times d} \to \{0, 1\}^d$ that takes as its input C_S for a generating matrix C and produces a watermark sequence w that is feasible for S. (So we will require security even against pirates who are able to determine the watermarks in their movie copies.)

Definition 7.5.17 (Fingerprinting codes, security). *A fingerprinting code* (Gen, Trace) *is secure if, for every n, every $S \subseteq \{1, \ldots, n\}$ and every randomized pirating algorithm $\mathcal{P}$: $\{0, 1\}^{|S| \times d} \to \{0, 1\}^d$, we have*

$$\Pr_{\substack{C \leftarrow \mathsf{Gen}(1^n) \\ w \leftarrow P(C_S)}} [w \text{ is feasible for } C \text{ and } S, \text{ and } \mathsf{Trace}(C, w) \notin S] \le \mathrm{neg}(n).$$

(Recall that $\mathrm{neg}(n)$ denotes a negligible probability, i.e., $n^{-\omega(1)}$.)

An optimal construction of fingerprinting codes was given by Tardos [101]:

Theorem 7.5.18 (Optimal fingerprinting codes [101]). *For every n, there is a fingerprinting code of length $d = \tilde{O}(n^2)$ for n users.*

We will not prove this theorem, but will instead show a simpler but suboptimal construction from the original paper of Boneh and Shaw [15].

A fingerprinting code of length $\tilde{O}(n^3)$: $\mathsf{Gen}(1^n)$ outputs a matrix obtained by *randomly permuting* columns of the matrix

$$
\begin{array}{cccccc}
\text{0 block} & \text{1st block} & \text{2nd block} & \cdots & \text{n-th block} \\
\end{array}
$$
$$
\begin{pmatrix}
111 \ldots 111 & 111 \ldots 111 & 111 \ldots 111 & & \\
000 \ldots 000 & 111 \ldots 111 & 111 \ldots 111 & & \\
 & 000 \ldots 000 & 111 \ldots 111 & & \\
0 \quad\quad 0 \quad\quad 0 & & & \cdots & 1 \\
 & & & 000 \ldots 000 & \\
\end{pmatrix}
$$

Each block spans $\tilde{O}(n^2)$ identical columns. For such a randomly generated matrix, a coalition S that does not include the i-th user cannot distinguish columns that come from the $(i - 1)$-th and the i-th blocks of the matrix, as these columns are identical in the submatrix C_S. The tracing algorithm takes advantage of this observation. The tracing algorithm $\mathsf{Trace}(C, w)$ outputs the first i such that

$$\underset{j \text{ in block } i}{\mathrm{Avg}} [w_j] - \underset{j \text{ in block } i-1}{\mathrm{Avg}} [w_j] \ge \frac{1}{n},$$

where $\mathrm{Avg}_{j \in T} f(j)$ denotes the average of $f(j)$ over j in set T. For a feasible codeword w, such an index i is guaranteed to exist since $\mathrm{Avg}_{j \text{ in block } 0}[w_j] = 0$ and

$\text{Avg}_{j \text{ in block } n}[w_j] = 1$. The correctness of the tracing algorithm follows from the following claim, which ensures that the probability we falsely accuse a user outside the coalition S is negligible:

Claim 7.5.19. *For a given coalition S and pirate $\mathcal{P}$, a randomly generated $C \leftarrow \text{Gen}(1^n)$ and $w \leftarrow \mathcal{P}(C_S)$, with probability greater than $1 - \text{neg}(n)$, for all $i \notin S$, we have*

$$\underset{j \text{ in block } i}{\text{Avg}} [w_j] - \underset{j \text{ in block } i-1}{\text{Avg}} [w_j] < \frac{1}{n}.$$

Proof: Fix $i \notin S$, and condition on the codeword $w \leftarrow \mathcal{P}(C_S)$. Since columns from block i and $i - 1$ are identical in C_S, it is still not determined which permuted columns are from block i and which are from block $i - 1$. More precisely, if we condition additionally on the entire submatrix C_S of the (permuted) codebook C as well as the permuted locations of all columns other than those from blocks i and $i - 1$, then the blocks i and $i - 1$ are still a uniformly random partition of their union into two equal-sized sets. The averages $\text{Avg}_{j \text{ in block } i}[w_j]$ and $\text{Avg}_{j \text{ in block } i-1}[w_j]$ have the same expectation over the choice of the partition (namely $\text{Avg}_{j \text{ in block } i \text{ or } i-1}[w_j]$). Since each is the average over $\tilde{O}(n^2)$ coordinates (selected without replacement from the union), Chernoff-type bounds imply that, with all but negligible probability (depending on the choice of the polylog(n) factor in the $\tilde{O}(\cdot)$), they will each deviate from the expectation by less than $1/2n$ (and hence will differ from each other by less than $1/n$). ∎

While the analysis of optimal fingerprinting codes, with $d = \tilde{O}(n^2)$, is more involved, the description of the codes is very simple. Following generalizations and simplifications given in Dwork et al. [47], for every $j \in [d]$, we can pick a bias $p_j \leftarrow [0, 1]$ uniformly at random, and then generate the j-th column as n independent samples from the Bernoulli distribution with expectation p_j. In fact, any sufficiently "smooth" and "spread out" distribution on the p_j's can be used.

Now, we will use fingerprinting codes to derive lower bounds on differential privacy, following Bun et al. [21]:

Theorem 7.5.20 (Fingerprinting codes $\Rightarrow$ for attribute means [21]). *If there is a fingerprinting code with codewords of length d for $n + 1$ users then there is no $(1, 1/10n)$-differentially private mechanism $\mathcal{M} : (\{0, 1\}^d)^n \rightarrow [0, 1]^d$ for answering all d attribute means (i.e., the counting queries $Q^{means}(d)$) with error $\alpha < 1/2$.*

Proof: Suppose for contradiction that there exists a $(1, 1/10n)$-differentially private mechanism $\mathcal{M}$ for answering attribute means with error $\alpha < 1/2$. Without loss of generality, we may assume that, for every dataset x, the output distribution of $\mathcal{M}(x)$ does not depend on the order of the rows of x (else $\mathcal{M}$ can randomly permute them first).

Use the hypothesized fingerprinting code to generate a (random) codebook C for $n + 1$ users. Let $S = \{1, \dots, n\}$ (i.e., the coalition consisting of all users except user $n + 1$). Let $(a_1, \dots, a_d)$ be attribute means obtained from $\mathcal{M}$ on the data set C_S. Define a vector $w \in \{0, 1\}^d$ by rounding vector $(a_1, \dots, a_d)$ to the nearest integer. Since $\mathcal{M}$ makes error less than $1/2$ (with high probability), w is a feasible pirated codeword for C_S. That is, we think of $\mathcal{P}(\cdot) = \text{Round}(\mathcal{M}(\cdot))$ as the pirate for the fingerprinting code. Since $\mathcal{M}$ is differentially private, so is $\mathcal{P}$.

By the properties of the fingerprinting code

$$\Pr[\text{Trace}(tk, \mathcal{P}(C_S)) \in \{1, \dots, n\}] \geq 1 - \text{neg}(n),$$

where the probability is taken over $(C, tk) \leftarrow \text{Gen}(1^{n+1})$ and the coin tosses of $\mathcal{P}$.

Hence, for n large enough, there is an i^* such that

$$\Pr[\text{Trace}(tk, \mathcal{P}(C_S)) = i^*] \geq \frac{1}{2n}.$$

Let $S' = \{1, \dots, n + 1\} - \{i^*\}$. Since C_S and $C_{S'}$ are neighboring datasets (after an appropriate permutation of the rows), the differential privacy of $\mathcal{P}$ tells us that

$$\Pr[\text{Trace}(tk, \mathcal{P}(C_S)) = i^*] \leq e^1 \cdot \Pr[\text{Trace}(tk, \mathcal{P}(C_{S'})) = i^*] + \frac{1}{10n}.$$

Thus, we have

$$\Pr[\text{Trace}(tk, \mathcal{P}(C_{S'})) = i^*] \geq \frac{1}{2en} - \frac{1}{10en} \geq \Omega(1/n),$$

which contradicts the security of the fingerprinting code, as with nonnegligible probability we are accusing someone not in the coalition S'.   ∎

Notice that the "good guys" and "bad guys" have switched roles in this relation between fingerprinting codes and differential privacy. The mechanism $\mathcal{M}$, which is supposed to protect privacy, plays the role of the adversarial pirate $\mathcal{P}$ for the fingerprinting code. And the Trace algorithm from the fingerprinting code (corresponding to the "authorities") plays the role of the privacy adversary. Tracing attacks (determining whether an individual was in the dataset or not) are not quite as devastating as the reconstruction attacks, but they still can be quite significant—for example, if the dataset consists of a collection of individuals who were all diagnosed with a particular disease. Indeed such tracing attacks (on releases of exact rather than approximate statistics) led the US National Institutes of Health to remove online access to summary statistics of certain genomic datasets [63, 110]. For a fingerprinting code to give a "realistic" attack, the tracing should not require extensive auxiliary information (captured by the tracing key tk) and should be fairly robust to the distribution according to which the codebook was generated. These issues are explored in [47].

Combining Theorems 7.5.18 and 7.5.20, we see that estimating d attribute means on a dataset of size $n = \tilde{\Omega}(\sqrt{d})$ requires an error of $\alpha \geq 1/2$ for $(1, 1/10n)$-differential privacy. Simple reductions imply that, in general, we need error $\alpha > \tilde{\Omega}(\sqrt{d})/\varepsilon n$. Steinke and Ullman [99] have tightened the lower bound to nearly match Theorem 7.2.7 (up to a factor of $O\left(\sqrt{\log \log d}\right)$):

Theorem 7.5.21 (Fingerprinting lower bound for attribute means [99]). *The following holds for every $d \in \mathbb{N}$, $\varepsilon \in (0, 1)$, and $\delta \in (2^{-d}, 1/n^{1.1})$. Suppose*

$\mathcal{M} : (\{0,1\}^d)^n \to [0,1]^d$ *is an* (ε, δ)-*differentially private mechanism that with high probability answers every attribute mean query in* $\mathcal{Q}^{means}(d)$ *with error at most* α. *Then*

$$\alpha \geq \Omega\left(\min\left\{\frac{\sqrt{d\log(1/\delta)}}{\varepsilon n}, 1\right\}\right).$$

Recall from Table 7.4 that partial discrepancy gave a lower bound of $\Omega(\sqrt{d}/n)$ when $d < n$, and otherwise gave a lower bound no better than $\sqrt{(\log d)/n}$. Packing (Theorem 7.5.14) gave a lower bound of $\Omega(\min\{d, \log(1/\delta)\}/\varepsilon n)$. Theorem 7.5.21 subsumes all of these bounds.

The fingerprinting lower bound above is for a particular family of counting queries—attribute means—in which the number of queries ($|\mathcal{Q}^{means}(d)| = d$) is logarithmic in the size of the data universe ($\mathcal{X} = \{0,1\}^d$), but it can be composed with reconstruction attacks of Section 7.5.1 to also yield nearly tight lower bounds for the case in which the number $|\mathcal{Q}|$ of queries is much larger:

Theorem 7.5.22 (Lower bounds for arbitrary counting queries [21]). *For every* $d, n, k \in \mathbb{N}$ *such that* $n^{2.1} \leq k \leq 2^{2^{d/3}}$, *there is a family* $\mathcal{Q}$ *of* k *counting queries on data universe* $\mathcal{X} = \{0,1\}^d$ *such that the following holds: If* $\mathcal{M} : (\mathcal{X})^n \to \mathbb{R}^{\mathcal{Q}}$ *is an* $(\varepsilon, 1/10n)$ *differentially private mechanism that with high probability answers all queries in* $\mathcal{Q}$ *within error at most* α, *then*

$$\alpha \geq \tilde{\Omega}\left(\frac{\sqrt{\log|\mathcal{X}| \cdot \log(|\mathcal{Q}|)}}{\varepsilon n}\right)^{1/2}.$$

This theorem mostly closes the gap between the largest discrepancy-based lower bounds (Theorem 7.5.12) and the upper bound given by private multiplicative weights (Theorem 7.4.3). So, we have a nearly tight understanding of the accuracy with which we can answer a worst-case set $\mathcal{Q}$ of counting queries, as a function of $|\mathcal{X}|$, $|\mathcal{Q}|$, n, and the privacy parameters. In fact, a similar lower bound is also known for the special case of t-way marginals, by composing the fingerprinting lower bound for attribute means with reconstruction lower bounds for marginals [14, 66, 29]:

Theorem 7.5.23 (Lower bound for t-way marginals [21]). *For every constant* $\ell \in \mathbb{N}$, *the following holds for all* $d, n, t \in \mathbb{N}$ *such that* $n \leq d^{2\ell/3}/\varepsilon$ *and* $\ell + 1 \leq t \leq d$: *If* $\mathcal{M} : (\{0,1\}^d)^n \to \mathbb{R}^{\mathcal{Q}_t^{conj}(d)}$ *is an* $(\varepsilon, 1/10n)$-*differentially private mechanism that with high probability answers all queries in* $\mathcal{Q}_t^{conj}(d)$ *to within error at most* α, *then*

$$\alpha \geq \min\left\{\tilde{\Omega}\left(\frac{t\sqrt{d}}{\varepsilon n}\right)^{1/2}, \Omega(1)\right\}.$$

However, as we have seen for point functions (Proposition 7.2.8 and Theorem 7.3.5), for some families of queries $\mathcal{Q}$, one can do much better than these bounds. Ideally, we would understand the best accuracy achievable in terms of the

combinatorial structure of the query family, similarly to what the hereditary dfis-
crepancy bounds (Theorems 7.5.9 and 7.5.10) give, but for a given value of n and
ideally without extra polylog($|Q|$) factors.

Open Problem 7.5.24. For an arbitrary family $Q = \{q : \mathcal{X} \rightarrow \{0, 1\}\}$ of counting
queries, $n \in \mathbb{N}$, $\varepsilon > 0$, and $\delta = o(1/n)$, characterize (to within "small" approximation factors) the smallest achievable error by (ε, δ)-differentially private mechanisms
$\mathcal{M} : \mathcal{X}^n \rightarrow \mathbb{R}^Q$.

A potentially easier task, advocated by Beimel et al. [10], is to characterize the
"sample complexity" for constant error, as we did for pure differential privacy in
Theorem 7.5.15:

Open Problem 7.5.25. For an arbitrary family $Q = \{q : \mathcal{X} \rightarrow \{0, 1\}\}$ of counting
queries, $\varepsilon > 0$, and $\delta = o(1/n)$, characterize (to within "small" approximation factors) the sample complexity (i.e., smallest value of n) needed by (ε, δ)-differentially
private mechanisms $\mathcal{M} : \mathcal{X}^n \rightarrow \mathbb{R}^Q$ to answer all the queries in Q to within an
arbitrarily small constant error $\alpha > 0$.

We note that there is a partial converse to the connections between fingerprinting
codes and differential privacy [21]; that is, if answering a set Q of counting queries
is impossible with differential privacy for a given set of parameters $(\alpha, n, \varepsilon, \delta)$, this
implies a weak form of a fingerprinting code that is defined with respect to the
query family Q and the given parameters. It would be very interesting to tighten this
relationship; this would be one approach to Open Problems 7.5.24 and 7.5.25.

Open Problem 7.5.26. Identify a variant of fingerprinting codes whose existence is
equivalent to the impossibility of answering a family Q accurately with differential
privacy (up to some loss in parameters).

7.6 Computational Lower Bounds

Now we turn to *computational* lower bounds, giving evidence that some tasks
that are information-theoretically possible with differential privacy are nevertheless
computationally intractable. Specifically, recall that both the smallDB and private
multiplicative weights algorithms of Section 7.4 can accurately answer (many) more
than n^2 counting queries over data universe $\mathcal{X} = \{0, 1\}^d$ with differential privacy,
provided that n is large enough compared with d (e.g., $n \geq d^2$), but use computation
time exponential in d. Below we will see evidence that this exponential computation
is necessary in the worst case.

7.6.1 Traitor-Tracing Lower Bounds

Our first hardness results will be based on *traitor-tracing schemes*, which were introduced by Chor et al. [28] as a cryptographic tool for preventing piracy of digital
content, like fingerprinting codes. Their benefit over fingerprinting codes is that they

allow for distributing an unbounded amount of content over a broadcast channel (after a setup phase where private keys are sent to the users). The price is having computational rather than information-theoretic security. The notion of traitor-tracing schemes predated the notion of fingerprinting codes, and their application to lower bounds for differential privacy also came first, in Dwork et al. [40].

To motivate the definition of traitor-tracing schemes, imagine a video-streaming company that distributes software or hardware that is capable of decoding their (encrypted) streaming signal. Each customer gets his own decryption program that has a unique decryption key, so that copying can be detected. However, we are also concerned that S customers might collude to create (and sell) unauthorized pirate decryption programs. They can build their pirate program using the decryption keys found in their own decryption program in an arbitrary way, so we may not be able to explicitly read off any of the keys from the pirate program. The goal of the traitor-tracing scheme is to be able to identify at least one of the colluding customers who contributed his decryption key. We can formalize this setup as follows:

Definition 7.6.1. *A* traitor-tracing scheme *consists of four algorithms* (Gen, Enc, Dec, Trace) *as follows:*

1. *The (randomized) key generation algorithm* Gen$(1^d, 1^n)$ *takes as input* $1^d, 1^n$, *where d is a security parameter and n is a number of customers, and outputs* $(k_1, \ldots, k_n, bk, tk)$, *where* $k_i \in \{0, 1\}^d$ *is the* decryption key *for user i, bk is the* broadcast key, *and tk is the* tracing key.
2. *The (randomized) encryption algorithm* Enc$_{bk}(m)$ *takes as input the broadcast key bk and a message* $m \in \{0, 1\}$ *and outputs a ciphertext c.*
3. *The* decryption algorithm Dec$_{k_i}(c)$ *takes as input a user key* k_i *and a ciphertext c and outputs a message* $m \in \{0, 1\}$. *We require that it always holds that* Dec$_{k_i}($Enc$_{bk}(m)) = m$ *for keys* (k_i, bk) *that are output by* Gen.
4. *The syntax of the (randomized) tracing algorithm* Trace *will be described below (as there are two variants).*

We will consider two different scenarios for tracing, depending on the type of pirates that we wish to trace and the access that Trace has to those pirates. Each will give us different types of lower bounds for differential privacy.

Stateless pirates Here the tracer can run the pirate decryption program many times from its same initial state, but on different ciphertexts as input. For example, this models the scenario where the pirate decryption program is a piece of software whose code is given to the tracer. We want to be able to trace given any pirate program that is correctly able to decrypt proper encryptions with high probability (though the tracer will feed the pirate malformed ciphertexts that are neither encryptions of 0 or 1 to help in identifying one of the colluders). This is the original and most standard notion of traitor tracing in the literature.

Stateful but cooperative pirates Here the tracer can submit a sequence of ciphertexts to the pirate, but the pirate may answer them in a correlated fashion, for example, changing its behavior to evade tracing if it receives and detects a malformed ciphertext. However, we will only require tracing for "cooperative" pirates, which still correctly distinguish encryptions of 0 from 1 even if they receive some other malformed ciphertexts. Tracing stateful pirates is well-motivated for traitor tracing; the "cooperativeness" condition is less natural in that context, but arises naturally in our application to differential privacy lower bounds.

We now formalize these two requirements.

Definition 7.6.2 (Tracing stateless pirates). *A traitor-tracing scheme* (Gen, Enc, Dec, Trace) *is secure against stateless pirates if the following holds for every $n =$ poly(d) and every $S \subseteq [n]$: let $\mathcal{P}$ be a probabilistic poly(d)-time algorithm that given the keys $(k_i)_{i \in S}$ outputs a Boolean circuit $\tilde{P}$. Then,*

$$\Pr[\text{Trace}(\tilde{P}, tk) \notin S \text{ and } \tilde{P} \text{ is a useful decryptor}] \leq \text{neg}(d),$$

where the probabilities are taken over $(k_1, \ldots, k_n, bk, tk) \leftarrow$ Gen$(1^d, 1^n)$, $\tilde{P} \leftarrow \mathcal{P}((k_i)_{i \in S})$, and the coins of Trace *and* $\mathcal{P}$. *The condition that $\tilde{P}$ is a useful decryptor means that, for every $m \in \{0, 1\}$, $\Pr[\tilde{P}(\text{Enc}_{bk}(m)) = m] = 1$, where the probability is taken over the coin tosses of* Enc. *(In the literature, tracing is typically required even for pirates that have just a nonnegligible advantage in distinguishing encryptions of 0 from encryptions of 1, but tracing pirate decoders that always decrypt correctly will suffice for our purposes.)*

Definition 7.6.3 (Tracing stateful pirates). *A traitor-tracing scheme* (Gen, Enc, Dec, Trace) *is secure against stateful but cooperative pirates if there is a polynomial function $k(\cdot, \cdot)$ (called the* tracing query complexity*) such that, for every $n =$ poly(d) and every $S \subseteq [n]$, the following holds for $k = k(d, n)$: Let $\mathcal{P}$ be any probabilistic poly(d)-time algorithm that, given the keys $(k_i)_{i \in S}$ and a sequence $(c_1, \ldots, c_k)$ of ciphertexts, outputs a sequence $(m_1, \ldots, m_k) \in \{0, 1\}^k$. Then,*

$$\Pr[\text{Trace}^{\mathcal{P}((k_i)_{i \in S}, \cdot)}(tk) \notin S \text{ and } \mathcal{P} \text{ cooperates}] \leq \text{neg}(d),$$

where the probabilities are taken over $(k_1, \ldots, k_n, bk, tk) \leftarrow$ Gen$(1^d, 1^n)$ and the coins of Trace. *We require that* Trace *makes only one query $(c_1, \ldots, c_k)$ to $\mathcal{P}$ (amounting to feeding $k = k(d, n)$ nonadaptively chosen ciphertexts to $\mathcal{P}$), and say that $\mathcal{P}$ cooperates if, for every coordinate j where c_j is in the support of* Enc$_{bk}(b_j)$ *for some $b_j \in \{0, 1\}$, we have $b_j = m_j$.*

We note that tracing stateless pirates is easier than tracing stateful but cooperative pirates, because whenever $\tilde{P}$ is a useful decryptor, using it to decrypt each ciphertext will qualify as cooperating.

Theorem 7.6.4 (Traitor-tracing schemes against stateful pirates [28, 103]). *Assuming one-way functions exist, there exists a traitor-tracing scheme secure against stateful but cooperative pirates with tracing query complexity $k(n, d) = \tilde{O}(n^2)$.*

Proof sketch: The key generation, encryption, and decryption are as in the original construction of Chor et al. [28] (which was for stateless pirates). Fix a secure private-key encryption system $(\mathsf{Enc}^0, \mathsf{Dec}^0)$ (which exists if one-way functions exist). $\mathsf{Gen}(1^d, 1^n)$ generates independently keys $k_1, \ldots, k_n$ for the encryption system $(\mathsf{Enc}^0, \mathsf{Dec}^0)$ and sets $tk = bk = (k_1, k_2, \ldots, k_n)$. Encoding is given by

$$\mathsf{Enc}_{bk}(b) = (\mathsf{Enc}^0_{k_1}(b), \mathsf{Enc}^0_{k_2}(b), \ldots, \mathsf{Enc}^0_{k_n}(b))$$

and decryption for user i by

$$\mathsf{Dec}_{k_i}(c_1, \ldots, c_n) = \mathsf{Dec}^0_{k_i}(c_i).$$

The tracing algorithm is from Ullman [103], and utilizes fingerprinting codes in order to minimize the tracing query complexity and handle stateful but cooperative pirates. $\mathsf{Trace}^P(tk, bk)$ first generates a fingerprinting codebook, namely an $n \times k$ matrix $C \leftarrow \mathsf{Gen}_{\mathrm{f.p.}}(1^n)$. (Recall from Theorem 7.5.18 that we can take $k = \tilde{O}(n^2)$.) It then creates ciphertexts $c^{(1)}, c^{(2)}, \ldots, c^{(k)}$ by

$$c_i^{(j)} = \mathsf{Enc}^0_{k_i}(C_{i,j}).$$

The tracing algorithm queries its oracle $P((k_i)_{i \in S}, c^{(1)}, c^{(2)}, \ldots, c^{(k)})$ to get answers $w = (w_1, \ldots, w_k)$, and runs the tracing algorithm of the fingerprinting code $\mathsf{Trace}_{\mathrm{f.p.}}(C, w)$ to get a suspect i. It outputs this i.

We sketch the correctness of this tracing scheme: if the pirate algorithm is computationally bounded, then it cannot learn any information about the messages encrypted by private keys of users not participating in S, so w essentially depends only on the rows of C in S. We now observe that w is feasible when $\mathcal{P}$ is cooperative, except with negligible probability. Indeed, if all entries of column j of C_S agree on value b_j, then to $\mathcal{P}$, $c^{(j)}$ is indistinguishable from a valid encryption of b_j, and hence $w_j = b_j$ with all but negligible probability. ∎

We now show that such traitor-tracing schemes imply the hardness of answering many counting queries with differential privacy, a result due to Ullman [103].

Theorem 7.6.5. (Tracing stateful pirates⇒hardness of answering many queries [103]). *If there exists a traitor-tracing scheme secure against stateful but cooperative pirates with tracing query complexity $k(d, n)$, then every $(1, 1/10n)$-differentially private mechanism for answering $k = k(n + 1, d)$ efficiently computable counting queries with error $\alpha < 1/2$ on datasets with n individuals from $\mathcal{X} = \{0, 1\}^d$ must run in time superpolynomial in d. Here the queries are given as input to the mechanism, as Boolean circuits of size $\mathrm{poly}(n, d)$.*

Proof sketch: Suppose $\mathcal{M}$ is a differentially private mechanism like in the statement of the theorem. We will show how to construct a pirate for the traitor-tracing scheme using $\mathcal{M}$ and conclude from the security of the scheme that $\mathcal{M}$ must have a runtime big enough to break the scheme.

Start by setting up the traitor-tracing scheme with $n + 1$ users and take a dataset x containing the keys of a coalition of n users obtained by removing one user at ran-

dom. We consider counting queries on this dataset given by ciphertext decryption:
for a ciphertext c, the query q_c evaluates to $q_c(k_i) = \mathsf{Dec}_{k_i}(c)$, where we identify
the row corresponding to the i-th user with its key k_i. Therefore, when query q_c is
answered accurately by $\mathcal{M}$ on the dataset x we obtain an $\pm\alpha$-approximation a to
the number of users in x whose key decrypts c to 1. If c is a valid encryption of a
message $m \in \{0, 1\}$, then $|a - m| \le \alpha < 1/2$, so rounding a will equal m. With this
notation, we define our pirate as follows:

$$\mathcal{P}((k_i)_{i \in S}, c^{(1)}, \ldots, c^{(k)}) = \mathrm{Round}(\mathcal{M}(x = (k_i)_{i \in S}, q_{c^{(1)}}, \ldots, q_{c^{(k)}})),$$

where $\mathrm{Round} : [0, 1]^k \to \{0, 1\}^k$ denotes componentwise rounding.

As discussed above, the accuracy of $\mathcal{M}$ implies that $\mathcal{P}$ is cooperative. On the
other hand, the fact that $\mathcal{M}$ is differentially private implies that $\mathcal{P}$ is also differentially private. As in the proof of Theorem 7.5.20, tracing contradicts differential
privacy. Thus, $\mathcal{P}$ must not be traceable, and hence must have superpolynomial running time.   ∎

Combining the above two theorems we get:

Corollary 7.6.6 (Hardness of answering many counting queries). *Assume one-
way functions exist. Then for every $n = \mathrm{poly}(d)$, there is no polynomial-time
$(1, 1/10n)$-differentially private algorithm for answering more than $\tilde{O}(n^2)$ efficiently
computable counting queries with error $\alpha < 1/2$ (given as Boolean circuits input to
the mechanism) over data universe $\mathcal{X} = \{0, 1\}^d$.*

This lower bound is nearly tight, in that we can answer $k = \tilde{\Omega}(n^2)$ efficiently
computable counting queries in polynomial time with differential privacy using the
Laplace mechanism and advanced composition (or Theorem 7.2.7).

Let us review the above proof's translation between objects in the traitor-tracing
scheme and those in differential privacy:

$$\text{user keyspace } \{0, 1\}^d \mapsto \text{data universe } \mathcal{X} = \{0, 1\}^d$$
$$\text{ciphertext } c \mapsto \text{counting query } q_c(k) = \mathsf{Dec}_k(c)$$
$$\text{pirate } \mathcal{P} \leftrightarrow \text{mechanism } \mathcal{M}$$
$$\text{tracing algorithm Trace} \mapsto \text{privacy adversary}$$

In particular, mechanisms that take a sequence of counting queries as input and
produce a vector of answers correspond very naturally to stateful but cooperative
pirates. On the other hand, a common application of the algorithms of Section 7.4
is not to specify the queries as input, but rather to fix some large family of counting
queries over data universe $\{0, 1\}^d$ (for example, the family of 3^d conjunction queries)
and then take n large enough so that we can produce a compact representation of the
answers to all of these queries (e.g., a synthetic dataset). What does this translate
to in the traitor-tracing world? Since we are interested in a family $\mathcal{Q}$ of efficiently
computable counting queries, we ideally should have ciphertexts that are of length
$\mathrm{poly}(d)$ (so that the queries have polynomial description length), not growing linearly with n as in Theorem 7.6.4. Second, the pirate P should no longer directly

produce answers to the queries (i.e., decrypt ciphertexts), but rather it should use its keys $(k_i)_{i \in S}$ to produce a summary (which we can view as an algorithm or data structure) $\tilde{P}$ that can then be used to estimate the answer to any query in the class (i.e., decrypt any properly generated ciphertext). This leads us naturally to traitor tracing with stateless pirates, as used in the original connection of Dwork et al. [40]:

Theorem 7.6.7 (Tracing stateless pirates $\Rightarrow$ hardness of differentially private summaries [40]). *If there is a traitor-tracing scheme secure against stateful pirates with ciphertexts of length $\ell(n, d)$, then for every d and $n = \mathrm{poly}(d)$, there is a family $\mathcal{Q}$ of efficiently computable counting queries of description length $\ell(n + 1, d)$ (and size $2^{\ell(n+1,d)}$) over data universe $\{0, 1\}^d$, such that no polynomial-time $(1, 1/10n)$-differentially private mechanism can accurately summarize the answers to all of the queries in $\mathcal{Q}$ on datasets of size n.*

We note that this theorem is only interesting if $\ell \ll n$. Indeed, Theorem 7.5.2 shows that there is a family of 2^n efficiently computable counting queries over a data universe of size $2n$ that is information-theoretically impossible to answer accurately with differential privacy. So we need traitor-tracing schemes with ciphertext length that is smaller than n, the number of users, unlike in the construction of Theorem 7.6.4. At the time that Theorem 7.6.7 was proven, the best known construction of traitor-tracing schemes against stateless pirates had ciphertext length $\ell(n, d) = \sqrt{n} \cdot \mathrm{poly}(d)$ [17] (under hardness assumptions about bilinear maps on certain groups), and this already implied an interesting hardness result for differential privacy. But it left open the possibility that producing differentially private summaries is possible for any efficiently computable family $\mathcal{Q}$ of counting queries provided that $n \geq (\log |\mathcal{X}|) \cdot (\log |\mathcal{Q}|)^2$.

Recently, however, there are candidate constructions of traitor-tracing schemes with ciphertext length $\ell = \mathrm{poly}(d)$, independent of n, assuming the existence of one-way functions and either "secure multilinear maps" or "indistinguishability obfuscation" [51, 16]. This yields a family $\mathcal{Q}$ of $2^\ell = 2^{\mathrm{poly}(d)}$ counting queries over a data universe $\mathcal{X}$ of size 2^d for which no $\mathrm{poly}(d)$-time algorithm can produce an accurate differentially private summary (for any $n = \mathrm{poly}(d)$). More recently, Kowalczyk et al. [72] showed that the same hardness result holds when either $|\mathcal{Q}|$ or $|\mathcal{X}|$ is $\mathrm{poly}(n)$, by constructing traitor-tracing schemes where either the ciphertexts or the keys are of length $O(\log n)$, albeit with a weaker security property that still suffices to show hardness of differential privacy. Specifically, the theorem says:

Theorem 7.6.8 (iO $\Rightarrow$ hardness of differential privacy [72]). *Assuming the existence of indistinguishability obfuscation and one-way functions:*

1. *For every $d \in \mathcal{N}$ and every $n = \mathrm{poly}(d)$, there is a family $\mathcal{Q}$ of $O(n^7)$ efficiently computable counting queries over data universe $\mathcal{X} = \{0, 1\}^d$ (specified by a uniform $\mathrm{poly}(d)$-time evaluation algorithm that takes an ℓ-bit description of a query q, for $\ell = 7 \log n + O(1)$, and an input $y \in \{0, 1\}^d$ and outputs $q(y)$) such that no polynomial-time differentially private mechanism can accurately answer all of the queries in $\mathcal{Q}$ on datasets of size n.*

2. *For every $\ell \in \mathcal{N}$ and every $n = \text{poly}(\ell)$, there is a family $\mathcal{Q}$ of 2^ℓ efficiently computable counting queries over data universe $\mathcal{X} = \{0,1\}^d$ for $d = 7 \log n + O(1)$ (specified by a uniform $\text{poly}(\ell)$-time evaluation algorithm that takes an ℓ-bit description of a query q and an input $y \in \{0,1\}^d$ and outputs $q(y)$) such that no polynomial-time differentially private mechanism can accurately summarize the answers to all of the queries in $\mathcal{Q}$ on datasets of size n.*

We note that, when $|\mathcal{Q}|$ and $|\mathcal{X}|$ are *both* of size $\text{poly}(n)$, the algorithm of Theorem 7.4.3 can answer all of the queries in polynomial time (so we cannot hope to prove hardness in this case). If, in part 1, the $|\mathcal{Q}|$ could be reduced to $n^{2+o(1)}$, then the hardness result would be stronger than that of Corollary 7.6.6 (albeit under a stronger complexity assumption). Indeed, here the set of queries is fixed and each query is described by $O(\log n)$ bits, whereas in Corollary 7.6.6, the queries have description length larger than n and need to be provided as input to the mechanism. It would also be interesting to reduce $|\mathcal{X}|$ to $n^{2+o(1)}$ in part 2; this too would be optimal because, when $|\mathcal{X}| \leq n^{2-\Omega(1)}$, the Laplace histogram is a $\text{poly}(n)$-time computable summary that is simultaneously accurate for up to $2^{n^{\Omega(1)}}$ queries (Theorem 7.2.9).

Open Problem 7.6.9. Can either $|\mathcal{Q}|$ or $|\mathcal{X}|$ in Theorem 7.6.8 be reduced to $n^{2+o(1)}$?

The existence of "indistinguishability obfuscation", as assumed in Theorem 7.6.8, is still very unclear, and thus it would be significant to replace it with a more well-understood complexity assumption:

Open Problem 7.6.10. Can a hardness result like Theorem 7.6.8 be established under a more standard and widely believed complexity assumption? This is open even for the case where we do not require either $|\mathcal{Q}|$ or $|\mathcal{X}|$ to be of size $\text{poly}(n)$, but rather we allow n and the mechanism running time to be $\text{poly}(d, \ell)$.

Similarly to (but earlier than) the case with fingerprinting codes, there is a partial converse to the connection between traitor-tracing schemes and the hardness of differential privacy [40], and it would be very interesting to tighten this relationship.

Open Problem 7.6.11. Identify a variant of traitor-tracing schemes whose existence is *equivalent* to the hardness of answering (or summarizing) counting queries with differential privacy (up to some loss in parameters, but ideally having a relationship holding per-query family $\mathcal{Q}$).

7.6.2 Lower Bounds for Synthetic Data

The lower bounds of the previous section provide families of efficiently computable counting queries that are hard to answer with differential privacy. However, these families consist of rather complicated functions that evaluate cryptographic algorithms (namely, the decryption algorithm for traitor-tracing schemes). We do not know similar results for simple/natural function classes of interest, such as the set of all 3^d conjunctions on data universe $\{0,1\}^d$.

However, we can prove a hardness result for differentially private algorithms that work by producing a synthetic dataset, as do the algorithms of Section 7.4. (This is explicitly stated for the smallDB algorithm, and the private multiplicative weights algorithm can be modified to produce synthetic data.) In fact, the result will hold even for the family $\mathcal{Q}_2^{conj}$ of 2-way marginals.

Theorem 7.6.12 (Hardness of synthetic data for simple queries [104]). *Assuming one-way functions exist, there exists a constant $\alpha > 0$ such that there is no $n = \text{poly}(d)$ and polynomial-time $(1, 1/10n)$-differentially private mechanism that given a dataset with n individuals over $\mathcal{X} = \{0, 1\}^d$ outputs a synthetic dataset approximating all the counting queries in $\mathcal{Q}_2^{conj}(d)$ (i.e., all the 2-way marginals) to within additive error at most α.*

We note that the requirement that the mechanism produces a synthetic dataset cannot be removed from the theorem. Indeed, recall that the Laplace mechanism and advanced composition will approximate all $k = \Theta(d^2)$ 2-way conjunctions within error $\alpha = \tilde{O}(\sqrt{k})/\varepsilon n = \tilde{O}(d)/\varepsilon n$ in time $\text{poly}(n, d)$. So for $n = \text{poly}(d)$, we get vanishingly small error in polynomial time.

Proof: The main ingredients in the proof are digital signature schemes and probabilistically checkable proofs (PCPs). We will use digital signatures to construct datasets for which it is hard to generate synthetic data that preserves the answer to a cryptographically defined query, and then we will use PCPs to transform this cryptographic query into a collection of 2-way conjunctions.

Recall that a *digital signature scheme* is given by a triple of polynomial-time algorithms as follows:

1. A randomized *key generation* algorithm $\text{Gen}(1^d) = (pk, sk)$ that produces a public key pk and a private key sk given a security parameter d as input.
2. A randomized *signing* algorithm that, given a message $m \in \{0, 1\}^d$ and a secret key sk, produces a signature $\sigma = \text{Sign}_{sk}(m) \in \{0, 1\}^d$.
3. A deterministic *verification* algorithm $\text{Ver}_{pk}(m, \sigma)$ that always accepts a signature for m generated using the secret key sk corresponding to pk.

Informally, we say that the scheme is *secure* if, given access to examples $(m_i, \sigma_i = \text{Sign}_{sk}(m_i))$ signed with the same secret key, any algorithm running in time $\text{poly}(d)$ cannot generate a new message $m' \notin \{m_i\}$ and a signature σ' such that $\text{Ver}_{pk}(m', \sigma') = 1$.

We now describe how to use digital signatures to construct datasets for which it is hard to generate synthetic data preserving the answer to a cryptographically defined counting query. This construction is due to Dwork et al. [40]:

The dataset: Generate $(pk, sk) \leftarrow \text{Gen}(1^d)$ and construct a dataset x with n individuals, where each row contains a pair (m_i, σ_i) with m_i selected uniformly at random from $\{0, 1\}^d$ and $\sigma_i \leftarrow \text{Sign}_{sk}(m_i)$.
The query: Consider the counting query $q(\cdot) = \text{Ver}_{pk}(\cdot)$. This query is efficiently computable and evaluates to 1 on the whole dataset.

The hardness: Now suppose for contradiction that there exists a polynomial-time
differentially private mechanism $\mathcal{M}$ that given x produces a synthetic dataset
$\hat{x} \in (\{0,1\}^d)^{\hat{n}}$ which is accurate with respect to q with high probability. By
accuracy, $\hat{x}$ must contain at least one row $\hat{x}_j = (\hat{m}_j, \hat{\sigma}_j)$ such that $\mathsf{Ver}_{pk}(\hat{m}_j, \hat{\sigma}_j) =
q(\hat{x}_j) = 1$. To derive a contradiction, we consider two cases:

- If $\hat{m}_j \notin x$, then $\mathcal{M}$ succeeded in creating a forgery for the signature scheme
  in polynomial time, contradicting its security.
- If $\hat{m}_j \in x$, then $\mathcal{M}$ intuitively has violated privacy, as it has copied part
  of a row (which is independent from all other rows) entirely in the output.
  More precisely, for every $i \in [n]$, the probability that an (ε, δ)-differentially
  private mechanism $\mathcal{M}$ outputs m_i is at most $e^\varepsilon/2^d + \delta$, since it could output
  m_i with probability at most $1/2^d$ if we replaced the i-th row with all zeroes.
  Thus, the probability $\mathcal{M}$ outputs any m_i is at most $n \cdot (e^\varepsilon/2^d + \delta) < 1/20$ for
  $\varepsilon = 1$ and $\delta = 1/10n$.

We now describe how to use PCPs to replace the cryptographic query Ver_{pk} with
2-way conjunctions. Actually, we will only describe how to get a result for 3-way
conjunctions, as it uses a more familiar type of PCP theorem.

Recall that *Circuit SAT* is an NP-hard problem. Then, by a strong form of the
PCP theorem there exist a constant $\alpha > 0$ and three polynomial time algorithms
Red, Enc, Dec satisfying the following:

1. Red is a randomized reduction that, given a circuit C, outputs a 3-CNF formula
   $\mathsf{Red}(C) = \phi = \phi_1 \wedge \ldots \wedge \phi_m$ such that if C is satisfiable then ϕ is satisfiable, and
   otherwise there is no assignment satisfying more than $(1 - \alpha)m$ clauses of ϕ.
2. If w is a satisfying assignment for C, then $z = \mathsf{Enc}(C, w)$ is a satisfying assignment for ϕ.
3. If z is an assignment for ϕ satisfying more than $(1 - \alpha)m$ clauses, then $w =
   \mathsf{Dec}(C, z)$ is a satisfying assignment for C.

Item 1 is the standard formulation of the PCP theorem in terms of the hardness
of approximating MAX-3SAT; it asserts a Karp reduction from Circuit SAT to the
promise problem Gap-MAX-3SAT. Items 2 and 3 are saying that this reduction is
actually a Levin reduction, meaning we can efficiently transform witnesses between
the Circuit SAT instance and the corresponding Gap-MAX-3SAT instance.

Here is our modified construction:

The dataset: Let x be the dataset constructed above using digital signatures. We
write z for the dataset with n individuals obtained by encoding each row x_i of
x with the encoding algorithm given by the PCP theorem, relative to the circuit
$C = \mathsf{Ver}_{pk}$. That is, $z_i = \mathsf{Enc}(\mathsf{Ver}_{pk}, x_i)$.
The queries: Our set of queries is all 3-way conjunctions, but we will only exploit
accuracy with respect to the clauses of the 3-CNF formula $\phi = \phi_1 \wedge \cdots \wedge \phi_m$
output by $\mathsf{Red}(\mathsf{Ver}_{pk})$. Note that for every row z_i in z we have $\phi(z_i) = 1$ (since
$\mathsf{Ver}_{pk}(x_i) = 1$), so for every clause ϕ_j in ϕ we have $\phi_j(z) = n^{-1} \sum_{i \in [n]} \phi_j(z_i) = 1$.
The hardness: Suppose for contradiction that $\mathcal{M}$ is a polynomial-time differen-
tially private mechanism that produces synthetic datasets that are α-accurate

with respect to 3-way conjunctions and let $\hat{z} = \mathcal{M}(z)$. Then for every $j \in [m]$ we have $\phi_j(\hat{z}) \geq 1 - \alpha$. By averaging, this implies that there exists some row $\hat{z}_i$ of $\hat{z}$ that satisfies at least $(1 - \alpha) \cdot m$ clauses from ϕ. Therefore, using this row from the sanitized dataset we can obtain $(\hat{m}, \hat{\sigma}) = \text{Dec}(\text{Ver}_{pk}, \hat{z})$ such that $\text{Ver}_{pk}(\hat{m}, \hat{\sigma}) = 1$. Now the same argument used earlier shows that either $(\hat{m}, \hat{\sigma})$ is a forgery (in case $\hat{m} \notin x$) or a violation of privacy (in case $\hat{m} \in x$).

∎

The hardness results we have seen either apply to contrived (cryptographic) queries (Corollary 7.6.6 and Theorem 7.6.8) or constrain the form of the mechanism's output to synthetic data (Theorem 7.6.12). Obtaining a hardness result for *any* "natural" family of queries without restricting the form of the mechanism's output remains an intriguing open problem.

Open Problem 7.6.13. Give evidence of hardness of accurately answering any "natural" family of counting queries under differential privacy, without constraining the form of the mechanism's output.

At the same time, the lack of such a hardness result should provide some hope in looking for algorithms, and suggests that we should look for output representations other than synthetic data. We can gain hope from computational learning theory, where proper learning (where the learner's output is constrained to come from the same representation class as the concept it is learning) is often computationally harder than unconstrained, improper learning. Indeed, we will see the benefits of moving beyond synthetic data for conjunctions in the next section.

7.7 Efficient Algorithms for Specific Query Families

In this section, we will see that, for some specific, natural families of queries, one can in fact obtain efficient algorithms for answering more than n^2 queries.

7.7.1 Point Functions (Histograms)

We have already seen that, for the class $\mathcal{Q}^{\text{pt}} = \mathcal{Q}^{\text{pt}}(\mathcal{X})$ of point functions on $\mathcal{X}$, we can achieve a better accuracy–privacy tradeoff than is possible with an arbitrary class $\mathcal{Q}$ of efficiently computable queries. Indeed, Proposition 7.2.8 and Theorems 7.3.5 and 7.5.14 show that the optimal error achievable for $\mathcal{Q}^{\text{pt}}(\mathcal{X})$ is $\Theta(\min\{\log |\mathcal{X}|, \log(1/\delta), \varepsilon n\}/\varepsilon n)$, whereas for an arbitrary query family with $|\mathcal{Q}| = |\mathcal{X}|$, there is a lower bound of $\Omega((\log |\mathcal{X}|)^{3/2}/\varepsilon n)^{1/2}$ for a wide range of parameters (Theorem 7.5.22).

Now we will see that in fact the optimal algorithms for point functions can be implemented in polynomial time, and can be modified to generate synthetic data.

Theorem 7.7.1 (Point functions with differential privacy [2]). *For every data universe $\mathcal{X}$, $n \in \mathbb{N}$, and $\varepsilon, \delta > 0$ such that $\delta < 1/n$, there is a* $\text{poly}(n, \log |\mathcal{X}|)$*-time*

(ε, δ)-differentially private algorithm that takes a dataset of n rows from data universe $\mathcal{X} = \{0,1\}^d$ and outputs a synthetic dataset approximating the value of all counting queries in $\mathcal{Q}^{pt}(\mathcal{X})$ up to an additive error of

$$\alpha = O\left(\min\left\{\frac{\log|\mathcal{X}|}{\varepsilon n}, \frac{\log(1/\delta)}{\varepsilon n}, 1\right\}\right)$$

with high probability.

Proof sketch: The stability-based histogram of Theorem 7.3.5 with error $O(\log(1/\delta)/\varepsilon n)$ already runs in polynomial time, as it outputs nonzero values only for points that occur in the dataset. However, the basic Laplace-based histogram of Proposition 7.2.8 adds noise Lap$(2/\varepsilon)$ to the value of all $|\mathcal{X}| = 2^d$ point functions, and thus does not run in polynomial time. Thus, to obtain a polynomial-time algorithm with error $\alpha = O(\log|\mathcal{X}|/\varepsilon n)$, first we consider a modification of the Laplace-based histogram algorithm that only uses the largest $O(1/\alpha)$ noisy fractional counts and treats the rest as zero. This modification maintains differential privacy by closure under postprocessing, and can be shown to maintain error $O(\log|\mathcal{X}|/\varepsilon n)$. (Note that there can only be at most $1/\beta$ points whose exact fractional counts are at least $\beta = \Omega(\alpha)$, and outputting zero for the remaining points introduces an error of at most β.) With this modification, to implement the mechanism efficiently, we can first add (discrete) Laplace noise to the $m \leq n$ point functions q_y for the points y that occur at least once in the dataset, and then sample the distribution of the top $\lceil 1/\alpha \rceil$ values of $|\mathcal{X}| - m$ discrete Lap$(2/\varepsilon)$ random variables. Sampling the latter distribution to within sufficient accuracy to maintain differential privacy (with some additional modifications to the mechanism) can be done in time poly$(\log|\mathcal{X}|, 1/\varepsilon, \lceil 1/\alpha \rceil) = $ poly$(n, \log|\mathcal{X}|)$.

To obtain synthetic data in both cases, we can simply use the noisy answers to determine how many copies of each point to put in the synthetic dataset. With a synthetic dataset of size $O(1/\alpha)$, the errors due to rounding will only increase the error by a constant factor. ∎

7.7.2 Threshold Functions (CDFs)

For the class of threshold functions $\mathcal{Q}^{thr}([2^d])$ on domain $[2^d]$, for pure differential privacy ($\delta = 0$), again the best possible accuracy is $\Theta(d/\varepsilon n)$, matching the lower bound of Theorem 7.5.14, and it can be achieved in polynomial time:

Theorem 7.7.2 (Thresholds with pure differential privacy [41, 45]). *For every* $n, d \in \mathbb{N}$, $\varepsilon > 0$, *there is a* poly(n, d)-*time* $(\varepsilon, 0)$-*differentially private algorithm that takes a dataset of n rows from data universe* $\mathcal{X} = [2^d]$ *and outputs a synthetic dataset maintaining the value of all threshold-function counting queries up to an error of*

$$\alpha = \max\left\{\frac{O(d)}{\varepsilon n}, \tilde{O}\left(\frac{1}{\varepsilon n}\right)\right\}$$

with high probability.

Interestingly, in the case of approximate differential privacy, there is an inherent dependence on $\log^* d$ in the error.

Theorem 7.7.3 (Thresholds with approximate differential privacy [9, 22]). *For every $n, d \in \mathbb{N}$, $\varepsilon, \delta > 0$ such that $\exp(-\varepsilon n / \log^* n) \leq \delta \leq 1/n^2$:*

1. *There is a poly(n, d)-time (ε, δ)-differentially private algorithm that takes a dataset of n rows from data universe $\mathcal{X} = [2^d]$ and outputs a synthetic dataset maintaining the value of all threshold-function counting queries up to an error of*

$$\alpha = \max\left\{ \frac{2^{(1+o(1))\log^* d} \cdot \log(1/\delta)}{\varepsilon n}, \tilde{O}\left(\frac{1}{\varepsilon n}\right) \right\}.$$

2. *Every (ε, δ)-differentially private algorithm for answering all threshold functions on datasets of n rows from data universe $\mathcal{X} = [2^d]$ must incur an error of at least*

$$\alpha = \Omega\left(\min\left\{ \frac{(\log^* d) \cdot \log(1/\delta)}{\varepsilon n}, 1 \right\} \right).$$

We will not cover the proofs of these results, except to note that the $\log^* d$ lower bound has a Ramsey-theoretic proof [18], raising the possibility that there is a more general Ramsey-theoretic combinatorial quantity that can help in characterizing the optimal accuracy or sample complexity for differentially private algorithms (Open Problems 7.5.24 and 7.5.25).

Note that our understanding of threshold functions is not as tight as for point functions, and it would be interesting to close the gap between the upper and lower bounds. In particular:

Open Problem 7.7.4. Does the optimal error for releasing threshold functions over $\mathcal{X} = [2^d]$ with approximate differential privacy grow linearly or exponentially with $\log^* d$, or something in between?

7.7.3 Conjunctions (Marginals)

Unlike point functions and thresholds, the class $\mathcal{Q}^{\text{conj}}$ of conjunctions is unlikely to have a polynomial-time differentially private algorithm for generating synthetic data, by Theorem 7.6.12. This suggests that we should look to other ways of summarizing the answers to conjunction queries.

Indeed, we will sketch two algorithms that beat the barrier of Theorem 7.6.12 by avoiding synthetic data. One algorithm summarizes the answers to *all* conjunction queries in subexponential ($2^{\tilde{O}(\sqrt{d})}$) time (using a subexponential-sized dataset), using low-degree approximations to Boolean functions. (Assuming the existence of digital signature schemes with exponential security and nearly linear-time verification, the proof of Theorem 7.6.12 can be extended to show that generating synthetic data requires time at least $2^{d^{1-o(1)}}$, even when $n = 2^{d^{1-o(1)}}$.) The other algorithm answers all $k = \Theta(d^2)$ 2-way conjunctions in polynomial time with error $\tilde{O}(\sqrt{d})/\varepsilon n$, in particular allowing us to answer $k = \tilde{\Omega}(n^4) \gg n^2$ such queries, using ideas from convex geometry and optimization.

Theorem 7.7.5 (Marginals via low-degree approximation [102]). *There is a constant c such that for all $\varepsilon, \alpha > 0$, $d, n, t \in \mathbb{N}$ with $d \geq t$ and $n \geq d^{c \cdot \sqrt{t} \cdot \log(1/\alpha)} / \varepsilon$, there is an ε-differentially private algorithm running in time $\mathrm{poly}(n)$ that takes a dataset $x \in (\{0, 1\}^d)^n$ and, with high probability, outputs a "summary" (say, as a Boolean circuit) that allows for approximating the answer to all the queries in $\mathcal{Q}_t^{conj}(d)$ to within additive error α.*

A more sophisticated algorithm from [26] reduces the amount of data needed to nearly optimal ($n = O(t \cdot d^{0.51})$) at the cost of a larger (but still slightly subexponential) running time of $2^{o(d)}$.

Proof sketch: Starting with our dataset x with n rows in $\mathcal{X} = \{0, 1\}^d$, the mechanism $\mathcal{M}$ will produce a "summary" S that will approximate the function f_x defined as $f_x(q) = q(x)$. S will be a polynomial of low degree.

By introducing new variables for negative literals and negating our functions, it suffices to handle *monotone t-way disjunctions*, which can conveniently be specified by bit strings $y \in \{0, 1\}^d$:

$$q_y(w) = \bigvee_{i : y_i = 1} w_i, \qquad w \in \mathcal{X}. \tag{7.6}$$

For a t-way disjunction, y has Hamming weight t, and the value of $q_y(w)$ is determined by the value of $\sum_{i=1}^t w_i y_i \in \{0, \ldots, t\}$. Specifically

$$q_y(w) = \begin{cases} 1 & \sum_{i=1}^t w_i y_i \in \{1, \ldots, t\}, \\ 0 & \sum_{i=1}^t w_i y_i = 0. \end{cases} \tag{7.7}$$

Given a dataset x, we are interested in producing a (differentially private) approximation to the function $f_x(\cdot)$ defined as

$$f_x(y) = q_y(x) = \frac{1}{n} \sum_{i=1}^n q_y(x_i) = \frac{1}{n} \sum_{i=1}^n f_{x_i}(y).$$

We will approximate f_x by a low-degree polynomial by approximating each f_{x_i} by a low-degree polynomial. We do the latter using a standard technique based on Chebychev polynomials:

Fact 7.7.6 *For all $t \in \mathbb{N}$ and $\alpha > 0$, there exists a univariate (real) polynomial g of degree at most $s = O(\sqrt{t} \log(1/\alpha))$ such that $g(0) = 0$ and for all $i \in \{1, \ldots, t\}$, $1 - \alpha \leq g(i) \leq 1 + \alpha$. Moreover, g can be constructed in time $\mathrm{poly}(t, \log(1/\alpha))$ and all of the coefficients of g have magnitude at most 2^s.*

Given g as in the fact and a row $w \in \mathcal{X}$, consider the following function:

$$h_w(y) = g\left(\sum_{j=1}^d w_j y_j \right), \tag{7.8}$$

where g is from Fact 7.7.6. h_w is a multivariate polynomial of degree $O(\sqrt{t} \cdot \log(1/\alpha))$. It has at most $C = d^{O(\sqrt{t} \cdot \log(1/\alpha))}$ coefficients of magnitude at most $M = d^{O(\sqrt{t} \cdot \log(1/\alpha))}$.

By construction, we have that, for all $w \in \mathcal{X}$ and all $y \in \mathcal{X}$ of Hamming weight at most t,

$$|h_w(y) - f_w(y)| \le \alpha.$$

Thus, if we define

$$h_x = \frac{1}{n} \sum_{i=1}^{n} h_{x_i},$$

we have that

$$|h_x(y) - f_x(y)| \le \alpha.$$

To obtain differential privacy, we can now add Laplace noise to each coefficient of h_x. Each coefficient is an average of the corresponding coefficients of the h_{x_i}'s, so has global sensitivity at most $2M/n$. By the Laplace mechanism and basic composition, it suffices to add noise $\mathrm{Lap}(2MC/\varepsilon n)$ to each of the C coefficients for the resulting vector of coefficients to be differentially private. With high probability, none of the coefficients will have noise more than $(\log C) \cdot 2MC/\varepsilon n$, which will add up to an error of at most $C \cdot \log C \cdot 2MC/\varepsilon n = d^{O(\sqrt{t})}/(\varepsilon n)$ when evaluating on any input y.
∎

Now we turn to a different approach, which runs in polynomial time and can answer nearly n^4 low-order marginals.

Theorem 7.7.7 (Marginals via SDP projection [46]). *Let $t \in \mathbb{N}$ be an even constant. For all $n, d \in \mathbb{N}$, $\varepsilon, \delta > 0$, there is a polynomial-time (ε, δ)-differentially private algorithm that takes a dataset $x \in (\{0,1\}^d)^n$ and answers all counting queries in $\mathcal{Q}_t^{conj}(d)$ on x to within additive error*

$$\alpha = \left(\tilde{O}(d^{t/4}) \cdot \sqrt{\log(1/\delta)}/\varepsilon n\right)^{1/2}.$$

The most interesting case of this theorem is $t = 2$, when the error is $(\tilde{O}(\sqrt{d}) \cdot \sqrt{\log(1/\delta)}/\varepsilon n)^{1/2}$, matching the lower bound of Theorem 7.5.23 up to a factor of poly$(\log d, \log(1/\delta))$ [21].

Proof sketch: The starting point for the algorithm is a beautiful geometric approach of Nikolov, Talwar, and Zhang [85] that was used to prove the hereditary discrepancy upper bound (Theorem 7.5.10). We will use an instantiation of their algorithm that provides near-optimal error bounds in terms of $|\mathcal{Q}|$, like the private multiplicative weights algorithm, but for ℓ_2 or ℓ_1 error rather than ℓ_∞.

We know that adding independent noise of magnitude $O(\sqrt{|\mathcal{Q}|}/\varepsilon n)$ to the answers to all the counting queries in a family $\mathcal{Q}$ provides privacy, but gives useless results (that lie outside $[0, 1]$) when $|\mathcal{Q}| > n^2$. Remarkably, it turns out that simply projecting these answers back to be consistent with *some* dataset yields highly accurate results.

To formalize this, recall the convex body K used in the packing characterization of sample complexity (Theorem 7.5.15). That is, $K = \text{ConvexHull}(\{a_w : w \in \mathcal{X}\})$, where $a_w = (q(w))_{q \in \mathcal{Q}}$ is the vector in $\mathbb{R}^{\mathcal{Q}}$ giving all the query answers on row $w \in \mathcal{X}$. Recall that, for every dataset $x \in \mathcal{X}$, the tuple of answers on x is $a_x = (1/n) \sum_{i=1}^n a_{x_i} \in K$.

This leads to the following algorithm $\mathcal{M}(x, \mathcal{Q})$:

1. Calculate the exact answers

$$y = a_x = (q(x))_{q \in \mathcal{Q}} \in K.$$

2. Add *Gaussian* noise to the coordinates of y:

$$\tilde{y} = y + \frac{O(\sqrt{|\mathcal{Q}| \cdot \log(1/\delta)})}{\varepsilon n} \cdot \mathcal{N}(0, 1)^{|\mathcal{Q}|}.$$

(This can be shown to achieve (ε, δ)-differential privacy, and is more convenient than Laplace noise for the geometric arguments we are about to make.)

3. Project back to K: Let

$$\hat{y} = \text{argmin}_{z \in K} \|z - \tilde{y}\|_2.$$

This step maintains (ε, δ)-differential privacy by postprocessing.

Let us analyze the error introduced by this algorithm. Consider the line ℓ through y and $\hat{y}$, and let p be the orthogonal projection of $\tilde{y}$ onto ℓ. On ℓ, p must be on the ray from $\hat{y}$ to infinity. (If p were on the segment between y and $\hat{y}$, then p would be a point in K closer to $\tilde{y}$ than $\hat{y}$. If p were on the ray from y to infinity, then y would be a point in K closer to $\tilde{y}$ than $\hat{y}$.)

$$
\begin{aligned}
\|y - \hat{y}\|_2^2 &= \langle \hat{y} - y, \hat{y} - y \rangle \\
&\leq \langle \hat{y} - y, p - y \rangle && \text{(because p is on the ray from $\hat{y}$ to infinity)} \\
&= \langle \hat{y} - y, \tilde{y} - y \rangle && \text{(because $\tilde{y} - p$ is orthogonal to $\hat{y} - y$)} \\
&\leq (|\langle \hat{y}, \tilde{y} - y \rangle| + |\langle y, \tilde{y} - y \rangle|) && \text{(triangle inequality)} \\
&\leq 2 \max_{z \in K} |\langle z, \tilde{y} - y \rangle|.
\end{aligned}
$$

Taking expectations, and writing $\tilde{y} - y = O(\sqrt{|\mathcal{Q}| \cdot \log(1/\delta)}/\varepsilon n) \cdot g$ for $g \sim \mathcal{N}(0, 1)^{|\mathcal{Q}|}$, we have

$$\text{E}\left[\|y - \hat{y}\|_2^2\right] \leq \frac{O\left(\sqrt{|\mathcal{Q}| \cdot \log(1/\delta)}\right)}{\varepsilon n} \cdot \text{E}_g\left[\max_{z \in K} |\langle z, g \rangle|\right].$$

The quantity

$$\ell^*(K) \stackrel{\text{def}}{=} \text{E}_g \max_{z \in K} |\langle z, g \rangle|$$

is known as the *Gaussian mean width* of the polytope K, an important and well-studied quantity in convex geometry.

Let us upper bound it for K defined by an arbitrary set $\mathcal{Q}$ of counting queries. For every choice of g, the maximum of $|\langle z, g \rangle|$ over $z \in K$ will be obtained at one of the vertices of K. Recalling the definition of K, we have

$$\max_{z \in K} |\langle z, g \rangle| = \max_{w \in \mathcal{X}} |\langle a_w, g \rangle|.$$

By rotational symmetry of Gaussians, the random variable $\langle a_w, g \rangle$ is distributed as $\mathcal{N}(0, \|a_w\|_2)$. We have $\|a_w\|_2 \leq \sqrt{|\mathcal{Q}|}$ since a_w is a $\{0, 1\}$ vector. Thus, with probability at least $1 - \beta$ over g, we have $|\langle a_w, g \rangle| \leq O(\sqrt{|\mathcal{Q}| \cdot \log(1/\beta)})$. Taking a union bound over $w \in \mathcal{X}$, we have

$$\max_{w \in \mathcal{X}} |\langle a_w, g \rangle| \leq O\left(\sqrt{|\mathcal{Q}| \cdot \log(|\mathcal{X}|/\beta)} \right).$$

with probability at least $1 - \beta$, for every $\beta > 0$. This implies that

$$\mathop{\mathrm{E}}_g \left[\max_{z \in K} |\langle z, g \rangle| \right] = \mathop{\mathrm{E}}_g \left[\max_{w \in \mathcal{X}} |\langle a_w, g \rangle| \right] \leq O\left(\sqrt{|\mathcal{Q}| \cdot \log|\mathcal{X}|} \right).$$

Putting it all together, we have

$$\mathrm{E}\left[\|y - \hat{y}\|_2^2 \right] \leq \frac{|\mathcal{Q}| \cdot O(\sqrt{\log|\mathcal{X}| \cdot \log(1/\delta)})}{\varepsilon n}.$$

So if we look at the average error (averaged over the $|\mathcal{Q}|$ queries), we have

$$\mathop{\mathrm{E}}_{\text{coins of } \mathcal{M}, q \in \mathcal{Q}} \left[|y_q - \hat{y}_q| \right] \leq \left(\mathop{\mathrm{E}}_{\text{coins of } \mathcal{M}, q \in \mathcal{Q}} |y_q - \hat{y}_q|^2 \right)^{1/2}$$

$$= \left(\mathop{\mathrm{E}}_{\text{coins of } \mathcal{M}} \left[\frac{1}{|\mathcal{Q}|} \cdot \|y - \hat{y}\|_2^2 \right] \right)^{1/2}$$

$$= O\left(\frac{\sqrt{\log(1/\delta)}}{\sqrt{|\mathcal{Q}|} \cdot \varepsilon n} \cdot \ell^*(K) \right)^{1/2}$$

$$\leq O\left(\frac{\sqrt{\log|\mathcal{X}| \cdot \log(1/\delta)}}{\varepsilon n} \right)^{1/2}.$$

This exactly matches the (optimal) bound from the private multiplicative weights algorithm, except that we only achieve small error on average for a random query from $\mathcal{Q}$. However, it can be generalized to obtain small average-case error on any given distribution of queries (just weight the coordinates in $\mathbb{R}^{\mathcal{Q}}$ according to the distribution), and then combined with a differentially private algorithm for "boosting" [42] to obtain small error on all queries with high probability (paying a factor of $\mathrm{polylog}(|\mathcal{Q}|)$ in the error).

Our interest in this algorithm, however, is that it does not appear to generate synthetic data, and thus is not subject to the computational complexity lower bounds of Theorem 7.6.12. Converting the output $\hat{y}$ to synthetic data would amount to decomposing $\hat{y}$ into a convex combination of the $|\mathcal{X}|$ vertices of K, which could take time proportional to $|\mathcal{X}|$. Unfortunately, this same reason means that the "Project back to K" step might take time proportional to $|\mathcal{X}|$, as the given description of K is in terms of its $|\mathcal{X}|$ vertices. Indeed, projection onto a convex set is known to be polynomially equivalent to optimizing linear functions on the set, and as we will see below, optimizing over K is NP-hard for the cases we are interested in.

Let us see how to make this process more efficient for the case of 2-way marginals. For t-way marginals with $t > 2$, the theorem follows by reduction to 2-way marginals. (Create $\binom{d}{t/2} \leq d^{t/2}$ variables representing the conjunctions on every subset of $t/2$ variables; and then every t-way conjunction in the original variables can be written as a 2-way conjunction in the new variables.)

Actually, releasing conjunctions of width at most 2 is equivalent to releasing parities of width at most 2, so let us focus on the latter problem. It will also be useful to work in ± 1 notation, so the parity function $q_{ij} : \{\pm 1\}^d \to \{\pm 1\}$ on variables i and j is given by $q_{ij}(v) = v_i v_j$. Thus we see that

$$K = \mathrm{ConvexHull}(\{v \otimes v : v \in \{\pm 1\}^d\}).$$

Unfortunately, projecting onto and optimizing over K is known to be NP-hard, so we will take a cue from approximation algorithms and look at a semidefinite programming relaxation.

It is NP-hard to do this optimally. So instead, we will find a nicer L "close" to K (where $K \subseteq L$) and optimize over L. We need to ensure that the Gaussian mean width of L is comparable to that of K (or at least the bound we used on the Gaussian mean width of K).

First, we will relax to:

$$L_0 = \mathrm{ConvexHull}(\{v \otimes v' : v, v' \in \{\pm 1\}^d\}).$$

To bound the Gaussian mean width of K, we only used the fact that K is the convex hull of $|\mathcal{X}| = 2^d$ vectors whose entries have magnitude at most 1, and the bound was linear in $\sqrt{\log |\mathcal{X}|} = \sqrt{d}$. L_0 is now the convex hull of 2^{2d} such vectors, so we only lose a constant factor in our bound.

Optimizing over L_0 is still NP-hard, but it has polynomial-time approximation algorithms. Indeed, if we relax L_0 to

$$L = \{V \in \mathbb{R}^{d^2} : \exists \{u_i\}_{i=1}^d, \{u'_j\}_{j=1}^d \text{ unit vectors with } V_{ij} = \langle u_i, u'_j \rangle\},$$

then we can optimize linear functions on L by semidefinite programming, and consequently we can project onto L. Moreover, Grothendieck's inequality (see [71]) says that the maximum of any linear objective function on L is at most a factor of $K_G < 1.783$ larger than on L_0, which implies that

$$\ell^*(L) \leq K_G \cdot \ell^*(L_0) = O(\sqrt{|\mathcal{Q}| \cdot d}).$$

To summarize, the algorithm for the set $\mathcal{Q}$ of 2-way parities operates as follows:

1. Calculate the exact answers

$$y = a_x = (q(x))_{q \in \mathcal{Q}} \in K \subseteq \mathbb{R}^{d^2}.$$

2. Add *Gaussian* noise to the coordinates of y:

$$\tilde{y} = y + \frac{O(\sqrt{|\mathcal{Q}| \cdot \log(1/\delta)})}{\varepsilon n} \cdot \mathcal{N}(0,1)^{|\mathcal{Q}|}.$$

3. Project back to L: Let

$$\hat{y} = \operatorname{argmin}_{z \in L} \|z - \tilde{y}\|_2.$$

By the analysis we did earlier, the average error per query we obtain is at most

$$\mathop{\mathrm{E}}_{\text{coins of } \mathcal{M}, q \in \mathcal{Q}} \left[|y_q - \hat{y}_q|\right] \leq O\left(\frac{\sqrt{\log(1/\delta)}}{\sqrt{|\mathcal{Q}|} \cdot \varepsilon n} \cdot \ell^*(L)\right)^{1/2}$$

$$\leq O\left(\frac{\sqrt{d \cdot \log(1/\delta)}}{\varepsilon n}\right)^{1/2},$$

as desired. ∎

The theorems above show that we can bypass the intractability of producing differentially private summaries by focusing on specific, structured query classes, and by avoiding synthetic data. We summarize the state of knowledge about t-way marginals in Table 7.5. (Results for all marginals, i.e., $\mathcal{Q}^{\text{conj}}(d)$, roughly correspond to the case $t = d$, but in some cases will be off by a logarithmic factor, and we do not include the result based on the hereditary partial discrepancy of $\mathcal{Q}^{\text{conj}}(d)$ being $\tilde{\Theta}((2/\sqrt{3})^d)$ [77].)

As can be seen from the table, there are still important gaps in our state of knowledge, such as:

Open Problem 7.7.8. Is there a polynomial-time differentially private algorithm for estimating all (higher-order) marginals with vanishing error $\alpha = o(1)$ on a dataset with $n = \text{poly}(d)$ rows from data universe $\mathcal{X} = \{0,1\}^d$? Or at least all t-way marginals for some $t = \omega(1)$?

Open Problem 7.7.9. Is there a polynomial-time differentially private algorithm for estimating all 3-way marginals with vanishing error $\alpha = o(1)$ on a dataset with $n = o(d)$ rows from data universe $\mathcal{X} = \{0,1\}^d$?

Open Problem 7.7.10. For what other classes of queries can one bypass the intractability of generating differentially private synthetic data and answer more than n^2 queries with polynomial- or subexponential-time algorithms?

7.8 Private PAC Learning

We now examine the possibility of machine learning in Valiant's PAC model [106], under differential privacy. (See [70] for background on the PAC model.)

Table 7.5: Error bounds for $Q_t^{\text{conj}}(d)$ when $t \ll d$ with (ε, δ)-differential privacy on a dataset of size n. Computational lower bounds hold under plausible cryptographic assumptions (e.g., exponentially secure digital signatures with linear-time verification). "Synth?" indicates whether the entry refers to algorithms that generate synthetic data.

Type	Bound	Constraints	Runtime	Synth?	Ref.
Upper	$O\left(\frac{d^{t/2}\cdot\sqrt{\log(1/\delta)\cdot\log\log d}}{\varepsilon n}\right)$		$\text{poly}(n, d^t)$	no	Thm. 7.2.7
Upper	$O\left(\frac{t\log d\sqrt{d\log(1/\delta)}}{\varepsilon n}\right)^{1/2}$		$\text{poly}(n, 2^d)$	yes	Thm. 7.4.3
Upper	α	$n \geq d^{c\sqrt{t}\cdot\log(1/\alpha)}/\varepsilon$	$\text{poly}(n)$	no	Thm. 7.7.5
Upper	$\left(\tilde{O}(d^{t/4})\cdot\sqrt{\log(1/\delta)}/\varepsilon n\right)^{1/2}$	t even	$\text{poly}(n, d^t)$	no	Thm. 7.7.7
Lower	$\min\left\{\frac{\tilde{\Omega}(d^{t/2})}{n}, \tilde{\Omega}\left(\frac{1}{\sqrt{n}}\right)\right\}$	$t = O(1)$	any	no	[66]
Lower	$\Omega\left(\min\left\{\frac{t\log(d/t)}{n}, 1\right\}\right)$		any	no	[14]
Lower	$\min\left\{\tilde{\Omega}\left(\frac{t\sqrt{d}}{\varepsilon n}\right)^{1/2}, \Omega(1)\right\}$	$n \leq d^{O(1)}/\varepsilon$	any	no	Thm. 7.5.23
Lower	$\Omega(1)$	$t \geq 2$	$\leq 2^{d^{1-o(1)}}$	yes	Thm. 7.6.12

7.8.1 PAC Learning vs. Private PAC Learning

Recall that PAC learning considers, for each input length d, two sets of functions:

- A concept class $C = C_d = \{c : \{0,1\}^d \to \{0,1\}\}$, from which the unknown concept c we are trying to learn comes.
- A hypothesis class $\mathcal{H} = \mathcal{H}_d = \{h : \{0,1\}^d \to \{0,1\}\}$, which contains the functions we will use to try to represent our learned approximation of c.

Definition 7.8.1 (PAC learning). *A concept class C is PAC-learnable if there exist an algorithm L (called the* learner*) and a number n polynomial in d (called the* sample complexity*) such that, for every distribution D on $\{0,1\}^d$ and every $c \in C$, if we sample points $x_1, \ldots, x_n, x_{n+1}$ chosen independently according to D, with high probability $L(x_1, c(x_1), \cdots, x_n, c(x_n))$ returns a function $h \in \mathcal{H}$ such that $h(x_{n+1}) = c(x_{n+1})$.*

If $\mathcal{H} = C$, we call L a proper learner *and say that C is* properly PAC-learnable*. If L is poly-time computable as are the functions in $\mathcal{H}$ (given a $\text{poly}(d)$-bit description of a function $h \in \mathcal{H}$ as output by L and an input $w \in \{0,1\}^d$, we can evaluate h(d) in time $\text{poly}(d)$), then we say that L is an* efficient learner *and say that C is* efficiently PAC-learnable*.*

Definition 7.8.2 (Private PAC learning). *Private PAC learning is defined in the same way as PAC learning, but with the additional requirement that L is differentially private. That is, for all sequences $(x_1, y_1), \ldots, (x_n, y_n)$ and $(x_1', y_1'), \ldots, (x_n', y_n')$ that differ in one coordinate $i \in [n]$, $L((x_1, y_1), \ldots, (x_n, y_n))$ and $L((x_1', y_1'), \ldots, (x_n', y_n'))$*

are (ε, δ)-indistinguishable for some constant ε (e.g., $\varepsilon = 1$) and δ negligible in n and d.

Taking ε to be a constant is without loss of generality due to a generic reduction for improving ε (increase the sample size by a factor of ε/ε', and run the original learner on random subsample of the dataset). The success probability of the learner can also be amplified via "boosting", which has a differentially private analogue [42].

Note that, while the definition of PAC learning only speaks of inputs that consist of i.i.d. samples from an unknown distribution that is consistent with some concept $c \in C$, we require privacy on all (worst-case) pairs of neighboring input sequences. Indeed, if our modeling assumptions about the world are wrong, we naturally expect that our learner might fail, but we do not want the privacy promises to the data subjects to be broken. Also note that we consider the output of the learner to be the entire description of the hypothesis h, not just its prediction $h(x_{n+1})$ on the challenge point.

Amazingly, there is no gap between PAC learning and Private PAC learning, if we do not care about computation time:

Theorem 7.8.3 (Generic private learner [67]). *If C is (nonprivately) PAC-learnable (equivalently, $\mathrm{VC}(C) \leq \mathrm{poly}(d)$), then it is privately and properly PAC-learnable with sample complexity $O(\log |C|) \leq O(d \cdot \mathrm{VC}(C)) = \mathrm{poly}(d)$.*

The relation $\log |C| \leq d \cdot \mathrm{VC}(C)$ is the Perles–Sauer–Shelah lemma. (See [70].)
Proof: We use the exponential mechanism (Proposition 7.4.2). Let $\mathcal{H} = C$. On input $(x_1, y_1) \cdots (x_n, y_n)$, we

$$\text{output } h \in \mathcal{H} \text{ with probability } \propto e^{-\varepsilon \cdot |\{i : h(x_i) \neq y_i\}|}.$$

Since $\mathrm{score}(x, h) = -|\{i : h(x_i) \neq y_i\}|$ has sensitivity 1 as a function of the dataset x, Proposition 7.4.2 tells us that this mechanism is 2ε-differentially private.

To prove that the learner succeeds with high probability, consider $x_1, \cdots, x_n$ that are taken according to some unknown distribution D, and let $y_i = c(x_i)$.

If $n \geq O(\mathrm{VC}(C) \cdot \log(1/\alpha)/\alpha^2)$, then Occam's razor from learning theory (cf. [70]) tells us that with high probability over $x_1 \cdots x_n$, we have

$$\forall h \in C \qquad \left| \frac{\#\{i : h(x_i) = c(x_i)\}}{n} - \Pr_{w \sim D}[h(w) = c(w)] \right| \leq \alpha.$$

Combining this with Proposition 7.4.2, we know that with high probability the hypothesis h we output satisfies

$$\Pr_{w \sim D}[h(w) = c(w)] \geq \frac{\#\{i : h(x_i) = c(x_i)\}}{n} - \alpha$$

$$\geq \frac{\operatorname{argmax}_{h^*} \#\{i : h^*(x_i) = c(x_i)\} - O(\log |\mathcal{C}|)/\varepsilon}{n} - \alpha$$

$$= \frac{n - O(\log |\mathcal{C}|)/\varepsilon}{n} - \alpha$$

$$\geq 1 - 2\alpha,$$

provided $n \geq O(\log |\mathcal{C}|)/\varepsilon\alpha$.

We are done when taking

$$n = O\left(\max\left\{\frac{\log |\mathcal{C}|}{\varepsilon\alpha}, \frac{\mathrm{VC}(\mathcal{C}) \cdot \log(1/\alpha)}{\alpha^2}\right\}\right) \ll 1.$$

∎

7.8.2 Computationally Efficient Private PAC Learning

Unfortunately, as is often the case with the exponential mechanism, Theorem 7.8.3 does not produce computationally efficient private learners. Thus, we now investigate what can be learned in polynomial time under differential privacy.

Nonprivately, most examples of computationally efficient PAC learners are learners in the *statistical query model* of Kearns [69]. This is a model where the learner does not get direct access to labeled samples $(x_i, c(x_i))$, but is allowed to obtain additive approximations to the expectation of any (efficiently computable) function $f : \{0, 1\}^d \times \{0, 1\} \to [0, 1]$ on the labeled distribution. That is, on specifying statistical query f, the learner obtains an answer in the range $E_{w \leftarrow D}[f(w, c(w))] \pm 1/\operatorname{poly}(n)$. Efficient statistical query learners can be simulated by efficient PAC learners because expectations $E_{w \leftarrow D}[f(w, c(w))]$ can be estimated to within $\pm 1/\operatorname{poly}(n)$ by taking the average of $f(x_i, c(x_i))$ over $m = \operatorname{poly}(n)$ random samples $x_i \leftarrow D$. Such estimations are also easily done with differential privacy, as an average of $f(x_i, y_i)$ over m samples (x_i, y_i) has global sensitivity at most $2/m$ as a function of the dataset, and thus can be estimated via the Laplace mechanism. Thus, we have the following:

Theorem 7.8.4 (Private SQ learning [13]). *Every concept class that is efficiently PAC learnable in the statistical query model (which includes Q^{pt}, Q^{thr}, and Q^{conj}) is efficiently and privately PAC learnable.*

In fact, Kasiviswanathan et al. [67] showed that (efficient) statistical query learners are *equivalent* to (efficient) private learners in the "local model" of privacy (which will be discussed more in the next section).

However, there are some concept classes that are efficiently PAC learnable that are provably not learnable in the statistical query model, most notably the class of parity functions, that is, the class of functions $\{0, 1\}^d \to \{0, 1\}$ of the form $x \mapsto c \cdot x$, where $c \cdot x$ is taken modulo 2. It turns out that there is an elegant, efficient private learner for this class, showing that efficient private learning goes beyond the statistical query model:

Theorem 7.8.5 (Private learning of parities [67]). *The class $Q^{par} = Q^{par}(d)$ of parity functions on $\{0, 1\}^d$ is efficiently and privately PAC learnable, with sample complexity $n = O(d/\varepsilon)$ for $(\varepsilon, 0)$-differential privacy.*

Since the class of parity functions on $\{0, 1\}^d$ has VC dimension d, the sample complexity for private learning is within a constant factor of the sample complexity for nonprivate learning.

Proof: We have a dataset (x, y) with n rows (x_i, y_i), where $x_i \in \{0, 1\}^d$ and $y_i \in \{0, 1\}$. Assume that $x_1, \ldots, x_n$ are drawn independently from some distribution D, and that there is some $c \in \{0, 1\}^d$ such that $y_i = c \cdot x_i$ for all $1 \le i \le n$. We wish to determine a hypothesis $h \in \{0, 1\}^d$ such that, if x is drawn from D, then $h \cdot x = c \cdot x$ with probability at least 0.99.

A simple (nonprivate) algorithm is to take any h such that $y_i = h \cdot x_i$ for all i. We can do this by using Gaussian elimination to solve the system of linear equations $y = h \cdot x$. Standard calculations show that this succeeds with $n = O(d)$ samples.

Now let us consider private learning, keeping in mind that we need to ensure privacy even when the data is inconsistent with the concept class. Indeed, we need to make sure that we do not leak information by revealing whether or not the data is consistent! For instance, we need to make sure that the algorithm's output distribution only changes by ε (multiplicatively) if we add a single row (x_i, y_i) such that $y_i \ne c \cdot x_i$.

Our mechanism $\mathcal{M}$ works as follows; we use $\bot$ to denote failure. We will start by succeeding with probability about $1/2$, and amplify this probability later.

1. Take $n = O(d/\varepsilon)$ samples.
2. With probability $1/2$, output $\bot$.
3. For each $1 \le i \le n$, set $\hat{x}_i, \hat{y}_i$ independently as follows:

$$(\hat{x}_i, \hat{y}_i) = \begin{cases} (0^d, 0) & \text{with probability } 1 - \varepsilon, \\ (x_i, y_i) & \text{with probability } \varepsilon. \end{cases}$$

   Call the resulting dataset $(\hat{x}, \hat{y})$. This is effectively a random sample of the original dataset, containing an expected fraction ε of the rows. The zero entries $(\hat{x}_i, \hat{y}_i) = (0^d, 0)$ will have no effect on what follows.
4. Using Gaussian elimination, determine the affine subspace V of hypotheses h that are consistent with $(\hat{x}, \hat{y})$, i.e.,

$$V = \{h \mid \forall i : \hat{y}_i = h \cdot \hat{x}_i\}.$$

   Output an h chosen uniformly from V. If $V = \emptyset$ (i.e., if no consistent h exists), then output $\bot$.

Since the nonprivate algorithm described above succeeds with probability 0.99, if the data is consistent then $\mathcal{M}$ succeeds with probability at least 0.49. We can amplify by repeating this t times, in which case the sample complexity is $n = O(td/\varepsilon)$.

Now we analyze $\mathcal{M}$'s privacy. We willfully identify $1 \pm \varepsilon$ with $e^{\pm\varepsilon}$, neglecting $O(\varepsilon^2)$ terms.

Claim 7.8.6. $\mathcal{M}$ is $(2\varepsilon, 0)$-differentially private.

Proof of claim: Let $x \sim x'$ be two neighboring datasets that differ at one row i. Assume that $(x_i', y_i') = (0^d, 0)$. Since we can get from any x to any x'' by going through such an x', if we can show that $\mathcal{M}(x)$ and $\mathcal{M}(x')$ are $(\varepsilon, 0)$-indistinguishable, then $\mathcal{M}$ will be $(2\varepsilon, 0)$-differentially private.

With probability $1 - \varepsilon$, we replace (x_i, y_i) with $(0^d, 0)$ in step 3 (assuming we make it past step 2). In that case, $(\hat{x}, \hat{y}) = (\hat{x}', \hat{y}')$, and the output probabilities are the same. Thus for all possible outputs z,

$$\Pr[\mathcal{M}(x) = z] \geq (1 - \varepsilon)\Pr[\mathcal{M}(x') = z]. \tag{7.9}$$

But we are not done. The problem is that x' is special (by our assumption) so the reverse inequality does not automatically hold. We also need to prove

$$\Pr[\mathcal{M}(x) = z] \leq (1 + \varepsilon)\Pr[\mathcal{M}(x') = z]. \tag{7.10}$$

To prove (7.10), start by fixing $(\hat{x}_j, \hat{y}_j) = (\hat{x}_j', \hat{y}_j')$ for all $j \neq i$. (Thus, we are coupling the algorithm's random choices on the two datasets.) Let V_{-i} be the affine subspace consistent with these rows:

$$V_{-i} = \{h \mid \forall j \neq i : \hat{y}_j = h \cdot \hat{x}_j\}.$$

As before, if we fail or if we set $(\hat{x}_i, \hat{y}_i) = (0^d, 0) = (\hat{x}_i', \hat{y}_i')$, the output probabilities are the same. On the other hand, with probability $\varepsilon/2$ we pass step 2 and set $(\hat{x}_i, \hat{y}_i) = (x_i, y_i)$ in step 3. In that case, $\mathcal{M}(x')$ is uniform in V_{-i} (or $\mathcal{M}(x') = \perp$ if $V_{-i} = \emptyset$), while $\mathcal{M}(x)$ is uniform in

$$V = V_{-i} \cap \{h \mid y_i = h \cdot x_i\}$$

(or $\mathcal{M}(x) = \perp$ if $V = \emptyset$).

Let us compare the probabilities that $\mathcal{M}(x)$ and $\mathcal{M}(x')$ fail. If $V_{-i} = \emptyset$, then $\mathcal{M}(x) = \mathcal{M}(x') = \perp$. But if $V_{-i} \neq \emptyset$ but $V = \emptyset$, the probability that $\mathcal{M}(x)$ fails is at most $1/2 + \varepsilon/2$; and since $\mathcal{M}(x')$ fails with probability at least $1/2$, we have

$$\Pr[\mathcal{M}(x) = \perp] \leq \frac{1 + \varepsilon}{2} \leq (1 + \varepsilon) \cdot \Pr[\mathcal{M}(x') = \perp].$$

Finally, we come to the most interesting case: comparing the probabilities that $\mathcal{M}(x)$ and $\mathcal{M}(x')$ output some hypothesis h, where both V_{-i} and V are nonempty and contain h. Since V is obtained by adding one linear constraint to V_{-i}, we have

$$|V| \geq \frac{1}{2}|V_{-i}|.$$

Since $\mathcal{M}(x)$ and $\mathcal{M}(x')$ are uniform in V and V_{-i}, respectively, for every $h \in V_{-i}$ we have

$$\Pr[\mathcal{M}(x) = h] \le \frac{1}{2}\left(\frac{1-\varepsilon}{|V_{-i}|} + \frac{\varepsilon}{|V|}\right) \le \frac{1}{2} \cdot \frac{1+\varepsilon}{|V_{-i}|} = (1+\varepsilon)\Pr[\mathcal{M}(x') = h],$$

which completes the proof.   ∎   ∎

Since linear algebra was essentially the only known technique for efficient private learning outside the statistical query model, this result suggested that perhaps every concept that is efficiently PAC learnable is also efficiently and privately PAC learnable. Bun and Zhandry [20] recently gave evidence that this is not the case.

Theorem 7.8.7 (Hardness of private learning [20]). *If "indistinguishability obfuscation" and "perfectly sound noninteractive zero-knowledge proofs for NP" exist, then there is a concept class that is efficiently PAC learnable but not efficiently PAC learnable with differential privacy.*

7.8.3 The Sample Complexity of Private PAC Learning

Another gap between PAC learning and private PAC learning is in sample complexity. The sample complexity of nonprivate learning is characterized by $\Theta(\mathrm{VC}(\mathcal{C}))$, whereas for private learning we have the upper bound $O(\log|\mathcal{C}|)$ from Theorem 7.8.5, which can be as large as $d \cdot \mathrm{VC}(\mathcal{C})$ on a domain of size 2^d. Two classes that illustrate this gap are the classes of point functions and threshold functions ($\mathcal{Q}^{\mathrm{pt}}$ and $\mathcal{Q}^{\mathrm{thr}}$). In both cases, we have $\mathrm{VC}(\mathcal{C}) = 1$ but $\log|\mathcal{C}| = d$.

For the class $\mathcal{C} = \mathcal{Q}^{\mathrm{pt}}(d)$ of point functions on $\{0,1\}^d$ and $(\varepsilon, 0)$-differentially private *proper* learners, Beimel, Brenner, Kasiviswanathan, and Nissim [10] showed that the best possible sample complexity is $\Theta(d)$, similarly to the situation with releasing approximate answers to all point functions (Proposition 7.2.8 and Theorem 7.5.14). If we relax the requirement to *either* improper learning or approximate differential privacy, then, similarly to Theorem 7.3.5, the sample complexity becomes independent of d, namely $O(1)$ or $O(\log(1/\delta))$, respectively [10, 9].

For the class $\mathcal{C} = \mathcal{Q}^{\mathrm{thr}}([2^d])$ of threshold functions on $\{1, \ldots, 2^d\}$, again it is known that $\Theta(d)$ sample complexity is the best possible sample complexity for $(\varepsilon, 0)$-differentially private proper learners [10], similarly to Theorem 7.7.2. In contrast to point functions, however, it is known that relaxing to either (ε, δ)-differential privacy or to improper learning is *not* enough to achieve sample complexity $O(1)$. For (ε, δ)-differentially private proper learners, the sample complexity is somewhere between $2^{(1+o(1))\log^* d} \cdot \log(1/\delta)$ and $\Omega(\log^* d)$, similarly to Theorem 7.7.3. For $(\varepsilon, 0)$-differentially private learners, the sample complexity was recently shown to be $\Omega(d)$ by Feldman and Xiao [50]. We present the proof of this result, because it uses beautiful connections between VC dimension, private learning, and communication complexity.

Every concept class $\mathcal{C}$ defines a one-way communication problem as follows: Alice has a function $c \in \mathcal{C}$, Bob has a string $w \in \{0,1\}^d$, and together they want to compute $c(w)$. The *one-way communication complexity* of this problem is the length of the shortest message m that Alice needs to send to Bob that lets him compute $c(w)$. We will consider randomized, distributional communication complexity, where the inputs are chosen according to some distribution μ on $C \times \{0,1\}^d$, and Bob should compute $c(w)$ correctly with high probability over the choice of the inputs and the (shared) randomness between Alice and Bob. We write $\mathrm{CC}_{\mu,\alpha}^{\to,\mathrm{pub}}(C)$ to denote the minimum message length over all protocols where Bob computes $c(w)$ with probability at least $1 - \alpha$.

It was known that maximizing this communication complexity over all *product distributions* characterizes the sample complexity of nonprivate learning (i.e., VC dimension):

Theorem 7.8.8 (CC characterization of nonprivate learning [73]). *For every constant $\alpha \in (0, 1/8)$,*

$$\mathrm{VC}(C) = \Theta\left(\max_{\mu_A,\mu_B} \mathrm{CC}_{\mu_A \otimes \mu_B, \alpha}^{\to,\mathrm{pub}}(C)\right),$$

where μ_A and μ_B are distributions on C and $\{0,1\}^d$, respectively.

Building on Beimel et al. [8], Feldman and Xiao [50] showed that the sample complexity of learning C with pure differential privacy is related to the one-way communication complexity maximized over all *joint* distributions on $C \times \{0,1\}^d$.

Theorem 7.8.9 (CC characterization of learning with pure differential privacy [50]). *For all constants $\varepsilon > 0$, $\alpha \in (0, 1/2)$, the smallest sample complexity for learning C under $(\varepsilon, 0)$-differential privacy is $\Theta(\max_\mu \mathrm{CC}_{\mu,\alpha}^{\to,\mathrm{pub}}(C))$.*

We note that, by Yao's minimax principle, $\max_\mu \mathrm{CC}_{\mu,\alpha}^{\to,\mathrm{pub}}(C)$ is simply equal to the worst-case randomized communication complexity of C, where we want a protocol such that, on every input, Bob computes the correct answer with probability at least $1 - \alpha$ over the public coins of the protocol. Returning to threshold functions, computing $c_y(w)$ is equivalent to computing the "greater than" function. Miltersen et al. [80] showed that for this problem the randomized communication complexity is $\Omega(d)$, proving that learning thresholds with pure differential privacy requires sample complexity $\Omega(d)$.

Proof sketch of Theorem 7.8.9: We begin by showing that the communication complexity is upper-bounded by the sample complexity of private learning. Let L be an $(\varepsilon, 0)$-differentially private learner for C with a given sample complexity n; we will use L to construct a communication protocol. Using their shared randomness, Alice and Bob both run L on the all-zeroes dataset $x^{(0)}$. They do this M times for M to be determined in a moment, giving a list of shared functions $h_1, \ldots, h_M \in \mathcal{H}$.

Since L is $(\varepsilon, 0)$-differentially private, by group privacy, the distribution of functions returned by L "covers" the distribution on every other dataset $x \in \mathcal{X}^n$, in the sense that, for each $h \in \mathcal{H}$,

$$\Pr[L(x^{(0)}) = h] \ge e^{-\varepsilon n} \Pr[L(x) = h].$$

Thus with $M = e^{O(\varepsilon n)}$ samples, Alice and Bob can ensure that, with high probability, at least one h_i in their shared list is a good hypothesis for any particular dataset.

In particular, let μ be a distribution on pairs (c, w), and let $c_0 \in C$ be Alice's function. Then there is some $1 \leq i \leq M$ such that h_i is a good hypothesis for the dataset x we would get by sampling the rows of x from the conditional distribution $\mu(w \mid c = c_0)$: that is, $h_i(w) = c_0(w)$ with high probability in w. Alice can send Bob this index i with communication complexity $\log M = O(\varepsilon n)$.

Conversely, suppose that we have a randomized, public-coin protocol for C with communication complexity at most n. Every setting r of the public randomness and message m from Alice defines a hypothesis $h_{r,m}$ which Bob uses to compute the output of the protocol (by applying it to his input w). Given a dataset $(x_1, y_1), \ldots, (x_n, y_n)$, our differentially private learner will choose r uniformly at random, and then use the exponential mechanism to select an m approximately maximizing $|\{i : h_{r,m}(x_i) = y_i\}|$, similarly to the use of the exponential mechanism in the proof of Theorem 7.8.3. The sample complexity n required by the exponential mechanism is logarithmic in the size of the hypothesis class $\mathcal{H}_r = \{h_{r,m}\}$, so we have $n = O(|m|)$. $\blacksquare$

While this provides a tight characterization of the sample complexity of learning with pure differential privacy, the case of approximate differential privacy is still very much open.

Open Problem 7.8.10. Does every concept class C over $\{0, 1\}^d$ have an (ε, δ)-differentially private learner with sample complexity $n = O(\text{VC}(C) \cdot \text{polylog}(1/\delta))$ (for δ negligible in n and d)? Or are there concept classes where the sample complexity must be $n = \Omega(d \cdot \text{VC}(C))$?

These questions are open for both proper and improper learning. In the case of proper learning, there are concept classes known where the sample complexity is at least $\Omega(\log^* d \cdot \text{VC}(C) \cdot \log(1/\delta))$, such as threshold functions [22], but this does not rule out an upper bound of $n = O(\text{VC}(C) \cdot \text{polylog}(1/\delta))$ when δ is negligible in n and d.

7.9 Multiparty Differential Privacy

7.9.1 The Definition

We now consider an extension of differential privacy to a multiparty setting, where the data is divided among some m parties $P_1, \ldots, P_m$. For simplicity, we will assume that m divides n and each party P_k has exactly n/m rows of the dataset, which we will denote by $x_k = (x_{k,1}, x_{k,2}, \ldots, x_{k,n/m})$. (Note the change in notation; now x_k is a subdataset, not an individual row.) We consider the case that P_k wants to ensure the privacy of the rows in x_k against an adversary who may control the other parties.

As in the studies of secure multiparty computation (cf. [52]), there are many variants of the adversary model that we can consider:

- Passive versus active: for simplicity, we will restrict to passive adversaries — ones that follow the specified protocol — but try to extract information from the communication seen (also known as "honest-but-curious" adversaries). Since

our emphasis is on lower bounds, this only strengthens the results. However, all
of the upper bounds we mention are also known to hold for active adversaries.

- Threshold adversaries: we can restrict the adversary to control at most t parties
  for some $t \leq m - 1$. For simplicity, we will only consider the case $t = m - 1$.
  Consequently we may assume without loss of generality that all communication
  occurs on a broadcast channel, as the adversary would anyhow see all communication on point-to-point channels.
- Computationally bounded versus unbounded: as in the basic definition of differential privacy, we will (implicitly) consider computationally unbounded adversaries. In the next section, we will discuss computationally bounded adversaries.

A *protocol* proceeds in a sequence of rounds until all honest parties terminate.
Informally, in each round, each party P_k selects a message to be broadcast based on
its input $x^{(k)}$, internal coin tosses, and all messages received in previous rounds. The
output of the protocol is specified by a deterministic function of the transcript of
messages exchanged. (As in secure multiparty computation, one can also consider
individual outputs computed by the parties P_k, which may depend on their private
input and coin tosses, but we do not do that for simplicity.) Given a particular ad-
versary strategy A, we write $\text{View}_A((A \leftrightarrow (P_1, \ldots, P_m))(x))$ for the random variable
that includes everything that A sees when participating in the protocol $(P_1, \ldots, P_m)$
on input x. In the case we consider, where A is a passive adversary controlling
$P_{-k} = (P_1, P_2, \ldots, P_{k-1}, P_{k+1}, \ldots, P_m)$, $\text{View}_A(A \leftrightarrow (P_1, \ldots, P_m)(x))$ is determined
by the inputs and coin tosses of all parties other than P_k as well as the messages sent
by P_k.

Definition 7.9.1 (Multiparty differential privacy [7]). *For a protocol $P = (P_1,
\ldots, P_m)$ taking as input datasets $(x_1, \ldots, x_m) \in (\mathcal{X}^{n/m})^m$, we say that P is (ε, δ)-
differentially private (for passive adversaries) if, for every $k \in [m]$ and every two
datasets $x, x' \in (\mathcal{X}^{n/m})^m$ that differ on one row of P_k's input (and are equal otherwise), the following holds for every set T:*

$$\Pr[\text{View}_{P_{-k}}(P_{-k} \leftrightarrow (P_1, \ldots, P_m)(x)) \in T]$$
$$\leq e^{\varepsilon} \cdot \Pr[\text{View}_{P_{-k}}(P_{-k} \leftrightarrow (P_1, \ldots, P_m)(x')) \in T] + \delta.$$

7.9.2 The Local Model

Constructing useful differentially private multiparty protocols for $m \geq 2$ parties is
harder than constructing them in the standard centralized model (corresponding to
$m = 1$), as a trusted curator could just simulate the entire protocol and provide
only the output. An extreme case is when $m = n$, in which case the individual data
subjects need not trust anyone else, because they can just play the role of a party in
the protocol. This is the *local model* that we've alluded to several times in earlier
sections. While this is the hardest model of distributed differential privacy, there are
nontrivial protocols in it, namely *randomized response* (as in Section 7.1.5):

Theorem 7.9.2 (Randomized response). *For every counting query* $q : \mathcal{X} \to \{0, 1\}$, $n \in \mathbb{N}$, *and* $\varepsilon > 0$, *there is an* $(\varepsilon, 0)$-*differentially private n-party protocol in the local model for computing q to within error* $\alpha = O(1/(\varepsilon \sqrt{n}))$ *with high probability.*

This can be extended to estimating statistical queries $q : \mathcal{X} \to [0, 1]$ over the dataset—first randomly round $q(x_k)$ to a bit $b_k \in \{0, 1\}$ with expectation $q(x_k)$ (i.e., set $b_k = 1$ with probability $q(x_k)$), and then apply randomized response to b_k. This gives some intuition for why everything that is PAC learnable in the statistical query model is PAC learnable in the local model, as mentioned in Section 7.8.

Note that the error in Theorem 7.9.2 is significantly worse than the error $O(1/\varepsilon n)$ we get with a centralized curator. Building on [7, 78], Chan et al. [25] proved that the $1/\sqrt{n}$ decay is in fact optimal:

Theorem 7.9.3 (Randomized response is optimal in the local model [25]). *For every* nonconstant *counting query* $q : \mathcal{X} \to \{0, 1\}$, $n \in \mathbb{N}$, *and* $(1, 0)$-*differentially private n-party protocol P for approximating q, there is an input dataset* $x \in \mathcal{X}^n$ *on which P has error* $\alpha = \Omega(1/\sqrt{n})$ *with high probability.*

Proof sketch: We first prove it for $\mathcal{X} = \{0, 1\}$, and q being the identity function (i.e., we are computing the average of the input bits). Consider a uniformly random input dataset $X = (X_1, \dots, X_n) \leftarrow \{0, 1\}^n$, let $R = (R_1, \dots, R_n)$ denote the randomness of the n parties, and let $T = T(X, R)$ be the random variable denoting the transcript of the protocol. Let $t \in \mathrm{Supp}(T)$ be any value of T. We claim that, conditioned on $T = t$:

1. The n random variables $(X_1, R_1), \dots, (X_n, R_n)$ are independent, and in particular $X_1, \dots, X_n$ are independent.
2. Each $\Pr[X_i = 1] \in (1/4, 3/4)$.

Item 1 is a general fact about interactive protocols—if the parties' inputs start independent, they remain independent conditioned on the transcript—and can be proven by induction on the number of rounds of the protocol. Item 2 uses $(\varepsilon = 1, 0)$-differential privacy and Bayes' rule:

$$\frac{\Pr[X_i = 1 | T = t]}{\Pr[X_i = 0 | T = t]} = \frac{\Pr[T = t | X_i = 1] \cdot \Pr[X_i = 1] / \Pr[T = t]}{\Pr[T = t | X_i = 0] \cdot \Pr[X_i = 0] / \Pr[T = t]}$$
$$= \frac{\Pr[T = t | X_i = 1]}{\Pr[T = t | X_i = 0]}$$
$$\in [e^{-\varepsilon}, e^{\varepsilon}].$$

This implies that

$$\Pr[X_i = 1 | T = t] \in \left[\frac{1}{e^{\varepsilon} + 1}, \frac{e^{\varepsilon}}{e^{\varepsilon} + 1} \right] \subset (1/4, 3/4)$$

for $\varepsilon = 1$.

Consequently, conditioned on $T = t$, $(1/n) \cdot (\sum_i X_i)$ is the average of n independent $\{0, 1\}$ random variables with bounded bias. In particular, the standard deviation of

$\sum_i X_i$ is $\Omega(1/\sqrt{n})$, and by anticoncentration bounds, with high probability we will have

$$\left| (1/n) \sum_i X_i - \text{output}(t) \right| = \Omega(1/\sqrt{n}),$$

where output$(\cdot)$ is the output function of the protocol. Since the protocol has error $\Omega(1/\sqrt{n})$ on a random dataset with high probability, there is some fixed dataset on which it has error $\Omega(1/\sqrt{n})$ with high probability.

To obtain the result for general nonconstant counting queries $q : \mathcal{X} \to \{0, 1\}$, fix two inputs $w_0, w_1 \in \mathcal{X}$ such that $q(w_b) = b$, and restrict to datasets of the form $(w_{b_1}, \ldots, w_{b_n})$ for $b_1, \ldots, b_n \in \{0, 1\}$. Estimating the counting query q on such datasets with differential privacy is equivalent to estimating the average function on datasets of the form $(b_1, \ldots, b_n)$ with differential privacy. ∎

Effectively, what the above proof is using is a "randomness extraction" property of the SUM function. Specifically, for every source Y consisting of n independent bits $Y = (Y_1, \ldots, Y_n)$ that are not too biased, $\sum_i Y_i$ has a lot of "randomness"—it is not concentrated in any interval of width $O(\sqrt{n})$. (In the proof, $Y_i = X_i|_{T=t}$.) In fact, a stronger statement is true: $\sum_i Y_i \mod k$ can be shown to be almost uniformly distributed in $\mathbb{Z}_k$ for some $k = \Omega(\sqrt{n})$. In the language of randomness extractors (see [94, 105]), we would say that "the sum modulo k function is a (deterministic) randomness extractor for the class of sources consisting of n independent bits with bounded bias."

7.9.3 Two-Party Differential Privacy

Now let us look at the case of $m = 2$ parties each holding $n/2$ rows of the dataset, which seems closer to the trusted curator case than to the local model. Indeed, in this model, any counting query can be computed with error $O(1/\varepsilon n)$: each party just adds $\text{Lap}(1/(\varepsilon \cdot (n/2)))$ noise to the counting query on her own dataset and announces the result; we average the two results to estimate the overall counting query. However, there are other simple queries where again there is a quadratic gap between the single curator ($m = 1$) and two-party case, namely the (normalized) inner product function $\text{IP} : \{0, 1\}^{n/2} \times \{0, 1\}^{n/2} \to [0, 1]$ given by $\text{IP}(x, y) = \langle x, y \rangle / (n/2)$. IP has global sensitivity $2/n$, and hence can be computed by a single trusted curator with error $O(1/n)$). But for two parties (one given x and one given y), the best possible error is again $\tilde{\Theta}(1/\sqrt{n})$:

Theorem 7.9.4 (Two-party DP protocols for inner product [81, 78]).

1. *There is a two-party differentially private protocol that estimates* IP *to within error* $O(1/\varepsilon \cdot \sqrt{n})$ *with high probability, and*
2. *Every two party* $(1, 0)$-*differentially private protocol for* IP *incurs error* $\tilde{\Omega}(1/\sqrt{n})$ *with high probability on some dataset.*

Proof sketch: For the upper bound, we again use randomized response:

1. On input $x \in \{0, 1\}^{n/2}$, Alice uses randomized response to send a noisy version $\hat{x}$ of x to Bob.

2. Upon receiving $\hat{x}$ and his input $y \in \{0, 1\}^{n/2}$, Bob computes

$$z = \frac{2}{n} \sum_{i=1}^{n/2} \frac{y_i}{\varepsilon} \cdot \left(\hat{x}_i - \frac{(1-\varepsilon)}{2} \right),$$

which will approximate $\mathrm{IP}(x, y)$ to within $O(1/\varepsilon \sqrt{n})$.

3. Bob sends the output $z + \mathrm{Lap}(O(1/\varepsilon^2 n))$ to Alice, where this Laplace noise is to protect the privacy of y, since z has global sensitivity $O(1/\varepsilon n)$ as a function of y.

For the lower bound, we follow the same outline as Theorem 7.9.3. Let $X = (X_1, \ldots, X_{n/2})$ and $Y = (Y_1, \ldots, Y_{n/2})$ each be uniformly distributed over $\{0, 1\}^{n/2}$ and independent of each other. Then, conditioned on a transcript t of an $(\varepsilon, 0)$-differentially private protocol, we have:

1. X and Y are independent, and
2. For every $i \in [n/2]$, $x_1, \ldots, x_{i-1}, x_{i+1}, \ldots, x_n$,

$$\Pr[X_i = 1 | X_1 = x_1, \ldots, X_{i-1} = x_{i-1}, X_{i+1} = x_{i+1}, \ldots, X_n = x_n] \in (1/4, 3/4),$$

and similarly for Y.

Item 2 again follows from differential privacy and Bayes' rule. (Consider the two neighboring datasets $(x_1, \ldots, x_{i-1}, 0, x_{i+1}, \ldots, x_n)$ and $(x_1, \ldots, x_{i-1}, 1, x_{i+1}, \ldots, x_n)$.) In the literature on randomness extractors, sources satisfying item 2 are known as "Santha–Vazirani sources" or "unpredictable-bit sources", because no bit can be predicted with high probability given the others. (Actually, the usual definition only requires that item 2 hold when conditioning on past bits $X_1 = x_1, \ldots, X_{i-1} = x_{i-1}$, so the sources we have are a special case.)

One of the early results in randomness extractors is that the (nonnormalized) inner product modulo 2 function is an extractor for Santha–Vazirani sources [107]. This result can be generalized to the inner product modulo $k = \tilde{\Omega}(\sqrt{n})$, so we know that $\langle X, Y \rangle$ mod k is almost uniformly distributed in $\mathbb{Z}_k$ (even conditioned on the transcript t). In particular, it cannot be concentrated in an interval of width $o(k)$ around output(t). Thus the protocol must have error $\Omega(k)$ with high probability. $\blacksquare$

The above theorems show there can be a $\tilde{\Theta}(\sqrt{n})$ factor gap between the worst-case error achievable with a centralized curator (which is captured by global sensitivity) and multiparty (even two-party) differential privacy. Both lower bounds extend to (ε, δ)-differential privacy when $\delta = o(1/n)$. When $\delta = 0$, the largest possible gap, namely $\Omega(n)$, can be proven using a connection to *information complexity*. Before defining information-complexity, let us look at an information-theoretic consequence of differential privacy.

Theorem 7.9.5 (Differential privacy implies low mutual information [78]). *Let* $\mathcal{M} : \mathcal{X}^n \to \mathcal{Y}$ *be an* $(\varepsilon, 0)$-*differentially private mechanism. Then for every random variable X distributed on $\mathcal{X}^n$, we have*

$$I(X; \mathcal{M}(X)) \leq 1.5\varepsilon n,$$

where $I(\cdot;\cdot)$ denotes mutual information.

Note that, without the DP constraint, the largest the mutual information could be is when X is the uniform distribution and $\mathcal{M}$ is the identity function, in which case $I(X;\mathcal{M}(X)) = n \cdot \log_2 |\mathcal{X}|$, so the above bound can be much smaller. We remark that, for approximate differential privacy, one can bound the mutual information $I(X;\mathcal{M}(X))$ in case the rows of X are independent [78, 92], but these bounds do not hold for general correlated distributions [29].

Proof: The mutual information between X and $\mathcal{M}(X)$ is the expectation over $(x,y) \leftarrow (X,\mathcal{M}(X))$ of the following quantity:

$$\log_2 \left(\frac{\Pr[\mathcal{M}(X) = y | X = x]}{\Pr[\mathcal{M}(X) = y]} \right).$$

By group privacy (Lemma 7.2.2), the quantity inside the logarithm is always at most $e^{\varepsilon n}$, so the mutual information is at most $(\log_2 e) \cdot \varepsilon n < 1.5\varepsilon n$.   ∎

To apply this to two-party protocols, we can consider the mechanism $\mathcal{M}$ that takes both parties' inputs and outputs the transcript of the protocol, in which case the mutual information is known as *external information cost*. Or we can fix one party's input x, and consider the mechanism $\mathcal{M}_x(y)$ that takes the other party's input y and outputs the former party's view of the protocol, yielding a bound on *internal information cost*. The information cost of two-party protocols has been very widely studied in recent years (with initial motivations from communication complexity), and there are a number of known, explicit Boolean functions f and input distributions (X,Y) such that any protocol computing f on (X,Y) has information cost $\Omega(n)$. These can be leveraged to construct a low-sensitivity function g such that any two-party differentially private protocol for g incurs error $\Omega(n \cdot \mathrm{GS}_g)$ [78]. This is within a constant factor of the largest possible gap, since the range of g has size at most $n \cdot \mathrm{GS}_g$. It is open to obtain a similar gap for approximate differential privacy:

Open Problem 7.9.6. Is there a function $f : \mathcal{X}^n \rightarrow \mathbb{R}$ such that any multiparty (ε,δ)-differentially private protocol (with constant ε and $\delta = \mathrm{neg}(n)$) for f incurs error $\omega(\sqrt{n} \cdot \mathrm{GS}_f)$ with high probability on some dataset? What about $\Omega(n \cdot \mathrm{GS}_f)$? These are open in both the two-party and local models.

More generally, it would be good to develop our understanding of multiparty differential privacy computation of specific functions such as IP and towards a more general classification.

Open Problem 7.9.7. Characterize the optimal privacy–accuracy tradeoffs for estimating a wide class of functions (more generally, solving a wide set of data analysis tasks) in two-party or multiparty differential privacy.

As the results of Section 7.9.2 suggest, we have a better understanding of the local model than for a smaller number of parties, such as $m = 2$. (See also [4] and the references therein.) However, it still lags quite far behind our understanding of the single-curator model, for example, when we want to answer a set $\mathcal{Q}$ of queries (as opposed to a single query).

7.10 Computational Differential Privacy

7.10.1 The Definition

The basic definition of differential privacy provides protection even against adversaries with unlimited computational power. It is natural to ask whether one can gain from restricting to computationally bounded adversaries, given the amazing effects of such a restriction in modern cryptography.

To obtain a computational analogue of differential privacy, we can simply take the inequalities defining differential privacy, namely

$$\forall T \subseteq \mathcal{Y}, \ \Pr[\mathcal{M}(x) \in T] \leq e^{\varepsilon} \cdot \Pr[\mathcal{M}(x') \in T] + \delta$$

and restrict our attention to tests T defined by feasible algorithms.

Definition 7.10.1 (Computational differential privacy [7]). *Let* $\mathcal{M} = \{\mathcal{M}_n : \mathcal{X}_n^n \to \mathcal{Y}_n\}_{n \in \mathbb{N}}$ *be a sequence of randomized algorithms, where elements in* $\mathcal{X}_n$ *and* $\mathcal{Y}_n$ *can be represented by* poly(n)*-bit strings. We say that* $\mathcal{M}$ *is* computationally ε*-differentially private if there is a superpolynomial function* $s(n) = n^{\omega(1)}$ *and a negligible function* $\delta(n) = n^{-\omega(1)}$ *such that, for all n, all pairs of datasets* $x, x' \in \mathcal{X}^n$ *differing on one row, and all Boolean circuits* $T : \mathcal{X}^n \to \{0, 1\}$ *of size at most* $s(n)$, *we have*
$$\Pr[T(\mathcal{M}(x)) = 1] \leq e^{\varepsilon} \cdot \Pr[T(\mathcal{M}(x')) = 1] + \delta(n).$$

We make a few remarks on the definition:

- We always allow for a nonzero $\delta = \delta(n)$ term in the definition of computational differential privacy. If we did not do so, then the definition would collapse to that of ordinary (information-theoretic) $(\varepsilon, 0)$-differential privacy, because the latter is equivalent to requiring $(\varepsilon, 0)$-differential privacy for sets T of size 1, which are computable by Boolean circuits of size poly(n).
- We generally are only interested in computationally differentially private mechanisms $\mathcal{M}$ that are themselves computable by randomized polynomial-time algorithms, as we should allow the adversary T to invest more computation time than the privacy mechanism.
- For simplicity, we have used the number n of rows as a security parameter, but it is often preferable to decouple these two parameters. We will often drop the index of n from the notation, and make the asymptotics implicit, for sake of readability.

7.10.2 Constructions via Secure Multiparty Computation

The most significant gains we know how to get from computational differential privacy are in the multiparty case. Indeed, by using powerful results on secure multiparty computation, everything that is achievable by a differentially private centralized curator can also be emulated by a multiparty protocol with computational differential privacy.

Theorem 7.10.2 (Computational differential privacy via cryptography [38, 7]).
*Assume that oblivious transfer protocols exist. Let $\mathcal{M} : \mathcal{X}^n \to \mathcal{Y}$ be computationally
ε-differentially private for $\varepsilon \le 1$ and computable in time $\mathrm{poly}(n)$. Then for every $m|n$,
there is an m-party protocol $P = (P_1, \ldots, P_m) : (\mathcal{X}^{n/m})^m \to \mathcal{Y}$ such that:*

1. *P is computationally ε-differentially private,*
2. *For every input $x \in \mathcal{X}^n$, the output distribution of $P(x)$ is the same as that of
$\mathcal{M} : (\mathcal{X}^{n/m})^m \to \mathcal{Y}$,*
3. *P is computable in time $\mathrm{poly}(n)$.*

Proof sketch: By classic results on secure multiparty computation [109, 53], there
exists an m-party protocol P for evaluating $\mathcal{M}$ that is secure against passive adversaries, assuming the existence of oblivious transfer protocols. (See [? 52] for
full definitions and constructions of secure multiparty computation.) Items 2 and
3 are immediately guaranteed by the properties of secure multiparty computation
protocols. For item 1, we recall that each party learns nothing from a secure multiparty computation protocol other than what is implied by their own input and the
output of the function being evaluated (in this case $\mathcal{M}$). More precisely, for every
$\mathrm{poly}(n)$-size adversary A, controlling all parties other than P_k, there is a $\mathrm{poly}(n)$-size
simulator S such that $\mathrm{View}_A(A \leftrightarrow (P_1, \ldots, P_m(x))$ is computationally indistinguishable from $S(\mathcal{M}(x), x_1, \ldots, x_{k-1}, x_{k+1}, \ldots, x_m)$. Thus, for every x and x' that differ
only by changing one row of the input to party j, and every $\mathrm{poly}(n)$-size T, we have

$$\Pr[T(\mathrm{View}_A(A \leftrightarrow (P_1, \ldots, P_m)(x))) = 1]$$
$$\le \Pr[T(S(\mathcal{M}(x), x_1, \ldots, x_{k-1}, x_{k+1}, \ldots, x_m)) = 1] + \mathrm{neg}(n)$$
$$= \left(e^\varepsilon \cdot \Pr[T(S(\mathcal{M}(x'), x'_1, \ldots, x'_{k-1}, x'_{k+1}, \ldots, x'_m)) = 1] + \mathrm{neg}(n)\right) + \mathrm{neg}(n)$$
$$\le e^\varepsilon \cdot (\Pr[T(\mathrm{View}_A(A \leftrightarrow (P_1, \ldots, P_m)(x'))) = 1] + \mathrm{neg}(n)) + \mathrm{neg}(n) + \mathrm{neg}(n)$$
$$= e^\varepsilon \cdot \Pr[T(\mathrm{View}_A(A \leftrightarrow (P_1, \ldots, P_m)(x'))) = 1] + \mathrm{neg}(n).$$

∎

In particular, with computational differential privacy, we have n-party protocols for
computing any counting query or the normalized inner product function with error
$O(1/\varepsilon n)$, significantly better than the $\tilde{\Theta}(1/\sqrt{n})$ error achievable with information-
theoretic differential privacy. It is interesting to understand to what extent general
secure multiparty computation (whose existence is equivalent to oblivious transfer)
is necessary for such separations between information-theoretic and computational
differential privacy. Haitner et al. [57] showed that black-box use of one-way functions does *not* suffice to construct two-party protocols for the inner product function
with error smaller than $\tilde{\Theta}(1/\sqrt{n})$, but a tight characterization remains open.

Open Problem 7.10.3. What is the minimal complexity assumption needed to construct a computational task that can be solved by a computationally differentially
private protocol but is impossible to solve by an information-theoretically differentially private protocol?

Recent works have made progress on understanding this question for computing *Boolean* functions with differential privacy, for example showing that achieving

near-optimal accuracy requires oblivious transfer in some cases [54], but it remains open whether there can be a separation based on a weaker assumption, and whether oblivious transfer is needed to have an asymptotic separation in accuracy for a more natural statistical task (e.g., estimating a function with bounded global sensitivity, such as normalized inner product).

7.10.3 Usefulness with a Trusted Curator?

For the single-curator case ($m = 1$), computational and information-theoretic differential privacy seem closer in power. Indeed, Groce et al. [56] showed that, in the case of real-valued outputs, we can often convert computational differentially private mechanisms into information-theoretically differentially private mechanisms.

Theorem 7.10.4 (From computational to information-theoretic differential privacy [56]). *Let $\mathcal{M} : \mathcal{X}^n \to \mathbb{R}$ be an ε-computationally differentially private mechanism with the property that, for every dataset $x \in \mathcal{X}^n$, there is an interval I_x of width at most $w(n)$ such that $\Pr[\mathcal{M}(x) \notin I_x] \leq \mathrm{neg}(n)$, and the endpoints of I_x are rational numbers with $\mathrm{poly}(n)$ bits of precision. Define $\mathcal{M}'(x)$ to be the mechanism that runs $\mathcal{M}(x)$ and rounds the result to the nearest multiple of $\alpha(n) = w(n)/n^c$, for any desired constant c. Then $\mathcal{M}'$ is $(\varepsilon, \mathrm{neg}(n))$-differentially private.*

Thus, the error incurred is an arbitrary polynomial small fraction of the "spread" of $\mathcal{M}$'s outputs.

Proof: Let I'_x denote the rounding of all points in I_x to the nearest multiple of $\alpha(n)$; notice that $|I'_x| \leq w(n)/\alpha(n) + 1 \leq n^c + 1$. $\mathcal{M}'$ is computationally differentially private because $\mathcal{M}$ is, and we will use this to show that it is actually information-theoretically differential private: For every $x, x' \in \mathcal{X}^n$ that differ on one row and every $T \subseteq \mathbb{R}$, we have

$$
\begin{aligned}
\Pr[\mathcal{M}'(x) \in T] &\leq \left(\sum_{y \in I'_x \cap T} \Pr[\mathcal{M}'(x) = y] \right) + \Pr[\mathcal{M}'(x) \notin I'_x] \\
&\leq \left(\sum_{y \in I'_x \cap T} (e^\varepsilon \cdot \Pr[\mathcal{M}'(x') = y] + \mathrm{neg}(n)) \right) + \mathrm{neg}(n) \\
&\leq e^\varepsilon \cdot \Pr[\mathcal{M}'(x') \in T] + (n^c + 1) \cdot \mathrm{neg}(n) + \mathrm{neg}(n) \\
&= e^\varepsilon \cdot \Pr[\mathcal{M}'(x') \in T] + \mathrm{neg}(n),
\end{aligned}
$$

where the second inequality uses the fact that testing equality with a fixed value y or testing membership in an interval can be done by polynomial-sized circuits, provided the numbers have only $\mathrm{poly}(n)$ bits of precision. ∎

This proof technique extends to low-dimensional outputs (e.g., answering a logarithmic number of real-valued queries) as well as outputs in polynomial-sized discrete sets [56, 23]. So to get a separation between computational and information-theoretic differential privacy with a single curator, we need to use large or high-dimensional output spaces, or measure utility in a different way (not by a low-dimensional metric). Such a separation was recently obtained by Bun et al. [23]:

Theorem 7.10.5 (Separating computational and information-theoretic differentially private curators [23]). *Assuming the existence of subexponentially secure one-way functions and "exponentially extractable noninteractive witness indistinguishable (NIWI) proofs for NP", there exists an efficiently computable utility function* $u : \mathcal{X}^n \times \mathcal{Y} \to \{0, 1\}$ *such that*

1. *There exists a polynomial-time CDP mechanism* $\mathcal{M}^{\text{CDP}}$ *such that, for every dataset* $x \in \mathcal{X}^n$*, we have* $\Pr[u(x, \mathcal{M}^{\text{CDP}}(x)) = 1] \geq 2/3$.
2. *There exists a computationally unbounded differentially private mechanism* $\mathcal{M}^{\text{unb}}$ *such that, for every dataset* $x \in \mathcal{X}^n$*, we have* $\Pr[u(x, \mathcal{M}^{\text{unb}}(x)) = 1] \geq 2/3$.
3. *For every polynomial-time differentially private* $\mathcal{M}$*, there exists a dataset* $x \in \mathcal{X}^n$ *such that* $\Pr[u(x, \mathcal{M}(x)) = 1] \leq 1/3$.

Note that this theorem provides a task where achieving information-theoretic differential privacy is infeasible—not impossible. Moreover, it is for a rather unnatural, cryptographic utility function u. It would be interesting to overcome either of these limitations:

Open Problem 7.10.6. Is there a computational task that is solvable by a single curator with computational differential privacy but is *impossible* to solve with information-theoretic differential privacy?

Open Problem 7.10.7. Can an analogue of Theorem 7.10.5 be proven for a more "natural" utility function u, such as one that measures the error in answering or summarizing the answers to a set of counting queries?

7.10.4 Relation to Pseudodensity

The definition of computational differential privacy is related to concepts studied in the literature on pseudorandomness. For random variables Y, Z taking values in $\mathcal{Y}$ and $\rho \in [0, 1]$, we say that Y has *density at least* ρ in Z if, for every event $T \subseteq \mathcal{Y}$, we have

$$\rho \cdot \Pr[Y \in T] \leq \Pr[Z \in T].$$

For intuition, suppose that Y and Z are uniform on their supports. Then this definition says that $\text{Supp}(Y) \subseteq \text{Supp}(Z)$ and $|\text{Supp}(Y)| \geq \rho \cdot |\text{Supp}(Z)|$. Additionally, if Z is the uniform distribution on $\mathcal{Y}$, then Y having density at least ρ in Z is equivalent to Y having "min-entropy" at least $\log(\rho|\mathcal{Y}|)$. Notice that a mechanism $\mathcal{M}$ is $(\varepsilon, 0)$-differentially private iff, for every two neighboring datasets $x \sim x'$, $\mathcal{M}(x)$ has density at least $e^{-\varepsilon}$ in $\mathcal{M}(x')$.

Just like computational analogues of statistical distance (namely, computational indistinguishability and pseudorandomness) have proven to be powerful concepts in computational complexity and cryptography, computational analogues of density and min-entropy have also turned out to be quite useful, with applications including additive number theory [55], leakage-resilient cryptography [49], and constructions of cryptographic primitives from one-way functions [62].

One of the computational analogues of density that has been studied, called *pseudodensity* (or sometimes *metric entropy* when Z is uniform on $\mathcal{Y}$) [3, 90], is precisely the one used in the definition of computational differential privacy, namely that, for every polynomial-sized Boolean circuit T, we have

$$\rho \cdot \Pr[T(Y) = 1] \leq \Pr[T(Z) = 1] + \text{neg}(n).$$

When considering a *single pair* of random variables (Y, Z), the dense model theorem of [55, 100, 90] says that pseudodensity is *equivalent* to Y being computationally indistinguishable from a random variable $\tilde{Y}$ that truly has density at least ρ in Z. Mironov et al. [81] asked whether something similar can be said about (computationally) differentially private mechanisms, which require (pseudo)density *simultaneously* for all pairs $\mathcal{M}(x), \mathcal{M}(x')$ where $x \sim x'$:

Open Problem 7.10.8. For every ε-computationally differentially private and polynomial-time computable mechanism $\mathcal{M} : \mathcal{X}^n \to \mathcal{Y}$, is there an $(O(\varepsilon), \text{neg}(n))$-differentially private mechanism $\tilde{\mathcal{M}} : \mathcal{X}^n \to \mathcal{Y}$ such that, for all datasets $x \in \mathcal{X}^n$, $\mathcal{M}(x)$ is computationally indistinguishable from $\tilde{\mathcal{M}}(x)$?

A positive answer to this question would imply a negative answer to Open Problem 7.10.6.

7.11 Conclusions

We have illustrated rich connections between the theory of differential privacy and numerous topics in theoretical computer science and mathematics, such as learning theory, convex geometry and optimization, cryptographic tools for preventing piracy, probabilistically checkable proofs and approximability, randomness extractors, information complexity, secure multiparty computation, and notions of pseudoentropy. There have also been very fruitful interactions with other areas. In particular, in both game theory and in statistics, differential privacy has proved to be a powerful tool for some applications where privacy is not the goal—such as designing approximately truthful mechanisms [79, 87] and preventing false discovery in adaptive data analysis [44]. Remarkably, both positive and negative results for differential privacy (including both information-theoretic and computational lower bounds as we have seen in this tutorial) have found analogues for the false discovery problem [44, 60, 98, 6], suggesting that it will also be a very fertile area for complexity-theoretic investigation.

We now mention some more directions for future work in differential privacy, beyond the many open problems stated in earlier sections. As illustrated in previous sections, there has been a thorough investigation of the complexity of answering *counting queries* under differential privacy, with many algorithms and lower bounds that provide nearly matching results. While there remain numerous important open questions, it would also be good to develop a similar kind of understanding for other types of computations. There is now a wide literature on differentially private algorithms for many types of data analysis tasks, but what is missing are negative results to delineate the border between possible and impossible.

Open Problem 7.11.1. Classify large classes of problems (other than counting queries) in differential privacy according to their privacy–utility tradeoffs and their computational tractability.

Two areas of particular interest, both in theory and in practice, are:

Statistical inference and machine learning. In this tutorial, we have mostly been measuring accuracy relative to the particular (worst-case) dataset that is given as input to our differentially private algorithm. However, in statistical inference and machine learning, the goal is usually to infer properties of the *population* from which the dataset is (randomly) drawn. The PAC model studied in Section 7.8 is a theoretically appealing framework in which to study how such tasks can be done with differential privacy, but there are many inference and learning problems outside the PAC model that are also of great interest. These problems include tasks like hypothesis testing, parameter estimation, regression, and distribution learning, and a variety of utility measures such as convergence rates, p values, risk minimization, and sizes of confidence intervals. Moreover, the data distributions are often assumed to have a significant amount of structure (or enough samples are taken for central limit theorems to provide such structure), in contrast to the worst-case distributions considered in the PAC model. Some broad positive results are provided in Smith [95] and Bassily et al. [5] and some negative results in [32, 21, 5], but our understanding of these types of problems is still quite incomplete.

Graph privacy. As mentioned in Section 7.3, there has been some very interesting work on differentially private graph analysis, where our dataset is a graph and we are interested in protecting either relationships (edge-level privacy) or everything about an individual/vertex (node-level privacy). We refer to Raskhodnikova and Smith [88] for a broader survey of the area. Again, most of the work to date has been algorithmic, and we still lack a systematic understanding of impossibility and intractability.

If the existing study of differential privacy is any indication, these studies are likely to uncover a rich theoretical landscape, with even more connections to the rest of theoretical computer science.

Acknowledgements This tutorial was written starting from notes taken during a minicourse given at the 26th McGill Invitational Workshop on Computational Complexity in February 2014, at the Bellairs Institute in Holetown, Barbados [1]. Special thanks go to Kunal Talwar for giving several of the lectures (leading to material in Sections 7.5.1 and 7.7.3 here), to the workshop attendees who wrote up the lecture notes (Eric Allender, Borja Balle, Anne-Sophie Charest, Lila Fontes, Antonina Kolokolova, Swastik Kopparty, Michal Koucký, Cristopher Moore, Shubhangi Saraf, and Luc Segoufin), to Alexander Russell for collecting and editing the notes, to Denis Thérien for organizing the workshop, to all of the participants for illuminating comments during the workshop, and to Sammy Innis for surfing lessons.

I am grateful to Cynthia Dwork, Ilya Mironov, and Guy Rothblum, who got me started on differential privacy during a month-long visit to the wonderful (sadly, now defunct) Microsoft Research Silicon Valley lab in 2008, and numerous collaborators and students since then, whose insights are reflected throughout this tutorial.

I thank Mark Bun, Iftach Haitner, Jack Murtagh, Sasho Nikolov, Adam D. Smith, and Uri Stemmer for extensive comments and corrections that have improved the tutorial. I also thank Yehuda Lindell for his leadership in producing this volume of tutorials in Oded's honor, and for his patience with all of my delays.

References

[1] Lecture notes for the 26th McGill Invitational Workshop on Computational Complexity, February 2014. Lectures given by Salil Vadhan and Kunal Talwar. Notes edited by Alexander Russell.

[2] Victor Balcer and Salil Vadhan. Efficient algorithms for differentially private histograms with worst-case accuracy over large domains. Manuscript, February 2017.

[3] Boaz Barak, Ronen Shaltiel, and Avi Wigderson. Computational analogues of entropy. In *Approximation, randomization, and combinatorial optimization*, volume 2764 of *Lecture Notes in Comput. Sci.*, pages 200–215. Springer, Berlin, 2003. doi: 10.1007/978-3-540-45198-3_18. URL http://dx.doi.org/10.1007/978-3-540-45198-3_18.

[4] Raef Bassily and Adam Smith. Local, private, efficient protocols for succinct histograms. In *STOC'15—Proceedings of the 2015 ACM Symposium on Theory of Computing*, pages 127–135. ACM, New York, 2015.

[5] Raef Bassily, Adam Smith, and Abhradeep Thakurta. Private empirical risk minimization: efficient algorithms and tight error bounds. In *55th Annual IEEE Symposium on Foundations of Computer Science—FOCS 2014*, pages 464–473. IEEE Computer Soc., Los Alamitos, CA, 2014. doi: 10.1109/FOCS.2014.56. URL http://dx.doi.org/10.1109/FOCS.2014.56.

[6] Raef Bassily, Kobbi Nissim, Adam Smith, Thomas Steinke, Uri Stemmer, and Jonathan Ullman. Algorithmic stability for adaptive data analysis. In *48th Annual Symposium on the Theory of Computing (STOC'16)*, June 2016. Preliminary version available at http://arxiv.org/abs/1511.02513.

[7] Amos Beimel, Kobbi Nissim, and Eran Omri. Distributed private data analysis: simultaneously solving how and what. In *Advances in cryptology— CRYPTO 2008*, volume 5157 of *Lecture Notes in Comput. Sci.*, pages 451–468. Springer, Berlin, 2008. doi: 10.1007/978-3-540-85174-5_25. URL http://dx.doi.org/10.1007/978-3-540-85174-5_25.

[8] Amos Beimel, Kobbi Nissim, and Uri Stemmer. Characterizing the sample complexity of private learners. In *ITCS'13—Proceedings of the 2013 ACM Conference on Innovations in Theoretical Computer Science*, pages 97–109. ACM, New York, 2013.

[9] Amos Beimel, Kobbi Nissim, and Uri Stemmer. Private learning and sanitization: Pure vs. approximate differential privacy. In *Approximation, Randomization, and Combinatorial Optimization. Algorithms and Techniques*, pages 363–378. Springer, 2013.

[10] Amos Beimel, Hai Brenner, Shiva Prasad Kasiviswanathan, and Kobbi Nissim. Bounds on the sample complexity for private learning and private data release. *Machine Learning*, 94(3):401–437, 2014. ISSN 0885-6125. doi: 10.1007/s10994-013-5404-1. URL http://dx.doi.org/10.1007/s10994-013-5404-1.

[11] Aditya Bhaskara, Daniel Dadush, Ravishankar Krishnaswamy, and Kunal Talwar. Unconditional differentially private mechanisms for linear queries.

In *STOC'12—Proceedings of the 2012 ACM Symposium on Theory of Computing*, pages 1269–1283. ACM, New York, 2012. doi: 10.1145/2213977. 2214089. URL http://dx.doi.org/10.1145/2213977.2214089.

[12] Jeremiah Blocki, Avrim Blum, Anupam Datta, and Or Sheffet. Differentially private data analysis of social networks via restricted sensitivity. In *ITCS'13—Proceedings of the 2013 ACM Conference on Innovations in Theoretical Computer Science*, pages 87–96. ACM, New York, 2013.

[13] Avrim Blum, Cynthia Dwork, Frank McSherry, and Kobbi Nissim. Practical privacy: the SuLQ framework. In *Proceedings of the 24th ACM SIGMOD-SIGACT-SIGART Symposium on Principles of Database Systems*, pages 128–138. ACM, 2005.

[14] Avrim Blum, Katrina Ligett, and Aaron Roth. A learning theory approach to noninteractive database privacy. *Journal of the ACM*, 60(2):Art. 12, 25, 2013. ISSN 0004-5411. doi: 10.1145/2450142.2450148. URL http://dx.doi.org/10.1145/2450142.2450148.

[15] Dan Boneh and James Shaw. Collusion-secure fingerprinting for digital data. *IEEE Transactions on Information Theory*, 44(5):1897–1905, Sep 1998.

[16] Dan Boneh and Mark Zhandry. Multiparty key exchange, efficient traitor tracing, and more from indistinguishability obfuscation. In *Advances in cryptology—CRYPTO 2014. Part I*, volume 8616 of *Lecture Notes in Comput. Sci.*, pages 480–499. Springer, Heidelberg, 2014. doi: 10.1007/978-3-662-44371-2_27. URL http://dx.doi.org/10.1007/978-3-662-44371-2_27.

[17] Dan Boneh, Amit Sahai, and Brent Waters. Fully collusion resistant traitor tracing with short ciphertexts and private keys. In *Advances in cryptology—EUROCRYPT 2006*, volume 4004 of *Lecture Notes in Comput. Sci.*, pages 573–592. Springer, Berlin, 2006. doi: 10.1007/11761679_34. URL http://dx.doi.org/10.1007/11761679_34.

[18] Mark Bun. *New Separations in the Complexity of Differential Privacy*. PhD thesis, Harvard University, August 2016.

[19] Mark Bun and Thomas Steinke. Concentrated differential privacy: Simplifications, extensions, and lower bounds. *CoRR*, abs/1605.02065, 2016. URL http://arxiv.org/abs/1605.02065.

[20] Mark Bun and Mark Zhandry. Order-revealing encryption and the hardness of private learning. In *Theory of Cryptography Conference (TCC '16A)*, pages 176–206. Springer, 10–13 January 2016. Full version available at https://eprint.iacr.org/2015/417.

[21] Mark Bun, Jonathan Ullman, and Salil Vadhan. Fingerprinting codes and the price of approximate differential privacy. In *Proceedings of the 46th Annual ACM Symposium on Theory of Computing*, STOC '14, pages 1–10, New York, NY, USA, 2014. ACM.

[22] Mark Bun, Kobbi Nissim, Uri Stemmer, and Salil Vadhan. Differentially private release and learning of threshold functions. In *Proceedings of the 56th Annual IEEE Symposium on Foundations of Computer Science (FOCS*

2015), pages 634–649. IEEE, 18–20 October 2015. Full version posted as arXiv:1504.07553.

[23] Mark Bun, Yi-Hsiu Chen, and Salil Vadhan. Separating computational and statistical differential privacy in the client-server model. In Martin Hirt and Adam D. Smith, editors, *Proceedings of the 14th IACR Theory of Cryptography Conference (TCC '16-B)*, Lecture Notes in Computer Science. Springer-Verlag, 31 October–3 November 2016. Full version posted on *Cryptology ePrint Archive*, Report 2016/820.

[24] Mark Bun, Kobbi Nissim, and Uri Stemmer. Simultaneous private learning of multiple concepts. In *Innovations in Theoretical Computer Science (ITCS '16)*, pages 369–380. ACM, 14–16 January 2016. Full version available at http://arxiv.org/abs/1511.08552.

[25] T.-H. Hubert Chan, Elaine Shi, and Dawn Song. Optimal lower bound for differentially private multi-party aggregation. In Leah Epstein and Paolo Ferragina, editors, *Algorithms - ESA 2012 - 20th Annual European Symposium, Ljubljana, Slovenia, September 10-12, 2012. Proceedings*, volume 7501 of *Lecture Notes in Computer Science*, pages 277–288. Springer, 2012. ISBN 978-3-642-33089-6. doi: 10.1007/978-3-642-33090-2_25. URL http://dx.doi.org/10.1007/978-3-642-33090-2_25.

[26] Karthekeyan Chandrasekaran, Justin Thaler, Jonathan Ullman, and Andrew Wan. Faster private release of marginals on small databases. In *ITCS*, pages 387–402, 2014. doi: 10.1145/2554797.2554833.

[27] Shixi Chen and Shuigeng Zhou. Recursive mechanism: Towards node differential privacy and unrestricted joins. In *Proceedings of the 2013 ACM SIGMOD International Conference on Management of Data*, SIGMOD '13, pages 653–664, New York, NY, USA, 2013. ACM. ISBN 978-1-4503-2037-5. doi: 10.1145/2463676.2465304. URL http://doi.acm.org/10.1145/2463676.2465304.

[28] Benny Chor, A Fiat, M. Naor, and B. Pinkas. Tracing traitors. *IEEE Transactions on Information Theory*, 46(3):893–910, May 2000.

[29] Anindya De. Lower bounds in differential privacy. In *Theory of cryptography*, volume 7194 of *Lecture Notes in Comput. Sci.*, pages 321–338. Springer, Heidelberg, 2012. doi: 10.1007/978-3-642-28914-9_18. URL http://dx.doi.org/10.1007/978-3-642-28914-9_18.

[30] Irit Dinur, editor. *IEEE 57th Annual Symposium on Foundations of Computer Science, FOCS 2016, 9-11 October 2016, New Brunswick, New Jersey, USA*, 2016. IEEE Computer Society. ISBN 978-1-5090-3933-3. URL http://ieeexplore.ieee.org/xpl/mostRecentIssue.jsp?punumber=7781469.

[31] Irit Dinur and Kobbi Nissim. Revealing information while preserving privacy. In *Proceedings of the Twenty-second ACM SIGMOD-SIGACT-SIGART Symposium on Principles of Database Systems*, PODS '03, pages 202–210, New York, NY, USA, 2003. ACM. doi: 10.1145/773153.773173.

[32] John C. Duchi, Michael I. Jordan, and Martin J. Wainwright. Privacy aware learning. *Journal of the ACM*, 61(6):Art. 38, 57, 2014. ISSN 0004-5411. doi: 10.1145/2666468. URL http://dx.doi.org/10.1145/2666468.

[33] Cynthia Dwork. Differential privacy. In *Automata, languages and programming. Part II*, volume 4052 of *Lecture Notes in Comput. Sci.*, pages 1–12. Springer, Berlin, 2006. doi: 10.1007/11787006_1. URL http://dx.doi.org/10.1007/11787006_1.

[34] Cynthia Dwork and Jing Lei. Differential privacy and robust statistics. In *STOC'09—Proceedings of the 2009 ACM International Symposium on Theory of Computing*, pages 371–380. ACM, New York, 2009.

[35] Cynthia Dwork and Kobbi Nissim. Privacy-preserving datamining on vertically partitioned databases. In *Advances in Cryptology–CRYPTO 2004*, pages 528–544. Springer, 2004.

[36] Cynthia Dwork and Aaron Roth. The algorithmic foundations of differential privacy. *Foundations and Trends in Theoretical Computer Science*, 9(34): 211–407, 2013. ISSN 1551-305X. doi: 10.1561/0400000042. URL http://dx.doi.org/10.1561/0400000042.

[37] Cynthia Dwork and Sergey Yekhanin. New efficient attacks on statistical disclosure control mechanisms. In *Advances in cryptology—CRYPTO 2008*, volume 5157 of *Lecture Notes in Comput. Sci.*, pages 469–480. Springer, Berlin, 2008. doi: 10.1007/978-3-540-85174-5_26. URL http://dx.doi.org/10.1007/978-3-540-85174-5_26.

[38] Cynthia Dwork, Krishnaram Kenthapadi, Frank McSherry, Ilya Mironov, and Moni Naor. Our data, ourselves: privacy via distributed noise generation. In *Advances in cryptology—EUROCRYPT 2006*, volume 4004 of *Lecture Notes in Comput. Sci.*, pages 486–503. Springer, Berlin, 2006. doi: 10.1007/11761679_29. URL http://dx.doi.org/10.1007/11761679_29.

[39] Cynthia Dwork, Frank McSherry, and Kunal Talwar. The price of privacy and the limits of LP decoding. In *Proceedings of the 39th Annual ACM Symposium on Theory of Computing (STOC)*, pages 85–94, San Diego, California, USA, June 2007. Association for Computing Machinery, Inc. URL http://research.microsoft.com/apps/pubs/default.aspx?id=64343.

[40] Cynthia Dwork, Moni Naor, Omer Reingold, Guy N. Rothblum, and Salil Vadhan. On the complexity of differentially private data release: Efficient algorithms and hardness results. In *Proceedings of the Forty-first Annual ACM Symposium on Theory of Computing*, STOC '09, pages 381–390, New York, NY, USA, 2009. ACM.

[41] Cynthia Dwork, Moni Naor, Toniann Pitassi, and Guy N. Rothblum. Differential privacy under continual observation. In *STOC'10—Proceedings of the 2010 ACM International Symposium on Theory of Computing*, pages 715–724. ACM, New York, 2010.

[42] Cynthia Dwork, Guy Rothblum, and Salil Vadhan. Boosting and differential privacy. In *Proceedings of the 51st Annual IEEE Symposium on Foundations of Computer Science (FOCS 2010)*, pages 51–60. IEEE, 23–26 October 2010.

[43] Cynthia Dwork, Moni Naor, and Salil Vadhan. The privacy of the analyst and the power of the state. In *Proceedings of the 53rd Annual IEEE Symposium on Foundations of Computer Science (FOCS 2012)*, pages 400–409. IEEE, 20–23 October 2012.

[44] Cynthia Dwork, Vitaly Feldman, Moritz Hardt, Toniann Pitassi, Omer Reingold, and Aaron Roth. Preserving statistical validity in adaptive data analysis [extended abstract]. In *STOC'15—Proceedings of the 2015 ACM Symposium on Theory of Computing*, pages 117–126. ACM, New York, 2015.

[45] Cynthia Dwork, Moni Naor, Omer Reingold, and Guy N. Rothblum. Pure differential privacy for rectangle queries via private partitions. In Tetsu Iwata and Jung Hee Cheon, editors, *Advances in Cryptology - ASIACRYPT 2015 - 21st International Conference on the Theory and Application of Cryptology and Information Security, Auckland, New Zealand, November 29 - December 3, 2015, Proceedings, Part II*, volume 9453 of *Lecture Notes in Computer Science*, pages 735–751. Springer, 2015. ISBN 978-3-662-48799-0. doi: 10.1007/978-3-662-48800-3_30. URL http://dx.doi.org/10.1007/978-3-662-48800-3_30.

[46] Cynthia Dwork, Aleksandar Nikolov, and Kunal Talwar. Efficient algorithms for privately releasing marginals via convex relaxations. *Discrete Comput. Geom.*, 53(3):650–673, 2015. ISSN 0179-5376. doi: 10.1007/s00454-015-9678-x. URL http://dx.doi.org/10.1007/s00454-015-9678-x.

[47] Cynthia Dwork, Adam Smith, Thomas Steinke, Jonathan Ullman, and Salil Vadhan. Robust traceability from trace amounts. In *Proceedings of the 56th Annual IEEE Symposium on Foundations of Computer Science (FOCS '15)*, pages 650–669. IEEE, 18–20 October 2015.

[48] Cynthia Dwork, Frank McSherry, Kobbi Nissim, and Adam Smith. Calibrating noise to sensitivity in private data analysis. *Journal of Privacy and Confidentiality*, 7(3), 2016. To appear. Preliminary version in *Proc. TCC '06*.

[49] Stefan Dziembowski and Krzysztof Pietrzak. Leakage-resilient cryptography. In *FOCS*, pages 293–302. IEEE Computer Society, 2008. ISBN 978-0-7695-3436-7. URL http://ieeexplore.ieee.org/xpl/mostRecentIssue.jsp?punumber=4690923.

[50] Vitaly Feldman and David Xiao. Sample complexity bounds on differentially private learning via communication complexity. In *Proceedings of COLT 2014*, pages 1000–1019, 2014.

[51] Sanjam Garg, Craig Gentry, Shai Halevi, Mariana Raykova, Amit Sahai, and Brent Waters. Candidate indistinguishability obfuscation and functional encryption for all circuits. In *Foundations of Computer Science (FOCS), 2013 IEEE 54th Annual Symposium on*, pages 40–49. IEEE, 2013.

[52] Oded Goldreich. *Foundations of cryptography. II*. Cambridge University Press, Cambridge, 2004. ISBN 0-521-83084-2. doi: 10.1017/CBO9780511721656.002. URL http://dx.doi.org/10.1017/CBO9780511721656.002. Basic Applications.

[53] Oded Goldreich, Silvio Micali, and Avi Wigderson. How to play any mental game or a completeness theorem for protocols with honest majority. In Alfred V. Aho, editor, *Proceedings of the 19th Annual ACM Symposium on Theory of Computing, 1987, New York, New York, USA*, pages 218–229. ACM, 1987. ISBN 0-89791-221-7. doi: 10.1145/28395.28420. URL http://doi.acm.org/10.1145/28395.28420.

[54] Vipul Goyal, Dakshita Khurana, Ilya Mironov, Omkant Pandey, and Amit Sahai. Do distributed differentially-private protocols require oblivious transfer? *IACR Cryptology ePrint Archive*, 2015:1090, 2015. URL http://eprint.iacr.org/2015/1090.

[55] Ben Green and Terence Tao. The primes contain arbitrarily long arithmetic progressions. *Annals of Mathematics. Second Series*, 167(2):481–547, 2008. ISSN 0003-486X. doi: 10.4007/annals.2008.167.481. URL http://dx.doi.org/10.4007/annals.2008.167.481.

[56] Adam Groce, Jonathan Katz, and Arkady Yerukhimovich. Limits of computational differential privacy in the client/server setting. In *Theory of cryptography*, volume 6597 of *Lecture Notes in Comput. Sci.*, pages 417–431. Springer, Heidelberg, 2011. doi: 10.1007/978-3-642-19571-6_25. URL http://dx.doi.org/10.1007/978-3-642-19571-6_25.

[57] Iftach Haitner, Eran Omri, and Hila Zarosim. Limits on the usefulness of random oracles. *Journal of Cryptology*, 29(2):283–335, 2016. ISSN 0933-2790. doi: 10.1007/s00145-014-9194-9. URL http://dx.doi.org/10.1007/s00145-014-9194-9.

[58] Moritz Hardt and Guy N. Rothblum. A multiplicative weights mechanism for privacy-preserving data analysis. In *Proceedings of the 51st Annual IEEE Symposium on Foundations of Computer Science (FOCS)*, pages 61–70, Oct 2010. doi: 10.1109/FOCS.2010.85.

[59] Moritz Hardt and Kunal Talwar. On the geometry of differential privacy. In *STOC'10—Proceedings of the 2010 ACM International Symposium on Theory of Computing*, pages 705–714. ACM, New York, 2010.

[60] Moritz Hardt and Jonathan Ullman. Preventing false discovery in interactive data analysis is hard. In *Symposium on Foundations of Computer Science (FOCS '14)*, pages 454–463. IEEE, Oct 18–21 2014.

[61] Moritz Hardt, Katrina Ligett, and Frank Mcsherry. A simple and practical algorithm for differentially private data release. In F. Pereira, C. J. C. Burges, L. Bottou, and K. Q. Weinberger, editors, *Advances in Neural Information Processing Systems 25*, pages 2339–2347. Curran Associates, Inc., 2012.

[62] Johan Håstad, Russell Impagliazzo, Leonid A. Levin, and Michael Luby. A pseudorandom generator from any one-way function. *SIAM Journal on Computing*, 28(4):1364–1396 (electronic), 1999. ISSN 1095-7111.

[63] Nils Homer, Szabolcs Szelinger, Margot Redman, David Duggan, Waibhav Tembe, Jill Muehling, John V. Pearson, Dietrich A. Stephan, Stanley F. Nelson, and David W. Craig. Resolving individuals contributing trace amounts of DNA to highly complex mixtures using high-density SNP genotyping microarrays. *PLoS genetics*, 4(8):e1000167, 2008.

[64] Peter Kairouz, Sewoong Oh, and Pramod Viswanath. The composition the-
     orem for differential privacy. In Francis R. Bach and David M. Blei, edi-
     tors, *Proceedings of the 32nd International Conference on Machine Learn-
     ing, ICML 2015, Lille, France, 6-11 July 2015*, volume 37 of *JMLR Pro-
     ceedings*, pages 1376–1385. JMLR.org, 2015. URL http://jmlr.org/
     proceedings/papers/v37/kairouz15.html.

[65] Shiva P. Kasiviswanathan and Adam Smith. On the 'semantics' of differential
     privacy: A bayesian formulation. *Journal of Privacy and Confidentiality*, 6
     (1), 2014.

[66] Shiva Prasad Kasiviswanathan, Mark Rudelson, Adam Smith, and Jonathan
     Ullman. The price of privately releasing contingency tables and the spectra
     of random matrices with correlated rows. In *STOC'10—Proceedings of the
     2010 ACM International Symposium on Theory of Computing*, pages 775–
     784. ACM, New York, 2010.

[67] Shiva Prasad Kasiviswanathan, Homin K. Lee, Kobbi Nissim, Sofya
     Raskhodnikova, and Adam Smith. What can we learn privately? *SIAM J.
     Comput.*, 40(3):793–826, 2011. doi: 10.1137/090756090.

[68] Shiva Prasad Kasiviswanathan, Kobbi Nissim, Sofya Raskhodnikova, and
     Adam Smith. Analyzing graphs with node differential privacy. In *TCC*,
     pages 457–476, 2013. doi: 10.1007/978-3-642-36594-2_26. URL http:
     //dx.doi.org/10.1007/978-3-642-36594-2_26.

[69] Michael J. Kearns. Efficient noise-tolerant learning from statistical queries.
     Journal of the Association for Computing Machinery, 45(6):983–1006,
     1998. doi: 10.1145/293347.293351. URL http://doi.acm.org/10.
     1145/293347.293351.

[70] Michael J. Kearns and Umesh V. Vazirani. *An introduction to computational
     learning theory*. MIT Press, Cambridge, MA, 1994. ISBN 0-262-11193-4.

[71] Subhash Khot and Assaf Naor. Grothendieck-type inequalities in combi-
     natorial optimization. *Communications on Pure and Applied Mathematics*,
     65(7):992–1035, 2012. ISSN 0010-3640. doi: 10.1002/cpa.21398. URL
     http://dx.doi.org/10.1002/cpa.21398.

[72] Lucas Kowalczyk, Tal Malkin, Jonathan Ullman, and Mark Zhandry. Strong
     hardness of privacy from weak traitor tracing. In Martin Hirt and Adam D.
     Smith, editors, *Theory of Cryptography - 14th International Conference,
     TCC 2016-B, Beijing, China, October 31 - November 3, 2016, Proceedings,
     Part I*, volume 9985 of *Lecture Notes in Computer Science*, pages 659–689,
     2016. ISBN 978-3-662-53640-7. doi: 10.1007/978-3-662-53641-4_25. URL
     http://dx.doi.org/10.1007/978-3-662-53641-4_25.

[73] Ilan Kremer, Noam Nisan, and Dana Ron. On randomized one-round com-
     munication complexity. In *Proceedings of STOC 1995*, pages 596–605, 1995.

[74] Yehuda Lindell and Benny Pinkas. Secure multiparty computation for
     privacy-preserving data mining. *Journal of Privacy and Confidentiality*, 1
     (1), 2009. URL http://repository.cmu.edu/jpc/vol1/iss1/5.

[75] Jiří Matoušek. *Geometric discrepancy*, volume 18 of *Algorithms and
     Combinatorics*. Springer-Verlag, Berlin, 2010. ISBN 978-3-642-03941-6.

doi: 10.1007/978-3-642-03942-3. URL http://dx.doi.org/10.1007/ 978-3-642-03942-3. An illustrated guide, Revised paperback reprint of the 1999 original.

[76] Jiří Matoušek and Jan Vondrák. The probabilistic method (lecture notes). http://kam.mff.cuni.cz/~matousek/lectnotes.html, March 2008.

[77] Jiří Matoušek, Aleksandar Nikolov, and Kunal Talwar. Factorization norms and hereditary discrepancy. arXiv:1408.1376 [math.CO], August 2014.

[78] Andrew McGregor, Ilya Mironov, Toniann Pitassi, Omer Reingold, Kunal Talwar, and Salil Vadhan. The limits of two-party differential privacy. In *Proceedings of the 51st Annual IEEE Symposium on Foundations of Computer Science (FOCS '10)*, pages 81–90. IEEE, 23–26 October 2010.

[79] Frank McSherry and Kunal Talwar. Mechanism design via differential privacy. In *Proceedings of the 48th Annual IEEE Symposium on Foundations of Computer Science*, FOCS '07, pages 94–103, Washington, DC, USA, 2007. IEEE Computer Society. doi: 10.1109/FOCS.2007.41.

[80] P. B. Miltersen, N. Nisan, S. Safra, and A. Wigderson. On data structures and asymmetric communication complexity. *J. Computer & System Sciences*, 57 (1):37–49, 1998.

[81] Ilya Mironov, Omkant Pandey, Omer Reingold, and Salil Vadhan. Computational differential privacy. In S. Halevi, editor, *Advances in Cryptology—CRYPTO '09*, volume 5677 of *Lecture Notes in Computer Science*, pages 126–142. Springer-Verlag, 16–20 August 2009.

[82] Jack Murtagh and Salil Vadhan. The complexity of computing the optimal composition of differential privacy. In Eyal Kushilevitz and Tal Malkin, editors, *Proceedings of the 13th IACR Theory of Cryptography Conference (TCC '16-A)*, volume 9562 of *Lecture Notes in Computer Science*, pages 157–175. Springer-Verlag, 10–13 January 2016. ISBN 978-3-662-49095-2. doi: 10.1007/978-3-662-49096-9. URL http://dx.doi.org/10.1007/ 978-3-662-49096-9. Full version posted on *CoRR*, abs/1507.03113, July 2015.

[83] S. Muthukrishnan and Aleksandar Nikolov. Optimal private halfspace counting via discrepancy. In *Proceedings of the Forty-fourth Annual ACM Symposium on Theory of Computing*, STOC '12, pages 1285–1292, New York, NY, USA, 2012. ACM. doi: 10.1145/2213977.2214090.

[84] Arvind Narayanan, Joanna Huey, and Edward W. Felten. A precautionary approach to big data privacy. In *Computers, Privacy & Data Protection*, 2015.

[85] Aleksandar Nikolov, Kunal Talwar, and Li Zhang. The geometry of differential privacy: the small database and approximate cases. *SIAM Journal on Computing*, 45(2):575–616, 2016. ISSN 0097-5397. doi: 10.1137/ 130938943. URL http://dx.doi.org/10.1137/130938943. Preliminary version in *Proc. STOC 2013*.

[86] Kobbi Nissim, Sofya Raskhodnikova, and Adam Smith. Smooth sensitivity and sampling in private data analysis. In *STOC'07—Proceedings of the 39th Annual ACM Symposium on Theory of Computing*, pages 75–84. ACM, New

York, 2007. doi: 10.1145/1250790.1250803. URL http://dx.doi.org/10.1145/1250790.1250803.

[87] Mallesh M. Pai and Aaron Roth. Privacy and mechanism design. *SIGecom Exch.*, 12(1):8–29, June 2013. ISSN 1551-9031. doi: 10.1145/2509013.2509016. URL http://doi.acm.org/10.1145/2509013.2509016.

[88] Sofya Raskhodnikova and Adam Smith. In Ming-Yang Kao, editor, *Encyclopedia of Algorithms*, chapter Private Analysis of Graph Data, pages 1–6. Springer Berlin Heidelberg, Berlin, Heidelberg, 2014. ISBN 978-3-642-27848-8. doi: 10.1007/978-3-642-27848-8_549-1. URL http://dx.doi.org/10.1007/978-3-642-27848-8_549-1.

[89] Sofya Raskhodnikova and Adam D. Smith. Lipschitz extensions for node-private graph statistics and the generalized exponential mechanism. In I. Dinur [30], pages 495–504. ISBN 978-1-5090-3933-3. doi: 10.1109/FOCS.2016.60. URL http://dx.doi.org/10.1109/FOCS.2016.60.

[90] Omer Reingold, Luca Trevisan, Madhur Tulsiani, and Salil Vadhan. Dense subsets of pseudorandom sets. In *Proceedings of the 49th Annual IEEE Symposium on Foundations of Computer Science (FOCS '08)*, pages 76–85. IEEE, 26–28 October 2008.

[91] Renato Renner and Stefan Wolf. Simple and tight bounds for information reconciliation and privacy amplification. In *Advances in cryptology—ASIACRYPT 2005*, volume 3788 of *Lecture Notes in Comput. Sci.*, pages 199–216. Springer, Berlin, 2005. doi: 10.1007/11593447_11. URL http://dx.doi.org/10.1007/11593447_11.

[92] Ryan M. Rogers, Aaron Roth, Adam D. Smith, and Om Thakkar. Max-information, differential privacy, and post-selection hypothesis testing. In I. Dinur [30], pages 487–494. ISBN 978-1-5090-3933-3. doi: 10.1109/FOCS.2016.59. URL http://dx.doi.org/10.1109/FOCS.2016.59.

[93] Aaron Roth. The algorithmic foundations of data privacy (course lecture notes). http://www.cis.upenn.edu/~aaroth/courses/privacyF11.html, Fall 2011.

[94] Ronen Shaltiel. An introduction to randomness extractors. In *Automata, languages and programming. Part II*, volume 6756 of *Lecture Notes in Comput. Sci.*, pages 21–41. Springer, Heidelberg, 2011. doi: 10.1007/978-3-642-22012-8_2. URL http://dx.doi.org/10.1007/978-3-642-22012-8_2.

[95] Adam Smith. Privacy-preserving statistical estimation with optimal convergence rates. In Lance Fortnow and Salil P. Vadhan, editors, *Proceedings of the 43rd ACM Symposium on Theory of Computing, STOC 2011, San Jose, CA, USA, 6-8 June 2011*, pages 813–822. ACM, 2011. ISBN 978-1-4503-0691-1. doi: 10.1145/1993636.1993743. URL http://doi.acm.org/10.1145/1993636.1993743.

[96] Adam D. Smith and Abhradeep Guha Thakurta. Differentially private feature selection via stability arguments, and the robustness of the lasso. *Journal of Machine Laerning Research: Workshop and Conference Proceedings*, 30: 1–32, 2013.

[97] Joel Spencer. Six standard deviations suffice. *Transactions of the American Mathematical Society*, 289(2):679–706, 1985. ISSN 0002-9947. doi: 10. 2307/2000258. URL http://dx.doi.org/10.2307/2000258.

[98] Thomas Steinke and Jonathan Ullman. Interactive fingerprinting codes and the hardness of preventing false discovery. In *Proceedings of The 28th Conference on Learning Theory (COLT 2015), Paris, France, July 3-6*, pages 1588–1628, 2015. URL http://jmlr.org/proceedings/papers/v40/Steinke15.html. Preliminary version posted as arXiv:1410.1228 [cs.CR].

[99] Thomas Steinke and Jonathan Ullman. Between pure and approximate differential privacy. *Journal of Privacy and Confidentiality*, 7(2):3–22, 2016. Special Issue on TPDP '15. Preliminary version posted as arXiv:1501.06095.

[100] Terence Tao and Tamar Ziegler. The primes contain arbitrarily long polynomial progressions. *Acta Mathematica*, 201(2):213–305, 2008. ISSN 0001-5962. doi: 10.1007/s11511-008-0032-5. URL http://dx.doi.org/10.1007/s11511-008-0032-5.

[101] Gábor Tardos. Optimal probabilistic fingerprint codes. In *Proceedings of the Thirty-fifth Annual ACM Symposium on Theory of Computing*, STOC '03, pages 116–125, New York, NY, USA, 2003. ACM.

[102] Justin Thaler, Jonathan Ullman, and Salil P. Vadhan. Faster algorithms for privately releasing marginals. In *ICALP (1)*, pages 810–821, 2012. doi: 10.1007/978-3-642-31594-7_68.

[103] Jonathan Ullman. Answering $n^{2+o(1)}$ counting queries with differential privacy is hard. In *Proceedings of the 45th annual ACM Symposium on Theory of Computing*, pages 361–370. ACM, 2013.

[104] Jonathan Ullman and Salil Vadhan. PCPs and the hardness of generating private synthetic data. In *Theory of Cryptography*, pages 400–416. Springer, 2011.

[105] Salil P. Vadhan. *Pseudorandomness*, volume 7 (1–3) of *Foundations and Trends in Theoretical Computer Science*. now publishers, December 2012. 336 pages.

[106] Leslie G. Valiant. A theory of the learnable. *Communications of the ACM*, 27(11):1134–1142, 1984.

[107] Umesh V. Vazirani. Strong communication complexity or generating quasirandom sequences from two communicating semirandom sources. *Combinatorica*, 7(4):375–392, 1987.

[108] Stanley L. Warner. Randomized response: A survey technique for eliminating evasive answer bias. *Journal of the American Statistical Association*, 60 (309):63–69, 1965.

[109] Andrew Chi-Chih Yao. Protocols for secure computations (extended abstract). In *23rd Annual Symposium on Foundations of Computer Science, Chicago, Illinois, USA, 3-5 November 1982*, pages 160–164. IEEE Computer Society, 1982. doi: 10.1109/SFCS.1982.38. URL http://dx.doi.org/10.1109/SFCS.1982.38.

[110] Elias A. Zerhouni and Elizabeth G. Nabel. Protecting aggregate genomic data. *Science*, 322(5898):44–44, 2008. ISSN 0036-8075. doi: 10.1126/

science.1165490. URL http://science.sciencemag.org/content/322/5898/44.1.

[111] Jun Zhang, Graham Cormode, Cecilia M. Procopiuc, Divesh Srivastava, and Xiaokui Xiao. Private release of graph statistics using ladder functions. In Timos K. Sellis, Susan B. Davidson, and Zachary G. Ives, editors, *Proceedings of the 2015 ACM SIGMOD International Conference on Management of Data, Melbourne, Victoria, Australia, May 31 - June 4, 2015*, pages 731–745. ACM, 2015. ISBN 978-1-4503-2758-9. doi: 10.1145/2723372.2737785. URL http://doi.acm.org/10.1145/2723372.2737785.

Nomenclature

$\text{Avg}_{j \in T} f(j)$ The average of $f(j)$ over j in the set T, page 396

$\mathcal{M}$ A (randomized) mechanism $\mathcal{M} : \mathcal{X}^n \times \mathcal{Q} \to \mathcal{Y}$ or $\mathcal{M} : \mathcal{X}^n \to \mathcal{Y}$, page 349

$\mathcal{Q}$ A $k \times |\mathcal{X}|$ matrix with $\{0, 1\}$ entries whose rows correspond to a set of counting queries over $\mathcal{X}$. Abusing notation, we also denote this set of counting queries by $\mathcal{Q}$, page 385

$\mathcal{Q}$ A set of queries $q : \mathcal{X}^n \to \mathcal{Y}$, page 349

$\mathcal{Q}_S$ The restriction of counting query family (i.e. $\{0, 1\}$ matrix) $\mathcal{Q}$ to the data universe elements (i.e. columns) in S, page 385

$\mathcal{X}$ A data universe for dataset rows, page 349

$\mathcal{Y}$ A (discrete) output space for a mechanism, page 349

δ The additive privacy parameter of differential privacy, page 351

$\text{Disc}(\mathcal{Q})$ The discrepancy of matrix $\mathcal{Q}$, i.e. $\min_{z \in \{\pm 1\}^n} \|\mathcal{Q}z\|_\infty$, page 383

$\ell^*(K)$ The Gaussian mean width of K: $\text{Exp}_g \max_{z \in K} |\langle z, g \rangle|$, page 414

ε The multiplicative privacy parameter of differential privacy, page 351

GS_q The global sensitivity of q, i.e. $\max_{x \sim x'} |q(x) - q(x')|$, page 353

$\text{HerDisc}(\mathcal{Q})$ The hereditary discrepancy of matrix $\mathcal{Q}$, i.e. $\max_{S \subseteq \mathcal{X}} \text{Disc}(\mathcal{Q}_S)$, page 387

$\text{HerPDisc}(\mathcal{Q})$ The hereditary partial discrepancy of matrix $\mathcal{Q}$, i.e. $\max_{S \subseteq \mathcal{X}} \text{PDisc}(\mathcal{Q}_S)$, page 386

$\text{Lap}(\sigma)$ The Laplace distribution with scale σ, page 353

$\ln$ The natural logarithm function, page 353

$\log$ Base 2 logarithm function, page 353

$\text{LS}_q(x)$ The local sensitivity of query q on dataset x, i.e. $\max_{x' \sim x} |q(x) - q(x')|$, page 367

$\|v\|_p$ The ℓ_p norm of vector v, i.e. $(\sum_i |v_i|^p)^{1/p}$, page 383

$\text{PDisc}(\mathcal{Q})$ The partial discrepancy of matrix $\mathcal{Q}$, i.e. $\min_{\substack{z \in \{0, +1, -1\}^n, \\ \|z\|_1 > n/10}} \|\mathcal{Q}z\|_\infty$, page 383

$\mathcal{Q}^{\text{conj}} = \mathcal{Q}^{\text{conj}}(d) \ \bigcup_{t=0}^{d} \mathcal{Q}_t^{\text{conj}}(d)$, page 351

$\mathcal{Q}_t^{\text{conj}} = \mathcal{Q}_t^{\text{conj}}(d)$ Set of t-way marginal queries, i.e. counting queries corresponding to t-way conjunctions on $\mathcal{X} = \{0, 1\}^d$, page 351

$\mathcal{Q}^{\text{means}} = \mathcal{Q}^{\text{means}}(d)$ Set of d attribute means on dataset with d boolean attributes, i.e. counting queries corresponding to coordinate functions on $\mathcal{X} = \{0, 1\}^d$, page 351

$\mathcal{Q}^{\text{pt}} = \mathcal{Q}^{\text{pt}}(\mathcal{X})$ Set of counting queries corresponding to point functions on $\mathcal{X}$, page 351

$\mathcal{Q}^{\text{thr}} = \mathcal{Q}^{\text{thr}}(\mathcal{X})$ Set of counting queries corresponding to threshold functions on totally ordered $\mathcal{X}$, page 351

$\text{SD}(Y, Y')$ The statistical distance between random variables Y and Y', page 354

$\sigma_{\min}(M)$ The smallest singular value of matrix M, i.e. $\inf_{z \neq 0} \|Mz\|_2 / \|z\|_2$, page 387

$\text{Supp}(Z)$ The support of random variable Z, i.e. $\{z : \Pr[Z = z] > 0\}$, page 356

$\text{VC}(\mathcal{Q})$ The Vapnik–Chervonenkis dimension of $\mathcal{Q}$, i.e. the largest number k such that there exist $x_1, \ldots, x_k \in \mathcal{X}$ for which $\{(q(x_1), \ldots, q(x_k)) : q \in \mathcal{Q}\} = \{0, 1\}^k$, page 374

$D(p\|q)$ The Kullback–Leibler divergence (a.k.a. relative entropy) between discrete probability measures p and q, i.e. $\sum_y p(y) \cdot \log(p(y)/q(y))$, page 363

$d(x, x')$ The Hamming distance between datasets $x, x' \in \mathcal{X}^n$, page 354

K The convex hull of the answer vectors $a_w = (q(w))_{q \in \mathcal{Q}} \in \mathbb{R}^{\mathcal{Q}}$ over $w \in \mathcal{X}$, page 392

n The number of rows in a dataset, page 349

$P_\alpha(K)$ The largest number of points that we can pack in K with all pairwise ℓ_∞ distances larger than α, page 393

$q : \mathcal{X} \to \{0, 1\}$ A predicate inducing a counting query $q : \mathcal{X}^n \to [0, 1]$, page 351

$q : \mathcal{X}^n \to \mathcal{Y}$ A query, page 351

$x = (x_1, \ldots, x_n) \in \mathcal{X}^n$ A dataset of n rows, page 349

$x \sim x'$ Datasets $x, x' \in \mathcal{X}^n$ differ in one row, page 351

Printed in the United States
By Bookmasters